HERMAN MELVILLE

a reference guide
1931–1960

A
Reference
Guide
to
Literature

Hershel Parker,
Editor

HERMAN MELVILLE

a reference guide
1931–1960

BRIAN HIGGINS

G.K. HALL &CO.
70 LINCOLN STREET, BOSTON, MASS.

Library of Congress Cataloging-in-Publication Data

Higgins, Brian, 1943–
  Herman Melville : a reference guide, 1931–1960.

  Includes index.
  1. Melville, Herman, 1819–1891—Bibliography.
I. Title.
Z8562.58.H52 1987 [PS2386]   016.813'3   87-19630
ISBN 0-8161-8671-5

This publication is printed on permanent/durable acid-free paper
MANUFACTURED IN THE UNITED STATES OF AMERICA

Contents

The Author

Brian Higgins is associate professor of English at the University of Illinois at Chicago. Among his publications are Herman Melville: An Annotated Bibliography. Volume 1: 1846-1930 (1979) and Critical Essays on Herman Melville's "Pierre; or, The Ambiguities" (1983; edited with Hershel Parker). Since 1984 he has written the annual chapter on Melville for American Literary Scholarship.

Acknowledgments

The preparation of this volume was made possible in part by a grant from the Research Division of the National Endowment for the Humanities, an independent federal agency. It was also aided by a research leave grant from the University of Illinois at Chicago.

Grateful acknowledgment is also made to all friends and members of the Northwestern-Newberry Melville Edition project who have helped to develop the unique collection of secondary materials in the Melville Collection of the Newberry Library, Chicago, where most of the work for this volume was carried out.

Introduction

Herman Melville's reputation as a major American author was founded in the 1920s by admirers of Moby-Dick, mainly nonacademic professional literary men and women--occasionally novelists and poets but predominantly literary journalists. Few American universities or colleges at that time offered courses in American literature, and very few professors of literature wrote about Melville. During the 1930s, when the teaching of American literature in universities and colleges became less rare though still not customary, Melville slowly entered the curriculum, and by the mid-1940s publication on Melville had become an accepted road to career advancement for young professors in the new field. As a result, the bulk of the writing on Melville in the years covered by this volume (1931-1960) was by academicians. Their labors consolidated Melville's position as a preeminent figure of American literature, despite the protests of a few critics and literary historians, both academic and nonacademic, who thought him overrated. During these three decades Moby-Dick was still generally regarded as Melville's single greatest achievement, though his accomplishments in his other works--particularly in Pierre, the tales (especially "Bartleby" and "Benito Cereno"), The Confidence-Man, and Billy Budd--won increasingly wider recognition.

Melville's life and personality continued to exercise the powerful fascination they had aroused in the 1920s, though biographical studies were now pursued with greater scholarly rigor. The biographers of the 1920s, Raymond M. Weaver (1921.A1), John Freeman (1926.A1), and Lewis Mumford (1929.A1), had all accepted Melville's books as reliably autobiographical. Short on facts, they had perforce been reticent or general about major parts of Melville's life, particularly his early years, his years in the Pacific, and his years after the publication of Moby-Dick. Beginning in the 1930s with Robert S. Forsythe's investigations into Melville's activities in the South Seas, new researchers (notably Charles R. Anderson, Willard Thorp, Leon Howard, Jay Leyda, Harrison Hayford, William H. Gilman, and Merrell R. Davis) established, through exhaustive use of archives, a fuller and more accurate record of the events in Melville's life and the composition of his books. In the process, they uncovered ways in which Melville's "autobiographical" books had departed from the facts of his own experiences and drawn freely on the work of other writers. In the early 1950s, some Melvilleans disparaged studies by the "new school" of biographers as mere registers of "external" facts and statistics that did little to illuminate Melville's mind and personality. More often scholars welcomed the fuller picture of Melville provided by the new studies, as well as their tendency to dispel "legends" about Melville that had accumulated during his lifetime and during his "Revival" in the 1920s (though the legends persisted in a good deal of subsequent Melville criticism).

By 1960 students of Melville had at their disposal a remarkable body of information about Melville unavailable in the 1920s, much of it collected in Jay Leyda's indispensable Melville Log (1951) and Leon Howard's biography (1951), which was based largely on source material in the Log. Melville's journals of his travels in 1849-1850 and in 1856-1857, previously extracted in Weaver's and Mumford's biographies, were published in their entirety in Journal of a Visit to London and the Continent, 1849-1850, edited by Eleanor Melville Metcalf, 1948; and in Journal Up the Straits, edited by Raymond M. Weaver, 1935, then retranscribed by Howard C. Horsford and retitled Journal of a Visit to Europe and the Levant, 1955. Melville's letters, most of them previously published but in a variety of places, were collected in The Letters of Herman Melville, edited by Merrell R. Davis and William H. Gilman (1960). Some Melville family papers not in the Log were made accessible in Eleanor Metcalf's Herman Melville: Cycle and Epicycle (1953). The texts of Melville's lectures were reconstructed in Merton M. Sealts, Jr.'s Melville as Lecturer (1957). Sealts's checklists of "Melville's Reading" (1948-1952; updated and published in book form in 1966) provided a meticulous record of the books Melville was known to have owned or borrowed. Melville's literary sources, ranging from nautical literature to Shakespeare and Carlyle, were extensively documented in numerous articles and in book-length studies, such as Howard P. Vincent's The Trying-Out of MOBY-DICK (1949), Nathalia Wright's Melville's Use of the Bible (1949), and Henry F. Pommer's Milton and Melville (1950).

The most pressing scholarly challenge unmet by 1960 was the publication of a definitive edition of Melville's works. One of the aims of the Melville Society, founded in 1945 by John H. Birss, Harrison Hayford, and Tyrus Hillway, was the publication of such an edition, an ideal that led to the projected fourteen-volume Hendricks House edition. From 1947 to 1960 only six volumes were published-- the Collected Poems (1947), The Piazza Tales (1948), Pierre (1949), Moby-Dick (1952), The Confidence-Man (1954), and Clarel (1960). These volumes failed to provide the standard texts envisaged by the founders of the Melville Society, though Moby-Dick, Pierre, The Confidence-Man, and Clarel were all landmark editions, invaluable for their notes and (in the case of the last three) introductions. Omoo, edited by Harrison Hayford and Walter Blair, remained in page proofs from 1957 to 1968.

The majority of critical books and articles on Melville during
these three decades inevitably reflect more specialized interests
than those in the appreciative essays of the 1920s, which tended
mainly to summarize his career and evaluate his works. Academic
Melvilleans were more apt to give detailed attention to such topics
as his narrative techniques, the function of specific scenes, his
language and imagery, his irony, his use of myth, his primitivism,
naturalism, or transcendentalism (or antitranscendentalism), as well
as to the psychological, philosophical, and moral implications of his
works, often in the 1940s and 1950s adopting (consciously or unconsciously) the assumptions and methods of the New Criticism. Melville criticism became largely the province of the academic journals,
though popular magazines and newspapers continued to publish reviews
of books about Melville and of new editions of his works, now often
written by academics. Richard Chase's polemical essays in the
Partisan Review and the Kenyon Review in the late 1940s addressed a
wider audience than most Melville criticism published between 1931
and 1960.

Commentary on Melville accumulated steadily during the 1930s and
the first half of the 1940s, then proliferated so rapidly in the
years following World War II that by 1950 Robert Spiller claimed that
Melville was "the most thoroughly studied of all American authors."
Throughout the 1950s the output of essays, notes, introductions to
new editions and reprints, chapters, and books continued unabated.
Critical guides to this increasingly overwhelming mass of secondary
material were in short supply, though Melville students were served
by a number of bibliographies. The earliest extensive listing of
writings about Melville was the twenty-nine page annotated selected
bibliography Willard Thorp published in his influential anthology
Herman Melville: Representative Selections (1938). Thereafter
Thorp's coverage was extended, without annotations, in listings
in the bibliography volume of the Literary History of the United
States (1948, 1959), Lewis Leary's Articles on American Literature,
1900-1950 (1954), Milton R. Stern's The Fine Hammered Steel of Herman
Melville (1957), and in mimeographed checklists compiled by John H.
Birss, Gordon Roper, and Stuart C. Sherman (1951, 1958) and by
Norman E. Jarrard (1958, 1959). (The Birss-Roper-Sherman lists and
Jarrard's 1959 list were circulated by the Melville Society.) By
1960 much of the work toward a comprehensive secondary bibliography
had been accomplished. Stanley T. Williams' chapter on Melville in
Eight American Authors, edited by Floyd Stovall (1956), provided the
first extensive critical survey of scholarship and criticism.

Not all the recognition accorded Melville in these three decades
was academic. Bibliophiles paid high prices for his scarcer first
editions, testimony to his literary standing as well as to the
scarcity of the editions. Novelists and poets continued to give
tribute to both the man and his work in essays, interviews, novels,
and poems. Nonacademic literary critics, such as Van Wyck Brooks,
Edmund Wilson, and Malcolm Cowley, still occasionally wrote about him
in their literary columns and books. Artists illustrated his works
and produced independent paintings and drawings inspired by them.
The most influential tributes, however, were undoubtedly the Broadway

and television productions and operatic version of <u>Billy Budd</u> and the
movie production of <u>Moby-Dick</u> in the early and middle 1950s--adapta-
tions through which, ironically, Melville achieved his greatest
popularity, reaching millions who had never actually read him. The
pages of this bibliography are testimony to the multifaceted fascination of Melville for those who did read him, academic and nonacademic
alike.

<u>Note</u>: Entries in the bibliography are arranged in chronological
order. Asterisks indicate items that I have not been able to locate.
Dissertations on Melville and books and articles on Melville in
foreign languages are not annotated or listed, though book reviews
in English are included. For dissertations, consult John Bryant's
<u>Melville Dissertations, 1924-1980: An Annotated Bibliography and
Subject Index</u> (Greenberg, 1983). For foreign language materials,
consult Leland R. Phelps's <u>Herman Melville's Foreign Reputation: A
Research Guide</u> (G.K. Hall, 1983), a full-scale bibliography of editions and scholarship in forty-eight languages.

References Abbreviated in the Text

Arvin (1966)	Arvin, Newton. _American Pantheon_. Ed. Daniel Aaron and Sylvan Schendler. New York: Delacorte Press, 1966.
Beebe, Hayford, and Roper	Beebe, Maurice, Harrison Hayford, and Gordon Roper, comps. "Criticism of Herman Melville: A Selected Checklist." _Modern Fiction Studies_, 8 (Autumn 1962), 312-346.
Berthoff (1962)	Berthoff, Warner. _The Example of Melville_. Princeton: Princeton University Press, 1962.
Browne and Light	Browne, Ray B. and Martin Light, eds. _Critical Approaches to American Literature. Volume 1: Roger Williams to Herman Melville_. New York: Thomas Y. Crowell, 1965.
Burnshaw	Burnshaw, Stanley, ed. _Varieties of Literary Experience: Eighteen Essays in World Literature_. New York: New York University Press, 1962.
Charvat (1968)	Charvat, William. _The Profession of Authorship in America, 1800-1870: The Papers of William Charvat_. Ed. Matthew J. Bruccoli. Columbus: Ohio State University Press, 1968.
Chase (1962)	Chase, Richard, ed. _Melville: A Collection of Critical Essays_. Englewood Cliffs, N.J.: Prentice-Hall, Inc., 1962.
Corrigan	Corrigan, Robert W., ed. _Tragedy: Vision and Form_. San Francisco: Chandler Publishing Co., 1965.
Cowley (1964)	Cowley, Malcolm, ed. _After the Genteel Tradition: American Writers, 1910-1930_. Carbondale: Southern Illinois University Press, 1964.
Dahlberg (1964)	Dahlberg, Edward. _Alms for Oblivion: Essays by Edward Dahlberg_. Minneapolis: University of Minnesota Press, 1964.
Doubloon	Parker, Hershel and Harrison Hayford, eds. _MOBY-DICK As Doubloon_. New York: W.W. Norton & Co., 1970.
Fadiman (1962)	Fadiman, Clifton. _Enter Conversing_. New York: The World Publishing Co., 1962.

References Abbreviated in the Text

Gilmore   Gilmore, Michael T., ed. Twentieth Century
          Interpretations of MOBY-DICK: A Collection of
          Critical Essays. Englewood Cliffs, N.J.:
          Prentice-Hall, Inc., 1977.

Goldberg and   Goldberg, G.J. and N.M. Goldberg, eds. The
Goldberg   Modern Critical Spectrum. Englewood Cliffs,
          N.J.: Prentice-Hall, Inc., 1962.

Gordon   Gordon, Walter K., ed. Literature in Critical
          Perspectives: An Anthology. New York:
          Appleton Century Crofts, 1968.

Gross   Gross, Seymour, ed. A BENITO CERENO Handbook.
          Belmont, Calif.: Wadsworth Publishing Co.,
          1965.

Gross and Hardy   Gross, Seymour L. and John Edward Hardy, eds.
          Images of the Negro in American Literature.
          Chicago and London: Chicago University Press,
          1966.

Hayford and Sealts Hayford, Harrison and Merton M. Sealts, Jr., eds.
          Billy Budd, Sailor (An Inside Narrative).
          Chicago and London: The University of Chicago
          Press, 1962.

Higgins   Higgins, Brian. "Supplement to Herman Melville:
(February 1979)   An Annotated Bibliography. Volume 1: 1846-
          1930." Melville Society Extracts, No. 37
          (February 1979), pp. 10-15.

Higgins and Parker Higgins, Brian and Hershel Parker, eds. Critical
          Essays on Herman Melville's PIERRE; OR, THE
          AMBIGUITIES. Boston: G.K. Hall & Co., 1983.

Inge   Inge, M. Thomas, ed. Bartleby the Inscrutable.
          A Collection of Commentary on Herman Melville's
          Tale "Bartleby the Scrivener." Hamden, Conn.:
          Archon Books, 1979.

Kazin (1961)   Kazin, Alfred. The Open Form: Essays for Our
          Time. New York: Harcourt, Brace & World,
          1961.

Kazin (1962)   Kazin, Alfred. Contemporaries. Boston: Little,
          Brown and Co., 1962.

Letters   Davis, Merrell R. and William H. Gilman, eds.
          The Letters of Herman Melville. New Haven and
          London: Yale University Press, 1960.

Lewis (1966)   Lewis, Sinclair. "The American Fear of Litera-
          ture," ed. Mark Schorer, in An American
          Primer. Ed. Daniel J. Boorstin. Chicago and
          London: Chicago University Press, 1966.

Log   Leyda, Jay, ed. The Melville Log. New York:
          Harcourt, Brace and Co., 1951. Reprint (with
          supplement). New York: Gordian Press, 1969.

Michel   Michel, Laurence A., ed. Tragedy: Modern Essays
          in Criticism. Englewood Cliffs, N.J.:
          Prentice-Hall, Inc., 1963.

Miller (1962)   Miller, James E., Jr. A Reader's Guide to Herman
          Melville. New York: Farrar, Straus and
          Cudahy; London: Thames and Hudson, 1962.

References Abbreviated in the Text

Miller (1967)	Miller, Perry. Nature's Nation. Cambridge, Mass.: Harvard University Press, 1967.
Norton The Confidence-Man	Parker, Hershel, ed. The Confidence-Man: His Masquerade. New York: W.W. Norton & Co., 1971.
Norton Moby-Dick	Hayford, Harrison and Hershel Parker, eds. Moby-Dick. New York: W.W. Norton & Co., 1967.
Oliver (1965)	Oliver, Egbert S. Studies in American Literature: Whitman, Emerson, Melville and Others. New Delhi: Eurasia Publishing House, 1965.
Olson (1965)	Olson, Charles. Human Universe and Other Essays. Ed. Donald Allen. San Francisco: The Auerhahn Society, 1965.
Olson (1966)	Olson, Charles. Selected Writings of Charles Olson. Ed. Robert Creeley. New York: New Directions, 1966.
Recognition	Parker, Hershel, ed. The Recognition of Herman Melville: Selected Criticism Since 1846. Ann Arbor: University of Michigan Press, 1967.
Ricks and Adams	Ricks, Beatrice and Joseph D. Adams, comps. Herman Melville: A Reference Bibliography 1900-1972. Boston: G.K. Hall & Co., 1973.
Rountree	Rountree, Thomas J. Critics on Melville: Readings in Literary Criticism. Coral Gables, Fla.: University of Miami Press, 1972
Runden	Runden, John P., ed. Melville's BENITO CERENO: A Text for Guided Research. Boston: D.C. Heath and Co., 1965.
Scott	Scott, Wilbur S., ed. Five Approaches of Literary Criticism: An Arrangement of Contemporary Critical Essays. New York: The Macmillan Co., 1962.
Sealts (1966)	Sealts, Merton M., Jr. Melville's Reading: A Check-List of Books Owned and Borrowed. Madison and London: University of Wisconsin Press, 1966.
Sealts (1982)	Sealts, Merton M., Jr. Pursuing Melville, 1940-1980: Chapters and Essays by Merton M. Sealts, Jr. Madison and London: University of Wisconsin Press, 1982.
Springer	Springer, Haskell S., ed. The Merrill Studies in BILLY BUDD. Charles E. Merrill Studies. Columbus, Ohio: Charles E. Merrill Publishing Co., 1970.
Stafford (1961)	Stafford, William T., ed. Melville's BILLY BUDD and the Critics. San Francisco: Wadsworth Publishing Co., 1961.
Stallman and Waldhorn	Robert W. Stallman and Arthur Waldhorn, eds. American Literature: Readings and Critiques. New York: G.P. Putnam's Sons, 1961.
Tuten	Tuten, Frederick, ed. Critical Reviews of MOBY-DICK. New York: Simon & Schuster, 1966.

References Abbreviated in the Text

Vickery   Vickery, John B., ed. <u>Myth and Literature:</u>
                   <u>Contemporary Theory and Practice</u>. Lincoln:
                   University of Nebraska Press, 1966.

Vincent (1969)   Vincent, Howard P., ed. <u>The Merrill Studies in</u>
                   <u>MOBY-DICK</u>. Charles E. Merrill Studies.
                   Columbus, Ohio: Charles E. Merrill Publishing
                   Co., 1969.

Vincent (1971)   Vincent, Howard P., ed. <u>Twentieth Century</u>
                   <u>Interpretations of BILLY BUDD: A Collection</u>
                   <u>of Critical Essays</u>. Englewood Cliffs, N.J.:
                   Prentice-Hall, Inc., 1971.

Willett   Willett, Ralph, ed. <u>The Merrill Studies in</u>
                   <u>PIERRE</u>. Charles E. Merrill Studies.
                   Columbus, Ohio: Charles E. Merrill Publishing
                   Co., 1971.

Writings about Herman Melville, 1931–1960

1931 A BOOKS

1   CURL, VEGA. <u>Pasteboard Masks: Fact as Spiritual Symbol in the Novels of Hawthorne and Melville</u>. Radcliffe Honors Theses in English, No. 2. Cambridge, Mass.: Harvard University Press, 50 pp.

      Under the influence of transcendentalism (though Melville opposed the optimism of the transcendentalists with "a Titanic pessimism"), Hawthorne and Melville introduced a new genre into American fiction, writing "not of the external world of men and manners, adventure, and petty moralizing, but of the more subtle, transcendental region of spiritual reality." They are not primarily concerned with appearance and fact: "these things are but the masks through which the real significance of life may be dimly apprehended." Hawthorne and Melville try to touch the reality behind the masks. Hawthorne is concerned with the psychological and moral, Melville with the metaphysical. Reviewed in 1932.B36.

1931 B SHORTER WRITINGS

1   ADAMS, JAMES TRUSLOW. <u>The Epic of America</u>. Boston: Little, Brown, and Co., pp. 234, 272.

      <u>Moby-Dick</u>, and its theme of evil in the universe, was disregarded in the mid-nineteenth century because Americans were preoccupied with work and getting rich.

2   BLANKENSHIP, RUSSELL. "Herman Melville (1819-1891)," in <u>American Literature As an Expression of the National Mind</u>. New York: Henry Holt and Co., pp. 377-386.

      Biographical sketch; brief survey. Hawthorne's romanticism kept him from offending most readers; Melville's realism repelled many. In "one of many impersonations," Melville appeared in <u>Moby-Dick</u> as Ishmael, the outcast, the wanderer.

3   BOAS, RALPH PHILIP. <u>The Study and Appreciation of Literature</u>. New York: Harcourt, Brace and Co., pp. 133, 144.

      Ahab used as illustration of "the simplest form of causation," in which the characters of a novel determine the action but are not changed by it. <u>Moby-Dick</u> used as example of a novel that secures vitality through its power over setting, through its "ability to produce a sense of a special world different from the reader's and hence more exciting." The sea "is there" in Moby-Dick as nowhere else except in Conrad.

4   BOYNTON, PERCY HOLMES. The Challenge of Modern Criticism. Chicago: Thomas S. Rockwell, p. 16.
       Claims that "No one ever paid serious attention to the writing of an obscure young man named Herman Melville until very modern times."

5   BROMFIELD, LOUIS. "Hawthorne," in American Writers on American Literature. Ed. John Macy. New York: Horace Liveright, pp. 97, 102.
       Melville's "title to greatness" remains in dispute (like that of Emerson, Mark Twain, and Howells) but Whitman, Poe, and Hawthorne "have passed the test of time and the perspective of distance and emerged as great men." For a short time Hawthorne shared "a fierce almost sinister intimacy" with Melville, "who, like himself, lived and wrote under a curse."

6   CANBY, HENRY SEIDEL. "Hawthorne and Melville," in Classic Americans: A Study of Eminent American Writers from Irving to Whitman. New York: Harcourt, Brace and Co., pp. 226-262. Reprint. New York: Russell & Russell, 1959.
       The difference between Hawthorne and Melville "is a difference between environments quite as much as a difference between men--a Salem bedroom and the seven seas, the moral liberalism of Concord and the memories of a man who had lived with savages, worked with brutes, and bent his untrained mind on ideas of life wherever and however he could find them." Yet Melville's skeptical relation to Emerson and Carlyle is curiously like Hawthorne's; Moby-Dick is Melville's answer to transcendentalism and his wildly imaginative comment on the intellectual pride of the nineteenth century. Melville's "rebellious skepticism is modern in its contradictions of hope, its dramatizations of will, and its projection of evil as nature." If Melville "went wild" after Moby-Dick, it was because he was both too late and too early to get the full effects of his genius. He "grew more metaphysical precisely at the moment when the age . . . was aswing toward materialism"; and in Pierre and other books he "was attempting to search out the psychology of motive a half century ahead of psychology, and by means of romantic, melodramatic narrative that only a Transcendentalist could have interpreted." The Scarlet Letter, Moby-Dick, and Emerson's Nature are "three climaxes of the religious obsessions of the American nineteenth century, different, but more than temporally related."

7   CROSS, TOM PEETE, REED SMITH, and ELMER C. STAUFFER. "Herman Melville," in American Writers. Good Reading for High Schools. Boston: Ginn and Co., p. 575.
       Biographical sketch. Extract (pp. 341-347) from Typee, chapter 30.

8   CURRIE, BARTON. Fishers of Books. Boston: Little, Brown and
     Co., pp. 33–35, 177–179, 274.
          A collector's reminiscences; prefers Conrad to Melville.
     Details of endpapers in Moby-Dick first editions; quotes prices
     paid for first editions. Illustration of first editions of Moby-
     Dick and The Whale.

9   GOHDES, CLARENCE L.F. The Periodicals of American Transcen-
     dentalism. Durham, N.C.: Duke University Press, pp. 9, 116.
          Notes "a tendency at present" to include among the number
     of transcendentalists "such literary figures as Melville and
     Whitman, who assuredly did not regard themselves as transcenden-
     talists." Quotes from the Harbinger review of Typee, attributing
     it to C.A. Dana. [See 1846.B40.]

10   HILLYER, ROBERT SILLIMAN, KENNETH BALLARD MURDOCK, and ODELL
     SHEPARD, eds. Prose Masterpieces of English and American
     Literature. New York: Harcourt, Brace and Co., p. 292.
          Headnote to extracts from Moby-Dick, chapters 28 and 135.
     In Moby-Dick, nature, the sea, the great whale are all symbols of
     the central forces shaping human life. At times Melville's prose
     is elaborately cadenced; at other times it "reminds one of the
     more restrained phrasing of Hawthorne."

11   LEWIS, SINCLAIR. "The American Fear of Literature," in Why
     Sinclair Lewis Got The Nobel Prize. Address by Erik Axel
     Karlfeldt, Permanent Secretary of the Swedish Academy, at the
     Nobel Festival, December 10, 1930, and Address by Sinclair
     Lewis before the Swedish Academy, December 12, 1930. New
     York: Harcourt, Brace and Co., p. 22.
          Mention: "all this time, while men like Howells were so
     effusively seeking to guide America into becoming a pale edition
     of an English cathedral town, there were surly and authentic
     fellows--Whitman and Melville, then Dreiser and James Huneker and
     Mencken--who insisted that our land had something more than tea-
     table gentility." Reprinted in Lewis (1966).

12   McFEE, WILLIAM. "Introduction," in Moby Dick (abridged).
     Notes by M.D. Holmes. Illustrated by Anton Otto Fischer.
     Philadelphia: The John C. Winston Co., pp. xi–xvii.
          Biographical sketch. Moby-Dick is a great spiritual expe-
     rience, a marvelous enlargement of our imaginative horizon.

13   MURRY, JOHN MIDDLETON. Son of Woman: The Story of D.H.
     Lawrence. New York: Jonathan Cape & Harrison Smith,
     pp. 255–256, 265–275, 277, 281.
          Discusses Lawrence's essays on Melville in Studies in
     Classic American Literature [see 1923.B3–4]. Lawrence projects
     himself through Melville; the "vicious, unmanly craving" for a
     perfect relationship that he attributes to Melville is in him-
     self. The sinking of the Pequod by the white whale symbolized to
     Lawrence the destruction of the ideal consciousness by the blood-
     consciousness--a destruction accomplished within himself.
     Lawrence's method in Studies in Classic American Literature is

a successive identification of great American books with events
in his own soul.

14   O'BRIEN, EDWARD J. "Notes," in The Twenty-Five Finest Short
      Stories. New York: Richard R. Smith, p. 507.
          Essentially the same note on "Benito Cereno" as in 1928.B25.
      Prints "Benito Cereno" (pp. 25–112).

15   OPPENHEIM, JAMES. "Whitman," in American Writers on American
      Literature. Ed. John Macy. New York: Horace Liveright,
      pp. 268, 270.
          Moby-Dick is not true tragedy, which is a purgation, leav-
      ing one whole and healed: the book "lets us down at the end,
      instead of heaving us up," since the only survivor is Ishmael
      (Melville), who is defeated by the world. Had the book been
      truer tragedy, it would have been truer poetry. Its vision of
      the world is not direct, like Whitman's vision, but comes
      "through the ageless fabulous atmosphere and images of the un-
      conscious." Moby Dick "is a gorgeous and terrible symbol of the
      dark, invisible devouring forces of life."

16   PERRY, RALPH BARTON. A Defence of Philosophy. Cambridge,
      Mass.: Harvard University Press, pp. 48–49.
          Brief quotation from the "philosophy" of Stubb and of
      Ishmael.

17   PETERSON, HOUSTON. The Melody of Chaos. New York: Longmans,
      Green, and Co., pp. 117–120.
          Places Melville (of Mardi, Moby-Dick, Pierre) in the line
      of modern writers, from Montaigne to Joyce, who developed the
      "disintegrating view of the unified soul, self, or ego." In
      Mardi Melville "constantly recurred to the ageless riddles of the
      self, playing variations on a number of traditional theories."
      Moby-Dick is "an allegory of the wild forces within the human
      psyche." Pierre presents "multiple ambiguities in the depths of
      the personality," which Melville does not describe or trace so
      much as point to in horror, repeatedly taking "refuge in violent
      rhetoric, in the most extravagant imagery, in order to give some
      hint of his fearful discovery." It is evident that "the full
      implications of modern psychopathology" would have been familiar
      to him.

18   PRESCOTT, FREDERICK C. and GERALD D. SANDERS. "Herman
      Melville," in An Introduction to American Prose. New York:
      Appleton-Century-Crofts, p. 499.
          Biographical sketch, with brief comments on Typee, Omoo,
      Moby-Dick, and Pierre. Long before the end of Moby-Dick, "the
      voyage is seen to be a mystical one, full of profound, if some-
      what cloudy meanings." Extracts (pp. 500–538) from Typee,
      chapter 18; Omoo, chapter 2; Moby-Dick, chapters 35 and 48; and
      sketches 1, 3, and 4 from "The Encantadas."

19   ROURKE, CONSTANCE. <u>American Humor: A Study of the National</u>
      <u>Character</u>. New York: Harcourt, Brace and Co., pp. 191–200,
      passim. Reprint. New York: Doubleday Anchor Books, 1953.
          The influence on Melville of tall tales of the west and sea
      lore, which would have reached him not only through almanacs and
      popular journals but through adventures of his own. <u>Moby-Dick</u> is
      concerned with "one of those illusory marked creatures of the
      natural world, magic and powerful, which had often appeared in
      western legends of the jet-black stallion or the white deer."
      Among "the tall tales of the West was one which ran close to the
      main outline of <u>Moby-Dick</u>, describing the comic adventures of a
      backwoodsman who sought a fabulously large bear, the Big Bear of
      Arkansas, in revenge for depredations." Legends of Mocha Dick
      were known before Melville used them. The <u>Pequod</u> seems to con-
      tain representatives of all the major characters who had figured
      largely in American comedy, and there are passages in the book
      that echo the comic interchanges of the current joke books and
      the stage. Even the movement of the narrative is that of comic
      travesty: "it soars, circles, and rises to the persistent native
      form of rhapsody." But the humor becomes sardonic: "that terror
      and sense of evil and impending death which had often been part
      of the comic legends of the country are relentlessly uncovered.
      Melville broke through the mask of comedy to find its ultimate
      secret, and gave to <u>Moby-Dick</u> the final element which creates the
      epic: an encounter between gods and men." Nothing in heroic
      literature before <u>Moby-Dick</u> had contained its deep and passionate
      stress on adventures of the mind.

20   ROGERS, STANLEY. <u>The Pacific</u>. London: George G. Harrap &
      Co., pp. 109, 128, 157–162, 187.
          Passing references to <u>Typee</u>, and in chapter on "The Liter-
      ary Pacific," a biographical sketch, summary of <u>Typee</u>, and com-
      mentary on <u>Moby-Dick</u>. Melville was essentially a man of one
      book--<u>Moby-Dick</u>. "Nothing else he wrote anywhere near reached
      its greatness, and, indeed, all that appeared thereafter was of
      such a trivial, inferior, opiniative, and eccentric nature that
      it can only be explained by a partial breaking down of the
      author's dark and mystic mind."

21   SCHWARTZ, JACOB. <u>1100 Obscure Points: The Bibliographies of</u>
      <u>25 English and 21 American Authors</u>. London: The Ulysses
      Bookshop, pp. 73–76.
          Descriptive bibliography of Melville's works.

22   UNTERMEYER, LOUIS. "Herman Melville," in <u>American Poetry</u>
      <u>From the Beginning to Whitman</u>. New York: Harcourt, Brace and
      Co., pp. 547–555.
          Biographical and critical. <u>Moby-Dick</u> synthesizes the
      various themes and variations of Melville's previous works.
      "Here, in one astonishing volume, is the luxuriance of <u>Typee</u>,
      the vivid unreality of <u>Omoo</u>, the allegory of <u>Mardi</u>, the sharp
      character-drawing of <u>White-Jacket</u>. But <u>Moby-Dick</u> not only com-
      bines these qualities, it transforms them; all is heightened in
      a kind of writing which is like nothing that ever came out of

America. To say that it is both Gargantuan and Biblical is to
suggest that . . . it has something of the rhapsody of Koheleth,
the wild imagery of Job, the swelling catalogues of Rabelais.
One is inevitably reminded of the Bible . . . . The power of the
sea is in Moby-Dick as the power of earth is in Leaves of Grass.
But Melville might easily have traded one element for another;
for it is the prodigious current, the unleashed but controlled
energy of his mind which speaks through Ahab's Shakespearian
soliloquies no less than through the crowded actions of this
colossal effort. . . . The structure of Moby-Dick is so vast and
complicated that the pattern is sometimes twisted askew; the
narration sprawls; the plot is submerged, reappears, and sinks in
a sea of troubled allegory. But, whatever its superficial defects, in spread and vigor, in sheer poetic movement (which, as
it rises, tends to swing into blank verse), in its vital 'digressions' Moby-Dick is an epic--and one of the world's greatest."
In Pierre "Melville's pessimism turns desperate and self-
defeating and the style becomes incredibly, even mawkishly
ornate. Its value as contribution to a case-history is obvious;
its value as literature is nil." The Confidence-Man is an unreadable and almost irrational satire. In Battle-Pieces the
"expression is direct; the impulse, even in the heat of conflict,
is generous; Melville's personal struggle is submerged in his
devotion to an impersonal cause." The essence of Clarel was
distilled from Melville's inherent Timonism. Though he could
sustain a prose work of any length, Melville was still an imperfect technician in verse; not until he was nearly seventy was he
at ease in the restricted forms he favored. The later poetry is
not only Melville's best but an unhampered expression of his
spirit, revealing peace although not complacency. Long unknown,
his verse will soon be "examined for the same quality found in
his prose, a delight in accumulated facts sharpened by a vigilant
scrutiny for the significant detail." Melville is the spiritual
opponent of Emerson and Whitman, but he measures up to them.
Prints (pp. 555-577) extracts from chapters 99, 93, 102, 36, 9,
and 119 of Moby-Dick and selections from Battle-Pieces, Clarel,
John Marr, Timoleon, Weeds and Wildings, and At the Hostelry.
The extracts from Moby-Dick "belong not to fiction but to major
poetry."

23   WEAVER, RAYMOND. "Melville," in American Writers on American
      Literature. Ed. John Macy. New York: Horace Liveright,
      pp. 190-206.
         Shortened version of 1928.B20, somewhat revised.

24   BROWN, E.K. "Hawthorne, Melville, and 'Ethan Brand.'"
      American Literature, 3 (March), 72-75.
         Refutes claim by Lewis Mumford [1929.A1] and Newton Arvin
      [1929.B1] that Hawthorne "drew a spiritual portrait" of Melville
      in "Ethan Brand." [See also 1929.B40.]

25 ROURKE, CONSTANCE. "Our Comic Heritage." Saturday Review of
    Literature, 7 (21 March), 678–679.
        Includes Melville material from 1931.B19, much abbreviated.

26 MURRAY, HENRY A., JR. "Book Reviews." New England Quarterly,
    4 (April), 333–337.
        Review of Knopf edition of Pierre [see 1930.B13]. Objects
    that Forsythe "in his accurate, thorough and most gentlemanly
    introduction does not mention the word incest," though incestuous
    passion is the nucleus of the book; and that Forsythe "takes
    special pains to dissociate the story of Pierre from the story of
    Melville," when Pierre is "to be taken as a spiritual biography,
    a modern counterpart . . . of the Confessions of St. Augustine."
    It was "due to the compelling and unresolvable character of
    Melville's personal conflicts that he was never able during this
    period to achieve the desired state of aesthetic detachment."
    The plot of Pierre is not unimportant, as Forsythe holds;
    Pierre's "ensuing sentiments are meaningless without it." The
    "value of the novel is the consummate sorcery of Melville's lan-
    guage." Reprinted in Higgins and Parker, pp. 188–191.

27 MORLEY, CHRISTOPHER. "The Bowling Green." Saturday Review of
    Literature, 7 (25 April), 775.
        Notes forthcoming auction sale of Melville's 8 January 1852
    letter to Sophia Hawthorne [Letters, pp. 145–147] and prints
    extract. [See 1931.B28–29.]

28 ANON. "Letter Reveals Author's Views on 'Moby Dick.'" New
    York Herald Tribune (26 April).
        Notes forthcoming sale of Melville's 8 January 1852 letter
    to Sophia Hawthorne [Letters, pp. 145–147] and prints extract.
    "The explicit explanation made by the author in this letter, says
    a note by the cataloguer, must set forever at rest the contro-
    versy over the part played by conscious symbolism in the writing
    of what perhaps is the greatest of American novels. The letter
    was discovered recently in a yellowing package of Hawthorne's
    papers, belonging to a grand-daughter of Hawthorne, 'a supreme
    fragment of a lost correspondence,' preserved, according to the
    cataloguer, by a strange and fortunate chance."

29 ANON. "Letter by Melville Sold Here for $3,100." New York
    Times (30 April), p. 48.
        Notes auction sale (to J.W. Bentley) of Melville's
    8 January 1852 letter to Sophia Hawthorne [Letters, pp. 145–147];
    and sale (to A.S.W. Rosenbach for $575) of first edition of
    Pierre, "which the author presented to the Hawthornes."

30 [DODGE, NORMAN L.]. "Dead Whale or Stove Boat." The Month at
    Goodspeed's, 2 (May), 251–268.
        Quotation from Moby-Dick, chapter 56; commentary on
    Ambroise Louis Garneray. Brief discussion of Owen Chase's
    Narrative and G.H. von Langsdorff's Voyages and Travels. Cites
    newspaper clipping (source unknown) quoting John Masefield "as

of the rather remarkable opinion that Michael Scott, Tom
Cringle's creator, is 'a much more brilliant writer' than
Marryat, Dana, or Melville."

31 HOWARD, LEON. "Melville and Spenser--A Note on Criticism."
    Modern Language Notes, 46 (May), 291-292.
        Identifies the sources of the quotations at the beginning
of each of the ten sketches of "The Encantadas." All the verses
are from Spenser, except for one stanza from Chatterton. "The
selections are more than conventional chapter headings or cap-
tions: they are presentations in verse of the same pictures that
are sketched in prose, and the closeness of the parallel is
emphasized by the fact that Melville changed several of them
slightly in order that they might correspond exactly with the
actual scenes." Melville "was an authority on the picturesque
whose literary appreciation was not directed by any formal tradition of reading, and when he chooses Spenser to illustrate the
sketches drawn largely from his own observations in the South
Seas, he is paying a high and sincere tribute to that poet's
art."

32 RIEGEL, O.W. "The Anatomy of Melville's Fame." American
    Literature, 3 (May), 195-203.
        Aims to correct "two erroneous conclusions" of Melville
enthusiasts: "first, that Melville's contemporaries were blind
to the significance of his work, and, second, that until the
beginning of the revival of the last decade Melville was completely forgotten." Names some of Melville's admirers during the
"dark" periods before 1919 and notes "at least four or five
movements which sought to reawaken a general interest in Melville." The recent revival of interest may be owing to the
1920s' "devotion to psychological history, to 'case histories' of
spiritual struggle and conflict, to the spectacle of man against
the world, to all evidences of psychological maladjustment: a
devotion induced by the recent enthusiasm for psychology as well
as by the post-war psychosis of futility, of futility and
defiance." The new interest is not so much bellestristic as
biographical; and the Melville cult may be limited "to those who
find in the 'Herman Melville' of the recent biographies a kindred
spirit, or a life which embodies their own psychological conflicts." [See 1934.B18.]

33 MORDELL, ALBERT. "Melville and 'White Jacket.'" [Letter to
    the Editor.] Saturday Review of Literature, 7 (4 July), 946.
        Identifies originals of some of the characters in White-
Jacket from the muster roll of the frigate United States. Muster
roll indicates that Melville enlisted in the navy on 17 August
1843 at Oahu.

34 MORLEY, CHRISTOPHER. "The Bowling Green." Saturday Review
    of Literature, 8 (1 August), 22.
        Reference to Melville's 25 October 1852 letter to
Hawthorne [Letters, pp. 161-162]. "It appears from an unpublished letter of Herman Melville to Hawthorne that H.M. liked to

consider symbolic the grains of sand left over from blotting his
script. 'If you find <u>sand</u> in this letter,' he wrote, 'regard it
as so many sands of my life, which ran out as I was writing it.'"
Asks for information about the book <u>Laughcomic</u> mentioned in the
letter. [<u>See</u> 1931.B36.]

35   MORRIS, LLOYD. "Melville: Promethean." <u>Open Court</u>, 45
     (September), 513-526.
          Biographical, indebted to Weaver [1921.A1] and Mumford
     [1929.A1]. Melville is "the peer of Milton, Bunyan, Dante,
     Goethe; and with them the superior of Shakespeare and Cervantes
     in the measure wherein all who deal transcendentally with the
     transcendental are superior to those who deal superlatively only
     with manners and morals." Continued in 1931.B37.

36   FORSYTHE, ROBERT S. "'Taghconic.'" [Letter to the Editor.]
     <u>Saturday Review of Literature</u>, 8 (19 September), 140.
          Reply to 1931.B34, giving information about <u>Taghconic</u> and
     the author, J.E.A. Smith. [<u>See</u> 1852.B4.]

37   MORRIS, LLOYD. "Melville: Promethean (II)." <u>Open Court</u>, 45
     (October), 621-635.
          Continued from 1931.B35. Biographical and critical. As a
     work of pure thought, <u>Mardi</u> is the greatest of Melville's books.
     Even the beginning of <u>Mardi</u> is symbolic: the ship representing
     Melville's first fifteen years of protected life; the sea, the
     ocean of social life; the sharks, the rigors of civilization
     from which he had been protected by parental care. The abrupt
     changes from calm opening to fantastic satire then allegory
     symbolize the abrupt transitions in Melville's own life and
     thought. Taji becomes Ahab, who exemplifies rationality carried
     to its logical extremity; Ahab-Melville "assails the Infinite
     with Promethean violence as the author of the mystery of
     iniquity." <u>Pierre</u>, "a psycho-analytical triumph," is the
     psychological sequel of <u>Moby-Dick</u>; its "thrasonical style" is
     "the only correct vehicle" for its material and is used "in
     savage scathing mockery of the times depicted." The social
     philosophy in <u>The Confidence-Man</u> is acrid and mordant, its satire
     picturesque and trenchant. It "contains passages of profound
     and original thought; and the brilliant shadow of a metaphysical
     truth that is exhilarating"; it "goes deeper than <u>Gulliver</u>; is
     more universal and less contemporary." "Bartleby" approaches
     Shakespeare's <u>Richard II</u> in conception and rivals Gogol's <u>Cloak</u>
     and Maupassant's <u>A Piece of String</u>. <u>Clarel</u>'s thought, "sometimes
     distinguished and wonderful, frequently mediocre and occasionally
     commonplace, often anticipates its future and has in part become
     valid today by progress." Melville's altruism never sprang from
     any depth of human tenderness but was the expression of intel-
     lectual dissatisfaction. The only way to a proper understanding
     of him is to take his works "in their constructive psychological
     sequence": <u>Redburn</u>, <u>Typee</u>, <u>Omoo</u>, <u>White-Jacket</u>, <u>Mardi</u>, <u>Moby-Dick</u>,
     <u>Pierre</u>, <u>The Confidence-Man</u>, "Bartleby." By so doing, we parallel
     his growth and experience.

38   NEWTON, A. EDWARD. "Books of One's Own." <u>Atlantic Monthly</u>,
148 (October), 447–448.
     Quotes Augustine Birrell talking about <u>Moby-Dick</u>. It "is
not one book, but two: there is the book which you may read at
a glance and a book written between the lines, as it were, a book
as psychical and as mystical as if it had been written by
Swedenborg, whose disciple, in a sense, its author surely was."
Reprinted in 1933.B16.

39   ARVIN, NEWTON. "Individualism and American Writers." <u>Nation</u>,
133 (14 October), 391–393.
     Historical survey of individualism in American writers. In
Emerson, Thoreau, and Whitman, "our individualism, on its brighter
side, attained its classic meridian. There was of course, even
then, a darker side; there were men for whom the gospel of self-
help--or the habit of estrangement, which is a form it may always
take--proved to be the path toward confusion, morbidity, and a
kind of impotence; and Poe, Hawthorne, and Melville, men of the
richest endowments, paid a tragic price for sitting on pumpkins
and effusing egotism. Their careers suggest that the principle,
from the artist's point of view, is at best a precarious one;
and that its spiritual fruitfulness is exhausted almost before
it is realized." The present heirs of Poe, Hawthorne, and
Melville "have retreated, in their despair of finding solid
ground on which to build a personal life, to an explicit philosophy of negation; and pitched here and there on the sands of the
Waste Land one descries the tents . . . of Jeffers and MacLeish,
of Krutch and Aiken, of Hemingway and Faulkner."

40   ANON. "$300 for First 'Moby-Dick.'" New York <u>Times</u>
(17 December), p. 21.
     Notes auction sale of a first edition of <u>Moby-Dick</u>.

<u>1932 A BOOKS--NONE</u>

<u>1932 B SHORTER WRITINGS</u>

1   ADAMS, JAMES TRUSLOW. <u>The March of Democracy: The Rise of</u>
<u>the Union</u>. New York: Charles Scribner's Sons, pp. 331, 335.
     Among all the men of his period, Melville alone had a
profound sense of evil, not as human sin as portrayed by
Hawthorne, but as something inherent in the very structure of the
universe. With a more passionate nature than any of his contemporaries in letters, he reacted more deeply against the conditions of American life as well as against the terms imposed
on man by the cosmos itself. Hawthorne was more of an artist
than Melville, but the reach and universality of his thought was
far more circumscribed.

2   BALCOM, LOWELL LEROY. "Introduction," in <u>Mocha Dick or the</u>
<u>White Whale of the Pacific</u>, by J.N. Reynolds. Illustrated by
Lowell Leroy Balcom. New York: Charles Scribner's Sons,
n.p.

Believes that Melville undoubtedly had heard of the White Whale many times by word of mouth and that he had also probably read Reynolds' account. Notes the great interest of Reynolds' story in throwing light on the legend from which Melville worked.

3   BOYNTON, HENRY WALCOTT. Annals of American Bookselling, 1638-1850. New York: John Wiley & Sons; London: Chapman & Hall, p. 174.
     During the years George Palmer Putnam was in London, John Wiley in New York "published much of the best American literary work of the period. The Wiley and Putnam 'Library of American Books,' unlike most assemblies of the kind, contained original material of high importance, Poe's 'Tales' and 'The Raven,' Hawthorne's 'Mosses from an Old Manse,' Melville's 'Typee.'"

4   CALVERTON, V.F. The Liberation of American Literature. New York: Charles Scribner's Sons, pp. 271-273.
     Typee "represented the revolt of an individual who hated the corruption of his own civilization, who saw through its shams and hypocrisies, and yet new no other way of dealing with it than to flee. The more serious, the more significant task of changing that civilization, staying with it to transform it, did not inspire him. Like Thoreau, he preferred to desert it, to build his fantasies where he could be free of it." Melville, "like Emerson, looked to the West for the coming of the new race--the native, the representative American race. It was the America of the East, of New England, that had repelled him and driven him from its shores." Moby-Dick, in symbolic form, indicts our whole capitalist society.

5   CARSWELL, CATHERINE. The Savage Pilgrim: A Narrative of D.H. Lawrence. New York: Harcourt, Brace and Co., p. 197.
     Lawrence never regarded Conrad's sea story at its best as equal to that of Melville's. "As compared with the true sea literature of Moby Dick, Lawrence dismissed the storm in Typhoon as descriptive journalism."

6   DE VOTO, BERNARD. Mark Twain's America. Boston: Little, Brown, and Co., pp. 159, 218, 268, 285, 289, 313, 317.
     Brief remarks on Melville's deficiencies in humor, characterization, structure, and style in contrast to Mark Twain. Exuberant vitality had no place in Melville's nature. The mates, harpooners, and sailors in Moby-Dick are "the book's disregarded possibility of great realism." A passage in Roughing It burlesques Moby-Dick, and in the same passage occurs what may be a jeer at Pierre. The minds of Melville and Mark Twain were antipathetic, though their careers had similarities. Passage on Moby-Dick reprinted in Norton Moby-Dick, p. 633.

7   DICKINSON, THOMAS H. "Herman Melville (1819-1891)," in The Making of American Literature. New York: The Century Co., pp. 490-498.
     Biographical and critical. All of Melville's great writing was done by the time he was thirty-three; the rest is anticlimax.

Hawthorne's "Ethan Brand" was inspired by Melville. [See 1929.B40 and 1931.B24.]

8   FULLERTON, B.M. "Melville, Herman (1819-1891)," in Selective
     Bibliography of American Literature, 1775-1900. New York:
     William Farquhar Payson, pp. 192-194.
         Partial list of Melville first editions, with brief bio-
graphical and critical notes. "With the completion of 'Moby-
Dick,' Melville's powers declined. The Transcendentalism which
had its first glimmering in 'Typee' and confessed its defeat in
'Mardi' and 'Moby-Dick' became despair. 'Pierre' is a welter of
extraordinary conjecture and save for a few war verses his subsequent work is almost unreadable."

9   GULICK, JOHN THOMAS. Evolutionist and Missionary John Thomas
     Gulick, Portrayed Through Documents and Discussions, by
     Addison Gulick. Chicago: University of Chicago Press,
     pp. 152-153; 163.
         Journal entry for 27 April 1859 records visit to Melville
and gives description of him. "Though it was apparent that he
possessed a mind of an aspiring, ambitious order, full of elastic
energy and illumined with the rich colors of a poetic fancy, he
was evidently a disappointed man, soured by criticism and dis-
gusted with the civilized world and with our Christendom in
general and in particular. The ancient dignity of Homeric times
afforded the only state of humanity, individual or social, to
which he could turn with any complacency. What little there was
of meaning in the religions of the present day had come down
from Plato. . . ." Omoo is listed in a memorandum of books
Gulick read in 1859. Journal entry reprinted in Log, pp. 604-
605.

10   HARVEY, SIR PAUL. "Melville, Herman," "Moby Dick," and
     "Pierre," in The Oxford Companion to English Literature.
     Oxford, England: At the Clarendon Press, pp. 510, 526, 616.
         Biographical sketch and brief notes on Moby-Dick and
Pierre.

11   HAWTHORNE, HILDEGARDE. Romantic Rebel: The Story of
     Nathaniel Hawthorne. New York and London: The Century Co.,
     pp. 153-154.
         Hawthorne's friendship with Melville, a "wild and wondrous
visitor."

12   HAWTHORNE, NATHANIEL. The American Notebooks by Nathaniel
     Hawthorne. Ed. Randall Stewart. New Haven: Yale University
     Press, pp. 131-132, 220-221, 225, 229, 231-232.
         Entries for 5, 7 August 1850; 4, 7, September 1850; and
1, 2, 5, 9 August 1851 record time spent with Melville or mention Melville.

13   HUXLEY, ALDOUS. <u>Texts & Pretexts: An Anthology With Commen-</u>
     <u>taries</u>. London: Chatto & Windus, pp. 33–35.
          Discusses Melville's commentary on Goethe in his 1[?] June
     1851 letter to Hawthorne [<u>Letters</u>, pp. 130–131]: "The <u>all</u> feel-
     ing is brief and occasional; but this is not to say that a meta-
     physical system based upon it must necessarily be untrue. Nor
     does the great predominance in our lives of not-all feelings
     necessarily invalidate an all-theory, any more than a theory of
     molecular movement is invalidated by our almost constant sense of
     the solidity and stability of matter. It is only in certain
     circumstances that we can observe the Brownian movement; at other
     times we observe stillness. Similarly, it is only in special
     circumstances that we have the all-feeling; at other times we
     have an immediate sense of separateness. We cannot help it; we
     are made that way. Melville is quite right, of course, in in-
     sisting that this immediate sense of separateness cannot be
     denied; an all-philosophy will not cure toothache, just as the
     molecular theory will not modify our native incapacity to be
     aware of molecules. On the other hand, toothache (Melville's
     expressive symbol of separateness) and the non-molecular life
     are, on their own plane, undeniable realities. Our experience is
     divided up into island universes. We jump from one to the
     other--there are no bridges. Because of their peculiar quality,
     we say that some of these experiences are more real, or at any
     rate more significant than others. But the others, nevertheless,
     continue to exist."

14   KNIGHT, GRANT C. <u>American Literature and Culture</u>. New York:
     Ray Long & Richard R. Smith, pp. 133, 205, 214–221, 244, 254.
          Survey. Transcendentalism enters <u>Mardi</u>: not the clear
     faith of Emerson or the rugged independence of Thoreau, but a
     recognition, distorted by Melville's fierce thinking, of the wide
     difference between what an individual wishes to be and what the
     world obliges him to become, between the idealist and his sur-
     rounding reality. In <u>Moby-Dick</u> the greatness of the allegory can
     be conceded, but the book "is as prodigal of emotional phrases
     as an Elizabethan novel or drama" and "suggests too much an
     experiment, a handling of material which gets out of bounds,
     the powerlessness to realize that the novel had advanced far
     with respect to form from the days of Queen Bess." Melville's
     architecture is consistently faulty: in none of his novels does
     he properly organize and plan. The style of <u>Pierre</u> is so hys-
     terical and morbid, so full of poetic affectations that no pub-
     lisher today would give such a manuscript a second glance.
     <u>Israel Potter</u> is "done with inexcusable carelessness; its inci-
     dents are hurried and often pointless, its style also hurried
     and inferior." <u>The Confidence-Man</u> (first part of a two-volume
     work which was never completed) contains several autobiographical
     items, as does <u>Pierre</u> "and is another intense parable upon the
     collision of ideals and actualities, another effort of an intel-
     ligent man to erect illusions for himself." Melville's volumes
     of poetry can be dismissed without discussion; but <u>The Piazza</u>
     <u>Tales</u> contains at least two of the best American short stories,

"Benito Cereno" and "Bartleby." If sheer strength, Dantesque
glooms, wild self-examination, reckless condemnations of the
spirit of the world make a great writer Melville was indubitably
one. His tone pleases the dismayed "intelligent minority" of the
1920s and 1930s, the postwar disillusioned; but Melville now
probably runs the risk of being overpraised where he was formerly
underrated. As a great American romantic he stands secure;
judged "by exacting standards of restraint and actuality in
action and dialogue, by the maxim that to conceal art is to
reveal it, Melville falls somewhat short of the noblest company."

15   LAWRENCE, D.H. The Letters of D.H. Lawrence. Ed. Aldous
      Huxley. New York: The Viking Press, p. 322.
           In a letter to Lady Ottoline Morrell, 7 February 1916: "I
      am reading Moby Dick. It is a very odd, interesting book: to me
      interesting, the others can't bear it."

16   LEWISOHN, LUDWIG. Expression in America. New York and
      London: Harper & Brothers, pp. 154, 186–193, 266. Reprinted
      as The Story of American Literature (New York: The Modern
      Library, 1939).
           Melville's reaction to his "overpowering fixation on his
      mother"--continual flight from home, from his own soul and life,
      from reality and outward experience--accounts for the fragmen-
      tary, chaotic, explosive, and unguided character of all his work
      and for its atmosphere of homelessness, emptiness, and desolate-
      ness of heart. The final image that arises from all the work "is
      that of a big bearded violently excited man trying to shout down
      the whimpering, lonely child in his soul." Melville was a weak,
      querulous, fretful man, one who adopted all his life the regres-
      sive attitude of the neurotic as is evident even in Moby-Dick.
      Typee and Omoo are morose books, without charm, like all of his
      books. The eloquence in Moby-Dick "is fierce and broken and
      sags every other minute into sheer jejune maundering or in-
      sufferable wordiness." The recent reestimate of Melville has
      overshot the mark: he is not even a minor master; his works
      constitute rather one of the important curiosities of litera-
      ture. "He will be chiefly remembered as the inventor of a
      somber legend concerning the evil that is under the sun. But to
      embody this legend in a permanently valid form he had only half
      the creative power and none of the creative discipline or
      serenity."

17   PASTON, GEORGE. At John Murray's: Records of a Literary
      Circle, 1843–1892. London: John Murray, pp. 51–54, 90–91.
           Details of the publication, reception, and sales of
      Murray's editions of Typee and Omoo. Prints letter from Sir
      Walter Farquhar to Lord Ashley forwarded to Murray, deploring
      the books' reprehensible tone. [Letter reprinted in Log,
      p. 265.] Quotes entries in Melville's journal for 23 November
      1849 and 20 December 1849 and extract of "The Paradise of
      Bachelors" from 1921.A1.

18   PIDGEON, HARRY. "The Marquesas Islands," in Around the World
     Single-Handed; The Cruise of the "Islander." New York and
     London: D. Appleton and Co., pp. 36-71.
          Recounts visit to the Typee valley; references to Typee and
     the following anecdote: "In the evening as we sat on the veranda
     of Sterling's house [at Hatiheu], listening to the low murmuring
     voices of the natives who had gathered around, I heard an old
     woman repeat the name, 'Tommo.' Sterling [an American mission-
     ary] questioned her, and he said she was talking about an Ameri-
     can, who long ago had lived with the Typees. We thought she
     spoke of Melville. Sterling told her of Melville and of the book
     he had written. After meditating over it for a time, she said,
     'This American came to our island in the old days, then he re-
     turned to his own country and wrote a book about what he saw, and
     now the Americans know more about the ways of our fathers than we
     do ourselves." A Typee (Poi Utu) showed Pidgeon "the pai-pai
     where once had stood the house of Tokuhi, a chief under whose
     protection two Americans had lived in the old days. He had made
     them tabu so they were safe to go and come about the valley where
     they would. They had lived for a time in Typee and then went
     away to Taiohae, but their names Poi did not know." Pidgeon
     speculates that Tokuhi was the Mehevi of Melville. Photographs
     of the Vale of Typee and Vaiahu Falls, where Melville and Toby
     descended into the valley, and other Marquesan scenes.

19   SHERMAN, STUART P. The Emotional Discovery of America and
     Other Essays. New York: Farrar & Rinehart, p. 19.
          Mention: "To take any part of the earth into your heart
     transfigures it for you and for all men whom you can persuade to
     use your eyes. And the transfiguring discovery of America has,
     in most periods, proceeded bit by bit, in the hearts of men like
     Cooper who took the forest into his heart, and Dana and Melville
     who took the sea into their hearts. . . ."

20   STEWART, RANDALL, ed. The American Notebooks by Nathaniel
     Hawthorne. New Haven: Yale University Press, pp. xcv,
     307-308, 337.
          Notes on Hawthorne's relationship with Melville.

21   VAN DOREN, MARK. "Preface," in The Oxford Book of American
     Prose. London and New York: Oxford University Press, p. x.
          Melville cited as one of the American "writers of prose
     who play upon intricate instruments of deep and mysterious
     sound." The three chapters (14, 41, and 42) from Moby-Dick used
     in the anthology (pp. 302-323) have speed and a color and com-
     plexity rarely to be found in American literature. "Even
     Melville goes like the wind, as Emerson does, however choppy his
     sentences and however many-hued his mind." The prose of Pierre
     is so little controlled as to be the best illustration, page
     after page, of Melville's besetting vice, blank verse; while
     Billy Budd is a narrative too organic in all its parts to admit
     abridgment.

22   WARD, A.C.   American Literature, 1880–1930.   New York:
     Lincoln Macveagh, The Dial Press, pp. 20–22.
         "Distinguished, by the infusion of a metaphysical element,
     from most other novels in which full-blooded physical action
     plays a large part, Moby-Dick is, as it were, a Day-of-Judgement
     fantasy, as well as a natural history of the whale, a manual of
     whaling, a whale anthology, and a collection of thrilling yarns.
     That Melville intended the protagonists, Captain Ahab and the
     White Whale, to be symbolic is evident; but apart from stirring
     a shadowy sense that some universal principle of antagonism is
     involved, the symbolism is obscure."   Melville's "stormily
     mystical outlook was in vivid contrast to the prevailing roseate
     New England transcendentalism; and he did nothing to encourage
     dogmatic notions that the recognition of truth, the propagation
     of virtue, and the practice of nobility are the natural preroga-
     tives of simple piety."

23   THOMAS, RUSSELL.   "Melville's Use of Some Sources in The
     Encantadas."   American Literature, 3 (January), 432–456.
         Examines Melville's "alterations and expansions of his
     source material in the light of what seems to have been his sole
     aim" in writing the sketches: to present the Enchanted Isles
     "as places of enchantment, of solitariness, and of inhospital-
     ity."   Identifies the sources of the quotations at the beginning
     of each of the ten sketches [cf. 1931.B31], including one quota-
     tion from William Collins's Dirge in Cymbeline, first printed in
     the 1856 edition of The Piazza Tales not in the Putnam's serial-
     ization.   Finds Melville indebted to Captain David Porter's
     Journal of a Cruise Made to the Pacific Ocean in at least a
     dozen passages, to Captain James Colnett's A Voyage to the South
     Atlantic and Round Cape Horn into the Pacific in two passages,
     and to the maps in both works; prints parallel passages and
     reproduces maps.   Compares versions of the story of Oberlus
     (Patrick Watkins) in Porter and in John Coulter's Adventures in
     the Pacific; finds that Melville follows Porter "rather closely"
     but thinks it "altogether possible" that he "had heard another
     version which differed to some extent from Porter's."

24   WAINGER, BERTRAND M.   "Herman Melville: A Study in Dis-
     illusion."   Faculty Papers of Union College, 3 [Union College
     Bulletin, 25] (January), 35–62.
         Biographical and critical survey, indebted to Weaver
     [1921.A1] and Freeman [1926.A1]; views Melville's works as
     factual or spiritual autobiography.   Melville's story is one "of
     disillusionment and defeat in man's struggle with society and
     in his struggle with nature."   Melville was one of those men
     "who find no rest from the torture of the ideal," an exile and
     an Ishmael "in search of the peace that never was."   In Mardi
     (where the social satire is the most effectively written element
     in the book), Melville's personal disillusionment for the first
     time is universalized into great literature; too often the satire
     lacks indirection, wit is sacrificed for enthusiasm, and the
     artist is lost in the preacher, but the "direct statements are so
     forceful, so sincere, so rational, the underlying sentiment is

so fine and noble, that the consciousness of lack of art is lost
in admiration of and enthusiastic assent to the message." In
Moby-Dick Melville reveals a new depth of thought and a continued
and strengthened independence of spirit. He is plagued by "the
indifference of the ultimate reality to man, and the ridiculous
insignificance of man's life and thoughts and feelings which is
logically deduced therefrom"; but the central allegory of Moby-
Dick is contained in Melville's reference, in his 16[?] April[?]
1851 letter to Hawthorne, to "the man who, like Russia or the
British Empire, declares himself a sovereign nature (in himself)
amid the powers of heaven, hell, and earth"; who "may perish; but
so long as he exists he insists upon treating with all powers
upon an equal basis" [Letters, pp. 124–125]. Faced in Pierre
with the problem of imbedding in the story the germs of subsequent events and character revelations, Melville often fell back
on more or less direct statement; he never achieved, or never
consolidated, the power of fusing matter and form. But, though
easily the worst written of Melville's books, in plot and human
insight and self-revelation, Pierre ranks, if not first, then a
close second to Moby-Dick. In Pierre Melville's disillusion is
completed. Academic critics have praised Israel Potter, The
Piazza Tales, and The Confidence-Man, even calling them Melville's best work, because they find in them the familiar and
comforting traditional elements of belles lettres. But one "who
searches in literature for the vital and personal experience
struggling toward universal expression will conclude that none
of these merits detailed attention. The old fire is gone."

25   WATSON, ARTHUR C. "The Ship On Which Herman Melville Sailed."
     Shipmodeler, 3 (January), 255–256.
          Information about the Acushnet, with reproduction of an
     illustration of the ship recently discovered in a logbook at the
     Widener Library, Harvard.

26   BIRSS, JOHN H. "Melville's Marquesas." [Letter to the
     Editor.] Saturday Review of Literature, 8 (2 January), 429.
          Reprints passage referring to Melville in Lieut. Henry A.
     Wise's Los Gringos. [See 1849.B2.]

27   BIRSS, JOHN HOWARD. "A Letter of Herman Melville." Notes
     and Queries, 162 (16 January), 39.
          Prints Melville's 19 December 1851 letter "in response to
     an invitation to attend commemorative proceedings in honour of
     [James Fenimore] Cooper." [Misdates letter 20 February 1852;
     see Letters, pp. 144–145.] Notes that Melville's interest in
     Cooper's sea tales was more than passing: he reviewed The Red
     Rover and The Sea Lions for the Literary World and used a quota-
     tion from chapter 17 of The Pilot in the "Extracts" in Moby-Dick.

28   ANON. "Wilde Manuscripts Removed from Sale." New York Times
     (10 February), p. 21.
          Notes sale of sourcebook for Moby-Dick, Owen Chase's
     Narrative of the Most Extraordinary and Distressing Shipwreck of
     the Whaleship Essex, for $1675. "This first edition was printed

in London in 1821" and "bears an inscription by Melville on the
front flyleaf and contains other autograph material by the famous
writer."

29   BIRSS, JOHN H. and ROBERT S. FORSYTHE. "A Melville Bibliog-
      raphy." [Letter to the Editor.] Saturday Review of Litera-
      ture, 8 (13 February), 525.
          Authors announce their undertaking of a Melville bibliog-
      raphy, proposing "to describe all editions (including revisions
      and reprints) of Melville's books and tales published prior to
      his death, and to catalogue all subsequent reprints by title with
      an indication of the source of the text used," expecting also "to
      include a calendar of Melville letters, published and unpublished;
      a description of existing manuscripts of the novels and tales; a
      list of portraits of Melville; a catalogue of such books as we
      can learn Melville to have possessed; and a list (more or less
      selective) of critical articles upon Melville and his writings."
      Authors would welcome information on such matters, "particularly
      in respect to unpublished letters and the like." [See also
      1932.B31, B39.]

30   WINTERICH, JOHN T. "Abhorred Shears," in "The Compleat
      Collector." Saturday Review of Literature, 8 (13 February),
      531.
          Comments on 1901.B10, in particular Mrs. Melville's note
      about Clarel. Melville's "suppression of the edition" must "go
      far toward explaining the scarcity" of Clarel. Wonders: "How
      large was the edition, how many copies made up the withdrawn
      fraction, and how did Melville effect their annihilation?"
      Quotes from 1900.B6; Peter Toft was "one of the earliest and most
      devout of Melvilleites."

31   BIRSS, JOHN H. and ROBERT S. FORSYTHE. "Herman Melville:
      Projected Bibliography." Notes and Queries, 162 (20 February),
      137.
          The same letter as in 1932.B29.

32   M[ABBOTT], T.O. "Herman Melville." Notes and Queries, 162
      (27 February), 151–152.
          Prints Melville's 24 July 1846 letter to Dr. William
      Sprague [Letters, p. 42]; notes that it was Byron who "woke one
      morning and found himself famous."

33   AMENT, WILLIAM S. "Bowdler and the Whale: Some Notes on the
      first English and American Editions of Moby-Dick." American
      Literature, 4 (March), 39–46.
          Examination of the first American edition of Moby-Dick and
      the first English edition of The Whale shows that the American
      edition "comes nearest to embodying Melville's final judgment;
      but fails in as far as it shows inconsistencies and inaccuracies
      in textual detail." The English edition "is an uninspired
      revision of the proof of the American. Many of the corrections
      of details are improvements, but most of the major changes are a
      weakening or unwarranted Bowdlerization of Melville's highly

colored style." In addition to 37 omissions of a sentence or
more, there are approximately 150 omissions or changes of less
than a sentence in length, and innumerable changes in spelling,
punctuation, and style. Bentley's copyreader tried to system-
atize the somewhat irregular punctuation, to correct American or
accidental misspellings, and to omit crude or blasphemous passages, not hesitating to rewrite whole sentences. There are more
typographical errors in the English edition than in the American.
The "Epilogue," which appears only in the American edition, was
evidently an afterthought, appended after the last proofs had
been mailed to England. A standard text of Moby-Dick, edited
with judgment and care, should be established. Forsythe's sane
and consistent standardization of the text of Pierre [see
1930.B13] is a model for future editors.

34   ANON. "Our Authors." Golden Book Magazine, 15 (March),
     287-288.
         Biographical details, introductory to "Sketch Eighth:
Norfolk Isle and the Chola Widow," extracted (pp. 248-256) from
"The Encantadas," sketches that "are serene, yet endowed with
purest imaginative life"; the story of Hunilla "is a romantic
idyll, touching, terrible and lovely."

35   [DODGE, NORMAN L.]. The Month at Goodspeed's, 3 (March),
     218-220.
         Announces copy of Amasa Delano's Narrative of Voyages and
Travels for sale. Its Melville association [see 1928.B26] merely
adds interest and value to an interesting and valuable book in
its own right. "Benito Cereno" and "The Encantadas" more closely
approach the artistry of Moby-Dick than anything else Melville
ever wrote.

36   ANON. Notice of Pasteboard Masks, by Vega Curl. London Times
     Literary Supplement, No. 1574 (31 March), p. 231.
         Curl "discusses Hawthorne and Melville, distinguishing, in
a simple but orderly argument, between the spiritual values with
which each was preoccupied, and examining their methods of using
the physical symbolically." [See 1931.A1.]

37   ADKINS, NELSON F. "A Note on Herman Melville's Typee." New
     England Quarterly, 5 (April), 348-351.
         Reprints passage referring to Melville and the publication
of Typee in Thomas L. Nichols' Forty Years of American Life.
[See 1864.B1.] Gives details of Dr. Nichols.

38   BIRSS, JOHN HOWARD. "A Book Review by Herman Melville." New
     England Quarterly, 5 (April), 346-348.
         Reprints Melville's "A Thought on Book-Binding," an un-
signed review of James Fenimore Cooper's The Red Rover that was
printed in the New York Literary World, No. 163 (16 March 1850),
pp. 276-277. "While there is internal indication of his
[Melville's] authorship, it has been definitely ascertained to
be his composition, the holograph manuscript having been found
among the Duyckinck Papers of the New York Public Library. The

manuscript and printed versions have been collated and a few
errors silently corrected, so that the text here reprinted for
the first time is considered to be nearest Melville's original
intentions."

39   BIRSS, JOHN H. and ROBERT S. FORSYTHE. "Herman Melville."
      [Letter to the Editor.] London Times Literary Supplement,
      No. 1575 (7 April), p. 250.
          The same letter as in 1932.B29.

40   BIRSS, JOHN H. "A Book of Melville Interest." Notes and
      Queries, 162 (21 May), 368.
          Draws attention to Melville material in 1932.B18.

41   AMENT, WILLIAM S. "Some Americanisms in Moby Dick." American
      Speech, 7 (June), 365–367.
          Records differences in spelling, idiom, and grammar, and
      other verbal variances between the Harper edition of Moby-Dick
      (1851) and the Bentley edition of The Whale (1851); lists errors
      in both.

42   PARRY, ELSIE A. "When Literature Went to Sea: Taken by Those
      Three Immortal Mariners, Cooper, Dana, Melville." Bookman, 75
      (June and July), 243–248.
          Cooper, Dana, and Melville demonstrate, each in his indi-
      vidual fashion, the possibilities of the sea as an integral part
      of a sustained narrative, not as a mere background (as in earlier
      writers), but as a controlling factor in men's lives. They
      represent three outstanding tendencies in sea writing: the
      romance, pure and simple; the literary "logbook"; and the
      psychological study. The tremendous gap between Cooper and
      Melville is the difference between objective and subjective,
      between running narrative and profound analysis; between a
      sloven, confused style and one with the richness of the early
      seventeenth century. The progression from Cooper to Melville
      reflects the nineteenth-century tendency of the novel, charting
      the transition from the novel of incident to that concerned with
      the study of character and with the conflict between nature and
      man; it is the evolution from the simple and spontaneous to the
      complex and self-conscious. Two Years Before the Mast occupies
      a strategic middle ground between Cooper's sea novel and Moby-
      Dick, "partaking to some degree of the qualities of each." In
      Moby-Dick there is a pathetic element in the white whale, a kind
      of helpless hugeness in spite of his powers of destruction; one
      is inclined to pity him as one pities Satan.

43   BIRSS, JOHN HOWARD. "A Note on Melville's 'Mardi.'" Notes
      and Queries, 162 (4 June), 404.
          Finds probable source of Queen Hautia's name in Rev. Daniel
      E. Tyerman and George Bennet's Journal of Voyages and Travels,
      vol. 1, p. 145, where Hautia "is mentioned not as a queen, but as
      an actual 'princely personage,' who is prime minister to Queen
      Pomare of Tahiti." Melville, however, may have heard of the
      historical Hautia at the time of his visit to the court of Queen

Pomare. That he "used the name more appropriately for a feminine rather than a masculine character, attests his feeling for language." Like Swift's Gulliver's Travels, Mardi contains a number of unusual verbal coinages employed as names for persons and places.

44 HUGHES, RAYMOND. "Melville and Shakespeare." Shakespeare Association Bulletin, 7 (July), 103–112.
      Finds similarities between Moby-Dick and Shakespeare's tragedies "in thought, imagery, dialogue, grammar, idioms, and philosophy, implied and expressed." Table of "echoes."

45 HOMANS, GEORGE C. "The Dark Angel: The Tragedy of Herman Melville." New England Quarterly, 5 (October), 699–730.
      Sees Mardi, Moby-Dick, and Pierre as "unautobiographical" (though many of their scenes may be drawn from life, their sequence of incidents is fictional), but as dramatizations of Melville's spiritual life. The three works form a tragedy in three acts, each of them dramatizing Melville's pursuit of the Ultimate or search for the secret of the universe; his ignorance whether the heavenly or earthly side of his spirit, idealism or disease, is driving him forward in the search; and his failure to find the secret. Pierre "suggests the tragedy of introspection, of the mind turning on itself, the last phase of the quest for the Ultimate." In all three works, the refusal of the hero's mind "to admit its mortal limitations in its pursuit of the Ultimate, implies a denial of any force higher than itself, a denial of God."

46 BIRSS, JOHN H. "An Obscure Melville Letter." Notes and Queries, 163 (15 October), 275.
      Reprints Melville's 15 December 1863 letter to George McLaughlin [Letters, p. 219] from History of the Great Western Sanitary Fair (Cincinatti: C.F. Vent, 1864), pp. 187–188. Notes that the same volume records (p. 438) sale of Melville's 6 February 1854 letter to George P. Putnam [Letters, pp. 219n, 313]. In his letter to McLaughlin, Melville "was merely replying to one of many requests for autographs and manuscripts with which celebrities were besieged for charitable purposes during the Civil War."

47 DULLES, FOSTER RHEA. "Sea Adventure." Saturday Review of Literature, 9 (19 November), 257.
      Review of Charles Scribner & Sons edition of Mocha Dick, by J.N. Reynolds. "There is no reason to believe that Melville either derived his inspiration or took any material from the earlier tale. The white whale existed; he must often have heard of it. And by the whalemen who told the saga of this whale's exploits, he was known both as Moby Dick and Mocha Dick."

48   HALE, PHILLIP.   "Melville Censored."   Boston <u>Herald</u>
     (26 December).
          Remarks that George Paston's history of John Murray [<u>see</u>
     1932.B17] "throws a light on the curious prudery of the Victorian
     period shown towards books that to this generation seem blame-
     less."   Notes that some readers found <u>Typee</u> and <u>Omoo</u> offensive
     and that <u>Typee</u> was "censored" for a revised edition.

1933 A BOOKS--NONE

1933 B SHORTER WRITINGS

1   ADAMS, JAMES TRUSLOW.   <u>From Civil War to World Power</u>.   Vol. 2
     of <u>The March of Democracy</u>.   New York: Charles Scribner's
     Sons, pp. 90–92.
          The civil war left a comparatively scant literary legacy.
     Melville's war poems are far below the level of his best work.

2   BENNETT, ARNOLD.   <u>The Journal of Arnold Bennett, 1896–1928</u>.
     New York: The Viking Press, pp. 862, 877, 882.
          Entry for 28 March 1926:   "After tea we went to the film
     <u>The Sea Beast</u> at the New Gallery; the idea being taken and
     slaughtered from <u>Moby Dick</u>.   A filthy and preposterous thing and
     humiliating to watch.   John Barrymore the chief interpreter.   A
     dreadful Hollywood girl as the heroine; obviously chosen for her
     looks, which were dreadful.   This film really did annoy me.   We
     didn't see it all."   Entry for 2 June 1926:   "I had ordered the
     complete works of Herman Melville on Monday.   They arrived
     yesterday in three large parcels, of which I only opened two,
     because I didn't want to begin reading <u>Pierre</u> (which was in the
     third parcel) immediately--not until I had assimilated <u>An Ameri-
     can Tragedy</u> a bit."   Entry for 27 June 1926:   "I finished reading
     <u>Pierre</u>.   This novel is not equal to <u>Moby Dick</u>; but it is full of
     very fine things, and a most remarkable book.   Melville's idea
     was the grand romantic manner, and when he succeeded in it, he
     <u>did</u> succeed.   His humour too is very rich.   I think he must have
     been influenced by Rabelais, though there is nothing Rabelaisian
     in the book.   The pity is he gets so many incidents improbable,
     when with a little more invention and trouble he might have made
     them quite probable.   Nevertheless, I think it is entitled to be
     called a great book--even if manqué here and there."

3   BOAS, RALPH PHILLIP and KATHERINE BURTON.   <u>Social Backgrounds
     of American Literature</u>.   Boston: Little, Brown, and Co.,
     pp. 105–106.
          Unrecognized in its day, <u>Moby-Dick</u> is now valued as the
     best record of the whaling ships that sailed from Nantucket.

4   BREWER, R.A. Six Hundred American Books Worth Money.
     Detroit: Rare Book Information Bureau, p. 17.
        Lists prices for first American editions of Melville's
     books: Typee ($75); Omoo ($75); Mardi ($65); Redburn ($85);
     White-Jacket ($65); Moby-Dick ($750); Pierre ($85); Israel
     Potter ($25); The Piazza Tales ($75); The Confidence-Man ($35);
     Battle-Pieces ($45); Clarel ($400). "The values given are
     the prices, as closely as can be estimated after consulting
     auction records and dealers' offerings, paid at retail by book
     collectors for the various items."

5   BRIGGS, THOMAS H., MAX J. HERZBERG, and EMMA MILLER BOLENIUS,
     eds. American Literature. Literature in the Senior High
     School. Boston: Houghton Mifflin Co., pp. 645–646.
        Brief comments on Moby-Dick. Prints (pp. 224–242) chap-
     ters 133–135 from Moby-Dick.

6   B[ROOKS], V[AN] W[YCK]. "Melville, Herman," in Dictionary of
     American Biography. Vol. 12. Ed. Dumas Malone. New York:
     Charles Scribner's Sons, pp. 522–526.
        Mainly biographical. Moby-Dick will undoubtedly continue
     to be regarded as Melville's masterpiece, "but all of his books
     published before his thirty-third year are sterling contributions
     to literature, notable for their clear, firm, classical style,
     their gusto, their vivid portraiture and their wealth of keen-
     eyed and well-organized observations." In Typee and Omoo
     Melville may be considered in some respects a disciple of
     Rousseau, for no one ever glorified more the natural, primitive,
     man. Mardi has many chapters of ethereal beauty, many pages of
     profound speculation, and two or three characters that are highly
     successful as grotesque portraits. The story in Moby-Dick would
     flow with more consistency if many of the whaling sections were
     omitted, for Melville's sense of form was very defective; but
     there is not a page of the book that is not richly rewarding.
     After Moby-Dick Melville's talent passed into a sort of eclipse
     that never resulted in actual extinction, though The Confidence-
     Man virtually touches the limit of absolute incomprehensibility.
     The love story in Pierre is fantastic and improbable, but the
     pages dealing with the struggles of the writer's soul have a
     splendid passion and veracity, equal to those of Moby-Dick. Most
     of Melville's verse is undistinguished. Billy Budd is based on
     the character of Jack Chase. Short bibliography of Melville
     studies.

7   DRIVER, LEOTA S. Fanny Kemble. Chapel Hill: University of
     North Carolina Press, p. 163.
        Notes that Melville lived several miles away from Kemble's
     cottage at Lenox while he was writing Moby-Dick and that some
     enthusiasts "claimed that Fanny made her first attempt as a
     Shakespearean reader with Catherine Sedgwick, Melville,
     Longfellow, and Hawthorne in her audience."

8 DULLES, FOSTER RHEA. <u>Lowered Boats: A Chronicle of American</u>
   <u>Whaling</u>. New York: Harcourt, Brace and Co., passim.
        References to and quotations from <u>Moby-Dick</u>; Melville used
   as an authority.

9 EDGAR, PELHAM. "Herman Melville and <u>Moby-Dick</u>," in <u>The Art of</u>
   <u>the Novel; From 1700 to the Present Time</u>. New York: The
   Macmillan Co., pp. 130–135.
        Notes much humor amidst Melville's seriousness and poetry.
   Ahab has a maniacal ferocity that has had no counterpart in literature since Lear stormed upon the heath. In his decay (after
   <u>Moby-Dick</u>), as in his development, there is something strangely
   abnormal about Melville. Though his mind kept its power, it had
   lost its tone. "Something between Hamlet's melancholy and
   Timon's misanthropy made expression savorless for him to the
   end." He had failed to find his spiritual bearings. Women in
   his books are almost ciphers, existing to whet his dissatisfac-
   tion; and there are no currents of sympathy cementing his men,
   nor even currents of hate to divide them. In <u>Moby-Dick</u> a
   dehumanized hate and defiance are pitted against an implacable
   impersonal malignity; there is no room for normal contacts. Biographical sketch and bibliography (pp. 440–442).

10 HAZLITT, HENRY. <u>The Anatomy of Criticism: A Trialogue</u>. New
    York: Simon and Schuster, pp. 52–53, 135.
        Young to Elder: "The function of the interpretative critic
    is not always to clarify mysteries; it is often to show that
    there is a mystery behind what was previously supposed to be
    clear. Two generations failed to understand 'Moby Dick' pre-
    cisely because they were sure they did understand it. To them
    it was only a sea story, a romance of whaling. It was not until
    critics saw that the huge white whale was not merely a white
    whale, but a symbol of Nature, or of the principle of evil, or
    what you will, that the greatness of 'Moby Dick' was recog-
    nized."
        Middleton to Elder: "When posterity does 'discover' an
    author, it is usually because he has previously had at least
    enough reputation to keep his books alive, and then later critics
    are able to raise him to a higher level in esteem. None of
    Melville's contemporaries, for example, realized that 'Moby Dick'
    was a great epic and a profound allegory, but many of them
    thought it a very good sea story for boys, and that modest
    reputation carried it along. If it had not been for that, it
    might have gone completely out of print, and there would have
    been nothing for later critics to 'discover.'"

11 HICKS, GRANVILLE. <u>The Great Tradition: An Interpretation of</u>
    <u>American Literature Since the Civil War</u>. New York: The
    Macmillan Co., pp. 7–8, passim.
        Melville did not state his preoccupation with the nature
    of evil and the mysteries of life and death in terms of contem-
    porary society. <u>Moby-Dick</u> failed to impress and influence the
    generation after the war because then men were wrestling with
    the problem of evil as it presented itself in concrete economic

phenomena. The terms in which Melville stated the problem were irrelevant. "This explains, in part, why Moby Dick, with all its virtues, is not comparable to the great metaphysical epics of the past, which have made room for all the principal varieties of experience in their eras."

12   LAING, ALEXANDER. "A Foreword Which Comes Last," in The Sea Witch. New York: Farrar & Rinehart; London: Thornton Butterworth, p. 486.
        Believes that Melville "would have written a great novel of the clipper ships, had public repudiation not caused him to fall silent at the very hour when he was turning from reminiscence of his adventurous youth to evaluate the world about him." In The Sea Witch Laing has tried "to evolve out of old records and imagination something of that pageant" that Melville "saw when he sailed the long sea road to California as a passenger in the clipper ship Meteor. . . ."

13   McDOWELL, TREMAINE. "The Romantic Triumph," in The Romantic Triumph: American Literature from 1830 to 1860. Ed. Tremaine McDowell. Vol. 2 of American Literature: A Period Anthology. Ed. Oscar Cargill. New York: The Macmillan Co., pp. 1–8, passim.
        Notes that Melville "burlesqued the rant and bombast of professional patriots" and "ventured into the realms of the anti-religious," even daring "to suggest that there are fallacies in world-faiths, including Christianity." Biographical sketch in "Notes," p. 727. Prints (pp. 377–416) extracts from Typee, chapters 18 and 32; Mardi, chapters 112, 113, 145, and 158; and Moby-Dick, chapters 40, and 133–135.

14   MILLER, EDWIN L. "Herman Melville (1819–1891)," in Explorations in Literature: American Writers. Philadelphia: J.B. Lippincott Co., pp. 215–216.
        Biographical sketch. Brief extracts (pp. 216–223) from Moby-Dick, chapters 1–3, 5–7, 9, 14, 17, 25, 29, 34, 48, 54, 60, 73–74, 81, 104, 135.

15   MILLER, LEON. American First Editions: Their Points and Prices. Kansas City: The Westport Press, pp. 57–58.
        Lists American first editions of Melville's books, noting bibliographical points and recent prices.

16   NEWTON, A. EDWARD. End Papers: Literary Recreations. Boston: Little, Brown and Co., pp. 25–26, 78, 197.
        Reprints Melville material in 1931.B38, slightly revised.

17   STARKE, AUBREY HARRISON. Sidney Lanier: A Biographical and Critical Study. Chapel Hill: University of North Carolina Press, pp. 318, 401.
        Nowhere in American literature "has orthodoxy been more severely trounced" than in Lanier's "Remonstrance"--"unless it be in the prose of Emerson and Melville." Lanier rebelled "as

strongly as Melville against the narrowness of Calvinistic theology and the complacent mediocrity of contemporary Christian practice."

18   VAN DOREN, CARL. American Literature: An Introduction. Westwood Village, Los Angeles: U.S. Library Association, pp. 48–53.

Though Melville might deal with other matters in his later books, "his mind was most at home when he turned it loose in the larger America which carried its frontiers with it on board its ships." In Moby-Dick, Ahab is the Yankee Lucifer, questing for a black grail. "The book was no more confused and turbulent than its age. That the age did not recognize its face in the mirror Melville held up means that America did not know what its face was like. For in Moby Dick a human will as reckless as America's fought a nature so defiant that it might be thought malignant, and fought it not in the quiet of thought but in the whirlwind and thunder of affairs."

19   WILLIAMS, STANLEY T. American Literature. Philadelphia and London: J.B. Lippincott & Co., pp. 90–93.

Brief survey. Melville's paramount intellectual worth is in his courage as he faces the age-old puzzles of life. His symbolism, as in the white whale standing for the malignity of nature, forces us, savagely, uncompromisingly, into considerations of problems more dear to Russian than to American literature. After Pierre his work betrayed slackening powers; both style and content fell under the spell of his abstruse speculations and his pessimism.

20   LEISY, ERNEST E. and JAY B. HUBBELL. "Doctoral Dissertations in American Literature." American Literature, 4 (January), 457.

Lists five Melville dissertations in progress.

21   COUCH, H.N. "Moby Dick and The Phaedo." Classical Journal, 28 (February), 367–368.

The comparison of men to "oysters observing the sun through the water, and thinking that thick water the thinnest of air" in Moby-Dick, chapter 7, was probably reproduced unconsciously from a passage in Plato's Phaedo.

22   KILHAM, LAWRENCE. "Ishmael in Revolt." Harvard Advocate, 119 (March), 12–16.

Focuses on Mardi and Pierre, which both represent a climax or turning point in Melville's emotional development. The idea of a quest for something indescribable is essential to an understanding of his work. His final cessation from authorship need not mean that he was defeated by the harsh realities of his generation, as critics have claimed: the "brooding pessimism of his soul resembled a sense of futility which comes to all men who attempt to grapple with the Infinite when restricted by the limitations of a finite mind." In Mardi everything seems transitory and futile; the idea of Fate was penetrating Melville's

mind. The ideas in the chapter on Serenia are similar to those
in the "Divinity School Address"; Melville was approaching
Emerson's doctrine that Christ's teaching should enable us to
find the Godlike within ourselves. As a psychological book
Pierre has never been, and probably never will be, adequately
criticized. Melville was one of the first American writers to
explain the activities of the mind in terms other than good and
evil, and to approach the more scientific conceptions of modern
thought. The defeat of Pierre was a demonstration of the in-
sufficiency of moral codes. Civilization and philosophy had
accomplished nothing. With publication of Pierre Melville was
probably glad to rid himself of his reading public, feeling that
he thereby added to his liberty.

23   BIRSS, JOHN HOWARD. "'Moby-Dick' Under Another Name." Notes
      and Queries, 164 (25 March), 206.
            Notes the influence of Moby-Dick on Péhe-Nú-e, The Tiger
      Whale of the Pacific by Captain Bill Barnacle [Charles Martin
      Newell] (Boston: D. Lathrop and Co., 1877). The Grolier Club
      sale catalogue of December 1911 stated that the book was "really
      'Moby-Dick' under a new name." Little attention has been given
      to Melville's influence on other writers.

24   BIRSS, JOHN HOWARD. "Whitman and Herman Melville." Notes and
      Queries, 164 (22 April), 280.
            Reprints review of Omoo in Brooklyn Daily Eagle, 5 May 1847
      [1847.B31], attributing it to Walt Whitman. Composed quite
      probably as a hurried and unrevised piece of paragraphing, it is
      not to be read as a well-considered judgment, though it shows to
      some extent Whitman's ability to form spontaneous and incisive
      critical opinion.

25   ANON. "Title-Page Proof of Next Colophon Imprint Stolen by
      Crier." Colophon Crier (June), n.p.
            Prepublication notice of Raymond Weaver's edition of
      Melville's Journal Up the Straits. [See 1935.B14.] "Any
      Melville journal or informal notebook ought to be mighty exciting
      reading. If Weaver is in on this, it ought to carry a double
      thrill. For from his introduction it may be possible to see how
      some of the material in the Journal actually found its way into
      later work." [See 1933.B28 and 1934.B21.]

26   WATSON, E.L. GRANT. "Melville's Testament of Acceptance."
      New England Quarterly, 6 (June), 319-327.
            Though it lacks the fine extravagance in style of the
      earlier books, Billy Budd is as rich, or even richer, in
      Melville's peculiar and elaborate symbolism, which becomes all
      the more effective for being presented in a dry and objective
      manner. Melville's ambitious purpose is "to portray those
      ambiguities of good and evil as the mutually dependent opposites,
      between which the world of realization finds its being." His
      philosophy has grown from rebellion to acceptance; the book's
      ending is very different from "the despairing acts of dissolu-
      tion" that mark the conclusions of Mardi, Moby-Dick, and

Pierre. Like Pontius Pilate, Vere "condemns the just man to a shameful death, knowing him to be innocent, but, unlike Pilate, he does not wash his hands, but manfully assumes the full responsibility, and in such a way as to take the half, if not more than the half, of the bitterness of the execution upon himself." At the moment of execution one feels that the souls of Vere and Billy are strangely one. In *Pierre* Melville discovered all the major complexes, peered as deep as any into the origins of sensuality; in *Billy Budd*, "from far behind the main pageant of the story," there "seem to fall suggestive shadows of primal, sexual simplicities." Problems almost as profound as those that puzzle us in the gospels are to be discovered in this work. Reprinted in part in Stafford, pp. 74-78; reprinted in Springer, pp. 12-17, and in Vincent (1971), pp. 11-16.

27   MENARD, WILMON. "A Forgotten South Sea Paradise." *Asia*, 33 (September-October), 459.
    Notes contrast between Typee past and present, remembering Melville's *Typee*. "A sense of desolation took possession of me as I rode on horseback through this beautiful valley, which is nine miles long, and felt its utter loneliness grow upon me. On all sides I could see the wreckage of paepaes which had been the foundations of the homes of the clan of Typee. . . . Once three thousand persons lived in this vale; now there were seven or eight."

28   ANON. "Melville Journal Progressing." *Colophon Crier* (October), n.p.
    Prepublication notice of Raymond Weaver's edition of Melville's *Journal Up The Straits*. [See 1935.B14.] Weaver's introduction and edited text have been delivered to the publishers. [See 1933.B25 and 1934.B21.]

29   ANON. "New Novels." *London Times Literary Supplement*, No. 1662 (7 December), p. 874.
    Review of *The Sea Witch* by Alexander Laing. [See 1933.B12.] Laing's "experiment has been on the whole a successful one, though Melville has been rather too obviously in his mind throughout. The imprint of the older writer's influence is evident in more ways than one, more particularly in the long monologues in which so many of the characters are given to indulging and the tendency to mystical disquisitions on the part of some of his sailormen on such things as the 'oversoul' and 'the atomics of Epicurus.'"

30   ANON. "$18,413 Paid for Books." New York *Times* (8 December).
    At auction Dr. A.S.W. Rosenbach "paid $475 for the dedication copy of Herman Melville's 'Omoo' with the presentation inscription by the author to his uncle."

31   BIRSS, JOHN HOWARD. "A Satire on Melville in Verse." *Notes and Queries*, 165 (9 December), 402.
    Reprints verses on Melville in 1855.B4; notes that an allusion to Paul Jones in the verses is to Melville's portrayal of him in *Israel Potter*.

1934 A BOOKS--NONE

1934 B SHORTER WRITINGS

1   BAKER, ERNEST A.   The Novel of Sentiment and the Gothic
    Romance. Vol. 5 of The History of the English Novel.
    London: H.F. & G. Witherby, pp. 5, 213.
        Novelists such as Poe, Hawthorne, Melville, and Henry James
    "have definitely contributed to the development of the English
    novel." Charles Brockden Brown (rude though his achievements
    were) was "the precursor of those American novelists, Poe,
    Hawthorne, Oliver Wendell Holmes, Herman Melville, Henry James,
    who were to explore strange mental cases with a more scientific
    or at least a surer understanding, often with effects upon the
    reader very similar to those produced by the novels of terror."
    Wieland gives "a glimpse of that kingdom of evil pitted against
    mankind whose terrors were to be so powerfully set forth by
    Melville in Moby Dick."

2   BOAS, RALPH P. and EDWIN SMITH. Enjoyment of Literature. New
    York: Harcourt, Brace and Co., p. 218.
        Notes that Cooper's Indians, Scott's knights, and Melville's
    whales have come to be more real to readers than their actual
    prototypes.

3   BRANCH, E. DOUGLAS. The Sentimental Years, 1836-1860. New
    York and London: D. Appleton-Century Co., p. 111.
        Mention in passages on the finances of writers: "Irving,
    in the Forties, got only a thousand dollars a year from his
    publisher. Emerson had a private income and his lecture fees.
    Hawthorne was barely sustained by a government appointment; Poe
    and Melville sought vainly for a like answer to the economic
    problem; Thoreau succeeded in managing his life so that his lack
    of money didn't matter."

4   COLE, ARTHUR CHARLES. The Irrepressible Conflict, 1850-1865.
    Vol. 7 of A History of American Life. Ed. Arthur M.
    Schlesinger and Dixon Ryan Fox. New York: The Macmillan
    Co., p. 220.
        A section on American literature in the 1850s refers to
    Melville as "a writer who stood aloof from the charmed circles
    of the New England intellectuals"; notes the "power and realism"
    of Ahab's pursuit of the white whale.

5   DAKIN, WILLIAM JOHN. Whalemen Adventurers: The Story of
    Whaling in Australian Waters and Other Southern Seas Related
    Thereto, From the Days of Sails to Modern Times. Sydney:
    Angus & Robertson, passim.
        References to and quotations from Moby-Dick; Melville used
    as an authority.

6　FINGER, CHARLES J. <u>After the Great Companions: A Free Fantasia on a Lifetime of Reading</u>. New York: E.P. Dutton & Co., pp. 256–258.

　　Brief comments on <u>Typee</u>, <u>Omoo</u>, and <u>Moby-Dick</u>. Finds in Melville "the geniality of a good seaman . . . of all out-of-door men," the "fullness of a man who says, 'Now I shall be generous and particular, missing nothing, harboring no curmudgeon spirit. There's a friendliness in leisureliness.'" Melville, "like Dana, and Marryat, and Dickens and Hudson, was not a book-man, but a real-life man."

7　HALLECK, REUBEN POST. "Herman Melville, 1819–1891," in <u>The Romance of American Literature</u>. New York: American Book Co., pp. 149–158.

　　High school textbook survey. Sees <u>Moby-Dick</u> as "an epic, not a novel," and, like <u>Paradise Lost</u>, "an epic of fighting against evil"; Moby Dick, the personification of "intelligent malignity," takes the place of Milton's Satan. <u>Pierre</u> "is an unpleasant psychological puzzle, popular with the few who love to risk making mistakes in trying to trace unpleasant thoughts to their supposed subconscious sources."

8　LOVETTE, LIEUTENANT COMMANDER LELAND P. <u>Naval Customs: Traditions and Usage</u>. Annapolis, Md.: United States Naval Institute, passim.

　　References to and quotations from <u>White-Jacket</u>. Melville used as an authority.

9　RYDER, ALICE AUSTIN. <u>Lands of Sippican, on Buzzards Bay</u>. New Bedford, Mass.: Reynolds Printing, pp. 115, 127–128.

　　Brief references to <u>Moby-Dick</u>.

10　STEWART, POWELL and MICHAEL BRADSHAW, JR. <u>A Goodly Company: A Guide to Parallel Reading</u>. New York: American Book Co., pp. 17–18.

　　Synopsis of <u>Moby-Dick</u>, which, "although not so exciting or romantic as the motion picture of the same name, will prove interesting to many, especially if read in the edition illustrated by Rockwell Kent." The white whale becomes the incarnation of evil.

11　SWINNERTON, FRANK. <u>The Georgian Scene: A Literary Panorama</u>. New York: Farrar & Rinehart, p. 155.

　　Notes that Conrad lacked Melville's apocalyptic grandeur, but also lacked Melville's fustian.

12　TOMLINSON, H.M. <u>South to Cadiz</u>. London: William Heinemann, pp. 224, 227–228.

　　Brief references to <u>Moby-Dick</u>. Melville went to sea in a whaler "as a way of escape from a reality he found irksome, and so enlarged his apprehension of Reality, the bounds of which are lost in mystery, as we see in <u>Moby Dick</u>." The humor in chapter 1 is "extravagantly sad," yet there is truth in Melville's "wild fun."

13   TOWNSEND, HARVEY GATES. <u>Philosophical Ideas in the United</u>
      <u>States</u>. New York: American Book Co., pp. 132–133.
            Mention: "Transcendentalism as a cultural episode in our
      history was largely an affair of the pulpit and the lecture plat-
      form. Its sources were literary rather than learned; its expres-
      sion was rhetorical. Of the literary figures, Herman Melville
      stands almost alone to represent a native tough-mindness."

14   UNTERMEYER, LOUIS and CARTER DAVIDSON. <u>Poetry: Its Apprecia-</u>
      <u>tion and Enjoyment</u>. New York: Harcourt, Brace and Co.,
      pp. 17–19, 64.
            Quotes passage from next to last paragraph in chapter 9 of
      <u>Moby-Dick</u> and a passage from Carlyle's <u>Sartor Resartus</u>; it would
      take little effort to rearrange the two passages into the line
      patterns of free verse. Melville's "realistic picture of life in
      the South Seas appeared highly romantic to New York and Boston."

15   VAN PATTEN, NATHAN. "Melville, Herman, 1819-1891," in <u>An</u>
      <u>Index to Bibliographies and Bibliographical Contributions,</u>
      <u>Relating to the Work of American and British Authors, 1923-</u>
      <u>1932</u>. Stanford, Ca.: Stanford University Press; London:
      Humphrey Milford, Oxford University Press, pp. 172–174.
            An index of Melville bibliographies and bibliographical
      contributions to the study of Melville.

16   WEEKLEY, MONTAGUE. <u>William Morris</u>. Great Lives. London:
      Duckworth, p. 85.
            Rates Morris's <u>Sigurd</u> as "a superb and unique achievement
      in modern literature" and <u>Moby-Dick</u> the one work of the nine-
      teenth century in any way comparable to it. Reminded of the
      final scene of <u>Moby-Dick</u> by the ending of <u>Sigurd</u>.

17   WHARTON, EDITH. <u>A Backward Glance</u>. New York and London:
      D. Appleton-Century Co., p. 68.
            Mention: "my parents and their group, though they held
      literature in great esteem, stood in nervous dread of those who
      produced it. Washington Irving, Fitz-Greene Halleck and William
      Dana were the only representatives of the disquieting art who
      were deemed uncontaminated by it; though Longfellow, they ad-
      mitted, if a popular poet, was nevertheless a gentleman. As for
      Herman Melville, a cousin of the Van Rensselaers, and qualified
      by birth to figure in the best society, he was doubtless excluded
      from it by his deplorable Bohemianism, for I never heard his name
      mentioned, or saw one of his books. Banished probably for the
      same reasons were Poe, that drunken and demoralized Baltimorean,
      and the brilliant wastrel Fitz James O'Brien, who was still
      further debased by 'writing for the newspapers.'"

18   BRASWELL, WILLIAM. "A Note on 'The Anatomy of Melville's
      Fame.'" <u>American Literature</u>, 5 (January), 360-364.
            Finds inaccuracies and exaggerations in Riegel's study of
      Melville's reputation. [<u>See</u> 1931.B32.] "The study of the re-
      views was not comprehensive and judicial, the motives of the
      reviewers were not sufficiently taken into account, and the

career of Melville's works in the commercial world was not considered." It is doubtful that there were as many revivals of
interest in Melville's work as Riegel claims. Riegel undervalues
the work of English critics throughout.

19   STEWART, RANDALL. "Hawthorne's Contributions to The Salem
      Advertiser." American Literature, 5 (January), 328–329.
          Reprints 1846.B19, with brief annotations.

20   BIRSS, JOHN HOWARD. "Herman Melville Lectures in Yonkers."
      American Book Collector, 5 (February), 50–52.
          Reprints 1858.B39, with brief commentary.

21   ANON. "Melville Journal Progressing." Colophon Crier
      (March), n.p.
          Prepublication notice of Raymond Weaver's edition of
      Melville's Journal Up the Straits [see 1935.B14], for which all
      the material has now been turned over to the printer. The book
      will constitute an important piece of Americana and will be a
      distinguished example of the typographer's and bookmaker's art.
      [See 1933.B25, B28.]

22   WEST, GEOFFREY. "William Morris—Man Creative: An Estimate
      of his Significance Today." Bookman, 85 (March), 472.
          Morris's view of art carries no metaphysical implications;
      hence Weekley's comparison of "Sigurd the Volsung" with Moby-Dick
      is fundamentally wrong: they are not in the same category. [See
      1934.B16.] Melville's is an esoteric work; there is little eso-
      tericism in Morris's productions, which are "straightforward in
      the best sense."

23   W., R.N. "October Mountains" [in "Queries and Answers"].
      New York Times Book Review (4 March), p. 27.
          "R.N.W. Wants to find 'October Mountains' (prose) by Herman
      Melville." (Complete item.) [See 1950.B65.]

24   LARRABEE, HAROLD A. "Herman Melville's Early Years in
      Albany." New York History, 15 (April), 144–159.
          History of Gansevoort family and account of economic con-
      ditions in Albany in the 1830s. By "dashing his boyish hopes
      and frustrating his earliest ambitions," Melville's economic
      hardships in Albany "struck the keynote of disaster which was to
      re-echo throughout his later life. What they supplied was the
      first, and in many ways the most crushing, of a series of re-
      fusals, the cumulative effect of which was to range him among the
      darker figures of American literature."

25   HOWARD, LEON. "A Predecessor of Moby-Dick." Modern Language
      Notes, 49 (May), 310–311.
          Joseph C. Hart's anonymous Miriam Coffin, or the Whale-
      Fisherman (New York, 1834) possibly helped form the plot of
      Moby-Dick. In Hart's book, "the account of a whaling voyage is
      brought to a sudden conclusion by the dramatic sinking of a ship
      by an unusually large whale," and "the drama of the event is

intensified by coupling it with the fulfillment of a prophecy."
(Thomas Starbuck sails on the Leviathan despite the prophecy of
a half-breed squaw that he is to die in a whale's jaws.)

26   BIRSS, JOHN H. "Herman Melville and Blake." Notes and
      Queries, 166 (5 May), 311.
          Birss recently located a first edition of Alexander
Gilchrist's Life of William Blake (1863), with Melville's signa-
ture and the date "June 4, '70." (Mumford [1929.A1], p. 335,
states that "Melville did not know Blake until 1874 at earliest.")
Suspects Blake's influence in Clarel and the verse that followed
later. Thinks it probable that Melville did not know Blake at
the time of writing Moby-Dick, for few in England, and fewer in
America, were acquainted with Blake as a poet in 1851.

27   LEWIS, JOSEPH WARD. "Berkshire Men of Worth." Pittsfield
      (Mass.) Berkshire County Eagle (18 July), p. 12.
          Biographical sketch, occasioned by the death of Hattie L.
Hawley [see 1924.B8] and the sale of Arrowhead to Madelaine
Cutting Hibbs [see 1927.B26 and 1937.B36]. Reports that
Melville's writings "are today among best sellers in the libraries
of classics."

28   BIRSS, JOHN H. "Herman Melville and the Atlantic Monthly."
      Notes and Queries, 167 (29 September), 223–224.
          Reprints Melville letter of 19 August 1857 from 1907.B9
[Letters, pp. 187–188], with introductory note.

29   BIRSS, JOHN HOWARD. "'Travelling': A New Lecture by Herman
      Melville." New England Quarterly, 7 (December), 725–728.
          Reprints what "appears to be a faithful digest" of Mel-
ville's lecture on "Travelling" from the Cambridge (Mass.)
Chronicle, 25 February 1860. [See 1860.B2.]

1935 A BOOKS

1   ANON. Prospectus of a Hitherto Unpublished Work by Herman
      Melville, Journal up the Straits, Now to be Published by the
      Colophon. New York: The Colophon, 14 pp.
          Mainly about the manuscript journal, which Weaver, "after
fifteen years of trial, error, and persistence, and with the
generous co-operation of specialists and friends," has transcribed and edited. Includes account by Weaver (pp. 7–13) of the
difficulties of the transcription. [See 1935.B14.]

1935 B SHORTER WRITINGS

1   ANON. "Melville, Herman," in The Columbia Encyclopedia. Ed.
      Clarke F. Ansley. Morningside Heights, N.Y.: Columbia Uni-
      versity Press, p. 1150.
          Biographical sketch. Notes that Moby-Dick is considered
Melville's masterpiece and that "Benito Cereno" has been included
in a list of the world's great short stories. [See 1928.B25 and
1931.B14.]

2   BENNETT, HENRY GARLAND. "The Romantic Period," in American
     Literature. New York: American Book Co., pp. 574-575.
        Anthology containing no Melville selection, but comments
on Moby-Dick. Moby-Dick "is thoroughly symbolic of man's brave
insignificance and the world's hugeness and mystery. . . . A confused, teeming book, majestic in its conceptions, it is one of
the classics of our literature . . . ."

3   BLACKMUR, R.P. "The Method of Marianne Moore," in The Double
     Agent: Essays in Craft and Elucidation. New York: Arrow
     Editions, p. 171.
        Mention: "It is provisionally worth noting that Miss Moore
is not alone but characteristic in American literature. Poe,
Hawthorne, Melville (in Pierre), Emily Dickinson, and Henry James,
all--like Miss Moore--shared an excessive sophistication of surfaces and a passionate predilection for the genuine--though Poe
was perhaps not interested in too much of the genuine; and all
contrived to present the conviction of reality best by making it,
in most readers' eyes, remote."

4   BREWER, REGINALD. The Delightful Diversion: The Whys and
     Wherefores of Book Collecting. New York: The Macmillan Co.,
     pp. 152, 292.
        Average prices of American first editions of Typee ($75),
Omoo ($75), Mardi ($65), Redburn ($85), White-Jacket ($65),
Moby-Dick ($750), Pierre ($85), Israel Potter ($25), The Piazza
Tales ($75), The Confidence-Man ($35), Battle-Pieces ($45),
Clarel ($400).

5   FREAR, WALTER F. Anti-Missionary Criticism, With Reference to
     Hawaii. Honolulu: Advertiser Publishing Co., pp. 3, 25-28.
        Claims that Melville grossly mispresented nearly every
phase of the Paulet episode in his appendix to Typee and that he
had an "innate inaptitude to investigate and weight facts."

6   GIBBINGS, ROBERT. "Introduction," in Narratives of the Wreck
     of the Whale-Ship Essex. London: Golden Cockerel Press,
     pp. 5-6.
        There can be "no doubt" that the story of the Essex "sup-
plied not only the original idea" for Moby-Dick, "but in addition
was drawn upon, in places almost word for word, for much of the
local colour" in the final chapter. The "intelligent malignity"
of Moby Dick is similar to the "malevolent premeditation" of the
whale Chase (first mate of the Essex) describes. The details of
the attack are also similar. Prints narratives by Owen Chase,
Thomas Chappel, second mate, and George Pollard, captain, of the
Essex.

7   HATCHER, HARLAN. Creating the Modern American Novel. New
     York: Farrar & Rinehart, p. 3.
        Mention: "Very little American fiction of the last century
has any life left in it. Hawthorne's The Scarlet Letter (1850),
despite its spare psychological dimensions and a point of view
toward a familiar material seldom shared by modern people, still

lives because of the perfection of its superb and living art.
Melville's <u>Moby-Dick</u> (1851) must be placed in the present century
where in spirit it really belongs and where it was first discovered. After we have mentioned these two memorable novels,
after we have acknowledged a mild interest in the pale contempo-
raneity of the earlier novels of Henry James and William Dean
Howells, and after we have declared with the authority of personal experience shared by everyone wlse that <u>Huckleberry Finn</u>
(1884) is a classic, we are confronted by the interesting fact
that American fiction of scope and distinction began with the
close of the last century."

8   HEMINGWAY, ERNEST. <u>Green Hills of Africa</u>. New York: Charles
     Scribner's Sons, p. 20.
        Mentions Melville in discussion of American writers: "we
have had, in America, skillful writers. Poe is a skillful
writer. It is skillful, marvelously constructed, and it is dead.
We have had writers of rhetoric who had the good fortune to find
a little, in a chronicle of another man and from voyaging, of how
things, actual things, can be, whales for instance, and this
knowledge is wrapped in the rhetoric like plums in a pudding.
Occasionally it is there, alone, unwrapped in pudding, and it is
good. This is Melville. But the people who praise it, praise it
for the rhetoric which is not important. They put a mystery in
which is not there."

9   JONES, HOWARD MUMFORD and ERNEST E. LEISY. "Herman Melville,
     1819-1891," in <u>Major American Writers</u>. New York: Harcourt,
     Brace and Co., pp. 1055-1057.
        Headnote to "Benito Cereno," pp. 1058-1116; text reprinted
from <u>The Piazza Tales</u>, with the "most important changes in substance" from the Putnam's text indicated in the footnotes. Includes chronology of Melville's life. To the nineteenth century
Melville was largely the teller of sea tales--an American rival
of Captain Marryat; to the twentieth he has become "the epitome
of the bitter fate of the artist under the industrial régime.
Pursuing this interpretation, critics have read into his novels
symbolic meanings which are perhaps not always intended; and,
fortified by large draughts of Freudian psychology, have developed what amounts to a Melville legend." The nineteenth century
overlooked the larger philosophical implications of works like
<u>Moby-Dick</u> and <u>Mardi</u>, and the twentieth, "intent upon reading its
own significances into these tales, has tended to overlook, minimize, or excuse the grave artistic blemishes (especially in point
of style) of Melville's novels." Like Borrow's, Melville's books
are neither fact nor fiction but a middle term between the two.
"His romances are a vast confession, but a confession veiled in
both deliberate and unconscious obscurities. These obscurities
arise from a number of causes, among which a certain wilfulness
must be counted; but they arise also from a certain confusion in
Melville himself. In his writing there is a perpetual tension
between romantic and realistic elements, between a thirst for
epic largeness and a vivid sense of the actual. Thus in 'Benito
Cereno' Melville bases his tale upon a highly factual record in

a forgotten travel book, but certain portions of the narrative are embroidered with much romantic and macabre detail; and not content to let his story speak for itself, he insists at the end on driving home its philosophic implications." Similar "threads of artistic method" are woven into Moby-Dick. "Touched by the transcendental atmosphere of his creative period, Melville was yet compelled to base what he wrote upon the actual, upon what he had himself seen and experienced and felt; and these 'realistic' elements, under the spell of his dilating imagination, frequently swell to abnormal proportions. Hence arise both the greatness and the failure of his method, and hence it is that the riddle of his personality and the enigma of his purposes have so fascinated the contemporary literary world." Lists a number of departures from Delano in "Benito Cereno." [See 1928.B26.]

10   LINN, JAMES WEBER and HOUGHTON WELLS TAYLOR. A Foreword to Fiction. New York and London: D. Appleton-Century Co., pp. 10-11.
     In Moby-Dick, Melville "presents a story romantic to all intents and purposes even though the scenes both on shore and on sea are sufficiently actual to be capable of being closely checked," for his "characterization represents a simplifying, a clarifying, an elevating of human motives to a level that is essentially fantasy." Moreover, "the rhapsodic and transcendental philosophy and the touches of symbolism which run through the narrative give even to the most actual of scenes and events a feeling of heightened, ideal existence."

11   O'NEILL, EDWARD H. A History of American Biography, 1800-1935. Philadelphia: University of Pennsylvania Press, pp. 267-269.
     Review of 1921.A1 and 1929.A1. Weaver's "is as complete a record of Melville's life as we shall ever have," and his criticism is quite as good as the biography. Mumford carries his theories of Melville's actions to the point of absurdity and distorts facts for the purpose of proving a preconceived point of view; but his criticism is immensely valuable and stimulating.

12   READ, HERBERT. "Melville," in Poems, 1914-1934. London: Faber & Faber, p. 120.
     Poem.

13   VAN DOREN, CARL. What is American Literature? New York: William Morrow and Co., pp. 69-70, passim.
     Reprint of 1933.B18.

14   WEAVER, RAYMOND. "Introduction," in Journal Up the Straits, October 11, 1856-May 5, 1857. New York: The Colophon, pp. iii-xxx.
     Mainly biographical. Melville "came to put the highest premium upon 'sincerity,' and the overwhelming bulk of his writing is 'self-expression' and satire; the hero is always himself, either in his own undisguised person or else thinly masked in all sorts of romantic and allegorical finery. Since he was so much

and so increasingly in earnest in his fiction, since he threw
himself so unreservedly into his creations, since his imagination
was so exclusively a vent for his personal preoccupations, rarely
could he portray emotion, which demands detachment; usually he
could but betray it." In Pierre and The Confidence-Man "he falls
dizzily from being a writer of seasoned experience and heavenly
inspiration," but, contra Julian Hawthorne [see 1926.B38],
Melville was not insane. Except for Billy Budd, "all that he
wrote after 1857 is, as achieved literature, negligible." Note
on the manuscript journals and Weaver's editorial policies. Reviewed in 1935.B23, B25-26, B28; [See also 1935.B24.]

15   WEAVER, RAYMOND. "Introduction," in Typee. Illustrated by
     Miguel Covarrubias. New York: The Limited Editions Club,
     pp. III-XXII.
        Account of activities of missionaries and the French in the
Marquesas and Tahiti. Notes that with the discovery of Moby-Dick
in the last decade, Typee has been unjustly neglected. The
essential interest of Typee is aside from its reflections on
church and state; rather it lies in its racy accounts of
Melville's and Toby's adventures.

16   WINTERICH, JOHN T. Early American Books & Printing. Boston
     and New York: Houghton Mifflin Co., The Riverside Press
     Cambridge, p. 152.
        Mention: "When the final part of The Sketch Book was
issued, Ralph Waldo Emerson was seventeen, Nathaniel Hawthorne
was sixteen, Henry Wadsworth Longfellow and John Greenleaf
Whittier were thirteen, Edgar Allan Poe and Oliver Wendell Holmes
were eleven, Henry David Thoreau was two, and James Russell
Lowell, Herman Melville, and Walt Whitman were a year old. What
an auspicious moment it would have been for a far-sighted book-
collector to choose to be born!"

17   FAGIN, N. BRYLLION. "Herman Melville and the Interior Mono-
     logue." American Literature 6 (January), 433-434.
        Refutes claim by Mary Colum that Edouard Dujardin was the
first to use the "interior monologue" in Les Lauriers sont coupés
(1886). Chapters 37-39 and many other passages in Moby-Dick "are
but lengthy soliloquies which, in modern parlance, we should call
interior monologues, since they are not spoken but represent the
thought processes" of characters. Melville's soliloquies pre-
figure the interior monologues of Joyce and his disciples, in
which the thoughts of characters are expressed "as subconscious
ruminations and impressions" and "remind one of dreams, which
sometimes they are."

18   FORSYTHE, ROBERT S. "Herman Melville in Honolulu." New
     England Quarterly, 8 (March), 99-105.
        Reprints 1873.B7; gives details of Isaac Montgomery. Con-
jectures that the arrival of the Acushnet, from which Melville
had deserted in the Marquesas the previous year, caused Melville's departure from Honolulu a few weeks after he had signed

his contract with Montgomery; and that Melville and Montgomery parted on amicable terms.

19   ANON. "Extremely Rare in Original Wrappers," in First Editions, Autograph Letters and Manuscripts, Association Books & Other Items of Outstanding Importance. [Catalogue for Public Sale, 24 and 25 April.] New York: American Art Association Anderson Galleries, p. 119.

      Lists first edition of Typee, with description. "This edition, as well as all subsequent American editions, does not contain the three vivid passages which appeared in the original printing of the work (London, 1846)."

20   ANDERSON, CHARLES R. "A Reply to Herman Melville's White-Jacket by Rear-Admiral Thomas O. Selfridge, Sr." American Literature, 7 (May), 123-144.

      Prints and annotates Selfridge's "twenty-one foolscap pages of detailed criticism" of White-Jacket, "dated July, 1850." Notes that S.R. Franklin's estimate of the influence of White-Jacket on the abolition of flogging "needs considerable qualification." [See 1898.B2.] The "fight to abolish flogging in the navy, which had begun in 1821 and had come to a head in the session of 1849-1850, was already substantially won when White-Jacket appeared"; Melville "simply got on the band-wagon of reform."

21   FORSYTHE, ROBERT S. "Herman Melville's 'The Town-Ho's Story.'" Notes and Queries, 168 (4 May), 314.

      The Harper's New Monthly Magazine text (October 1851) "is exactly the same as that of the chapter in the novel; probably it was put in type from a proof of the longer work." "The Town-Ho's Story" was also published in the Baltimore Weekly Sun (8 November 1851, p. 1), the text corresponding with that of the magazine, except for numerous typographical errors, and likely a reprint from it.

22   WEGELIN, OSCAR. "Herman Melville as I Recall Him." Colophon, NS 1 (Summer), 21-24.

      Wegelin saw Melville in the New York bookshop of John Anderson, Jr. (where Wegelin was an assistant) on a number of occasions in 1891-1892 and delivered books several times to Melville's house. A friendship developed between Melville and Anderson. Among the books Melville bought "were copies of his own sea tales, of which, oddly enough, he seemed to have had virtually no copies until Mr. Anderson supplied him." Melville did not seem a disappointed man, but one "who preferred being alive and neglected to being dead and famous."

23   CHAMBERLAIN, JOHN. "Books of the Times." New York Times (24 June).

      Review of 1935.B14. Taken in the setting Weaver provides, Melville's jottings help refute the imputation that he was insane and suggest that he was suffering from nothing more than a general sense of disillusion with the universe. Along with the

abortive writings of his years as a customs inspector, they are
evidence that Melville never got hold of the definite belief
Hawthorne thought he needed in order to be able to rest.

24   CHAMBERLAIN, JOHN. "Melville's Journal Again." New York
     Times (5 July).
        Chamberlain reported in 1935.B23 that Weaver spent fourteen
     years deciphering Melville's 1856–1857 journal; has since been
     informed "that the entire journal can be read through in an
     afternoon; that, in fact, it had been read through in an after-
     noon some six years ago"; that it is only difficult "for persons
     who are accustomed to a fine Spencerian hand," and once "the key
     to Melville's elisions is plain, the rest of the unraveling
     is . . . easy."

25   HUTCHISON, PERCY. "A New Book by Herman Melville." New York
     Times Book Review (7 July), pp. 2, 19.
        Review of 1935.B14. Because of Melville's "many steno-
     graphic short cuts," Weaver, in editing the journal, "was faced
     with a task comparable to that performed by the first editors of
     Samuel Pepys." It is evident from the brevity of statement and
     the hastiness of much of the spelling that Melville fully ex-
     pected to write up his journal when he was home again. But the
     fact that we have his narrative in its original bareness adds
     much to the attraction. In Freudian language, the journal is a
     continuous record of escape; hence, one sees the sadness that is
     so gloriously obscured by buoyancy.

26   ANON. "Melville's Last Voyage." London Times Literary
     Supplement, No. 1747 (25 July), p. 474.
        Review of 1935.B14. Weaver does not illuminate Melville's
     intellectual and moral crisis of the 1850s by putting the blame
     on Mrs. Melville; so far as we know, there is no evidence to
     suggest that her limitations were, in any sense, the cause of
     his trouble. The journal is a rather disappointing document,
     throwing no light on this crisis and showing no particular gift
     of observation; it may best be described as a long series of
     shorthand notes to refresh Melville's memory. Certain passages
     suggest that the "core" of his crisis "was religious in a some-
     what narrower and more definite sense than is generally sus-
     pected." There seems to have been at work in Melville "some grim
     combination of a childish terror of Jehovah and an adult terror
     at elemental Nature." One is conscious of a weariness pervading
     the journal.

27   ANON. "Your Taste and Your Typee." New York Monthly Letter
     of the Limited Editions Club, No. 75 (August), pp. 1–4.
        Notes that for his illustrations for Typee [see 1935.B15],
     Miguel Covarrubias "has studied the natives themselves, and has
     then taken himself to libraries for consultation of the get-up of
     the natives in the days when Melville was among them."

28   CHAMBERLAIN, JOHN. Current History, 42 (August), xiv.
         Review of 1935.B14. The journal does not add much to the
understanding of Melville. But only a sane man could have made
its prosaic notations.

29   AARON, DANIEL. "Melville and the Missionaries." New England
         Quarterly, 8 (September), 404–408.
         Reprints parts of articles and reviews in the Honolulu
Polynesian and Friend, which "reflect the antagonism which
Melville's Typee and Omoo provoked among the so-called respecta-
ble element of the islands of the South Seas." [See 1846.B94,
B96; 1847.B67; 1848.B9–10, 1848.B13; 1850.B63; 1853.B12.] Cites
earlier critics of the South Sea missionaries.

30   MacDONALD, ALLAN. "A Sailor Among the Transcendentalists."
         New England Quarterly, 8 (September), 317.
         Notes John Ross Dix's description of Father Edward Taylor's
church as "small and neat--the only ornament being a large painting at the back of the pulpit, representing a ship in a stiff
breeze off a lee shore." Comments: "This is strikingly close to
Melville's 'large painting representing a gallant ship beating
against a terrible storm off a lee coast of black rocks and snowy
breakers' [Moby-Dick, chapter 8]. In each was an angel, though
Taylor's threw down a realistic anchor; while Mapple's shed a
spot of radiance on the deck." There "never was a sermon like
Father Mapple's on land or sea, but if ever a preacher came close
to it in method, in the vivid retelling of a Bible story in terms
of what a sailor has lived, it was Taylor. Knowing, as we do,
how usual it was in Melville to imagine only by transcending
known facts and actual experience, it can hardly be doubted that
Taylor was to Mapple what Mocha Dick was to Moby Dick."

31   LARRABEE, STEPHEN A. "Melville Against the World." South
         Atlantic Quarterly, 34 (October), 410–418.
         "Melville wrote as he pleased because he was always a lit-
erary libertine. Robert Burton, Sir Thomas Browne, and Tobias
Smollett, his favorite writers (along with Plato and Shakespeare),
had been the same. Instead of choosing one of that trio for a
model, he tried ambitiously to unite in his work the merits of
all three--the realism of Smollett, the symbolism of Browne, the
erudition of Burton. . . . The inevitable result was the mixed
(not to say chaotic) style of the works of his maturity--a style,
unique to Melville while definitely of the nineteenth century; a
style ornate, diffuse, and overfull, yet one that often is not
only musical and profound but also concise. Carlyle, Emerson,
and Whitman exhibit similar phenomena." But the "imperfect blend
of rhetoric and simplicity" in Mardi and Moby-Dick "is, in the
final analysis, the result of Melville's alternation between his
fondness for allegorical interpretation and his interest in
actual men and their customs." He was half-transcendentalist,
half-scorner of "Neo-Platonic mist," his whole labor "an attempt
to reconcile the infinitely varied shades of vice and stupidity,
of weakness and virtue, that he discovered among landlubbers as
well as sailors with the idealism which he, born in 1819, had

absorbed like some atmospheric taint out of the early nineteenth-century sky. . . . Like many of his contemporaries, he wanted to believe that somewhere was hidden a philosopher's stone potent enough to compel the world to bow to the soul. Mardi is the first and, perhaps, clearest account of his quest for that talisman--the record of his search for some answer to the problem of evil that hounded him all his days." Mardi may be called the Gulliver's Travels of the mid-19th century; but though more inclusive in the objects of satire, it is decidedly inferior to Swift's work, principally because Melville "lacked the steel-like temper of the satirist," was never able to write in one mood for very long, and in this novel was only too eager to moralize his tale. He strives to be tolerant, and very often the presentation of both sides of a question weakens his criticism. In the Yillah story Melville is possibly restating Blake's major thesis: Taji, the revolutionary, rescues joy from the priest who, in the role of custom or superstition or reason, destroys beauty and mystery and passion.

32   ANON. "Rare Melville Book is Bid In at $1,575." New York
     Times (17 October), p. 21.
        The book was a copy of the first English edition of The
     Whale (auctioned at the American Art Association Anderson Gal-
     leries). Notes that the American edition, Moby-Dick, 1851,
     "contained thirty-five passages omitted from the English edi-
     tion."

33   AARON, DANIEL. "An English Enemy of Melville." New England
     Quarterly, 8 (December), 561-567.
        Reprints passages about Melville from Edward Lucett's
     Rovings in the Pacific. [See 1851.B3.] Concludes that Lucett's
     "identification of Melville as his attacker and ring-leader of
     the mutineers is extremely shaky," but Dr. Long Ghost might have
     been the ringleader. Rovings in the Pacific "is significant
     because it suggests two important facts, viz., the identity of
     the Julia [the Lucy Ann] and of Captain Guy [Captain Ventom] and
     the exact time of Melville's incarceration in the calliboose."

1936 A BOOKS--NONE

1936 B SHORTER WRITINGS

1   BEATTY, RICHARD CROOM. Bayard Taylor: Laureate of the Gilded
    Age. Norman: University of Oklahoma Press, p. 86.
       Records that Taylor dined one day with Sir Edward Belcher
    and Melville (September 1850). [See 1884.B5.]

2   BOYNTON, PERCY H. "Herman Melville," in Literature and Ameri-
    can Life. Boston: Ginn and Co., pp. 461-477.
       Slightly revised reprint of 1927.B3, with added short pas-
    sage on Melville after 1852. "Despair was to be the undercurrent
    in 'Benito Cereno,' 'Bartleby,' and 'The Encantadas' in 'The
    Piazza Tales,' the most skillful in this volume; but contempt was

to dominate 'The Confidence Man,' and may even account for the dull drabness in the execution of this cynical satire. In Melville's own external life the despair of the Ishmael and the exile was to give way to the contempt of the recluse, and this, in time, to a quiet acceptance of things that was nearer to happiness than to the mere resignation of defeat." In Clarel he "was more nearly reconciled to near circumstance than to the remoter problems, but he was not in either respect the pessimist that he has carelessly been called. He was a doubter, and in doubt there is always potential the element of hope."

3   BROOKS, VAN WYCK. The Flowering of New England, 1815–1865.
    New York: E.P. Dutton & Co., p. 534, passim.
       Cursory mentions of Melville. Claims that at the end of Hawthorne's life his "mind had grown like Melville's in Pierre, groping in a fog for the firm conceptions that turned to vapour as he tried to grasp them."

4   BRUSSEL, I.R. "Herman Melville," in West to East, 1786–1930.
    Part 2 of Anglo-American First Editions. London: Constable & Co.; New York: R.R. Bowker Co., p. 106.
       Lists books by Melville "issued in England prior to the "American Editions" (excluding Typee); gives English publication dates and dates the American printed books were received for copyright.

5   BURRELL, ANGUS and BENNETT A. CERF. "Introduction," in The Bedside Book of Famous American Stories. New York: Random House, p. xv.
       Mention: "There have been, of course, throughout our literary history, fine artists—Irving, Poe, Hawthorne, Melville, Henry James—whose emphasis in fiction has always been upon truth in characterization. . . . But the great writers always realize that fiction—short or long—is an attempt to 'render the visible world.'" Prints Billy Budd, Foretopman (pp. 141–206). Biographical sketch ("Herman Melville," p. 1247).

6   CANBY, HENRY SEIDEL. Seven Years' Harvest: Notes on Contemporary Literature. New York: Farrar & Rinehart, pp. 118, 143–144, passim.
       Sees "the tense transcendentalism of New England" leading to "the autobiographical fiction" of Moby-Dick. Views as decadent that fiction in which "the recessive abnormalities of character become the mainsprings of the plot"—which "is what Melville attempted in his violent reaction from the happy simplicities of 'Typee,' but lost himself in a maze of words." Asks: "whence comes this tension which, when the tragic imagination of Americans reaches a certain pitch, sends our best minds [Hawthorne, Poe, Melville, Bierce, Faulkner, Julian Green, O'Neill] taut and trembling into the depths of the macabre?" Presumes it is "the result of a triple struggle which has lasted longer than the United States:—an unexampled acquisitive energy bred of protestantism and pioneering; an unexampled idealistic optimism, the strain which Emerson and Whitman have lifted into literature; and

a violence of reaction against either or both of these native impulses which carries the sensitive and dissatisfied spirit (even a Mark Twain) into a search for something horrid enough to smite this complacent country into attention. . . ."

7   GILDER, RODMAN. The Battery. Boston: Houghton Mifflin Co., p. 171.
    Quotes "the diarist [Philip] Hone" on the arrival of the seventy-foot Robert F. Stockton in New York harbor from Gravesend in late May 1839: "It was fortunate that . . . this little cockle-shell . . . did not come across a whale, one of the descendants of 'Mocha Dick, the white whale of the Pacific.'"

8   HARTWICK, HARRY. "Herman Melville," in A History of American Letters, by Walter Fuller Taylor. New York: American Book Co., pp. 506-509.
    Lists of Melville's works; selective list of texts, biography, criticism, bibliography.

9   HUBBELL, JAY B. "Herman Melville (1819-1891)," in American Life in Literature. Vol. 1. New York: Harper & Brothers, pp. 642-644.
    Biographical sketch. The twentieth century has found Melville's pessimism "not uncongenial and has relished his attacks upon aspects of American life and thought which he disliked." But modern critics and biographers "have read into Melville perhaps more than is actually there," reading his books, particularly Pierre, "in the light of the Freudian psychology, of which Melville of course knew nothing." Yet even if some contemporary critics have overrated Melville, it now seems clear that Moby-Dick belongs among the great American novels, along with The Scarlet Letter and Huckleberry Finn. Headnote to "Poems" (p. 651) argues that Melville's "finest poetic passages are to be found in the prose of Moby-Dick, but his verse has qualities that remind one of Emily Dickinson's compact and powerful poems. If Melville never attained complete command of the poetic medium, he at least had something to say." Prints (pp. 644-654) Melville's letters of 29 June 1851 and 1[?] June 1851 to Hawthorne [Letters, pp. 132-133, 126-131]; chapters 36 and 111 from Moby-Dick; "A Utilitarian View of the Monitor's Fight"; "Rebel Color-Bearers at Shiloh"; "'Formerly a Slave'"; the "Epilogue" to Clarel; "To Ned"; and "Art."

10   JOINT COMMITTEE OF THE AMERICAN LIBRARY ASSOCIATION, NATIONAL EDUCATION ASSOCIATION, NATIONAL COUNCIL OF TEACHERS OF ENGLISH. NORA BEUST, Chairman. Graded List of Books for Children. Chicago: American Library Association, p. 92.
    Lists Moby-Dick, illustrated by Mead Schaeffer, (Dodd, 1922) and Typee (McKay, 1930) for grades 8-9.

11   LAING, ALEXANDER. "Foreword" and "Afterword," in The Life &
      Adventures of John Nicol, Mariner. New York and Toronto:
      Farrar & Rinehart, pp. 3-7, 207.
         Finds the prose in Nicol's book (first published in
      Edinburgh and London, 1822) unsurpassed, except by Melville.
      Notes two man-of-war narratives that "set the style" for White-
      Jacket: Life on Board a Man-of-War (anonymous; Glasgow, 1829)
      and Henry James Mercier's Life in a Man-of-War, or Scenes in "Old
      Ironsides," which demonstrably influenced Melville. Reviewed in
      1936.B36.
12   LAWRENCE, D.H. Phoenix: The Posthumous Papers of D.H.
      Lawrence. Ed. Edward D. McDonald. London: William
      Heinemann, pp. 342-343.
         Review of Gifts of Fortune by H.M. Tomlinson. [See
      1926.B13.] Though Tomlinsom claims that a talk with seamen in
      the forecastle of a ship has meant more to him than any book, it
      is obvious from these essays "that books like Bates's Amazon,
      Conrad's Nigger of the Narcissus, and Melville's Moby Dick have
      gone deeper into him than any talk with seamen in forecastles of
      steamers." Asks: What are we all after? "It is our yearning to
      land on the coasts of illusion, it is our passion for other
      worlds that carries us on. And with Bates or Conrad or Melville
      we are already away over the intangible seas. As Mr. Tomlinson
      makes very plain, a P. & O. liner will only take us from one
      hotel to another. Which isn't what we set out for, at all. That
      is not crossing seas."

13   MENCKEN, H.L. The American Language: An Inquiry into the
      Development of English in the United States. New York:
      Alfred A. Knopf, p. 261,n.
         Citing 1932.B33, B41, notes the many changes made in the
      text of the first English edition of Moby-Dick (The Whale, 1851)
      "in order to get rid of Americanisms and American spellings."

14   NEWTON, A. EDWARD. Bibliography and pseudo-Bibliography.
      London: Humphrey Milford, Oxford University Press, pp. 33-35.
         On the bowdlerizing of the text of Moby-Dick for The Whale,
      using 1932.B33. Records a recent purchase of The Whale for
      $1,575.

15   QUINN, ARTHUR HOBSON. "Herman Melville and the Exotic
      Romance," in American Fiction: An Historical and Critical
      Survey. New York and London: D. Appleton-Century Co.,
      pp. 149-158.
         Reprints much of the material in 1922.B43 and expands it;
      still finds the same weaknesses in Melville and Moby-Dick.
      Redburn is dull reading; Dana had done better with Two Years
      Before the Mast because he had more selective power. Pierre can
      hardly be taken seriously because of its total lack of construc-
      tion. Israel Potter "is not in any sense noteworthy, partly
      because of Melville's continued railing at life, but more espe-
      cially because of the absurdity of the pictures of historical
      characters, like George III and Benjamin Franklin." The
      Confidence-Man is Melville's dullest book, with tedious conversa-
      tions among stupid characters. "Benito Cereno" is a masterpiece,

though a briefer explanation might have been more effective than
the long deposition at the end. Except for "The Encantadas" and
"The Bell-Tower," the other stories in The Piazza Tales are not
so important. Billy Budd is written "with a clarity unsmirched
by any of Melville's earlier turgid style" and may rank just
below Doubloon, pp. 177-178. Revised version in 1951.B18.

16   SANTAYANA, GEORGE. The Last Puritan: A Memoir, in the Form
     of a Novel. New York: Charles Scribner's Sons, p. 179.
        Moby-Dick is kept on board the yacht Hesperus, apparently
     one of the "books that bear re-reading."

17   [TARG, WILLIAM]. Ten Thousand Rare Books and Their Prices:
     A Dictionary of First Editions and Valuable Books. Chicago:
     William Targ, pp. 239-240.
        Catalogue of Melville's books offered at auction and by
     dealers, 1927-1936, with prices.

18   TAYLOR, WALTER FULLER. "Herman Melville (1819-1891)," in
     A History of American Letters. New York: American Book Co.,
     pp. 131-140.
        Survey. Moby-Dick "was written out of the throes of a deep
     unrest." Melville "had loved heartily a few great ideal quali-
     ties of manhood--wisdom, justice, gaiety, purity, and tender-
     ness--and his mind was seared by a growing conviction that these
     qualities counted for little in nature's scheme. Men, at least
     in the usual American surroundings, were prevailingly stupid, or
     unjust, or morose, or vile, or cruel; and in the system of nature
     the ignoble man fared as well as the noble." Melville was simi-
     lar to the transcendentalists in his impulse "to seek and know
     the bare, elemental truth, heedless of the terrors it bore, and
     heedless of the conventions that might restrain him from it," but
     unlike the transcendentalists he had come to feel that "nature is
     at bottom heartless and inconceivably cruel." Moby-Dick "is in
     effect a great philosophical drama, concerned, like Byron's Cain
     and Shelley's Prometheus Unbound, with man's revolt against
     enthroned evil"; in it Melville "succeeded, like the ancient
     Greeks, in embodying his interpretation of life in an original,
     self-consistent myth, beautiful, terrible, and profoundly sug-
     gestive." Since 1919 Melville's greatness has been exaggerated
     and probably cannot be maintained.

19   THOMPSON, RALPH. American Literary Annuals & Gift Books,
     1825-1865. New York: The H.W. Wilson Co., p. 23.
        Notes that nearly every American writer of reputation was
     "pressed into service" of the gift books. "Of those who reached
     maturity by 1845 or earlier, only Melville, Thoreau, and Whitman
     escaped--and one cannot be sure that their work does not hide
     under pseudonymity or anonymity in any of a dozen volumes.

20   VAN DOREN, CARL. <u>Three Worlds</u>. New York and London: Harper & Brothers, pp. 195–196.
     Remembers: "Herman Melville had been unbelievably neglected. Having done, for the Cambridge History, the first detailed study and the first bibliography of his work, I set Raymond Weaver at Columbia to writing the first life of Melville. (But between 1915 and 1917 I saw several copies of the first edition of Moby Dick offered in New York bookstores for a dollar each, and, being short of money, bought only one, badly water-stained and cheaper still, and then cut that up to save myself the work of transcribing a long passage. A Melville letter which I bought for two dollars I later sold for a hundred.)"

21   WHITLOCK, BRAND. <u>The Letters and Journal of Brand Whitlock:</u> <u>The Journal</u>. Ed. Allan Nevins. New York and London: D. Appleton-Century Co., p. 652.
     Entry for 1 March 1921: "I am reading an amazing book, <u>Moby Dick, or the White Whale</u>, by Herman Melville, an American, who wrote and published it at New York in 1851, as <u>The White Whale, or Moby Dick</u>. It is one of the finest sea stories ever written, it has all the mystery, all the fascination, the very secret of the sea. Curious, too, it is, with long philosophizings, and almost scientific treatises on whales and whale-fishing, but a breathless tale of adventure at the same time. It might have been written in collaboration by Joseph Conrad, R.L. Stevenson, Carlyle, Shakespeare, and old Gus Wright, the whaleman I knew as a boy." Entry for 3 March 1921: "I am rapt away from everything in that wonderful book <u>Moby Dick</u>."

22   BRASWELL, WILLIAM. "The Satirical Temper of Melville's Pierre." <u>American Literature</u>, 7 (January), 424–438.
     A "demoniac comic spirit within Melville was responsible for some of the curious features" of <u>Pierre</u>. "The unusual style, the exaggerated characterization, the shockingly unconventional theme, and the mysterious nature of the book as a whole . . . may be partly accounted for as a manifestation of Melville's somewhat perversely humorous reaction" to his situation: his failure as a self-supporting author, his bad health and failing eyes, his increasing isolation, and his realization of the futility and harm of his excessive introspection. He expected <u>Pierre</u> to be his final publication; he was having his last fling, satirizing his own too idealistic self (Pierre symbolizes Melville's own spiritual being), and "giving a parting blow to a world that had struck him many a blow." He was deliberately "defying the literary conventions of a world that feted its clever authors and starved its geniuses," expecting such criticism of the book's theme, plot, and style as reviewers made and wishing to provoke it. Pierre's spitting on the manuscript and his unfinished book to get "the start of the wise world's worst abuse of it" is "symbolical of Melville's spirit in giving <u>Pierre</u> to the world." [<u>See</u> 1937.B30 and 1946.B34.]

23   FORSYTHE, ROBERT S. "Herman Melville in the Marquesas."
     Philogical Quarterly, 15 (January), 1–15.
         Examines the chronology of Typee and Omoo and concludes
     that Melville "did not spend four months among the natives of a
     valley of the Marquesas Islands. The dates fixed by means of
     external evidence . . . do not permit us to agree to Melville's
     estimate of the duration of his residence among the Typees." He
     was their guest for twenty-five days—or at most about fifty-
     four. Melville "rather innocently extended the term of his stay
     among the Typees in order to make his account more effective. A
     longer term of captivity than the probable twenty-five days in-
     creased the pathos of the situation of the young sailor who fled
     from the brutality of a tyrannical captain to become the prisoner
     of the redoubtable cannibals who had repulsed the attack of the
     heroic Porter. A somewhat dramatic period was put to the aimless
     cruise of the Julia, when as she sighted Papeete Harbor, the
     French frigate was seen and heard saluting the newly proclaimed
     protectorate over Tahiti, an event which actually took place
     almost two weeks before the real Julia's arrival." In defending
     the veracity of Typee, as in his unpublished 23 May 1846 letter
     [Letters, pp. 25–27], Melville was exclusively concerned with
     scenes and events; he never mentioned the matter of time.

24   KUMMER, GEORGE. "Herman Melville and The Ohio Press." Ohio
     State Archaeological and Historical Quarterly, 45 (January),
     34–36.
         Quotes from 1858.B8–9, B20–21, B26; reprints 1858.B24.
     Concludes that despite a measure of praise from his Ohio re-
     viewers, "it is apparent that Melville lacked most of the quali-
     ties of a popular lecturer."

25   THOMAS, RUSSELL. "Yarn for Melville's Typee." Philological
     Quarterly, 15 (January), 16–29.
         Prints passages from Typee parallel with passages from C.S.
     Stewart's A Visit to the South Seas, In the U.S. Ship Vincennes,
     During the Years 1829 and 1830, 2 Vols. (New York, 1831). Con-
     cludes that Melville "seems to have had Stewart's account before
     him, and to have taken material from it as he progressed chapter
     by chapter with Typee." Also finds Melville indebted in chap-
     ter 19 of Typee to a passage in volume 2 of John Hawkesworth's
     An Account of the Voyages Undertaken by the Order of His Present
     Majesty for Making Discoveries in the Southern Hemisphere,
     3 Vols. (London, 1773).

26   ROLLINS, CARL PURINGTON. "The Compleat Collector." Saturday
     Review of Literature, 13 (11 January), 21.
         Review of 1935.B14. The glimpses it gives of Melville's
     troubled years will compensate for the syncopated diary form of
     the text for Melville enthusiasts.

27   FORSYTHE, ROBERT S.   "Book Reviews."   American Literature, 8
      (March), 85–96.
           Review of 1935.B14.   Finds numerous errors in Weaver's
      annotation and transcription of the journal.

28   ANON.   The Library of John Edward Zahn.   [Catalogue for Public
      Sale, 21 and 22 April.]   New York: Rains Galleries, p. 63.
           Lists Typee (New York, 1849), The Piazza Tales (New York,
      1856), and The Confidence-Man (New York, 1857), with brief
      descriptions.

29   CURRIE, BARTON.   "182. Melville: Typee."   Bibliographical
      Notes and Queries, 2 (May), 11.
           Notes an assumption "in an American catalogue that the
      publication in England of the first part prior to its publication
      in America establishes priority for the whole book though the
      whole book was published in America prior to its publication in
      England.   Government copyright records establish positively that
      the whole book Typee was published first in the United States.
      Date, March 17th, 1846.   English publication (Murray's Home and
      Colonial Library), Part I, February 26th, 1846; Part II,
      April 1st, 1846."   Asks: "Is it not rather ridiculous to hold
      that the publication of a part of a book is of greater importance
      (where priority of dates is concerned) than the publication of
      the entire book?"   [See 1936.B32–33; 1937.B21.]

30   FORSYTHE, ROBERT S.   "Robert Elwes and the Schooner Caroline."
      Notes and Queries, 170 (23 May), 366–370.
           Notes that "during his twenty-seven day voyage from
      Honolulu to Papeete, one of Elwes's travelling companions was a
      living evidence of the fact that books containing derogatory
      allusions to living persons in the remote corners of the Pacific
      did not only come to the attention of those individuals but were
      also strenuously resented by them."   [See 1854.B1.]   This knowl-
      edge may have "led Elwes to conceal the identity of the schooner
      and her captain under the veil of pseudonymity" in his book, con-
      sidering the accusations he made against the captain.

31   CARPENTER, FREDERIC I.   "Puritans Preferred Blondes: The
      Heroines of Melville and Hawthorne."   New England Quarterly,
      9 (June), 253–272.
           Focuses on Mardi, Pierre, The Blithedale Romance, and The
      Marble Faun, where "blondeness is an ideal virtue and darkness a
      serious and sometimes unforgivable sin"; the maiden with blue
      eyes and blonde hair is invariably innocent, good, and pure,
      while the dark lady is impetuous, ardent, and passionate.   In
      Mardi Yillah is the embodiment of that innocence and purity that
      dreads the contamination of worldly experience; Hautia is worldly
      experience that cannot be attained without pain and loss of
      innocence.   "Through the acceptance of experience and the under-
      standing of it, the true Yillah might have been found and set
      free; for mere innocence can not endure for ever.   True purity
      does not imply the renunciation of experience, but rather the
      transformation of it.   But the hero will not, or can not, realize

this." In Pierre, even more clearly than in Mardi, the blonde
becomes the symbol of goodness, the dark the symbol of evil; but
Isabel, unlike Hautia, is truly beautiful and desirable.
"Although he has been unable to rid himself of his fixation on
purity, Melville has come to the realization that experience is
also desirable and necessary to the growth of the soul. But he
can not easily reconcile the two; so he describes Isabel as the
half-sister of Pierre--a relationship which makes any passionate
desires incestuous, and thwarts the very nature of the angel of
experience; while it allows Pierre to have his brunette and his
blonde, too. . . . Why is this natural desire for experience
made to seem so sinful? The answer lies, perhaps, in Melville's
failure to realize that purity, in the sense of inexperience, is
a temporary or adolescent ideal, and that true purity of heart
can be achieved only through the acceptance of experience and the
mature understanding and use of it for the purposes of spiritual
growth." Both Melville and Hawthorne proclaimed the ideal of
purity, emphasized the sense of sin, and refused to accept "their
dark ladies of experience."

32 M., P.H. "Query No. 182. Melville: Typee." Bibliographical
    Notes and Queries, 2 (July), 4.
        Reply to 1936.B29: "Mr. Currie gives no authority for the
    date February 26th, 1846, for the publication of Part I of the
    English edition. John Murray, the English publisher, says that
    his records give the month as March, but do not mention the day."
    [See also 1936.B33.]

33 WARBURTON, T. "Query No. 182. Melville: Typee."
    Bibliographical Notes and Queries, 2 (July), 4.
        Reply to 1936.B29: "Surely, importance has nothing to do
    with the entity of a first issue of a book. Is a book then 'not
    a book' because it consists of part of a larger work?" [See also
    1936.B32.]

34 ADAMS, FREDERICK B., JR. "The Crow's Nest." Colophon, NS 2
    (Autumn), 148-154.
        Notes Melville's debt in Moby-Dick to William Scoresby's
    An Account of the Arctic Regions, with a History and Description
    of the Northern Whale-Fishery (Edinburgh, 1820) and his humor at
    Scoresby's expense in chapter 35, "The Mast-Head."

35 WARREN, ROBERT PENN. "Some Recent Novels." Southern Review,
    1 (Winter), 624-629.
        The great classics of American fiction are something else
    before they are American. "By inspiration, Hawthorne and
    Melville are, for instance, of New England; then, almost by
    political and geographical definition only, or by a mystical
    hocus-pocus of definition, they are American. Moby Dick is, with
    very slight and mechanical qualification, quite as 'regional' as
    The Scarlet Letter. Its stage of action is the deck of a whaler
    and not a New England village, but the whaler is only New England
    afloat, New England with its edges whetted and its essence con-
    centrated by the valiant rigors of that calling in which it

discovered a special congeniality. The premises of the story of
Ahab and the White Whale afford a more metaphysical approach to
New England, and the tragedy of New England, than do those of the
story of the lovers in The Scarlet Letter. Or it might be put
otherwise: Melville tends to employ the religious and the mythical approach, Hawthorne, in The Scarlet Letter and elsewhere, the
social or allegorical. But the theme is finally the same: the
grandeur and the terrible incompleteness of the New England conception of man's rôle in the world brought into conflict with the
multiform, recalcitrant, seductive, and violent world. To the
modern writer, it may seem that Hawthorne and Melville were under
no necessity of hunting for a theme, that the theme, the fundamental idea, the obsession, was already theirs.

36   COLCORD, LINCOLN. "An Old-Time British Seaman." New York
      Herald Tribune Books (20 December), p. 6.
      Review of 1936.B11. Thinks it a mistake to make such extrava-
gant claims as Laing does in comparing Nicol with Melville at his
best and almost putting the book ahead of Dana's Two Years Before
the Mast.

1937 A BOOKS--NONE

1937 B SHORTER WRITINGS

1   ANDERSON, CHARLES ROBERTS. "Introduction" and "Notes," in
     Journal of a Cruise to the Pacific Ocean, 1842-1844, in the
     Frigate UNITED STATES, With Notes on Herman Melville. Durham,
     N.C.: Duke University Press, pp. 3-18, 118-140.
     The journal shows that for "the narrative part of White-
Jacket Melville made use of several methods in dealing with his
materials: first, expedient alterations of fact to suit the
exigencies of his tale; second, dramatic elaboration of certain
actual events; and, finally, deliberate invention of his most
powerful scenes. Yet he declares emphatically that he was
writing 'an impartial account . . . inventing nothing'; and his
biographers have taken him literally at his word." In fact
"little of what went into the making of White-Jacket was
straightforward autobiography. Following closely the route of
the homeward-bound cruise of the United States in 1844,
Melville's wholesale inventions multiply in a soaring crescendo,
from light comic preludes to the stirring and eloquent climaxes
by which White-Jacket is remembered. More than a dozen of the
most important scenes, making up almost half of the volume, were
manufactured out of whole cloth. Several of them, at least,
found their source in contemporary travel books; many more,
perhaps, were revampings of sailor-lore, garnered from the tall
tales he had heard in the maintop on pleasant nights." White-
Jacket was written primarily as propaganda, not as autobiography
or fiction. The anonymous author of the journal was probably
Melville's character Lemsford. Frequent mention of Melville in
"Notes." Reviewed in 1937.B41; 1938.B39; 1939.B17.

2   BARNES, HARRY ELEMER. "Literature and the Arts in the
    Nineteenth Century," in <u>An Intellectual and Cultural History</u>
    <u>of the Western World</u>. New York: Random House, pp. 1042–1043.
         Finds "profound searching into the mysteries of nature and
    man" in <u>Moby-Dick</u>. Melville stands with Hawthorne at the top of
    American fiction.

3   BASSO, HAMILTON. "Thomas Wolfe," in <u>After the Genteel Tradi-</u>
    <u>tion: American Writers Since 1910</u>. Ed. Malcolm Cowley. New
    York: W.W. Norton & Co., p. 207.
         Discussing the claim that Thomas Wolfe "has returned
    declamation to American literature," Basso remarks that "it was
    Herman Melville who introduced it." Reprinted in Cowley (1964),
    p. 162.

4   BOGGS, TOM. "Herman Melville," in <u>51 Neglected Lyrics</u>. New
    York: The Macmillan Co., pp. xxxii–xxxiii.
         Claims that Melville "wrote but one slim book of
    lyrics. . . . But while the foliage is scant, the roots are
    deep in the race. A man's poetry, like Hardy's, it is in direct
    descent of the earliest Saxon scalds; and all the true virtues
    preservative of poetry are there." Prints (pp. 66–68) "The
    Portent" and "The Martyr."

5   BROWN, STERLING. <u>The Negro in American Fiction</u>. Bronze
    Booklet Number 6. Washington, D.C.: The Associates in Negro
    Folk Education, pp. 11–13, 33.
         Melville's portrayal of Negroes. Pip's cowardice in <u>Moby-</u>
    <u>Dick</u> is not racial but naturally human; Negro sailors, generally
    courageous and praiseworthy, occur in Melville's other sea
    romances. In "Benito Cereno" the Negroes "bear witness to what
    Melville recognized as a spirit that it would take years of
    slavery to break." Although opposed to slavery, he does not make
    "Benito Cereno" into an abolitionist tract; he is more concerned
    with a thrilling narrative and character portrayal. The mutineers
    are bloodthirsty and cruel, but Melville does not make them into
    villains; they revolt as mankind has always revolted. Because
    Melville was unwilling to look upon men as "Isolatoes," wishing
    instead to discover the "common continent of man," he comes
    nearer the truth in his scattered pictures of a few unusual
    Negroes than do the other authors of the period. Notes Melville's
    "bitter antislavery protest and wise prophecy" in the Vivenza
    sections of <u>Mardi</u>.

6   CAPE, JONATHAN. "T.E. as Author and Translator," in <u>T.E.</u>
    <u>Lawrence, By His Friends</u>. Ed. A.W. Lawrence. London:
    Jonathan Cape, p. 467.
         By some of the letters he received from Lawrence, Cape is
    "reminded of an interest we shared in the works of Herman Mel-
    ville. <u>Moby Dick</u>, <u>Typee</u>, and <u>Omoo</u> he considered to be works of
    the greatest significance; as also <u>White Jacket</u>, that remarkable
    document of life in the United States Navy. <u>Mardi</u> he considered
    dull, while <u>Redburn</u>, he remarked, 'should have interest for
    Liverpudlians as a local curiosity.'"

7   CENTER, STELLA S. and MAX J. HERZBERG, eds. <u>Books for Home</u>
    <u>Reading for High Schools, Graded and Classified</u>. Chicago:
    The National Council of Teachers of English, pp. 26–27.
        Lists <u>Moby-Dick</u> for fourth year high school students and
    <u>Typee</u> for second, third, and fourth year high school students.

8   DIXON, ALEC. "Royal Tank Corps," in <u>T.E. Lawrence, By His</u>
    <u>Friends</u>. Ed. A.W. Lawrence. London: Jonathan Cape, p. 369.
        Lawrence "thought <u>The Mirror of the Sea</u> Conrad's best work,
    fine enough to stand with Melville's <u>Moby Dick</u> as the greatest
    sea book of our time."

9   GARNETT, EDWARD. "T.E. as Author and Critic," in <u>T.E.</u>
    <u>Lawrence, By His Friends</u>. Ed. A.W. Lawrence. London:
    Jonathan Cape, p. 460.
        Quotes from letter, dated 26 August 1922, from Lawrence:
    "I collected a shelf of titanic books, those distinguished by
    greatness of spirit, <u>Karamazov</u>, <u>Zarathustra</u> and <u>Moby Dick</u>. Well,
    my ambition was to make an English fourth."

10 GESSLER, CLIFFORD. <u>Hawaii: Isles of Enchantment</u>. New York
    and London: D. Appleton-Century Co., p. 191.
        Anecdote: "It was at Punahou that a shocked teacher dis-
    covered in Herman Melville's <u>Typee</u>, on the supplementary reading
    list, uncomplimentary references to the missionaries and to a
    king of Hawaii in Melville's time, whom that plain-spoken sailor
    described, rather unfairly, as 'an ugly, Negro-looking block-
    head.' The book was summarily banned until a contrite publisher
    hastily assembled a revised edition from which the offending
    passages had been removed."

11 GOODSPEED, CHARLES E. <u>Yankee Bookseller: Being the Reminis-</u>
    <u>cences of Charles E. Goodspeed</u>. Boston: Houghton Mifflin
    Co., p. 299.
        "If Herman Melville had not happened to be a mystic, I
    might not have cared for <u>Moby Dick</u>--but what would <u>Moby Dick</u> have
    been with the mysticism left out?"

12 HORTON, PHILIP. <u>Hart Crane: The Life of an American Poet</u>.
    New York: W.W. Norton & Co., pp. 26, 174, 195, 329–334,
    passim.
        Crane's reading in Melville. "In the work of both Melville
    and Crane there is a profound sea spell: eloquent evocations of
    the subterranean peace, of the mysterious and primeval life-
    forces, and the paradisaical beauty of the tropical ocean--a
    nostalgia, one suspects, for another world than the one from
    which they felt so deeply estranged." Possibly no other writer
    but Melville "has ever been able to express the mysteries and
    terrors of the sea with such eloquence and imagination" as Crane
    did in the "Voyages." Crane read <u>White-Jacket</u> with a view to
    material for <u>The Bridge</u>. Reprints Crane's letter to Harriet
    Monroe about "At Melville's Tomb." [<u>See</u> 1926.B42.]

13   JONES, B.V. "Royal Air Force, India," in T.E. Lawrence, By
     His Friends. Ed. A.W. Lawrence. London: Jonathan Cape,
     p. 413.
        Jones once asked Lawrence "which in his opinion were the
     world's five greatest books, to which he replied without hesita-
     tion, and in the following order: The Old Testament, Tolstoy's
     War and Peace, Don Quixote, Moby Dick, and C.M. Doughty's Arabia
     Deserta."

14   [LAWRENCE, A.W.]. "Books at Clouds Hill," in T.E. Lawrence,
     By His Friends. Ed. A.W. Lawrence. London: Jonathan Cape,
     pp. 476–510.
        Lawrence owned the Constable edition of Melville, volumes
     1–12 and 16, Israel Potter (London: Jarrolds, 1925) and Moby-
     Dick, illustrated by Rockwell Kent (London: Cassell, 1930).

15   PLOMER, WILLIAM. "Introduction," in Redburn. The New
     Library, No. 6. London: Jonathan Cape, pp. 11–18.
        Admires Melville's "vigour and vividness," the "lucidity
     and the narrative and pictorial qualities of his prose," and
     "his skilful display of the lost art of digression" in Redburn--
     a work of singular originality. Melville pities and mocks his
     younger self here but probably is not caricaturing that self;
     Melville's reason for sometimes disparaging the book may have
     been that it continued "to remind him in a disturbing way of
     early difficulties that he would fain have forgotten." In
     Redburn for the first time Melville is trying to get to grips
     with the "mysteries of iniquity" and the nature of evil.
     Reprinted in 1948.B25.

16   POWELL, LAWRENCE CLARK. "Studies in Classic American Litera-
     ture," in The Manuscripts of D.H. Lawrence: A Descriptive
     Catalogue. Los Angeles: The Public Library, pp. 60–61.
        Lists "Herman Melville's 'Typee' and 'Omoo'," typescript,
     12 pages, and "Herman Melville's 'Moby Dick'" typescript,
     19 pages. "Early, unpublished versions of two essays on Melville
     which appeared in different form in the Studies."

17   SMITH, BERNARD. "Van Wyck Brooks," in After the Genteel
     Tradition: American Writers Since 1910. Ed. Malcolm Cowley.
     New York: W.W. Norton & Co., p. 77.
        Brooks "has been the most influential critic of the past
     twenty years. His early work was the principal factor in the
     erection of the lofty cultural standards that have encouraged
     the rise of a mature, serious, philosophical criticism. The
     effect of his later work was not so praiseworthy, for it led to
     the embittered subjectivity of such books as Lewis Mumford's
     'Melville' and Matthew Josephson's 'Portrait of the Artist as
     American.' [See 1929.A1 and 1930.B15.] (Both men, by the way,
     have since rejected that mood.)" Reprinted in Cowley (1964),
     p. 66.

18   WARFEL, HARRY R., RALPH H. GABRIEL, and STANLEY T. WILLIAMS,
     eds. The American Mind: Selections From the Literature of
     the United States. New York: The American Book Co.,
     pp. 630–631.
         Headnote ("Herman Melville, 1819–1891") to extract from
     Moby-Dick. "Melville, in a period deeply affected by romanti-
     cism, was a man out of place in his century." Superficially he
     sometimes displayed the romantic mood, but even then he "never
     lost sight of realism"; this "tendency to see things as they
     were" made him unhappy in America. Melville "saw the world as a
     struggle between Captain Ahab and Moby Dick; that is, as a con-
     flict between good and evil. Man's only privilege was to fight
     dauntlessly." Melville's contemporaries rejected him because
     they were unwilling to listen to honest criticism of the institu-
     tions and ideas by which they lived. Yet Melville also was at
     fault: he "too often clothed his message in obscure allegory."
     Prints (pp. 631–653) chapters 132–135 of Moby-Dick; an extract
     from chapter 161 of Mardi; and chapters 4 and 5 in book 25 of
     Pierre.

19   WEAVER, RAYMOND. "Introduction," in Moby Dick. New York:
     Carlton House [1937?], pp. v–viii.
         Reprint of the 1926 Modern Library introduction. [See
     Higgins (February 1979), p. 13.]

20   WILLIAMS, STANLEY THOMAS. "The Literature of New York," in
     History of the State of New York. Volume Nine: Mind and
     Spirit. New York: Columbia University Press, pp. 249–251.
     Reprint. Port Washington, N.Y.: Ira J. Friedman, 1962.
         Sees "two strains" in New York literature in the era pre-
     ceding the Civil War: "the urban tradition, founded by Irving
     and sustained by his followers, and that of the unique and inde-
     pendent genius, illustrated by Cooper and Herman Melville, both
     untrammeled by the conventions of the cosmopolitan group."
     Melville's world of blue water and southern isle "is but his
     approach to a world of ideas. Here man, a battered, defiant
     Prometheus, wrestles with evil, and, though he cannot change his
     doom, meets it, unyielding. . . . In spirit, if not in art, he
     [Melville] rivals the great writers who, scorning conventional
     explanations of man's defeat in a rock-ribbed universe, have
     pictured him as a Titan, unconquered and morally triumphant."
     The early influence on Melville of the river and harbor at Albany
     is important.

21   CARTER, JOHN. "The London Publication of Typee." Biblio-
     graphical Notes and Queries, 2 (February), 2–3.
         Publication dates of the London edition of Typee, with
     evidence from advertisements. The one-volume edition was pub-
     lished after part I, before part II (and before the New York
     edition). [See also 1936.B29, B32–33.]

22   ANDERSON, CHARLES ROBERTS. "Contemporary American Opinions
     of Typee and Omoo." American Literature, 9 (March), 1-25.
         Anderson's account of the reception of Typee and Omoo is
     offered to help complete the "neglected early portrait of
     Melville as the romantic young raconteur who found authorship a
     delightful, stimulating, and reasonably profitable adventure, at
     least in the first few years after his return from the South
     Seas." In grooming Melville for "the doubtfully merited rôle of
     philosopher," the "legend-makers," such as Weaver [1921.A1], have
     denied him the popular success enjoyed by these books. Of the
     fifteen American magazine reviews Anderson consulted, "only three
     were hostile to Typee and but two of these were hostile to Omoo;
     however, these few did attack him roundly on three scores: dis-
     honesty, unfounded abuse of the missionaries, and personal im-
     morality. The remaining twelve were all favorable to both works
     in general; and, though a few of them were more or less non-
     committal as to the truth of one or the other as veracious travel
     books, seven were outspoken in their opinion that Typee was
     authentic and ten were converted upon the appearance of Omoo."
     In general the reaction of the newspapers paralleled that of the
     literary periodicals. Reprints comments on Typee and Omoo by
     Longfellow [see 1886.B3]; Hawthorne [see 1846.B19]; Whitman [see
     1846.B46 and 1847.B31]; Donald Grant Mitchell [see 1850.B3];
     Dr. John W. Francis [see 1852.B28]; William Ellery Channing [see
     1847.B2]; Nathaniel P. Willis [see 1849.B99]; and Lieutenant
     Henry A. Wise [see 1849.B2]. Conjectures that Lowell's lines
     containing a reference to "ludicrous Peck" in A Fable for Critics
     "may have been specifically inspired" by 1847.B71 and that Lowell
     "may have been paying an indirect compliment to Melville, whom he
     does not mention by name in his gallery of contemporary authors."

23   [DODGE, NORMAN L.]. "Roosevelt Writes of White Jacket." The
     Month at Goodspeed's Book Shop, 8 (March), 221-222.
         As Woodrow Wilson's assistant secretary of the Navy,
     Franklin D. Roosevelt wrote a reply to "a well-known author who
     had inquired about Melville's naval service," giving the infor-
     mation that Melville enlisted at Honolulu on 17 August 1843 and
     served on board the United States till 14 October 1844, when he
     was discharged.

24   HART, JAMES D. "Melville and Dana." American Literature,
     9 (March), 49-55.
         Quotes letters and journal entries pertaining to the
     relationship between Melville and Dana. Concludes that the two
     could never have been very intimate. To Melville "Dana was
     seemingly more a powerful political aid than a friend. Dana
     evidently admired Melville as a man, but there is no indication
     that he was acquainted with his books, other than Typee, although
     White-Jacket must certainly have come to his notice. Melville,
     on the other hand, probably admired Dana as an author more than
     as a man." The two sea authors "were brought together by the
     mutual love of their subject, but kept apart by their different
     temperaments." Discounts the possibility that Dana's Two Years

Before the Mast influenced Melville's sea-going. [See 1892.B5, p. xviii and 1929.A1, p. 40; see also 1944.B16.]

25   JAFFÉ, DAVID. "Some Sources of Melville's Mardi." American Literature, 9 (March), 56-69.
        Proposes Melville's indebtedness to Daniel Tyerman's and George Bennet's Journal of Voyages and Travels (Boston, 1832); William Ellis's Polynesian Researches (New York, 1833); Frank Debell Bennett's Narrative of a Whaling Voyage Round the Globe (London, 1840); and Charles Wilkes's Narrative of the United States Exploring Expedition (Philadelphia, 1845). At "the very least, Melville borrowed two passages from F.D. Bennett, two from Wilkes, one from Tyerman and Bennet, and ten from Ellis. In some instances he selected factual information which he used by way of background; but in most cases he took the most extraordinary and most bizarre of the accounts he found; and these he embellished for purposes of satire."

26   MANSFIELD, LUTHER STEARNS. "Glimpses of Herman Melville's Life in Pittsfield, 1850-1851: Some Unpublished Letters of Evert A. Duyckinck." American Literature, 9 (March), 26-48.
        Prints letters Duyckinck wrote to his wife during his visits to Pittsfield in August 1850 and August 1851, which draw "a picture of Melville as jolly and sociable during the first year or more of his life at Pittsfield." Also prints Melville's letter of 28 July 1851 to Duyckinck [Letters, pp. 135-136]. Prints in part Duyckinck's letter of 7 August 1850 to George L. Duyckinck, reporting that Melville had "a new book mostly done"; William Allen Butler's letters of 20 August 1850 and 24 August 1850 to George L. Duyckinck, mentioning Melville; and Sarah Morewood's letters of 21 November 1851 and 28 December 1851 to George L. Duyckinck, the latter showing that "Melville the gay excursionist and Melville the recluse are different men." Mansfield remarks: "Did seclusion in the country away from the brisk cultural activities of New York, did the absence of close and stimulating contact with literary friends have some part in effecting this change in Melville? Duyckinck's information about Melville's life in Pittsfield is valuable as possible aid in answering this question and achieving a fuller understanding of Melville as a man and as an author." Letters by Duyckinck and Butler, and Morewood's 28 December 1851 letter reprinted in part in Log, pp. 382-387, 391, 419-426, 441.

27   FORSYTHE, ROBERT S. "Herman Melville's Father Murphy." Notes and Queries, 172 (10 April), 254-258.
        Focuses mainly on Father Murphy's activities in the South Sea islands prior to Melville's encounter with him. [See Omoo, chapter 37.] Continued in 1937.B28.

28   FORSYTHE, ROBERT S. "Herman Melville's Father Murphy." Notes and Queries, 172 (17 April), 272-276.
        Continued from 1937.B27. Concludes that Melville's portrait of Father Murphy appears to be on the whole fairly accurate,

without "expressing an opinion as to the grounds for certain innuendoes of Melville regarding Father Murphy's personal conduct."

29   FORSYTHE, ROBERT S. "An Oversight by Herman Melville." Notes and Queries, 172 (24 April), 296.
    Notes disparity between the reference to the Pequod's tiller, carved from the jawbone of a sperm whale in chapters 16 and 96 of Moby-Dick, and the reference to "the spokes" of the helm in chapter 61, in which it seems evident that Melville "forgot that he had equipped the vessel with a tiller, and for the time being at least supplied her with the type of steering device to which he had become accustomed in his own service on merchant ships, whalers, and men-of-war."

30   THORP, WILLARD. "Herman Melville's Silent Years." University Review, 3 (Summer), 254-262.
    Melville's "habits and activities during his silent years," particularly his literary and social activities and family life. Stresses that "in the decade following the failure of Pierre, Melville continued to think of himself as an author by profession." Views the years 1851-1861 as "the most bitter" in Melville's life, the few surviving letters of that period revealing "the desolation of his spirit from which he suffered." Portions of the book of poems Mrs. Melville attempted to publish for Melville in 1860 are "probably imbedded" in Timoleon.

31   QUERCUS, P.E.G. [MORLEY, CHRISTOPHER]. "Trade Winds." Saturday Review of Literature, 16 (26 June), 24.
    Reprints J.M. Barrie's reference to Fayaway in 1922.B35.

32   PETERS, HAROLD. "The 'Pilgrim' Sails the Seven Seas." National Geographic Magazine, 72 (August), 228.
    Photograph of Bay of Taï-o-Haé, with caption "'Loveliest View I Ever Beheld'--Thus Herman Melville Described the Bay of Taï-o-Haé Nearly 100 Years Ago."

33   MULLER, HERBERT J. "The New Psychology in Old Fiction." Saturday Review of Literature, 16 (21 August), 3-4, 11.
    The strange symbols in Pierre, more plainly than in Moby-Dick, have a psychological significance, "representing the deep, obscure, unconscious tendencies in the human mind that carry one beyond good and evil, finally beyond self." Melville "set out consciously to explore the innermost recesses of the human soul; and no explorer has been more daring" [cf. 1930.B31]. On the whole, nineteenth-century writers approached psychology in a different spirit from the moderns: their interest was ethical, not scientific. Except for Melville, "they kept a gentlemanly distance from the underground world"; although "they were becoming more and more conscious of the complexities of mental experience, they were not yet obsessed by these complexities or greatly troubled by their implications."

34   GOHDES, CLARENCE. "Gossip About Melville in the South Seas."
      New England Quarterly, 10 (September), 526–531.
          Reprints 1868.B4. Stresses that the "gossip about Fayaway
  and Melville's child . . . was reported merely as hearsay."

35   FORSYTHE, ROBERT S. "Herman Melville in Tahiti." Philologi-
      cal Quarterly, 16 (October), 344–357.
          Examines the chronology of events in Omoo and finds it more
  reliable than the "time-system" in Typee, though there are some
  discrepancies. [See 1936.B23.] Continued in 1938.B24.

36   ANON. "Arrowhead Estate Sold to Mr. and Mrs. Francis."
      Pittsfield (Mass.) Berkshire County Eagle (4 October),
      pp. 1–2.
          Reports sale of Arrowhead to Mr. and Mrs. J. Dwight
  Francis. [See 1934.B27.] "None but minor alterations will be
  made, in order to preserve the original features of the literary
  shrine as far as possible"; the buyers "plan to instal a tennis
  court." [See 1938.B40.] Reports that Melville and Oliver
  Wendell Holmes "were intimate" during the time Melville lived at
  Arrowhead.

37   ANON. "Melville's Chimney Intact in Old House." New York
      Times (10 October), section 2, p. 3.
          Occasioned by sale of Arrowhead by Mrs. Russell A. Hibbs.
  Describes chimney and quotes from "I and My Chimney." [See
  1937.B36.]

38   BRASWELL, WILLIAM. "Melville as a Critic of Emerson."
      American Literature, 9 (November), 317–334.
          Discusses Melville's annotations in his copies of
  Emerson's Essays: First Series, Essays: Second Series, and
  The Conduct of Life, treating them under three topics--comments
  on Emerson's ideas about the poet; praise of Emerson's views of
  life; and unfavorable criticism of Emerson's ideas about the
  problem of evil. Annotations show that Melville, like Emerson,
  was more concerned with thought in literature than craftsmanship
  and agreed with Emerson that poets are "liberating gods" who
  open new worlds for other men; he did not share Emerson's beliefs
  that a man's ambitions and powers are commensurate and that in-
  toxicants are harmful to poets or his belief in the poet's ability to reconcile man to the deepest mysteries of the universe.
  Melville agreed with Emerson that great truth is learned only
  through suffering and was delighted by the importance Emerson
  attached to veracity, honesty, and self-trust, but felt that
  Emerson went too far when he spoke disparagingly of the benefits
  to be derived from the study of foreign cultures. He objected to
  a suggestion by Emerson that man is responsible for the origin of
  his ills and was perturbed by Emerson's belief that man attains
  goodness by obeying immutable natural laws at one with a benefi-
  cient tendency of the universe and becomes depraved by disobeying
  them. He was not nearly so sanguine as Emerson about man's
  ability to overcome evil and objected to Emerson's tendency to
  dispose of disagreeable facts and to minimize some of the harsher

facts of nature. He found in Emerson intellectual smugness and an imperfect appreciation of the suffering of mankind. The gulf between the two men's interpretations of truth can be accounted for by the differences in the types of people they associated with as young men, in their religious training, and in their temperaments. Claims that Melville "apparently did not express himself in print on either Emerson or the Transcendentalists as a school" and believes Van Vechten's theory that The Confidence-Man is a satire on the transcendentalists to be unfounded. [See 1922.B12.]

39 HASLEY, LOUIS. "The Stream-of-Consciousness Method." Catholic World, 146 (November), 211.
        Notes that the "method was used to a greater or less degree among some of the older writers of fiction," as in chapters 37-39 of Moby-Dick.

40 HIRSCH, KATHERINE F. "Moby Dick, or The Whale: An Enduring Monument." Reading and Collecting, 1 (November), 19-20.
        Biographical sketch and account of critical reception of Moby-Dick. "The tragedy of Melville's career was not in its outward aspects of discouragement and want of appreciation, but rather in the utterly drab circumstances that surrounded his entire life," except for his few brief years of adventure. Bibliographical description of Moby-Dick, 1851, and reproduction of title page.

41 TINKER, EDWARD LAROCQUE. "New Editions, Fine & Otherwise." New York Times Book Review (21 November), p. 20.
        Review of 1937.B1, noting the journal's relevance to White-Jacket and the subject of flogging.

42 BIRSS, JOHN HOWARD. "Charles Reade's Copy of 'Moby-Dick.'" Notes and Queries, 173 (27 November), 390.
        Asks for information about "the present locus of this copy," mentioned in 1922.B9, p. 218, n. "This copy has faded from sight and Mr. Sadleir has informed me that it must have been fifteen years ago when he saw the book, 'three volumes in one, and bound in scarlet cloth, in a little shop kept by Everard Meynell off Piccadilly, which shop shortly disappeared for its owner went to California and there died'" [cf. 1938.B35].

43 ALMY, ROBERT F. "J.N. Reynolds: A Brief Biography with Particular Reference to Poe and Symmes." Colophon, NS 2 (Winter), 227-245.
        Biographical details of Reynolds, with notes on "Mocha Dick."

44 BIRSS, J.H. "International Copyright: A New Letter of Herman Melville." Notes and Queries, 173 (4 December), 402.
        Reports that four London publishers who refused White-Jacket before Bentley accepted it were all "much vexed at the current state of international copyright." Reprints 1850.B11.

1   GLEIM, WILLIAM S. The Meaning of MOBY DICK. New York: The
     Brick Row Bookshop, 149 pp. Reprint. New York: Russell &
     Russell, 1962.
          Expansion of allegorical reading in 1929.B50. Ahab, in
     addition to being "a composite of all the historical and mythical
     rebels against Destiny," assumes "the character of a savior"
     aiming "to save the world." He also personifies ego, will, soul,
     and intellect. In Moby-Dick, doctrinal religion is the object of
     "allegorical satire." Reviewed in 1938.B49 and 1939.B35.

2   MANSFIELD, LUTHER STEARNS. Herman Melville: Author and New
     Yorker, 1844–1851. Chicago: private edition; distributed by
     the University of Chicago Libraries.
          Chapter 8 ("Some Aspects of Melville's Reading") of
     Mansfield's 1936 dissertation of the same title. An account of
     Melville's reading in the period 1844-1851, drawn from Melville's
     works, letters and 1849-1850 journal, and Evert Duyckinck's
     record of "Books Lent."

1   ALBION, ROBERT GREENHALGH. Square-Riggers on Schedule: The
     New York Sailing Packets to England, France, and the Cotton
     Ports. Princeton: Princeton University Press; London:
     Humphrey Milford, Oxford University Press, pp. 141, 143-145,
     151-152.
          Redburn quoted as illustrative of the packets. "Numerous
     accounts describe the Atlantic shuttle of that day from the
     viewpoint of the passenger or captain, but no other approaches
     this [Redburn] in describing the seaman's experiences on that
     particular run."

2   ALCOTT, BRONSON. The Journals of Bronson Alcott. Ed. Odell
     Shepard. Boston: Little, Brown and Co., p. 185.
          Entry for 9 December 1846: "Read Typee, by Melville--a
     charming volume, as attractive even as Robinson Crusoe. I almost
     found myself embarked to spend the rest of my days with those
     simple islanders of the South Seas."

3   ANON. "Melville, Herman," in American Authors, 1600–1900: A
     Biographical Dictionary of American Literature. Ed. Stanley
     J. Kunitz and Howard Haycraft. New York: The H.W. Wilson
     Co., pp. 524-527.
          Biographical sketch, stressing Melville's disillusionment,
     mysticism, and solitude. Moby-Dick is the only American novel
     worthy to stand on the pinnacle with Wuthering Heights. Melville
     might be called the American Blake.

4   ARMSTRONG, MARGARET. <u>Fanny Kemble: A Passionate Victorian</u>.
     New York: The Macmillan Co., pp. 324-325.
        Mention: So "many great men were gathered there that Lenox
     has been called 'a jungle of literary lions.' An uncomfortable
     simile for the colony and its mild inhabitants--Hawthorne,
     Holmes, G.P.R. James, Catherine Sedgwick--less inappropriate for
     Herman Melville, busily writing 'Moby Dick' in his old house with
     its 'purple prospect; Greylock, with all his hills about him,
     like Charlemagne among his peers.' But Melville was not yet
     grown into a lion, and most of Fanny's neighbors were so quiet
     in their tastes that they found her a trifle alarming. The allu-
     sions to Mrs. Kemble in their letters and reminiscences are dep-
     recating, admiration tinged with awe. . . ."

5   ARVIN, NEWTON. <u>Whitman</u>. New York: The Macmillan Co.,
     pp. 12, 18, 69, 92, 255, 267, 281.
        Brief comparative references to Melville. Notes that
     Whitman "had really been exhilarated again and again, as men
     like Thoreau and Melville had never been, by the great, dis-
     sonant, heady blare of American material prosperity." Reviewed
     in 1938.B48.

6   AUDEN, W.H. "Introduction," in <u>The Oxford Book of Light</u>
     <u>Verse</u>. Oxford: At the Clarendon Press, p. ix, n.
        Notes that a few pieces, such as Blake's <u>Auguries of</u>
     <u>Innocence</u> and Melville's <u>Billy in the Darbies</u>, do not really fall
     into any of the categories of "light" verse as used in the
     anthology, consisting of (1) poetry written for performance;
     (2) poetry intended to be read, but having for its subject matter
     the everyday social life of its period or the experiences of the
     poet as an ordinary human being; (3) nonsense verse. But "their
     technique is derived so directly from the popular style that it
     seemed proper to include them."

7   BABCOCK, ROBERT WITBECK, ROBERT DEWEY HORN, and THOMAS HOPKINS
     ENGLISH. <u>Creative Writing for College Students</u>. New York:
     American Book Company, pp. 23-24, 42-44, 135.
        Extracts from <u>Moby-Dick</u>, chapter 84, to illustrate exposi-
     tion, and from chapter 32 to illustrate classification. See
     hints of the stream-of-consciousness technique in the soliloquies
     in <u>Moby-Dick</u>.

8   BEATTY, RICHMOND CROOM. <u>Lord Macauley: Victorian Liberal</u>.
     Norman: University of Oklahoma Press, p. 339.
        Quotes entry in Macauley's journal (no date given):
     "Began a queer book called 'The Whale,' by Herman Melville--
     Absurd."

9   BELL, FREDERICK J. <u>Room to Swing a Cat: Being Some Tales of</u>
     <u>the Old Navy</u>. New York: Longmans, Green and Co., pp. 82-83,
     134.
        Quotations from <u>White-Jacket</u> to illustrate life on a man-
     of-war. Melville used as an authority.

10   BENÉT, WILLIAM ROSE and NORMAN HOLMES PEARSON. "Herman
     Melville (1819-1891)," in The Oxford Anthology of American
     Literature. Vol. 1. New York: Oxford University Press,
     pp. 793-794.
          Biographical sketch, with brief comments on the books; in
     Moby-Dick the white whale stands for "the insoluble and evil
     mystery of the universe." Melville was the most versatile Ameri-
     can writer of prose in the nineteenth century, his dexterity dis-
     played especially in his constant manipulation of style for par-
     ticular emotional effects. The freshness and vigor of his poetry
     has not yet received its due attention. Prints (pp. 690-746)
     chapters 10-11 from Typee; chapters 60-63 from White-Jacket;
     chapter 121 from Mardi; book 21, chapter 1, and book 22 from
     Pierre; chapters 132-135 from Moby-Dick; and selections of poems
     from Mardi, Battle-Pieces, Clarel, John Marr, Timoleon, and Weeds
     and Wildings.

11   CARTER, JOHN. "Melville, Herman," in More Binding Variants.
     Contributions by Michael Sadleir. London: Constable & Co.,
     pp. 23-24.
          Bibliographical description of The Whale (London: Richard
     Bentley, 1851). "Only 500 copies were printed of this
     book. . . . The A binding [cobalt blue cloth sides] is, I think,
     undoubtedly the primary; and it is incidentally the most stunning
     and successful piece of bravura treatment on any mid-century
     three-decker of my experience. B [brown ripple-grain] is a
     dismal testimony to the book's commercial failure. It might well
     be taken for a jobber's or remainder binding if it were not for
     the square spine panels, which are characteristic of Bentley
     books of the middle 'fifties (e.g. Reade Peg Woffington, 1853,
     and It's Never Too Late to Mend, 1856)."

12   COLUM, MARY M. From These Roots: The Ideas That Have Made
     Modern Literature. New York and London: Charles Scribner's
     Sons, pp. 288-289.
          The New England literary men "left behind them few seminal
     ideas such as might yield a harvest for their descendants or for
     the greater America that was coming in. They worked effectively
     and even nobly with the ideas they took over and made their own,
     but they really added little to them, and they produced neither
     literary philosophies nor speculative philosophies as did the
     Germans and the French of the same period. Herman Melville, the
     one man among them who might have come out with a speculative
     philosophy expressive of a country that persistent men had con-
     quered or half conquered, tamed or half tamed from the wild, had
     no real contacts with the others or with the life around him; he
     was more alone, more undirected than any of them. . . . It is
     hardly surprising that Americans, demanding some profounder view
     of life out of their history than their literary men as a whole
     had given them, turned to this anarchical epic [Moby-Dick] and
     perhaps overestimated its significance." Poe, Whitman, and Henry
     James are the three writers "who left behind them the most pene-
     trating influences, who impregnated their epochs with a set of
     literary values that have been felt all over the world."

13   FERGUSON, DE LANCEY, HAROLD A. BLAINE, and WILSON R. DUMBLE.
     "Adventure" and "Notes on Contributors," in Theme and Varia-
     tion in the Short Story. New York: The Cordon Co., pp. 17,
     544.
          In "The Town-Ho's Story," Melville exhibits a more primi-
     tive use of the "frame" than Kipling does in "The Man Who Would
     Be King." The opening paragraphs "are merely the clumsy device
     by which Melville lugged a previously written short story into
     the vast fabric" of Moby-Dick. "Here the whole tale is related
     at second hand, but the auditors are kept before the reader
     throughout, and a contrast is always suggested between the
     savage actions and emotions of the tale itself and the civilized
     setting in which it is told." Melville is the greatest and most
     uneven of American romancers. "The sterility of his later years,
     for which sentimental biographers seek explanations in psychology
     and sociology, probably means only that his creative imagination
     had to be fired by personal experience. He had emptied all he
     had into the magnificent chaos of Moby Dick." Prints (pp. 19–41)
     "The Town-Ho's Story."

14   HASTINGS, LOUISE. "The Hawthorne-Melville Friendship: A
     Chronological Analysis," in A Reader for Writers. Ed. Henry
     Holland Carter and Frank Davidson. Boston: D.C. Heath and
     Co., pp. 238–253.
          Attempts to refute ideas of incompatibility and a final
     breach between Melville and Hawthorne by using "concrete evidence
     among the available letters, journals, and personal reminis-
     cences." Melville's letters to Hawthorne, read chronologically,
     tell the story of a close friendship, ripening into a spiritual
     intimacy; from the first letter it is plain that the friendship
     had become unquestioned and unlimited. Melville was just as
     aware of Hawthorne's reticence as he was of his own prolixity,
     laughing openly at both traits; his overeagerness is followed
     usually by self-conscious apology, the puritan's reprimand of
     the romantic. Melville discusses in his letters at least four
     subjects that seem to be mutual interests: the power behind the
     universe, Truth, fame, and democracy. Miles rather than in-
     compatibility might have separated the two men after the Haw-
     thornes left Lenox; with his editing of The Heart of Hawthorne's
     Journals, [see 1929.B5], Newton Arvin has done much to establish
     the fact that no breach existed. Melville's letter of 12 February
     1851 to Evert Duyckinck [Letters, pp. 119–122] shows that
     Melville became a more exacting critic of Hawthorne's work as he
     came to know Hawthorne better.

15   HAWTHORNE, JULIAN. The Memoirs of Julian Hawthorne. Ed.
     Edith Garrigues Hawthorne. New York: The Macmillan Co.,
     p. 42.
          Mention, after anecdote in which Julian at age six is
     embarrassed at inadvertently appearing naked in front of male
     and female visitors: "In my friend Herman Melville's 'Typee' or
     'Omoo' the episode would have passed unnoticed; but I realized
     thus early the pains of the White Man's Burden."

16   KINGSMILL, HUGH [LUNN, HUGH KINGSMILL]. <u>D.H. Lawrence</u>.
        London: Methuen & Co., pp. 145–146.
            Discusses Lawrence's commentary on <u>Moby-Dick</u>. [See
        1923.B3.] "As the <u>Pequod</u> symbolizes for Lawrence the mental,
        spiritual consciousness he condemns, it is not clear why he
        should be upset by its sinking. But it is useless to expect
        clarity from Lawrence when he starts clashing his symbols."

17   LAWRENCE, T.E. <u>The Letters of T.E. Lawrence</u>. Ed. David
        Garnett. London: Jonathan Cape, pp. 360, 402, 458–459, 467,
        548, 797.
            Letter of 28 August 1922 to Edward Garnett: "Do you re-
        member my telling you once that I collected a shelf of 'Titanic'
        books (those distinguished by greatness of spirit, 'sublimity'
        as Longinus would call it): and that they were <u>The Karamazovs</u>,
        <u>Zarathustra</u>, and <u>Moby Dick</u>. Well, my ambition was to make an
        English fourth. You will observe that modesty comes out more in
        the performance than in the aim!" With letter of 10 March 1923
        to A.E. Chambers, Lawrence sends copy of <u>White-Jacket</u> and writes:
        "I hope you will like it: had it not been meant to improve the
        American Navy it would have been a better book: but at least
        that is an honourable fault, & the particular aim was achieved.
        I would willingly have done something in this manner upon the
        R.A.F.--a much finer show that the States' Navy of 1820:--but
        that's another of the undone things. ¶ The book is part of a set,
        so I hope you'll be able to return it eventually." (Garnett
        records in a footnote that "Lawrence had been reading Melville
        about this time: the previous autumn he had given an inscribed
        copy of <u>Redburn</u> to Edward Garnett.") Letter of 21 March 1923
        to A.E. Chambers: "To start <u>Sartor</u> requires courage. To finish
        it is pretty near folly, to my mind. I don't think Carlyle was
        quite the best possible (as H.M. was) and I don't think he has
        much to say to the mind of 1923." Letter of 19 March 1924 to
        Sydney Cockerell: "<u>Moby Dick</u> . . . ah, there's a titan of a book.
        Do you know <u>Redburn</u>, & <u>Pierre</u>, two of the less common ones?
        <u>Whitejacket</u> very good: <u>Mardi</u> dull: two early S.Sea adventures
        (<u>Omoo</u> & <u>Typee</u>), fair. One of his finest works is <u>Clarel</u>, in
        verse: but it isn't as fine verse as his War Stuff. That's
        magnificent. Melville was a great man. ¶ I got £20 for my
        <u>Piazza Tales</u> the other day. Someone is working a Melville boom,
        & I've sold all my early editions profitably." Letter of 29
        September 1924 to E.M. Forster: "A critic told me 'that E.M.F.
        plays exquisitely on the flute: more exquisitely than any solo-
        ist we have today . . . but that he longed to hear an orchestra
        again'. It would make a good subject for a thesis. 'Quote
        examples of an orchestral nature' etc. etc. I can't think
        of one. My 'big' books, <u>Leaves of Grass</u>, <u>War & Peace</u>, <u>The
        Brothers Karamazoff</u>, <u>Moby Dick</u>, Rabelais, <u>Don Quixote</u>, are
        all solo performances." In his letter of 1 December 1927 to
        Edward Garnett, Lawrence commented on Herbert Read's statement,
        in his <u>Criterion</u> review of <u>Seven Pillars of Wisdom</u>, that "Great
        books are written in moods of spiritual light and intellectual
        certainty": "I would maintain against him that these moods never

produced an imaginative work the size of a mouse from any of the
people sterile enough to feel certain. My notion of the world's
big books are <u>War and Peace</u>, <u>The Brothers Karamazoff</u>, <u>Moby Dick</u>,
Rabelais, <u>Don Quixote</u>. Of course we treat of prose. There's a
fine set of cores of darkness!" Letter of 12 April 1934 to
Lincoln Kirstein: "I am glad you like Melville. He is not
enough praised by Americans."

18   LONG, HANIEL. <u>Walt Whitman and the Springs of Courage</u>. Santa
      Fe: Writers' Editions, p. 85.
         Characterizes Melville in passage on Whitman's contempo-
raries: "whatever drove him restlessly over the earth and the
seas, whatever demon he faced in his solitude, he was not the
victor; and his works, though strange and often grand, are empty
of food for the heart, and too chaotic for the intelligence to
linger with."

19   MOTT, FRANK LUTHER. <u>A History of American Magazines, 1850–
      1865</u>. Cambridge, Mass.: Harvard University Press, pp. 169,
      173, 395, 420, 423, 424, 508.
         Brief references to Melville as a magazine writer and to
his reputation.

20   POWYS, JOHN COWPER. "Melville and Poe," in <u>Enjoyment of
      Literature</u>. New York: Simon and Schuster, pp. 379–390.
         Claims to be "a congenital disciple of the particular kind
of imagination, both mystic and realistic, both monstrous and
grotesque, that was so natural to Melville." The imagination
displayed in <u>Moby-Dick</u> is a model for all time of the most penetrating form of imagination; it "makes use of that deepest of all
kinds of metaphor, the kind that sinks down into the very substance, essence, and occult life of the thing described, indicating its inmost esoteric affinity, . . . its spiritual identity,
with some kindred emanation from the world-reservoir, whose
external appearance is different, but whose root in the great
underlying Noumenon is the same." The gross neglect of Melville
may have resulted from this deep imagination, combined with his
Diogenes-like philosophy, which scorned all competition, rivalry,
and ambition, and his peculiar brand of humor, which is of the
kind more likely to alienate than to attract and to the average
mind is not humor at all. One of its hallmarks is "a fierce
malicious urge to lead this whole business of 'being funny' such
a dance that it will hardly be able to recognize its own features
in the circus-mirror"; another is its huge and unashamed naïveté,
a tremendous simplicity of buffoonery; another, Melville's
abysmal pessimism, which is a mystical pessimism. Almost all
mystics are by nature happy; but the mysticism of Melville is a
dark satanic mysticism.

21   RASCOE, BURTON. "Introduction: Publishing in America," in
      An American Reader: A Centennial Collection of American
      Writings. . . . Selected From the Publications of the House
      of Putnam, 1838–1938. New York: G.P. Putnam's Sons,
      pp. xvii–xix.
          Commentary on Charles Wiley and George Palmer Putnam, Wiley
      & Putnam in the 1840s, and Putnam's Monthly in the 1850s. Men-
      tions of Melville. Brief note (p. 1025) identifies Melville as
      "perhaps the chief contributor of shorter fiction to the early
      Putnam's," though except for "Benito Cereno" it was "not in his
      best vein." Prints (pp. 741–813) "Benito Cereno."

22   THORP, WILLARD. "Introduction," "Bibliography," and "Notes,"
      in Herman Melville: Representative Selections, with Intro-
      duction, Bibliography, and Notes. American Writers Series.
      New York: American Book Co., pp. xi–cxxix, cxxxiii–clxi,
      405–437.
          Thorp's 119-page introduction is divided into six parts.
      1. "Formative Influences" finds "five determining influences in
      Melville's youth and the years of his greatest creative period:
      the religious orthodoxy of his home, which left its imprint
      though he revolted from it; his contact with the brutalities of a
      sailor's life and with savage societies which impelled him to
      question the premises of western civilization; his reading in
      philosophy and belles-lettres which, though unmethodical, was
      prodigious between 1846 and 1851; his friendships with artists
      and men of letters in New York who advanced his interests and
      educated him in his craft; and the sympathy of Hawthorne, which
      more than any other factor contributed to the fruition of his
      genius." Weaver [1921.A1] and Mumford [1929.A1] have exaggerated
      Hawthorne's aloofness in their effort to dramatize Melville's
      loneliness. Hawthorne's immediate influence is seen in "the dark
      and intense story of intimate human relationships in Pierre," a
      "new departure" for Melville.
      2. "Melville as Artist" rejects the view of Melville as "a natural
      genius who never understood the art he practiced, but wrote out
      of the fullness of experience, and then, when memory and emotion
      were exhausted, could write no more" in favor of "the truer pic-
      ture of a writer who from the beginning of his career was occu-
      pied with the theme of the artist's problems and brooded over the
      nature of his own creative powers and their relation to the vital
      center of his spiritual life, until in much of his finest work
      [particularly in Mardi, Pierre, and The Confidence-Man] this
      theme is deeply involved in the other mysteries with which he
      wrestled." In discussing Typee, Omoo, Redburn, White-Jacket,
      Israel Potter, and The Piazza Tales, Thorp focuses on Melville's
      artistic use of his literary sources and finds developing archi-
      tectural skill and mastery of technique, "Benito Cereno" being
      the culmination of Melville's art of transmuting sailors' yarns
      and travelers' tales into fiction. In Mardi, Moby-Dick, and
      Pierre, Melville is seen as setting himself deliberately against
      the main currents of fiction-writing of his time, and his con-
      ception of what constitutes reality in fiction as totally at
      variance with midcentury realism. His heterodoxy on the subject

of character (as expounded in Pierre, book 7, chapter 8 and in The Confidence-Man, chapters 14, 33, and 44) is strikingly modern, his thought akin to ideas of D.H. Lawrence and Aldous Huxley.   In Moby-Dick and Pierre his ambition was to create "originals" of the stature of the original described in The Confidence-Man, chapter 44.   The prose of Moby-Dick resulted from the convergence of two styles he had been perfecting since he began to write: one realistic, rapid, lucid, in the manner of Defoe, relying for its charm on picturesque details and appeal to the eye; the other depending for its effect solely on the music of its rhythms.   Three patterns are commonly found within a single passage of the mature prose: a sequence of short phrases or clauses of nearly equal length; variations of the Old Testament antiphonal verse; and a tripartite arrangement of rising clauses that drop to a weighted close.
3. "The Trilogy: Mardi, Moby-Dick, Pierre" sees Melville engaged in a search for a master key to "the chronic problems of philosophy," a quest for the Ultimate or Absolute, his mood changing from the recklessness of Taji to partial sympathy with vengeful Ahab to the desponding and skeptical mood of Pierre, as he fails to find any such key.   In Billy Budd, where he achieves unsurpassable tragedy, Melville's "passionate rage at the inscrutableness of the universe" is at last spent.
4. "Melville's Poetry" suggests that despite Melville's habitual depreciatory tone when referring to his poetry, his real feeling for his poems can be inferred from his frequent reworking of them. Battle-Pieces (unified in spite of its differing moods) exploited extensively the Rebellion Record. Mumford [1929.A1, p. 299] may well be right in suggesting that Melville's sense of the inexorability of the war relieved for a time his mood of extreme skepticism, giving him a temporary sense of purpose. Clarel is the key to Melville's thought in his later years but has all the faults of a "private" poem and should not be read till one is familiar enough with the genesis of Melville's dominant moods to understand the significance of its innumerable allusions.   The feud between what Derwent and Ungar represent becomes the dominant theme in the poem, which shows Melville's struggle toward the affirmation of faith in the "Epilogue."   In John Marr the final note is reconciliatory, and in Timoleon the fundamental tone is again one of tranquility and peace.   In his poetry Melville coveted chiefly clarity of expression and concision of thought, and only a few of the poems achieve the unity of rhythmical exactness, propriety of image and melodic beauty that the best poetry possesses; their juxtaposition of colloquial language and the rags of eighteenth-century and romantic diction is often ludicrous.   But his verse has strength, sobriety, and almost embarrassing sincerity, and will be congenial to those who admire Landor, Hardy, and Housman. A few poems, such as "The Portent," "Malvern Hill," and the "Epilogue" to Clarel, must be included with the best American contributions to the world's store of memorable verse.
5. "Melville's Social Ideas" views every serious book or article Melville wrote as a variation on the social theme and sees

Melville opposed to the fundamental social tenets of his age.
Surveys his views on the state of nature and the social state,
the fundamental problem of social organization, the American
political system and Constitution, liberty, democracy, and the
Civil War; and his opposition to the expansionist movement,
slavery, the new competitive society and plutocracy, the factory
system, and war, as illustrated in his prose works, Battle-Pieces,
and Clarel. Finds Melville's passion for social justice and
hatred of all forms of tyranny rooted in his sense of our common
humanity and sees a change from confidence in mankind in Moby-
Dick to misanthropy in The Confidence-Man (which teaches a lesson
about man the reverse of that in Moby-Dick, chapter 26, "Knights
and Squires").
6. "Melville's Reputation" surveys Melville's reputation from
1846 to the 1920s. Disputes the legend that contemporary reviewers "demolished" Moby-Dick and that Melville, defeated and
defiant, wrote Pierre with a mad desire to revenge himself on the
critics. "Enough was said which was obtuse and narrow-minded but
as much was said which should have enheartened any author, and
even the most adverse judgments were in many instances uttered
with a show of respect for Melville's talents." Claims, however,
that Melville could have expected nothing but abuse for Pierre.
    The five sections of the "Selected Bibliography" are
devoted to (1) bibliography, (2) texts, (3) biography, (4) contemporary reviews and criticism, (5) criticism and scholarship.
In addition to explanatory notes, the "Notes" contain details of
the publication of the books extracted and of Melville's revisions in surviving manuscripts. The volume itself contains
lengthy selections from Typee, Omoo, Mardi, White-Jacket, and
Moby-Dick; Melville's review of J. Ross Browne's Etchings of a
Whaling Cruise and Captain Ringbolts's Sailor's Life and Sailor's
Yarns (reprinted here for the first time); "Hawthorne and His
Mosses"; "To Daniel Shepherd" (previously unpublished); selections from Battle-Pieces, John Marr, and Timoleon; and a selection of letters by Melville (including five previously unpublished, three from which "only fragments" had been previously
published and nine which had "not before been given in a correct
and complete text"). Section 3 of the "Introduction" is reprinted in Recognition, pp. 207-223, and reprinted in part in
Higgins and Parker, pp. 191-196. Reviewed in 1939.B15, B33.

23   WINTERS, YVOR. "Herman Melville and the Problems of Moral
     Navigation," in Maule's Curse: Seven Studies in the History
     of American Obscurantism. Norfolk, Conn.: New Directions,
     pp. 53-89.
        Treats Moby-Dick, "Benito Cereno," "The Encantadas,"
Pierre, The Confidence-Man, Billy Budd, Typee, Omoo, Mardi,
White-Jacket, Redburn, and Israel Potter (in that order). In
Winters' exposition of the symbolism in Moby-Dick, the land
represents the known, the mastered in human experience; the sea,
the half-known, the obscure region of instinct, uncritical feeling, danger, and terror. The sea is also the home of demons and
symbols of evil, especially Moby Dick, the chief symbol and
spirit of evil; it is the home, too, of the great white squid,
the symbol of chance in life. Man cannot merely stay on land,

lest he perish of imperception, but must venture on the sea
without losing his relationship to the land; thus judgment is
required. Symbolically, the "Lee Shore" chapter represents the
process of living by judgment, "by perception trained in principle, in abstraction, to the point where it is able to find its
way amid the chaos of the specific." The harpooneers represent
the basic pagan virtues of strength, accuracy, and absolute
fidelity; but they are below the level of reason, so that they
are governed unquestioningly by Ahab. The mates represent
various levels of normal human attitudes toward physical and
spiritual danger, the highest being that of Starbuck, who represents the critical intelligence; Starbuck's struggle with Ahab
represents the unsuccessful rebellion of sanity and morality
against a dominant madness; after his defeat the brutal instincts
of the crew are progressively loosened in the chapter "Midnight,
Forecastle." Ahab's ivory leg represents the death that has
become a part of the living man as a result of his struggle with
evil; it is the numb wisdom that is the fruit of experience.
Ahab is conceived in terms similar to Jonathan Edward's opposition of the predestined and sinning will and the understanding
soul; Fedallah is perhaps the sinning mind as distinct from the
whole man. Ahab is Promethean in defying the gods, but goes
beyond Prometheus in seeking to destroy a god; he represents,
essentially, the ultimate distillation of the Calvinistic temperament. Moby-Dick is one of the most carefully and successfully
constructed of all the major works of literature. It is less a
novel than an epic poem, the plot too immediately interpenetrated
with idea to lend itself easily to the manner of the novelist;
its language is closer to the poetry of Paradise Lost or Hamlet
than to the prose of the realistic novelist and is essentially as
original and powerful an invention as the blank verse of Milton.
The epic hero, except in Paradise Lost, is normally a successful
figure; but Ahab, though epical in dimensions, obeys the traditional law of tragedy and destroys himself by allowing himself
to be dominated by a heroic vice. In writing a tragic instead of
a traditionally heroic epic, Melville displayed a thorough understanding of his material: the Calvinistic view led to sin and
catastrophe, not to triumph, though at times to sin and catastrophe on an inspired and heroic scale; Ahab is the magnificent
fruition of Maule's curse. Melville himself escaped the curse
by comprehending it. Moby-Dick is a profoundly American epic,
typifying the adventurous spirit of the nation as a whole at the
period.

The idea of Pierre is the same as that governing Moby-Dick,
namely the relationship of principle to perception and the difficulty of adjusting principle to perception in such a manner as
to permit a judgment that will be a valid motive to action. But
there is a shift in emphasis: in Moby-Dick Melville assumed that
such judgment was possible; in Pierre and The Confidence-Man he
assumed that valid judgment is impossible, for every event, fact,
person, is too fluid, too unbounded to be known; the final truth
is absolute ambiguity and nothing can be judged. A work of art,
like each detail comprising it, is by definition a judgment, and
so it is small wonder that Pierre is so unsatisfactory as a whole

and in detail. The Confidence-Man is unsatisfactory as philosophy and tediously repetitious as narrative; but the prose, unlike
that of Pierre (which is excited and inflated) is crisp and hard,
and in a few passages the comment is brilliant. The Winsome-
Egbert section is a very biting commentary on Emerson and on the
practical implications of Emersonian philosophy.
    Melville's greatest works, aside from Moby-Dick, are
"Benito Cereno," "The Encantadas," and Billy Budd. In "Benito
Cereno" the morality of slavery is not an issue; the story is a
portrait of fundamental evil in action and of the effect of the
action. In Billy Budd, the most profound of the later works
though not the best written, the problem posed in Pierre and The
Confidence-Man received its answer. Vere's solution (to act
according to established principle, which supports public order,
and to accept the margin of difference between established principle and the facts of the particular situation as private
tragedy) is at once unanswerable, dignified, and profound--
though, as Melville asserted in Moby-Dick, there may be cases in
which the problem of moral navigation, though not insoluble, is
a subtler one in which the exact relevance of any single principle is harder to establish, and in which there may appear to be
the claims of conflicting principles. In Mardi the theme is
immature and romantic, yet many of the parts possess extraordinary beauty; in chapters 71-85, the most extraordinary part of
the book, and in other shorter passages the epic prose of Moby-
Dick is already highly developed. Israel Potter is one of the
few great novels of pure adventure in English and probably sur-
passes all the works before Moby-Dick except, possibly, Mardi.
Reprinted in 1947.B22.

24   FORSYTHE, ROBERT S. "More Upon Herman Melville in Tahiti."
      Philological Quarterly, 17 (January), 1-17.
       Continued from 1937.B35. More on Melville's chronology in
Omoo, concluding that Melville's stay at Tahiti was a little
less than seven weeks, from 26 September to 9 November 1842.
Agrees with Aaron [1935.B33] that Lucett's identification of
Melville as his assailant [see 1851.B3] is "extremely shaky";
nominates Salem instead. Melville may not have even been present
at the scene; the best proof that he did not witness Lucett's
discomfiture is that there is no such scene in Omoo. Other
accounts indicate that Melville has probably not been altogether
fair in his portrayal of Dr. Johnston, but seems to have dealt
justly with Consul Wilson. It seems safe to say that in Omoo
Melville "incorporates, on the whole, much less fiction with his
facts than in Typee, and that, in consequence, the book is much
more nearly a literal autobiography than is its predecessor."

25   GARY, LORENA M. "'Rich Colors and Ominous Shadows.'" South
      Atlantic Quarterly, 37 (January), 41-45.
       Finds that Melville "produces animation and magic force
chiefly through the use of two of the special senses, sight and
sound."

26   MANSFIELD, LUTHER STEARNS. "Melville's Comic Articles on
      Zachary Taylor." American Literature, 9 (January), 411–418.
          Gives evidence of Melville's authorship of "Authentic
Anecdotes of 'Old Zack,'" published 24 July to 11 September 1847
in Yankee Doodle and information about the magazine's chief con-
tributors; summarizes the articles and reprints "Anecdote,
No. III." There is "no indication that Melville had any direct
information from Taylor's camp; apparently, like many other
periodical writers of the day, he was largely dependent on newspaper accounts for his knowledge of the man, and was manufactur-
ing the anecdotes. His readers were probably as well aware as he
that there was nothing 'authentic' about his material. Factual
accuracy would hardly be expected, certainly not demanded, of
articles appearing in Yankee Doodle. Taylor was good copy; the
anecdotes served to illustrate his virtues and his humanity."
There is little literary merit in the anecdotes; they "are important chiefly as showing the range of Melville's interests, his
keen awareness of the life of his time, and his knowledge of the
current humorous conventions. In themselves hastily written hack
work, they appear to point the way toward the political comment
of Mardi and the satirical or comic temper of Pierre."

27   THORP, WILLARD. "'Grace Greenwood' Parodies Typee." American
      Literature, 9 (January), 455–457.
          Reprints 1847.B93. This parody of Melville's style, in-
cluded in a series of imitations of the most popular authors of
the day and appearing little more than a year after the publication of his first book, is significant proof of Melville's sudden
fame.

28   McAVOY, MARY CAREY. "Melville's 'Fair Piazza' Where He Wrote
      'Moby-Dick' Will Be Preserved in New Jersey." Springfield
      (Mass.) Sunday Union and Republican (30 January).
          Biographical, focusing on Melville's Berkshire days. Won-
ders if Melville ever attended the meetings of pioneer educator
Horace Mann in Pittfield when he was a "boy-teacher"; despite his
youth and his lack of formal education, he harbored the same
ideas as Mann for improving the school system. In content,
Melville's 30 December 1837 letter to his uncle Peter Gansevoort
[Letters, pp. 4–7] is not unlike one written by John Adams when
he was a schoolmaster in Worcester. Arrowhead belongs to Moby-
Dick and Moby-Dick to it. Reports that Judge Robert Pitney of
Mendham, New Jersey, will attach the "hallowed piazza" to his
home.

29   ANON. "Herman Melville." Princeton University Library
      Biblia, 9 (February), n.p.
          Notes gift of American first editions of Melville's works
to the library by Dr. Frank Jewett Mather, Jr.; notes other
items in the Princeton Melville collection. John Marr and
Timoleon "are among the outstanding rarities in American
literature."

30   ANDERSON, CHARLES ROBERTS. "The Romance of Scholarship: Tracking Melville in the South Seas." Colophon, NS 3 (Spring), 259–279.

     Account of Anderson's research for 1937.B1 and 1939.A1. Discovers that C.S. Stewart's Visit to the South Seas (1831) and Captain David Porter's Journal of a Cruise to the Pacific Ocean (1815) were "the sources of wholesale plagiarisms, some verbatim and many more closely paraphrased" in Typee. With "his sources open before him, Melville could have written the entire book without ever leaving New York"; as autobiography Typee was true only in a broad and general sense. In Omoo almost half of the material was again borrowed, but Melville now relied less on literary sources and more on his own experiences; nearly all the major episodes were based on actual occurrences and at least a dozen of the principal characters were actual persons. White-Jacket was more nearly a straightforward autobiographical record than any of Melville's previous books, but a larger proportion of it was fiction; some of the episodes were exaggerated, and several of the most thrilling passages were invented. In Mardi and Moby-Dick Melville dropped almost all pretense at autobiographical veracity, plunging headlong into creative fiction.

31   BLACKMUR, R.P. "The Craft of Herman Melville." Virginia Quarterly Review, 14 (Spring), 266–282.

     Concerned mainly with Melville's "malpractice" as a novelist in Moby-Dick and Pierre, "his two most interesting works." Melville never influenced the direction of the art of fiction, though in Pierre he evidenced its direction; he added nothing to the novel as a form, and his work nowhere showed conspicuous mastery of the formal devices of fiction. There was nothing formally organized enough in his work for others to imitate or modify or perfect; his lack of influence arose, at least partly, from a series of technical defects in persuasive craft—from his inefficient relation to the formal elements of his medium. Melville was "only a story teller betimes," for illustrative or apologetic or evangelic purposes; when Pierre proved that the material of illustration had been exhausted in Moby-Dick, there was no longer any need to tell a story. Melville controlled Moby-Dick and Pierre haphazardly, being as careless of what he thought important as of what he thought trivial, and not always seeing that after taking one series of steps one's choice of further directions is narrowed. But the mode of Ishmael in Moby-Dick is a success exactly where the mode of Pierre is wrong: Ishmael is looking on and able to see; Pierre is in the center of his predicament and lost in the action. The mates and crew of Moby-Dick, however, are not in the book substantially: their real use is to divide up the representation of the image of Ahab, but they are not given enough to do to seem everywhere natural; and Ahab comes out a great figure probably more because of the eloquence of Melville's putative conception of him and Ishmael's feeling for him than from any representational aids from the crew; the result is a great figure, not a great character. Unlike Ahab, Pierre is seen without the intervening focus of any sensibility whatever: the White Whale exists entirely in his

own inadequate perception of it; the book has no compositional
center, its real weight--what it is really about: tragedy by
unconsidered virtue--being left for Melville's digressions and
soliloquies to carry. The center of Moby-Dick lies in the suspense attached to the character of Ahab and in the half-imputed,
half-demonstrated peril of the White Whale. The book's compositional form is a long, constantly interrupted but as constantly
maintained suspense, using as nexuses or transitions the recurring verbal signs of Melville's allegory, Ahab's character, and
the business of whaling. The business of whaling takes the most
space, provides the most interest, and is a compositional device
mounting to the force of drama. Pierre lacks special material of
objective interest, such as sea, ship, whale, unique tradition of
behavior, or unusual daily life. Melville had to depend more
than ever before on the actual technique of fiction to make the
book hang together. Its tragedy fails to come off as well as
that of Moby-Dick only because it lacks the extraneous interest
of whaling; the two books share weaknesses in plot, narrative,
dramatic motive on the subordinate level, dialogue, and delineation of character. The force and nobility of conception, the
profundity of theme, are as great in either book--not because of
the dramatic execution but in spite of it; they lie in the simple
strength of the putative statement and in the digressive apo-
logues or sermons Melville made from the drama. When he really
had something to say, Melville resorted to the mode of the liberal Emersonian sermon, the moral apologue on the broad Christian
basis; his natural aptitude lay there. He made only the loosest
efforts to tie his sermons into his novels, being content if his
novels illustrated his sermons (and reasonably content if they
did not). He preached without scruple, and with full authority,
because he felt in full command of the mode he used, believing in
its conventions and the deeper convention of its relation to
society. Father Mapple's sermon and Plinlimmon's lecture are the
two sustained examples of self-complete form in his work. The
vices of his style either disappear or reveal themselves as
virtues when he used the sermon because he had found a mode that
suited his themes, allowed the putative statement to reach its
full glory without further backing, made room for rhetoric, and
demanded digression. In Moby-Dick and Pierre Melville adopted
the Gothic convention of language with all its archaisms and
rhetorical inflations as the means of popularizing his material;
what is often called the Elizabethan influence in his prose might
more accurately be called the Gothic influence heightened by the
greatness of his intentions; though the prose has been called
Websterian, it more often contains Marlovian tropes. Melville
wrote nothing of major significance after Pierre (though the
later books are not uninteresting); he was left impotent for
forty years of mature life not because of the injuries inflicted
on him by the age, but because of his radical inability to master
a technique--that of the novel--radically foreign to his sensibility. Melville's was nonetheless the only great imagination
in the middle period of the American nineteenth century. Reprinted in 1940.B2; reprinted in part in Higgins and Parker,
pp. 196-201.

32   BRASWELL, WILLIAM. "Book Reviews." <u>American Literature</u>, 10
      (March), 104-107.
          Review of <u>Herman Melvilles Gedankengut: Eine kritische
      Untersuchung seiner weltanschaulichen Grundideen</u> by K.H.
      Sundermann [Berlin, 1937]. Sundermann, as he himself admits,
      wrote on too broad a subject to be able to treat it exhaustively.
      One wonders here and there why he chose to discuss this topic and
      omit that (there is no section on Melville's knowledge of British
      philosophy; Hume is barely mentioned). Some authors he might
      have examined more carefully in searching for possible influences,
      while too much is made of the parallelism of certain ideas in
      Melville, Emerson, and Carlyle. The book too rarely traces fully
      the development of Melville's thought on the subject discussed
      but is a very worthwhile contribution to scholarship on Melville.
      Synopsis.

33   BIRSS, JOHN HOWARD. "Melville and James Thomson ('B.V.')."
      <u>Notes and Queries</u>, 174 (5 March), 171-172.
          Records some of the markings in Melville's copy of
      Thomson's <u>A Voice from the Nile</u>, a gift from J.W. Barrs in 1886.
      The verses underscored are typical of the moods of Melville's
      later years.

34   MATHER, FRANK JEWETT, JR. "Reminiscences of a Melvillian."
      <u>Princeton Alumni Weekly</u>, 38 (25 March), 555-556.
          Reminiscences of forty-five years of reading and collecting
      Melville by one of the forerunners of the "revival." [<u>See</u>
      1919.B18-19.] Tells of visiting Melville's daughter Elizabeth
      and reading Melville letters and manuscripts, including <u>Billy
      Budd</u>, kept in "a japanned tin cake-box." [<u>See</u> 1929.B39 for a
      similar account.] Reprinted in <u>Doubloon</u>, pp. 180-182.

35   BIRSS, JOHN H. "Charles Reade's Copy of <u>Moby-Dick</u>."
      <u>Bibliographical Notes and Queries</u>, 2 (April), 12.
          The same query as in 1937.B42.

36   BRIGGS, WALTER B. "The Herman Melville Manuscripts." <u>Harvard
      Library Notes</u>, 3 (May), 172-173.
          List of Melville manuscripts donated to Harvard College
      Library by Mrs. Eleanor Melville Metcalf in February 1937.

37   BLANCK, JACOB. "News from the Rare Book Shops." <u>Publishers'
      Weekly</u>, 133 (28 May), 2119-2120.
          "It becomes more apparent that unless a first edition of
      Herman Melville's 'Moby Dick' contains the orange end-papers it
      will be difficult to sell on the grounds that the 'real' first
      edition is so marked. That there is no basis for the claim that
      the orange end-papers are the mark of first issue has been
      pointed out innumerable times but the legend persists to the
      detriment of desirable first editions of the book."

38   AARON, DANIEL. "Short Notices." New England Quarterly, 11
     (June), 434.
         Review of Cruelty to Seamen by Richard Henry Dana, Jr.
     (Berkeley, Ca.: Wilder and Ellen Bentley Press, 1937). Dana
     anticipated here many of the arguments Melville was to state more
     dramatically in White-Jacket.

39   FORSYTHE, ROBERT S. "Reviews." Modern Language Notes, 53
     (June), 446-448.
         Review of 1937.B1. Points out minor errors and omissions
     and takes issue with Anderson's claim that Melville invented his
     most powerful scenes: the loss overboard of the cooper was not
     invented. But this is the best preface as yet to White-Jacket.

40   ANON. "Herman Melville House Has Retained Historic Features."
     Pittsfield (Mass.) Berkshire County Eagle (25 June), pp. 6,
     22.
         Reports that the piazza "was taken from the building
     earlier this year and transported, piece by piece, to New
     Jersey," since it was not part of the original house. Inside
     "the House of Melville is retained." The old corn crib was moved
     from its place near the red barn to the front of the newly con-
     structed red clay surfaced tennis court. [See 1937.B36.]

41   ANON. "'There She Blows!': A Condensation from 'Moby Dick.'"
     Reader's Digest, 33 (July), 115-132.
         Condenses chapters of Moby-Dick, giving a firsthand picture
     "of the gallant days of American whaling--of New Bedford in the
     1850's; of hardy sailors and wild harpooners; of cockleshell
     boats attacking great whales," which is part of the American lit-
     erary heritage. Concluding note recalls that "the narrative
     tends increasingly toward the mystical, becoming at the last the
     symbolic and incredible tale of the pursuit of Moby Dick. . . ."
     Biographical sketch ("Herman Melville"), p. 136.

42   FORSYTHE, ROBERT S. "Book Reviews." Philological Quarterly,
     17 (July), 317-319.
         Review of Herman Melvilles Gedankengut: Eine kritische
     Untersuchung seiner weltanschaulichen Grundideen by K.H.
     Sundermann. A work of considerable importance, the first book
     devoted exclusively to Melville's opinions, their sources and
     their value. The last section, with little more than page-long
     discussions of such topics as "Civilization, South Sea Islanders,
     and Indians," "Social Criticism, the Machine, Industrialism,
     Social Distress," and "Poverty and Riches," is the least satis-
     factory part of the book. Sundermann attributes to Emerson a
     direct influence on Melville, but "it is hard to estimate accu-
     rately how much of Emerson Melville had read during his whole
     lifetime and to say when he had done that reading. The fact is
     that one might be safest in saying that many of Emerson's ideas
     were in the air to be grasped by alert and intelligent young men
     like Herman Melville." New England transcendentalism, moreover,
     "was rather an attitude of mind than a system of thought or even

a body of ideas. Having acquired this mental attitude, Melville not unnaturally brought forth ideas which now and again parallel those of the Concord-Boston group." To the collector, Sundermann's "solid work should appeal as offering for the first time in book form three prose pieces by Melville"--his Literary World reviews of Parkman's The California and Oregon Trail, Cooper's The Sea Lions, and Hawthorne's The Scarlet Letter. [For discussion of Melville's alleged authorship of this review of The Scarlet Letter, see 1942.B25.]

43   BROOKS, PHILIP. "Notes on Rare Books." New York Times Book Review (17 July), p. 19.
       Résumé of 1938.B1.

44   CARTER, JOHN. "Best Sellers and the Atlantic." Spectator 161 (16 September), 446.
       Claims that Melville, "one of the first really American writers," made very little mark in England and that Moby-Dick was remaindered.

45   OLSON, CHARLES. "Lear and Moby-Dick." Twice A Year, No. 1 (Fall-Winter), 165-189.
       Analyzes Melville's annotations and markings in his set of Shakespeare and his jottings on the last flyleaf of the last volume. Sees Lear at the heart of the relation of Melville and Shakespeare and directly behind the creation of Moby-Dick, throwing Melville back on his preoccupation with the origins of evil. (Melville's copy of Lear is marked more heavily than any of the other plays but Antony and Cleopatra.) Madness and "right reason," the flyleaf jottings indicate, seek "converse with the Intelligence, Power, the Angel," and in the Ahab world (closer to the world of Macbeth than of Lear) there is no place for such converse; Melville's assumption is that a league with evil closes the door to truth. Ahab's art is black, and "the black art Goetic," unlike white "Theurgic magic," does not seek true converse; Pip, through madness, achieves this converse, which Ahab denies himself by his blasphemy. Bulkington and the choric Ishmael correspond to "right reason" (the highest range of the intelligence and the other way to true converse). Ishmael tells the crew's story and tragedy and thus creates the Moby-Dick universe in which the Ahab world is included. With Ahab, Melville draws on the Faust legend but alters it by creating a relation between Ahab and Pip like that between Lear and the Fool and between Lear and Edgar. Moby-Dick is a prose tragedy, a novel organized not epically but dramatically, with the rise and fall comparable to an Elizabethan tragedy and with many of the devices of drama, including Ahab's Elizabethan soliloquy to the skull. Ahab's speech in his soliloquies, contrasting the "long ease and sea swell" of Ishmael's narrative, is staggered and broken like that of a Shakespearean tragic hero in the fourth and fifth act; and after the "Candles" chapter Ahab comes to repose in his fate like a Shakespearean hero in the fifth act. The whaling chapters function like the comic plot of an Elizabethan play. Yet the concept of prose tragedy Melville worked

out in <u>Moby-Dick</u> is democratic. Shakespeare helped Melville to
the free articulation of his own vision.

46   BERKELMAN, ROBERT G. "<u>Moby Dick</u>: Curiosity or Classic?"
      <u>English Journal</u>, 27 (November), 742-755.
          Attempts to mediate between extremes of praise and abuse of
      <u>Moby-Dick</u> (as in 1929.A1, 1932.B6, B16), arguing that it is not a
      novel and should not be judged as one: like the Bible it moves
      toward one large purpose using a free variety of means, including
      narrative, biography, essay, lyric, drama, and epic. Melville's
      many faceted style (which "resembles the architecture of Frank
      Lloyd Wright in that it transcends ready-made molds and strives
      to make the design of each structure suit its function and its
      environment"), though sometimes inept, tries to harmonize the
      spirit of each passage with its material. His sheer narrative
      power is unsurpassed in modern literature. Ahab is not less real
      than Huck Finn for being a physical-symbolic being. The whole
      story is an interpenetration of outer world and inner signifi-
      cance, its blend of fact and fantasy one of its chief distinc-
      tions, not its flaw; nonetheless, too much of Melville's
      philosophy comes from outside the drama, from the intruding
      author, unlike Shakespeare's, which comes from within the drama.
      In <u>Moby-Dick</u> two forces that tugged at Melville most of his
      life--Byronic independence and a craving for understanding and
      warm sympathy--are to be seen in equilibrium. Melville identi-
      fies with Ahab's defiance, yet makes clear its folly. In <u>Pierre</u>
      he deliberately chose the woe that is madness. Besides the
      structure of allegory, <u>Moby-Dick</u> has two deep and broad founda-
      tions of form: the numerous well-planned foreshadowings of the
      tragic conclusion and the <u>Pequod</u>'s meetings with other ships,
      which serve as omens or as foils to Ahab's philosophy.

47   CROLL, MORRIS W. "Brief Mention." <u>Modern Language Notes</u>, 53
      (November), 551-552.
          Review of <u>Herman Melville, eine Stilistische Untersuchung</u>
      by Walter Weber [Basel, 1937]. Weber's "procedure, though pre-
      cise and formal, is not pedantic, and it serves to clarify Mel-
      ville's relations with German romanticism, his affinities with
      Rabelais, the Elizabethan dramatists, Sterne, and Carlyle, and
      his essential originality."

48   GREGORY, HORACE. "Was Walt Whitman a Socialist?" New York
      <u>Herald Tribune Books</u> (6 November), p. 8.
          Review of 1938.B5. Finds the core of one of Arvin's dif-
      ficulties in his "unserious dismissal" of Melville.

49   FREEMAN, F. BARRON. "Book Reviews." <u>New England Quarterly</u>,
      11 (December), 850-853.
          Review of 1938.A1. Gleim is occasionally overingenious,
      though on the whole logical. But he needed to "go outside"
      <u>Moby-Dick</u> for evidence to verify his assumptions of Melville's
      beliefs and his theories of Melville's use of symbols. Gleim's
      interpretation still seems more safely entitled "A Theory of
      <u>Moby-Dick</u>." [<u>See</u> 1929.B50.]

50   THORP, WILLARD. "Redburn's Prosy Old Guidebook." <u>PMLA</u>, 53 (December), 1146-1156.

     Melville's debt to <u>The Picture of Liverpool; or Stranger's Guide</u> (Liverpool: Jones and Wright, 1808). The guide gives Redburn something to do during his stay in Liverpool, and provides Melville with several easily designed chapters, in which he pillages many facts from his source, usually without hint of their origin, while satirizing its ornate title page, "reverential" preface, and pompous style. Melville's most important use of the guidebook is to emphasize Redburn's forlorn situation through his reliance on the book. Identifies seven of the nine guidebooks Redburn lists in chapter 30; in almost every instance, Melville humorously exaggerates some pretentious phrase in the title page or invents some feature for the book.

1939 A BOOKS

1   ANDERSON, CHARLES ROBERTS. <u>Melville in the South Seas</u>. New York: Columbia University Press, 522 pp. Revised ed. New York: Dover Publications, 1966.

     Reconstruction of Melville's years in the South Seas (1841-1844), "the most significant part of his life for the literary biographer, for it furnished the experiences which make up the great body of his published works." Employing hitherto unused documentary evidence, the book offers a "more detailed and more authentic" account of Melville's experiences in those years "than previous biographers [such as Weaver (1921.A1) and Mumford (1929.A1)] have been able to draw from supposedly autobiographical passages in his writings." Works on the South Seas by other authors are used to corroborate or contradict Melville's records of his experiences. Anderson is concerned throughout with Melville's "technique of composition," his combination of autobiography, invention, and use of literary sources in ("beyond question") his best books as literature, <u>Typee</u>, <u>Omoo</u>, <u>White-Jacket</u>, and <u>Moby-Dick</u>, and in <u>Mardi</u> and <u>The Piazza Tales</u> insofar as they relate to the South Seas. [<u>See also</u> 1937.B1, 1938.B30.] The books are "set forth less as masterpieces of creative imagination than as deliberately manufactured travel records—on the whole joyous—partly borrowed from the writings of other voyagers, partly fictionized autobiography, embellished and pointed for the sake of propaganda." Anderson's portrait of Melville "contains slight touch of foreboding gloom or impending tragedy, small hint of the 'mystic' or the philosopher, no trace of the beard which later muffled the lamentations of America's mid-Victorian Jeremiah." Despite the claims of the "legend-makers," Melville's philosophic offering is a rather meager one; he made a mistake when he abandoned the romantic genre he had fashioned to his peculiar talents, the semi-autobiographical, semifictitious travel-book. The "survival value" of his reputation lies in the fact that he was the literary discoverer of the South Seas. Indexed. Reviewed in 1939.B14, B19, B20, B22, B24, B26, B27, B30, B32, B34, B36; 1940.B18, B28, B29.

2   GEIST, STANLEY. Herman Melville: The Tragic Vision and the
    Heroic Ideal. Harvard Honors Theses in English, No. 12.
    Cambridge, Mass.: Harvard University Press, 76 pp. Reprint.
    New York: Octagon Books, 1966.
        In both Moby-Dick and Pierre a dominant theme is the impor-
    tance and greatness of the tragic vision. To be truly heroic is
    to attain this vision--by diving deeply within oneself and becom-
    ing aware of the blackness at the heart of life. Melville called
    fate the irresistible power--internal or external--that drove an
    individual deeper and deeper into himself. In the Melvillean
    superman, greatness means not power but profundity and conquest
    over one's surface-skimming self. Democracy in Melville's
    thought is simply the equal privilege of all men to achieve this
    heroism within themselves. For Melville, to see profoundly is to
    see mournfully; grief and greatness are inseparable. Ahab be-
    comes a demigod only after he is maddened with grief and hatred;
    Pierre becomes "divine," "Christ-like," a "demigod," a "Titan,"
    and "Prometheus" by attaining the vision of tragedy and mystery
    through Isabel. In its theme of the inseparability of grief and
    greatness and in the imagery through which the motive of heroic
    suffering is expressed, Moby-Dick closely resembles the work that
    inspired it, King Lear.
        By descending into the depths of himself and attaining the
    tragic vision, man becomes sorrowful and acquires a heart; by
    heart Melville means the richness of spirit that can be gained
    in this way only. Promethean defiance of the gods and intense
    pride are other elements in the nature of the tragic hero; his
    pride is the corollary to the belief that man becomes godlike
    through tragic vision and springs not out of conceit or vanity
    but out of suffering. In becoming a demigod by his descent into
    himself, the tragic hero isolates himself from other men while
    remaining incapable of complete godhead; he is cut off from men
    and gods. Melville's works are a commentary on his descent into
    his own heart; his "unfolding" within himself is his own attain-
    ment of the tragic vision. The extreme inwardness of his self-
    scrutiny and the extreme outwardness of his scrutiny of the
    universe are identical: the universe comes to reside in his own
    identity; world and self fuse. Self being synonymous with world,
    Melville's concept of the soul is dominated by the gigantic: He
    can describe the soul only by reference to what is most enormous
    in the physical world. He uses interchangeably images contrast-
    ing land and sea to represent either the world or the soul.

1939 B SHORTER WRITINGS

1   BAKER, ERNEST A. Yesterday. Vol. 10 of The History of the
    Novel. London: H.F. & G. Witherby, pp. 13, 15, 28, n.
        Brief comparisons of Conrad with Melville. Suggests that
    Conrad may have evolved the Nigger and Donkin in The Nigger of
    the Narcissus out of Jackson in Redburn.

2   BOLITHO, HECTOR and JOHN MULGAN. "Wainewright and Herman Melville," in The Emigrants: Early Travellers to the Antipodes. London: Selwyn & Blount, pp. 162–167.

Reprints passage about Melville in 1851.B3. Believes that the "forgotten notes of Lafcatt's [Lucett's] wanderings reveal him as a bully and a swashbuckler and a liar"; but accepts that Melville and Lucett met in the calliboose at Tahiti. [See 1938.B24.]

3   DAVIDSON, DONALD. American Composition and Rhetoric. New York: Charles Scribner's Sons, pp. 75–77, 340–344.

Extract from Moby-Dick, chapter 84, to illustrate "simple expository writing," followed by questions; and from chapter 28, illustrate "descriptive writing." In each of Davidson's illustrations, "the point of view or the dominant impression provides some nucleus or core of description, which serves as a kind of topic for the description as a whole."

4   HEARN, LAFCADIO. "Tropical Literature," in Literary Essays. Ed. Ichiro Nishizaki. Japan: The Hokuseido Press, p. 14.

Notes that cultivated men who have visited the tropics have generally touched only slightly on their poetic aspects; they have been mostly men of science or practical pursuits, seldom novelists or poets. Melville and Kingsley are exceptions. The ideals of tropical life created for English readers have been largely the work of men who have not themselves visited the tropics.

5   LAWRENCE, T.E. The Letters of T.E. Lawrence. Ed. David Garnett. New York: Doubleday, Doran & Co., pp. 360, 402, 458–459, 467, 548, 797.

First American edition. [See 1938.B17.]

6   MEMBERS OF THE FEDERAL WRITERS' PROJECT OF THE WORKS PROGRESS ADMINISTRATION FOR MASSACHUSETTS. The Berkshire Hills. New York and London: Funk & Wagnalls Co., pp. 70, 73–75, 76, 85, 120–121.

Details of Melville in the Berkshires.

7   PELTZ, W.L.L. The Top Flight at Number One La Fayette Street. Albany: privately printed, passim.

Details of Melville's Gansevoort relatives; portraits of Peter Gansevoort (p. 44) and General Peter Gansevoort (p. 127).

8   SMITH, BERNARD. Forces in American Criticism: A Study in the History of American Literary Thought. New York: Harcourt, Brace and Co., pp. 264–265.

Notes the failure of prewar academics to appreciate Mark Twain, Melville, Dickinson, and Whitman, while they took very seriously Irving, Longfellow, Holmes, and Lowell. "What the academy feared, in brief, was realism. Broadly defined, the term summarizes all the abominated subjects, emotions, and styles. Americans were not supposed to be disillusioned about the human body and human society. The existing economic order had to be maintained, the church supported, the gentlemanly ideal vindicated."

9   WRIGHT, LYLE H.   "Melville, Herman," in <u>American Fiction,</u>
    <u>1774-1850: A Contribution Toward A Bibliography</u>. San Marino,
    Ca.: The Huntington Library, pp. 140-141.
        Bibliographical entries for <u>Mardi</u>, <u>Omoo</u>, <u>Redburn</u>, <u>Typee</u>,
    and <u>White-Jacket</u>, with selective list of libraries owning the
    editions noted. Revised version in 1948.B34.

10   PARKS, AILEEN WELLS.   "Leviathan: An Essay in Interpreta-
    tion." <u>Sewanee Review</u>, 47 (January-March), 130-132.
        Satirical account of criticism of "<u>Leviathan</u>." Critics
    have unanimously missed the true meaning: Ahab "undoubtedly
    represents the finance-capitalist, with a symbolic missing leg
    which shows that sensibility has been amputated from his make-up
    in the bitter struggle with the brute whale, industrialism."

11   MABBOTT, T.O.   "A Letter of Herman Melville." <u>Notes and</u>
    <u>Queries</u>, 176 (28 January), 60.
        Prints letter by Melville, dated 29 November 1857,
    "recently presented to the British Museum" [<u>Letters</u>, p. 190.]

12   ANON.   "New Acquisitions by British Museum." London <u>Times</u>
    (15 February), p. 17.
        Notes gift of Melville letter by Dr.T.O. Mabbott. [<u>See</u>
    1939.B11.]

13   ANDERSON, CHARLES.   "Melville's English Debut." <u>American</u>
    <u>Literature</u>, 11 (March), 23-38.
        Examination of fifteen major British periodicals shows that
    Weaver [1921.A1] "violently distorted" the facts of the British
    reception of <u>Typee</u> and <u>Omoo</u>, in characterizing it as uniformly
    hostile, as he did those of the American reception. [<u>See</u>
    1937.B22.] "The proportion of favorable and unfavorable reviews
    was surprisingly similar in the two countries. The only notice-
    able difference between Melville's reception on the two sides of
    the Atlantic was just what one would expect: the seasoned and
    urbane British critics were not so extravagant in their praise or
    so long-faced in their censure. They took Melville's measure
    more accurately as a light-hearted raconteur of picaresque travel-
    fiction." The one exception was the hostile piece in the
    <u>Eclectic Review</u> [1850.B110], which Weaver quoted as typical.
    Melville's debut abroad was, if anything, even more favorable
    than it was at home--only one out of the fifteen reviews examined
    being actually unfavorable. American reviews were heavy and
    patriotic in their praise of Melville; the English light and
    urbane. America was proud of Melville; England enjoyed him.

14   FORSYTHE, ROBERT S.   "Book Reviews." <u>American Literature</u>, 11
      (March), 85–92.
          Review of 1939.A1. Anderson has done two things: given us
      the fullest account to date of Melville's journeyings in 1841–
      1844, the most important years of his life; and come much closer
      than any preceding scholar to determining the proportions of
      autobiography, borrowing, and pure invention in the novels and
      tales based on Melville's South Sea adventures. The most impor-
      tant publication on Melville since Weaver's biography [1921.A1],
      it is concerned almost entirely with a period of Melville's life
      that Weaver touches very lightly. Anderson's carefully docu-
      mented and inescapable conclusions correct Weaver's tendency to
      treat the South Sea narratives as highly autobiographical. Per-
      haps Anderson's chief contribution to criticism of <u>Typee</u> as a
      novel, besides his identification of several literary sources, is
      the clear fashion in which he points out its domination by
      Melville's clever use of suspense. Anderson "has undoubtedly
      given most of his readers a new and surely a pretty exact picture
      of Herman Melville at work."

15   FORSYTHE, ROBERT S.   "Book Reviews." <u>American Literature</u>, 11
      (March), 92–95.
          Review of 1938.B22. An excellent book with helpful notes,
      its introduction practically free of factual errors, "the sanest
      and soundest discussion of Melville's life and works which has
      been published up to this time," treating Melville "not as a
      psychological case, but as a fundamentally pretty normal human
      being, whose experiences, intelligence, imagination, and unusual
      power of expression set him far above the ordinary run of men of
      his day." Thorp's selections from Melville's letters are ir-
      refutable evidence of Melville's soundness and healthiness of
      mind. <u>Mardi</u>, <u>Moby-Dick</u>, <u>Pierre</u>, and <u>The Confidence-Man</u> might be
      treated as a tetralogy.

16   GOHDES, CLARENCE.   "Reviews." <u>Modern Language Notes</u>, 54
      (March), 204–205.
          Review of <u>Herman Melvilles Gedankengut: Eine kritische
      Untersuchung seiner weltanschauerlichen Grundideen</u> by K.H.
      Sundermann. The most important part of the work is its discus-
      sion of Melville's religion, which is well considered and com-
      plete, giving for the first time in print a complete analysis of
      <u>Clarel</u>, "a work which with <u>Mardi</u> and <u>Moby-Dick</u> appears to be the
      chief pabulum for the investigation of Melville's ideas."
      Sundermann has not altogether escaped the proneness of Weaver
      [1921.A1] and Mumford [1929.A1] to consider Melville's works
      primarily as autobiography--the chief weakness of his study,
      other than the limitations natural to any attempt to extract
      philosophy from fiction.

17   OLSON, CHARLES J., JR.   "Book Reviews." <u>New England Quarterly</u>,
      12 (March), 148–149.
          Review of 1937.B1. The journal has interest only in that
      it "supplies the actual and until now unknown framework within
      which Melville moved for fourteen months of his sea life," and

"reveals what is literal and what is fictitious in the incidents and characters of White-Jacket."

18   OLSON, CHARLES J., JR. "Book Reviews." New England Quarterly, (March), 154-156.
      Review of Herman Melvilles Gedankengut: Eine kritische Untersuchung seiner weltanschauerlichen Grundideen by K.H. Sundermann. Never before has Melville's thought been so orga-nized; the freshest and probably the most interesting sections are those in which Melville's views on art and his criticism of society are catalogued. But a number of distortions follow from Sundermann's search for the Philosoph in Melville (whom he labels ein Dichterphilosoph): "the statements of Clarel become more important than the perceptions of Moby-Dick: the bulk of the quotations used in the book are drawn from Clarel. The influence of Plato and Emerson on Melville is exaggerated and that of Hawthorne and Shakespeare is ignored." No one will go to this book to illuminate his own experience with Melville, but a man possessed of his own judgment will make it useful.

19   ANON. "Lies-cum-Art." Time, 33 (20 March), 76.
      Review of 1939.A1. Observes that since 1919, "the 'Melville Revival' has provoked several biographies, some 500 essays, a flood of new Melville editions (54 U.S. and English editions of Moby Dick alone), and a consuming curiosity about Melville's scantily documented life." Concludes: "Author Anderson pretty well clinches his proof that Melville wrote fic-tion. All his hammering does not chip an inch off Melville's stature as one of the major figures of U.S. letters."

20   ANON. "Books in Brief." Christian Century, 56 (29 March), 418.
      Review of 1939.A1. "Besides giving a corrected and factual life of Melville with exhaustive documentation, the author has thrown light upon many related matters having to do with the South Seas, the whalers, the missionaries and the navy in the second quarter of the nineteenth century."

21   WRIGHT, LYLE H. "A Statistical Survey of American Fiction, 1774-1850." Huntington Library Quarterly, No. 3 (April), 317.
      Includes "Omoo (1847). 5th ed. in 1847" and "Typee (1846). 4th ed. in 1849" in list of best sellers. "Because the figures for copies sold were not available, the list has been based on the number of editions."

22   ANON. "A Wandering Genius." London Times Literary Supplement, No. 1943 (29 April), p. 246.
      Review of 1939.A1. It is doubtful that Anderson has over-looked one extant relevant item bearing on Melville's life in the South Seas. But research can never result in explaining what brings about such a chapter as "The Try Works" in Moby-Dick. Anderson's effort all the time is directed to bringing Melville down to earth; he will not even allow that Melville was a philosopher. Melville was perhaps in no way suitable for a

university chair, "but at least he was sufficient of a philosopher to understand, without alarm, what philosophers, meta-
physicians and theologians have always talked about since men
began to wonder."

23   RUBIN, JOSEPH JAY. "Melville's Reputation, 1847." Notes and
      Queries, 176 (29 April), 298.
          Reprints 1847.B13.

24   SMITH, DANE FARNSWORTH. "College Books." New Mexico
      Quarterly, 9 (May), 115-117.
          Review of 1939.A1. The importance of Anderson's book lies
      not so much in its sound scholarship or in its new light on
      Melville's life and writings shed by careful research as in a
      corrected emphasis on Melville's significance. While recent
      apologists have tried to present him as a mystic and a prophet,
      Anderson proves that "the survival value of Melville's reputation
      rests on the fact that he was the literary discoverer of the
      South Seas."

25   WAINGER, BERTRAND M. "Descriptive Notices." Philosophical
      Review, 48 (May), 340.
          Review of Herman Melvilles Gedankengut: Eine kritische
      Untersuchung seiner weltanschauerlichen Grundideen by K.H.
      Sundermann. "The book has value for the student in that it
      brings together Melville's scattered statements on various sub-
      jects, thus supplying a convenient reference manual. Beyond that
      its contribution lies in the critical analysis of the characters
      in Melville's obscure poem Clarel. . . . One is struck in this
      naked and schematic array of Melville's thought by the triteness
      of his conceptions: that truth is everlastingly elusive, that
      experience fails to measure up to romantic anticipation, that
      the ideal and the real are in irreconcilable contradiction and
      the divine laws cannot be brought into harmony with the expe-
      rience of this world, that the human will is powerless against
      fate, and so on. Two conclusions are basic to his pessimism:
      that the divine attributes cannot be reconciled with the
      existence of evil, and that the universe is indifferent to man's
      moral and ethical ideals. In his early creative stage Melville
      represents the Promethean protest of the self-conscious individ-
      ual against this universal meaninglessness; in his later passive
      stage he represents the tragic submission of the same individual
      to his fate."

26   GORMAN, HERBERT. "New Light on the Life of Herman Melville."
      New York Times Book Review (21 May), p. 2.
          Review of 1939.A1. Anderson has uncovered the most impor-
      tant portion of Melville's life, which "has hitherto been mostly
      assumption by his biographers," finding enough new material to
      tive us an authentic and conclusive picture of Melville--to give
      us a new Melville. We see that Melville depended to a greater
      extent than was believed before on the contemporary writings of
      his day. The importance of Anderson's book is that, besides
      giving us a huge amount of new biographical material, he has

shown us, as no writer before has done, how Melville transformed
the rough substance of life as he saw it into art. He also provides a sound argument in favor of Melville's seabooks as opposed
to his "overwrought satire and metaphysical nonsense."

27   ANON. "Books in Brief. Biography." North American Review,
     247 (Summer), 399–400.
        Review of 1939.A1. "Altogether a valuable volume for the
literary historian."

28   OLSON, CHARLES J., JR. "Book Reviews." New England Quarterly,
     12 (June), 389–390.
        Review of Arctic Harpooner: A Voyage on the Schooner Abbie
Bradford, 1878–1879 by Robert Ferguson, edited by Leslie
Dalrymple. Three of the book's tales "have to do with the
brutality of mates, the best of which, about a bruiser named
Badger Higgins, is a rough 'Town-Ho Story.'" The third mate of
the Abbie Bradford was the son of George Pollard, captain of the
Essex, rammed by a whale and sunk in 1819; he "has a significant
story to tell, and whaling historians will want to add it to the
three versions of the Essex tragedy already known."

29   STROUT, EDITH BAUER. "At Home on the Oceans." National
     Geographic Magazine, 76 (July), 33–86.
        Includes account of visit to the Galapagos Islands and
Marquesas Islands, with photographs; brief references to
Melville.

30   SHEPARD, ODELL. "Melville and His Sources." Saturday Review
     of Literature, 20 (8 July), 11–12.
        Review of 1939.A1. Sees Anderson concerned not so much
with "an analysis of Melville's technique of composition" as with
"gathering the materials upon which that technique acted."
Anderson "finds an amazing quantity of facts, many of which are
really pertinent to our understanding of a strange and enigmatic
figure" and enable us to distinguish, for the first time, between
those materials of Typee, Omoo, and White-Jacket derived from
personal experience and those drawn from Melville's reading. No
other book has added in a comparable degree to the little we
know about Melville's life and the raw materials of his writing.
Anderson brings before us a less imposing Melville than the one
presented by other recent commentators; but Melville remains a
man of mystery.

31   WEST, GEOFFREY. "Biography and Herman Melville." Adelphi
     15 (August), 551–556.
        Discussion of biography—a dual process, beginning in in-
dustry, completing itself only by intuition. "The two are interdependent. . . . What happens when either seeks to stand alone
has seldom been better illustrated than in a consideration of
certain earlier biographies of Herman Melville set in conjunction
with" Anderson's "scholarly and extraordinarily revealing
Melville in the South Seas" [1939.A1]. Continued in 1939.B34.

32 FISHER, H.H. "Reviews of Books." Pacific Historical Review,
      8 (September), 356–357.
         Review of 1939.A1. A "valuable contribution to our knowl-
   edge of one of the most fascinating figures in the history of
   American literature." Melville "emerges from the aura of mysticism in which his personality has been enveloped, a more human
   and vivid figure." Anderson effectively deflates the theory that
   Moby-Dick is fable or allegory.

33 FREEMAN, F. BARRON. "Book Reviews." New England Quarterly,
      12 (September), 609–610.
         Review of 1938.B22. Thorp gives the much-needed straight-
   forward summary of Melville's life, clarifying through the use of
   new material and an objective approach, some of the questionable
   statements that earlier biographers have made. One might object
   to the selection from Mardi, which gives the impression that the
   novel is only a political allegory, and to the curious omission
   of Billy Budd; but these objections are almost balanced by the
   inclusion of previously unpublished material. Notes "the excel-
   lently selected critical bibliography."

34 WEST, GEOFFREY. "Biography and Herman Melville." Adelphi, 15
      (September), 583–588.
         Continued from 1939.B31. Review of 1939.A1. Synopsis of
   Anderson's findings. Contrary to Anderson, believes that the
   "early" Melville who now emerges seems more of a piece with the
   "later" Melville than he ever seemed before. "Gone is the picture of the simple sailor-wanterer spinning his yarns of the
   world as he has found it, and only later, in pride of this
   accidental authorship, lifted to higher realms of aspiration if
   not always of achievement. Instead we have the man who had
   (however briefly and ineffectively) sought literary fame before
   ever he sailed on the 'Acushnet,' and whose books written after
   his return were literary works in intention as well as in fact."
   Part of the merit of Anderson's book is to show how genuinely
   Melville's work was a true organic development. Up to a point it
   may be said that Melville's previous biographers "accepted his
   account because they lacked the means of verifying or refuting
   it. But it is also true up to a point that they lacked the means
   because, accepting the account, they did not go looking for them.
   Much material was waiting all the time for the sufficiently
   patient and persistent researcher."

35 FORSYTHE, ROBERT S. "Book Reviews." American Literature, 11
      (November), 308–309.
         Review of 1938.A1. Finds Gleim no more convincing here
   than in his article. [See 1929.B50.] Rejects the idea that in
   Moby-Dick every character personifies some abstraction and that
   every action was intended to convey some secret lesson; Gleim
   has abused his ingenuity in proposing "such a formless tangle of
   allegory." Suggests that in Moby-Dick, as in Mardi, "Melville
   was often simply swept along by his inventive powers and his
   tendency toward rhapsodical prose into the composition of

passages over which the modern student may puzzle himself but in which there really is little that is hidden."

36   WELLS, HENRY W. "The White Wale's Wake." New York <u>Herald</u> <u>Tribune Books</u> (3 December), p. 41.
     Review of 1939.A1. Anderson's "book is a thoroughly entertaining specimen of minute research in naval history and biography. No volume on Melville approaches it in abundance of factual material." But Anderson's scholarship "cannot in itself satisfy the reader who seeks the fruition of a psychological, a reflective or an esthetic approach to literature."

37   FORSYTHE, ROBERT S. "Emerson and 'Moby-Dick.'" <u>Notes and</u> <u>Queries</u>, 177 (23 December), 457–458.
     Quotes 19 February 1834 entry in Emrson's journal; five years before J.N. Reynolds published "Mocha Dick" (1839), Emerson heard of a ferocious white sperm whale named Old Tom. The tale told by the seaman Emerson encountered "would seem to show that when Melville was a boy in Albany, New York, the legend of the vengeful white whale had already taken shape."

<u>1940 A BOOKS--NONE</u>

<u>1940 B SHORTER WRITINGS</u>

1   BATES, ERNEST SUTHERLAND. <u>American Faith: Its Religious,</u> <u>Political, and Economic Foundations</u>. New York: W.W. Norton & Co., p. 202.
     Melville's satiric portrait of Captain Bildad in <u>Moby-Dick</u> expresses "the common driving force of all the Protestant sects," the "desire to unite worldly and spiritual advantage, to insure at the same time both a good life on earth and a better one in heaven." The Quakers nonetheless "were more ready to sacrifice pecuniary gain to religious principle than were any of the others."

2   BLACKMUR, R.P. "The Craft of Herman Melville: A Putative Statement," in <u>The Expense of Greatness</u>. New York: Arrow Editions, pp. 139–166.
     Reprint of 1938.B31, with additional passage (pp. 142–149). Melville either refused or was unable to use the available fictitional conventions of his time as if they were real; he worked not on the representative, dramatic level but on the "putative" level: his work constantly <u>said</u> what it was doing or going to do, and then, as a rule, stopped short. Preferring the non-dramatic mode, he did not write of characters in action but "employed the shells of stock characters, heightened or resounding only by the eloquence of the author's voice, to witness, illustrate, decorate, and often . . . to impede and stultify an idea in motion." The elaboration of his allegorical intentions in <u>Moby-Dick</u> "was among the causes that prevented him from the achievement of enacting composition and the creation of viable characters"; he mistook allegory as "a sufficient enlivening

agent for the form of the novel." Reprinted in 1954.B3 and
1955.B3.

3   CALHOUN, DOROTHY C. Typee: 15-Minute Radio Play, in One
     Hundred Non-Royalty One-Act Plays. Ed. William Kozlenko.
     New York: Grosset & Dunlap, pp. 794-802.
       Begins with Melville reminiscing to "his young grandson."

4   ELLIS, MILTON, LOUISE POUND, and GEORGE WEIDA SPOHN. "Herman
     Melville," in A College Book of American Literature. Vol. 2.
     New York: American Book Co., pp. 89-91.
       Biographical sketch, with brief comments on the books.
Melville "was more conscious of his artistic powers and problems
than has been believed of one who wrote so copiously and so
easily," as is clear from a reading of Pierre. Prints (pp. 92-
112) chapters 41 and 133-135 of Moby-Dick.

5   ELLIS, MILTON, LOUISE POUND, and GEORGE WEIDA SPOHN. "Herman
     Melville," in A College Book of American Literature, Briefer
     Course. New York: American Book Co., pp. 517-519.
       The same headnote and the same extracts (pp. 520-540) as
in 1940.B4.

6   GABRIEL, RALPH HENRY. "Melville, Critic of Mid-Nineteenth
     Century Beliefs," in The Course of American Democratic
     Thought: An Intellectual History Since 1815. New York:
     The Ronald Press Co., pp. 67-77.
       Melville questioned the doctrines of Protestant Christian-
ity and the democratic faith--the God-given moral law, progress,
the free individual, and the destiny of America--which together
provided for Americans of his time the socially sanctioned
answers to questions of belief and conduct. He viewed the
security they offered as false and most of their basic assumptions as illusions. He found no security in religion and none
in science; he was the supreme individualist of the nineteenth
century, founding his philosophy of individualism on the doctrine
that security is an illusion. God and man he viewed as mysteries; the purpose and significance of human life as the last
mystery. For Melville, the fundamental moral law derives from
the dualism between good and evil that is the essence of the
world: man must fight evil wherever he finds it, alone, with
whatever weapons are at hand, and without compromise and respite.
This is the theme of Moby-Dick, Pierre, and Billy Budd. As early
as 1851, Melville formulated a philosophy of morals founded on
naturalism in a generation whose thought was permeated with
romanticism and theism. Reviewed in 1940.B32.

7   GUÉRARD, ALBERT. "Survey of the Genres," in Preface to World
     Literature. New York: Henry Holt and Co., pp. 247, 249.
       Moby-Dick cited as an instance of the exotic romance.
Mardi cited as an instance of the philosophical romance "in the
form of the Fantastic Voyage."

8   MATHER, EDWARD. <u>Nathaniel Hawthorne: A Modest Man</u>. New
     York: Thomas Y. Crowell, pp. 178, 199–201.
          Discusses Melville's friendship with Hawthorne. Both
     "based their fiction on a reserve of specialized knowledge.
     Melville's was practical, visual and exotic: Hawthorne's was
     obsessional, observative and narrow. And both were much affected
     by the early death of a father, a loss which was not compensated
     by transference of affection to a mother." Melville was over-
     enthusiastic in "Hawthorne and His <u>Mosses</u>," his hyperbole un-
     fortunate; some contemporary readers found his eulogies ridicu-
     lous.

9   ORIANS, G. HARRISON. <u>A Short History of American Literature,</u>
     <u>Analyzed by Decades</u>. New York: F.S. Crofts & Co., pp. 132,
     133, 148, 167–168, 181.
          Brief comments on Melville's books to 1866. In <u>Typee</u> and
     <u>Mardi</u> "Utopian thought is by implication: Melville measures the
     known nations, creeds, philosophies, cultures in terms of ideal
     truth and happiness, revealing their shortcomings as active
     forces in the world." Melville is parodying sentimental novels
     of the 1840s in <u>Mardi</u> when Babbalajanja goes down into the cata-
     combs to see Oh-Oh's manuscripts. <u>Moby-Dick</u> has in it "some of
     the spirit of Ecclesiastes, the Odyssey and Rabelais, mingled,
     too, with something of the madness of William Blake." The story
     "speedily verges into man's symbolic struggle with the forces of
     nature, pessimistically viewed as a horrible vulturism." The
     crew of the <u>Pequod</u>, "cosmopolitan in character, represents man-
     kind's feeble force hurtled against an infinite and baffling
     power." In Ahab Melville gives "an expressionist interpretation
     of the skeptic's spiritual torture." <u>The Piazza Tales</u> are well
     written but cling too definitely to the loose, discursive type of
     short story then popular in America. Everything Melville wrote
     after 1855, with the possible exception of <u>The Confidence-Man</u>, is
     anticlimax.

10   PATTEE, FRED LEWIS. "Melville and Whitman," in <u>The Feminine</u>
     <u>Fifties</u>. New York and London: D. Appleton-Century Co.,
     pp. 28–37.
          Survey through 1851. Melville is great in fragments, never
     in wholes. He never completely found himself; two natures warred
     in him: Gansevoort-Melville, New York-Boston, and neither
     reached the powers that might have been his. The feminine fif-
     ties rejected him: <u>Moby-Dick</u> had no love story, no feminine
     characters, no humor, no religion even remotely orthodox. It was
     Hawthorne who undoubtably ruled that <u>Moby-Dick</u> must be more than
     a mere record of adventure, must be like a Greek tragedy.

11   [RUSSELL, FRANK ALDEN]. "Herman Melville," in <u>Ted Malone's</u>
     <u>Mansions of Imagination Album. A Listener's Aid to "American</u>
     <u>Pilgrimage."</u> New York: Columbia University Press (for the
     National Broadcasting Company), n.p.
          Biographical sketch and photograph of Arrowhead; a supple-
     ment to radio broadcast about Melville on 3 November 1940.

12   TARG, WILLIAM. "Moby Dick," in Adventures in Good Reading.
Chicago: The Black Archer Press, pp. 23-24.
     Notes that Moby-Dick has been made into a new American
opera. The book "is a superbly eloquent incantation of man's
struggle against space and time and the dark, infinite sea from
whence there is no return."

13   [TARG, WILLIAM]. Ten Thousand Rare Books and Their Prices:
A Dictionary of First Editions and Valuable Books. Chicago:
William Targ, pp. 239-240.
     Lists mainly first editions, with prices.

14   VAN DOREN, CARL. "Herman Melville," in The American Novel,
1789-1939. Rev. and enlarged ed. New York: The Macmillan
Co., pp. 84-102.
     Revises opinions in 1917.B3 and 1921.B6 and draws on new
scholarship. Mardi is now seen as a magnificent failure, lacking
a large, clear, powerful subject, but continually achieving the
epic prose of Moby-Dick, and containing one of the wittiest
chapters in English (that on the College of Physicians and
Surgeons) and one of the most beautiful (that on dreams). "The
Encantadas" are superb description, and for suspense and unity
"Benito Cereno" is unsurpassed by any other short novel in any
language. Melville keeps close to his original for roughly a
third of Israel Potter, but gives free rein to his powerful
bitter imagination in the rest of the book. Nevertheless,
Melville lived the great chapter of his life in the Pacific and
when he exhausted his memories of that, or lost interest in them,
his vitality fell off and his imagination found no other theme
large enough to rouse him to action. In Billy Budd he came at
last to a full mastery of himself, his imagination, and the
materials it worked on, producing a work with all his early
freshness and with a profound and realistic wisdom that was new
to him--a stern understanding beyond the reach of the romancer
who had imagined Ahab. The entire story is closely and beautifully reasoned, full of the most arresting insights into the
human heart. Discussion of Moby-Dick, "the epic of America's
unquiet mind," draws on 1925.B20. Selective bibliography
(pp. 373-374).

15   VON HAGEN, VICTOR WOLFGANG. "Introduction," "Epilogue:
Source Material of the Encantadas," and "Bibliographical
Notes," in The Encantadas. Burlingame, Ca.: William P.
Wreden, pp. v-xxiii, 101-113, 115-119.
     The "Introduction" contains an account of the Galapagos
Islands and their early discoverers and explorers. Von Hagen
recounts that his interest in "The Encantadas" began when he
conducted an expedition to the Galapagos; reading "these haunting
sketches in the very midst of the inferno that inspired them,"
he judged them "the finest descriptive pieces of writing" about
the archipelago; other accounts are more accurate, he adds, but
"I know of nothing that describes the islands as poetically and,
I am almost tempted to say, as realistically," as "The

Encantadas." Von Hagen notes in his "Epilogue" that Melville's method with his sources [Colnett, Cowley, and Porter (see 1932.B23)] is to take the "skeleton of fact" from one, some lines from another, to quote verbatim or alter lines to suit the mood he would create--all with superb balanced artistry, transforming the most prosaic of factual material into literature. With the single exception of a quotation from Cowley, none of the prose quotations follows the actual quoted text. "The Encantadas" also contain descriptions that did not then exist elsewhere in the literature of the Galapagos and could not have occurred to observers with less acute powers than Melville's. Nonetheless, while Melville creates the impression that he visited several of the islands, it is obvious to one who has checked him "on the spot" that he never visited more than perhaps the northern tip of Albemarle Island. His reliance on Colnett causes him to err in describing Barrington Island. The first four sketches are "doubtless" written out of his own experience and are the best in the book, though Sketch Eighth is the most masterful and most original (for this sketch alone Von Hagen cannot locate the source). In the last six sketches, Melville attempts to move from the general to the particular and to create for distinct islands a legend peculiar to them. Von Hagen identifies the "Dog King" of Sketch Seventh as General Jose Villamil, who was a Creole, though born in New Orleans not Cuba, and who fought not for Peru but for Ecuador in 1810 in its War of Independence. The "Bibliographical Notes" specify some of the differences between the Putnam's Monthly text of "The Encantadas" and The Piazza Tales text. Reviewed in 1940.B36.

16   WELLS, HENRY W. New Poets from Old: A Study in Literary Genetics. New York: Columbia University Press, p. 201.
     Believes that an "age numbering Joyce and Yeats, Lawrence and Melville, among its literary guides and sitting at the feet of Frazer and Freud is not likely to witness a diminution in allegorical poetry or lack of attention to earlier English masters of the symbolical technique."

17   KELLOGG, REMINGTON. "Whales, Giants of the Sea." National Geographic Magazine, 77 (January), 35–90.
     Article on whales and whaling, with many photographs and reproductions of paintings; brief reference to Moby-Dick.

18   LANDIS, PAUL. "Book Reviews." Journal of English and Germanic Philology, 39 (January), 157–158.
     Review of 1939.A1. Anderson's book amplifies rather than alters our knowledge of Melville's method of writing, but in doing so gives us a more comprehensible and more convincing porrait of Melville than we have been accustomed to, enhancing rather than diminishing his power. His fiction never got far from autobiography; his biography, as Anderson demonstrates, was always partly fiction. "Melville was a poet in everything but the artistic discipline required by poetry. His genius was lyric, but he lived at a time which directed lyric intensity

towards problems of justice, happiness, and evolutionary progress. These problems, always a chief occupation of Melville's mind, finally dominated it completely." Approves of Anderson's judgment that Melville is not important as a thinker.

19   LANDIS, PAUL. "Book Reviews." Journal of English and Germanic Philology, 39 (January), 159–160.
     Review of Herman Melvilles Gedankengut: Eine kritische Untersuchung seiner Weltanschauerlichen Grundideen by K.H. Sundermann. A thorough study of Melville's religious, metaphysical, and social ideas with a somewhat less satisfactory treatment of his theories of art. It serves chiefly to emphasize again the chaos of Melville's genius. Although "the influence of his reading is obvious, all of Melville's philosophical ideas are rooted in his own romantic and non-conformist nature and nourished not by logic but by the intensity of his own feelings. It is this subjectivity, expressed often in a language of powerful suggestion, which gives to much of Melville's prose its fiery lyricism. The same qualities, however, reduce his stature as a thinker."

20   SACKMAN, DOUGLAS. "The Original of Melville's Apple-Tree Table." American Literature, 11 (January), 448–451.
     Melville "added the touch of the literary artist" to a familiar story he might have read in the Rev. Timothy Dwight's Travels in New England and New York (New Haven, 1821), in Chester Dewey's article "Remarkable Fact" in the Literary and Philosophical Repertory (March 1816), or in A History of Berkshire County, Mass., ed. D.D. Field (Pittsfield, 1829). Compares versions of the bug-in-the-table story.

21   WATTERS, R.E. "Melville's Metaphysics of Evil." University of Toronto Quarterly, 9 (January), 170–182.
     Interprets Melville's works as his mental struggles on paper. In an imaginative cosmos, Melville placed protagonists that symbolized in concrete form his abstract questions, the chief problems that tormented him being Time and Eternity, the afterlife, the relation of man to God, divine ethics, and the rationale of evil and suffering. Mardi might be called his sociology of evil (the evil of man toward man); Moby-Dick his metaphysics of evil (the evil of Nature and God toward man); and Pierre his psychology of evil (evil seen as inseparable from man's highest aspirations). In Melville's interpretation of the universe, there seems to be a dichotomy of good and evil; but while he saw clearly the evil demonism immanent in the universe (and in the soul) he seems to see no God there, unless it be the capricious Jehovah of the Old Testament who works both evil and good. Melville favored necessitarianism over fatalism because he saw no evidence of any final purpose in the universe. His trilogy of evil was impelled by his own bitterness. Not until he wrote Billy Budd did he see clearly that love and all it implies--spiritual creation, growth, life itself--can alone give value or human significance to the pattern man imprints on the blackness of the cosmos.

22   MAUGHAM, W. SOMERSET. "The Classic Books of America."
     Saturday Evening Post, 212 (6 January), 29, 64–66.
          Considers Moby-Dick a great book, in which the style
     wonderfully suits the theme. Melville's "tumbles may be condoned
     when you consider how splendidly, with what a noble force, with
     what a sustained splendor of phrase, he writes his best pas-
     sages." Finds the chapters of antiquarian lore tedious; but in
     the scenes at New Bedford, when he describes events, the killing
     of whales and the incidents on shipboard; when he deals with men,
     harpooners, mates, and above all the tremendous Ahab, Melville is
     magnificent. Melville's culture was European, and his book does
     not have "the American tang." Though his important characters
     are American, they are so by accident. They "are a little larger
     than life size and they are inhabitants really of no definite
     country, but native to that thrilling and strange land in which
     live and torture one another the persons of Dostoevski's novels
     and the stormy creatures of Wuthering Heights."

23   RANDALL, DAVID A. and JOHN T. WINTERICH. "Old & Rare Books.
     One Hundred Good Novels: Melville, Herman: 'Moby Dick.'"
     Publishers' Weekly, 137 (20 January), 255–257.
          Collations by Randall of Moby-Dick, 1851, and The Whale,
     1851; notes by Winterich about Harpers after the 1853 fire.

24   BRASWELL, WILLIAM. "Melville's Use of Seneca." American
     Literature, 12 (March), 98–104.
          Melville adapted freely from his copy of Sir Roger
     L'Estrange's Seneca's Morals by Way of Abstract, 15th ed.
     (London, 1746) in the passages quoted from an "antique Pagan"
     in Mardi, chapter 124. Seneca confirmed Melville's admiration
     for the religious ideals depicted in the chapters on Serenia.

25   EBY, E.H. "Herman Melville's 'Tartarus of Maids.'" Modern
     Language Quarterly, 1 (March), 95–100.
          Melville "constructed out of experiences and scenes around
     Pittsfield a story in which he presents the biological and social
     burdens of women contrasted to men. On one level the unfortunate
     maids who are the drudges at the bleak paper mill are contrasted
     to the lucky bachelors at Temple Court. At a deeper level the
     sketch contrasts men exempt from the biological burdens of
     childbirth to women, victims of the gestation process. The
     meaning . . . is thinly veiled by symbolism and implication but
     such a disguise was necessary if Melville wished to escape the
     censorship which had already prevented the publication of a much
     less daring sketch" ["The Two Temples"]. This interpretation
     "discloses methods and ideas completely consistent with all that
     we know about Melville even though it reveals that he ranged
     farther and more daringly in idea and treatment than had been
     previously suspected."

26   O'BRIEN, JUSTIN. "American Books and French Readers."
     College English, 1 (March), 486.
      Notes that the publishing house of the Nouvelle revue
française has issued several of Melville's novels in the last
three years and that the most recent volume, Pierre, has been
receiving favorable reviews.

27   SCOTT, SUMNER W.D. "Some Implications of the Typhoon Scenes
     in Moby Dick." American Literature, 12 (March), 91–98.
      Melville wrote for an audience familiar with ordinary
nautical facts and maneuvres and generally refrained from
explicit nautical detail. With the era of sail over, most
readers are in danger of missing the nautical implications of
passages such as the typhoon scenes in Moby-Dick (chapters 118–
125). The reversals of the Pequod's course there may be read as
indicating the alternating ascendencies of Ahab and Starbuck; so
read, they make exciting drama, remarkably suggestive of the
quick progressions and reversals that occur near the climaxes of
many classical tragedies. Nature allies herself with Starbuck in
placing hindrances in Ahab's way, the Pequod turning at each
obstacle to the westward or northward, only to be brought back by
Ahab to his southeasterly heading--toward the "Season-on-the-
Line." The typhoon scenes are not incomprehensible, as Colcord
claimed. [See 1922.B38–39.] Gives diagram and explanation of
the Pequod's movements.

28   JONES, C.E. "Reviews." Modern Language Notes, 55 (April),
     318.
      Review of 1939.A1. The chief values of the study are:
Anderson's organization and the discoveries made during the
course of his research, particularly in the Navy Department's
Naval Records and Library and in the Old Dartmouth Historical
and Whaling Museum. Anderson's most radical departure from the
methods of previous writers on Melville "lies in his purely
inductive technique, in his basing his work on secondary sources
rather than on the novels themselves." The "parallels adduced
to show the effect of Melville's reading on his own work, the
personal contacts and influences suggested, all are plausible."
An excellent piece of scholarly work.

29   THOMAS, W.D. "Reviews." Modern Language Review, 35 (April),
     248.
      Review of 1939.A1. Anderson has probably accumulated all
the sources Melville used in Typee, Omoo, White-Jacket and Moby-
Dick, "and by their aid the genuinely autobiographical is sifted
from the imaginary, and the story of these years of wandering is
set forth in as exact detail as seems possible." A distinct
contribution to knowledge.

30   LAWRENCE, ROBERT. "'Moby Dick' to Music." New York Herald
     Tribune (7 April), section 6, p. 6.
      Report of interview with Bernard Herrmann, composer of the
cantata "Moby Dick." Notes that Moby-Dick has been set to music

previously by Douglas Moore "in the shape of a tone poem" and that the late Henry F. Gilbert once contemplated an opera on the subject.

31   WRIGHT, NATHALIA. "Biblical Allusion in Melville's Prose."
     American Literature, 12 (May), 185-199.
        Finds approximately 650 references to biblical characters, places, events, and books in the thirteen volumes of Melville's prose (Constable edition). The number of references by volume are: Typee 6; Omoo 8; Mardi 75; Redburn 51; White-Jacket 52; Moby-Dick 155; Pierre 70; The Piazza Tales 37; Israel Potter 31; The Confidence-Man 63; Billy Budd 95. Two thirds of the references, some 430, are to the Old Testament, 200 are to the New Testament, and about 12 are to the Apocrypha. By far the greater number are to persons and events rather than to chapters and verses (the amount of direct quotation is slight; only about 50 passages are enclosed in quotation marks). Melville alludes to more than 100 biblical characters: Jonah is mentioned most often, then Adam, Jesus, Noah, Solomon, Job, Abraham, Moses, and Paul. The events most frequently referred to are, in order, the Flood, the Creation, the Last Judgment, and the destruction of Sodom and Gomorrah. Melville's use of biblical material is most evident in his imagery, mostly in simile and metaphor. In characterization he is indebted to the Bible for certain prototypes: except for Benito Cereno and Billy Budd all his heroes are manifestations of one character--Ishmael. A group of characters in Moby-Dick have prototypes in the story of King Ahab in the first book of Kings. Melville also drew on the Bible for certain themes, never adopting an entire story, but rather patterns of thought and action. Four such themes or motifs may be distinguished: the motif of prophecy in Moby-Dick; the theme of the Gospels in Pierre; the motif of crucifixion in Billy Budd; and the theme of the Wisdom Literature of the Old Testament that appears cursorily from Mardi to Billy Budd. Melville's indebtedness to the Bible is distinguishable finally in his style: he is particularly successful in imitating three biblical strains: the apocalyptic, the prophetic, and the tradition of the Psalms; he adopts many biblical idioms and certain Hebraisms, and paraphrases individual verses. Biblical allusion is Melville's chief method of creating an extensive background for his narratives; it magnifies his characters and themes, which are essentially simple and mundane, so that they appear larger and more significant than life, and invests his events with a certain timeless quality. Biblical lore is indiscriminately mixed with ancient and medieval history in Melville's attempt to create an "indefinite, infinite background" and finally loses its separate identity, being but part of the great past, undistinguished otherwise in the sum of human experience.

32   ANON. "Faith and Democracy." Time (6 May), 88–90.
         Review of 1940.B6. Melville "could stomach neither
Transcendentalism nor the common democratic optimism of his
day. . . . Democracy he saw as a moment in history, not as
history's goal. He had two absolutes: the eternal duality of
good and evil, the eternal mission of the individual, a lonely
Ahab, to fight invincible evil wherever he found it." Such
hardihood was not welcome to Melville's time; but Melville had
a spiritual successor in William Graham Sumner.

33   HOWARD, LEON. "Melville's Struggle with the Angel." Modern
         Language Quarterly, 1 (June), 195–206.
         Survey of the developments and limitations of Melville's
craftsmanship. His first major literary device, which he used
with increasing emphasis and eventually with considerable skill,
was suspense. The second, most skillfully cultivated in a new
method of characterization in Mardi, was allusiveness, "or the
use of the incident and phraseology for the purpose of giving
intellectual significance to the story and of achieving imaginative coherence." Later, looking at Shakespeare through the
medium of Coleridge, during the composition of Moby-Dick ("his
one successful struggle with the art of the novel"), Melville
discovered an artistry that enabled him to create, instead of
fictitious "humor" characters, a lifelike tragic hero and thereby
a new dramatic intensity. In creating Ahab, Melville remembered
Coleridge's dictum in his lecture on Hamlet that "one of
Shakespeare's modes of creating characters is to conceive any
one intellectual or moral faculty in morbid excess, and then to
place himself . . . . thus mutilated or diseased, under given
circumstances." Ahab's disease has many symptoms of that
diagnosed by Coleridge: he is a man with a "craving after the
indefinite," who "looks upon external things as hieroglyphics,"
and whose mind, with its "everlasting broodings," is "unseated
from its healthy relation" and "constantly occupied with the
world within, and abstracted from the world without--giving substance to shadows, and throwing a mist over all commonplace
actualities." Although the literary art which makes Moby-Dick
different from Melville's earlier works was "an art learned from
Shakespeare under the tutelage of Coleridge," it was "adjusted to
Melville's own peculiar temperament and to the requirements of
the novel according to the example set by Hawthorne," in whom
Melville found a contemporary master "of the great Art of Telling
the Truth" during the summer of 1850. The plot of Moby-Dick is
that of the "quest" story, unified by its complete dependence on
the character of the protagonist. "It is the sort of plot found
in the stories of Hawthorne rather than the casual quest plot
found in Mardi. The plot is further unified by a parabolic significance which, again, is more like the stories of Hawthorne
than anything hitherto achieved by Melville; and, to make the
similarity even closer, Melville seems to have been attempting to
illustrate the same 'profound' and 'appalling' moral found in
'Earth's Holocaust'--a story which he particularly admired in the
Mosses from an Old Manse." In Pierre Melville tried almost to
duplicate his achievement in Moby-Dick, but his Elizabethan

tragic hero was unconvincing in the commonplace environment of
Victorian New York. Melville "attempted Hawthorne's more restrained manner in a number of short stories, tried dramatic
tale-telling without a parable in Israel Potter, and made an
effort towards a parable without a dramatic hero in The
Confidence-Man--but with no real success in any instance. When
he found a story ready to hand that needed only the element of
suspense and the development of its incidental 'significances,'
as in Benito Cereno, he could accomplish remarkable results. But
his later artistic struggles produced no new skill that would
enable him to continue his career." At thirty-seven he closed
his early career as a writer of fiction, with his artistic
craftsmanship "little more than that of an extraordinarily
talented amateur--effective only when external influences and
personal experiences were united in a fortunate, but largely
fortuitous, combination." Reprinted in Recognition, pp. 223-237.

34   POTTER, DAVID. "Reviews of Moby-Dick." Journal of the
      Rutgers University Library, 3 (June), 62-65.
            Presents evidence from hitherto unmentioned reviews to help
      dispel "the unfounded, but remarkably persistent, belief that
      Melville's novels and, especially Moby-Dick, were unfavorably
      received by the American public." Despite numerous objections to
      Melville's style, philosophy, and irreverence, Moby-Dick still
      retained for him much of the popular favor his earlier works had
      won.

35   LEESON, IDA. "The Mutiny of the Lucy Ann." Philological
      Quarterly, 19 (October), 370-379.
            Prints documents relating to the mutiny kept at the British
      Consulate at Papeete, and now at the Mitchell Library, Sydney,
      Australia, which Anderson lacked. [See 1939.A1.]

36   ANDERSON, CHARLES. "Book Reviews." American Literature, 12
      (November), 374-376.
            Review of 1940.B15. A book at once deluxe and authorita-
      tive. Von Hagen provides a valuable introduction to the study of
      Melville's text, navigating the perilous water of Melville schol-
      arship with commendable skill.

37   ANDERSON, CHARLES. "The Genesis of Billy Budd." American
      Literature, 12 (November), 329-346.
            No materials for Billy Budd can be found in any of the
      records of the British Navy's Great Mutiny of 1797. But specific
      details in Lieutenant H.D. Smith's "The Mutiny on the Somers,"
      American Magazine, 8 (June 1888), 109-114, are echoed in the
      story, and Gail Hamilton's "The Murder of Philip Spencer,"
      Cosmopolitan Magazine, 7 (June, July, August 1889) may have been
      of considerable help to Melville. Melville might also have taken
      note of a number of points in Fenimore Cooper's argument in The
      Cruise of the Somers (New York, 1844). His cousin Guert
      Gansevoort, who played "a leading and somewhat ambiguous role"
      in the Somers affair, may have told Melville enough about
      Commander Mackenzie of the Somers to furnish a model for

Claggart. The portrayal of Claggart may also have been influenced by details in Smith and Hamilton, but Claggart owes
something to the actual master-at-arms on the frigate United
States in 1843-1844. Bland in White-Jacket seems like the first
draft of the more complex villain in Billy Budd. Billy may be
an idealization of Jack Chase; and Captain Edward Fairfax Vere
seems clearly to have been modeled on Sir William George Fairfax.
Melville may have had the British warship Indefatigable in mind
in naming the Indomitable. The setting of the story in British
naval history, at the outset of the Napoleonic War in the summer
after the Great Mutiny of 1797, was for dramatic effect, but was
probably also influenced by Melville's recollections of Jack
Chase. The story hints that Billy was the natural son of Vere,
who was thus faced with the historic dilemma of choosing between
patriotic duty and paternal love. Billy Budd shows a considerable advance in the technique of composition from the cruder beginnings in Typee; borrowing is reduced to a minimum, and imaginative invention counts for almost everything.

38   RAHV, PHILIP. "The Cult of Experience in American Writing."
      Partisan Review, 7 (November-December), 415-417.
          The literature of early America was a sacred rather than a
profane literature, which largely left untouched the two chief
experiential media, the novel and the drama--Brockden Brown,
Cooper, Hawthorne, and Melville being romancers rather than
novelists and "incapable of apprehending the vitally new principle of realism by virtue of which the art of fiction in Europe
was in their time rapidly evolving toward an hitherto incon-
ceivable condition of objectivity and familiarity with existence."
No American fiction writer before James was able to sympathize
with and hence take advantage of the methods of Thackeray, Balzac,
and Turgenev. "Since the principle of realism presupposes a
thoroughly secularized relationship between the ego and experience, Hawthorne and Melville could not possibly have appre-
hended it. Though not religious men themselves, they were
nevertheless held in bondage by ancestral conscience and dogma,
they were still living in the afterglow of a religious faith
that drove the ego, on its external side, to aggrandize itself by
accumulating practical sanctions while scourging and inhibiting
its intimate side." The "unutterable confusion that reigns in
some of Melville's narratives (Pierre, Mardi), and that no amount
of critical labor has succeeded in clearing up, is primarily due
to his inability either to come to terms with experience or else
wholly and finally to reject it." Poe, Hawthorne, and Melville
all display a healthy resistance to the sentimentality and vague
idealism of their contemporaries; they also display "morbid
qualities that, aside from any specific biographical factors,
might perhaps be accounted for by the contradiction between the
poverty of the experience provided by the society they lived in
and the high development of their normal [moral], intellectual,
and affective natures." The dilemma that confronted them
"chiefly manifests itself in their frequent failure to integrate
the inner and outer elements of their world so that they might
stand witness for each other by way of the organic linkage of

object and symbol, act and meaning." The defects of <u>Moby-Dick</u> include "dispersion, a divided mind: its real and transcendental elements do not fully interpenetrate, the creative tension between them is more fortuitous than organic." Many changes had to take place in America before its spiritual and material levels could fuse in a work of art in a more or less satisfactory manner. Reprinted in 1949.B16.

39 ROSENHEIM, FREDERICK, M.D. "Flight from Home: Some Episodes in the Life of Herman Melville." <u>American Imago</u>, 1 (December), 1-30.
    Freudian interpretation relating <u>Mardi</u> and <u>Redburn</u> to Melville's "flights from home" (his voyages to Liverpool and the South Seas). The "journey to Liverpool was an imitation of father, an attempt to become the father and occupy the desired position at home. Mother would welcome Herman as the new father figure and Gansevoort would be relegated to obscurity." This "trend" involved guilty wishes, sexual desires for mother, and murderous wishes towards father and brothers. In <u>Mardi</u> Yillah represents Melville's mother, her disappearance the trauma of his weaning; the slain priest represents his father, the avenging sons his brothers; Hautia represents both the sexual temptation in the marriage relationship and the sexual element in the bond with mother. Guilt, remorse, and dread of retribution made Melville's journey from home a flight, a self-banishment; the hardships and privations were balm for a bad conscience. Melville's agonies in writing were also a working off of guilt feelings, punishments for evil wishes. Another strong trend in Melville was to give up his fight for mother, to renounce his masculinity and atone for the "murder" of his father; in going to Liverpool he not only imitated his father but tried to bring him back to life. In the second flight another motive can be seen, a denial of anxiety, helplessness, and dependency; it is an overly brave feeling of the world's worst terrors; it is also a suicidal gesture. Melville also reveals tendencies to infantile regression (wanting the world to be a breast offered to him unfailingly and unstintedly) and feminine identification (in his writing identifying himself with the mother whose breasts are full of milk). His crippled leg in <u>Typee</u> symbolizes his sexual inhibition, much of the anxiety relating to fear of castration; in paradise Melville must have remained a puritan and must have been miserable.

1941 A BOOKS

1 MATTHIESSEN, F.O. <u>American Renaissance: Art and Expression in the Age of Emerson and Whitman</u>. London and New York: Oxford University Press, pp. 119-132, 284-291, 371-514, passim.
    According to Matthiessen, the "one common denominator" of the five writers he studies--Emerson, Thoreau, Whitman, Hawthorne, and Melville--"was their devotion to the possibilities of democracy." In his sections on Melville, Matthiessen traces

the course of his career, analyzing his themes, his "dominant
symbols" and language, and the structure of his works. Matthies-
son pays considerable attention to literary influences--notably
to Sir Thomas Browne, Shakespeare, the Bible, and Carlyle--to
their influence on Melville's language especially, and to
Shakespeare's influence on his concept of tragedy, particularly
in Moby-Dick. Matthiessen also emphasizes Melville's reaction
against Emersonian individualism, especially in Moby-Dick.
Indexed. Reviewed in 1941.B28-30, B32-34, B37-39, B41; 1942.B10.

1941 B SHORTER WRITINGS

1   AUDEN, W.H. New Year Letter. London: Faber and Faber,
     pp. 70, 153.
         In the modern condition Auden finds: "Each subway face the
     Pequod of / Some Ishmael hunting his lost love, / To harpoon his
     unhappiness / And turn the whale to a princess." Observes in
     "Notes to Letter": "The American literary tradition, Poe,
     Emerson, Hawthorne, Melville, Henry James, T.S. Eliot, is much
     nearer to Dostoievski than to Tolstoi. It is a literature of
     lonely people. Most American books might well start like Moby
     Dick, 'Call me Ishmael.' . . . Melville's sea is not a real sea
     nor his whale a real whale. Most American novels are parables,
     their settings even when they pretend to be realistic, symbolize
     settings for a timeless and unlocated (because internal) pscyho-
     mania." Verses, but not the notes, reprinted in 1945.B2.

2   BENNETT, WHITMAN. "Boston, Mass. 1851: Herman Melville 1819-
     1891," in A Practical Guide to American Book Collecting (1663-
     1940). New York: The Bennett Book Studios, pp. 108-109.
         Bibliographical details of the American first edition of
     Moby-Dick and the English first edition of The Whale.

3   BENNETT, WHITMAN. "New York, N.Y. 1846: Herman Melville
     1819-1891," in A Practical Guide to American Book Collecting
     (1663-1940). New York: The Bennett Book Studios, pp. 95-96.
         Bibliographical details of the English and American first
     editions of Typee; publication details. Notes that the English
     edition "contains a few phrases censored from the American ver-
     sion, having to do with the dalliance of sailors and native
     maidens."

4   BROCKWAY, WALLACE and BART KEITH WINER. "Herman Melville, at
     Work on Moby Dick, Spills out His Artist's Soul to his
     Neighbor and Friend, Nathaniel Hawthorne," in A Second
     Treasury of the World's Great Letters. Ed. Wallace Brockway
     and Bart Keith Winer. New York: Simon and Shuster,
     pp. 405-412.
         Biographical notes; details of Melville's friendship with
     Hawthorne (pp. 405-406, 411-412). Prints (pp. 406-411)
     Melville's letter of 1[?] June 1851 to Hawthorne [Letters,
     pp. 126-131].

5   BURKE, KENNETH. The Philosophy of Literary Form: Studies in
    Symbolic Action. Baton Rouge: Louisiana State University
    Press, p. 88.
        A passage in chapter 2 of Moby-Dick exemplifies the
    "serial" quality--or "withinness of withinness"--found in the
    "to the end of the line" mode.

6   CARGILL, OSCAR. Intellectual America: Ideas on the March.
    New York: The Macmillan Co., pp. 280, 508.
        Finds suggestions of the "mad prose" of Mardi in the "Cutty
    Sark" section of Hart Crane's The Bridge. Carl Van Vechten's
    essay on the later work of Melville in Excavations [1926.B14] is
    an excellent piece of special pleading.

7   COAN, OTIS W. and RICHARD G. LILLARD. America in Fiction: An
    Annotated List of Novels That Interpret Aspects of Life in the
    United States. Stanford, Ca.: Stanford University Press,
    pp. 99, 113.
        Brief annotations of Israel Potter and Moby-Dick. Moby-
    Dick is a chaotic masterpiece, which may be taken as a pessi-
    mist's reply to Emerson and the optimistic transcendentalists.

8   DAHLBERG, EDWARD. Do These Bones Live. New York: Harcourt,
    Brace and Co., pp. 31-34, 106-110, 112-116.
        The effects of puritanism on Melville's life and works.
    Many passing references to Melville.

9   HART, JAMES D. "Melville, Herman (1819-91)," in The Oxford
    Companion to American Literature. London and New York:
    Oxford University Press, pp. 475-476.
        Mainly biographical. Finds it noteworthy that Pierre was
    published at the same time as Hawthorne's The Blithedale Romance
    because both deal with idealists who are crushed in their
    attempts to pursue the ways of heaven on earth. Melville "is now
    considered to be not only an outstanding writer of the sea and a
    great stylist who mastered both realistic narrative and a rich,
    rhythmical prose, but also a shrewd social critic and philosopher
    in his fiction, which, through penetrating allegory and symbol-
    ism, ground away at the core of the universe in his search for an
    Absolute to reconcile heaven and earth." The alphabetically
    arranged volume also contains synopses of Melville's books, with
    occasional brief comments.

10 HAWTHORNE, NATHANIEL. The English Notebooks by Nathaniel
    Hawthorne. Ed. Randall Stewart. New York: Modern Language
    Association of America; London: Oxford University Press,
    pp. 98, 432-437.
        Entries for 25 December 1854 and 20 November 1856 with the
    full account of Melville's visit to Hawthorne at Liverpool and
    their visit together to Chester (cf. 1870.B3). [See also
    1941.B17.]

11   HOLMES, OLIVER WENDELL and SIR FREDERICK POLLOCK. <u>Holmes-Pollock Letters: The Correspondence of Mr Justice Holmes and Sir Frederick Pollock, 1874–1932</u>. Vol. 2. Ed. Mark DeWolfe Howe. Cambridge, Mass.: Harvard University Press, pp. 68, 70, 227.

     Holmes, in letter to Pollock, 18 May 1921: "It seems an age since I last wrote. Did I mention <u>Moby Dick</u>, by Herman Melville? I remember him in my youth. It seemed to me a great book—as ten years later may some of George Borrow's things, possibly influenced by him—but I should think a much greater man. It shook me up a good deal. It is wonderful already that a book published in 1851 doesn't seem thin, now. Hawthorne did when last I read <u>The Scarlet Letter</u>. Not so <u>Moby Dick</u>." Pollock replied, 29 May 1921: "<u>Moby Dick</u> never came in my way: I remember seeing something about it a while ago." Holmes, in letter to Pollock, 30 August 1928: "I . . . always had scruples lest I was wasting time when I read the classics. I am thinking now of re-reading <u>Moby Dick</u> which for several reasons would come nearer to me than to you and which seemed to me great when I half read it. I am trying to feel unscrupulous and to read it for amusement but it comes very hard."

12   INGLIS, REWEY BELLE, et al. "Hawthorne and Melville—New England Writers of Fiction," in <u>Adventures in American Literature</u>. Standard Third Edition. Ed. Rewey Belle Inglis et al. New York: Harcourt, Brace and Co., pp. 576–578.

     Brief general commentary. Notes that Melville has greatly risen in reputation on the strength of his masterpiece, <u>Moby-Dick</u>, which is one of our great American novels. No Melville selection in the anthology (designed for senior high school students).

13   LEVIN, HARRY. <u>James Joyce: A Critical Introduction</u>. Norfolk, Conn.: New Directions Books, pp. 57, 93.

     Notes that the sermon in chapter 3 of <u>A Portrait of the Artist as a Young Man</u> provides an ethical core for the book, as Father Mapple's sermon does for <u>Moby-Dick</u>; and that Ahab in chapter 37, "Sunset," has a curious resemblance to Stephen in his soliloquy by the shore in <u>Ulysses</u>. Within the traditions of the novel, the internal monologue appears to be less of an innovation than Joyce or Dujardin would have liked to believe. [<u>See also</u> 1944.B7.]

14   MASEFIELD, JOHN. <u>In the Mill</u>. London and Toronto: William Heinemann, pp. 47–48.

     Masefield remembers in his youth liking <u>White-Jacket</u> and "that masterly account of New Bedford" in <u>Moby-Dick</u>.

15   PAYNE, LEONIDAS WARREN, JR., MARK A. NEVILLE, and NATALIE E. CHAPMAN, eds. <u>Enjoying Literature: Voices of America</u>. New York: Rand McNally & Co., pp. 298–303, 652.

     Teaching and class discussion aids for <u>Moby-Dick</u> (abridged, pp. 203–298) in high school text. Brief biographical and critical sketch.

16   SMITH, BERNARD. "Herman Melville," in The Democratic Spirit:
      A Collection of American Writings from the Earliest Times to
      the Present Day. Ed. Bernard Smith. New York: Alfred A.
      Knopf, p. 336.
            Biographical and critical sketch. Prints (pp. 337–350)
      "Poor Man's Pudding and Rich Man's Crumbs."

17   STEWART, RANDALL. "Notes," in The English Notebooks by
      Nathaniel Hawthorne. Ed. Randall Stewart. New York: Modern
      Language Association of America; London: Oxford University
      Press, p. 651.
            Quotes extracts from entries in Melville's journal [see
      1935.B14] dated Monday, 10 November, through Friday, 14 November
      1856, and comments: "It is curious that Melville did not mention
      the excursion to Chester with Hawthorne on Saturday or his seeing
      Hawthorne again on Monday. His final comment in the Journal
      before sailing was, 'Tired of Liverpool.'" [See 1941.B10.]

18   THOMPSON, HAROLD W. "Introduction: Bearings and Scrimshaw-
      ing," in The Last of the LOGAN: The True Adventures of Robert
      Coffin, by Robert Coffin. Ed. Harold W. Thompson. Ithaca,
      N.Y.: Cornell University Press, p. 4.
            Regards Coffin's previously unpublished narrative as one of
      the best supplements to Melville we are likely to have, narrating
      events that occurred just after the publication of Moby-Dick.

19   THORP, WILLARD, MERLE CURTI, and CARLOS BAKER, eds. The
      Social Record. Vol. 1 of American Issues. Philadelphia:
      J.B. Lippincott Co., pp. 426–427, 584.
            Headnotes (both titled "Herman Melville, 1819–1891") to
      "The Tartarus of Maids" (pp. 427–433) and "Supplement" to Battle-
      Pieces (pp. 585–588). Sees "The Tartarus of Maids" as an attack
      on the devastating effect of the machine on the lives of mill
      operatives and notes many other bitter judgments on the indus-
      trial system, the new form of slavery, in Clarel. Melville "saw
      clearly that only so long as America continued to be a land of
      opportunity could we expect to be free from the horrors of indus-
      trial war." In Battle-Pieces he shows a magnanimity that is
      probably unique among Northern poets. He hated slavery even more
      than he hated war.

20   THORP, WILLARD, MERLE CURTI, and CARLOS BAKER, eds. The
      Literary Record. Vol. 2 of American Issues. Philadelphia:
      J.B. Lippincott Co., pp. 431–433.
            Headnote ("Herman Melville, 1819–1891") to Mardi, chap-
      ter 161; White-Jacket, chapters 60–63; Moby-Dick, chapters 133–
      135; "The Encantadas," Sketches First and Eighth; poems from
      Battle-Pieces, John Marr, Timoleon; and the "Epilogue" from
      Clarel (pp. 433–471). Biographical and critical sketch.
      Melville's great quest was for some answer to the nature of ulti-
      mate reality. "The Whiteness of the Whale" in Moby-Dick raises
      the whole question whether ultimate reality, seemingly incarnate
      in the monster, may not be a void and an illusion. In Billy
      Budd, which was all but completed at his death, Melville came

finally to that full realization of the tragic sense of life felt
by men like Sophocles and Shakespeare.

21   WALPOLE, HUGH R. <u>Semantics: The Nature of Words and Their</u>
      <u>Meanings</u>. New York: W.W. Norton & Co., pp. 58–62.
         Three attempts to interpret the first paragraph of <u>Moby-</u>
      <u>Dick</u> "by means of analytical paraphrases."

22   WEEKS, EDWARD. "Introduction" to <u>Billy Budd, Foretopman</u>, in
      <u>Great Short Novels: An Anthology</u>. New York: The Literary
      Guild of America, pp. 643–646.
         Biographical sketch and critical note on <u>Billy Budd</u>. In
      this story Melville "was essentially more interested in exploring
      the psychology of seamen and in coping with the ageless conflict
      between good and evil than in harking back to a more direct nar-
      rative of life aboard ship"; he deliberately subordinates action
      to concentrate on the antagonism between Claggart and Billy.
      Like Milton's <u>Paradise Regained</u>, it was written in the calm after
      a stormy life and reaffirms "essential truths, which soak into
      you slowly and are not soon forgotten."

23   DAVIS, MERRELL R. "Melville's Midwestern Lecture Tour, 1859."
      <u>Philological Quarterly</u>, 20 (January), 46–57.
         Newspaper reviews indicate that Melville's lecture tour in
      the Midwest was not a success. In the four cities in which he
      spoke, critics objected both to his delivery and his subject
      matter; only two accounts give an independent and favorable
      criticism. The "bookish" quality objected to in his lecture on
      the South Seas was the result of his reliance on historical
      accounts of the islands and descriptive scenes from his own
      books. The failure of the tour shows that Melville could not
      achieve public success even when he avoided the metaphysical
      speculations that have sometimes been held responsible for his
      literary downfall. In large part it may be attributed to the
      fact that he had so completely exhausted his personal experiences
      that his attempts to please the public led him into commonplace
      generalities and verbal repetitions of himself. Reprints
      1859.B24, the most nearly complete report of the lecture.

24   QUERCUS ASSOCIATES, P.E.G. "Trade Winds." <u>Saturday Review of</u>
      <u>Literature</u>, 23 (18 January), 14–15.
         Report of ballot organized by the Heritage Press to deter-
      mine the ten greatest classics of American literature. (Fifty
      leading critics were asked to name the ten books they considered
      the greatest.) <u>Moby-Dick</u> placed second, after <u>Huckleberry Finn</u>
      and <u>Tom Sawyer</u>, which were considered as one work.

25   AUDEN, W.H. "The Wandering Jew." <u>New Republic</u>, 104
      (10 February), 185–186.
         In article on Kafka, Auden notes that after the Reformation
      "the Sacred Object (the concrete material incarnation of the
      Absolute)" vanishes from the quest genre, <u>Moby-Dick</u> being the
      unique exception. There the "motif of salvation is absent and

the whale is a fusion of the Sacred Object with the Malevolent Guardian."

26   SEALTS, MERTON M., JR. "Herman Melville's 'I and My
      Chimney.'" American Literature, 13 (May), 142-154.
          In pondering over his chimney, Melville "is introspectively
surveying his own soul" and stating "that introspection is an
endless, empty-handed search." His portrayal of the chimney also
"depicts perfectly the enigma Herman Melville presented to his
acquaintances, who were anew astonished every now and then by
what he said and did." "I and My Chimney," further, "is Melville's account of the examination of his mind made a few years
before the story was written, at the instigation of his family.
This meaning is conveyed in disguised form by the plot itself,
with the aid of symbolism parallel to that of Pierre though the
terms are dissimilar. The examination was made because of
anxiety over Melville's nervous condition, represented by the
speculation concerning the chimney, and with the knowledge of
the tragic circumstances surrounding the death of his father,
represented by the mystery concerning the late kinsman of the
story" [Dacres, an anagram for "sacred"]. The characterization
of the story "points to Melville's mother as the person responsible for the consultation of physicians, one of whom [Scribe] may
have been Dr. Oliver Wendell Holmes. The examination revealed
that Melville's nervous condition was not a manifestation of
insanity. . . ." Reprinted in Recognition, pp. 238-251, and
Sealts (1982), pp. 13-22.

27   LEAF, MUNRO. "Moby Dick by Herman Melville." American
      Magazine, 131 (June), 58.
          Humorous summary.

28   ANON. "American Masterpieces." Time, 37 (2 June), 84, 86.
          Review of 1941.A1. By far the most exciting pages are
those devoted to Melville.

29   DEUTSCH, BABETTE. "Caviar for the People." Nation, 152
      (7 June), 672-673.
          Review of 1941.A1. A veritable seed bin for future Ph.D.
theses. Matthiessen's detailed scrutiny of the many problems
presented has somewhat obscured the main structure of his work;
but he elucidates with discriminating scholarship the enduring
values that make these writings live. He makes a nice distinction between Hawthorne's allegories and Melville's symbols and
offers throughout a fruitful discussion of the organic style that
Emerson desired.

30   FADIMAN, CLIFTON. "Thomas Mann--F.O. Matthiessen." New
      Yorker, 17 (7 June), 74, 76.
          Review of 1941.A1. Not a book of literary essays but a
carefully reasoned study in interrelations, American Renaissance
is so full of stimulating judgments, thoughtful insights, and
deep scholarship that it cannot fail to affect the way we think
about our culture. Especially fruitful is the constant

reference to other arts. Matthiessen's argument about his
authors' common devotion "to the possibilities of democracy" is,
however, feeble. Matthiessen writes well but very solemnly.

31   WHITE, WILLIAM. "Herman Melville: A New Source?" Notes and
      Queries, 180 (7 June), 403.
              Cites parallels between Melville's works and a penny-
      dreadful, Harry Martingale: or, Adventures of a Whaleman in the
      Pacific Ocean, by Dr. Louis A. Baker (Boston: F. Gleason, 1848),
      though "in almost every case they are either typical of whaling
      stories or are common literary devices."

32   HELLMAN, GEORGE S. "'They Are the Mountains in Our Range of
      Letters.'" New York Times Book Review (15 June), p. 4.
              Review of 1941.A1. In all five of the authors Matthiessen
      treats, the characteristically American trait of individualism
      is apparent. All, "though in varying degree, shared in the in-
      tuition of super-sensuous truth connoting the divine—the basis
      of the transcendental philosophy . . . which Melville in some
      moods seemed almost fiercely to reject." All of them were
      artists. Matthiessen has succeeded in proving anew what they so
      richly offer.

33   KAZIN, ALFRED. "On Our Nineteenth Century Literature." New
      York Herald Tribune Books (13 July), p. 3.
              Review of 1941.A1. Matthiessen's is the first attempt of
      its kind, based on every possible resource in modern scholarship
      and criticism, to study our representative nineteenth-century
      classics as works of art. One of the richest and most intensive
      studies of American literature and culture ever written, it is an
      extraordinarily sound and unusual introduction to our understand-
      ing of American character and development. It is the fraternalism
      of the book, an appreciation of the democratic spirit in the
      authors considered, joined to his own awareness of the problems
      and needs of democratic men in a democratic society, that gives
      Matthiessen's insights such acuteness and flexibility. Matthies-
      sen has so many points to make, so many applications and annota-
      tions of insights first realized by others, that he seems
      occasionally at the mercy of his material. He has given new
      dimensions to our familiar conceptions of the spiritual and
      intellectual world his authors moved in and has shown the
      "renaissance" of 1850–1855 to be the cornerstone of the imagina-
      tive experience in America, and, if deeply felt and closely
      understood, a guide to whatever we may call the American expe-
      rience itself.

34   RICHARDSON, E.P. "Criticism." Commonweal, 34 (25 July), 330.
              Review of 1941.A1. A thoughtful book, useful, and reward-
      ing. Matthiessen's method is a little like that of a skilled
      cross-examiner who approaches a subject by asking questions from
      every possible angle. If the book has a predominant fault, it is
      that analysis has outrun synthesis, so that the five authors con-
      sidered tend to lose their human unity in the wealth of Matthies-
      sen's analysis of their art.

35   MABBOTT, T.O. "A Source for the Conclusion of Melville's
      'Moby Dick.'" Notes and Queries, 181 (26 July), 47–48.
         An extract in Southey's Commonplace Book (1st Series, 1850,
      p. 430), "A Coffin used as a Boat," ascribed to Mandelslo, tells
      of a sailor marooned on St. Helen's Island using a coffin as a
      boat. Melville may have drawn on the extract in Southey or on
      the original in Mandelslo. [See 1941.B36 and B43.]

36   VISIAK, E.H. "A Source for the Conclusion of Melville's
      'Moby Dick.'" Notes and Queries, 181 (9 August), 80.
         Finds 1941.B35 exceedingly interesting, like all of
      Mabbott's source notes. But in nearly all such discoveries, one
      can never make sure that it is a source; it may be a parallel.

37   ANON. "800 Literature." Booklist, 38 (September), 6.
         Review of 1941.A1. "The books of Emerson, Hawthorne,
      Melville, Thoreau, and Whitman are appraised as works of art and
      studied in detail, with evident scholarship, to discover their
      relations to one another and their bearing on the development of
      American literature. Solid, important material." Complete
      review.

38   HICKS, GRANVILLE. "Book Reviews." New England Quarterly, 14
      (September), 556–566.
         Review of 1941.A1. Finds a lack of clarity because
      Matthiessen does not always make clear his own literary, philo-
      sophical, and religious positions, but can think of no American
      book in which both knowledge and insight are so sharply focused
      on a series of literary problems. Matthiessen is magnificent on
      Melville; no one has come so close to getting out of Moby-Dick
      what is in it. At least a generation of students of American
      literature will draw on this book and be influenced by it.

39   K, B.M. "New Books." Catholic World, 153 (September),
      762–763.
         Review of 1941.A1. Objects to the term "Renaissance" as an
      anomaly when applied to this period because there was no cultural
      heritage in this country to revive. For lack of such heritage,
      the writers Matthiessen considers were under the necessity (or
      thought they were) of discovering for themselves a theory of art,
      a set of principles whose practice would inevitably lead to
      aesthetic achievement comparable to that of the great masters of
      Europe. Matthiessen devotes 656 pages to their earnest but
      pathetic efforts in this direction; the very bulk of his book
      tends to emphasize their ultimate and inevitable failure, though
      their recognition of evil as an incontrovertible fact brought
      Hawthorne and Melville to the verge of greatness.

40   PURCELL, JAMES MARK. "Melville's Contribution to English."
      PMLA, 56 (September), 797–808.
         Lists 180 words to show the nature of Melville's contribu-
      tions to and his influence on the formation of the English lan-
      guage: (1) words not in either the New English Dictionary or the
      Dictionary of American English, or used by Melville with a

meaning not recorded in those dictionaries; (2) words and phrases used by Melville whose use is earlier or appreciably later than those examples quoted in the N.E.D. or D.A.E. The list of words include 10 from Typee, 21 from Omoo, 28 from Mardi, 29 from Redburn, 38 from White-Jacket, 36 from Moby-Dick, 6 from Pierre, 7 from Israel Potter, 6 from The Piazza Tales. The percentage of new words appears to have risen and fallen with Melville's genius.

41   WILLIAMS, STANLEY T. "In the Age of Emerson and Whitman." Yale Review, NS 31 (September), 200-202.
       Review of 1941.A1. A dynamic book, provocative and perceptive in its analysis of Emerson, Thoreau, Hawthorne, Melville, and Whitman, and boldly experimental in method. A solid volume of criticism on a high intellectual level and probably the most firmly fibered book ever written on a substantial period of American literature. The 144 pages on Melville form the most compact, most ingenious, and most complete study in existence.

42   RUKEYSER, MURIEL. "The Fear of Poetry." Twice a Year, No. 7 (Fall-Winter), 25-26.
       "Melville has given us a challenge which could stand as the core of a tradition--the phrase, 'the usable truth.' . . . The usable truth! That is Yankee enough to satisfy the most practical person shopping for common sense. Hard-headed and durable, and serving its own purpose, and calling for its own poetry, and not countenancing any kind of fear. It makes its own demands. It sets its own standards." Rather than beautiful, poetry should be usable and true. Reprinted in 1949.B18.

43   DUFFY, CHARLES. "A Source for the Conclusion of Melville's 'Moby Dick.'" Notes and Queries, 181 (15 November), 278-279.
       The "folk tale" of the dead, clad in shrouds and holding candles, sailing in their coffins, that Mabbott reports having heard from Robert S. Forsythe in 1941.B35 is reminiscent in some of its details of Thomas Campbell's "Death Boat of Heligoland" (1828).

44   DAVIS, MERRELL R. "The Flower Symbolism in Mardi." Modern Language Quarterly, 2 (December), 625-638.
       The Poetry of Flowers and Flowers of Poetry, ed. Frances S. Osgood (New York: J.C. Riker, 1841) provided Melville with the flower symbolism of Yillah and Hautia and may also have suggested the quest as a basis for the story of Mardi. Appends a "Floral Dictionary" for Mardi.

1942 A BOOKS--NONE

1942 B SHORTER WRITINGS

1   GEROULD, GORDON HALL. The Patterns of English and American
     Fiction. A History. Boston: D.C. Heath and Co., pp. 352-358.
          Survey. In "Benito Cereno" and Billy Budd Melville found
     a new way of dealing with human life, anticipating the work of
     Conrad. Like Conrad, he presents a sharply defined crisis in
     which the essential qualities of the actors can be revealed.
     Melville never more completely fused his thought with his story,
     and never--even in Moby-Dick--exhibited more powerfully the
     imagination of genius.

2   HONE, JOSEPH. W.B. Yeats, 1865-1939. London: Macmillan &
     Co., p. 181.
          W.B. Yeats's brother Jack and John Masefield were joint
     owners of a little fleet; their first boat was named Moby Dick.

3   KAZIN, ALFRED. On Native Grounds: An Interpretation of
     Modern American Prose Literature. New York: Harcourt, Brace
     and Co.; New York: Reynal & Hitchcock, passim.
          Brief references to Melville; brief comments (pp. 158, 163)
     on Parrington's "unfortunate" discussion of Melville in 1927.B12.

4   MALONE, TED [RUSSELL, FRANK ALDEN]. "Herman Melville," in
     American Pilgrimage. New York: Dodd, Mead and Co.,
     pp. 119-123.
          Biographical narrative, using Melville's books as auto-
     biography. The "real story of Moby Dick was Melville's own
     bitter battle against the white specter of man's inhumanity;
     his war against the smug conventions, the blind hypocrisy, the
     evil and ugliness that destroyed his world and, finally, Melville
     himself." Reprinted in 1943.B10.

5   RUKEYSER, MURIEL. "Three Masters: Melville, Whitman, Gibbs,"
     in Willard Gibbs. Garden City, N.Y.: Doubleday, Doran & Co.,
     pp. 353-357.
          Melville "was his own remote reflected self, Narcissus in
     conflict, but with the scope that made the twin images almost
     able between them to create a universe. Inclusive in hunger,
     inclusive in sexuality and in power, he would forever find his
     needs denied, until the terrible engendering desire to make
     fruitful whatever he touched was burned down to the last maso-
     chism of 'a fierce, a cannibal delight in the grief that shrieks
     to multiply itself.' . . ."

6   UNTERMEYER, LOUIS, ed. A Treasury of Great Poems English and
     American. New York: Simon and Shuster, pp. 916-920.
          Biographical and critical sketch ("Herman Melville"). In
     strength and amplitude Melville has only two equals in America:
     Emerson and Whitman. Prints the hymn from Moby-Dick (chapter 9),
     "The Martyr," and "The March into Virginia."

7   VAN DOREN, CARL. "Foreword," in <u>Billy Budd, Benito Cereno,</u> <u>and The Enchanted Isles</u>. New York: The Press of the Readers Club, pp. v–ix.
      Brief comments on the three works; whoever does not know them has not read Melville. Wilbert Snow first mentioned <u>Moby-Dick</u> to Van Doren, with excited praise, about 1911, but it was another year or so before he read it. Remembers secondhand bookstores before the "revival," "where Melville first editions usually sold for a dollar each and where I bought one rain-spotted copy of <u>Moby Dick</u> for a quarter, and Melville's brother's copy of <u>The Piazza Tales</u> for fifty cents, and a highly interest-ing Melville letter, with two signatures, for two dollars. (The letter and <u>The Piazza Tales</u> I later sold at about five thousand percent profit. The damaged <u>Moby Dick</u> I threw away, after I had cut out a passage to save myself the trouble of transcribing it!)"

8   GOHDES, CLARENCE. "British Interest in American Literature During the Latter Part of the Nineteenth Century as Reflected by Mudie's Select Library." <u>American Literature</u>, 13 (January), 356–362.
      In 1862 Mudie's annual library catalogue listed all of Melville's novels, except for <u>Redburn</u>, <u>White-Jacket</u>, and <u>Pierre</u>. The 1869 catalogue lists only <u>The Whale</u> and <u>Israel Potter</u>. (<u>Israel Potter</u> was probably his most widely read work in nineteenth-century England, appearing in a number of the cheap reprint series and sold at very low price.) The 1896 catalogue lists <u>Typee</u>, <u>Omoo</u>, <u>White-Jacket</u>, and <u>Moby-Dick</u>, the first two works classified as nonfiction. The decline of Melville's repu-tation as a novelist is indicated by the fact that his name is not separately listed in the section of the catalogue devoted to fiction.

9   LLOYD, FRANCIS V., JR. "Melville's First Lectures." American <u>Literature</u>, 13 (January), 391–395.
      Reprints 1857.B46, a review of Melville's first lecture (at Lawrence, Massachusetts, 23 November 1857); found no reviews of his second lecture (at Concord, New Hampshire, 24 November 1857). Notes omissions and errors in previous records of Melville's lectures.

10   SPILLER, ROBERT E. "Book Reviews." <u>American Literature</u>, 13 (January), 432–435.
      Review of 1941.A1. An important piece of historical writing, which should influence our concepts of how the history of American literature might be rewritten. Melville "confronts the dualism in life which Emerson sought to distil to a single essence and Hawthorne, in fright, to veil thinly. Art must accept the primitive depths of nature as well as the 'refined ascent of the mind.' In his acceptance of the whole of expe-rience he recalls Shakespeare, as he does in his development of original comic and tragic art forms. But he is finally an 'American Hamlet,' his conflict, like Hawthorne's, unresolved."

11   MYERS, HENRY ALONZO. "Captain Ahab's Discovery: The Tragic
     Meaning of Moby Dick." New England Quarterly, 15 (March),
     15–34.
          Critics of Moby-Dick have become absorbed in hidden mean-
     ings, in the interpretation of vague symbols and the ferreting
     out of concealed analogies. But Moby-Dick is primarily a tragic
     interpretation of an action, and one understands its tragic
     import by understanding the story, by grasping the relation of
     the hero's character to his fate. Moby-Dick is in spirit a
     tragic drama rather than a romantic novel, its action possessing
     all the perfections Aristotle found in the best tragic plots: it
     is complex and artfully combines the main reversal of fortune
     with a discovery and a reversal of intention. The hero, Ahab,
     achieves a final victory at the moment he loses his ship and his
     life, a victory of insight as well as of will. In discovering
     that his grief and his greatness are but the two sides of his
     nature, one impossible without the other, Ahab grasps the high
     principle of tragic morality, the principle that men pay for what
     they get. The end of the Pequod corresponds with Ahab's end:
     just as Ahab carries his unconquerable spirit into defeat, the
     Pequod carries a bit of heaven into the deeps. Reprinted in
     1945.B7; 1956.B18.

12   WAGGONER, HYATT HOWE. "A Possible Verse Parody of Moby-Dick
     in 1865." American Notes & Queries, 2 (April), 3–6.
          The possible parody, reprinted here, is "The Great Whaling
     Expedition" by Benny the Bo'sen, originally published in Comic
     Monthly (July 1865). The verses "must have seemed as pointless
     in 1865 as they do today, unless read as some kind of satire."
     [See 1942.B18-19 for replies.] Reports that in the 1860s Moby-
     Dick "was raided for a brochure on whaling printed in connection
     with a current whaling exhibition." [See 1942.B17.]

13   ARVIN, NEWTON. "Toward the Whole Evidence on Melville as a
     Lecturer." American Notes & Queries, 2 (May), 21–22.
          Suggests further search for contemporary reviews of the
     lectures. Highly evocative touches in all the known reviews
     "evoke a curiously complex image of Melville in his later
     thirties, and bear revealingly on his uneasy relations with his
     fellow-Americans of the time."

14   ASHLEY, CLIFFORD W. "The Original Crew List of the Acushnet."
     American Notes & Queries, 2 (May), 20.
          Reports that a page from the New Bedford Custom House
     record, containing the original crew list of the Acushnet, with
     Melville's signature, is framed and hanging in the New Bedford
     Whaling Museum.

15   MADDOX, NOTLEY S. "Literary Nationalism in Putnam's Magazine,
     1853–1857." American Literature, 14 (May), 118–119.
          The sort of material Putnam's received from such leading
     American authors as Longfellow, Lowell, Thoreau, Melville, and
     Cooper (posthumously), as well as lesser figures, supports F.L.
     Mott's opinion that the magazine "maintained consistently about

the highest level which an American magazine had reached up to
that time" [A History of American Magazines, vol. 2 (Cambridge,
Mass., 1938), pp. 423-424, 426]. It offered substantial en-
couragement to American authors by publishing their works and
paying for them promptly and liberally.

16   MILLS, GORDON. "The Significance of 'Arcturus' in Mardi."
      American Literature, 14 (May), 158-161.
         The star Arcturus, referred to several times in Mardi,
becomes the symbol of independence and critical detachment and
provides indirectly a statement of what Mardi is: an impartial
and detached criticism of the ways of mankind. In the "Prologue"
to the first number of the Duyckincks' magazine Arcturus (1840-
1842), Arcturus is characterized as "a star that shines high and
brightly, and looks down with a keen glance on the errors, fol-
lies, and mal-practices of men."

17   BELDEN, T. CYRUS. "Barnum Brochure on Whaling." American
      Notes & Queries, 2 (June), 41.
         Wonders if it is possible to identify P.T. Barnum's hand in
the brochure that borrowed so heavily from Melville. [See
1942.B12.]

18   VIETOR, ALEXANDER O. "A Possible Verse Parody of Moby-Dick."
      American Notes & Queries, 2 (June), 43.
         Reply to 1942.B12. The verse quoted there has nothing to
do with Moby-Dick but is a parody on whaling in general. Cites
differences between the verse and Moby-Dick.

19   ASHLEY, CLIFFORD W. "A Possible Verse Parody of Moby-Dick."
      American Notes & Queries, 2 (July), 62-63.
         Reply to 1942.B12. Notes that Benny the Bo'sen's piece
appears to be a literary version of a genuine folk song with
varying titles, such as "The Greenland Fishery," "The Whale," and
"The Greenland Whale." Whaling was tremendously popular in fiction and verse in that period, and such verses would not have
appeared pointless, however poor they may be as poetry. [See
1942.B23 for reply.]

20   DUFFY, CHARLES. "Toward the Whole Evidence on Melville as a
      Lecturer." American Notes & Queries, 2 (July), 58.
         Reprints 1858.B11.

21   [PILKINGTON, WALTER and B. ALSTERLUND]. "Melville and His
      Public: 1858." American Notes & Queries, 2 (August), 67-71.
         Reprints 1858.B21, B31. Concludes from these and other
accounts that (1) Melville's immediate public was little conscious of Moby-Dick; (2) he was not a "popular lecturer" on the
subject of "Statuary in Rome'; (3) his failure as a speaker in no
way harmed his reputation as an author; (4) his knowledge of his
subject was never doubted, but his choice was unfortunate and
his platform mannerisms were monotonous; and (5) both as a
speaker and as a writer he faced a very real dilemma: "what he
wanted to say would not sell well, and to say what he himself had

little will for was almost intolerable." Rejects Davis's contention [see 1941.B23] that public response to Melville's Midwest lectures suggests that he stopped writing because he could offer the public nothing new. Melville did not regard his lectures as any part of his seriously imaginative writing. The reviews suggest that Melville's criteria as a lecturer were moderation and restraint. Notes errors in Weavers's dating of Melville's lecture engagements in 1921.A1.

22 CARPENTER, FREDERIC I. "The Genteel Tradition: A Re-Interpretation." New England Quarterly, 15 (September), 429–430, 434–435.
Hawthorne and Melville illustrate the genteel tradition at its best, recognizing the beauty and the heroism of the transcendental ideal but denouncing its romantic extravagances. They both went beyond the genteel tradition to pay homage to the unknown God, but returned to tradition, arguing that men should follow a known god rather than seek a fancied perfection.

23 WAGGONER, HYATT HOWE. "A Possible Verse Parody of Moby-Dick." American Notes and Queries, 2 (September), 96.
Concedes that Ashley's reply "seems to settle the question." [See 1942.B19.]

24 P., A.S. "Toward the Whole Evidence on Melville as a Lecturer." American Notes & Queries, 2 (October), 111–112.
Finds advertisement and advance notice for lecture by Melville in New Haven on 30 December 1857 but no reviews; believes the lecture was withdrawn. Reprints 1857.B61. [See 1943.B22 for reply.]

25 THORP, WILLARD. "Did Melville Review The Scarlet Letter?" American Literature, 14 (November), 302–305.
The legend that Melville wrote the review of The Scarlet Letter in the Literary World, 30 March 1850, is rapidly attaining the status of a fact in Melville scholarship. But the weight of the evidence is decidedly against Melville's having written it. The tone of the reviewer is that of one long familiar with Hawthorne's work, whereas Melville's "Hawthorne and His Mosses," published five months later, makes a point of the fact that the writer has just discovered Hawthorne's qualities; and Hawthorne's letter of 26 April 1851 to E.A. Duyckinck implies that Duyckinck wrote the review. There can be little doubt that Duyckinck was the author; and it would be a dull ear that could mistake the conventional ideas and prim editorial sentences for the bold extravagances present in Melville's style even when he wrote notices for the Literary World.

26 HOWE, M.A. DeWOLFE. "The Tale of Tanglewood." Yale Review NS 32 (December), 323–324, 333–336.
Discusses Melville's friendship with Hawthorne. Melville's statement in "Hawthorne and His Mosses" that he "never saw the man" may have been as figurative as the "Virginian" in "Vermont," or, "as seems more likely, the article may have been written before August 5 [1850]."

 1   BRASWELL, WILLIAM. Melville's Religious Thought: An Essay
      in Interpretation. Durham, N.C.: Duke University Press,
      154 pp. Reprint. New York: Pageant Books, 1959; Folcroft,
      Pa.: Folcroft Library Editions, 1970; New York: Octagon
      Books, 1973.
          After an account of Melville's religious upbringing and "a
      brief, informal survey of his reading in religion and philosophy,"
      Braswell traces his developing concern with the nature of God,
      with the question why a benevolent God permits evil in the world,
      and with the question of man's divinity and immortality. By the
      time he wrote Moby-Dick, Melville was an "accuser of the Deity":
      his "inability to account for evil had made him conclude that
      the Christian conception of a wholly benevolent Deity is wrong,
      and he had arrived at the point where he could give full artistic
      expression to his heretical view without suffering pangs of con-
      science." Agonizingly conscious of the beauty of Christ's ideal-
      ism, he nonetheless asserted in Pierre the dangers of being
      guided entirely by spiritual values; he concluded that "a vir-
      tuous expediency" is all that God expects of mankind in general.
      At the time he completed Pierre, his "disillusionment in God and
      man had brought him to the nadir of despondency"--he was farther
      from religious peace than he had ever been before. His "failure
      to find any satisfactory religious or philosophical explanation
      of the universe" stands out as the most significant of the causes
      of his pessimism thereafter. "This last portion of his life
      presents the pathetic enigma of one who, unable to reconcile
      himself to the loss of his early faith, spent much time reason-
      ing on the same old problems." Yet "Christ's doctrine of love
      and his promise of immortality were among the lasting influences
      in Melville's life," as Clarel shows. Though "he did not accept
      the teachings of Christianity in their literalness, he was a
      sincere believer in the truth and the virtue of Christian ideals."
      In Billy Budd, Melville "counseled resignation to the inscrutable
      laws of the universe. Deeply as man may be grieved by the rigid
      and sometimes merciless working of these laws, his duty is to
      accept them and to lay about him doing the best he can." Braswell
      finds the key to the symbolism of Mardi and Pierre in Burton's
      account of the four souls in The Anatomy of Melancholy. Indexed.
      Reviewed in 1944.B15, B19, B26, B27, B33; 1945.B26, B29.

 1   ANON. "Herman Melville," in Americans Who Have Contributed
      to the History and Traditions of the United States Merchant
      Marine. Kings Point, N.Y.: The Educational Unit, U.S.
      Merchant Marine Cadet Corps, pp. 114-115.
          Brief note. Claims that Moby-Dick is an account of a
      whaling expedition in the Dolly and that White-Jacket was
      responsible for the abolition of flogging in the U.S. Navy.

2   ANON. "Melville, Herman." <u>Britannica Junior: An Encyclo-</u>
    <u>paedia for Boys and Girls</u>. Vol. 8. Chicago: Encyclopaedia
    Britannica Co.; London: Encyclopaedia Britannica Co.,
    pp. 235–236.
       Biographical and critical sketch.

3   BURKE, W.J. and WILL D. HOWE. "Melville, Herman," in <u>American</u>
    <u>Authors and Books, 1640–1940</u>. New York: Gramercy Publishing
    Co., p. 479.
       List of Melville's works.

4   CURTI, MERLE. <u>The Growth of American Thought</u>. New York and
    London: Harper & Brothers, pp. 305, 395–396.
       Sees Melville's "criticisms of the factory" as part of the
    transcendentalists' opposition to the idea that industrialism is
    democratic and desirable. Regards his distrust of democracy as
    both more theoretical and profound than Cooper's.

5   DE VOTO, BERNARD. <u>The Year of Decision: 1846</u>. Boston:
    Little, Brown and Co., pp. 26, 35–36, 123, 138–139, 230.
       Brief references to <u>Typee</u> and <u>Mardi</u>. In early 1846,
    Melville "sat down to write <u>Typee</u>'s successor, in Lansingburg,
    New York, and began to court the daughter of Lemuel Shaw. In the
    end he married her and found no tattooing on her shoulders; if
    she had breasts, no one crushed flowers between them. She is
    implacable in our literature. Her husband's work turned aside,
    after <u>Omoo</u>, into phantasies of incest and at last an orphic
    impotence that has too much in common with Bronson Alcott's
    noblest thoughts."

6   FADIMAN, CLIFTON. "Introduction," in <u>Moby Dick</u>. New York:
    The Heritage Press, pp. v–ix.
       Slightly expanded version of 1943.B24. Reprinted in 1950.B10.

7   FADIMAN, CLIFTON. "Introduction," in <u>Moby Dick</u>. New York:
    Limited Editions Club, pp. v–ix.
       Same as 1943.B6. Reprinted in 1955.B7.

8   LEWIS, CHARLES LEE. <u>Books of the Sea: An Introduction to</u>
    <u>Nautical Literature</u>. Annapolis, Md.: United States Naval
    Institute, pp. 29–31, passim.
       Brief survey. Identifies characters in <u>White-Jacket</u> with
    originals. Most of Melville's work after <u>Moby-Dick</u> is rather
    dreary reading, but "Benito Cereno" is an excellent sea tale.

9   MACY, GEORGE. <u>A Sailor's Reader</u>. New York: The Heritage
    Press, p. 402.
       Prefatory note to "Benito Cereno," one of the finest novels
    in America's literature. Melville's method anticipates Conrad's:
    the incidents are set down as they come to the attention of the
    surprised observer, and their significance only gradually reveals
    itself.

10   MALONE, TED [RUSSELL, FRANK ALDEN]. "Herman Melville," in
Should Old Acquaintance. Haddonfield, N.J.: Bookmark Press,
pp. 119–133.
     Reprint of 1942.B4 in retitled edition.

11   MILES, DUDLEY and ROBERT C. POOLEY, eds. Literature and Life
in America. Chicago: Scott, Foresman and Co., pp. 148–149.
     Biographical and critical sketch, "Herman Melville (1819–
1891)." In Moby-Dick the sea seems to stand for human life, Ahab
for the spirit of man struggling with the forces of evil. After
his thirty-second year Melville wrote nothing that seems likely
to survive. Prints (pp. 189–195) chapter 32 of Typee.

12   MURRAY, HENRY A. "Personality and Creative Imagination."
English Institute Annual, 1942. New York: Columbia University Press, pp. 140–144, 154–156.
     In an account of "experiments worked out at the Harvard
Psychological Clinic with the hope of throwing light on the
subtle matter of deducing the personality of an author from his
writings," Murray tells of the beginning of his interest in
Melville's personality and in the nature of his spiritual
pilgrimage. He sees the sixteen volumes of the complete works as
"chapters of a running commentary on the evolutions, the gains
and the afflictions" of Melville's spirit. The words "Call me
Ishmael" in Moby-Dick are an avowal that Melville feels himself
spiritually an orphan, a rejected, disinherited outcast of
society. A factor in the prevalence of the Orphan or Ishmael
theme in American literature is the generally low status, the
widespread neglect and belittlement of the artist in our culture.

13   PALTSITS, VICTOR HUGO. "Herman Melville's Background and New
Light on the Publication of Typee," in Bookmen's Holiday:
Notes and Studies Written and Gathered in Tribute to Harry
Miller Lyndenberg. Ed. Deoch Fulton et al. New York: The
New York Public Library, pp. 248–268.
     Biographical details to 1845. Questions Thomas L. Nichols'
account of his role in the publication of Typee. [See 1864.B1
and 1874.B2.] Quotes from an unpublished memoir of Frederick
Saunders (dictated to his grandson Walter Bobbette), formerly
first copyreader for Harper & Brothers, on their rejection of
Typee and acceptance of Omoo. Prints extracts from Gansevoort
Melville's diary relating to the publication of Typee, and, in
an "Appendix," a transcription of a manuscript draft of part of
chapter 14 of Typee against the text of the first London edition.

14   PLOMER, WILLIAM. "Introduction," in Selected Poems of Herman
Melville. Vol. 10. Ed. William Plomer. The New Hogarth
Library. London: The Hogarth Press, pp. 6–8.
     "Though rich in what may be called poetic feeling and a
master of romantic prose, Melville was an uneven and on the whole
an undeveloped poet. Much of his verse is flat and tedious, or
sprightly in a heavy way; it is full of the faults of the
period—trite poeticisms and mythological formulae, rhetorical
questions and so on; it often conveys the sense of strain

produced by a moralist's yearnings after hedonism; above all, it
is technically weak, monotonous and unresourceful. But when he
is strongly moved, especially by the sea, ships or sailors, the
images crystallize and a strange and unique light shines through
the crystals. . . . Nostalgia could bring out his powers as a
poet . . . and in a number of short gnomic or epigrammatic
pieces, sometimes embedded in versified prose, he also attains a
kind of perfection, though he very rarely achieves 'pure'
poetry." In Clarel, "the reader is left with an extraordinary
impression of a man of the nineteenth century trying to free himself from the incubus of conscience, the weight of tradition and
the lumber of a whole civilization, and to look backwards or
forwards, inwards or outwards, for living realities." Melville
disliked the way of the world in his day, "but he was in many
ways too much 'before his time' and too much of an artist to
prescribe reforms or to define, like some pamphleteer, what was
needed to bring in the millennium. His poetry, including Clarel
with all its faults and limitations, contains much of the essential Melville, that is to say, much that deserves to be better
known." Reviewed in 1944.B14.

15   STOVALL, FLOYD. American Idealism. Norman: University of
      Oklahoma Press, pp. 67-73. Reprint. Port Washington, N.Y.:
      Kennikat Press, 1965.
           Like Hawthorne, Melville felt an instinctive antagonism to
      the transcendental philosophy, although he was more than half a
      transcendentalist himself. The transcendentalists believed that
      the soul, whether of God or man, can be known by intuition.
      Melville denied that the soul can be known, and pointed out the
      danger of seeking knowledge of it, yet could not altogether re-
      sist the temptation himself. Scorning intuition, he tried to
      translate the soul's mysteries in terms of the intellect, failed,
      and fell into the state of skepticism and pessimism shown in The
      Confidence-Man. Melville stands midway between the faith of the
      transcendentalists and the extreme pessimism and determinism that
      developed in American thought a generation or two later.

16   VAN DOREN, CARL. "Introductory Remarks," in The Three
      Readers. Ed. Clifton Fadiman, Sinclair Lewis, and Carl Van
      Doren. New York: The Press of the Readers Club, p. 323.
           Introductory note to extract (pp. 381-383) from Mardi,
      chapter 119, "Dreams," retitled "Reverie of Space and Time."
      "Reading Herman Melville's Mardi during the First World War, and
      feeling lost in that wilderness of allegorical adventures, I
      came upon--and still remember coming upon--two chapters, one
      called 'Dedicated to the College of Physicians and Surgeons' and
      the other called 'Dreams,' which seemed to me like happy islands
      in a bewildering ocean. If the book as a whole is a gigantic
      cipher, 'Dreams' is Melville's signature candidly exposed in the
      narrative."

17   WELLS, HENRY W. "A Religious Quest," in <u>The American Way of Poetry</u>. New York: Columbia University Press, pp. 78–88.

     Revised version of 1943.B21. New passages stress the American qualities in the style and outlook of <u>Clarel</u>. The poem chiefly expresses the immense force of American transcendental idealism, under which Melville chafed severely but from which he never escaped. <u>Clarel</u> exists to stimulate rather than to convince. Melville owes his singular fair-mindedness, which leads him to find both good and evil in almost all systems and institutions, to American nineteenth-century liberalism, the philosophy he otherwise so thoroughly distrusts. Melville is most clearly a product of a land not of fixed dogma but of the very freest intellectual inquiry and thus one of the most profound embodiments of American freedom. With a vigor of mind belonging partly to himself and partly to his New England culture, he has digested the thought of many lands to a fresh and definite purpose and with the most enlivening consequences for his art.

18   WILSON, EDMUND. <u>The Shock of Recognition: The Development of Literature in the United States Recorded by the Men Who Made It</u>. New York: Doubleday, Doran & Co., pp. 185–186.

     Prefatory note to "Hawthorne and His Mosses." For the purposes of his essay Melville assumed a fictitious character. His remarks about Shakespeare, "uttered on the brink of his own great moment of creative energy, must have been inspired by his sense of his own genius rather than by any clear perception of the quality of Hawthorne's." Reprinted in 1955.B31.

19   ANON. "Manuscript Division Accessions During 1942." <u>Bulletin of the New York Public Library</u>, 47 (February), 96.

     Lists two holograph letters by Melville: "One, an A.L.S., August 10, 1885 [<u>sic</u>], to Dix & Edwards, publishers, acknowledges a check in payment for an article; the other, January 15, [n.d.] accepts an invitation from Mr. and Mrs. George S. Putnam [<u>sic</u>]." [<u>See</u> <u>Letters</u>, pp. 173–174, 304.]

20   BIRSS, JOHN H. "Toward the Whole Evidence on Melville as a Lecturer." <u>American Notes & Queries</u>, 3 (April), 11–12.

     Reprints 1858.B27, which seems to indicate that on occasion Melville could make a fairly pleasing impression as a speaker and tends to show that he could be felicitous in his critical appreciation of art as well as in fictional narration. Notes passages in Melville's 1856–1857 journal [<u>see</u> 1935.B14, pp. 125–144] relevant to his lectures on Roman statuary and a report by Henry Sanford Gansevoort on one of the lectures [<u>see</u> 1929.B52, pp. 14–16].

21   WELLS, HENRY W. "Herman Melville's <u>Clarel</u>." <u>College English</u>, 4 (May), 478–483.

     Praises the intellectual and artistic riches of <u>Clarel</u>, a work of the most deliberate and studied art. Its dry and vigorous style is typically American, akin to the best verse manner of Dickinson, Emerson, and Thoreau, as well as to much of the undoubted best of twentieth-century poetry. In <u>Clarel</u> style is

outwardly less glowing than in Moby-Dick but a greater fire burns
within. The style inclines to a certain coarseness, however, and
Clarel succeeds primarily by virtue of Melville's superb design,
his imaginative penetration into his theme, his great earnestness
and humanity, and his extraordinary gifts in symbolism. The
waste land of Palestine, figuring the spiritual aridity of the
modern world, denuded of religious faith, leaves other waste
lands in poetry well behind. The finest sustained passage of
poetic inspiration occurs in the last thirty pages of highly
symbolical verse in the third book, in which the five leading
characters come in contact with Cyril and the ancient, sacred
palm tree. Comparisons with the Divine Comedy. Revised in
1943.B17.

22 LLOYD, FRANCIS V., JR. "Toward the Whole Evidence on Melville
      as a Lecturer." American Notes & Queries, 3 (June), 40–41.
        Reply to 1942.B24. Absence of reviews of Melville's
30 December 1857 lecture at New Haven may be owing to the fact
that New Haven papers of the time, like many other newspapers,
did not usually report lectures. Melville's account book has a
$50 fee listed for the lecture, and it seems unlikely that the
fee would have been listed if the lecture had not been given.
[See also 1945.B12.]

23 GARNETT, EMILY. "New Books Appraised." Library Journal, 68
      (August), 621.
        Brief notice of 1943.A1. Melville was continually dis-
turbed by religious problems, never stopped questioning, and
always found the same negative answers.

24 FADIMAN, CLIFTON. "Herman Melville." Atlantic Monthly, 172
      (October), 88–91.
        Moby-Dick is a book about Evil, the nearest thing we have
to an un-Christian (though not anti-Christian) epic, the product
of unfaith, as Dante's epic was the product of faith. It is also
a book of metaphysical and personal despair (Melville was a sick,
worried, unhappily married man when he sat down to write it, and
some of the poison of his personal life was discharged into it,
veiled in symbols). A pessimism as profound as Melville's can
exist only in a man without humor; Melville had none, as chapter 100 of Moby-Dick proves. At times he shows a vast, grinning,
unjolly, sardonic humor (as in Ishmael's first encounter with
Queequeg); but this humor is bilious, not sanguine, and has no
power to uplift the heart. Ahab is an artist in suicide, deep in
hell even in the days when he stood on two feet of living bone.
The crew's fear of Ahab is fear of self, of the despair every man
knows at times to be within him. In the last two decades we have
discovered how Moby-Dick should be read: not as a novel but as a
myth, an expression of mankind's deepest terrors and longings.
The book's symbolism is no mere system of correspondences, but
rather the subtle atmosphere the whole story breathes. Reprinted
in 1943.B6–7.

25   CHARVAT, WILLIAM. "Melville's Income." <u>American Literature</u>,
     15 (November), 251–261.
          Details of Melville's income from 1846–1891. Melville's
     situation was not as bad as tradition suggests. Reprinted in
     Charvat (1968), pp. 190–203.

26   E., T.T. "Melville's <u>Billy Budd</u>." <u>Explicator</u>, 2 (December),
     item Q14.
          Early in the novel the disinterestedness of Vere's mental
     processes are noted (chapter 6), but his final argument at the
     trial (chapter 18) is concerned with the "practical consequences"
     if Billy is not immediately hanged. "Are we to regard this dis-
     parity as an oversight or as one of the essential ambiguities in
     the story? Does it perhaps point the way to regarding the novel
     as rather more concerned with social repercussions and less con-
     cerned with personal ethics than is customary? In this respect
     the 'Preface' deserves especial note." [<u>See</u> 1945.B32 for reply.]

1944 A BOOKS

1   SEDGWICK, WILLIAM ELLERY. <u>Herman Melville: The Tragedy of
     Mind</u>. Cambridge, Mass.: Harvard University Press, 255 pp.
     Reprint. New York: Russell & Russell, 1962.
          Considers Melville's books as the record, "in their inner-
     most recesses," of Melville's unfolding--"an unfolding of inward
     vision, a vision not so much of life as of what it is to be alive,
     and alive as a complete human being and not a mere two-thirds or
     three-quarters of one," a vision that "expands and deepens and
     rounds itself out" in the course of Melville's development from
     book to book. An "integral part of the story" is "the way
     Melville's inward vision requisitioned all his varied experiences
     of life" (though Sedgwick is not concerned with the details of
     Melville's "private or domestic life"). "The unfolding within
     Melville takes on the character of a drama in which his
     identity--or soul--is the protagonist. . . . Passing from the
     ruddy, solid-seeming world of very young manhood, the protagonist
     comes to feel himself assailed and ambushed by one shattering
     realization after another of the true nature of things. Instead
     of solid, stubborn familiarity, ambiguous strangeness is all
     around him. More terrible, he feels this same strangeness inside
     himself." His "drama of human growth" entails his effort to
     preserve his equilibrium, his "sovereign nature in himself," in
     the teeth of the tragic necessities the human mind is under, out
     of its own deepest nature, to apprehend "the absolute condition
     of present things," regardless of the desolation that this in-
     variably brings. "This drama of human growth is much more to the
     fore and directly before us in Melville's books from first to
     last than in Shakespeare's plays. It begins with <u>Typee</u> and
     closes with <u>Billy Budd</u> . . . which stands to <u>Moby Dick</u> and <u>Pierre</u>
     in much the same relation in which <u>The Tempest</u> . . . stands to
     Shakespeare's greatest tragedies." Indexed. Reviewed in
     1944.B35–39; 1945.B4, B10, B13, B14, B21–22, B24, B26, B30–31;
     1946.B17, B37. [<u>See also</u> 1947.B73.]

1944 B SHORTER WRITINGS

1   BROOKS, VAN WYCK. <u>The World of Washington Irving</u>. New York:
     E.P. Dutton & Co., pp. 20, 370–371, 376–377, passim.
        Notes that Charles Brockden Brown was a precursor, in more
than one respect, of Poe, Melville, Hawthorne, and James. Identifies the "wonderful Arabian traveller" in <u>Redburn</u>, chapter 1,
as John Lloyd Stephens, "the greatest of American travel-
writers." Notes similarities between Melville and Whitman, such
as their emotional amplitude, wholly new in American letters, and
their admiration for the "kingly commons." Reviewed in 1944.B28.

2   DEFERRARI, ROY J., SISTER MARY THERESA BRENTANO, and BROTHER
     EDWARD P. SHEEKY, eds. <u>American Profile: Book Three</u>. New
     York and Chicago: W.H. Sadleir, pp. 162–163.
        Biographical and critical sketch ("Herman Melville").
"Melville had experienced the latent cruelty of nature and of
man at first hand. He traced it to its source in original sin
and, realizing its inevitability, allowed it to drive him to a
cynical bitterness." Prints (pp. 199–206) chapter 135 of <u>Moby-
Dick</u>, with critical questions (pp. 206–207).

3   EKIRCH, ARTHUR ALPHONSE. <u>The Idea of Progress in America,
     1815–1860</u>. New York: Columbia University Press, pp. 179,
     184, 186.
        Finds in Hawthorne and Melville a pessimistic attitude
toward materialistic progress and the idea of progress.

4   GOHDES, CLARENCE. <u>American Literature in Nineteenth-Century
     England</u>. New York: Columbia University Press, passim.
        Brief references to Melville, especially in chapter on
"The Booktrade." Notes that in 1846 and 1847 publisher Murray
apparently did not succeed very well in selling <u>Typee</u> and <u>Omoo</u>
even at the low price of six shillings.

5   HALL, LAWRENCE SARGENT. <u>Hawthorne: Critic of Society</u>. New
     Haven: Yale University Press, p. vii.
        Melville cited as one of the few sympathetic critics who
understood (in "Hawthorne and His Mosses") that Hawthorne was
the product and spokesman of nineteenth-century American democratic society.

6   JONES, HOWARD MUMFORD. <u>Ideas in America</u>. Cambridge, Mass.:
     Harvard University Press, p. 219.
        Mention: "I hear much talk of <u>Moby Dick</u>, which was written
in Lenox almost a hundred years ago, and that book is supposed to
prove that the universe is evil. I had thought it had something
to do with the dauntless spirit of man."

7   LEVIN, HARRY. <u>James Joyce: A Critical Introduction</u>. London:
     Faber and Faber, pp. 46–47, 68–70.
        English edition of 1941.B13.

8　　MATTHIESSEN, F.O.　"Herman Melville (1819–1891)," in Herman
　　　Melville: Selected Poems.　The Poets of the Year.　Norfolk,
　　　Conn.: New Directions, n.p.
　　　　　Few of Melville's poems reveal anything like the mastery of
organic rhythm found in his best prose.　He had become an appren-
tice too late to a new craft.　Although he tried a variety of
metrical forms, he seldom progressed beyond an acquired skill.
Yet what he had to convey is impressive.　Clarel is in the tradition of those poetic debates of the mind common in Clough,
Arnold, and Tennyson.　It is impossible to determine from the
poem exactly what Melville believed.　To put the gloom of some
of his conjectures in proper perspective, we should remember that
the "Epilogue" dwells on Christian hope, and that "The Lake," the
most sustained poem Melville left in manuscript, celebrates the
theme of seasonal death and rebirth.　To counteract his forebodings of the possible degradation of democracy, we should recall his celebration of the heroic possibilities of the common
man--one of the most recurrent themes of his fiction, from Jack
Chase to Billy Budd.　Reviewed in 1944.B34, B38, B39; 1945.B30.
Reprinted in 1952.B19.

9　　PEYRE, HENRI.　Writers and Their Critics: A Study of Mis-
　　　understanding.　Ithaca, N.Y.: Cornell University Press,
　　　pp. 58–59, 62–63.
　　　　　Discusses the recurrent failure of critics to understand
important contemporary literature.　"In that utter lack of
sympathy between writers and their environment lies a partial
explanation of the paradox which has always struck European
observers of American letters: the youngest and most active
country in the northern hemisphere, where optimism is even more
of a religion than plumbing, sanitation, and 'having a good
time,' produces the most consistently gloomy literature of recent
centuries.　Stigmas of stifling sadness, a moral and imaginative
morbidity, a haunting pessimism mark Poe, Hawthorne, Melville,
Emerson himself, as well as Emily Dickinson, Henry Adams, Henry
James, and their successors: Eugene O'Neill, Robinson Jeffers,
Hart Crane, William Faulkner. . . ."　Briefly surveys Melville's
reputation; concludes that "far from having acquired a truer
perspective today, we probably over-estimate Melville's greatness
and thus prepare a new wave of reaction."

10　　WOLLE, FRANCIS.　Fitz-James O'Brien: A Literary Bohemian of
　　　the Eighteen-Fifties.　University of Colorado Studies.
　　　Series B.　Studies in the Humanities, 2 (1959), 57–60, 143.
　　　　　Summarizes 1853.B8 and 1857.B3; finds O'Brien's style
lively and entertaining, his comments discerning and discriminating.

11　　GOHDES, CLARENCE.　"Melville's Friend 'Toby.'"　Modern
　　　Language Notes, 59 (January), 52–55.
　　　　　Information about Richard Tobias Greene during his resi-
dence in Sandusky, Ohio, in the middle 1850s.　Greene's regular
column for the Sandusky Mirror indicates "that he was more of a

literary fellow than one would expect an ex-sailor, ex-telegraph
operator, or even a small-town editor to be. Like Jack Chase,
then, Greene had undoubtedly endeared himself to Melville through
his literary propensities." Reprints a letter of 20 December
1854 to Greene, which is possibly from Melville.

12   SEALTS, MERTON M. "The Publication of Melville's Piazza
     Tales." Modern Language Notes, 59 (January), 56–59.
        Details of the publication of The Piazza Tales, with sales
     figures to 28 August 1856. Prints Melville's previously un-
     published letter of 16 February 1856 to Dix, Edwards & Co.
     [Letters, p. 179], which suggests a date early in February 1856
     for the composition of "The Piazza"; and a previously unpublished
     letter of 30 August 1856 to Melville from Dix, Edwards & Co.,
     which accompanied their statement of sales of The Piazza Tales.

13   WELLS, HENRY W. "An Unobtrusive Democrat: Herman Melville."
     South Atlantic Quarterly, 43 (January), 46–51.
        Finds a moving and personal vision of democracy inspiring
     all Melville's most familiar books. He is fascinated with
     ships' crews chiefly because he finds in them a practical epitome
     of a social order. His primary concern is with the success or
     failure of men to live together in some sort of society; beneath
     his romantic exterior he proves fundamentally a sociologist. All
     Melville's tragic tales--Redburn, White-Jacket, Moby-Dick, and
     Pierre--were written during the four years following the republi-
     can revolutions in democracy's most fatal year, 1848. Although
     in no sense a doctrinaire Marxian, Melville became, as Pierre
     shows, a class-conscious man, hating the coldness and pride of
     the rich and almost instinctively defending the cause of the
     masses. Learning as early as his voyage to Liverpool that the
     rights of property were still vastly more powerful than the
     rights of man, he surveyed mankind as prey to misgotten social
     institutions. He is a democrat in that he is a great humani-
     tarian who seeks to ameliorate the hardships of the under-
     privileged and submerged classes and turns, with the great
     bitterness of his social vision at heart, for moral support
     chiefly to the severe and simple virtues that he finds among
     the people. He distrusted most of the political institutions of
     democracy and was no optimist on the subject of American society
     as he knew it. Yet in certain ways, more deeply than any other
     writer, Melville sounded the basis of our democratic idea. Out
     of the depths of his humanity, he made after his own light a
     religion of democracy.

14   STONIER, G.W. "Books in General." New Statesman and Nation
     [London], NS 27 (5 February), 95.
        Review of 1943.B14. Finds in Melville the "enigma of a
     very good, very bad writer." His greatness is confined to Moby-
     Dick; Typee and Omoo are readable, Mardi and Pierre unreadable.
     Melville is a curiously unsympathetic figure, "and it is with a
     weary distaste that one reaches the picture of his old age, when
     his own children back away from him. Lives of Melville are not

made easier by the fact that he is reverenced as a mystic." One
comes back to Moby-Dick doubting: "Can this inhibited and
fumbling man, with an instinct for third-rate poetics, really
have written a book as one remembers Moby Dick to have been
written?" Rereading shows Melville to be the master of high-
charged narrative; and though in general his "symphonic writing"
may fall short of De Quincey's in verbal subtlety and power, it
is put to vaster uses. In the nineteenth century only War and
Peace has scope and execution comparable to Moby-Dick. Plomer's
selection of poems reveals only a minor poet, but one whose
words, though unpractised, have still a cutting edge.

15   FREEMAN, F. BARRON. "Book Reviews." New England Quarterly,
     17 (March), 125–127.
          Review of 1943.A1. The conflict of heavenly and earthly
wisdom is the key to Melville's ideas on the nature of man, the
validity of the Bible, the integrity of the Church, the compassion of Christ, and the essence of God. In interpreting this
problem of dual wisdom, Braswell does an admirable, but occasionally over-simplified, job of condensing and clarifying its
complex manifestations in Melville's life, writing, and reading.
With the reading, Braswell does too little, perhaps, with
Melville's significantly marked copies of Schopenhauer, but more
with Bayle's "Gnostic influence" and "Manichaeistic insistence on
the evil principle," and is most illuminating in his analyses of
Melville's symbolic uses of Burton's "four souls"--vegetal,
sensible, rational, and spiritual. His analyses of the symbolic
meanings in Mardi and Pierre of "sea" and "land" and their relation to "father" and "mother," of "fire," and of the characters'
connection with the "four souls" of Burton is most revealing.

16   HAYFORD, HARRISON. "Two New Letters of Herman Melville."
     ELH: A Journal of English Literary History, 11 (March),
     76–83.
          Prints Melville's previously unpublished letters of
6 October 1849 and 1 May 1850 to Richard Henry Dana, Jr.
[Letters, pp. 92–93, 106–108]. The second letter "can take its
worthy place with the superb letters Melville wrote to Evert
Duyckinck and to Hawthorne, and, in the broader world of literature, with the letters of Lamb and Keats." But beyond their
intrinsic merit the letters illuminate aspects of Melville's life
and works. The second letter contains Melville's own testimony
that after his first voyage he read Dana's Two Years Before the
Mast, which may now be at least mentioned among the complex
influences leading to Melville's second voyage. [See 1939.A1,
pp. 12–21.] The two letters modify the picture of Melville's
personal relationship with Dana [see 1937.B24], showing that Dana
read and praised Redburn and White-Jacket and was sufficiently
interested in Melville's work to have suggested a man-of-war book
and a book about a whaling voyage (though in each case Melville
had anticipated the suggestion), and indicating on Melville's
side a feeling of friendly esteem for Dana and of warm admiration
for his book. Although still no intimate friendship is revealed,
at this period at least, Melville and Dana regarded each other

fraternally, as "sea-brothers." The second letter shows that,
unless Melville deliberately lied to Dana, the white jacket "was
a veritable garment" [see 1939.A1, pp. 417-418, where Anderson
concludes that it was fictitious]; perhaps Melville actually
owned such a jacket but for artistic purposes exaggerated its
role in the story. The second letter furnishes the earliest
allusion to Moby-Dick, though the white whale is not mentioned,
and is also interesting for the new light it casts on the composition of the book, revealing that Melville was "half way in the
work" as early as 1 May 1850 and did not begin it in the late
summer of 1850 as usually assumed [see 1921.A1, pp. 306, 311;
1926.A1, p. 50; 1929.A1, pp. 146, 154]. Between August 1850,
when Evert Duyckinck described the book as "mostly done" and
July 1851, Melville was possibly occupied not with completing it
but with refashioning it altogether. [See also 1940.B33.]
"Neither Melville's own bluff reference to the half-finished
book, in May, 1850--'. . . blubber is blubber, you know; tho' you
may get oil out of it, the poetry runs as hard as sap from a
frozen maple tree;--& to cook the thing up, one must needs throw
in a little fancy . . .'--nor Duyckinck's description of the
nearly finished book in August--'a romantic, fanciful & literal
& most enjoyable presentment of the Whale Fishery . . .'--affords
any hint of the titanic tragic hero, Ahab, or his mad hatred and
pursuit of the white whale, or of the pervasive allegory. Quite
different is the tone in which Melville later refers to 'the
hell-fire in which the whole book is broiled' and confesses to
Hawthorne, 'I have written a wicked book, and feel spotless as
the lamb.' Is it not possible that the 'whaling voyage' book
Melville wrote between February and August, 1850, was another
Redburn or White Jacket, with Ishmael as its narrator and protagonist and the whale fishery as its real subject, and that what
occupied him so painfully for nearly a year thereafter was the
creation of the whole drama and allegory of Ahab and the revision
of the earlier narrative to incorporate the Ahab theme?"

17   KIMPEL, BEN D. "Two Notes on Herman Melville." American
     Literature, 16 (March), 29-32.
          First note: "A Possible New Article by Melville?" argues
     that Melville may be the author of an article on "Lucian" in the
     British Cornhill Review, 36 (September 1877), 336, 342-343.
     Second note: "Melville's 'The Lightning-Rod Man'" interprets
     the story as a "vigorous attack on organized religion, and a
     declaration of independence of the orthodox creeds." The
     lightning-rod man represents a minister of orthodox religion,
     the lightning-rod his creed.

18   MUNSON, GORHAM. "Who Are Our Favorite Nineteenth-Century
     Authors?" College English, 5 (March), 294.
          Survey of "the favorites of the public who voluntarily
     went to bookstore and library for nineteenth-century reading
     matter and exercised a free taste" shows that Moby-Dick, "with
     some help from the moving picture," puts Melville among a group
     of nineteenth-century authors "whose popularity is very consid-
     erable."

19   THORP, WILLARD. "American Literary History." <u>Sewanee Review</u>,
       52 (Spring), 302-309.
          Review of 1943.A1. The first adequate discussion of
Melville's metaphysics. Braswell makes the kind of enlightened,
imaginative guess, based on facts, which leads to genuine understanding. He identifies Melville rather too closely with Ahab,
however (the key sentence of <u>Moby-Dick</u> is found in "The Try-
Works": "There is a wisdom that is woe; but there is a woe that
is madness"), and goes too far in the opposite direction by withdrawing Melville's support from the hero of <u>Pierre</u>. The chapter
on <u>Mardi</u> and <u>Pierre</u> overworks the system of symbols Braswell un-
covers; one feels that Melville's imagination is being settled
into a straight jacket. But the excellent final chapter gives
the best account yet written of Melville's resolution of the
question that had caused him, and his generation, so much agony
of mind.

20   NICHOLAS, WILLIAM H. "Nantucket--Little Gray Lady." <u>National</u>
       <u>Geographic Magazine</u>, 85 (April), 433-458.
          Includes details of Nantucket's whaling past; photographs.
Recounts story of the <u>Essex</u>; brief references to <u>Moby-Dick</u>.

21   WEIR, CHARLES, JR. "Malice Reconciled: A Note on Melville's
       <u>Billy Budd</u>." <u>University of Toronto Quarterly</u>, 13 (April),
       276-285.
          <u>Billy Budd</u> completes the pattern of Melville's work, a
pattern that is not to be understood without it. Melville's
preoccupation with the problem of sin, the difficulty of dis-
tinguishing good from evil, the arbitrary character of earthly
justice, is at work here, but in contrast to his earlier attempts
Melville has succeeded in formulating a solution to the problem,
which is both morally and artistically satisfactory. In <u>Billy</u>
<u>Budd</u> the tragedy of Pierre is repeated; but there is a final act
and another figure--that of Vere, Melville's final synthesis,
alone in Melville's works the complete moral man. In <u>Billy Budd</u>
Melville makes his climactic assertion of eternal justice,
establishing the paradox that injustice may find its place
within the pattern of a larger, all-embracing divine righteous-
ness. Reprinted in part in Rountree, pp. 121-126.

22   WALCUTT, CHARLES CHILD. "The Fire Symbolism in <u>Moby Dick</u>."
       <u>Modern Language Notes</u>, 59 (May), 304-310.
          Finds in chapter 119 the key that explains many paradoxical
and confusing references to fire and enables us to relate the
fire symbolism to the final, central meaning of the book. The
presence of Fedallah the Parsee suggests that Ahab has practiced
Zoroastrian rites assisted by him. Since fire represents
Ahmazd, the good, to the Zoroastrians, it is difficult to understand how it can also symbolize evil, as it does constantly, and,
in the scene of the corpusants, fire can be virtually identified
with the malign element in nature that Ahab is opposing. The
paradox can only be resolved by an understanding of Ahab's
spiritual development. Ahab first worshipped fire as the
destroyer of evil, in the authentic Zoroastrian manner,

considering it the principle of light. When doing so he was
struck by lightning: fire burned him. The burning was the
counterpart of his being maimed later by Moby Dick. His being
burned is the revelation--not yet understood by Ahab--that "evil"
and "good" are not separate but One. After this experience Ahab
hates the fire as he hates Moby Dick because he considers it
essential evil, alien to man and maliciously destructive. As the
voyage proceeds and Ahab grows wiser through speculation, he
brings his two polar attitudes toward fire together, realizing
that evil cannot be destroyed but that man rises to greatness in
struggling with it.

23   WILSON, EDMUND. "A Treatise on Tales of Horror." New Yorker,
       20 (27 May), 67.
       Review of several collections of horror tales aiming pri-
marily at popular entertainment and not pretending to a literary
standard. Suggests that "an anthology of considerable interest
and power could be compiled by assembling some horror stories
by really first-rate modern writers, in which they have achieved
their effects not merely by attempting to transpose into terms
of contemporary life the old fairy tales of goblins and phantoms
but by probing psychological caverns where the constraints of
that life itself have engendered disquieting obsessions." Wilson
would start with Hawthorne and Poe and include Melville and
Gogol. The Melville selection would be "Bartleby," which oddly
resembles Gogol in its vein of the sombre-grotesque, and "Benito
Cereno," a "more plausible yet still a nightmarish affair, which
ought to be matched farther on by Conrad's 'Heart of Darkness.'"
Reprinted in 1950.B32.

24   BOLTÉ, CHARLES GUY. "The White Whale and the War." Tomorrow,
       4 (September), 10-14.
       Moby-Dick is the great American novel because it demon-
strates why its protagonist must stand up and fight the power of
darkness. That fighting for life freed from the rule of darkness
seems the central fiber of the American genius. Ahab is "a
shadowing forth of the indomitable, the highly practical, and
the self-deprecating unknowable that distinguish the American
folk-hero and the American soldier-hero." He is the great American because he followed his primal bent to its savage end. In
his realization of "the world's opposing white whale" and on-
slaught against it, Ahab symbolizes the American awareness and
aggressivenews that could prosperously civilize a sprawling
continent; in his continuing battle he symbolizes the American
spirit that goes on trying to bring the American dream closer to
reality. At its best and fairest, America tries to set every
man free to follow his own white whale; Americans are fighting
the war in Europe for that purpose.

25 WILSON, EDMUND. "Nikolai Gogol--Greek Paideia." New Yorker, 20 (9 September), 65.

Notes Gogol's closeness to Melville and Poe. One "of the books that 'Dead Souls' most resembles, for all the differences between the ostensible subjects, is certainly 'Moby Dick,' in which Ahab's pursuit of the white whale is no more merely a fishing expedition than Chichikov's journey through Russia to buy up the titles to dead serfs is merely a swindling trip." Reprinted in 1950.B32.

26 BAKER, CARLOS. "Book Reviews." Theology Today, 1 (October), 409-411.

Review of 1943.A1. "The total effect of Braswell's book is that of abundant information perhaps unduly compressed through limitation of space. Melville scholars will need more convincing if they are to accept Braswell's interpretation of the symbol-pattern in Mardi and Pierre. Certain ideas, for example Melville's complex views on free will and predestination, need further development, and one inevitably misses the pervasive richness of Melville's mind in this redaction of it." But the seven chapters "provide a trustworthy chart of Melville's stormy course through Christian thought."

27 MANSFIELD, LUTHER S. "Recent Books." Journal of Religion, 24 (October), 295-296.

Review of 1943.A1. Braswell has amassed many pertinent facts and suggestive interpretations. The chapter on "Religious Background and Influences" is admirably complete, though, since Melville's religious outlook was constantly changing, more emphasis on the chronology of reading would prove helpful. The final chapter, "The Long Search for Peace," gives almost the first lucid account--and easily the best--of the religious phases of Melville's last forty years. The interpretation in "The Story in the Symbolism of Mardi and Pierre" is a genuine contribution, provocative and convincing; very possibly the four-soul theory of Paracelsus and Campanella will prove the key to these often baffling novels. As in earlier work, Braswell has shown himself the most profound and intelligible expositor of Pierre. Regrettably, he has contented himself with sketchy and conventional remarks about Moby-Dick, "seeming to accept uncritically the verdict of the early twenties about Melville's pessimism and to follow along with a too facile identification of Ahab with Melville." (Ishmael, more logically than Ahab, is to be identified with Melville.) Moby-Dick is perhaps best understood with reference to the Book of Job (which Braswell never mentions); verbal parallels, borrowing of metaphors, allusions, and quotations abound. Melville's treatment is more complex than Job's, but their problem was identical: the existence of evil.

28 WILSON, EDMUND. "A Fine Picture to Hang in the Library: Brooks's Age of Irving." New Yorker, 20 (7 October), 73.

Review of 1944.B1. Notes that if someone were to speak of "the noblest and most eloquent prose" in connection with a work

of fiction one might think of Melville, or Flaubert, or D.H.
Lawrence—but not of Fenimore Cooper, as Brooks does. Reprinted
in 1950.B32.

29   SCUDDER, HAROLD H.   "Hawthorne's Use of 'Typee.'" Notes and
     Queries, 187 (21 October), 184–186.
          Hawthorne drew on Typee for "The Paradise of Children" in
     A Wonder-Book for Boys and Girls.

30   CHARVAT, WILLIAM.   "James T. Fields and the Beginnings of Book
     Promotion, 1840–1855." Huntington Library Quarterly, 8
     (November), 88.
          Warns that to attempt to estimate Melville's reputation by
     counting up favorable reviews is simply naïve. "Melville himself
     was well aware of the value of such evidence, for he had the far
     more realistic figures of Harper's accounting office to tell him
     how popular he was with readers."

31   FREEMAN, F. BARRON.   "The Enigma of Melville's 'Daniel
     Orme.'" American Literature, 16 (November), 208–211.
          Questions Braswell's use of "Daniel Orme" as a "symbolic
     self-portrait, important for an understanding of Melville's
     [final] spiritual state." [See 1943.A1, p. 124.] The fragment
     went through four distinct stages of composition. Any wordplay
     in the title, such as the pun "Daniel, or me?" that Braswell
     finds, came only after the fragment was greatly extended, com-
     pletely revised, and retitled. Since the fragment was first
     written for Billy Budd, one could conclude that Melville did not
     first write it with possible autobiographical significations as
     his primary aim. There are specific parallels between Orme and
     the Danskar in Billy Budd and "Old Combustibles" in White-Jacket
     (and since the reader can fully understand the reasons for the
     Danskar's enigmatic reply to Billy only through a synthesis of
     their three closely related descriptions, Melville's suspicion
     of a flaw in Billy Budd, indicated in the manuscript, seems
     warranted). "Daniel Orme" reveals a fairly common attribute of
     Melville's last writings: a frequent harking back to the milieu
     of White-Jacket and, perhaps, to his own experiences aboard the
     United States.

32   HILLWAY, TYRUS.   "Taji's Abdication in Herman Melville's
     Mardi." American Literature, 16 (November), 204–207.
          At the end of Mardi Taji commits suicide. "Whether one
     interprets the flight through the reef barrier into the outer
     ocean as the symbol of Melville's appeal to metaphysics for the
     explanation of life's major mystery or sees in it more blasphe-
     mous implications, the belief that the search goes on in a world
     similar in form and substance to Mardi itself must be rejected."
     To seek his lost happiness, Taji is willing to sever all his ties
     with life. The ending of Mardi parallels the last stanza of
     Shelley's "Adonais."

33   THORP, WILLARD. "Book Reviews." <u>American Literature</u>, 16
      (November), 240–243.
          Review of 1943.A1. A brief but highly charged book, in
which Braswell grapples with the difficult problems of Melville
criticism, in nearly every instance scoring a victory or winning
a decision on points. He does not make full use of the conclusion Melville finally reached satisfactorily to himself in <u>Billy
Budd</u> on the question of human depravity. Braswell goes too far
in seeing in Ahab's accusation of the Deity the reflection of
Melville's blasphemous mood (Ishmael learns what Ahab is tragi-
cally incapable of learning, that "there is a wisdom that is woe;
but there is a woe that is madness"). And Braswell is too absolute in his contention that if Pierre had practiced the "virtuous
expediency" recommended in the Plinlimmon pamphlet he might have
escaped the consequences of his folly (Plinlimmon is just another
of those imposter philosophers who pretend to have got an answer
out of "that profound Silence, that only Voice of our God").
Brawell's hypothesis about Melville's use of Burton's theory of
the four souls is ingenious and, for <u>Mardi</u>, to a degree plausible, but many objections can be offered to it. Even if Melville's symbols were derived from this system, there is far more
meaning, in <u>Pierre</u> particularly, than is provided by Burton's
psychology. Melville was not bitter about the scientific spirit
as it is reflected in the works of Strauss and Niebuhr, as
Braswell claims. The journal of 1856–1857 "seems rather to indicate that he resented the historical criticism of the Bible for
the same reason he did the drabness of the Holy Land. It was not
that they killed faith. After one had read the criticism and
seen the dreary landmarks it was no longer possible for one's
imagination to flower in the Christian myth." But though one may
differ with Braswell on many points, he has written a thoughtful,
provocative book that does much to clarify dark passages in
Melville's writing.

34   ANON. "Verse." <u>New Yorker</u>, 20 (18 November), 87.
          Review of 1944.B8. Melville's talent for the verse medium
was not remarkable, but he was often able to frame poetic insights and emotions in compressed and compelling form. The
selections from <u>Clarel</u> have particular interest.

35   WILSON, EDMUND. "Books." <u>New Yorker</u>, 20 (25 November), 89.
          Review of 1944.A1. A careful and thoroughgoing study of
Melville's fundamental ideas as developed in his successive
works, by a sensitive and searching critic.

36   RAHV, PHILIP. "Purging the Real." <u>Nation</u>, 159 (2 December),
      694.
          Review of 1944.A1. Chides Sedgwick for adopting a critical
method that deliberately isolates the psychic content of
Melville's work from its philosophical content and the personal
crisis behind it from the crisis it imaginatively represents.
For Melville, writing was far more a means of personal expression
than of objective creation; figures like Ishmael, Ahab, and
Pierre are clearly psychological self-portraits, and such

heroines as Mrs. Glendinning, Lucy, and Isabel in <u>Pierre</u> and
Hautia and Yillah in <u>Mardi</u> are projections of his unresolved
emotional experience. Sedgwick handles his subject on so ideal
a plane as to make it altogether easy to discover in Melville's
career a pattern of unity and basic fulfillment that no other
critic has been able to discern. Typical of his approach is the
attempt to blur the psychosexual theme in <u>Pierre</u>, piling one
ethical abstraction on another till one loses all sense of the
reality of the incest motif. A solemn, high-minded, but essentially lifeless job of criticism.

37   THORP, WILLARD. "Spokesman for the Melvillists." <u>Saturday
      Review of Literature</u>, 27 (9 December), 11.
          Review of 1944.A1. No previous critic has comprehended and
      set forth so completely as Sedgwick the tragic drama that un-
      folds, act by act, from <u>Typee</u> to <u>Billy Budd</u>. Page after page is
      prodigal of new insights.

38   KAZIN, ALFRED. "The Inmost Leaf." <u>New Republic</u>, 111
      (18 December), 840-841.
          Review of 1944.A1, B8. Sedgwick's is an extremely alert,
      sensitive, and genially noncommittal commentary on Melville's
      ideas, but Melville himself is not in it. It is a superior
      academic book, fertile in its discussion of many problems in
      Melville's thought, but one lacking in essential personal refer-
      ence, esthetic interest, or those comparative judgments with
      other writers which Melville, by his peculiarly neo-Faustian
      leaps, demands more than most American writers. Sedgwick lacked
      even Parrington's feeling for social dynamics. One of the inci-
      dental faults of his method is that he ignores, except for a
      brief reflection on the cardinal loneliness of certain American
      minds, the whole problem of Melville as déclassé. One cannot
      properly study so extreme a sensibility under the rubric of gen-
      eral ideas in the Anglo-American tradition, as Sedgwick attempts.
      Melville's indebtedness to Shakespeare does not mean that they
      had the same problem. (Melville probably learned from Shake-
      speare the way young Communist poets used to learn from Eliot--
      learned a tone, that is.) If there is real indebtedness from
      one writer to another, it must at least be studied from the point
      of view of that disharmony in the individual and his tradition
      which seeks a forced harmony of style. In his inmost leaf
      Melville was a man before he was a writer, and a man whose con-
      viction of the inexpressible barrenness of life was such that he
      could relieve his alienation only by passing it off to the uni-
      verse. Without an awareness of Melville's obsession with sepa-
      rateness, the incidence and range of its images, we are cut off
      from what is deepest in his work. The "tragic necessity that the
      mind is under to reach for the infinite," Sedgwick's theme, is
      not general, and it was tragic in Melville's heroes, as it arose
      in him, for finite reasons. What were they, at least in the
      genus? Could some of them have arisen from the nature of Ameri-
      can society, the real loneliness of man in a new naturalistic
      epoch, and Melville's own deprivation of God the Father, God the

Mother, and His own resolver? Sedgwick did not ask these
questions.
        Melville's poems seem too often constrictions of his prose
habits; his poetic diction hangs like wax fruit. He never
bothered to make poems evolve; they were his conclusions. They
were the product of a man arguing with himself, convincing himself by laborious bareness that he was in port at last.

39   SCOTT, W.T. "Study of Herman Melville, and His Poems."
        Providence (R.I.) Sunday Journal (31 December).
        Review of 1944.A1, B8. Sedgwick's book is a brilliant
interpretation, a moving forward of our knowledge of literature
and even of our conception of it; undoubtedly the most profound
sustained criticism of Melville's Moby-Dick and other allegorical
romances. Its single basic flaw is its avoidance of biographical
material; such an extraordinary career as Melville's cannot be
explained by mind alone. But Sedgwick's criticism transmits a
passionate excitement. In his preface Matthiessen shows more
than one indebtedness to Sedgwick. In a somewhat crabbed,
attractively Hardyesque style of verse, Melville wrote many a
plain, good poetic line.

1945 A BOOKS--NONE

1945 B SHORTER WRITINGS

1   AUDEN, W.H. "Herman Melville," in The Collected Poetry of
        W.H. Auden. New York: Random House, pp. 146-147.
        Poem.

2   AUDEN, W.H. New Year Letter, in The Collected Poetry of W.H.
        Auden. New York: Random House, p. 312.
        The same Moby-Dick allusion as in 1941.B1.

3   CRAWFORD, BARTHOLOW V., ALEXANDER C. KERN, and MORRISS H.
        NEEDLEMAN. "Herman Melville," in An Outline-History of Ameri-
        can Literature. New York: Barnes & Noble, pp. 70-73.
        Biographical sketch and brief notes on the books, with
selective references to scholarship and criticism.

4   EBY, E.H. "The Tragedy of Mind." Interim, 1 (No. 4), 34-37.
        Review of 1944.A1. There are qualities in Sedgwick's
thinking that make his work provocative and exciting; he has
avoided irrelevant issues and considered final questions; his
thesis is essentially sound and adequate. But he has weakened
the force of his work by special pleading. He arbitrarily labels
the first half of Melville's quest radical Protestantism, imply-
ing that the search ended in defeat and frustration barely short
of self-annihilation because of the inadequacies of the Protestant philosophy; he then suggests that Melville's rehabilitation
was made possible through the rejection of Protestantism and an
"inclination to Catholicism." This use of labels distorts the
essential truth about Melville; his difficulties were those of

much nineteenth-century thought, but the issue of Catholicism versus Protestantism was not at the core of the matter. Melville wanted to believe in the tenets of the age, its philosophical idealism and individualism as instanced by Emerson, but was compelled to discard them because they were contradicted by his own experience. A more insidious distortion by Sedgwick, never forthrightly expressed, is the suggestion that Melville was not in agreement with the North in the Civil War, that he believed slavery a wrong but opposed the abolition movement because the effort to abolish slavery would itself cause another evil. Anyone familiar with his Civil War poems knows this is not his true position. Sedgwick argues, moreover, that in Billy Budd Melville is in accord with Vere's reasoning about the necessity to hang Billy; so Melville now supports conduct that produces evil even though the act performed is not done to right some wrong. Sedgwick does not notice the inconsistency. Sedgwick's latent motivation is an urgent desire for certainty and security, which he gets by accepting established authority and repudiating any questioning or rebellion. Sedgwick hides this from himself and the world under the label of Catholicism.

5 JONES, JOSEPH. "Humor in Moby Dick." University of Texas Studies in English, 25 (1945-1946), 51-71.
    Refutes Fadiman's contention that Moby-Dick contains no humor [see 1943.B24]; finds "many threads of humor which brighten the entire dark fabric and which are woven inseparably into its texture." Melville's greatest achievement in the humor of Moby-Dick is the character Stubb; chapter 64, "Stubb's Supper," is probably the best humorous passage in the book. Flask is a blank, a purely comic character in most of the scenes he figures in; Stubb is a laughing philosopher, with ideas and a point of view.

6 MATTHEWS, WILLIAM, with ROY HARVEY PEARCE. American Diaries: An Annotated Bibliography of American Diaries Written Prior to the Year 1861. Berkeley: University of California Press, p. 320.
    Brief summaries of Melville's journals, with publication details.

7 MYERS, HENRY ALONZO. "Captain Ahab's Discovery: The Tragic Meaning of Moby Dick," in Are Men Equal? An Inquiry into the Meaning of American Democracy. New York: G.P. Putnam's Sons, pp. 45-56.
    Reprint of 1942.B11.

8 OSBORNE, WALTER. "Melville--A Family Portrait," in Program Note accompanying Decca Album No. DA-401, Moby Dick, with Charles Laughton as Captain Ahab, adapted by Brainerd Duffield.
    The "portrait" consists mainly of recollections of Melville by Frances T. Osborne, Osborne's mother and one of Melville's granddaughters.

9   UNTERMEYER, LOUIS. Program Note accompanying Decca Album
     No. DA-401, <u>Moby Dick</u>, with Charles Laughton as Captain Ahab,
     adapted by Brainerd Duffield.
          The reason for <u>Moby-Dick</u>'s rediscovery, its continuing and
     ever-growing appeal: it catches hold of the imagination and
     fastens upon the mind because it seems so many different things
     to so many different people. It is an adventure in excitement,
     a symbolic narrative, a mighty fable, a myth in terms of action,
     and a myth that is also a biblical legend. It is a work of sus-
     taining inspiration, a glorification of man's indomitable courage
     and spirit, which is not only energetic but noble.

10   WILLIAMS, STANLEY T. "Profiles of Melville." <u>Quarterly</u>
     <u>Review of Literature</u>, 2 (No. 2), 149–150.
          Review of 1944.A1. Whether we study the trilogy <u>Mardi</u>,
     <u>Moby-Dick</u> and <u>Pierre</u>, or "Bartleby," we soon become centripe-
     tal--find ourselves within the consciousness of a thinker strug-
     gling with the mysteries that confronted Plato or St. Paul (who
     are omnipresent in Melville's writing); thus Sedgwick is wise in
     thinking in terms of no particular book, but rather of Melville's
     mind itself. His study of <u>Typee</u> is especially illuminating in
     suggesting the indelible character of such experiences for
     Melville and also for us. But Sedgwick contributes most in his
     three final chapters.

11   F[ALL], J[OHN]. "A Melville Tradition." <u>American Notes &</u>
     <u>Queries</u>, 4 (January), 151.
          Is there any basis "for even a part-truth" in the legend
     that Melville wrote <u>Moby-Dick</u> at Sailors' Snug Harbor on Staten
     Island? [<u>See</u> 1945.B16, B19 for replies.]

12   HILLWAY, TYRUS. "A Note on Melville's Lecture in New Haven."
     <u>Modern Language Notes</u>, 60 (January), 55–57.
          Documentary proof that Melville lectured in New Haven on
     30 December 1857 is provided in an official report by the execu-
     tive committee of the Young Men's Institute, dated 19 May 1858.
     [<u>See</u> 1942.B24, 1943.B22.] In 1904.B5 Borden "tells of difficul-
     ties which arose during the eighteen-fifties after certain lec-
     turers had offended the conservative citizenry by speaking out on
     racial and religious issues." This throws light on the insis-
     tence in 1857.B61 that Melville's subject "is purely artistic,
     and of course can arouse no jealous solicitude in regard to any
     possible connection between it and questions of current politics,
     or the vexed questions of theological dispute."

13   WHICHER, GEORGE F. "The Unfolding of a Personality." New
     York <u>Herald Tribune Weekly Book Review</u> (7 January), p. 4.
          Review of 1944.A1. A thoughtful attempt to comprehend the
     unfolding of a great writer's personality. Melville's books, as
     Sedgwick convincingly demonstrates, were reports rendered at
     various stages of a spiritual progress comparable to Dante's or
     Shakespeare's, but expressed in terms that are vividly fresh and
     entirely American.

14   MUMFORD, LEWIS. "The Tragic Mind of Herman Melville." New
     York Times Book Review (21 January), p. 3.
         Review of 1944.A1. Sedgwick's book will not merely take a
     high place in the canon of Melville criticism; it will also be
     valued as the expression of a sound type of criticism, whose
     thesis derives not from the preoccupations of the critic but from
     the nature of his subject. Sedgwick did well to emphasize, as
     the most characteristic fact about Melville's mature books, a
     forward pull into the contemporary scene and a backward pull into
     the universal and the eternal, at which point he is at one with
     the religious minds of every age. What his study finally estab-
     lishes is the soundness of Melville's ultimate vision of life
     (as seen in Clarel and Billy Budd), "a vision that suddenly
     seems contemporaneous because it is true, as Shakespeare's and
     Dostoievsky's visions are true, . . . but as so many of the more
     smug and hopeful writers of the last century definitely are not."
     Mumford notes that Melville's life still awaits a final charting
     by Dr. Henry A. Murray, who "alone has the key to important data
     on the most critical moments of Melville's life--material that is
     not known--to any of his other biographers."

15   ANON. The Frank J. Hogan Library: Part One. [Catalogue for
     Public Auction Sale, 23-24 January.] New York: Parke-Bernet
     Galleries, pp. 110-124.
         Descriptions of Melville items for sale, including
     Melville's nine letters to James Billson [Letters, pp. 275-283,
     287-289]; his annotated copy of Thomas Beale's The Natural His-
     tory of The Sperm Whale; his annotated copy of Owen Chase's
     Narrative of the Most Extraordinary and Distressing Shipwreck of
     the Whale-Ship Essex; and his first editions, which include
     Melville's presentation copy of Mardi to Allan Melville and his
     presentation copy of John Marr to James Billson. Extracts from
     Melville's annotations in Beale and Chase. The "beautifully
     written" letters to Billson "abound in memorable phrases, bril-
     liant bits of criticism, and implications of biographical impor-
     tance" and "disclose, too, in every line, the gracious tranquil
     spirit of the man who wrote them."

16   BIRSS, JOHN H. "A Melville Tradition." American Notes &
     Queries, 4 (February), 170.
         The erroneous tradition that Melville wrote Moby-Dick at
     Sailors' Snug Harbor [see 1945.B11] probably originated among the
     old salts there. Melville occasionally visited the harbor while
     his brother Thomas was governor (1867-1883). [See also 1945.B19.]

17   POMMER, HENRY F. "Melville as Critic of Christianity."
     Friends Intelligencer: A Quaker Weekly, 102 (24 February),
     121-123.
         By their kneeling in tribute to Serenia's "remarkably
     Quaker-like doctrine and deed," Babbalanja, Mohi, Yoomy, and
     Media (who represent, respectively, Melville's rational mental
     processes, memory, imagination, and extrovert interests) indicate
     that Serenia's was the way Melville would have liked the whole
     world to live. The source of the disappointment in which

Melville wrote his attack on the church in <u>Pierre</u> and on our whole race in <u>The Confidence-Man</u> was the fact that Serenia remained an unrealized ideal. Yet even if Melville had found an actual Serenia, he would not have been completely happy in it; Taji, who represents Melville's most deeply rooted drives and intuitions, does not kneel in tribute to Serenia or wish to live there. Melville's soul demanded more knowledge than just an ideal of conduct; Serenia could not solve the ultimate problems he never ceased to ponder. Early on Melville became an agnostic concerning God but only gradually cleared his writing of stock religious phrases at strange variance with the main current of his thought--a symptom of long-continued mental struggle. The ascendency in Melville's mind and in his writings during the 1850s of two important beliefs traditionally opposed by Christianity--that the universe is not dominated by God and that the practice of the highest Christian ideals often leads directly to great evil--largely accounts for the intellectual, physical, and financial difficulties that harrassed him in that decade. <u>Clarel</u> is rewarding to those concerned with the ambiguities of religion, the attractiveness of faith, and the compulsion of skepticism; it is also an admirable mirror of the thought-currents that swept over Christianity in the wake of Darwinism and objective historical studies of the Bible.

18   FOSTER, ELIZABETH S. "Melville and Geology." <u>American Literature</u>, 17 (March), 50-65.
     Although "his knowledge of geology was spotty and amounted by no means to mastery in any area, nevertheless, early in his career Melville had studied, with enough care and interest to reproduce at least a part of the data with extraordinary accuracy, precisely those discoveries of the new science which were proving most dangerous to religious faith in the nineteenth century: the vast antiquity of our planet; the gradual changes of the earth through the operation of natural causes; the rise and extinction of species in era after era; the appearance, in succeeding ages, of related forms and increasingly higher forms, which tended to discredit doctrines of special creation; and perhaps the theory that species were not fixed but were developed from common antecedent types." Geology "added a little to Melville's literary resources; it gave him opportunities for humor in <u>Mardi</u>, and in <u>Moby-Dick</u> it supplied some of that characteristic imagery the largeness of which, with its constant suggestion of cosmic sweep and grandeur, sustains the sense of vastness, timelessness, and deeper significance in that novel. But what geology contributed to the development of his mind was doubtless much more. . . . [T]he story that the rocks had to tell of the nature of Nature, of the mindless, planless, fortuitous, and wasteful change and development in the material universe, could not lie comfortably in his courageous and open mind along with a creed of universal intelligence and benevolence." At the end of <u>Mardi</u> Melville begins his long search for a place for faith and the ethics of the Sermon on the Mount in a heartless universe.

19   HAYFORD, HARRISON. "A Melville Tradition." <u>American Notes &</u>
     <u>Queries</u>, 4 (March), 186.
         Recent scholarship has shown that much of <u>Moby-Dick</u> was
     written before Melville moved to Arrowhead in September or early
     October 1850. It is geographically and chronologically possible
     that he wrote some of the book on Staten Island, but there is no
     evidence for this. [<u>See</u> 1945.B11, B16.]

20   HUNTRESS, KEITH. "Melville's Use of a Source for <u>White-</u>
     <u>Jacket</u>." <u>American Literature</u>, 17 (March), 66–74.
         Some of the episodes in <u>White-Jacket</u> that Anderson thought
     fictional [<u>see</u> 1939.A1, pp. 395–399] were borrowed from <u>Life in a</u>
     <u>Man-of-War or Scenes in "Old Ironsides" During her Cruise in the</u>
     <u>Pacific</u>, by a Fore-Top-Man (Philadelphia, 1841). Melville's
     borrowings from the book fall into four categories: incidents
     for chapters, short passages of description or dialogue, names
     of characters, and a single verse. Melville improved his bor-
     rowed material artistically and made changes in incidents and
     viewpoint to emphasize the weight and arbitrary enforcement of
     authority in the navy.

21   MANSFIELD, LUTHER S. "Book Reviews." <u>American Literature</u>, 17
     (March), 90–93.
         Review of 1944.A1. More sharply than any previous inter-
     preter, Sedgwick has defined the main problem Melville was
     everywhere concerned with: why in the drama of human growth does
     the application of thought produce an inward desolation? Wisely
     eschewing all concern with Melville's private and domestic life,
     he has shown how out of this question Melville shaped a new form,
     "the tragedy of mind." A more thorough consideration of the
     relation of Melville's thought to that of his American contempo-
     raries may have been more revealing for Sedgwick's purpose than
     his numerous analogies with Shakespeare, in view of Melville's
     assertion apropos Shakespeare that "the Declaration of Inde-
     pendence makes a difference." Sedgwick fails to note many
     resemblances between Emerson and Melville, which may not argue
     indebtedness but may serve to clarify Melville's meaning.
     Melville was concerned with "the theological problems of original
     sin, origin of evil, predestination and the like," though his
     interest in them was not theological but human, as was Emerson's.
     Sedgwick's emphasis on a duality in man's nature (the head
     against the heart) giving rise to a conflict reconcilable only in
     submission or acceptance makes Melville's works tragedies of
     futility, although, with the possible exception of <u>Pierre</u>,
     Melville never so conceived them; such an emphasis also produces
     a probable misreading of <u>Clarel</u> in the implied attraction of
     Melville to Catholicism. More than previous interpreters,
     Sedgwick recognizes the significance of Ishmael and Starbuck in
     the structure of <u>Moby-Dick</u>; Starbuck is not, however, "mere
     intellectual coinage" or "simply a counterpiece." Sedgwick some-
     times uses the term "humanity" ambiguously in reference to Ahab,
     so that it is not always clear whether he means the "heart"
     quality in man or the human attribute of often finding the head

and the heart in apparent conflict. Despite some failures,
Sedgwick has written a powerful and provocative book.

22   THORP, WILLARD. "Book Reviews." New England Quarterly, 18
      (March), 101-104.
          Review of 1944.Al. Sedgwick shows a rare sensitiveness to
the meaning of Melville's texts and a scrupulous regard for the
known facts, physical and psychological, of Melville's life. But
the definitive work on Melville will have to take more account of
Melville's appropriation of the experience of other men (from his
reading) and the way in which he subordinated this experience, as
well as that which came to him immediately, to his preoccupation
with ultimate truth. In Billy Budd, Melville is ready to submit
to a moral order in which we fight at command. The passage dis-
tinguishing between Claggart's "natural depravity" and the false
dogma of total depravity is one of the most significant in his
work. Here, at last, he succeeds in answering the problem of
evil, but his answer also includes the redemptive quality of
Billy's execution. Claggart's evil is accidental and temporary
in its effect; Billy's goodness lives after him. That the men
respond naturally to Billy, as they are repelled by Claggart,
shows the "constitutional soundness of humanity." In the end
Melville returned to his earlier democratic idealism.

23   WATTERS, R.E. "Melville's 'Sociality.'" American Literature,
      17 (March), 33-49.
          Melville opposed Emerson's "self-reliant doctrine of insu-
lated individualism" with a belief in the individual's debt to
the "racial community of mankind" and to the social community in
which he lived. He repeatedly portrayed the distortion of the
individual and the destruction of the group that followed upon
voluntary repudiation or involuntary neglect of the social debt.
The "individual is unavoidably caught up in both a cosmic and
social context whether or not he recognizes or likes the fact.
The cosmic limitations of the individual's self-reliant freedom
is a kind of Over-Soul--but an evil one. The social limitation
springs from the inescapable bonds of the social fabric."
Chiefly responsible for "insulated" individualism is the excessive development of intellect at the expense of the heart. Billy
Budd portrays the balance of head and heart in Vere, who unites
the cold truth of Billy's case with a warm human love that purges
it of all its cerebral harshness and redeems its earthly
injustice.

24   WILSON, JAMES SOUTHALL. "Henry James and Herman Melville."
      Virginia Quarterly Review, 21 (Spring), 285-286.
          Review of 1944.Al. Believes that Sedgwick's will be
accorded position as the best book on Melville. A kinship
between the "turbulent" Melville and the "temperate" Henry James
might be found in the origins of the "transcendental morality"
prevalent in the work of each.

25   HEALY, J.V. "Melville's Poetry." <u>Poetry: A Magazine of
     Verse</u>, 66 (April–September), 47–48.
          Melville's poetry has negligible merit. Its flatness is
     due to a contorted syntax, a pompous diction, and a great deal of
     fumbling with symbolism. It has, nevertheless, the merit of
     imaginative concern with the larger problem of good and evil.
     The imagery is often interesting and echoes Melville's prose.

26   HILLWAY, TYRUS. "Reviews." <u>Modern Language Notes</u>, (May),
     339–341.
          Review of 1943.A1; 1944.A1. Because of Melville's lifelong
     preoccupation with religion and ideas essentially religious in
     character, there could hardly be a subject of greater signifi-
     cance for Melville students than his religious thought. In
     studying the development of his attitude on moral and spiritual
     problems, both Braswell and Sedgwick have shed new light on his
     genius in strikingly different ways. Braswell's conclusions
     agree pretty consistently with those of earlier critics and
     biographers, but his is the first published study of the nature,
     significance, and sources of the religious elements in Melville's
     work as a whole. Besides bringing to light a number of new,
     though minor, biographical details, the book makes a notable
     contribution to Melville scholarship in its discussion of the
     symbolism in <u>Mardi</u> and <u>Pierre</u>. The rather elaborate interpreta-
     tions of their allegories seem plausible and amazingly consistent;
     but all such interpretations are weakened by the danger of
     assuming that Melville's plots accurately represent his own men-
     tal and spiritual conflicts. Sedgwick's is a book of remarkable
     power spotted with a few pathetic weaknesses. His principal
     theme is a profound and suggestive one; and for the first time
     Melville is studied as an American, as a critic of the nation's
     ills, as a patriot profoundly affected by the Civil War. Re-
     grettably, there is almost no discussion of Melville's relation
     to the literary movements of his day in Sedgwick's work; and the
     tendency to isolate Melville's thinking and study it in vacuo
     (avoided so far as his political ideas are concerned) seriously
     weakens the whole study. Sedgwick seems to have been unaware of
     the work on Melville being done by other scholars between 1939
     and 1942. Some of his opinions are presented in far greater
     detail in, for example, Foster's and Bezanson's dissertations.

27   OLIVER, EGBERT S. "A Second Look at 'Bartleby.'" <u>College
     English</u> 6 (May), 431–439.
          "Bartleby" presents a picture of Thoreau abstracted from
     "Resistance to Civil Government," probably embellished and en-
     larged by Melville's conversations with Nathaniel and Sophia
     Hawthorne. Bartleby parallels Thoreau in many ways, inwardly and
     outwardly, and is a reductio ad absurdum of Thoreau's convictions.
     Melville's satire shows that "to squat somewhere and live within
     yourself is to refrain from living"; the persistent attempt to
     cut oneself off from society leads only to self-destruction. The
     story is an important clue from 1853 "pointing toward Melville's
     wholesome sanity, his objective searching of social relation-
     ships, his active interest in his contemporaries and their

writings. In 'Bartleby' we see him looking outward, not in any
spirit of despairing rebellion searching his own heart." Reprinted in Oliver (1965), pp. 40–53, and Inge, pp. 61–74.

28   HUNTRESS, KEITH. "A Note on Melville's Redburn." New England
      Quarterly, 18 (June), 259–260.
         Two of the books mentioned in Redburn, chapter 18, may be
      Delirium Tremens by Andrew Blake (1830), and Interesting and
      Authentic Narratives of the most Remarkable Shipwrecks, Fires,
      Famines, Calamities, Providential Deliverancies, and Lamentable
      Disasters on the Seas, in most Parts of the World by R. Thomas
      (1835). Melville may have first learned of the wreck of the
      Essex through Thomas's anthology and been led to Owen Chase's
      Narrative as a result.

29   HILLWAY, TYRUS. "Book Reviews." Philological Quarterly, 24
      (July), 285–286.
         Review of 1943.A1. The first half of the review essen-
      tially corresponds to Hillway's review of Braswell in 1945.B26.
      The impression Braswell conveys that Melville for a time totally
      rejected Christianity is dangerous: Braswell's evidence cannot
      be called conclusive, particularly when much of the contrary
      evidence is omitted or explained away as inconsequential.
      Braswell gives well-deserved consideration to the effect of
      science on Melville's thought; without much doubt it was from
      science as well as from biblical scholarship that Melville first
      learned to question the institutions of religion. Braswell might
      have made the point that Melville, nevertheless, deplored the
      tendency of science to destroy religious belief. In the years
      after Darwin and Lyell published their views, Melville dis-
      tinctly denied the truth of organic evolution and ridiculed the
      scientists who were promising a new world free of superstition.

30   BLACKMUR, R.P. "The Sphinx and the Housecat." Accent, 6
      (Autumn), 60–63.
         Review of 1944.A1; 1944.B8; Henry James: The Major Phase
      by F.O. Matthiessen; Stories of Writers and Artists by Henry
      James, ed. F.O. Matthiessen; The Great Short Novels of Henry
      James, ed. Philip Rahv. In reference to 1944.A1 and 1944.B8,
      Blackmur observes that after Moby-Dick Melville "struggled
      chiefly in his mind, in an impasse of mind, and never worked it
      out in any form involving so much acceptance as tragedy," as "is
      illustrated amply enough in his verse where the stricture of form
      was never able to secure from him for its own purposes either the
      force of intellect or of sensibility. Thus we read the verse
      either as exercises to pass the mind's time or as clues to the
      impasse: that is, as data of Melville's defects." Matthiessen's
      and Rahv's texts show "both the particular abjectness of Melville
      and James faced with their own society except at their peaks of
      commitment, and the general prospect of similar abjectness for
      any artist who by nature finds himself,--not so much transplanted,
      exiled, or ignored--as deliberately self-pruned at the roots
      rather than at the branch: the prospect of wilt, self-pity, and
      flagging histrionics; things which are indeed part of the modern

story, the story of rejection, denial, and passionate preening
agony thereafter." Something of this abject posture is also
taken in some part of their lives and in a great part of their
works by Poe, Whitman, Hawthorne, Dickinson, and Mark Twain. The
interesting question is whether the inadequacy lay radically in
American society or accidentally in the writers themselves. Why
did American society as a going concern never occupy any of these
writers for long if at all? Why did none of them, except Whitman
by excess, exhibit sex as the force it universally is? Why in
both respects were their European and Russian contemporaries an
opposite case? A feature common to all our distinguished American writers through the end of the last century is the relative
absence of overarching intellect and the virtual absence of sustained dramatic or narrative power. The absence of intellect
prevented the fullness of feeling from getting into the writing,
for intellect, in the arts, furnishes capable forms for which no
perfection of mere superficial or "technical" forms can substitute. What we call ambiguity in "The Turn of the Screw" or "The
Figure in the Carpet" and what Melville called ambiguities in
Pierre both arise from this negative cause. The superficial
forms to which Melville and James were addicted--the allegory in
Moby-Dick and Mardi, the sermons in Moby-Dick and Pierre, the
"Gothic froth" in Pierre; the fables and ghost stories and frantic fantasies in James--could not use the full force of their
minds, but centrifugally dissipated it.

31   R., P.B. "Melville's Imagination." Kenyon Review, 7
      (Autumn), 703-705.
         Review of 1944.A1. Sedgwick has brought us to the thresh-
old of that fuller understanding of Melville that another generation should give us. In his discussion of Moby-Dick he "might
have added that the Whale is Spinoza's Deus sive Natura (Melville's debt to Spinoza is yet to be acknowledged), at the level
of Natura naturata. . . . It is no necessary repudiation of a
Spinozistic metaphysic, but rather a building upon it of a
Christian superstructure, that Melville in his later life should
have achieved, through an emotional attachment to the person of
Christ, a period of 'recognition, restoration and return.'"

32   HILLWAY, TYRUS. "Melville's Billy Budd." Explicator, 4
      (November), item 12.
         Reply to 1943.B26. Vere's "disinterestedness" is discussed
(in chapter 6) chiefly in relation to the social and political
reforms of his day; he is anything but disinterested in the main
problem of the story, which he quickly recognizes as the conflict
between the world, or necessity, and the human heart. Because
Vere believes men to be ruled by the "forms" or institutions of
society, he also sees at once the inevitable result of that conflict in Billy's instance: "the angel must hang!" It is the
suffering of Vere, far greater than that of Billy, that makes
Billy Budd a great work of art. The social questions discussed
in Billy Budd, though Melville was clearly aware of their importance, form only a vivid backdrop to the spiritual drama.

33   OLIVER, EGBERT S. "Melville's Goneril and Fanny Kemble."
     New England Quarterly, 18 (December), 489–500.
        Goneril in The Confidence-Man is a caricature, the most
savage in all of Melville's work, of "a widely known contemporary
woman, the Shakespearean actress and dramatic reader, Fanny
Kemble," Melville's neighbor for the six years preceding the
writing of The Confidence-Man. Melville's use of the name
Goneril "had a double barb: it carried associations with Lear's
violent and unfeminine daughter and it also related to the most
widely discussed interpreter of Shakespeare's women of that generation." Fanny Kemble was not the kind of woman to win Melville's admiration, and through Goneril he voiced his extreme
disapproval of her qualities. He not only used Fanny as the
basis for Goneril; he also used a biased interpretation of the
proceedings of her divorce and the circumstances leading up to it.
Almost all that he wrote of Goneril's husband could have been
said of Pierce Butler, Fanny's husband. The Goneril story is part
of The Confidence-Man's general theme and brings into focus the
two opposites around which most of the book is built. Goneril's
husband tries to use reason with her when he should have used
something more persuasive—love. Melville's caricature of Fanny
is aimed at presenting a woman who is entirely lacking in those
qualities he associated with the "heart." The Goneril story is
a small part of The Confidence-Man; but it, at least, shows
Melville looking outwardly at the drama around him rather than
brooding in bitter discontent. Reprinted in Oliver (1965),
pp. 105–115.

34   WATTERS, R.E. "Melville's 'Isolatoes.'" PMLA, 60 (December),
     1138–1148.
        Critics who see in Ahab the personification of Melville's
individualism are mistaken. Throughout his works, Melville "displayed his belief that happiness is not obtainable by the individual in isolation, but may be found in shared experiences—in a
community of thought and action and purpose. The man whose solitude is thrust upon him is to be deeply pitied. The man whose
isolation is self-imposed through repudiation of his social ties
creates sorrow for himself and pain for others." Examples from
Typee through John Marr. Reprinted in 1960.A6.

35   AUDEN, W.H. "The Christian Tragic Hero." New York Times Book
     Review (16 December), pp. 1, 21.
        Contrasts Greek tragedy (of necessity) with Christian
tragedy (of possibility). Ahab is at the beginning what in a
Greek tragedy he could only be at the end—exceptionally unfortunate. What to the Greeks could only have been a punishment
for sin is here a temptation to sin, an opportunity to choose; by
making the wrong choice and continuing to make it, Ahab punishes
himself. His career is at every point a "negative parody" of
the possibility of becoming a saint; just as the saint never
ceases to be tempted to forsake his calling, so Ahab is never
free from the possibility of renouncing his refusal to surrender
his will to God's. Like the chorus in Greek tragedy, Ishmael in
Moby-Dick is the only survivor. But Ishmael is not, like the

Greek chorus, the eternal average man: he is not a character at
all. "Ishmael has no will, only consciousness; he does not act,
he only knows, and what he knows is good <u>and</u> evil, i.e., possibility. He cannot die because he has not yet begun to live, and
he ends the book as a baby reborn from the sea in Queequeg's
coffin, thrust back into life as an orphan with his first choice
still to make." Reprinted in Michel, pp. 234-238, and Corrigan,
pp. 143-147.

1946 A BOOKS--NONE

1946 B SHORTER WRITINGS

1   ARVIN, NEWTON. "Introduction," in <u>Hawthorne's Short Stories</u>.
     New York: Alfred A. Knopf, p. xv.
        Symbols utterly unnatural to Hawthorne--a trackless sea,
violent tempests, water spouts and tornadoes, the monstrous animal life of the ocean, hunting, combat, and slaughter--"are wonderfully expressive of Melville's wilder, more passionate, more
deeply demoniac nature." Melville's "talismanic language," too,
with its "telltale words <u>wild</u>, <u>barbarous</u>, and <u>savage</u>; <u>vengeful</u>,
<u>cunning</u>, and <u>malignant</u>; <u>noble</u>, <u>innocent</u>, and <u>grand</u>; <u>inexorable</u>,
<u>inscrutable</u>, and <u>unfathomable</u>," is revealingly unlike Hawthorne's
vocabulary, with its favorite adjectives <u>dusky</u>, <u>dim</u>, and <u>shadowy</u>,
or <u>cold</u>, <u>sluggish</u>, and <u>torpid</u>; its favorite verbs, <u>separate</u>,
<u>estrange</u>, and <u>insulate</u>; its favorite nouns, <u>pride</u> and <u>egotism</u>,
<u>guilt</u>, and <u>intellect</u>, <u>heart</u>, and <u>sympathy</u>.

2   BELGION, MONTGOMERY. "Introduction," in <u>Moby Dick</u>. London:
     The Cresset Press, pp. vii-xxvii.
        If we are to enjoy the book to the utmost, "we must tear
off the accretions it has acquired like coral through the com-
mentating activity of latter-day literary polyps, and undergo its
effect directly." If a reader approached <u>Moby-Dick</u> for the first
time imfluenced by an interpretation such as Sedgwick's, his
enjoyment would be gravely marred: he "would be looking all
the time for symbols and their meaning when he ought to let the
charm and spell which Melville casts work stealthily upon him."
Every allegation that the book has a concealed meaning must be
avoided. The book has strong American affinities--in its sardonic humor and reflections--and English derivations--in particular from the Bible, Sir Thomas Browne, and Shakespeare. In the
Shakespearean influence lies the key to what happens to the
reader of <u>Moby-Dick</u>: Shakespeare's language creates feelings of
exaltation; the contents of <u>Moby-Dick</u> have an analogous effect.
[See 1947.B73 for a more developed version of this argument.]
Reviewed in 1952.B16.

3   BOAS, FREDERICK S. "The Nineteenth Century and After." <u>The
     Year's Work in English Studies, 1944</u>, 25 (1946), pp. 200-201.
        Brief synopses of 1944.B11-12, B16, B22.

4   BOOTH, EDWARD TOWNSEND. "Berkshire Loam: Melville," in <u>God Made the Country</u>. New York: Alfred A. Knopf, pp. 220-245.
     Account of Melville in the Berkshires, drawn mainly from his writings. Finds "many striking similarities" in the "background" of <u>Moby-Dick</u> and <u>War and Peace</u>.

5   HOWE, HELEN. <u>We Happy Few</u>. New York: Simon and Schuster, p. 87.
     A group of characters in the novel are all said to be writing books on Melville with such titles as <u>Melville: Schizophrenic or Manic-Depressive</u> and <u>The Mysticism of Melville; Its Seventeenth-Century Sources</u>. Melville "had them all in thrall."

6   LOWELL, ROBERT. "Christmas Eve Under Hooker's Statue," in <u>Lord Weary's Castle</u>. New York: Harcourt, Brace and Co., p. 17.
     Quotation from "The March into Virginia" ("All wars are boyish").

7   LOWELL, ROBERT. "The Quaker Graveyard in Nantucket," in <u>Lord Weary's Castle</u>. New York: Harcourt, Brace and Co., pp. 8-9.
     Allusions to <u>Moby-Dick</u>.

8   PHILLIPS, WILLIAM. "Introduction," in <u>Great American Short Novels</u>. New York: Dial Press, p. ix.
     "Benito Cereno" can be said to be the first really distinguished short novel produced by an American author. There is no doubt of its impeccable structure, its superbly controlled pace, and its quality of complete self-containment. Of Melville's shorter works only <u>Billy Budd</u> is comparable in stature.

9   PLOMER, WILLIAM. "Introduction," in <u>Billy Budd, Foretopman</u>. London: John Lehmann, pp. 7-10.
     Plomer sees <u>Billy Budd</u> not as an attempt to "justify the ways of God to man" [see 1928.B20], but "rather as Melville's final protest against the nature of things--that is to say, against fate and against human institutions, of which the apparent necessity is itself ascribable to fate." Two particularly significant features of <u>Billy Budd</u> are Melville's effort to understand evil by exploring the unconscious and his belief in the virtues of aristocracy.

10   SCHNEIDER, HERBERT W. "At Sea," in <u>A History of American Philosophy</u>. New York: Columbia University Press, pp. 293-301.
     Melville was "thoroughly infected with the transcendental temper" and therefore haunted by the realm of absolutes. His "basic intellectual program was to approach God by means of the 'heart' rather than the 'head,' imagining that though both men and God are eternal mysteries to themselves and each other, they enter together into a tragedy which both can feel and act." His "chief transcendental insight consisted precisely in his realization that absolute and relative standards are necessary to each other, neither being intelligible in itself."

11   SHORT, RAYMOND W.   "Introduction," in <u>Four Great American</u>
      <u>Novels</u>. New York: Henry Holt and Co., pp. xxviii-xxxiii.
         Biographical sketch and introduction to <u>Billy Budd</u>. After
      "the completeness of the spiritual inferno of <u>Moby-Dick</u>, with its
      penitude of Delphic ambiguities, it is a relief to have the
      essential problem extracted from its attendant involvements and
      stated in stark, laconic terms." Vere is the true hero of the
      novel: in him natural goodness has been fortified by the kind
      of virtue that civilization may teach. Melville's ultimate con-
      clusion was that we must accept the world's conditions. Like
      Hawthorne, Melville "explored the conscious and subconscious pits
      of human nature in order to discover, not the quirks of person-
      ality, but the abstractions from which behavior springs. His
      faith, his religion, consisted in the conviction that such ab-
      stractions exist. His relentless purpose was to track them down
      and represent them." The effects of homely, day-by-day life are
      missing from <u>Billy Budd</u>, but moments in the story have the
      dramatic poignancy of the Old Testament. Even more remarkable
      is the flashing penetration of the book's symbolism. Reviewed
      in 1948.B41.

12   SMITH, CHARD POWERS. <u>The Housatonic: Puritan River</u>. New
      York: Rinehart & Co., pp. 337-359.
         Biographical; Melville and Hawthorne in the Berkshires.
      Perpetuates legend that "Ethan Brand" contains Hawthorne's por-
      trait of Melville [<u>see</u> 1929.A1, B40; 1932.B7]; the story was
      Melville's "destruction" and "sentence to hell."

13   STEWART, RANDALL. "Herman Melville: Explorer of the World
      and Enigmas," in <u>The Literature of the United States: An</u>
      <u>Anthology and a History</u>. Vol. 1.   Ed. Walter Blair, Theodore
      Hornberger, and Randall Stewart. Chicago: Scott, Foresman
      and Co., pp. 736-738.
         Section of introduction to chapter 3, "The American
      Renaissance." Like Hawthorne, "Melville was concerned with the
      darker side of human fate. Both insisted upon the reality of
      evil in the world; both were skeptical of the optimism of Emerson
      and his benevolent theory of the Universe; both presented the
      tragedies of the mind and soul." Like Hawthorne, Melville was a
      philosophical pessimist and a political optimist.

14   STEWART, RANDALL. "Herman Melville, 1819-1891," in <u>The</u>
      <u>Literature of the United States: An Anthology and a History</u>.
      Vol. 1.   Ed. Walter Blair, Theodore Hornberger, and Randall
      Stewart. Chicago: Scott, Foresman and Co., pp. 1063-1066.
         Headnote to extracts (pp. 1066-1115) from <u>Mardi</u> (chap-
      ters 158, 161, and 162) and "Benito Cereno." Biographical and
      critical survey.

15 WARREN, ROBERT PENN. <u>All the King's Men</u>. New York: Harcourt,
    Brace and Co., p. 294.
        "That was how the nights became Anne Stanton, too. For
    that night in the roadster, Anne Stanton had done her trick very
    well. It was a wordless and handless trick, but it didn't need
    words or hands. She had rolled her head on the leather seat back,
    and touched her finger to her lips to say, 'Sh, sh,' and smiled.
    And had sunk her harpoon deeper than ever. Queequeg sunk it,
    through four feet of blubber to the very quick, but I hadn't
    really known it until the line played out and the barb jerked in
    the red meat which was the Me inside of all the blubber of what I
    had thought I was. And might continue to think I was."

16 McCLOSKEY, JOHN C. "<u>Moby Dick</u> and the Reviewers." <u>Philo-
    logical Quarterly</u>, 25 (January), 20-31.
        Examines a number of British and American contemporary
    reviews. Concludes that "the notion that in its own day <u>Moby-
    Dick</u> was greeted with a little respect and a great deal of
    derision [<u>see</u>, e.g., 1921.A1; 1926.A1; 1929.A1] is not in accord
    with the facts. Although British critical opinion was about
    evenly divided, American critical opinion was predominantly
    favorable. . . . Melville's genius was recognized by both
    British and American contemporary reviewers."

17 ANON. "Melville's Journey: The Conflict of Heart and Mind."
    London <u>Times Literary Supplement</u>, No. 2293 (12 January),
    p. 18.
        Review of 1944.A1. Sedgwick's is the most penetrating book
    on Melville yet written. The search for truth over the sea of
    consciousness seems to have left Melville with the conviction
    that evil is a necessity of creation, that good and evil maintain
    the balance of life--a not very helpful conclusion. Melville's
    poetry deserves to be better known, for its own fine blossoming
    and for the fuller autobiography of a great mind.

18 COLLINS, CARVEL. "Melville's <u>Moby Dick</u>." <u>Explicator</u>, 4
    (February), item 27.
        In the part of chapter 47 ("The Mat-Maker") after the
    asterisks, "the ball of free will" is ironically made to drop
    from Ishmael's hands. Perhaps it is here that he begins to learn
    that even his conservative compromise with Fate, evolved while
    weaving, is illusion only. [<u>See</u> 1946.B28 for reply.]

19 WARREN, ROBERT PENN. "Melville the Poet." <u>Kenyon Review</u>, 8
    (Spring), 208-223.
        Occasioned by publication of 1944.B8, offering "a few
    remarks" supplementary to Matthiessen's preface and treating
    poems he was unable to include in his limited collection. Though
    Melville did not master his craft, "the violences, the distor-
    tions, the wrenchings in the versification of some of the poems"
    are perhaps to be interpreted not so much as the result of mere
    ineptitude as the result of a conscious effort to develop a
    nervous, dramatic, masculine style--to create a poetry of some
    vibrancy, range of reference, and richness of tone. The craft

Melville "did not learn was not the same craft which some of his
more highly advertised contemporaries did learn with such glib-
ness of tongue and complacency of spirit." His poems again and
again reflect his "concern with the fundamental ironical dualities of existence: will against necessity, action against idea,
youth against age, the changelessness of man's heart against the
concept of moral progress, the bad doer against the good deed,
the bad result against the good act, ignorance against fate,
etc." Melville's effort to resolve these dualities manifests
itself in three different terms: nature, history, and religion.
Illustrations from Battle-Pieces, Clarel, John Marr and Other
Sailors, Timoleon. Reprinted in 1960.A6 and Chase (1962),
pp. 144–155.

20   GURKO, LEO. "American Literature: The Forces Behind Its
     Growing Up." College English, 7 (March), 319.
        Between the Revolutionary War and 1914 American literature
was a satellite of English literature. "Individual exceptions,
such as James or Melville, might be argued, but the collective
bulk was all on the other side of the Atlantic."

21   HILLWAY, TYRUS. "Taji's Quest for Certainty." American
     Literature, 18 (March), 27–34.
        The adventure of the fifth pilgrim on the isle of Maramma,
the youth who wishes to scale the mountain Ofo, roughly parallels
Taji's experience in the pursuit of Yillah. Hints suggest that
Ofo represents Truth or a pathway by which Truth may be sought;
Yillah represents Ultimate Truth (though when Taji possesses
Yillah, what he possesses is not really Truth but merely an in-
stinctive and youthful philosophy that he had mistaken for it).
Both Taji and the pilgrim commit the same crime--rejection of
traditional institutions (especially organized religion) and
reliance upon an inner consciousness of truth. Taji's search for
Yillah embodies the futility of searching in the human mind for
Ultimate Truth.

22   JONES, JOSEPH. "Ahab's 'Blood-Quench': Theater or Metal-
     lurgy?" American Literature, 18 (March), 35–37.
        The spectacular episode of the blood-quench at the forge in
Moby-Dick, chapter 113, has a long tradition of practice behind
it: human blood was long regarded as a very good quench for
steel--considerably better than plain water. In other respects,
theoretically and practically, Ahab seems to have been an expert
smith.

23   MARTIN, EDWIN T. "The Melville Society." South Atlantic
     Bulletin, 12 (April), 15.
        Reports that the Melville Society, organized in February
1945 by John H. Birss, Harrison Hayford, and Tyrus Hillway, now
numbers among its members most of the leading active Melville
scholars of the United States. The objectives of the Melville
Society are "to stimulate the exchange of information among students of Melville, to secure the publication of a satisfactory

American edition of Melville's works, and to establish in some
large university library a center where all materials necessary
for the study of Melville will be gathered and made accessible
to scholars."

24   HOLLIS, SOPHIE. "Moby Dick: A Religious Interpretation."
     Catholic World, 163 (May), 158–162.
       Moby-Dick "is an allegory; the green land is the oasis of
faith (a bucolic, non-thinking faith); the sea is the tree of
knowledge which is fraught with dangers to the peace of the soul;
and the whale is the hand of God." The main theme is that "Ahab
was foredoomed to pursue his destiny, his damnation." The
"counterpoint--which is swallowed up and lost in the main theme--
is the story of the possibility of free will, of man's being
master of his fate, of being damned only by aping God. In a
word, it is the story of the fall of the angels." If man is
bound to his fate, pursued by a malignant God, the whale is that
evil God; if man shapes his destiny by his will, the whale is
under orders, "moved by God to smite the proud Lucifer who dares
to ape God." Both interpretations are possible in Moby-Dick, but
Melville's "dyspeptic Protestantism" inclines him to the former
view. His tragedy is that he was neither believer nor infidel.

25   McGRAVES, DONALD E. "The Steering Gear of the 'Pequod.'"
     American Notes & Queries, 6 (May), 25.
       Notes the discrepancy between the reference to the tiller
in chapter 16 and the spokes of the helm in chapter 61. [Cf.
1937.B29.]
26   NICHOLAS, WILLIAM H. "American Pathfinders in the Pacific."
     National Geographic Magazine, 89 (May), 625, 632, 639.
       Brief Melville references; photograph of Nuka Hiva harbor.

27   WATTERS, R.E. "Boston's Salt-Water Preacher." South Atlantic
     Quarterly, 45 (July), 350–361.
       Details of the life and works of Edward Thompson Taylor,
who seems most likely to be remembered under the alias of Father
Mapple. The chapel Ishmael attends in Moby-Dick, chapter 8, "is
unmistakably a duplicate of a painting which hung at the back of
Father Taylor's pulpit" in the Seamen's Bethel in Boston. Melville was familiar with Boston, "and it would be incredible if he
had not heard Father Taylor."

28   GIOVANNINI, G. "Melville's Moby Dick." Explicator, 5
     (October), item 7.
       Reply to 1946.B18. The context of "the ball of free will"
dropping might suggest Melville's characteristic whimsicality,
used here to ease the shift from the abstractly allegorical to
the business of narrating. If allegory is intended, the incident
may be interpreted not as a negation but as a confirmation of the
limited freedom of will, limited by necessity and chance.

29   HILLWAY, TYRUS. "Historical Note." <u>Melville Society News-</u>
      <u>letter</u>, 2 (30 October), n.p.
          Quotes Wilbert Snow, candidate for the governorship of
      Connecticut, member of the Melville Society, and frequently
      called the originator of the Melville revival: "I ran across
      Melville's books in the stacks of the Bowdoin College Library in
      1905 and 1906; read them through, and became an enthusiast. One
      night at Columbia I told Carl Van Doren that <u>Omoo</u> was as good as
      <u>Robinson Crusoe</u>. Carl replied, 'What in hell is Omoo?' That
      conversation marks the beginning of the Melville revival, because
      Carl wanted to do something about it and got some Melville mate-
      rial published in Everyman's Library."

30   OLIVER, EGBERT S. "Melville's Picture of Emerson and Thoreau
      in 'The Confidence-Man.'" <u>College English</u>, 8 (November),
      61–72.
          Argues that Melville "used Emerson as the pattern of the
      mystic" in <u>The Confidence-Man</u>. Winsome "resembles Emerson in
      posture and physical appearance, in manner and in public asso-
      ciations." His argument "in practically every point comes from
      <u>Nature</u>--by suggestion, by association of ideas, by direct con-
      densation, or by distorted synopsis." In using <u>Nature</u>, Melville
      offered a criticism of the nature of transcendentalism, a criti-
      cism he extended by "explicitly" basing Winsome's disciple,
      Egbert, on Thoreau and caricaturing the section on friendship in
      <u>A Week on the Concord and Merrimack Rivers</u>. Melville exposes the
      cold heartlessness in Emerson and Thoreau, their abstract
      approaches to life's problems. Reprinted in Oliver (1965),
      pp. 86–104.

31   RODMAN, SELDEN. "Boston Jeremiads." New York <u>Times Book</u>
      <u>Review</u> (3 November), pp. 7, 32.
          Review of <u>Lord Weary's Castle</u> by Robert Lowell. Lowell
      has expertly adapted the angry mythologies of Melville and Milton
      to his strictly modern sensibility. Like Melville, Lowell is
      filled with fury at the spectacle of mankind beating its brains
      out in a spurious race after the unattainable, "and like Melville,
      he comes to endow the symbolism of this chase, inhuman and homi-
      cidal, with a greater reality than those who have seemed to lose
      their humanity in its madness."

32   GILMAN, WILLIAM H. "Melville's Liverpool Trip." <u>Modern</u>
      <u>Language Notes</u>, 61 (December), 543–547.
          Maria Melville's 1 June 1839 letter to Gansevoort Melville
      (in the New York Public Library Gansevoort-Lansing Collection)
      and the official papers of the merchantman <u>St. Lawrence</u> show that
      "Melville made his first voyage in 1839, not 1837 as has been
      supposed. He was a man of twenty and not the boy of seventeen
      whom his biographers have assumed him to be. In writing <u>Redburn</u>
      he reproduced certain elements of time and place, like the
      schedule of the ship which took him to Liverpool and back, and
      he used men from real life for the basis of his portraits. But
      he changed materially the whole story of his leaving home and
      getting the job on the <u>St. Lawrence</u>, as a comparison between his

mother's letter and the opening chapters of <u>Redburn</u> will readily show. Furthermore, he made his hero a young boy and gave him all the callowness, exaggerated sensitivity, and naiveté which suited his years. Unless Melville's psychological development was arrested to an incredible degree, he must at the age of twenty have long outgrown the character he creates for Wellingborough Redburn." The materials presented in this article "provide grounds for a vigorous challenge to the school which identifies Melville with Redburn and accepts <u>Redburn</u> as Melville's autobiography."

33   HAYFORD, HARRISON. "Hawthorne, Melville, and the Sea." <u>New England Quarterly</u>, 19 (December), 435–452.
     Hawthorne's own experience with matters of the sea may have been among the subjects he and Melville discussed and may have contributed largely to his pleasure in Melville's company. Hawthorne was linked to the sea by family, by his own interest, by his reading, and even by a number of his own writings; he had also edited two full-length works dealing in good part with the sea (Horatio Bridge's <u>Journal of an African Cruiser</u> and Benjamin F. Browne's "Papers of an Old Dartmoor Prisoner") and had once very nearly set off for the South Seas himself.

34   HAYFORD, HARRISON. "The Significance of Melville's 'Agatha' Letters." <u>ELH</u>, 13 (December), 299–310.
     The "significant point" about the proposed story in Melville's "Agatha" letters to Hawthorne [<u>Letters</u>, pp. 153–163] is that "unlike Ahab and Pierre, the heroine does not assert her ego, pit herself against the evil, and assault heaven, but innocent and submissive, accepts the cruelties of life with 'great patience, & endurance, & resignedness.' Had Melville carried out his resolution to write this story we would almost certainly hold a rather different idea than we now entertain of his attitude toward evil at the period directly following the publication of <u>Pierre</u>." Melville's 16 April 1852 letter to Richard Bentley [<u>Letters</u>, pp. 149–151] proves that he "neither deliberately provoked nor accurately foresaw the critical castigation and public neglect that <u>Pierre</u> received." [<u>See</u> 1936.B22.] The "Agatha" letters prove that he "neither meant <u>Pierre</u> to be his last word, nor, on completing it, found himself 'without internal urgings to write.'" [<u>See</u> 1921.A1, pp. 343–344, and 1936.B22.]

35   LEISY, ERNEST E. "Folklore in American Literature." <u>College English</u>, 8 (December), 122–129.
     Brief passage on Melville's awareness of folk material in <u>Moby-Dick</u>. "The legend of the white whale is truly fabulous, as fabulous as the big bear sought by the backwoodsmen of Arkansas, and a great deal more significant. Ahab is a legendary figure, and throughout the narrative appear such references as the white steed of the prairies, the Erie Canallers, the Heidelburgh Tun, Tamerlane, Perseus and Andromeda, Jupiter and Europa, St. Elmo Lights, St. George and the Dragon."

36   OPITZ, EDMUND A. "Herman Melville: An American Seer."
      Contemporary Review 170 (December), 348-353.
          Biographical sketch and appreciation of Moby-Dick.
      Melville will live as a great seer, one "whose vision penetrated
      to the core of things and matched the blackness he found there
      with an unconquerable soul."

37   WENDEL, TOM. "The Meaning of Melville." Yale Literary
      Magazine, 113 (December), 5-6.
          Review of 1944.A1. Through all Melville's works there is
      one underlying idea giving them their "startling unity"--the
      postulate that spiritual introspection is the greatest ability of
      man; Melville celebrates the desire to probe. The works are less
      a continuing development of a theme than variations on a theme.
      Mardi explores the never ending possibilities of the mind of man;
      Moby-Dick is completely concerned with the process of thought
      itself; Pierre stresses the ambiguities that appear from deep
      probing into the mind's labyrinth (and again the vastness and
      unending possibilities of the mind). Melville's closest literary
      ancestor is not Shakespeare but the author of Ecclesiastes.

38   MABBOTT, T.O. "Possible Melville MS." Melville Society News-
      letter, 2 (14 December), n.p.
          Remembers having seen many years ago in a bookseller's
      catalogue "some kind of old schoolbook, described as having some
      MS poetry by Melville," but no longer has the catalogue. [See
      1947.B26 for reply.]

1947 A BOOKS

1   BROOKS, VAN WYCK. "Melville the Traveller" and "Melville in
      the Berkshires," in The Times of Melville and Whitman. New
      York: E.P. Dutton & Co., pp. 142-161, 162-175.
          Partial account of Melville's life, with general commentary
      on the works. Melville "was an instance of the well-known fact
      that when artists take to theorizing it is often because their
      creative power is gone." Great writer though he was, Melville
      "lacked the developing sense of a craft that might have sustained
      him in the loss of other powers. He was one of the writers, like
      Whitman, who prove that the rules of an art are of small impor-
      tance when the mind and the grasp of life are large enough, whose
      genius far outstrips their talent, . . . and who triumph solely
      by virtue of their magnitude and depth." These anomalous spirits
      "can break with impunity every rule, and yet, when their genius
      fails them, they are all but helpless." For Melville, "an un-
      stable writer, always in a sense an amateur, the collapse or the
      frustration of his genius was catastrophic"--as Pierre and The
      Confidence-Man bear witness. "What he lacked especially was an
      interest in society, in actual people in all the concreteness of
      their lives, that objective feeling for human nature, the founda-
      tion of a novelist's life, which alone could have corrected his
      tendency to the abstract and the subjective." Reviewed in
      1947.B61, B66, B68-69, B71-72, B76; 1948.B37-38, B46, B48, B60,
      B64, B77; 1949.B26, B48.

2   OLSON, CHARLES. <u>Call Me Ishmael</u>. New York: Reynal &
     Hitchcock, 119 pp. Reprint. New York: Grove Press, [1958];
     San Francisco: City Lights Books, [1958], 1966.
         Typographically and stylistically idiosyncratic study of
     influences on <u>Moby-Dick</u>, in particular America (defined as
     "space"), whaling (considered as "frontier" and "industry"), and
     Shakespeare (this section a revised version of 1938.B45). In-
     cludes a transcription of Melville's notes in his copy of Owen
     Chase's <u>Narrative</u> of the <u>Essex</u> (published here for the first
     time). According to Olson, <u>Moby-Dick</u> "was two books written
     between February, 1850 and August, 1851"; the "first book did not
     contain Ahab" and "may not, except incidentally, have contained
     Moby-Dick." Shakespeare, in particular, and Hawthorne caused the
     "ferment" in Melville that led him to compose the second book
     after the summer of 1850. Melville's notes on the flyleaf of the
     last volume in his edition of Shakespeare were "rough notes for
     the composition of <u>Moby-Dick</u>": they "involve Ahab, Pip,
     Bulkington, Ishmael, and are the key to Melville's intention with
     these characters." Olson interprets these notes and discusses
     the influence of Shakespeare in general, and of <u>King Lear</u> and
     <u>Antony and Cleopatra</u> in particular, on <u>Moby-Dick</u>, with citations
     from Melville's markings and annotations in the plays [cf.
     1938.B45]. The last quarter of the book gives an account of
     Melville's journeyings in 1856-1857 (with lengthy quotation from
     <u>Journal Up the Straits</u> [1935.B14]), during which, according to
     Olson, Melville became "Christ's victim": the "result was
     creatively a stifling of the myth power in him." Reviewed in
     1947.B33-36, B38, B41, B44, B58-59; 1948.B35, B40, B43; 1958.B54.

<u>1947 B SHORTER WRITINGS</u>

1   AIKEN, CONRAD. "The Last Vision," in <u>The Kid</u>. New York:
     Duell Sloan and Pearce, pp. 29-32.
         Poem with section on Melville.

2   BARRIE, J.M. <u>Letters of J.M. Barrie</u>. Ed. Viola Meynell. New
     York: Charles Scribner's Sons, p. 28.
         Letter of 20 November 1893 to Maarten Maartens: "I suppose
     you know Herman Melville's <u>Typee</u> and <u>Omoo</u>. If not, the mere
     telling you to get them is giving you a handsome present."

3   BRILL, A.A. "Introduction," in <u>Leonardo da Vinci: A Study</u>
     <u>in Psychosexuality</u>, by Sigmund Freud. Trans. A.A. Brill.
     New York: Random House, pp. 24-25.
         Quotes passage in <u>Mardi</u>, chapter 3, about Jarl's attachment
     to the narrator "to illustrate the fact that between normal and
     abnormal there are many gradations." Continues: "To my knowl-
     edge, Melville led a normal psychosexual existence; there was
     never any intimation that he was anything but sexually normal.
     Yet, judging by his attitude toward men, not only as expressed
     in this quotation but from many of his other works, notably from
     his idealization of Jack Chase, a fellow sailor to whom he dedi-
     cated his last work, one is justified in saying that Melville's

normal homosexual component was more or less accentuated. Having
endured the hardships of a sailor on a merchantman, whaler and
man-of-war in the beginning of the last century, his mind must
have often yearned for that period of his existence when he was
in a nice home surrounded by the love and protection of parents,
especially of a mother. During such stress one can easily empa-
thize himself back into the early stage of life and gladly
accept the love of an old sailor who would guide and protect him.
Some might call his idealization of Jack Chase homosexual, in the
sense that we all have a normal homosexual component which enables us to carry on philanthropic relations and friendships with
our own sex. In other words, Melville's feelings represent a
higher degree of homosexuality than one ordinarily encounters in
daily life, but contains no taint of abnormality."

4   CANBY, HENRY SEIDEL. American Memoir. Boston: Houghton
    Mifflin Co., pp. 94, 219, 319, 347, 415.
        Brief Melville references. Among Canby's objections to
"that windbag Thomas Carlyle is the harm his vaporous sermonizing
on society did to . . . Moby Dick. Melville, who knew men and
events better than philosophy, was impressed by Carlyle's
rhetoric, and swashed paint by the bucketfuls on his magnificent
story, which should have been as stark and meaty as a late
Shakespearean tragedy."

5   FREUND, PHILIP. "Sea and Sky: Melville," in How to Become a
    Literary Critic. New York: The Beechhurst Press, pp. 80–96.
        Finds in Billy Budd an even better story than Moby-Dick.
Although Billy Budd lacks the sweep of Moby-Dick, it shows
greater humanity, more penetrating psychology, couched in exalted
prose, and a more steadfast philosophy of life, accomplishing a
tragic catharsis, which Moby-Dick does not. The stories are
essentially the same, except that in Billy Budd the symbolism has
been translated into human terms: the struggle of innocence and
evil is retold, with Claggart fulfilling the role of Moby Dick.

6   INGLIS, REWEY BELLE, et al. "Herman Melville," in Adventures
    in American Literature. 4th ed. Ed. Rewey Belle Inglis et
    al. New York: Harcourt, Brace and Co., pp. 518–520.
        Biographical sketch and brief commentary on Moby-Dick,
unquestionably one of the great American books. A sense of
mystery broods over the book--mysterious predictions, magical
sights and sounds, strange and inexplicable happenings--as though
Melville were trying to take his readers into the mystery of life
itself. Perhaps no other American book has in it so much sustained excitement, so much elemental terror and beauty. No
Melville selection in the anthology [cf. 1941.B12].

7   LEARY, LEWIS. Articles on American Literature Appearing in
    Current Periodicals, 1920–1945. Durham, N.C.: Cuke Univer-
    sity Press, pp. 81–87.
        Bibliography of articles on Melville, 1920–1945.

8   LEVIN, HARRY. "'Don Quixote' and 'Moby Dick,'" in <u>Cervantes Across the Centuries</u>. Ed. Angel Flores and M.J. Benardete. New York: The Dryden Press, pp. 217–226.

Discusses Melville's annotations and markings in his copy of <u>Don Quixote</u> (Philadelphia, 1853), his references to <u>Don Quixote</u> in his works, and its influence on <u>Moby-Dick</u>. "The relation of <u>Moby-Dick</u> to <u>Don Quixote</u> is neither close nor similar; it is complementary and dialectical." For example, "One proposes worldly wisdom as the touchstone for an outworn set of ideals; the other, abandoning economic values, goes questing after a transcendental faith." <u>Don Quixote</u> must have furnished "more than a hint" for "Benito Cereno," with its "atmospheric tension of mingled races and its sense of grim realities smouldering beneath romantic surfaces." Reprinted with revisions in 1957.B20.

9   MOTT, FRANK LUTHER. <u>Golden Multitudes: The Story of Best Sellers in the United States</u>. New York: The Macmillan Co., pp. 131–132, 307, 319.

Not until the Melville renaissance, thirty years after Melville's death, did <u>Moby-Dick</u> sell the hundreds of thousands necessary for it to be included in Mott's list of best sellers. Considerably more than half a million copies of the book have been distributed in the United States in the past twenty-five years.

10 PARKES, HENRY BAMFORD. <u>The American Experience: An Interpretation of the History and Civilization of the American People</u>. New York: Alfred A. Knopf, pp. 200–205.

Of Melville's three major books, two--<u>Moby-Dick</u> and <u>Pierre</u>--dealt with the problem of the American will; the third--<u>Billy Budd</u>--may be described as a resolution of the problem. "Having carried the drive of the individual will to its furthermost limits, Melville had found that it ended in the sinking of the <u>Pequod</u> and in the death of Pierre; but in his old age he passed beyond individualism and beyond its inevitable defeat. <u>Billy Budd</u>, unlike any other work by a major American writer, is based on the belief in an underlying social order and harmony that gives meaning to the lives of those who participate in it and that transcends the struggle between the will and the environment."

11 RAHV, PHILIP. "Herman Melville: What Redburn Saw in Launcellot's-Hey," in <u>Discovery of Europe</u>. Ed. Philip Rahv. Boston: Houghton Mifflin Co., p. 128.

Headnote to extracts from <u>Redburn</u> (chapters 37, 38, and 33). "It is not by chance that the account of the unspeakable misery and pauperism that Redburn saw is followed by a description of the German emigrants to America which is at once an extraordinarily moving celebration of the hopes lodged in the New World and one of the noblest pleas in our literature for the extinction of national hatreds and racial prejudice."

12   REED, HENRY. "Ishmael," in A Map of Verona and Other Poems.
      New York: Reynal & Hitchcock, pp. 79-88.
          The "lyric interludes" from Reed's adaptation of Moby-Dick
      for radio. [See 1947.B13.]

13   REED, HENRY. "Preface," in Moby Dick: A Play for Radio from
      Herman Melville's Novel. London: Jonathan Cape, pp. 5-11.
          Moby-Dick has a Shakespearean capacity, which Melville's
      other books wholly lack, for standing in one's life as a major
      experience (despite its at times overromantic prose, arch
      heartiness, and sentimentality--faults of Melville's age). In
      Moby-Dick everything fits into an ambitious and comprehensive
      picture of a particular world in all its completeness. (Some of
      Melville's devices--the potted encyclopedia, the sermon, the
      dialogues in play form--and his intent to describe a small world
      and make it stand for a large one--remind the reader of Joyce.)
      But a dramatic adaptation has largely to omit the technical chap-
      ters on whaling, whaling history, and the history of whales and
      concentrate on the book's symbolism and tragedy alone. Moby Dick
      and the element in which he lives are little less than the face
      and the unquestionable judgment of God. At times Melville seems
      to say that the face of God has sometimes an expression that
      appears evil to us. It is clear that God's judgments have a
      frequent brutality; but Melville is also saying that it is not
      man's part to strike out or to rebel against God's judgments, as
      Mapple's sermon teaches. Cuts and changes have been made for the
      adaptation, but the destruction of Ishmael with the rest of the
      crew is the only deliberate falsification of the story, in which
      Ishmael is saved not so much because of his own spiritual intui-
      tions but because someone must survive to tell the story.

14   SNELL, GEORGE. "Herman Melville: The Seeker," in The Shapers
      of American Fiction, 1798-1947. New York: E.P. Dutton & Co.,
      pp. 60-78.
          Survey. Places Melville in the "apocalytical tradition" of
      American fiction. Comparisons with Poe. Reviewed in 1949.B25.

15   STORM, COLTON and HOWARD PECKHAM. Invitation to Book Collect-
      ing: Its Pleasures and Practices. New York: R.R. Bowker Co.,
      pp. 10-11, 14-15, 55, 231.
          Brief discussion of Melville's indebtedness to Owen Chase's
      Narrative and the copy he owned and annotated. Lists prices of
      Moby-Dick first editions.

16   THORP, WILLARD. "Introduction," in Moby-Dick. New York:
      Oxford University Press, pp. ix-xviii.
          Brief treatment of the book's "deeper meanings" and symbols.
      Ahab stands for all men who rebel so furiously against evil that
      they seek to destroy it and to find the reason why the world was
      formed in evil and not in good. Ishmael survives because he has
      not been a party with his entire consent to the blasphemous pur-
      suit of the white whale. Reviewed in 1949.B79.

17   TRILLING, LIONEL. <u>The Middle of the Journey</u>. New York: The
Viking Press, pp. 153–157.

The character Gifford Maxim publishes an essay on <u>Billy
Budd</u>. According to Maxim, the modern mind, in its radical or
liberal intellectual part, is not really capable of understanding
the story. "For such people, Billy Budd will be nothing more
than an oppressed worker, and a very foolish one, an insufficiently activated one, nothing more than a 'company man,' weakly
acquiescent to the boss. And Captain Vere will seem as at best
but a conscience-ridden bourgeois, sympathetic to a man of the
lower orders but committed to carrying out the behests of the
established regime." But <u>Billy Budd</u> is the tragedy of Spirit
(Billy) and the tragedy of Law (Vere) in the world of Necessity.
The modern progressive believes that Spirit should find its
complete expression at once; he cannot believe in Spirit unless
it is established in institutions, matched exactly in external
forms. But "it is the <u>weakness</u> of the inner life that will not
tolerate any discrepancy between what Spirit can conceive and
what Necessity can tolerate. Melville's perception is that
Spirit and the Law that is established in the world of Necessity
are kin, yet discontinuous. . . . Spirit blesses Law, even when
Law has put the noose around his neck, for spirit understands the
true kinship." Vere's is the tragic choice of God the Father,
who must condemn his own son to death; but not "as a sacrifice
and an atonement, but for the sake of the Son himself, for the
sake of Spirit in humanity. For Billy Budd is not only Christ,
he is Christ in Adam, and is therefore imperfect, subject to
excess."

18   UZZELL, THOMAS H. <u>The Technique of the Novel: A Handbook on
the Craft of the Long Narrative</u>. Philadelphia: J.B.
Lippincott Co., pp. 33n, 85, 134, 154, 253, 273–274.

<u>Moby-Dick</u> and <u>Billy Budd</u> used to illustrate advice to
would-be writers.

19   VINCENT, HOWARD P. "Preface," "Introduction," "Explanatory
Notes," and "Textual Notes," in <u>Collected Poems of Herman
Melville</u>. Ed. Howard P. Vincent. Chicago: Packard and Co.,
Hendricks House, pp. v–vi, vii–xii, 445–489, 491–536.

"Introduction" gives a brief account of Melville's career
as a poet. Yoomy's poems in <u>Mardi</u> may be mocking parodies of
Melville's own youthful poetry. By 1859 Melville had grown to
the conviction that the poet should be not only a Yoomy but a
Babbalanja, that the spontaneous overflow of Yoomy should be
tempered by Babbalanja's critical penetration. The new appreciation of Melville in the last twenty-five years, Vincent notes,
is limited among most people to three or four novels; few are
aware that he was also a poet. This first American edition of
his collected poems will be of value in rounding out our understanding of Melville's mind and art. "Explanatory Notes" include Melville's preface and "Supplement" to <u>Battle-Pieces</u>; his
notes to individual poems; the dedicatory letters to W. Clark
Russell in <u>John Marr</u> and to Elizabeth Shaw Melville in <u>Weeds and
Wildings</u>; and an extract from the manuscript of Melville's

Burgundy Club sketches. "Textual Notes" attempt to "indicate exactly what appears in the Melville verse manuscripts by way of changes and corrections" and "to show how and where the manuscripts differ from the printed text." Reviewed in 1947.B49–50, B52, B65; 1948.B36, B54.

20   WILSON, CARROLL A. "Herman Melville: Moby-Dick, New York, 1851," in One Hundred Influential American Books Printed Before 1900: Catalogue and Addresses, by the Grolier Club. New York: The Grolier Club, pp. 93–94.
      Notes on the first editions of Moby-Dick and The Whale (part of an exhibition at the Grolier Club, 18 April–16 June 1946) and on Melville's reputation.

21   WILSON, RUFUS ROCKWELL and OTILIE ERICKSON WILSON. New York in Literature: The Story Told in the Landmarks of Town and Country. Elmira, N.Y.: The Primavera Press, pp. 12–13, 72, 135–136.
      Biographical sketches.

22   WINTERS, YVOR. "Herman Melville and The Problems of Moral Navigation," in In Defense of Reason. New York: The Swallow Press & William Morrow and Co., pp. 200–233.
      Reprint of 1938.B23.

23   WITHAM, W. TASKER. "Herman Melville (1819-1891)," in Panorama of American Literature. New York: Stephen Daye Press, pp. 132–136.
      Biographical and critical sketch. With the twentieth-century admiration for the unusual and the expressionistic, critics are now inclined to assign Melville a higher place in literature than he deserves.

24   WOOD, JAMES PLAYSTED. "Omoo, A Narrative of Adventures in the South Seas," in One Hundred Years Ago: American Writing of 1847. New York: Funk & Wagnalls Co., pp. 385–387.
      Introduction to extracts from Omoo, chapters 19–24, 27, 30–31, 33, 36, 39, 43, 49, 51, 81, 82. Biographical sketch and brief commentary on Omoo (three parts story, one part sharp-spoken iconoclastic comment).

25   BIRSS, JOHN H. "Another, but Later, 'Redburn.'" American Notes & Queries, 6 (January), 150–151.
      Notes the anonymous book of poetry Redburn: or, The Schoolmaster of a Morning (1845), which contains descriptive passages that parallel events in Melville's youth, though there is strong argument to support the contention that it is not Melville's; the novel Redburn by Henry Ochiltree (1896); and the short story "Maria Redburn" by Ruth Kimball Gardiner (1906).

26   POMMER, HENRY F. "Melville's 'The Gesture' and the Schoolbook Verses." American Notes & Queries, 6 (January), 150–151.
     Reply to 1946.B38. The volume in question is almost certainly The London Carcanet (New York, 1831). [See Sealts (1966), pp. 75–75, No. 331.] The copy Melville owned in his youth does contain manuscript verses, but Pommer has identified them as the work of other writers. Pommer also records having seen an autograph manuscript poem by Melville called "The Gesture," which was in the style of the shorter poems of Timoleon and John Marr.

27   ANON. "Fiction Reprints." London Times Literary Supplement, No. 2347 (25 January), p. 55.
     Notice of 1946.B2. Brief synopsis of Belgion's introduction.

28   HOPE-WALLACE, PHILIP. "Critic on the Hearth." Listener [London], 37 (30 January), 215.
     Review of performance of Henry Reed's adaptation of Moby-Dick for radio. "This 'Moby Dick' was not only a perfectly valid projection in another medium of Melville's splendid book; it was as independently and sensually 'alive' as a new film or opera or play, catching and holding imagination from start to finish." Henry Reed is the hero: the "feel" of the original was there. Melville was not betrayed.

29   HILLWAY, TYRUS. "Melville and the New-York Historical Society." American Notes & Queries, 6 (February), 169.
     "Among the Melville papers in the New York Public Library is a statement for annual dues sent to Melville by the New-York Historical Society, probably about 1848. Is there any additional evidence that Melville was a member? The Society does not find Melville's name on its membership lists. . . ."

30   WRIGHT, NATHALIA. "A Source for Melville's Clarel: Dean Stanley's Sinai and Palestine." Modern Language Notes, 62 (February), 110–116.
     Borrowings from Stanley's book are scattered through Clarel, many of them corroborated by the markings in Melville's 1863 edition. Melville's most obvious borrowings are from passages in Stanley that describe what he himself never saw, though he also relied on Stanley to help him describe places he had seen. Some of Stanley's geological descriptions of Palestine, too, are recognizable in Clarel. Melville found much biblical history in Stanley, some of which is also to be found in Clarel. Parallel passages quoted.

31   ANON. "Fiction Reprints." London Times Literary Supplement, No. 2350 (15 February), p. 96.
     Notes that Billy Budd is published for the first time as a separate volume in the Lehmann edition and that Plomer sees the book as "Melville's final protest against the nature of things" [see 1946.B9].

32   FAST, HOWARD. "American Literature and the Democratic Tradi-
      tion." College English, 8 (March), 279–284.
          "Prior to the Civil War, although our literature frequently
      reflects an American scene, there is nothing uniquely American
      about the form, and often the same holds true of the content.
      Even though agrarian democracy and Christian utopian socialism
      are major threads running from Paine, Franklin, Jefferson, and
      Freneau to Emerson and Melville and Stowe, one never has an
      overwhelming sense of an American condition." There is an
      enormously static quality in early American literature: Irving,
      Poe, Hawthorne, and Melville live in a changeless world. "It was
      a fruitful land they occupied, a land content with itself. The
      working class was just a germ of something still aborning; the
      militant minority of Abolitionists had not yet a mass following,
      and respectable people of antecedents did not move westward."

33   WALBRIDGE, EARLE F. "New Books Appraised." Library Journal,
      72 (15 March), 460.
          Review of 1947.A2. A stimulating study. Olson "writes in
      a style which is elliptical, gnomic, and occasionally rather
      heavily loaded with social significance."

34   GREENSLET, FERRIS. "Melville and the Genesis of Moby Dick."
      New York Herald Tribune Weekly Book Review (23 March), p. 5.
          Review of 1947.A2. The book is not only important but
      apocalyptic. Olson has a gift for the explosive collocation of
      small, apparently unrelated facts; his gnomic style is marked "by
      flashings forth of intuitive truth, quick probings of the very
      axis of reality." Even in Billy Budd Melville never found the
      serenity that was beyond the "blackness" of Shakespeare. Accord-
      ing to Greenslet, "in the last thirty years in this country more
      and better brains have been more profitably employed in the study
      of the life and work of Herman Melville than in any other single
      field for the exercise of the literary intelligence."

35   ANON. "Shakespeare and Moby Dick." Newsweek, 29 (31 March),
      97.
          Review of 1947.A2. A brilliant essay that is as much a
      prose poem as a critique; one of the most knowing books about
      Melville, his times, and his influence ever written.

36   MAYBERRY, GEORGE. "Inside the Whale." New Republic, 116
      (31 March), 33.
          Review of 1947.A2. The most important contribution to
      Melville criticism since Weaver's biography [1921.A1]. Olson
      has done a great deal to explain how out of the welter of
      Melville's writing a masterpiece emerged.

37   SPILLER, ROBERT E. "Critical Standards in the American
      Romantic Movement." College English, 8 (April), 352.
          In "the perspective of a century, such writers as Long-
      fellow and Lowell, who seemed in their own day to represent the
      culmination of the struggle toward a national literature in the
      romantic mode, appear to us in their truer colors as spokesmen

for the culture of Europe transplanted to these shores. And such
writers as Emerson, Thoreau, Melville, and Whitman, who seemed to
their contemporaries to be eccentrics in many respects, protest-
ing against currents of the times, reveal to us today the deeper
forces of a romanticism at once indigenous and universal."   ·

38   MUMFORD, LEWIS. "Baptized in the Name of the Devil." New
      York Times Book Review (6 April), p. 4.
          Review of 1947.A2. After Olson's record of scholarly re-
search (tracking Melville's dispersed library), Call Me Ishmael
is something of an anomaly, mainly following the intuitive line
of D.H. Lawrence and Edward Dahlberg and forcing the reader to
take or leave its thesis without benefit of persuasion or scholarly argument. The special typographical arrangement was perhaps
intended to make the book look more original and challenging than
it actually is.

39   CHASE, RICHARD. "An Approach to Melville." Partisan Review,
      14 (May-June), 285-294.
          If we see Melville's work as a whole, a total concept of
his personality begins to emerge, of which Ahab and Pierre repre-
sent only one of several parts (the wounded Titan), one person
in a multiple personality that also includes Pip, Bartleby,
Benito Cereno, Bulkington, Jack Chase, the Confidence Man, and
Billy Budd. Recurrent figures in Melville's books are "The
Maimed Man in the Glen," such as the narrator in Typee, Donjalolo
in Mardi, Ahab, Pierre, the "kind of invalid Titan" in The
Confidence-Man; the "Divine Inert," such as Pip, Bartleby,
Benito Cereno, and the "Handsome Sailor," such as Bulkington,
Jack Chase, Billy Budd. All of Melville's maimed heroes have
affinities with the saint and the savior--with Christ, Adonis,
the magician, the shaman--but their fate, as we see from Ahab
and Pierre, is to rush headlong into violent action, betraying
whatever is creative within them and submitting themselves to
everything that is mechanical, corrupting, repressive, and death-
wishing. In doing so, they kill themselves and all whose fate is
in their hands; they are the Tragic Suicides. The Divine Inert
are superior to the Tragic Suicides, figures whose withdrawal
from the world has been uncompromising and complete and who have
gained the spiritual illumination that comes from dying out of
life without dying into death. The Handsome Sailor encompasses
and reconciles both the Suicide and the Divine Inert, though
this figure remains so inadequately objectified in Melville's
books that it cannot fully serve as synthesis. Bulkington, Jack
Chase, and Billy Budd "are direction, force, potentiality rather
than completed forms. They are the stuff and energy of an heroic
American personality in the act of setting forth toward fulfill-
ment--the Titanic body of America stirring out of the uncreated
Night and passing ponderously into motion and consciousness."
Prometheus is Chase's name for the total personality encompassing
the Suicide, the Divine Inert, and the Handsome Sailor. The
Suicide is a false Prometheus because of the blind violence to
which he is driven by his neurosis; the Divine Inert is a false
Prometheus because his compact with death and the unconscious is

irrevocable. The Promethean man has attained the spiritual illumination of the Divine Inert without losing the capacity for
action of the Suicide whose action is creative, like the Handsome
Sailor's; he is a man able to use the rhythms of life and death,
Withdrawal and Return, toward creative ends. Melville symbolizes
these rhythms in several ways: sea versus land, valley versus
mountain, stasis versus motion, time versus space, narcissism
versus genius, dark versus light, night versus day, and so on.
Melville seems to be making approximately the same point as
Toynbee in Study of History. All creativity, whether individual
or social, proceeds from individuals who can uncompromisingly
embark on the transit of Withdrawal and Return and who can ride
out the rhythms without coming into conflict with them. The
Divine Inert fail because they respond only to Withdrawal; the
Tragic Suicides fail because they allow themselves to be caught
and mangled between Withdrawal and Return. Pierre's burning of
his father's portrait symbolizes the function of allegory in
Melville's novels: allegory is the fire that consumes the
Father, every hypostatization of experience that inhibits creativity and destroys personality. No account of Melville can
afford to ignore or underestimate The Confidence-Man, a great
book, a buoyant, energetic piece of writing, on the whole free
of Melville's often clumsy rhetoric, a book of folkore (like
Israel Potter), and a wonderfully perceptive study of the American character, done at the folklore level. The Confidence Man is
another false Prometheus, a do-gooder, a Progressive, and an
emotional-intellectual-spiritual cutpurse. Melville's books have
enough energy, coherence, and intelligence to justify our calling
him an artist; his moral intelligence must not be underestimated
either. It is wrong to let our liberal political scruples keep
us from fully understanding his ideas of the Heroic American.
Incorporated in 1949.A1. Reprinted in 1951.B3.

40 GILMAN, WILLIAM H. "A Note on Herman Melville in Honolulu."
    American Literature, 19 (May), 169.
        Quotes from letter written by H.R. Hawkins in Honolulu,
    10 December 1849, to his father, Captain Esek Hawkins, Jr., of
    Lansingburgh, New York. Hawkins states: "All that Melville ever
    told about the missionaries in this part of the world, you may
    take for gospel." He adds, "I was conversing with a gentleman
    the other day about Typee and Omoo when he stated that he was
    well acquainted with their author, and knew him at a time when
    he was setting up pins in a ball alley." In view of Melville's
    vagabonding career in the South Pacific, there seems little
    reason to doubt the "gentleman's" story.

41 H., Z. "More Books." Bulletin of the Boston Public Library,
    22 (May), 192.
        Review of 1947.A2. The tone of the book is baffling. Imi-
    tating Melville, who imitated Shakespeare, Olson tries to talk
    the language of genius, and his effort becomes irksome. The
    substance of the volume could have been communicated just as
    well, and perhaps better, in a simple and unaffected way. Yet
    the substance is valuable.

42   ARMS, GEORGE. "'Moby-Dick' and 'The Village Blacksmith.'"
      Notes and Queries, 192 (3 May), 187-188.
           Finds allusions in Moby-Dick, chapter 112, "The Black-
      smith," to Longfellow's "The Village Blacksmith." Parallels
      suggest that Melville presented his pessimistic story as a
      satiric counterpoise to Longfellow's.

43   ANON. "Have You Any Material on Melville? Jay Leyda,
      Biographer, Can Use It." Pittsfield (Mass.) Berkshire
      Evening Eagle (16 May), section 2, p. 1.
           Reports that Leyda is doing research among old volumes of
      the newspaper in the basement of the circulation department of
      the Eagle and "is anxious for a look at the relevant material
      that must be in some Pittsfield attics. He has appealed for old
      family albums and old journals, manuscripts or letters in which
      Melville might have received mention, however small. Books owned
      by Melville or given by him to friends, even a ledger entry,
      showing receipt of a payment by him, would help."

44   THORP, WILLARD. "More About Melville." Saturday Review of
      Literature, 30 (24 May), 36.
           Review of 1947.A2. A book to rejoice those admirers of
      Melville who identify him with Ahab, it will have "a quite dif-
      ferent impact on the scholars and critics who have been trying to
      disperse the fogs which the myth-makers have been sending up
      around Melville for the past quarter of a century." The asser-
      tion that Melville wrote two Moby-Dicks needs careful scrutiny.
      Howard [1940.B33] and Hayford [1944.B16] offered the idea only as
      a conjecture. There is little in the evidence [Melville's letter
      of 1 May 1850 (Letters, pp. 106-108) and Evert Duyckinck's letter
      of August 1850 to George Duyckinck (see 1944.B16)] to warrant the
      guess that Melville's delay in finishing Moby-Dick was caused by
      a rewriting of the book on a new plan under the influence of
      Shakespeare. The two letters suggest sufficiently well that the
      book was not going to be a simple, factual account of the whale
      fishery. There are more satisfactory ways than Olson's to account
      for Melville's delay in finishing Moby-Dick--such as the state of
      his eyes during the winter of 1850-1851.

45   REED, HENRY. "Books in General." New Statesman and Nation
      [London], 33 (31 May), 397.
           Occasioned by publication of 1946.B9. Billy Budd exempli-
      fies many virtues modern fiction has lost or discarded: it is a
      good story and well written. The uncertainties of its manuscript
      text do not greatly matter. Its most striking feature for the
      reader of today is its discursive comments on character, the
      generalizations about psychology evoked by the development of the
      story itself. Modern novelists tend more and more to suppress
      such commentary. Melville's discernment of the ways and means of
      a hate like Claggert's is one of his many profound intuitions.
      "At school one sometimes dimly recognized something ineffably
      horrible when one saw a perverted schoolmaster bullying an
      angelic-looking boy; Melville allows us dimly to recognise a
      perversion of much the same kind here." Melville's mind is free

from the allegorical impulse that takes a spiritual theme and impresses objects into the illumination of it. He sees the object first, and from it a "purpose breaks." In Billy Budd, Melville gives expression to a feeling he has perhaps not before acknowledged or understood; once more he comes to understand it by way of real objects and people.

46   HARASZTI, ZOLTÁN. "Melville Defends Typee." Bulletin of the Boston Public Library, 22 (June), 203-208.
         Prints Melville's letter of 23 May 1846 to Alexander W. Bradford [Letters, pp. 25-27] in response to 1846.B48, and "Toby's" deposition in 1846.B74. Comparison of the revised and original texts of Typee "shows that the changes were far more substantial than a casual reading of the new preface might suggest. They involve the omission of the entire third chapter, also long sections from Chapters IV, XVII, XXIV, and XXVI, and the whole appendix--all the attacks on the missionaries, the French, and the misery which civilization had spread among the savages. . . . Nor are the modifications of style as 'slight' as one would suspect them to be from the preface. They include the expurgation of many sections about the sexual life of the savages." Melville yielded to his critics in the press, and his book suffered real loss in the resulting "mutilations." Regrettably, all later editions have been reprints of the revised edition.

47   ROUSE, H. BLAIR. "Democracy, American Literature, and Mr. Fast." English Journal, 36 (June), 321-323.
         Reply to 1947.B32. In Moby-Dick, as in his other writings, Melville is fully aware of his times, though he transcends the concrete limitations of his material and his age.

48   VINCENT, HOWARD P. "The Rediscovery of Herman Melville: Comment from the General Editor of the Definitive Edition of His Works." Chicago Sun Book Week (6 July), p. 1.
         Occasioned by publication of the first volume of the projected fourteen-volume Hendricks House edition of the Complete Works of Herman Melville. [See 1947.B19.] Stresses the current inaccessibility of Melville texts; such texts as have been reprinted are unreliable. There are still in Melville literary valleys as little known as his own Typee glen. Mardi is still unexplored, largely because it is unpurchasable; Clarel "is an uncharted jungle unvisited save by two or three scholars"; The Confidence-Man is similarly unknown, and out of print; the poems have yet to meet the test of careful reading and honest, intelligent criticism. With all of the novels, poetry, and the essays before us, we may now see Melville in his largeness and variety; he will be recognized as an author of varied styles, techniques, subject matter. Scheduled for publication in the next three years are a biography by Henry Murray and the bibliography and the letters, both edited by John Birss. "Publication Schedule" (1947-1948) for the Complete Works.

49   FRANKENBERG, LLOYD. "Herman Melville's Poems." New York
      Times Book Review (20 July), pp. 4, 22.
            Review of 1947.B19. As a poet Melville comes nowhere near
      Emily Dickinson or Whitman; nor can he compare with Poe; but his
      rightful place in American poetry is higher than Longfellow's.
      What he has, "inside quite commonplace metrics, might be
      described as flashes of eccentric insight." The virtues of his
      poetry go with a nineteenth-century prolixity, the tendency to
      write reams of what can only be called competent verse.

50   GRAY, JAMES. "Books in the News." Chicago Daily News
      (30 July).
            Review of 1947.B19. In his lyrics Melville was self-
      consciously determined to be musical and to seduce the ear. What
      one likes about him as a poet, at a first meeting, is that any
      mood seems spontaneous, inspired by the moment's hearty candor.
      A first reading also assures one that he was a better poet than
      several who were cherished in his day.

51   LEYDA, JAY. "White Elephant vs. White Whale." Town &
      Country, 101 (August), 68–69, 114d, 116–118.
            Account of Melville's life at Arrowhead, which became
      increasingly a physical and mental burden to him. "Cock-A-
      Doodle-Doo!" which concerns a handsome piece of property and a
      Shanghai rooster that the farmer's whole family slaves, starves,
      and finally dies to maintain, seems clearly to reflect this
      "Arrowhead strain." Prints "Report of the Committee on Agricul-
      ture" for the first time as Melville's and prints his diary
      jottings for 18–20 July 1850.

52   BENÉT, WILLIAM ROSE. "Poet-in-Prose." Saturday Review of
      Literature, 30 (2 August), 17.
            Review of 1947.B19. In this volume, Melville appears,
      except in unusual instances, a second-rate and often tedious
      rhymester. The "Battle-Pieces" are mostly not good; we have a
      touchstone for them in the extraordinary poems of Henry Howard
      Brownell, the most authentic poet of the Civil War. The good
      work includes "The Portent," "The Martyr," "In the Prison Pen."
      "Rebel Color-Bearers at Shiloh," "Sheridan at Cedar Creek," and
      among the sailor poems "The Haglets." "Monody" is an immortal
      poem; "Lone Founts" is wise and beautiful.

53   HART, JAMES D. "Two References to Melville." Melville
      Society Newsletter, 3 (8 August), 1–2.
            Reprints 1863.B4 (giving 1893 as date). Records experiment
      by G.P.R. James at Stockbridge in growing seed from the pyramids.
      [See Melville's letter of 1[?] June 1851 to Hawthorne (Letters,
      p. 130).]

54   BAKER, CARLOS. "Of Art and Artifacts." New York Times Book
      Review (10 August), p. 2.
            Like all great novels, Moby-Dick vitalizes both "the sub-
      stance of things and the substance of thought." Its bias is for
      "the unvanquishable man."

55   BLANCK, JACOB. "News from the Rare Book Sellers."
     Publishers' Weekly, 152 (23 August), section 2, B122.
          Reports that Whitman Bennett has discovered a first edition
     of Moby-Dick in the third issue binding with the "original waxed
     yellow end papers attached." Until the discovery of this third
     issue with the yellow endpapers, only copies of the first issue
     binding were known to exist with colored endpapers; later issues
     invariably turned up with plain white endpapers. If put on the
     sheets after 1853 this third issue binding would prove that not
     all the sheets of Moby-Dick were destroyed in the Harper's fire.
     Summary of the three known bindings.

56   ELIOT, ALEXANDER. "Melville and Bartleby." Furioso, 3
     (Fall), 11–21.
          Bartleby is Melville. The lawyer's chambers are the prison
     of Melville's life. The "dead letters" are Melville's manu-
     scripts, and the "flames" are "the same that gutted the quarters
     of his publisher, Harpers, in the year the story was written,
     destroying the plates of all his novels, and almost all the
     printed copies of his books." Melville guessed that even his
     greatest books would be forgotten soon.

57   HULL, WILLIAM. "Moby Dick: An Interpretation." Etc.: A
     Review of General Semantics, 5 (Autumn), 8–21.
          Moby-Dick for the student of general semantics.

58   BEZANSON, WALTER E. "Book Reviews." New England Quarterly,
     20 (September), 410–413.
          Review of 1947.A2. Olson has written a prose poem in the
     modern manner, a personal book, the very best that he could do
     "to tell what it has been like living with Melville between two
     wars and up through Project Manhattan"; it is "Olson's version,
     all fire and ice at once, of Melville's vision." In spite of
     difficulties and excesses, it needs to be read and pondered.
     Olson's newly added thesis to 1938.B45 that Melville wrote Moby-
     Dick twice is overasserted in terms of what is known. Part IV,
     in which Clarel is badly plundered and Billy Budd is dismissed in
     a footnote, is a completely private rationalization of Melville's
     loss of power in his later years.

59   WANNING, ANDREWS. "Melville and His Myth." Partisan Review,
     14 (September–October), 542–543.
          Review of 1947.A2. A "remarkably interesting and remarka-
     bly baffling book," which gives the impression "that it has some-
     how been put together in layers corresponding to different
     critical methods. The first part works by suggestions through
     the statement of fact; the second comes the nearest to the
     respectable academic methods of the study of influence and formal
     structure; while the last elicits a variety of symbols which,
     taken together, embody a kind of Melvillean historical myth."
     The second part is the most fully articulated in its argument,
     the most convincing. The opposing symbols of the third part
     "ramify in a number of directions: they begin as a comparative
     study of the earlier and the later Melville, they involve a

psychology of the man himself, and they end as a kind of master
clue to human history, if more particularly American history."
Olson's symbols seem "finally at work on a myth whose embodiment
is Melville, but whose function is not so much the explicating
of Melville himself as the vitalizing of a way of grasping the
experience of America, or even the world."

60   BROOKS, VAN WYCK. "Melville in the Berkshires." Tiger's Eye
       1 (October), 47–52.
           Chapter 8 of 1947.A1, minus footnotes.

61   SHIRER, WILLIAM L. "Books and Things." New York Tribune
       (31 October), p. 19.
           Review of 1947.A1. Brooks's history of the literary life
       in America becomes also a history of the social, economic, and
       political life of our civilization.

62   FELTENSTEIN, ROSALIE. "Melville's 'Benito Cereno.'" American
       Literature, 19 (November), 245–255.
           Examines Melville's treatment of his source to show his
       mastery of technique. It is inaccurate to say, as Scudder does
       [in 1928.B26] that Melville found his story ready-made in
       Delano. He "changes the names of the two ships from the
       Perseverance and the Tryal to the Bachelor's Delight and the
       San Dominick; he invents the oakum pickers and the hatchet
       polishers, the shaving of Cereno by Babo, the appearance of the
       giant Atufal in chains, the luncheon aboard the Spanish ship, the
       attack of the two Negroes upon the Spanish seaman, the glimpse
       of the sailor with the jewel, the incident of the sailor and the
       knot, and finally, Don Benito's death in a monastery. He also
       makes Babo, the leader of the revolt, the Spaniard's devoted ser-
       vant, rather than one Muri, and extends the period of Delano's
       isolation aboard the Spanish vessel. Instead of suppressing
       'just a few items,' he omits the whole second half of the narra-
       tive, which deals with the quarrel between the two captains."
       This large omission is part of the procedure by which Melville
       everywhere elevates the character of Benito Cereno and turns Babo
       into a manifestation of pure evil. Other small but significant
       changes show how deliberately Melville shaped the rambling source
       into a beautiful design. The episodes he adds increase the help-
       less purity of Don Benito and the wickedness of Babo, deepen the
       central mystery, intensify the sinister atmosphere, increase the
       suspense, and add powerful irony. The work's most powerful
       symbols are related to the two themes that obsessed Melville:
       the nature of evil and the ambiguity of appearances, especially
       as related to evil. Melville is no longer asking why evil should
       exist and be so mighty; instead he is examining in the actions of
       the Negroes how evil operates and, in Don Benito and Delano, what
       its effects are. Reprinted in Runden, pp. 124–133.

63   HILLWAY, TYRUS. "Melville's Art: One Aspect." Modern
     Language Notes, 62 (November), 477–480.
        After 1851, Melville "never quite regained, until forty
     years later, the subtle mastery of his materials which he ex-
     hibited in varying degrees between Typee and Moby-Dick." The
     reason: Melville was not a literary inventor but an assimilator;
     he recorded rather than devised most of the incidents in his
     major works, drawing on his own experience and his reading. By
     1852 he had exhausted his own experience, and his art gradually
     became less effective, until he added Billy Budd to his "bril-
     liant galaxy of sea stories."

64   VON ABELE, RUDOLPH. "Melville and the Problem of Evil."
     American Mercury, 65 (November), 592–598.
        Melville's dilemma was how to respond to the fact of evil
     in the world, to the problem of man's survival in an alien, in-
     different universe. In Moby-Dick no answers are given; in the
     next books Melville concludes that answers are impossible or
     nonexistent. Virtue itself, in the face of the malignancy of the
     universe, becomes irrelevant; adherence to the moral law ensures
     destruction in a world to which the moral law is meaningless. In
     his old age Melville became reconciled to the universe and to
     man's precarious position in it. In Billy Budd Melville accepts
     the world as it is, recognizing the tragic limitations within
     which men must live and act. He understands that no action,
     however rational, can be entirely free of evil, that the effort
     must be to choose those actions that result in the least evil,
     and that the "basic criterion must be the welfare of the whole
     social body, considered as an aggregate of interdependent
     individuals."

65   ANON. "A Poet of Strange Vision." London Times Literary
     Supplement, No. 2387 (1 November), p. 562.
        Review of 1947.B19. The exclusion of Clarel, "the overlong
     philosophical travelogue of Palestine in which Melville sums up
     his search for religious faith, was inevitable; but it cannot be
     neglected in any attempt to obtain a full view of the poet in his
     quest for an answer to the universal riddle. It traverses some
     very flat and monotonous tracts, but the oases are rewarding, the
     self-communings profound. There are Janus-faced decisions, but
     no wavering attitude in his disbelief in progress, civilization
     and politics as roads to redemption." The lyrics in "Weeds and
     Wildings" are the "spontaneous aftergrowth" that disproves the
     notion that Melville had exhausted his powers in Moby-Dick. The
     poems in Timoleon are rich in feeling, matured thought and ex-
     pression; Melville had overcome the technical difficulties that
     marred his earlier ventures in poetry.

66   WHICHER, GEORGE F. "Mr. Brooks' History of Our Literary
     Life." New York Herald Tribune Weekly Book Review (2 Novem-
     ber), p. 3.
        Review of 1947.A1. The rhetorical contrasts Brooks makes
     between Melville and Whitman ("One gave the dark side of the
     planet, the other the bright") are striking as characterization

but do little to explain the divergence of the two writers. Nor
is it enough to say that Melville, like the painters Page and
Duvenek, had a taste for the somber effects attained by the use
of "literary bitumen," suggestive as the analogy is. There is
often a fine imaginative lift in Brooks' writing, but he avoids
inward probings as if they were lethal.

67   ANON. "Topics of the Times." New York Times (8 November),
      p. 16.
          Appreciation of Moby-Dick occasioned by rereading. A
"bafflingly compounded masterpiece," a "reckless attempt to
blend the unblendable." Comparisons with Poe, Wagner, and
Shakespeare.

68   MUMFORD, LEWIS. "Our Rich Vein of Literary Ore." Saturday
      Review of Literature, 30 (8 November), 11–13.
          Review of 1947.A1. For the first time Brooks places Ameri-
can writers in the mainstream of American life, and in so doing
adds an extra dimension to all that we know about political,
economic, and military affairs. Yet there is an effect of glib-
ness in his prose, which would be rectified if he halted his
narrative long enough to introduce the books he refers to and
let the authors speak occasionally in their proper person,
instead of through his own ventriloquial mouth. His method has
the effect of making Holmes as important as Thoreau, or Bayard
Taylor almost as interesting as Melville.

69   COMMAGER, HENRY STEELE. "Writers Who Discovered America."
      New York Times Book Review (9 November), pp. 5, 57.
          Review of 1947.A1. The theme that animates Brooks's books,
most notably this one and its immediate predecessor, is the discovery of America. "It is a bit harder to fit Melville [rather
than Whitman] into this general pattern of the discovery of
America and the passion for democracy, and it is interesting that
Mr. Brooks emphasizes not the later Melville, with his deep sense
of the tragic, but the earlier Melville who thought America 'the
Israel of our time' and Americans the 'chosen people,' who was
closer to the Transcendentalists, perhaps, than to Hawthorne,
whose faith in the plain people was still lively."

70   HILLWAY, TYRUS. "Berkshire Athenaeum." Melville Society
      Newsletter, 3 (10 November), 2.
          Reports that Agnes Morewood, Melville's grandniece,
"remembers a Christmas card received by Melville from Hawthorne,
on the back of which were comments about The Confidence-Man; the
card, unfortunately, seems to have been mislaid and is perhaps
permanently lost."

71   SCHLESINGER, ARTHUR, JR. "America in Pastels." Nation, 165
      (29 November), 598.
          Review of 1947.A1. Brooks has long since abandoned any
recognizable critical function in favor of lengthy and tender
exercises in nostalgia. His method and his prose have a peculiar
effect of eviscerating the past—of divesting it of its dark and

tragic strains and making it something graceful and innocuous. His recoil from trauma inevitably wrecks his treatment of his main figures. Thus we have a Melville almost indifferent to the problem of evil, a Whitman whose ambiguities are muted and denied, a Lincoln without internal agonies.

72   WILSON, EDMUND. "Van Wyck Brooks on the Civil War Period." New Yorker, 23 (29 November), 130, 132, 134, 137, 138.
Review of 1947.A1. With Melville, Brooks seems never to have got into his subject; it can almost be said that he simply passes Melville by--or at least that he sees him only in relation to the national idealism. He skims over the depths and intensities of Melville with less insight than he had for Poe's. "The systole and diastole of Melville, the alternations of attraction and repulsion, of ecstatic rapture with horror, that supply the dark fable of 'Benito Cereno' as well as that of 'Moby-Dick,' do not pulse" in Brooks's pages. Brooks sidesteps real discussion of Moby-Dick, never making clear what he supposes the book's "innermost meaning" to be. He does not come to terms with the "ordeal" of Herman Melville. Reprinted in 1950.B32.

73   BELGION, MONTGOMERY. "Heterodoxy on Moby Dick?" Sewanee Review, 55 (Winter), 108–125.
Argues against Sedgwick's claim [1944.A1] that in Moby-Dick Ahab, the whale, and the sea are symbols and against his interpretation of the alleged symbols. A reader must shun every allegation that the book holds a concealed meaning. If, "for a monomaniac but individual Ahab pursuing a definitely given whale over the everyday sea, we substitute Man pursuing the mystery of creation over the tossing waters of truth: the plot of Moby Dick will not have been made more exciting to us; it will have been less exciting. Far from having been enriched, the experience of reading the book will have been impoverished." The whale does not grow more sinister and dreadful through being accepted as "the mystery of creation," and the sea is only belittled in being translated into the waters of truth. Sedgwick's theory, and any other theory of a concealed meaning, is a hindrance to a reader's fullest enjoyment and appreciation of Moby-Dick , which requires his acceptance of the "reasonableness of the whole story," his putting himself imaginatively in the place of the characters, and his awareness of the book's American affinities and European derivations. The American philosophizing, leisured and deliberate, rustic and eccentric, affirms Melville's affinities with Thoreau, Emerson, Hawthorne, Whitman, Poe, and Mark Twain. It is the philosophizing that gives Moby-Dick its uniqueness and makes it one of the world's great books, not through imparting knowledge but by moving us in our feelings. Three of the book's prominent derivations are the Bible, Sir Thomas Browne, and Shakespearean drama, the latter the key to the book's extraordinary power. The language of a Shakespeare play fills auditor or reader with a swarm of exalted feelings; in Moby-Dick, "what fires our sensibility and casts over us an exalting enchantment, is the flash in a philosophizing phrase."

74 BIRSS, JOHN H. "The Story of Toby, a Sequel to Typee ."
    Harvard Library Bulletin, 1 (Winter), 118-119.
         Bibliographical data of the sixteen-page pamphlet, The
    Story of Toby, A Sequel to "Typee," published by John Murray in
    England in 1846. Birss reports that a copy of this item is now
    part of the Melville holdings of the Harvard College Library;
    until recently no copy had been traced.

75 WILLIAMS, STANLEY T. "'Follow Your Leader': Melville's
    'Benito Cereno.'" Virginia Quarterly Review, 23 (Winter),
    61-76.
         Examines the craftsmanship of "Benito Cereno," including
    its highly original method of narration and the still more
    impressive perfections in technique, the unities of time and
    place, the suspense, the representation of the three contrasting
    temperaments of Delano, Benito, and Babo, the constant identifi-
    cation of the reader with Delano, the exact manipulation of
    incident enhanced by a definitiveness of language designed to
    create a mood of darkness, mystery, and tragic loneliness. Two
    dominant themes of the story are the fading glories of the
    Church and the disintegration of the Spanish grandeur of the past;
    counterpointed with these is the brutal arrogance of the blacks.
    The symbols in "Benito Cereno," from the humblest, such as the
    jolly whaleboat Rover afoul in the riptide, to the most complex,
    such as the character of Babo, equate ideas in the moral or meta-
    physical world, yet these symbols never withdraw their own hard
    identities in the matter-of-fact experience of Delano. Not only
    is there in "Benito Cereno" an "amazing union of fact and fancy,
    simple event impinging upon the invisible world, but most of the
    meanings are fluid, almost indeterminate, or localized only by
    the particular experience of the reader," as in some twentieth-
    century writing. Thus Benito represents more than the decadence
    of mighty Spain. The three protagonists in their various ways
    confront merciless evil. If Delano stands remotely for the
    energy of a new civilization, he suggests also the genial com-
    placence of the everyday mind toward the mysteries of good and
    evil; Melville admires and perhaps envies Delano but regards him
    as philosophically and ethically immature. Delano is a wicked
    decoy for readers of the story; in showing his comfortable illu-
    sions concerning evil, Melville underlies our own. Benito has
    the weaknesses of the introvert; he is also, unlike Delano, a
    conscious, reflective being to whom the fact of evil is more
    devastating than its manifestations. Benito is linked with
    church and state, the tottering bulwarks of the past, that have
    proved valueless in his crisis. The problem of evil is the inner
    theme of "Benito Cereno," its symbol Babo, through whom, as
    through Claggart in Billy Budd, Melville reexamines "the mystery
    of iniquity." Its mystery is partly its outward simulation of
    the good, its ambiguity, and use of masks, but more its hatred
    for the happiness of hatred, evil for the sake of evil. "Every-
    thing on the San Dominick proclaims the ascendancy in the uni-
    verse of natural, primitive, evil man and his easy victory over
    the obsolete armor of the past. Without recording conclusions,

Babo, like the other two characters, opens the doors of wider and more rueful speculation."

76   MAYNARD, THEODORE. "New Books." Catholic World, 166
     (December), 278–279.
          Review of 1947.A1. Brooks treats Melville and Whitman with
     affection and insight.

77   P., B.A. "Ageless and Edible." American Notes & Queries, 7
     (December), 141.
          Draws attention to 1947.B53 and summarizes the information
     there about G.P.R. James's experiment with seed from the
     pyramids.

78   POTTER, DAVID. "The Brodhead Diaries 1846–1849." Journal of
     the Rutgers University Library, 11 (December), 23–24.
          John Romeyn Brodhead, Secretary of the United States Lega-
     tion to the Court of St. James, acted as Melville's literary
     agent in the London Publication of Omoo and Mardi. Details from
     diary entries.

79   ANON. "The Spoken Word." London Times Literary Supplement,
     No. 2392 (6 December), p. 632.
          Review of Moby Dick, A Play for Radio from Herman
     Melville's Novel by Henry Reed. Moby-Dick "is a novel which owes
     everything to the unifying force of the first person singular--a
     force which excuses the hollow boom of its weaker passages.
     Melville's style swells easily to an organ volume; but like the
     organ it has a tendency to cipher. Only the tone of voice which
     he imposes immediately on the teller of the tale can make a
     fitting amalgam of the majestic and the absurd in what is to
     come." Reed has recast the central drama of the story, using as
     far as possible Melville's own words.

1948 A BOOKS--NONE

1948 B SHORTER WRITINGS

1   ARVIN, NEWTON. "Introduction," in Moby Dick. New York:
     Rinehart & Co., pp. v–x.
          Brief account of Moby-Dick's success in Melville's first-
     hand experience as a whaler and in his reading of whaling and
     travel literature and Elizabethan drama, particularly of
     Shakespeare. Also gives an account of the book's affiliations
     with epics (rather than with tragedy). Moby-Dick is not liter-
     ally an epic but a work of nineteenth-century fiction with a
     character of its own, its warp a tough, prosaic realism, its weft
     a metaphysical symbolism. In making the white whale the central
     symbol, Melville was instinctively turning to a Primordial Image,
     the "image of a creature that must be regarded with mingled
     terror and veneration, with alternating gratitude and resentment,
     as a paradoxical source of much good (of food, of light, of
     fragrance) and of much evil and suffering." To see in Moby Dick

only a quasi-human malignity is a great and tragic error.
Ishmael survives because he has risen to a truer sense of the
good and evil in Moby Dick than Ahab has and to a capacity for
human fellowship to which Ahab is lost.

2   BENÉT, WILLIAM ROSE, ed. The Reader's Encyclopedia. New
     York: Thomas Y. Crowell, p. 710.
        Two-paragraph biographical and critical sketch. Melville's
"work at its best is marked by realism, rich and poetic prose,
the use of allegory and symbolism, and an effort to express the
philosophical and religious meanings the author felt he had found
in the world."

3   BLAIR, WALTER and JOHN C. GERBER.   "'Fiction Versus Fact,'" in
     Literature: Better Reading Two. Chicago: Scott, Foresman
     and Co., pp. 8–9.
        Commentary on extract from Chapter 61 of Moby-Dick, "Stubb
Kills A Whale."

4   BOWERS, DAVID.   "Democratic Vistas," in Literary History of
     the United States.   Vol. 1.   Ed. Robert E. Spiller et al.
     New York: The Macmillan Co., pp. 345–357.
        Enumerates concerns, perspectives, and assumptions shared
by Emerson, Thoreau, Hawthorne, Melville, and Whitman, affinities
attributable to the influence of transcendentalism. By "reawaken-
ing--even among its critics--an interest in the great problems of
human nature and destiny, transcendentalism conferred upon
American literature a perspective far wider and deeper than that
proposed by its own formulated doctrines, the perspective of
humanity itself. This perspective it is which gives common
purpose and meaning to the otherwise divergent achievements of
Emerson, Thoreau, Hawthorne, Melville, and Whitman, and accounts
in great part for their manifest superiority to predecessors like
Irving and Bryant whose interests were less profound and more
superficially literary."

5   CARTER, JOHN.   Taste and Technique in Book-Collecting: A
     Study of Recent Developments in Great Britain and the United
     States.   New York: R.R. Bowker Co., p. 158.
        Notes that after the success of Typee and Omoo the Harpers
printed a large edition of Mardi; because the book was a dismal
failure, it is today easily the commonest of all Melville first
editions.

6   COMMITTEE ON THE COLLEGE STUDY OF AMERICAN LITERATURE AND
     CULTURE.   American Literature in the College Curriculum.
     Chicago: National Council of Teachers of English, pp. 22–31.
        Melville was included in fifty-two out of ninety survey
course syllabi examined. Most often included in courses restricted to the study of five or fewer American writers were
Emerson, Whitman, Hawthorne, Poe, Thoreau, Clemens, and Melville.

7   COWIE, ALEXANDER. "Herman Melville (1819-1891)," in The Rise
     of the American Novel. New York: American Book Co.,
     pp. 363-411.
         Biographical and critical survey. For each book, a
     synopsis, critical analysis and evaluation. Sections on Melville
     as "Mariner," "Mystic," "Thinker," "Critic," and "Artist."

8   DAVIS, JOE LEE, JOHN T. FREDERICK, and FRANK LUTHER MOTT, eds.
     American Literature: An Anthology and Critical Survey.
     Vol. 1. New York: Charles Scribner's Sons, pp. 990-1003.
         Biographical and critical survey ("Herman Melville").
     Headnote to extract from "Hawthorne and His Mosses"; "Benito
     Cereno"; selections from Battle-Pieces, Clarel (the "Epilogue"),
     John Marr, and Timoleon; and Billy Budd, Foretopman.

9   FREEMAN, F. BARRON. "Preface," "Introduction: Background for
     Billy Budd," and "Bibliography," in Melville's BILLY BUDD.
     Ed. F. Barron Freeman. Cambridge, Mass.: Harvard University
     Press, pp. vii-xii, 3-126, 373-381.
         Freeman's book is "an attempt to present the first accurate
     transcription, with all variant readings, of the manuscripts of
     Billy Budd; the first publication of Melville's previously un-
     discovered short story, 'Baby Budd, Sailor,' out of which he
     wrote his last novel. "Appendix I" prints "Related Fragments
     Found in the Manuscripts" and "Appendix II" prints "Unrelated
     Fragments of Verse and Prose Found in the Manuscripts." The
     "Introduction" gives an account of Melville's "life, reading, and
     writing, after 1886"; his sources for Billy Budd, both "factual"
     borrowings and sources in philosophy, psychology, and creative
     literature, including his own White-Jacket; and the book's struc-
     ture, characters, style, and themes, emphasizing in the discus-
     sion of its "religious level" Melville's affinities with
     Schopenhauer. The "Bibliography" includes a checklist of
     Melville manuscripts and books owned by Melville in the Harvard
     College Library. [Hayford and Sealts, pp. 16-23, point
     out "the shortcomings and errors" of Freeman's edition, while
     acknowledging the value of his introduction, and from their own
     analysis of the manuscript conclude that at "no stage of the
     composition of Billy Budd did Melville have a version constitut-
     ing, corresponding to, or even approximating the text Freeman
     mistakenly presented under the title 'Baby Budd, Sailor.'"] Re-
     viewed in 1948.B81; 1949.B39, B49, B59, B62, B79, B83, B91, B110;
     1950.B22. [See also 1949.B87.]

10   FULLER, ROY. "Introduction," in The Confidence-Man. London:
     John Lehmann, pp. v-xiii.
         The violence of Melville's antipathy to modern commercial
     society is shown most clearly in The Confidence-Man. Melville's
     inexplicitness about its plot has been one reason for the book's
     neglect. We are never told, as his contemporaries would have
     told us, that the book is about a rogue who assumes a number of
     different disguises for the purpose of extracting money from the
     ship's passengers. This inexplicitness resembles Kafka's. The
     book resembles Kafka too in that there is hardly any attempt to

exploit its ingenious plot for the sake of entertainment or
neatness. It is steadfastly used for Melville's moral purpose.
There is a power, a control, a vision, a singular intelligence,
behind The Confidence-Man. We can never at any time during its
course proclaim it a great novel, but we can never forget that
its author was a great novelist. Reading the book for the first
time, we await in vain the appearance of the sympathetic character, on whose judgments of the action and the other protagonists
we can base our own. "It is as though in Gulliver's Travels
Swift had left out Gulliver. . . . [T]he eighteenth-century
reasonable man has disappeared. In the mid-nineteenth-century
world of America, a violently commercial world, in which men have
based their morality on money--so runs Melville's inexorable
logic and terrible honesty--there can be no person outside the
struggle capable of making a valid moral judgment of it."

11   FURNAS, J.C. Anatomy of Paradise: Hawaii and the Islands of
      the South Seas. New York: William Sloane Associates,
      pp. 434-436.
       Melville set the pattern for all his successors in creative
interpretation of the South Seas. Fayaway is the durable prototype of the South Sea enchantress, with numerous offspring:
Pierre Loti's Rarahu, Robert Keable's Numerous Treasure, and the
thronging heroines of Nordhoff and Hall. Her effect on the
aesthetic world is well illustrated by John La Farge's watercolor
of her standing in a canoe. "He painted her with the attenuated
figure of an Ingres model and a face of somewhat pre-Raphaelite
cast. The blue cloth swirling ahead of her is the identical
piece of flowing studio drapery that appears in every third academic painting of the nineteenth century. She looks not at all
like a Marquesan, but is a synthesis of beauties as understood in
the salons of 1880." Yet La Farge did Melville no violence:
Fayaway is a whimsical and cryptically voluptuous abstraction.
Typee is good reading but dismally unconvincing. It should have
been R.H. Dana who stayed in the Typee valley: there would have
been much less condescending cuteness about the savages and much
more pithy life in the observations. Reprinted in 1948.B49.

12   GUERARD, ALBERT J. "Introduction," in The Cannibal, by John
      Hawkes. New York: New Directions, p. xv.
       The Cannibal's "total reading of life and vision of desola-
tion" is "as terrible as that of Melville's Encantadas."

13   HUDDLESTONE, LINDEN. "An Approach to Dylan Thomas," in The
      Penguin New Writing. Ed. John Lehmann. London: Penguin
      Books, pp. 157-158.
       There are interesting parallels between Melville's symbol-
ism and Thomas's. The first two paragraphs of chapter 132 in
Moby-Dick gives the substance of thought underlying several passages of Thomas's work. Possibly Thomas was influenced by Melville, but the personal experiences "onto which he loaded the
symbolism" must have been of the rivers, weather, and sea of his
native Glamorgan.

14   HYMAN, STANLEY EDGAR. The Armed Vision: A Study in the
      Methods of Modern Literary Criticism. New York: Alfred A.
      Knopf, pp. 56-57, 59-60.
           Evaluation of 1938.B23. Winters deserves particular
      praise for his treatment of Melville, "to whom (almost alone of
      contemporary critics, with the honorable exception of F.O.
      Matthiessen) he has at last given his rightful due as America's
      greatest writer and one of the world's supreme novelists.
      Winters is weak, or at least too limited, in interpreting the
      deeper meanings of Moby Dick, but in detailed symbolic inter-
      pretation of passages he is invaluable. He seems to be totally
      unaware, for example, of the elaborate homosexual imagery running
      through Melville, especially concentrated in his favorite short
      novel, Billy Budd. . . . Winters' study of Melville is never-
      theless a remarkable piece, if only for its full and excellently
      chosen quotations, and despite the possibility, as in the case of
      his Poe study, that Winters is actually evaluating the man accu-
      rately for the wrong reasons, for a 'morality' that seems to be
      his chief interest in all of the works of Melville's he praises."

15   JOHNSON, THOMAS H. "Herman Melville, 1819-1891," in Literary
      History of the United States. Ed. Robert E. Spiller et al.
      New York: The Macmillan Co., pp. 647-654.
           Selective bibliography, divided into "Separate Works,"
      "Collected Works," "Edited Texts and Reprints," "Biography and
      Criticism," "Primary Sources," and "Bibliography."

16   JONES, HOWARD MUMFORD. The Theory of American Literature.
      Ithaca, N.Y.: Cornell University Press, passim.
           The effect of changing critical fashions on Melville's
      reputation.

17   LASKI, HAROLD J. The American Democracy: A Commentary and an
      Interpretation. New York: The Viking Press, p. 15, passim.
           Like Emerson, Thoreau, Hawthorne, and Mark Twain, Melville
      is profoundly American, always puts his ultimate allegiance in
      the American tradition.

18   LEYDA, JAY. "The Army of the Potomac Entertains a Poet." Art
      and Action (10th Anniversary Issue of Twice A Year),
      pp. 259-272.
           Biographical, treating the period 1857-1866 and focusing on
      Melville's new career as a poet; relates aspects of poems in
      Battle-Pieces to Melville's own experiences. Prints Melville's
      letters of 10 May 1864 to Henry Sanford Gansevoort [Letters,
      pp. 224-226] and 21 July 1864 to Brigadier General Robert O.
      Tylor [Letters, pp. 226-227].

19   MAILER, NORMAN. The Naked and the Dead. New York: Rinehart
      and Co., p. 345.
           "For his thesis he [the protagonist] has been given a
      magna: A Study of the Cosmic Urge in Herman Melville."

20   MAUGHAM, W. SOMERSET. "Herman Melville and Moby Dick," in Great Novelists and Their Novels: Essays on the Ten Greatest Novels of the World, and the Men and Women Who Wrote Them. Philadelphia: The John C. Winston Co., pp. 211–232.

     To biographical material drawn from Weaver [1921.A1], Mumford [1929.A1], and Anderson [1939.A1], Maugham adds the suggestion that marital disappointment and homosexual frustration ("instincts, perhaps even unrecognized, and if recognized angrily repressed and never, except perhaps in imagination indulged in") turned "the commonplace, undistinguished writer of Typee into the darkly imaginative, powerful, inspired and eloquent author of Moby Dick." Observations on allegorical interpretations of Moby-Dick (which Maugham distrusts); on the book's style ("copious magnificence"), faulty construction, magnificent descriptions of action, and "intensely real" and "enchantingly romantic" early chapters; and on "the sinister and gigantic figure" of Ahab: "I can think of no creature of fiction that approaches his stature. You must go to the Greek dramatists for anything like that sense of doom with which everything that you are told about him fills you, and to Shakespeare to find beings of such terrible power. It is because Herman Melville created him that, notwithstanding all the reservations one may make, Moby Dick is a great, a very great book." Reprinted in 1948.B56, 1949.B10; revised version in 1954.B14, 1955.B19.

21   METCALF, ELEANOR MELVILLE. "Preface," "Introduction," and "Notes," in Journal of a Visit to London and the Continent by Herman Melville, 1849–1850. Ed. Eleanor Melville Metcalf. Cambridge, Mass.: Harvard University Press, pp. vii–xi, xvii–xx, 89–175.

     The "Preface" explains Metcalf's principles in editing the journal, published here in its entirety for the first time. The "Introduction" characterizes the journal as "the record of a quick and varied response to historical and natural scenes, rich accumulations of the arts, social life, and literary and philo-sophical discussions" and briefly relates it to Melville's circumstances in the fall of 1849. The "Notes" identify persons and places mentioned in the journal, explain allusions, and draw connections between journal entries and many of Melville's "later works, even poems published in the last year of his life." The notes also contain the letters of introduction written for Melville by Edward Everett and R.H. Dana and quotations from letters concerning Melville by George Duyckinck, Sir Walter Farquhar, Edward Everett, George Adler, and David Davidson. Indexed. Reviewed in 1948.B74–75, B80, B82; 1949.B42, B52, B59, B79, B83, B91, B106, B107, B113; 1950.B54. [See also 1949.B11.]

22   NEIDER, CHARLES. "Introduction," in Short Novels of the Masters. Ed. Charles Neider. New York: Rinehart and Co., pp. 7–11.

     Melville's influence on Joyce has been underrated. There are stylistic affinities and such striking similarities as the use of interior monologue and the play form in Moby-Dick and Ulysses. "Benito Cereno" is the architectural delight of

Melville's fiction. Its one flaw is the mass of depositions,
which are anticlimactic after the running narrative. Melville
"was so absorbed in the symbolistic aspects of his theme that he
allowed himself to be guilty of meretriciousness in deviating too
far from the truth." He "glosses over extenuating circumstances
in an effort to blacken the blacks and whiten the whites, to
create poetic images of pure evil and pure virtue. The result is
sometimes unfortunate in the feelings it arouses against the
Negroes." Melville "is swept away by artistic and thematic considerations to a point where he seems to lack compassion and an
acute awareness of the truth." The language of "Benito Cereno"
is "restrained and formal, possessing a dry beauty, yet perilously
close to Melville's last unhappy style. . . . Melville's real
tragedy is not that he withdrew from his early subjects into the
metaphysical mists of Pierre and The Confidence Man, but that he
permitted himself to stiffen inwardly in recoiling from the
public's misunderstanding of him, and let his language grow
formal and stale."

23   O'CONNOR, WM. VAN. Sense and Sensibility in Modern Poetry.
     Chicago: University of Chicago Press, pp. 97-98, passim.
         Brief references to Melville's influence on modern writers,
     particularly on Hart Crane, who carried into modern poetry the
     "awful heritage of evil," which Melville caught in his symbols of
     the sea. The last seven poems of White Buildings are about
     Melville and the sea, and throughout The Bridge one senses the
     presence of Melville.

24   OLIVER, EGBERT S. "Introduction," "Explanatory Notes," and
     "Textual Variations," in The Piazza Tales. Ed. Egbert S.
     Oliver. New York: Hendricks House, Farrar Strauss,
     pp. ix-xii, 225-250, 251-256.
         "Introduction" includes details of publication, sales, and
     contemporary reception of The Piazza Tales. "Explanatory Notes"
     include Melville's letters of 7 January, 16 February, and
     24 March 1856 to Dix & Edwards regarding publication of The
     Piazza Tales [Letters, pp. 176-177, 179-180], that of 7 January
     published here for the first time; and extracts from chapter 18
     of Amasa Delano's Narrative, Melville's source for "Benito
     Cereno." Reviewed in 1948.B79; 1949.B39, B47, B69, B79, B83,
     B90; 1950.B40.

25   PLOMER, WILLIAM. "Introduction," in Redburn. London:
     Jonathan Cape, pp. 11-18.
         Reprint of 1937.B15.

26   ROUTH, H.V. "The Nineteenth Century and After." The Year's
     Work in English Studies, 1946, 27 (1948), 254.
         Summaries of 1946.B32, B34.

27   RUKEYSER, MURIEL. "Rari from the Marquesas," in The Green
     Wave. Garden City, N.Y.: Doubleday & Co., pp. 55-65.
          Examples of the rari, or love chant (until 1925 the popular
     song, the poetry of the Marquesas, "fought relentlessly by the
     missionaries because of the 'erotic symbolism of some of the
     words'"), by Moa Tetua and others, translated by Samuel Elbert
     and Muriel Rukeyser. "These songs are like the songs that
     Melville heard."

28   STEWART, RANDALL. Nathaniel Hawthorne: A Biography. New
     Haven: Yale University Press, pp. 107-112, passim.
          The relationship between Hawthorne and Melville. The two
     men "had much in common: an intellectual honesty and disinter-
     estedness, a skepticism, a distrust of fashionable panaceas, a
     sense of the humor as well as the tragedy of life, and an appre-
     ciation also of life's good things. Both could be at once
     Olympian and down to earth. Although Hawthorne was tempera-
     mentally less ebullient than Melville and philosophically less
     rebellious, and although the two men were separated by the dis-
     tance between middle age and youth, their friendship, by any
     reasonable standards, was an eminently successful one. . . . It
     is impossible to determine precisely the effects which the
     friendly association of Hawthorne and Melville had upon their
     literary productions, but it seems certain that each stimulated
     the other to the happiest exertion of his creative powers."

29   TEDLOCK, E.W., JR. The Frieda Lawrence Collection of D.H.
     Lawrence Manuscripts: A Descriptive Bibliography.
     Albuquerque: University of New Mexico Press, pp. 159-160.
          Descriptions of the typescripts of Lawrence's essays on
     Melville in Studies in Classic American Literature [1923.B3-4].
     The typescript of the essay on Typee and Omoo "represents an
     early version of the text of the chapter of the same title in the
     book. In general the cardinal points of the typescript are pres-
     ent in the book, but the two parallel each other in wording only
     occasionally and then not for long. The ending in the book in
     its analysis of Melville's search for the perfect human relation-
     ship, the ideal, has no counterpart in the typescript. Like the
     style in the book the paragraphs of the typescript are broken up
     into short, provocative statements." The typescript of the essay
     on Moby-Dick "is closest of all those described here to the text
     of the book, yet it too underwent change. From approximately the
     tenth paragraph to the end it is used with only minor revisions
     in the book. Typical of the final style Lawrence gave to the
     essays, some twenty-eight short paragraphs are added at the end
     of the published text and some twenty at the beginning."

30   THORP, WILLARD. "Herman Melville," in Literary History of the
     United States. Ed. Robert E. Spiller et al. New York: The
     Macmillan Co., pp. 441-471.
          Biographical and critical survey. For each book, a synop-
     sis, critical analysis, and evaluation. Reprinted in 1960.B36.

31   VON HAGEN, WOLFGANG. "The Encantadas," in <u>Green World of the</u>
     <u>Naturalists</u>. Ed. Wolfgang Von Hagen. New York: Greenberg
     Press, pp. 201–202.
         Headnote to excerpts from "The Encantadas." Melville's
     visit to the Galapagos Islands "first awakened in him a feeling
     for the pathos of life."

32   WEBER, BROM. <u>Hart Crane: A Biographical and Critical Study</u>.
     New York: The Bodley Press, passim.
         Brief references to Crane's reading of Melville. "Black
     Tambourine" was probably inspired by Pip in <u>Moby-Dick</u>, as well as
     by Crane's own experiences with Negroes in his father's factories
     and warehouses.

33   WELLS, HENRY W. <u>Where Poetry Stands Now</u>. Toronto: The
     Ryerson Press, pp. 40–43.
         It is tempting to find in Melville a sound and auspicious
     directive for poetry today, reconciling the extremes of person-
     alism (seen in Emily Dickinson) and impersonalism (seen in Walt
     Whitman). Melville never forgets that in his philosophy two
     conditions are essential to a good life: a degree of excellence
     in both personal and social life, and harmony between the two.
     All his books fuse personal and social concerns. Probably no
     American poem of the latter half of the nineteenth-century is so
     rich in social imagination as <u>Clarel</u> or so profoundly religious
     and spiritual; there are no poetical meditations on war so
     original and so forceful as Melville's battle poems. By organic
     development, the Shakespearean little volume <u>John Marr and Other</u>
     <u>Poems</u> passes from a rugged ballad style in the early pieces to
     the shy and elusive beauty of the imagistic closing poems. "But
     the whole volume is clearly intended as one poem, and its parts
     are far more consciously and successfully harmonized than the
     sections into which Whitman's 'Song of Myself' falls. This study
     in integration is fundamental to Melville's mental and aesthetic
     processes. He endeavours to unite what others rest content to
     leave divided." Hart Crane is the most distinguished heir of
     Melville's centralized position.

34   WRIGHT, LYLE H. "Melville, Herman," in <u>American Fiction,</u>
     <u>1774–1850: A Contribution Toward a Bibliography</u>. Rev. ed.
     San Marino, Ca.: The Huntington Library, pp. 197–198.
         Bibliographical entries for <u>Mardi</u>, <u>Omoo</u>, <u>Redburn</u>, <u>Typee</u>,
     and <u>White Jacket</u>, with selective list of libraries owning the
     editions noted. Revised version of 1939.B9.

35   ANDERSON, CHARLES. "Book Reviews." <u>American Literature</u>, 19
     (January), 376–377.
         Review of 1947.A2. Two brief passages will be of some
     interest to scholars: Melville's notes in his copy of Owen
     Chase's <u>Narrative</u> of the <u>Essex</u> and the rehashing of 1938.B45,
     mostly built up around a forty-two-word annotation made by
     Melville in the last volume of his Shakespeare set. The two
     documents "are then squeezed dry of every possible, and impossi-
     ble, drop of significance they contain." We are not informed in

either case whether the annotations are printed entire. The
present evidence does not bear upon the speculation (stated as
fact) that Moby-Dick was written as two books, for we have
Melville's own word that he read Chase in 1841 and "discovered"
Shakespeare in 1849, both before the date now assigned for the
beginning of the first draft of Moby-Dick, February 1850.
Olson's expression of critical ideas in the remaining two-thirds
of the book is usually lacking in clarity and coherence, and at
times even in sanity.

36   BRASWELL, WILLIAM. "Book Reviews." American Literature, 19
       (January), 366-368.
         Review of 1947.B19. Vincent's "Introduction" is a good
concise account of Melville's activities as a productive poet
and his efforts toward having his poems published; the "Explanatory Notes" are a valuable aid to the understanding of the poems;
and the "Textual Notes" afford a view of Melville in the throes
of composition such as one could otherwise get only by going to
the manuscripts themselves. Questions a number of Vincent's
readings and regrets that the book was so carelessly printed--has
spotted forty-four errors beyond the seventy-three listed on the
errata sheet.

37   EBY, E.H. "Reviews of Books." Pacific Northwest Quarterly,
       39 (January), 70-71.
         Review of 1947.A1. Brooks has failed because his materials
are not put together in any really significant synthesis. Brooks
"is more interested in colorful aspects of personality or scene
than in causes which evoke them, more concerned with the external
facts of literary associations and friendships than with the significant similarities which often underlie them. The broader
aspects of history within which this literary history is a part
are mentioned only incidentally and sporadically." The treatment
of Melville is particularly disappointing. Brooks discounts
Melville's intellectual attainments, yet the author of Moby-Dick
was the most intense and searching thinker of all the writers
included in the volume.

38   TRILLING, LIONEL. "Family Album." Partisan Review, 15
       (January), 105-106, 108.
         Review of 1947.A1. Brooks is not writing literary criti-
cism, nor literary history as it is usually understood. He is
engaged in an act of unselective, undiscriminating family piety.
His enterprise is to be harshly judged because it sets out to
fill a genuine lack but fills it so badly, "for with a high
devotion and a really grandiose ideal of scholarship it supplies
America with a literary past of the blandest and most genteel
sort, calculated to give pleasure only to the Philistine and to
draw the mind and heart of no one, not even of the Philistine."

39   WILLIAMS, MENTOR L. "Horace Greeley Reviews Omoo." Philo-
       logical Quarterly, 27 (January), 94-96.
         Prints 1847.B70, with brief commentary.

40   THORP, WILLARD. "Reviews." <u>Modern Language Notes</u>, 63
     (February), 141-142.
          Review of 1947.A2. Makes the same points against Olson's
     "baffling" book as in 1947.B44.

41   WEGELIN, CHRISTOF. "Brief Mention." <u>Modern Language Notes</u>,
     63 (February), 143-144.
          Review of 1946.B11. Regrets that Short was not able to
     base his text of <u>Billy Budd</u> on F.B. Freeman's variorum edition
     (unpublished dissertation, Harvard, 1942), since Weaver's text of
     1928, which he evidently followed, is often inaccurate.

42   FOOTE, ELLIS. "Hail Whalemocked The Damned." <u>Neurotica</u> 1
     (Spring), 29-30.
          Poem with allusions to <u>Moby-Dick</u> (begins "call me
     ashmeal / some years ago spurning pistol and balls / i went to
     sea").

43   HYMAN, STANLEY EDGAR. "The Critic as Narcissus." <u>Accent</u>, 8
     (Spring), 187-191.
          Review of 1947.A2. Treats Olson with other critics who
     reduce writers to their own image. The first two thirds of his
     book "is bursting with new material he never gets a chance to
     discuss, including Melville documents here published for the
     first time and new historical and whaling material of enormous
     relevance," but Olson "goes wild" in the last third "and goes
     chasing after Moses the Myth, Christ the Anti-Myth, the Pacific
     as HEART SEA, Ulysses as Atlantic Man, and page after page of
     similar half-coherent mumbo-jumbo." Yet even in this "stew of
     eccentricities" Olson's use of the patterns of myth, tragedy,
     and ritual as clues to Melville stand out as extraordinarily
     fruitful.

44   SEALTS, MERTON M., JR. "Melville's Reading: A Check-List of
     Books Owned and Borrowed." <u>Harvard Library Bulletin</u>, 2
     (Spring), 141-163.
          Introduction to the checklist: The "study is intended to
     bring together all that has been learned to date concerning the
     disposition of Melville's library. It also assembles the further
     evidence of his reading afforded by his correspondence and jour-
     nals and by booksellers' statements, library ledgers, and similar
     contemporary documents, including the titles of 93 books which he
     is recorded as borrowing. Part II, which traces chronologically
     Melville's life-long interest in books and reading, is a survey
     of this evidence. Part III is an alphabetical check-list of all
     books except those of Melville's own authorship which are known
     to have survived or which are referred to in the documents men-
     tioned." Part I includes an account of the disposal of Melville's
     library after his death. Continued in 1948.B65; 1949.B43, B89,
     B120; 1950.B115; 1952.B50. Revised and enlarged in Sealts
     (1966).

45   ARVIN, NEWTON. "A Note on the Background of Billy Budd."
American Literature, 20 (March), 51–55.
     The Autobiography of Thurlow Weed (Boston, 1883) contains
an account of the inquiry on the Somers given by Guert Gansevoort
to his cousin Passed Midshipman Gansevoort. If, as seems extremely likely, Melville heard from Gansevoort a similar version
of the inquiry, it is not difficult to imagine that the narrative
would have lingered in his memory when he was writing chapter 18
of Billy Budd. The impression we get from Weed of Gansevoort's
demeanor after the tragedy confirms the portrait Melville
sketched of his cousin (under the name "Tom Tight") in "Bride-
groom Dick." In creating Captain Vere, Melville can hardly have
been unaffected by his memory of Gansevoort's painful dilemma on
the Somers, his division between professional obligation and
humane feeling, his inner struggles at the time, and his sufferings then and afterward. "God bless the flag!" the exclamation
of Elisha Small ("a great favorite with the crew" on the Somers)
at the moment he was run up to the yardarm strongly suggests
Billy's final words and tempts one to speculate on the possibility of Melville's having heard the story from his cousin or from
Weed himself.

46   STEWART, RANDALL. "A Populous World." Yale Review, 37
(March), 542–544.
     Review of 1947.A1. Brooks's "associationism," the constant
association of writers with other writers, and books with other
books, results in the blurring of distinctions. The approach
becomes least satisfactory perhaps in the passages where Brooks
tries to make allies of Melville and Whitman, emphasizing their
resemblances and passing over their differences, for where in all
literature could more radical opposites be found than these
two--the one rebellious, questioning, the other acquiescent,
believing? But the grand idea of a confraternity of American
writers imbued with democratic ideals is both inspiring and
useful.

47   GOODSPEED, GEORGE T. "The Home Library." Papers of the
Bibliographical Society of America, 42 (2d Quarter), 110–118.
     Background to Wiley and Putnam's Library of American Books,
which introduced to the American reader major books by Hawthorne,
Poe, and Melville.

48   BRADDY, HALDEEN. "Reviews." Journal of American Folklore, 61
(April-June), 222–223.
     Review of 1947.A1. Notes folklore elements in the works
of several of the authors Brooks discusses, including "hearsay
from adventurous skippers" in Moby-Dick.

49   FURNAS, J.C. "Fayaway's Children." Town and Country, 102
(April), 60ff.
     Reprints 1948.B11.

50   VIETOR, ALEXANDER O. "Five Inches of Books." Yale University
     Library Gazette, 22 (April), 124–128.
          Describes Melville's markings and annotations in four
     books: The London Carcanet (New York, 1831); La Bruyère's works
     2 Vols. (London, 1776); Sady's Gulistan, or Rose-garden, trans.
     Francis Gladwin (London, 1822); and William Hazlitts's The Round
     Table (Edinburgh, 1817). A quotation from Gay's Beggar's Opera
     written by Melville in The London Carcanet (which he won as a
     school prize in 1831) suggests that his early knowledge of this
     work could have been one of the influences on "Fragments from a
     Writing Desk." Melville's markings in La Bruyère and Sady re-
     flect his depressed state of mind in 1862 and 1868, when he
     bought the books.

51   LEARY, LEWIS. "Doctoral Dissertations in American Literature,
     1933–1948." American Literature, 20 (May), 189–190.
          Lists twenty-two completed Melville dissertations and seven
     in progress. [See 1933.B20.]

52   HOWARTH, R.G. "Melville and Australia." Notes and Queries,
     193 (1 May), 188.
          The world of Mardi apparently does not contain Australia,
     but the name of the god Roo (Mardi, chapter 105) may come from
     kangaroo, and Hooloomooloo (chapter 174) may be a recollection of
     Woolloomooloo, on the waterfront in Sydney.

53   ARVIN, NEWTON. "Counterfeit Presentments." Partisan Review,
     15 (June), 673–680.
          On the use of portraits in eighteenth- and nineteenth-
     century fiction, which is illuminated by Freud's essay on "The
     Uncanny," where "the word 'uncanny' does not apply to all
     frightening things whatever, but only to the kind of things that
     not only frighten us but carry us back to something long known
     to us, something once familiar but 'forgotten' with the lapse of
     time, buried below the drifting accumulations of later expe-
     ience, or actually repressed by an inner censor which cannot
     allow them to obtrude into consciousness directly." Notes the
     conspicuous role played by the "chair portrait" in Pierre, a
     "somewhat Radcliffean novel."

54   DUNCAN, HARRY. "Melville, Definitive." Poetry, 72 (June),
     167–170.
          Review of 1947.B19. As a poet, Melville "didn't much
     question poetic techniques current in his day. His ear, often
     sound, was never nervous or delicate; and his quarrel with
     Emerson or other New England worthies entered no issues of
     prosodic form--Bryant or Longfellow might have written some of
     these lines and stanzas. That Melville is the better poet
     testifies to his more candid, just mind and keener sense of
     responsibilities. If Walt Whitman and Emily Dickinson realized
     more than he, they did so in personal, even eccentric idioms.
     But Melville assumed rhyme as handed down, like a vestment for
     public ritual. These trappings never fitted him quite well or
     allowed him to move comfortably; he never selected from them one

useful piece to alter, as Frederick Goddard Tuckerman chose and
re-cut the sonnet." In Battle-Pieces few of the poems succeed
like "The Portent," which achieves a compact, intense ambiguity
adequate to the occasion. Melville could not discover in his
equivocal sympathies an informing order; shifting from one point
of view to another or merely leaving the point of view out cannot
achieve the formal integrity he wanted. Many of the poems,
through this technical failure, seem to get nowhere. John Marr
realizes more of the Civil War or of historical meaning than
Battle-Pieces. Melville had read Browning's dramatic monologues
to his profit. In Timoleon, "official" poetic style serves
Melville as well as possible; the subjects are for the most part
"high" and narrow, that is, suitable. The rest of the poems all
show that poetic shrinkage into methodism which Emily Dickinson
nowhere allows. Verse was not Melville's central concern, but he
wrote poems of probity and cultivated solicitude that allowed his
manly mind to perceive and judge, though never greatly to form,
some experiences essential to his time and place.

55 FIEDLER, LESLIE. "Come Back to the Raft Ag'in, Huck Honey!"
   Partisan Review, 15 (June), 664–671.
      Moby-Dick, along with the Leatherstocking Tales, Two Years
   Before the Mast, and Huckleberry Finn, embodies the American myth
   of a chaste mutual love between a white man and a colored man.
   Reprinted in 1955.B9 and in Scott, pp. 303–312.

56 MAUGHAM, W. SOMERSET. "Moby Dick." Atlantic, 181 (June),
   98–104.
      Reprint of 1948.B20.

57 OLIVER, EGBERT S. "'Cock-A-Doodle-Doo!' and Transcendental
   Hocus-Pocus." New England Quarterly, 21 (June), 204–216.
      "Cock-A-Doodle-Doo!" is a companion piece to "Bartleby,"
   a reductio ad absurdum of the transcendental disregard of
   materialism. [See 1945.B27.] "In 'Bartleby' the principle of
   self-reliance, the complete individualism of turning inwardly
   upon oneself and withdrawing from the obligations and associations of the outward world, is considered and exposed as leading
   only to the negation of death. 'Cock-A-Doodle-Doo!' explores
   the outward-turning transcendent reaches of that doctrine which
   would put itself in tune with the infinite, even to the fateful
   disregard of the individual's physical need. This kind of withdrawing into the evanescent, too, ends in the negation of the
   grave. The two stories thus complement each other as they reduce
   to the ultimate extreme of ridiculousness the anthithetical
   extremes of transcendentalism." Specifically, the story
   burlesques the passage in "Monday" in A Week on the Concord and
   Merrimack Rivers in which Thoreau discusses the Laws of Menu.
   Reprinted in Oliver (1965), pp. 54–64.

58   BIRSS, JOHN H., ed. "'A Mere Sale to Effect' with Letters of
      Herman Melville." New Colophon, 1 (July), 239-255.
           Prints correspondence by Melville, John R. Brodhead, and
      John Murray, concerning the English publication of Omoo, includ-
      ing Melville's letters of 30 December 1846 and 31 March 1847 to
      Brodhead [Letters, pp. 48-50, 56-58]; Melville's letter of
      August 1849 to the secretary of the American Legation, London
      [Letters, pp. 89-90]; and Melville's letters of 5 June 1849,
      20 July 1849, 27 June 1850, 20 July 1851, and 16 April 1852 to
      Richard Bentley [Letters, pp. 85-87, 87-89, 109-110, 133-135,
      149-151].

59   DIX, WILLIAM S. "Herman Melville and the Problem of Evil."
      Rice Institute Pamphlet, 35 (July), 81-107.
           A "brief and superficial survey" of Melville's developing
      concern in his works with the problem of evil.

60   LEARY, LEWIS. "Book Reviews." South Atlantic Quarterly, 47
      (July), 418-419.
           Review of 1947.A1. Perhaps a major feature of the book "is
      that Melville and Whitman and Twain settle so easily into the
      background of George W. Curtis, Ik Marvel, Constance Fenimore
      Woolson, and others usually considered of estimable but dis-
      tinctly minor achievement that it may sometimes be difficult for
      the reader to distinguish between them. Perhaps this is Mr.
      Brooks's intention, for so it must have seemed to American
      readers during the latter half of the nineteenth century." His
      book is a reassembling of the cultural background, much as it
      must have seemed to people of that day, against which a few
      major literary figures rose to maturity.

61   WEAKS, MABEL. "Long Ago and 'Faraway': Traces of Melville in
      the Marquesas in the Journal of A.G. Jones, 1854-1855."
      Bulletin of the New York Public Library, 52 (July), 362-369.
           Prints extracts from Jones's journal, with introductory
      note. Jones visited the Typee valley in 1855. His interpreter,
      Moreta, who had lived on the island for twenty-five years, re-
      membered Melville and "had seen the personages alluded to in his
      book, but there was no one of the name of 'Faraway'. Indeed
      their language does not admit of such a name." Jones learned
      that Mehevi had been killed by Te Moana (Mowanna in Typee), and
      that Kory Kory, Tinor, and the one-eyed chief, Mow-Mow, had once
      existed, but were now dead and their houses abandoned or
      destroyed. Jones was convinced that the Typees "were cannibals
      until a very late period" and concluded that Melville "had a
      truthful basis for his book but that his imagination was very
      largely drawn upon for the attractive features of the same."

62   HILLWAY, TYRUS. "The Unknowns in Whale-Lore." American Notes
      & Queries, 8 (August), 68-69.
           Explanation of "why whales occasionally beach themselves."

63   JONES, JOSEPH. "Melville: A 'Humorist' in 1890." <u>American Notes & Queries</u>, 8 (August), 68.
     Draws attention to 1890.B4. Lukens dredged up so many forgotten names that no great significance attaches to his mention of Melville, unless it is to remind literary historians that Melville was, among other things, a humorist.

64   CHASE, RICHARD. "The Times of Brooks and Gorer." <u>Sewanee Review</u>, 56 (Autumn), 703–706.
     Review of 1947.A1 and <u>The American People</u> by Geoffrey Gorer. In "ordealism" there is a tendency to destroy the objective values we need in order to judge art and artists. "The ordealist critic cannot help reducing Melville to the stature of Jack London, and Mark Twain to the stature of Artemus Ward. Criticism becomes not the study of books but the study of suffering and failure, of which the artist is often wrongly alleged to be as conscious as his critic." Brooks "is still a captive of the ordealist myth. The values are inverted: whereas he used to assert alienation, suffering, and failure, he now asserts connection, happiness, and success. His misjudgment of art and his underestimation of the great remain constant."

65   SEALTS, MERTON M., JR. "Melville's Reading: A Check-List of Books Owned and Borrowed." <u>Harvard Library Bulletin</u>, 2 (Autumn), 378–392.
     Continuation of 1948.B44. Continued in 1949.B120.

66   SHORT, R.W. "Melville as Symbolist." <u>University of Kansas City Review</u>, 14 (Autumn), 38–46.
     Melville's method "allows his symbols to accumulate meanings in the course of their use, as they knock about in his myth-world, and so a single meaning attached to them often has at least a partial validity. Allegorical interpretation of a medieval or puritanic sort, however, defeats the larger aspect of the work, for Melville's view of reality is a more oriental view, based upon a sense of the ultimate interdependence, rather than the isolation, of experiential units. By devices which serve his ends, even though they involve a considerable dehumanization of his characters, he makes his symbols blur through one another and take shape at that vanishing point where the one and the many become indivisible."

67   ANON. "Forgotten Man." New York <u>Times Book Review</u> (26 September), p. 8.
     Announces forthcoming publication of 1948.B9, B21, B24; 1949.A3; and notes the publication of 1947.B16; 1948.B10. The Melville boom, under way since the appearance of the Weaver and Mumford biographies [1921.A1 and 1929.A1] is gaining rather than losing force and makes quainter reading than ever of 1891.B19.

68 CONNOR, C.H. "Moby Dick." <u>CEA Critic</u>, 10 (October), 3.
      The whale is a symbol of the true nature of man, "our
deepest blood nature"; Ahab is the incarnation of the "maniacal
fanaticism" of man's mental consciousness [cf. 1923.B3]. When
Ahab set his course for the white whale, he had conquered the
Moby Dick of his "deepest blood-being."

69 WEAKS, MABEL CLARE. "A Miniature of Herman Melville's
      Mother." <u>Antiques</u>, 54 (October), 259.
      Describes and reproduces a miniature of Maria Gansevoort,
painted by Anson Dickinson in 1813. The miniature was presented
in April 1946 to the New York Public Library Gansevoort-Lansing
Collection by "a granddaughter of Mrs. Melville."

70 CHASE, RICHARD. "Dissent on <u>Billy Budd</u>." <u>Partisan Review</u>, 15
      (November), 1212–1218.
      There has been a great temptation to see in <u>Billy Budd</u>
Melville's final "testament of acceptance." But Melville made
his definitive moral statement in <u>Moby-Dick</u>, <u>The Confidence-Man</u>,
and <u>Clarel</u>. The moral situation in <u>Billy Budd</u> is deeply equivocal. Vere's "examination and defense of law in a man-of-war
world and his decision that a human life must be sacrificed to
this law is impeccable, irrefutable, and fully conscious of the
pathetic irony of the situation. The flaw in the book is that
Melville does not fully conceive of that which, in a genuine
tragedy, has to be opposed to law." The weakness is in the
central character himself. "He <u>ought</u> to be 'deep' and in some
inescapable human way a 'man-trap.' Otherwise he cannot function
meaningfully in a tragedy which tries to demonstrate the opposition between human nature and the heart on the one hand and law
on the other. Otherwise he cannot possibly be the Handsome
Sailor. . . . Billy Budd is the final, and almost the first--
first <u>crucial</u>--self-indulgence of a great intelligence." By
portraying him, "not as Isaac or the fallen Adam or Oedipus, but
as the innocent hermaphrodite Christ who ascends serenely to the
yardarm of the frigate, Melville made it impossible for us to
see the tragedy we ought to see in the betrayal of the young hero
to the man of power and law by the man of 'retributive righteous-
ness.' [Claggart "is another version of Melville's self-
righteous Liberal, the Confidence Man. He is the Confidence Man
plus an actively evil nature."] Billy Budd is pre-eminently the
beatified boy of the liberal-progressive myth, the figure who
gets 'pushed around,' the figure 'to whom things happen.' His
suffering and death are without moral content." Melville "is
possibly our greatest critic of the liberal-progressive ethos.
But this we must see <u>in spite of Billy Budd</u>."

71 HEFLIN, WILSON L. "The Source of Ahab's Lordship Over the
      Level Loadstone." <u>American Literature</u>, 20 (November), 323–327.
      Melville was indebted to William Scoresby, Jr.'s <u>Journal of
a Voyage to the Northern Whale-Fishery</u> (Edinburgh and London,
1823) for the idea of having the lightning of the typhoon reverse
the polarity of the <u>Pequod</u>'s compass and for the dramatic solution of Ahab's navigational difficulties.

72   L., R.M. "Melville's ART." Explicator, 7 (November),
      item Q6.
        Requests explication of "Art." Do the early versions con-
tribute insight into its own art?

73   POMMER, HENRY F. "Herman Melville and the Wake of The Essex."
      American Literature, 20 (November), 290–304.
        "The story of the Essex was highly important to the author
of Moby-Dick; Owen Chase's printed version of that story was not
of any great importance to the story Melville used. Nevertheless, Melville's copy of the Narrative did contribute some things
to Moby-Dick--material for parts of two chapters of cetology
["The Affadavit" and "The Battering-Ram"], and six quotations. . . . There was time between April [when Melville
acquired his copy] and October of 1851 to bolster the probability
of an ending already determined." Most of Melville's subsequent
use of the Essex and her survivors, in his "Agatha" letters to
Hawthorne [Letters, pp. 153–163] and in Clarel, I, xxxvii, stems
from his meeting Pollard in 1852. Melville changes details of
the Essex disaster and Pollard's life for various purposes.

74   ARVIN, NEWTON. "Melville in Europe." Nation, 167 (6 Novem-
      ber), 524–525.
        Review of 1948.B21. Melville's journal has by no means the
kind of rich literary interest that Hawthorne's and James's notebooks have, but it abounds in biographical interest, nevertheless. Melville's first remarks on Mrs. Lawrence do not seem
characteristic of his ordinary tenor but "tell us what a tiger
pit of irritable emotionality lay concealed, for the most part,
in his nature." One's impressions of Melville at this time are
not of nervous irritability but of a still youthful and outgoing
lightheartedness, springiness, and eagerness for new experience.
Metcalf has provided full and valuable notes and a text that we
may be sure is accurate. (Weaver's reading of Melville's manuscript [1921.A1] was impressionistic and cavalier.)

75   THORP, WILLARD. "Melville's Notebooks." New York Herald
      Tribune Weekly Book Review (28 November), p. 26.
        Review of 1948.B21. Though Melville's frankly stated
impressions of London publishers form a kind of theme in the
journal and will greatly interest future Melville biographers,
the journal is fascinating for many other reasons. It is a
record of sharp impressions of men and cities and "a veritable
seedpod of ideas, scenes and characters which would germinate in
his later works." Metcalf's minute knowledge of Melville's
career and his family life illuminates many obscure passages; her
excellent notes provide new information about Melville drawn from
manuscript collections not before explored by scholars. The text
is a model of accurate editing; and Metcalf has dealt sensibly
with such problems as Melville's loose punctuation and misspellings of place names.

76   COOK, REGINALD L.   "Big Medicine in 'Moby Dick.'"   Accent, 8
      (Winter), 102-109.
         Seeing no particular efficacy in Christian conciliation of
      a force that permits evil to prevail, Ahab rejects the Christian
      way and turns by reversion to the forms of magic--"big medicine"--
      to achieve his "supernatural revenge," by infusing his will upon
      his men and the elemental forces of the universe. Ahab's magic
      (displayed in incidents such as his ceremonial rituals with the
      harpooneers and his magnetizing the compass needle) does not fol-
      low the usual pattern of the primitive magician--he did not seek
      for supernatural power in a dream or vision, to be effected by
      fasting, stimulants or flagellant torture; but he dies with the
      overweening pride and arrogance typical of primitive medicine men.
      He is physically destroyed but spiritually triumphant. In his
      physical defeat, he betrays not the lack of skill but the limita-
      tion of all men before superior animate forces; his fallibility is
      a token of the inadequacy of magic. Reprinted in 1960.A6 and
      Vickery (1966), pp. 193-199.

77   LEISY, ERNEST E.   "Mid-Century America."   Southwest Review, 33
      (Winter), 87-89.
         Review of 1947.A1. A remarkably well-integrated, brilliant
      account of the era.

78   VIRTANEN, REINO.   "Emile Montégut as a Critic of American
      Literature."   PMLA, (December), 1273.
         Montégut "noted only Israel Potter [in 1855.B32], and
      allowed himself to be superseded by E.D. Forgues, whose article
      on Moby Dick [1853.B9] is perhaps more sensitive and penetrating
      than that of any non-American of the time." There is no indica-
      tion that any of Melville's greater works made a strong impres-
      sion on Montégut.

79   BREIT, HARVEY.   "Repeat Performances, Reappraised."   New York
      Times Book Review (5 December), p. 61.
         Notice of 1948.B24. Notes the "temperate and qualified"
      enthusiasm of contemporary reviewers for The Piazza Tales, a
      "melancholy response" to such stories as "Benito Cereno," "The
      Encantadas," and the "fantastic and contemporary" "Bartleby."

80   WADE, MASON.   "Books."   Commonweal, 49 (10 December), 234.
         Notice of 1948.B21. A very human document that affords
      some interesting insights on Melville and his books. The journal
      is notable for its scanty attention to the familiar incidents of
      voyage, its rich picture of London literary life, and a few sug-
      gestive notes of ideas and books that anticipate Moby-Dick and
      Pierre.

81   BIRSS, JOHN H.   "The Four Stages of the Tragic Tale of Billy
      Budd."   New York Times Book Review (26 December), p. 4.
         Review of 1948.B9. Freeman has met the challenge of the
      difficult and haphazard manuscript of Billy Budd and surmounted
      it. Critically and textually the volume is a sound contribution

to exact knowledge about Melville. In Billy Budd Melville is
concerned not with the question of why evil exists but of how man
should accept its intricate devastating effect.

82   HICKS, GRANVILLE. "Melville's Log of a Visit to Europe." New
     York Times Book Review (26 December), p. 4.
          Review of 1948.B21. The journal is as nonliterary as any-
thing written by a great novelist could well be and shows us the
thirty-year-old Melville as his contemporaries may have seen him;
his fellow-passengers must have thought him unspoiled, sociable,
quite normal. Melville recorded events in a style appropriate
to a ship's log; the records are for the most part bare and even
commonplace; the accounts of the people he met are as a rule
equally meager, though there is an astonishingly violent description of Mrs. Abbott Lawrence and an amusingly vicious picture of
J.G. Lockhart. Far from being dull, the journal is rather charm-
ing in a brisk, casual way, and is certainly revealing, reminding
us that there was a sociable, hopeful, practical, "normal"
Melville who had wagered everything on his ability to support a
family by his writing.

1949 A BOOKS

1   CHASE, RICHARD. Herman Melville: A Critical Study. New
     York: The Macmillan Co., 305 pp.
          Rejecting the view that Melville was primarily engaged in
a philosophic quest for ultimate truth [see 1938.B22, 1944.A1],
Chase claims that Melville was not so much interested in philosophical truths as in man and his culture. Chase's method is
"partly biographical," but his main concern is with Melville's
"recurring and developing images, symbols, ideas, and moral attitudes." According to Chase, Melville created in his works a
historical-cultural myth with two recurring themes: the Fall and
the Search for what was lost in the Fall; and with three central
characters: Ishmael and a true and a false Prometheus. Ishmael
is cast out, disinherited, bereaved, searching--and symbolic of
Young America, the revolutionary nation in quest of its destiny.
Seeking some human embodiment of the lost patrimony of nobility,
splendor, and virtue, Ishmael meets an array of Promethean figures. The false Prometheus "betrays his humanity through some
monstrous pride, some titanic quest for moral purity, some
obsessed abdication from the natural ambiguities of life in quest
of the absolute and the inviolable, or some moral treachery which
involves his companions as well as himself in a final catastrophe." The true Prometheus is the hero Melville came to call "the
Handsome Sailor." He is Prometheus in a state of becoming
Oedipus. Melville's ideal human hero must not only be the young
Promethean revolutionary, he must also be Oedipus, the man who
has accepted the full moral responsibility of his fallible
humanity and so makes himself the symbol of a culture formed in
wisdom and love. Exemplars of the true hero are Marnoo, Jack
Chase, Bulkington, and Ethan Allen.

Ishmael's search is conducted within the recurring symbolic polarities of Light, Space, Mountain, Tower, Fire, Phallus, Life, and Dark, Time, Valley, Cave, Stone, Castration, Death--polarities he must reconcile, through the "spiritual transit of withdrawal and return," if he is to become the true Promethean hero. "In Melville's books the young man who cannot reconcile these antinomies is doomed to spiritual, moral, and aesthetic failure. The young man who can reconcile them is the true Promethean hero." The symbolic polarities represent the extremes of attitude and behavior out of the tensions of which the true hero learns to evolve consciousness and morality. The true hero commits himself to the rhythms of life and achieves a creative mobility among extremes. The false hero cannot achieve this mobility but commits himself to the extremes themselves, trying to derive consciousness and morality from absolute values. The Prometheus complex Melville delineates and the Oedipus complex have much in common, and Melville makes use of many specifically Oedipal themes: the fear of castration (symbolized by cannibalism, decapitation, the injured leg, the horror of women), homoeroticism, narcissism, incest, and parricide. Most of Melville's protagonists are Prometheus-like men shown in the act of failing to become the American Oedipus--the fully moral, fully wise, and fully tragic American. It is the failure of the progressive American liberal. In addition to analyzing the works in these terms, Chase extensively examines Melville's use of American folk culture. Indexed. Reviewed in 1949.B111, B114, B127-128, B130; 1950.B36-38, B42, B44, B50, B71, B87, B94, B105, B110, B114; 1951.B30; 1954.B7.

2   STONE, GEOFFREY. <u>Melville</u>. Great Writers of the World. New York: Sheed & Ward, 336 pp. Reprint. New York: Octagon Books, 1976.
    A biographical and interpretive study, "addressed to the general reader." Roman Catholic in bias, it attributes Melville's personal difficulties and artistic failures to his Calvinist-romantic "attitude of mind," which led him to find and to revolt against a "contradiction at the heart of things," before which the intellect was ultimately helpless. In Stone's view, Melville never "departed very far from the Calvinist attitude, whose incipient Manichaeanism . . . colored what doctrines he . . . held as well as his revolt against other doctrines. A large measure of his anguish [was] caused by his demand that all those things which he discretely observed and experienced in the universe be correlated in some rationally coherent scheme; but the basic irrationality with which he gave primacy to his own will made that scheme impossible. The deepest experience, his books insisted, showed some inscrutable malice sinewing the universe. How else could be explained the will's defeat in its constant aspiration--inherent in its nature--to realize the ideal?" Indexed. Reviewed in 1949.B114, B128-130; 1950.B42, B96, B109, B114.

3   VINCENT, HOWARD P. The Trying-Out of MOBY-DICK. Boston:
     Houghton Mifflin Co., 400 pp. Reprint. Carbondale and
     Edwardsville: Southern Illinois University Press, 1965;
     Kent: Kent State University Press, 1980.
        A "study of the whaling sources of Moby-Dick with an
     account of its composition, and suggestions concerning interpre-
     tation and meaning." Vincent contends that Moby-Dick, begun in
     February 1850, "was first intended to be a whaling story pure and
     simple, much as White-Jacket had been a naval yarn with plot
     secondary to the description of shipboard life." The "whaling
     voyage" was almost ready for publication by late summer of 1850,
     but Moby-Dick was not published till October 1851. Only the
     hypothesis of an important revision can adequately account for
     the year's delay. The "revolution within Melville's mind which
     led him to his genius" may be seen "first as the result of forces
     long gathering within Melville as he brooded on life and read
     Shakespeare; second, as the sudden and magnificent release of
     those Shakespearean forces when Melville met Nathaniel Hawthorne"
     [in early August 1850]. Melville's spiritual response to
     Hawthorne's Mosses from an Old Manse and his review for the
     Literary World "were unquestionably responsible for the birth of
     the great Melville in the revised and great Moby-Dick," compel-
     ling him to rewrite almost in entirety his "whaling voyage." The
     original plot of this "whaling voyage" was quite possibly "The
     Town Ho's Story" [chapter 54 of Moby-Dick]. The white whale
     probably did not enter Melville's manuscript till March or April
     1851, because he did not possess a copy of Owen Chase's Narrative
     of the Essex till April 1851 and "would not work on such an
     important subject without consulting the main source," which he
     first read on the Acushnet.
        In his detailed discussion of Melville's use of his "fish
     documents" (works such as Thomas Beale's Natural History of the
     Sperm Whale, Frederick Debell Bennett's A Whaling Voyage Round
     the Globe, J. Ross Browne's Etchings of a Whaling Cruise, Henry
     T. Cheever's The Whale and His Captors, Francis Allyn Olmstead's
     Incidents of a Whaling Voyage, and William Scoresby, Jr.'s An
     Account of the Arctic Regions and Journal of a Voyage to the
     Northern Whale Fishery), Vincent cites parallel passages, illus-
     trating Melville's transformation of routine exposition into
     dramatic incidents, metaphysical commentary, and symbolism.
        Vincent sees Ishmael as the chorus character in Moby-Dick,
     as Melville's surrogate, and as Everyman; moreover, Melville "has
     atomized the various selves of Everyman-Ishmael, projecting each
     of them in a separate character within the novel": Ahab,
     Starbuck, Queequeg, Fedallah, Flask, and Pip "are phases of
     Ishmael's total self"--all "add up together with the other char-
     acters to total Ishmael." Moby-Dick "is a study of both single
     and multiple personality; it is concerned with the psychological
     phase of the problem of the One and the Many." Composed during
     a period of rampant individualism, it is also a study of alone-
     ness and isolation, a criticism of the individualistic American
     pattern of life. While Father Mapple establishes the Christian
     paradox that the fullest selfhood may be won only by annihilation
     of self, Ahab carries out his search in self-assertion, not in

self-submission, and illustrates the fatality of rampant self-reliance. Indexed. Reviewed in 1949.B30, B74–76, B80–85, B88, B92, B98, B101, B115; 1950.B87, B108, B114, B118; 1951.B74.

4   WRIGHT, NATHALIA. Melville's Use of the Bible. Durham, N.C.: Duke University Press, 203 pp. Reprint. New York: Octagon Books, 1969.
       A more developed version of the study in 1940.B31, discovering in Melville's prose and verse more than fourteen hundred allusions to the Bible. Chapters explore the influence of the Bible on Melville's imagery; characters and types; themes and plots; and style. Indexed. Reviewed in 1949.B86, B116; 1950.B50, B87, B106, B113. Reprint publication has a new appendix.

1949 B SHORTER WRITINGS

1   BEALS, FRANK L. "Introduction," in The Story of Moby Dick, adapted and retold by Frank L. Beals. Famous Story Series. Chicago: Benj. H. Sanborn & Co., p. v.
       "Where it was thought necessary to interpret the thought in language different from the original, I have employed my own method of expression freely," retelling the story in the third person, in about 38,000 words, divided into 32 chapters. For "the young, or less expert, reader."

2   BROOKS, CLEANTH and ROBERT PENN WARREN. Modern Rhetoric. New York: Harcourt, Brace and Co., pp. 48–51.
       Analysis of excerpt from "Sketch First" in "The Encantadas." The "whole passage is based on two things, the image of the cinder heap and the idea of sin and punishment, which combine to give the notion of a world after the Judgment, the final desolation."

3   CADY, EDWIN HARRISON. The Gentleman in America: A Literary Study in American Culture. Syracuse, N.Y.: Syracuse University Press, p. 56.
       Notes that Melville, "who had an eye for a gentleman," made Pierre "a Christian gentleman to show how terribly the abysses of moral ambiguity opened beneath even the man conventionally recognized as humanly perfect."

4   CONNER, FREDERICK WILLIAM. Cosmic Optimism: A Study of the Interpretation of Evolution by American Poets from Emerson to Robinson. Gainesville: University of Florida Press, pp. 139–140, 146–147.
       Lyell's Geological Evidences of the Antiquity of Man and Pope Pius IX's Syllabus of Errors appeared respectively in 1863 and 1864; in "The New Ancient of Days" Melville "appears to have taken a kind of unholy glee in their incongruity. . . . However, though the obvious object of Melville's satire was the discord between science and priestcraft, his poem cannot be regarded as an attack on faith in the name of evolution, for it ends, as the Epilogue of Clarel was to begin, with an apprehensive question

concerning the consequences of the philosophy suggested by the
new-found skulls" (in the caves of Engis in Belgium, discussed
by Lyell). Clarel is an important document in the soul-searching
of the age of Arnold and Clough, yet surprisingly "contains
almost no direct comment on the theory of evolution. Darwin's
name is mentioned only three times, twice insignificantly, and
the few references to the general idea of evolution are for the
most part merely tangential and so closely identified with individual characters that it is difficult to tell when they express
Melville's own views. And yet, not only does the whole poem
revolve around questions brought to a head by The Origin of
Species, but in the Epilogue Darwin's name is used to symbolize
these questions."

5   COOK, ALBERT. The Dark Voyage and the Golden Mean: A
     Philosophy of Comedy. Cambridge, Mass.: Harvard University
     Press, passim.
         Passing references to Moby-Dick, Pierre, and Billy Budd.

6   GEISMAR, MAXWELL. "Introduction," in Moby Dick (abridged).
     Ed. Maxwell Geismar. The Pocket Library. New York: Pocket
     Books, pp. v-x.
         The central legend of Moby-Dick is "that of Lucifer, the
dark angel, who conspires against God for possession of the
universe. But Ahab is not content with taking into his own hands
the question of good and evil. Through his plan to track down
and destroy the white whale, he wants, as it were, to destroy the
principle of life itself, which is beyond good and evil." The
central symbols of the novel are consistently those of birth and
death, of the primeval origins of the individual and of the
race. As we read, "we have the sense of unfolding layer upon
layer of human consciousness." The voyage of the Pequod "is a
voyage into the night thoughts of the race; the violent and
shameless past which still haunts us, and that black mood of
cosmic insubordination and defiance to which all of us are subjected. . . . Ahab's sin--the destruction not merely of the
primitive father, but of the seminal source of the life impulse--
is the one deviation that cannot be tolerated; it is the original
sin."

7   GROSSMAN, JAMES. James Fenimore Cooper. The American Men of
     Letters Series. New York: William Sloane Associates,
     pp. 192-193, 235.
         Melville and Cooper both used, in Billy Budd and Ned Myers,
one of the most striking incidents in the Somers affair, the
seaman Small's reported words, "God bless that flag and prosper
it!" In his pamphlet on the Somers affair, Cooper "from his
study of the facts arrives at a fine statement . . . that as a
matter of sheer worldly wisdom and practicality the processes of
law must be just if they are to work at all. Melville's fiction
seems to move in the very opposite direction from Cooper's
rational optimism; to maintain law in this world, a man whom all
feel to be innocent must be punished summarily for a formal

transgression of the law, and the condemned man himself agrees. Melville, at the very moment that he has won our sympathy for the reluctant yet insistent Captain Vere, cites the Somers affair and, without justifying it, suggests that her officers felt the same urgency for their deed." In his brief review of The Sea Lions, Melville erred on the side of generosity.

8   HOHN, MAX T. and GRACE A. BENSCOTER. "Life of Herman Melville," in Moby Dick, adapted by Max T. Hohn and Grace A. Benscoter. Chicago: Laidlow Brothers, pp. 263-270.
       Biographical sketch. Introductory note, "To the Teacher" (pp. viii-ix) explains that "without adaptation, the average high-school reader cannot get through Moby Dick at all," and so "we have felt obliged to omit much of the technical lore, and most of the symbolism, but very little of the story. It has been necessary also to modify the vocabulary," though "so far as possible, in what remains of the original text, we have left the poetry intact. For without the rhythms and imagery (and at least a touch of the symbolism), the product would not be Melville at all."

9   LEYDA, JAY. "An Introduction" and "Notes on Sources, &c," in The Complete Stories of Herman Melville. Ed. Jay Leyda. New York: Random House, pp. ix-xxxiv, 455-472.
       The introduction supplies details of the stories' composition, publication, and reception and comments on aspects of Melville's imagination and craftsmanship. Leyda sees Melville's "Agatha" letters to Hawthorne [see 1946.B34 and Letters, pp. 153-163] as "our most substantial proof of the methods and intentions" beneath all the stories in the volume and stresses the stories' personal "undercurrents" and significances, veiled by Melville's "policy of concealment." Much of the stories' "materiality seems a minutely painted and deceptive screen erected across what is really taking place behind it--in Melville's mind. We are compelled to regard these stories as an artist's resolution of that constant contradiction--between the desperate need to communicate and the fear of revealing too much. In these stories the contradiction is expressed on various levels of tension--the fiercer the pull, the higher the accomplishment. There is also a level, closer to the surface, of game, for in 'The Tartarus of Maids' Melville gives one the impression of seeing how close he can dance to the edge of nineteenth century sanctities without being caught." Both "An Introduction" and "Notes" point to sources for the stories in Melville's own experience and to literary sources. Reviewed in 1949.B57-58, B61, B69, B78, B83, B90, B99, B103, B123; 1951.B42, B46. Reprinted in part in Norton The Confidence-Man, pp. 284-285. [See also 1951.B11.]

10 MAUGHAM, W. SOMERSET. "Introduction," in Moby-Dick. Philadelphia: The John C. Winston Co., pp. xi-xxviii.
       Reprint of 1948.B20. Reviewed in 1949.B97.

11   METCALF, ELEANOR MELVILLE. "Preface," "Introduction," and "Notes," in Herman Melville: Journal of a Visit to London and the Continent, 1849-1850. London: Cohen & West Ltd.
     English edition of 1948.B21.

12   MORLEY, CHRISTOPHER. The Man Who Made Friends With Himself. Garden City, N.Y.: Doubleday & Co., pp. 9, 28, 61.
     Allusions to Moby-Dick, referred to by the narrator as the most dangerous book in American literature.

13   MURDOCK, KENNETH B. Literature & Theology in Colonial New England. Cambridge, Mass.: Harvard University Press, pp. 196-198.
     In all his best work from Mardi to Billy Budd, Melville drew something from Puritan thought, as in his use of concrete symbols to express ideal reality. Melville, Hawthorne, Emerson, and Thoreau all echoed something closely akin to the Puritan's personal belief that the foundation of holiness was the personal search for truth.

14   MURRAY, HENRY A. "Preface," "Introduction," "Explanatory Notes," and "Textual Notes," in Pierre. New York: Hendricks House, Farrar Strauss, pp. v-viii, xiii-ciii, 429-504, 505-514.
     Pierre "is a literary monster, a prodigious by-blow of genius whose appearance is marred by a variety of freakish features and whose organic worth is invalidated by the sickness of despair." But despite its dislocations of emotional logic, eccentricities of language, and atmosphere of unreality, it contains rare virtues. Melville wrote Pierre while still exhausted by his labors on Moby-Dick. His spiritual state included moral conflict that had resulted in an inflexible dualism wherein every significant object had become ambivalent to him (the source of the "ambiguities"--almost synonymous with ambivalences--in Pierre) and "an underlying will to wreck his self." Melville was fighting for spiritual survival and his reason was losing ground.
     Melville's impelling intention in writing Pierre was to write his spiritual autobiography in the form of a novel, the biography of his self-image. Thus Pierre "is Oedipus-Romeo-Hamlet-Memnon-Christ-Ishmael-Orestes-Timon-Satan-Cain-Manfred, or, more shortly, an American Fallen and Crucified Angel." The models of the principal characters were all persons to whom Melville was affectionately attached during some period of his life, including Hawthorne, the model for Plinlimmon. Melville should be commemorated as the literary discoverer of the Darkest Africa of the mind; as depth psychologist he belongs with Dostoeveski and Nietzsche and Freud, a claim not easily supported without Pierre. Though narcissism bulked large in his personality, it would be a mistake to regard his autobiographical writings mainly as egotistical exhibitions of purely personal experiences. By "opening his mind to the spontaneities of the impersonal unconscious and identifying with a procession of archetypal figures, he succeeded in memorably portraying dispositions that are universal."

   In calling <u>Pierre</u> his "book of sacred truth" Melville meant
by truth (1) autobiographical truths, driven as he was at this
time "by a veritable compulsion to cast forth his inmost self";
(2) psychological generalizations, most of which pertain to man's
sinister and tragic shadow self; (3) moral sentiments or statements of value that he strongly endorses; (4) divinely right
conduct, obedience to a moral imperative, a creed in action--this
last in <u>Pierre</u> truth in its supremest sense, synonymous with
virtue. These different truths "are <u>all</u> culturally unacceptable.
They either are shocking or depressing facts about man's hidden
self, or scathing condemnations of civilization, or offensive
references to Deity; or they are positive truths, in agreement
with the Sermon on the Mount, which are 'ridiculous to men.'"
Partly to avoid "a barrage of gun shots" from "public sharp-
shooters," Melville concealed his truths in symbols, allegories,
and myths in such a way that only a worthy reader can get at
them.
   Murray interprets Pierre's "spiritual dilemmas and trans-
formations" and his relationships with Mrs. Glendinning, Lucy,
and Pierre in psychological and mythical terms. In act 1
Melville set forth the "myth of Paradise" at Saddle Meadows,
representing, in Pierre's relationship with Mrs. Glendinning, the
Oedipus complex "as it would flower in the wishful fantasy of a
victimized adolescent." One of Melville's archetypal themes "was
that of Paradise Lost and he evidently wished to have his hero's
fall complete in all particulars, not only spiritual but mate-
rial--from wealth to penury, from leisure to toil, from the
romance of chivalry to the mechanics of profit, from the bene-
dictions of the country to the city without grace." The description of the effect of Isabel's face on Pierre is the best in
literature of the autonomous inward operation of the aroused
soul-image, or anima. Isabel is both Pierre's dark, or tragic,
anima, and personification of his unconscious. From her he
acquires the tragic sense of life, a value and an outlook the
Glendinnings have never included in their system.
   In act 2, which begins with Pierre's reception of Isabel's
letter, Melville describes with consummate talent and verisimili-
tude another great archetypal situation, the discovery of un-
suspected evil in the revered object. Pierre's passion for
Isabel is a fusion of Eros and Agape. His plan of a pretended
marriage with Isabel was not chiefly motivated by desire to save
her: "It was motivated by a consuming romantic passion of the
fateful anima type, the blind Dionysian compulsion of the mystery
religions. Pierre conceived of his love in the most glorified
terms, first because no other terms could do justice to the
redeeming nature of the experience and second because he had to
defend his resolution before the high court of conscience. Since
there was no authority to which he could refer and since he was
not in a position to create his own justifying myth--partly
because his head had abdicated in favor of his heart--, he had to
assimilate his course of action as best he could to Platonic and
Christian ideals. This accounts for the impression one gets of
Melville's quoting scripture in support of Pierre's demonic
purpose."

The scenes in the city comprise act 3. After the one "tumultuous uprising and definitive suppression of instinct" on the third night in the city, Pierre's love for Isabel begins to fade. None of his pledges to Isabel are carried out; in a few days he becomes wholly involved in the writing of a book. Having "devoured what Isabel had to give him," he withdraws "libido (interest, love) from her as a person" and uses it to nurture "embryoes of thought and to feed a precipitant ambition." Creativeness "in sacramental action gives way at once to creativeness in writing; the religionist is routed by the artist; the potential mythology of relationship is blighted by the traditional mythology of ambition."

Throughout the last phase of Pierre's career, Melville's imagination "is enthralled by a cluster of embattled figures" of the same substance with Ahab--"Titan, Prometheus, Satan, Lear, Timon, Cain, and Manfred, with images from Isaiah and the un-Christian author of Ecclesiastes hovering in the background," and at the center of this circle of heroic sufferers and malcontents "Byron in person, prototype of the Romantic genius, as celebrated by his biographer Thomas Moore." The pervading temper of Pierre is that of German romanticism. "Throughout the drama, but more especially in the last act, the spirit of Byron--nobility of sentiment, sublime stretching, pride, defiance, revenge, contempt, and misanthropy--determines the course of events." Pierre is the first of Melville's books in which the resilient humorist is incapacitated.

In his introduction and notes, Murray cites further sources and analogues in works by Shakespeare, Burton, Browne, Walpole, Radcliffe, Scott, Keats, Shelley, Mary Shelley, Fenimore Cooper, Carlyle, De Quincey, Bulwer-Lytton, and others. Reviewed in 1949.B41, B50, B69, B83, B94; 1950.B37, B60.

15   POCHMANN, HENRY A. and GAY WILSON ALLEN, eds. Masters of American Literature. Vol. 2. New York: The Macmillan Co., pp. 174-180.
     Biographical headnote ["Herman Melville (1819-1891)"]; brief synopses and evaluations of the major works. Prints "Hawthorne and His Mosses," Melville's letters of 16? April[?], 1[?] June, and 17[?] November, 1851, to Hawthorne [Letters, pp. 123-131, 141-144], selections from Battle-Pieces, and Billy Budd, Foretopman.

16   RAHV, PHILIP. "The Cult of Experience in American Writing," in Image and Idea: Fourteen Essays on Literary Themes. Norfolk, Conn.: New Directions Books, pp. 13-15.
     Reprint of 1940.B38, with the reference to the "normal, intellectual, and affective natures" of Poe, Hawthorne, and Melville corrected to "moral, intellectual, and affective natures."

17   ROUTH, H.V. "The Nineteenth Century and After." The Year's
     Work in English Studies, 1947, 28 (1949), 259, 261-262.
          Notes publication of 1947.B16, with Thorp's "crisp schol-
     arly introduction." Brief synopses of 1947.B30, B42, B63.

18   RUKEYSER, MURIEL. The Life of Poetry. Current Books. New
     York: A.A. Wyn, pp. 67-74, 76, 86.
          Reprints 1941.B42. Melville defined as "the poet of out-
     rage of his century in America," while Whitman is "the poet of
     possibility."

19   RUSK, RALPH L. The Life of Ralph Waldo Emerson. New York and
     London: Columbia University Press, pp. 276, 300-301, 425.
          In a notebook entry, Emerson's brother Charles identifies
     himself with others in a manner suggestive of later passages in
     Melville and Whitman. Emerson's essay "The Poet" brought
     "occasional sharp cries of dissent" from Melville, "along with
     approval for the nobility of certain passages." In 1864 Emerson
     was among twenty prospective members of a projected National
     Academy of Literature and Art; Melville and Whitman were not.

20   SEALTS, MERTON M., JR. "Melville and The Shakers." Studies
     in Bibliography, 2 (1949-1950), 105-114.
          Melville's markings (and one annotation) in the anonymous
     work A Summary View of the Millenial Church, or United Society of
     Believers, Commonly Called Shakers. "Melville's interest in the
     Shakers as indicated by the pattern of his markings is fairly
     clear. He checked key incidents in the general story of Shaker-
     ism, perhaps in order to qualify himself as a better guide when
     conducting his visiting New York friends to the Shaker villages
     [in the summer of 1850], as he did again in the summer of 1851.
     The character of Mother Ann and the governing principles of the
     Shaker communities were other topics of interest. But what
     seemingly attracted him most was the prophetic strain in the
     Shaker religion, with its association of exalted bodily and
     mental states. Despite his evident skepticism toward Shaker
     sanity and the Shaker creed, he apparently agreed with their
     pessimistic outlook upon this earthly life, and was sympathetic
     toward their intuitive yearning for a better life to come. In
     his personal knowledge of the sect and in A Summary View lay the
     material for his characterization of the Shaker Gabriel in one
     of the most striking and portentous chapters of Moby-Dick."

21   VAN DOREN, MARK. Nathaniel Hawthorne. The American Men of
     Letters Series. New York: William Sloane Associates, p. 178,
     passim.
          Melville's friendship with Hawthorne. In "Hawthorne and
     His Mosses," Melville saw as far into Hawthorne as anyone has
     seen.

22   VON HAGEN, VICTOR WOLFGANG. <u>Ecuador and the Galápagos</u>
<u>Islands</u>. Norman: University of Oklahoma Press, p. 237,
passim.
      References to Melville's visit to the Galápagos Islands
and quotations from "The Encantadas." "Although an eclectic and
great borrower, Melville was able to envelop the Galapagos in a
mood which has never been quite equaled since. And it helped to
inspire new explorers."

23   COWIE, ALEXANDER. "Symbols Ahoy." <u>CEA Critic</u>, 11 (January),
7–8.
      Argues "(1) that in the teaching of <u>Moby-Dick</u> it is best to
begin not with symbol-reading but with the stuff that gave rise
to the symbols [the factual aspects of the book] and (2) that
rich as symbols are as tokens of Melville's being––his feelings
and perceptions––they are by their very nature unavailable for
use as keys to a coherent system of thought." Melville's symbols
are not so much fixed representations of a philosophical scheme
as fragmentary notations of his momentary attitude or outlook or
emotion; they are also sometimes contradictory on a literal
level. Melville did not think important books had answers––
hence Schneider's bafflement in his attempt to interpret him
satisfactorily. [<u>See</u> 1946.B10.] Melville's symbols bring us
close to what we feel are centers of his thought but do not
render up the final secret.

24   HILLWAY, TYRUS. "Melville and the Spirit of Science." <u>South</u>
<u>Atlantic Quarterly</u>, 48 (January), 77–88.
      Influenced by the scientific thinking of his day, Melville
saw nature as indifferent to man's welfare and silent as to his
goal. But, while rejecting the romantic idea of nature as a
benevolent goddess, Melville "did not, except in his blacker
literary moods, regard her simply as the source of evil. Science
provided him with a more harrowing paradox: Nature breeds both
good and evil but is equally indifferent to both." Evidence
cited from <u>Mardi</u>, <u>Moby-Dick</u>, and <u>The Confidence-Man</u>.

25   MURDOCK, KENNETH B. "Book Reviews." <u>American Literature</u>, 20
(January), 461–465.
      Review of 1947.B14. The title "apocalyptics" can be made
to fit Brown, Poe, Melville, Bierce, Hearn, and Faulkner, but
are there no other authors, classified separately by Snell, who
have in most ways stronger ties with Melville or Brown or Poe,
than Faulkner or Hearn? If so, the "apocalyptics" category is
a possible source of confusion rather than help to understanding.

26   SPILLER, ROBERT E. "Book Reviews." <u>American Literature</u>, 20
(January), 459–461.
      Review of 1947.A1. Anyone searching here for a key to the
personalities of the thwarted geniuses Melville and Whitman will
be disappointed. Brooks understands them both and discusses
their strengths and weaknesses with warmth and tolerance, but he
nowhere becomes involved in their inner lives. The lives of even
great writers here merge into the life of a nation in civil war

and reconstruction and become important only as they express the
vitality and uniqueness of that nation. Relatively minor authors
receive illuminating treatment while the greatness of the great
remains largely unexplained.

27   VARLEY, H. LELAND. "Heroic Failure." CEA Critic, 11
        (January), 8.
            Reports Harry Levin's inclusion of Moby-Dick in the
humanities course at Harvard as a portrayal of "heroic failure."

28   VINCENT, HOWARD P. "Brief Mention." American Literature, 20
        (January), 484.
            Review of 1947.B16. The notes are clear, accurate, infor-
mative, restrained in number. Thorp has appropriately adopted
the first American edition as the basis of his text because it
had the authority of Melville's own supervision, but he might
have made use of some of the interesting variants in the first
English edition, especially the attractive footnote on the verb
"to gallow" (chapter 87).

29   WHITMAN, RUTH. "Century on the Sea." Christian Science
        Monitor (8 January), 5.
            On nineteenth-century transatlantic sailing packets. In
Melville's journal [see 1948.B21] one finds a few last glimpses
of travel across the Atlantic under sail before the steamers
ended it. (Picture of the Devonshire, a sister ship of the
Southhampton, on which Melville sailed to London in 1849, and
reproduction of the first page of Melville's journal.)

30   TILTON, ELEANOR M. "Story Behind Moby Dick." Philadelphia
        Inquirer (16 January).
            Review of 1949.A3. Wishes that Vincent had not undermined
his own authority (his scholarly labor is evident) by insisting
at the start on his theory that there were originally two very
different versions of Moby-Dick. He builds this elaborate fiction on a phrase, "whaling story"; that the phrase is not
grandiloquent is no evidence that the manuscript referred to is
slight. The phrase is apparently not even Melville's own: he
seems to be quoting Dana. The letter from which Vincent deduces
two versions accurately describes the one Moby-Dick that exists
in fact. Vincent's claim that Melville could not have gotten
halfway through the book, as we know it, when he wrote to Dana
rests on two unsupported assumptions: one about the time
Melville began writing and the other about the speed with which
he worked. Vincent's book is, nevertheless, a much needed addition to earlier studies of Melville's sources.

31   SEALTS, MERTON M., JR. "Melville's 'Friend Atahalpa.'" Notes
        and Queries, 194 (22 January), 37–38.
            Atahalpa's attempt to hatch a fairy in a jar (Mardi, chap-
ter 98) is based on a quotation from Isaac D'Israeli's Curiosi-
ties of Literature, which Melville read in the dition of Sir
Thomas Browne's Works he borrowed from Evert Duyckinck in 1848.

32   ANON. "Radio and Television." New York <u>Times</u> (28 January).
      List of novels to be dramatized for radio as part of the
"NBC University Theatre" spring semester includes <u>Moby-Dick</u>.

33   ATKINSON, BROOKS. "At the Theatre." New York <u>Times</u>
      (31 January).
      Review of production (by the Experimental Theatre at the
Lenox Hill Playhouse) of <u>Uniform of Flesh</u>, a dramatization of
<u>Billy Budd</u> by Louis O. Coxe and R.H. Chapman. The climax is
savagely ironic--as brutal an attack on the complacence of the
world as <u>Moby-Dick</u>. There are imperfections: <u>Uniform of Flesh</u>
is too gaudy a title for so austere a play; some of the dialogue,
probably transposed from the novel, is ridiculously archaic; the
last two scenes carry some of Melville's metaphysical obscurity
to the stage, where it is less tolerable than in a novel; and the
play never specifically establishes Claggart's sadistic villainy
toward the crew--his sin seems to be intellectual or spiritual.
The play needs some physical horror to establish his evil dramatically. But these are minor flaws in a play "that reaps the
whirlwind and rushes on to a climax of incredible though deliberate tragedy."

34   ARVIN, NEWTON, ROBERT GORHAM DAVIS, and DANIEL AARON.
      "Liberalism and Confusion." [Letter to the Editors.]
      <u>Partisan Review</u>, 16 (February), 221-222.
      The authors object to Chase's statement in 1948.B70 that
Claggart in <u>Billy Budd</u> "is another version of Melville's self-
righteous Liberal, the Confidence Man." They wonder if liberalism has become interchangeable with natural depravity. [See
1949.B35 for reply.]

35   CHASE, RICHARD. "Reply." [Letter to the Editors.] <u>Partisan
      Review</u>, 16 (February), 223.
      Reply to 1949.B34. Unable to defend his reading of
Melville or use of words like "liberal" in the space allotted,
Chase refers interested persons to the texts at issue. Hopes
that "the Confidence Man of the 1940's has not turned out to be
the Liberal Who Has Officially Reassessed Liberalism And Found It
Good."

36   PARKES, HENRY BAMFORD. "Poe, Hawthorne, Melville: An Essay
      in Sociological Criticism." <u>Partisan Review</u>, 16 (February),
      157-165.
      The most essential resemblance among Poe, Hawthorne, and
Melville "is that they all assume the individual to be isolated
and regard this isolation as a problem. What is lacking in their
framework of experience is any sense of society as a kind of
organic whole to which the individual belongs and in which he has
his appointed place. And lacking the notion of social continuity
and tradition, they lack also the corresponding metaphysical conception of the natural universe as an ordered unity which harmo-
nizes with human ideals. In this respect their view of life
differs from that of most European writers; . . . for the Americans there is no underlying order, and each individual must find

his own way of dealing with chaos." Melville "differs from both Poe and Hawthorne in that he has a positive conception of solidarity. This solidarity, however, can be found only in the miniature world of the ship, which is transitory and artificial, and ceases as soon as the sailor goes ashore. Ashore, as in the Liverpool scenes in Redburn, in the concluding chapters of Israel Potter, and in Pierre, the individual is utterly and hopelessly alone. This aloneness is not glorified, as in Poe, or attributed to sin, as in Hawthorne; it is simply stated as an inescapable part of the general misery of human existence." The ultimate relationship between man and the universe is, for Melville, one of conflict; and whether the individual asserts his will or denies it, he is, in the end, alone. All three writers present individuals who lack the sense of belonging to a social organism and whose relationships with other men are, in consequence, disturbed and insecure. In their relationships with women, this feeling of insecurity becomes even stronger and more compulsive. What is significant is not merely the lack of normal sexual emotion but the dubious or abnormal quality of such emotion as does manifest itself. These writers were presumably concerned with the problem of isolation because they lived in a society that was violently competitive, composed predominantly of individuals who were on the make and whose values were acquisitive and pecuniary, a society lacking in the sense of continuity, tradition, and human solidarity, but exalting individualism. In their writings, we find a statement of the psychological costs of individualism and a foreshadowing of the neurotic personality of the twentieth century.

37   P[OWELL], L[AWRENCE] C[LARK]. "My Melville." Hoja Volante, No. 22 (February), pp. 5-7.
       Anecdotal, personal appreciation of Melville, with accounts of Powell's first reading of Moby-Dick, of a Frenchman who wrote an essay on Melville during his pre-World War I student days at the Sorbonne, and of Melville editions owned by Powell. Powell particularly values Melville as a diarist, "for his entries are the man himself, entirely unselfconscious." The edition he turns to most is Thorp's [1938.B22]: "of all the essential Melville which it contains, the quintessence is the series of wonderful confessional letters which Melville wrote to his neighbor Hawthorne at the creative zenith which he reached in the writing of Moby Dick." Alongside Melville's "rich experience, nobility of person and the passion of his style, how cautious seems Emerson, how tricky Poe, Hawthorne anemic, and Whitman how florid!" Reprinted in 1951.B17; 1960.B30.

38   FRIEDRICH, GERHARD. "Postscript to 'Moby Dick.'" Saturday Review of Literature, 32 (12 February), 42.
       Sonnet. Reprinted in 1957.B9; 1958.A1.

39   KAZIN, ALFRED. "Ishmael in His Academic Heaven." <u>New Yorker</u>,
      24 (12 February), 84, 87–89.
          Mainly a review of 1948.B9, B24. Although we owe much to
      the new Melville scholars, "some of them are not as sensitive to
      his individual quality as those first enthusiasts they condescend
      to. They tend to build up a Melville who never had any religious
      doubts that cannot be explained away by the death and transfig-
      uration of innocent Billy Budd, who was as alert to all the
      implications of his thoughts as a psychoanalyst, who was never
      disorderly in his writing except on purpose--a Melville in whom
      we miss Ishmael's enduring wrath, 'his maddened heart and
      splintered hand.'" Kazin disputes Oliver's identification of
      Bartleby with Thoreau; claims there is no reason to suppose that
      Melville thought Thoreau's life one of final negation; sees
      Bartleby as "the stranger in the city, in an extreme condition
      of loneliness, and the story a fable of how we detach ourselves
      from others to gain a deeper liberty and then find ourselves so
      walled up by our own pride that we can no longer accept the love
      that is offered us." The irony in the story is directed not
      against Bartleby but against the narrator. It is a story of the
      ultimate difficulty human beings have in reaching each other.
      Melville was not writing about anyone, except as he drew on his
      own situation and his bitter understanding of himself. Kazin
      finds Freeman's introduction "exceedingly useful" and accepts his
      findings about the manuscript; regrets the presence of footnotes
      and lists of variants on every page, but acknowledges they were
      "called for by Melville's hesitations and corrections, by the air
      the manuscript gives out of having been written in secrecy, and
      for his own pleasure, by an old man." In <u>Billy Budd</u> Melville
      accepts authority and man's dependence on it; but Freeman's
      proofs that Melville made through Billy's rapturous death an
      affirmation of Christian belief are not very convincing. Melville
      had agreed to accept the whole mysterious creation at last, but
      "it does not follow from this that he forgave God for just possi-
      bly not existing." Reprinted in part in Inge, pp. 75–77.

40   CAVENDISH, HENRY. "Melville's Bread and Butter Tales."
      Chicago <u>Sunday Tribune Magazine of Books</u> (13 February), p. 12.
          Review of 1948.B24. The tales themselves, while hardly of
      the morbidity inferred by Hawthorne in his journal entry for
      20 November 1856, are nonetheless reflective of Melville's great
      symbolic preoccupation: man's struggle with the opposing forces
      within the universe in which he finds himself. For sixty years
      after initial publication, <u>The Piazza Tales</u> were so consistently
      neglected that even today the standard reference works, for the
      most part, make no mention of them. Their inclusion now as the
      second volume in the Hendricks House edition will come not only
      as belated recognition of their literary merit but as a dis-
      tinguished contribution to American scholarship.

41   ANON. "Reprints, New Editions." New York <u>Herald Tribune</u>
     <u>Weekly Book Review</u> (27 February), p. 16.
         Review of 1949.B14. Murray's introduction is a valuable
     study of this dark and tormented novel. "It took a trained
     psychologist to show how far Melville in this book moved on the
     level of reason, and how far he was affected by the levels of
     passion and instinct out of which the book came, not merely out
     of the reason."

42   LEISY, ERNEST E. "New Melville Journal." <u>Southwest Review</u>,
     34 (Spring), 205.
         Review of 1948.B21. Already there were stirrings of no
     common sort within this "pondering man," as a result of which the
     journal he kept during his seventeen weeks' trip is helpful in
     understanding his genius. Metcalf's editorship is excellent.
     Summary of the journal's contents.

43   SEALTS, MERTON M., JR. "Melville's Reading: A Check-List of
     Books Owned and Borrowed." <u>Harvard Library Bulletin</u>, 3
     (Spring), 268-277.
         Continuation of 1949.B120. Continued in 1949.B89.

44   ARVIN, NEWTON. "Melville and the Gothic Novel." <u>New England</u>
     <u>Quarterly</u>, 22 (March), 33-48.
         Traces elements of Gothic fiction (wild landscapes, haunted
     castles, ruined towers, subterranean vaults, musical instruments
     and imagery of music, magic portraits, incest, romantic victims,
     and "majestic monsters") in Melville's works from <u>Typee</u> to <u>Billy</u>
     <u>Budd</u>. Reprinted in Arvin (1966), pp. 106-122; reprinted in part
     in Willett, pp. 12-15.

45   GIOVANNINI, G. "Melville's <u>Pierre</u> and Dante's <u>Inferno</u>."
     <u>PMLA</u>, 64 (March), 70-78.
         About half of <u>Pierre</u>, books 2-9, "pivots on references to
     the <u>Inferno</u>, which in a powerfully symbolical manner underscore
     the pervasive tragic gloom and develop on an emotive level the
     hero's reactions to the existence of evil. Relying on some
     knowledge of the <u>Inferno</u> on the reader's part, Melville adopts
     the technique of literary allusion and quotation functioning in
     place of formal exposition, the literary reference itself becom-
     ing contextually an expository symbol of the hero's internal
     states and of the ubiquity and universality of evil. Melville
     adopts this technique in other works [such as <u>Israel Potter</u>], but
     never so extensively as in <u>Pierre</u>, nor so effectively at crucial
     moments in the development of character and theme." Reprinted in
     part in Willett, pp. 15-19.

46   HILLWAY, TYRUS. "Melville's Use of Two Pseudo-Sciences."
     <u>Modern Language Notes</u>, 64 (March), 145-150.
         Survey of Melville's use of physiognomy and phrenology in
     "Authentic Anecdotes of 'Old Zack,'" <u>Mardi</u>, <u>White-Jacket</u>, <u>Moby-</u>
     <u>Dick</u>, <u>Pierre</u>, <u>The Confidence-Man</u>, and <u>Billy</u> Budd. "The signifi-
     cant thing is that he was not, like others of his time, deceived
     by the pretensions of these two pseudo-sciences to respectability,

but instead recognized the limitations of their methods and
theories. His use of the jargon of these two studies added
sometimes humor and sometimes irony to his writing; now and again
his literary skill in such instances was effective enough to make
him appear nearly, but never quite, serious."

47　　SPILLER, ROBERT E. "Brief Mention." American Literature, 21
　　　　(March), 138.
　　　　　　Review of 1948.B24. Chiefly valuable because it again
makes available the full text of the first edition of what
Melville may have regarded, with The Confidence-Man, as his fare-
well to prose authorship. One could wish for a more detailed and
perceptive discussion of Melville's art, here at a moment of firm
but precarious balance, and of the bearing of the tales upon the
problem of collapse of the artist so soon.

48　　ANON. "Strange, Wondrous Times." London Times Literary
　　　　Supplement, No. 2458 (12 March), p. 170.
　　　　　　Review of 1947.A1. Melville and Whitman are symbols in
Brooks's narrative of a national work for freedom, freedom being
the preponderating tendency in the two decades before the Civil
War, when we can see the pattern of American literature changing
from that set by the English classics. Like Whitman, Melville
found the American voice--but lost it. White-Jacket's notion of
Americans as the "chosen people--the Israel of our time," bearing
"the ark of the liberties of the world," has the note made
familiar and monotonous now by Moscow. But Melville retired from
the busy uprush to brood on the chosen peoples of all lands making wealth and spreading misery.

49　　THORP, WILLARD. "Definitive 'Billy Budd.'" New York Herald
　　　　Tribune Weekly Book Review (13 March), p. 4.
　　　　　　Review of 1948.B9. Praise of new "definitive text";
accepts Freeman's account of the relationship between "Baby Budd"
and Billy Budd; finds his introduction "packed with new information about the sources which Melville used, in his old characteristic fashion to give scope and depth and ambiguity to his
theme." Billy Budd is Melville's greatest work after Moby-Dick;
in articulation of theme and control of language it in fact out-
ranks Moby-Dick.

50　　BREIT, HARVEY. "Repeat Performances." New York Times Book
　　　　Review, (20 March), p. 22.
　　　　　　Review of 1949.B14. Murray chooses to ignore many of the
aesthetic questions the book inevitably raises and to concentrate
on psychological analysis, which he accomplishes with excellent
taste and graciousness. Despite Murray's claim that the American
today is largely absorbed in technical problems, Melville is
enjoying perhaps more favor than at any other time--it is the
period of the second revival of Melville.

51   HEFLIN, WILSON L.   "Melville's Third Whaler."   Modern Language
     Notes, 64 (April), 241-245.
          Melville's last whaling cruise, from Eimeo in the Society
     Islands to Lahaina on the island of Maui in the Sandwich Island
     group, was in the Charles and Henry, a Nantucket ship, under the
     command of Captain John B. Coleman.

52   ANDERSON, CHARLES.   "Book Reviews."   American Literature, 21
     (May), 250-251.
          Review of 1948.B21.   The liberties Metcalf has taken in
     transcribing the journal appear to be minimal and sensible; the
     few evidences that this is the work of an amateur rather than a
     trained scholar are trivial; on the whole the editing has clearly
     been done with painstaking care and intelligent industry.   The
     journal "is not a literary one in the sense of James's, or even
     Hawthorne's.   It is the sprightly log of a good traveler, an
     observant sightseer, and a bon vivant--further evidence that
     Melville was not a dedicated artist."

53   HILLWAY, TYRUS.   "Melville's Geological Knowledge."   American
     Literature, 21 (May), 232-237.
          Melville may have been indebted to John Reinold Forster's
     Observations Made During a Voyage round the World, Oliver
     Goldsmith's Animated Nature, John Mason Good's The Book of
     Nature, and Robert Chambers's Vestiges of the Natural History of
     Creation for geological information and misinformation.   [See
     also 1945.B18; see 1951.B23 for reply.]

54   HILLWAY, TYRUS.   "Pierre, The Fool of Virtue."   American
     Literature, 21 (May), 201-211.
          "If Melville attempts to prove anything in Pierre, it is
     simply that virtue cannot be, as Milton pretended in Comus, a
     protection in itself against evil; and this, Melville implies,
     is true because the nature of both good and evil turns out upon
     close inspection to be ambiguous."

55   HOWE, IRVING.   "The Confidence Man."   Tomorrow, 8 (May),
     55-57.
          Review of the John Lehman edition of The Confidence-Man.
     The Confidence-Man is the Salesman par excellence, the bloodless
     symbol of the encroaching Salesman's Civilization, to which every
     object and value must become a commodity for sale; he is the
     salesman as Melville bitterly apprehends his function: to sell
     short goods and watered stock.   He is essentially featureless,
     lacking either character center or peripheral eccentricities
     because, as a series of restless manifestations of social func-
     tion, he cannot exist as a person.   The only thing that "happens"
     in the book physically and socially is the exchange of money.
     The hard-fact consequence of the Confidence Man's jabber is that
     he almost always emerges from his conversations richer than he
     was before; he can never enter into the slightest social rela-
     tionship without an ulterior motive.   By strewing commercial-
     business images through its pages, Melville sustains the book's
     monetary skein and effect of flinty depersonalization and

anonymity. While the Confidence Man preaches the doctrine of
"confidence," Melville suggests that what men really need is intelligent skepticism. If the Confidence Man triumphs, life will
become completely mechanized and banalized; no basic experience
will ever be met or grappled with, for he has a "certain cure for
any pain in the world." Expropriating the language of all belief
and value--liberalism, faith and science--he goes about his
business: the making, that is, the taking of money. Hardly a
novel, and not much of an allegory, The Confidence-Man is rather
a dialectical Punch-and-Judy Show, intended to burlesque American
morality. But its dialectic of ideas is too repetitive to sustain the book all the way through; for once we know that each
forthcoming episode will reveal the Confidence Man in another act
of deceit, the possibility of dramatic development is destroyed.
Individual sections are brilliantly done; the writing is almost
always sharply sour, as tart as the mind behind it; yet the book
is eventually tedious. It fails as a novel because its structure
is inadequate to its reserve of thought. Nonetheless, The
Confidence-Man is of first importance for anyone interested in
the development of Melville's mind; and, as an antidote to the
kind of chauvinism now clouding the American literary arena, the
book is of incalculable value.

56   PAUL, SHERMAN. "Melville's 'The Town-Ho's Story.'" American
      Literature, 21 (May), 212-221.
          "The Town-Ho's Story" contains Melville's germ of comedy
      and his portrayal of the retributive justice of the white whale
      (an alternative and variant meaning of the whale's significance).
      It also affirms the sanctity of personality and the kind of
      democracy that recognizes kings in commoners. Radney goes beyond
      the law of the ship and the divine law and brings down upon him-
      self the force of divine justice. Steelkilt displays traits
      associated with the "heart" and Christ; Radney displays the cold
      intellectuality of Claggart, Bland, and Jackson. The central
      meaning of "The Town-Ho's Story" is the reaffirmation of the
      heart with which Melville arms his reader for the greater tragedy
      to come. Through the Erie Canal, Melville portrays the out-
      running of the religious support of democracy and the ever-
      grasping, ever-extending rapaciousness of American life, an
      apparent failure in the basis of American democracy that has its
      counterpart in the mutiny on the Town-Ho. Reprinted in 1960.A6.

57   McFEE, WILLIAM. "The Complete Stories of Herman Melville."
      New York Sun (4 May), p. 22.
          Review of 1949.B9. The volume is for Melville enthusiasts
      only; the resurrection of Melville's fugitive pieces will be of
      more interest to professors than to the younger generation. It
      is doubtful that Melville's stories would rate the attention
      lavished upon them if they were not by the author of Moby-Dick.
      It will be surprising if the present generation of fiction read-
      ers thinks they compare as stories with such works as Stephen
      Crane's "The Open Boat" or Ambrose Bierce's "The Horseman in the
      Sky" or Ring Lardner's "Haircut."

58   BREIT, HARVEY. "Herman Melville's Short Stories." New York
      Times Book Review (8 May), pp. 4, 26.
          Review of 1949.B9. A reader unbaptized in Melville would
      see in the stories more promise than fulfillment, except in the
      three great ones, "Bartleby," "The Encantadas," and "Benito
      Cereno." A baptized reader would see an irony of chronology, a
      reversal, as though the boy had come after the man; he would be
      all the more moved, having come from the profound and controlled
      universe of demonic struggle in Moby-Dick, by the excesses of
      "The Happy Failure," the disproportions of "Cock-A-Doodle-Doo!,"
      "by the spectacle of the sensibility overcrowding the small frame
      and the intellectuality overflowing the objects meant to contain
      it." In Melville's short pieces, there are "cunning glimpses" of
      Truth, but in them he is not so much a Truth teller as a tale
      teller; he was not "at the very axis of reality." In any one of
      them, despite imperfections, there is great reward; each has an
      extraordinarily fertile idea, charm, urbanity, unflagging
      thought, and language "too rich to be incisive, and too incisive
      not to dazzle."

59   SPILLER, ROBERT E. "Problem of Melville." Saturday Review of
      Literature, 32 (14 May), 19.
          Review of 1948.B9, B21. Briefly sketches the biographical
      background of the 1849 journal. Freeman's edition of Billy Budd
      "is important because it gives us for the first time a reliable
      text, because it offers incontrovertible evidence of Melville's
      normal method of composition (at least at that time), by lifting
      out and printing separately the narrative stage of the writing,"
      and because in his introduction Freeman "explores all the kinds
      of sources that Melville used, and reconstructs, in both literal
      and psychological terms, the actual workings of Melville's
      creative imagination." We may not agree with all of Freeman's
      conclusions, but here is the tool long needed for drawing our
      own.

60   'THERSITES.' "Talk on Parnassus." New York Times Book Review
      (22 May), pp. 7, 27.
          Humor. Melville, James, and Kafka discuss their current
      vogue.

61   VINCENT, HOWARD P. "Treasure of Melville Gems." Philadelphia
      Inquirer Book Review (29 May).
          Review of 1949.B9. There can be no doubt of the critics'
      final verdict: Melville was a master of the short story, ranking
      with Hawthorne. His stories sound the depths of the human heart
      and explore the far reaches of evil, both social and personal.
      Leyda deserves special praise for his editorial work; his skill
      in criticism is no less remarkable than his research, and his
      wealth of new facts does not interfere with the flow of intel-
      ligent interpretation.

62   ANDERSON, QUENTIN. "Second Trip to Byzantium." <u>Kenyon
       Review</u>, 11 (Summer), 516–520.
            Begins as review of 1948.B9 and goes on to general commen-
       tary on Melville's work. Freeman's readings are often, though
       not always, better than Weaver's and in some instances Freeman's
       readings correct Weaver's serious slips in transcription. Free-
       man is perhaps a little disingenuous in assuming that since the
       reader has the choices before him the editor need not take full
       responsibility for the use of one variant rather than another in
       the body of the text. Because Melville never put the manuscript
       in shape for the printer, both editors have had to act as inter-
       preters. The inclusion of "Baby Budd, Sailor" in the volume
       represents scholarly busywork and nothing more. <u>Billy Budd</u> is
       informed by a sort of primal moral wonder. "How could innocence,
       malignity and righteousness be housed in the soul? The book does
       not and could not contain an answer. Its theological references
       are designed to reinforce the wonder, never to lessen or dispel
       it. Christian doctrines are but the tropes of Melville's total
       feeling." Reprinted in part in Vincent (1971), pp. 97–98.

63   HUBBEN, WILLIAM. "Ahab, the Whaling Quaker." <u>Religion in
       Life</u>, 18 (Summer), 363–373.
            A Quaker's view of the contemporary relevance of Melville's
       "search after the meaning of evil," the "key problem in the
       religious confusion of our generation." Ahab "has become a com-
       panion to our generation because we are as perplexed as he was by
       the might of evil, the blind powers of catastrophe, and the con-
       spiracies of misfortune." We "share his fascination with evil,
       and may not be aware that man in attempting to destroy evil may
       find himself in unexpected partnership with its very essence."
       Ahab "is not an authentic Quaker. He has no other religion than
       that of a pathological self-deification, and a helpful, friendly
       God is entirely missing in the structure of his thinking." <u>Moby-
       Dick</u> holds a great teaching for our time: "The mad dictator of
       the <u>Pequod</u> is demonstrating an eternal law which the tyrants of
       all ages have unwittingly confirmed: that man whose reasoning
       has done away with God will soon set out to discard all mercy for
       his fellow men." Reprinted in 1949.B71.

64   SCOTT, W.B. "Chicago Letter." <u>Furioso</u>, 4 (Summer), 43.
            Regrets decline in the mean annual production of Melville
       books and articles in Cook County from 274 three years ago to
       scarcely 15 today. "Three years ago we were finding new hope in
       George Barnwell's 'Melville's Whale and M. de Charlus,' Hjalmar
       Ekdal's 'Melville's Tumor,' Bernard Mosher's 'Barnwell, Ekdal,
       and the Melville World.' Nowadays one encounters, at best--and
       it is simply not good enough--some Northwestern University
       pedant's cynical and barren, 'Smile When You Call Me Ishmael.'"

65   BARRETT, WILLIAM. "Art, Aristocracy, and Reason." <u>Partisan
       Review</u>, 16 (June), 659.
            In reply to Chase's designation of Claggart as "a fake
       liberal" [1948.B70], Barrett asks: "why could not Claggart
       equally well be a fake reactionary, conservative, communist,

fascist, or Catholic? Which is to say, that human evil can crop up in the camp of any ideology." [See also 1949.B34-35; see 1949.B66 for reply.]

66 CHASE, RICHARD. "Liberalism and Literature." Partisan Review, 16 (June), 651.
     Reply to 1949.B65 in defense of Chase's claim in 1948.B70 that Claggart in Billy Budd is another version of Melville's self-righteous liberal, the confidence man. Versions of the confidence man appear in several of Melville's books, including Israel Potter and Clarel: one is Claggart; another is Bland, the master-at-arms in White-Jacket, "a smooth-talking swindler with a remarkable array of masks and guiseful personalities." It is not indulgence in unwarranted moral preachments to suggest that Claggart resembles a modern type, the fake liberal and Pharisee who delivers the "common man" over to the man of power, or to suggest that our understanding of this type might be enhanced by reading Melville. [See also 1949.B34-35.]

67 HAYFORD, HARRISON and MERRELL DAVIS. "Herman Melville as Office-Seeker." Modern Language Quarterly, 10 (June), 168-183.
     Detailed, documented account of Melville's attempts to secure government appointments in 1839, 1847, 1853, 1857, 1861, and 1866. Concluded in 1949.B93.

68 PALTSITS, V.H. "Melville Letter." Melville Society Newsletter, 4 [5] (June), n.p.
     Brief comment on the connection between two letters Melville wrote on 10 December 1863 and 15 December 1863 in reference to the Cincinnati "Sanitary Fair" [Letters, pp. 218-219].

69 REDMAN, BEN RAY. "New Editions." Saturday Review of Literature 32 (4 June), 37.
     Review of 1948.B24, 1949.B9, B14. If the fact that Melville was a strangely flawed genius does not enhance his value in the eyes of ordinary readers, it obviously increases his fascination for literary and psychological investigators. These three volumes give a good idea of the kind of scholarly attention that is being devoted to him. Each has a carefully edited text, with authoritative introduction and learned notes; but Murray's is by far the most interesting, because of his remarkably fine ninety-five-page introduction. Pierre is one of the great freaks and failures of literature, and Murray explores Melville's intentions and frankly exposes the botch he made of them. A re-reading of Pierre confirmed Redman's opinion that, however interesting it may be as a case history, it is largely worthless as a work of imaginative fiction. [See 1929.B68.] Melville's tales and sketches, too, are sometimes more interesting as windows through which we glimpse the writer's psyche than as works of literary art. Most successful are "The Encantadas" sketches, but Melville's shorter fiction--including the teasing "Bartleby" and the gripping "Benito Cereno"--has been somewhat over-estimated.

70   PAUL, SHERMAN. "Morgan Neville, Melville and the Folk-Hero." Notes and Queries, 194 (25 June), 278.
     In "The Town-Ho's Story," chapter 54 in Moby-Dick, Melville gives his version of a tall tale. The transference of "western" feats of skill and strength to the inner realm of strength of will might be an indication of the way Melville alchemized western material. His description of Steelkilt suggests the first literary portrayal of Mike Fink, by Morgan Neville, in "The Last of the Boatmen" (The Western Souvenir, Cincinnati, 1828).

71   HUBBEN, WILLIAM. "Ahab, the Whaling Quaker." Friends Quarterly [London], 3 (July), 169–181.
     Reprint of 1949.B63.

72   STEVENS, HARRY R. "Melville's Music." Musicology, 2 (July), 405–421.
     Summarizes and quotes passages in Melville's works involving music.

73   JONES, HOWARD MUMFORD. "The American Malady." Saturday Review of Literature, 32 (6 August), 24–27.
     Cites Melville as part of the Gothic strain in American writing, from the sentimental novel of the 1790s to Sanctuary and The Naked and the Dead, a Gothicism of violence, brutality, and decadence; and sees his violent reaction against the course of popular culture in Clarel as part of a recurrent mood of cultural nihilism in American writing. Melville is also part of the "tradition of unhappiness" in American literature.

74   DUFFUS, R.L. "The Making of an Epic." New York Times Book Review (14 August), p. 7.
     Review of 1949.A3. Wonders if certain statements by Vincent on the "universal meaning" of Moby-Dick were what Melville had in mind. What scholarship can do Vincent has done; but "Melville was a mystic—and across that threshold scholarship may penetrate only to a measured distance."

75   THORP, WILLARD. "The Sources of Melville's Masterpiece." New York Herald Tribune Weekly Book Review (14 August), p. 4.
     Review of 1949.A3. The book offers illuminating discoveries but would possess more force and unity if Vincent had not tried to crowd so much into it. There was no need to digress into somewhat elementary discussions about the creative process or to insert so much critical observation on the narrative structure of the novel, its metaphysical meaning, and possible interpretation of particular characters. It would have been more to the point to treat these concerns only to the extent that Melville's transmutations of his sources affected them.

76   B[RADLEY], V[AN] A[LLEN]. "Melville's Method of Creation." Chicago Daily News (17 August), p. 32.
     Review of 1949.A3. The vigor and thoroughness with which Vincent has pursued his inquiries lend his book the fascination of a detective story. Layman and scholar alike will delight in

his comparisons of passages from Melville with their original versions in old whaling books, and no less valuable is Vincent's penetrating analysis of the emergence of the great spiritual theme that gave <u>Moby-Dick</u> its sweep and power.

77   ANON. "Writers Who Influenced Herman Melville." <u>Christian Science Monitor</u> (18 August), p. 11.
       Lists Shakespeare, Hawthorne, Thomas Browne, I Corinthians 13, Blake, the Old Testament, Homer, Carlyle, and Schopenhauer, with brief comments on their influence on Melville.

78   H., R.M. "The Short Stories of Melville." <u>Christian Science Monitor</u> (18 August), p. 11.
       Review of 1949.B9. Interest in the relation of Melville's personality to his work has led Leyda to overestimate the short stories. Except for "Bartleby" and "Benito Cereno," they are not of compelling interest. Too often in these years Melville's bitterness led him to write of man at his worst. In <u>Billy Budd</u> the reader feels Melville is more interested in Billy the symbol than Billy the man.

79   KALEM, THEODORE. "Why Is It That an Age Turns Back to a Past Writer?" <u>Christian Science Monitor</u> (18 August), p. 11.
       Review of 1947.B16, 1948.B9, B21, B24. It was Melville's destiny to propose answers to questions his age had not raised and to be haunted by dilemmas of which the mass of his contemporaries were unaware. What has taken place in his revival, what inevitably takes place in such instances, is a rediscovery of ourselves, a new awareness of certain areas of human experience and certain facts about human nature and man's destiny that we had somehow lost sight of, concerning which the rediscovered writer seems to have vital things to tell us. The present age has shown a predilection for writers who stress man's tragic situation, the psychologists of the soul in extremity, figures like Kierkegaard, Dostoevski, and Melville. Two devastating wars, rending social upheavals, moral inertia and decay, "and a profound crisis in every compartment of contemporary culture" have stimulated the tragic sense, and reintroduced twentieth-century man to the age-old problem of evil. Bartleby's disenchantment, alienation, and paralysis of will form a pattern of experience similar to that depicted in contemporary Existentialist literature; if he were a modern he might speak of the absurdity of the universe. In one mood Melville saw only a cruelly meaningless flux in the universe; but in another mood he was also capable of an almost mystical belief in a beneficent order in the universe; Billy's final words of forgiveness in <u>Billy Budd</u> are inconceivable except in terms of such a belief.

80   REYNOLDS, HORACE. "About 'What is Probably the Greatest Sea Novel Ever Written.'" <u>Christian Science Monitor</u> (18 August), p. 11.
       Review of 1949.A3. Much of this is a worthwhile addition to Melville scholarship, and the first half of the book holds the attention of the general reader. But by the middle of the

discussion of the whaling chapters, comparison begins to grow a bit tedious and repetitive. Vincent, moreover, refuses to face the simple fact that <u>Moby-Dick</u> is not a well-constructed book. His study adds to our understanding of what is probably the greatest sea novel ever written, however. More than mere source-hunting, it is a torch.

81   BREIT, HARVEY. "Books of the Times." New York <u>Times</u> (20 August), p. 9.
     Review of 1949.A3. Vincent's book does more than show why Melville changed his original plan for <u>Moby-Dick</u> and how he went about achieving it; his book becomes, as well, an insight into the mysterious phenomena we call the "creative process."

82   SPILLER, ROBERT E. "Browne, Beale, Bennett, et al." <u>Saturday Review of Literature</u>, 32 (20 August), 19.
     Review of 1949.A3. The most thorough analysis of the sources of <u>Moby-Dick</u> that we have yet had. It is unfortunate Vincent felt impelled to lash previous critics for their failure to appreciate just why the novel is great when he himself is so obviously indebted to them for his own insights. His book is more a synthesis and elaboration of the work of others than a pioneering study. The one real contribution to an understanding of Melville that the book provides is the proof that the wide range of reading suggested by Melville's sub-sub-librarian preface is largely window dressing.

83   DAICHES, DAVID. "Melville: A Survey of the New Volumes." <u>New Republic</u>, 121 (22 August), 18-19.
     Review of 1948.B9, B21, B24, 1949.A3, B9, B14. The diversity and breadth of Melville criticism is perhaps proof that he is a genuine classic, and not simply an able minor writer whose sensibility happens to attract the present generation. The short story was a salutory form for Melville, compelling him to come to grips with his inspiration and force his meaning into the narrative by sheer intensity rather than by the more dangerous method of piling up symbolic detail, a method magnificently successful in <u>Moby-Dick</u>, but a failure in <u>Pierre</u>. Melville did not always meet the challenge of the short story and learn from it, however. "Benito Cereno," one of the finest stories in the language, is a complete success; nowhere else does Melville achieve this perfection. "Bartleby" is a powerful story, with an impressive presentation of the central idea, but once Bartleby has been presented and his characteristic behavior described, Melville has nothing more to say. The story's significance is in Bartleby the character, not in the action in which he participates. Melville's concluding words are a confession of failure: Bartleby stands for an aspect of humanity, and does so long before the end of the story; to project the story to a narrative climax, which adds nothing to the essential meaning of the character, is to have failed to use the possibilities of narrative. Melville could achieve meaning through narrative, as "Benito Cereno" and <u>Billy Budd</u> demonstrate; but many of his short stories are not really narratives at all. They

are a kind of prose dithyramb in which a situation is projected and brooded over until it becomes a symbol of an aspect of man's fate. Read as such, "Bartleby" shows coherence and unity; read as such, stories like "The Paradise of Bachelors and the Tartarus of Maids" show skill and subtlety. Melville was not always able to correlate his imaginative excitement with his handling of narrative or description. For example, Pierre, though full of remarkable passages and moments of brilliant symbolic writing, has too much melodrama to come alive as a significant novel. Billy Budd, one of the cleanest cut of all Melville's later works, skillfully blends "symbolic expansion of meaning by comment and achievement of significance by the outcome of the narrative."

84   MACFALL, RUSSELL. "Scholarly 'Trying-Out' of Melville." Chicago Sunday Tribune Magazine of Books (28 August), p. 3.
        Review of 1949.A3. Vincent's particular contribution to scholarship and readership, aside from the close study of sources and contemporary intellectual influences, lies in a convincing exposition of Melville's use of many apparently diverse elements to achieve his single purpose.

85   ANON. "Track of the White Whale." Time, 54 (29 August), 84.
        Review of 1949.A3; an ingenious study in literary genetics.

86   G[ARRISON], W.E. "Books in Brief." Christian Century, 66 (31 August), 1013.
        Review of 1949.A4. Wright's book is concerned with the influence of the Bible on Melville and his use of biblical material. It "also involves a thoroughly intelligent statement of some important biblical ideas embodied in and illuminated by Melville's writings."

87   OLSON, CHARLES. "David Young, David Old." Western Review, 14 (Fall), 63-66.
        Occasioned by publication of 1948.B9. Considers Billy Budd "as something less than the latter-day gem it has been taken for"; finds chapters that dry up in futile digressions, sentences that ground on commonplace. Freeman's discovery of the short story "Baby Budd" makes it possible to see the reason: "between the original version of the tale and Melville's rewrite of it Hawthorne intervened, and stole a strength away." There are two levels of love operative in Billy Budd: that of the plot (and Freeman, more thoroughly than any previous commentator, has exhibited "the homsexuality resident to all three of the men of the tragedy"); and that implicit in the book's final presentation. The first version of the tale was "worked over and over as though the hand that wrote was Hawthorne's, with his essayism, his hints, the veil of his syntax, until the celerity of the short story was run out, the force of the juxtapositions interrupted, and the secret of Melville as artist, the presentation of ambiguity by the event direct, was lost in the Salem manner." Melville's interest in Billy Budd was more amorous than imaginative (Olson wonders if anyone can be moved by anything in it

other than "the myrrh of Melville's love for Billy"). If
Melville had not been prevented from joining his natural
imagination to his love, he would have written a major work.
Weaver transcribed <u>Billy Budd</u> more accurately than anyone,
including Freeman, if Freeman is to be judged by his errors of
reading from the longer of the two pages of the manuscript reproduced in his book. Reprinted in Olson (1965), pp. 105–108.

88   RUBIN, LOUIS D., JR. "Melville and His Material." <u>Hopkins</u>
     <u>Review</u>, 3 (Fall), 49–51.
       Review of 1949.A3. Vincent's study is of uncommon value in
helping to get at a problem present not only in Melville but in
any artist: the relationship between factual source material and
the creative use of it. It aids the student in examining not
only Melville's artistry but the nature of the creative process
itself. Vincent, however, is a bit too eager to make Melville a
conscious allegorist.

89   SEALTS, MERTON M., JR. "Melville's Reading: A Check-List of
     Books Owned and Borrowed." <u>Harvard Library Bulletin</u>, 3
     (Autumn), 407–421.
       Continuation of 1949.B43. Continued in 1950.B115.

90   THORP, WILLARD. "Reviews." <u>Furioso</u>, 4 (Fall), 104–106.
       Review of 1948.B24; 1949.B9. Thorp is grateful for
Oliver's and Leyda's texts, less so for the introductions and
notes, in which the editors do not seem to have been quite certain of what they could or should do. Neither provides an extended critical study of the significance and excellence of the
stories themselves; enough of the biographical evidence is now
in so that such an essay could be written. The sixteen prose
pieces Melville wrote between <u>Pierre</u> and <u>The Confidence-Man</u> are
now "the happy hunting ground of scholars and critics. The
scholars have discovered in them all manner of covert allusions
to Melville's state of mind during those obscure years of defeat.
The critics, surprised to find that his technical skill was not
diminished by his failure as a metaphysician and a provider for
his family, are swarming in the periodicals, dropping those
blessed words irony, myth, symbol, ambiguity, allusions to Henry
James, and comparisons between the allegorical methods of
Melville and Hawthorne."

91   VINCENT, HOWARD P. "From the Melville Archives." <u>Accent</u>, 10
     (Autumn), 58–60.
       Review of 1948.B9, B21. Many of Melville's jottings in his
journal are not much more than shorthand, but once understood
they lead us to the mind and art of genius; embedded in these
notes are little nuggets for later assay, primarily in the short
stories and in <u>Moby-Dick</u>. The journal reveals what an excellent
traveler Melville was, his alert eye, retentive brain, tolerant
humor (which made him appreciative of tribal peculiarities), and
above all his zest for life. It may be used profitably by editors of <u>White-Jacket</u> and <u>Moby-Dick</u> and for study of topics such
as Melville's interest in art. Metcalf's editing is skillful;

her annotations are detailed but not overloaded. Freeman makes a thorough examination of biographical, scholarly, and critical problems connected with Billy Budd, and his edition is an important step in Melville scholarship; criticism of Billy Budd may now really settle down to work (Weaver's 1924 edition left crucial readings uncertain). Freeman's introduction and the sections in Chase's and Stone's books [1949.A1-2] show that it already has. Whether Freeman's text is definitive only a close comparison of his transcription with the manuscripts can tell. His manuscript facsimile facing p. 262 shows that his set of symbols designed to indicate what the manuscript is like is totally inadequate to serve its purpose.

92   ANON. "The Larger Meanings of 'Moby-Dick.'" Think, 15
     (September), 24.
          Brief synopsis of 1949.A3.

93   HAYFORD, HARRISON and MERRELL DAVIS. "Herman Melville as
     Office-Seeker." Modern Language Quarterly, 10 (September),
     377-388.
          Conclusion of 1949.B67.

94   LEVENSON, J.C. "Book Reviews." New England Quarterly, 22
     (September), 419-421.
          Review of 1949.B14. At a time when the psychological
     approach to literature has been almost bankrupted by the mal-
     practice of amateurs, Dr. Murray's professional skill restores
     the credit of an illuminating field of literary study. Some of
     Melville's comments on Pierre's behavior seem to be culled from
     the latest text on psychoanalysis, but in 1851 Melville had
     neither the technical equipment nor the mental stability success-
     fully to navigate "the endless, winding way--the flowing river in
     the cave of man." Murray helps us, as Melville could not, to
     make coherent sense of the psychological novel in Pierre, and by
     that help we can arrive at a new assessment of the novel of ideas
     in Pierre. Murray's interpretation of Plotinus Plinlimmon must
     be questioned, however: if the face of Plinlimmon is the face of
     Hawthorne, his voice is the voice of Emerson. The prudential
     wisdom of Plinlimmon stands in the same relation to the ethics of
     the Reverend Falsgrave as Concord transcendentalism to the
     unitarianism that preceded it.

95   PALTSITS, V.H. "A Melville Letter." Melville Society News-
     letter, 4 [5] (September), n.p.
          Reproduces most of Melville's letter of 30 April 1872 to
     Samuel Adams Drake [Letters, pp. 238-239] and refers to a later
     letter Melville wrote to Drake.

96   VINCENT, HOWARD P. "'White-Jacket': An Essay in Interpreta-
     tion." New England Quarterly, 22 (September), 304-315.
          White-Jacket is Melville's hesitant experiment in symboli-
     cal expression. The jacket becomes the central symbol of the
     book as well as the chief means of structural unity, symbolizing
     White Jacket's refusal to participate in the ordinary life of

humanity and his pseudo-self-sufficiency, followed by his
spiritual growth and conversion to life. Through the jacket, the
book "tells of the coming of the knowledge of good and evil and
of the fall from innocence and from the unconscious grace of
childhood. It is a study of disenchantment." Reprinted in part
in Rountree, pp. 72–75.

97   ANON. "Reprints, New Editions." New York Herald Tribune
      Weekly Book Review (11 September).
         Review of 1949.B10. "So many sweating critics have lately
      panted over the mysteries in Herman Melville that it is restful
      to find W. Somerset Maugham quiet, expert and sensible on the
      subject" in his excellent introduction.

98   ANON. "Briefly Noted." New Yorker, 25 (24 September), 108.
         Review of 1949.A3. When Vincent is working as a "source
      hunter" or "geneticist," he is fascinating; when he moves to
      interpretation and analyzes Moby-Dick chapter by chapter, he is
      much less successful, even reaching the point of identifying the
      White Whale with the atomic bomb and Queequeg with Hawthorne.
      The book is not comparable to John Livingston Lowes' The Road to
      Xanadu, though the comparison is made on its jacket.

99   AARON, DANIEL. "Melville: Descent into Tartarus." Tomorrow,
      9 (October), 53–56.
         Review of 1949.B9. In The Complete Stories the signs of
      Melville's exhaustion are discernible. "It is not by accident
      that his narrators or protagonists are usually old or prematurely
      old men cut off from their friends or misunderstood or patron-
      ized. And it is perhaps even more significant that Melville
      seems to be obsessed with the theme of personal misfortune.
      These stories might well have carried the subtitle, 'The Descent
      into Tartarus, or the Self-Adjurations of a Failure.'" Melville
      obeys his own injunction (in "The Encantadas") and attempts to
      depict black's polar opposite, but his joviality is unconvincing
      and his rationalizations about the advantages of failure succeed
      neither as fiction nor as philosophy. His pink-cheeked bachelors,
      descendants of Bracebridge Hall, are both tedious and bogus; only
      the harassed drifter, darkened by experience, is his proper
      spokesman. When Melville discovered a suitable medium for his
      thoughts, as he did in "Bartleby," "Benito Cereno," and "The
      Encantadas," he could project his emotions unobtrusively and
      dramatically. In most of the stories and sketches in Leyda's
      excellent edition, Melville's ideas are pathetically clothed,
      however. Nevertheless, they are interesting as autobiography,
      for in them an unhappy man is rationalizing his misfortunes
      through his characters.

100   ARVIN, NEWTON. "Melville's Shorter Poems." Partisan Review,
      16 (October), 1034–1046.
         Focuses on the vocabulary of Melville's poems (the "power-
      fully prosaic" terms suggesting business, industry, law, mathe-
      matics; and the more frequent rare, learned, often archaic, and
      sometimes apparently invented terms) and on the imagery, which

"varies interestingly and revealingly from volume to volume of the three collections Melville published during his life and the collection he left in manuscript" (elemental naturalistic imagery in Battle-Pieces; imagery of nautical disaster in John Marr; imagery of sight-seeing in Timoleon; and "the homely imagery of countrified retirement and quiet domestic simplicity" in the manuscript poems.)

101   BREIT, HARVEY. "Reader's Choice." Atlantic, 184 (October), 76, 78-79.
      Review of 1949.A3. The most definitive work of its kind on Moby-Dick. The first sections, dealing with Melville's two different plans for Moby-Dick are the weakest. When Vincent advances from speculation to documentation, he is richly at home and his defects are shed.

102   LEYDA, JAY. "Ishmael Melvill: Remarks on Board of Ship Amazon." Boston Public Library Quarterly, 1 (October), 119-134.
      Piere François Henry Thomas Wilson Melvill (Thomas W.), son of Melville's uncle Thomas Melvill, cited as "a perfect person to sit for Melville's portrait of Ishmael." Extracts from a whaling log of the Amazon, on which Thomas W. made his penultimate voyage. (Ships sailed by Thomas usually took a route-- across the Atlantic and round the Cape of Good Hope to the Indian and Pacific oceans--exactly that of the Pequod, a route Melville never sailed.) Melville himself is the least reliable of all sources for information on his whaling experiences; although the Melville family was financially worse off than usual in the fall of 1840 and Herman needed a job badly, there is no foundation beyond his words, as a novelist, for dressing him in the mood and character of his Ishmael. A bare month before Herman signed the ship's articles of the Acushnet, his brother Gansevoort reported to the family at home that Herman was "in good health & tolerable spirits." The first lesson taught every Melville excavator is: Suspect everything.

103   OLIVER, EGBERT S. "The Complete Stories of Herman Melville." Advance, 141 (October), 27.
      Review of 1949.B9. "Melville does not write of slavery in those Uncle Tom's Cabin days; he writes of those social factors which enslave man's spirit. He looks for the dignity of man's individual nature and the integrity of his soul as he snipes with real marksmanship at those foibles and fads and social festers which deaden man." Melville "never lost his fo'cas'le point of view. He took his firm stand with the poor, the toiling, the anxiously insecure, as against the smugness of privilege and position." His "stories will gradually become a part of our national literature."

104   WEAKS, MABEL C. "Some Ancestral Lines of Herman Melville as Traced in Funeral and Memorial Spoons." New York Genealogical and Biographical Record, 80 (October), 194-197.

The ancient custom of presenting funeral or memorial spoons to near relatives of deceased persons at their funerals or some time thereafter was observed in Melville's family until the middle of the nineteenth century. The spoons Weaks describes and reproduces "constitute a documentary pedigree in silver of Herman Melville, his ancestors, and his descendants. They prove his descent from Olof Stevense Van Cortlandt and Jeremias Van Resselaer in a line that is unbroken except for the missing spoons of Hendrick Van Rensselaer and his daughter, Anna (Van Rensselaer) Douw."

105   WEBER, WALTER. "Some Characteristic Symbols in Herman Melville's Works." English Studies [Amsterdam], 30 (October), 217-224.
    Relates symbols Melville derived from the Bible, from Greek mythology, and Egyptian history and legend to his concept of himself as "an outcast both in the natural creation and the social world," to his lifelong "titanic assault to force Heaven to deliver its secrets," to his "recognition of man's impotence and defencelessness against Fate," and to his final "heroic resignation." Melville's "one central idea" is that the whole universe is a monstrous lie. He rapturously exalts the very few men (such as Solomon, Dante, and Shakespeare) bold and sharp-sighted enough for this discovery.

106   ANON. "The Listener's Book Chronicle." Listener [London], 42 (20 October), 688.
    Review of 1948.B21. "As journals go, it has no rare virtues of style or candour or revelation, . . . but because it is Melville's journal it is a little treasure," containing indications of "the way Melville's creative imagination worked--the magnetism, for instance, that drew him to relics of Nelson, or the marked sentence in some bought book that set up a radiation later contributory to the vast explosion and efflorescence of Moby Dick."

107   ANON. "Visitor to London." London Times Literary Supplement, No. 2491 (28 October), p. 698.
    Review of 1948.B21. A "light-hearted, pleasant journal," revealing Melville's "quick and bright response to people, scenes, history, art and thoughts, before the tides of philosophic doubt had risen to billows of pessimism and phrase." Summary of the journal's contents.

108   MABBOTT, T.O. "Melville's Moby Dick." Explicator, 8 (November), item 15.
    Brief explications of short passages in chapters 3, 18, 38, 71, 79, 99, 117.

109   NICHOL, JOHN W.   "Melville's 'Soiled Fish of the Sea.'"
      American Literature, 21 (November), 338-339.
         The phrase "soiled fish of the sea" (White-Jacket, chap-
      ter 92), which Matthiessen [1941.A1, p. 392] cites (from the
      Constable standard edition) as a felicitous example of discordia
      concors, contains a misprint. The American and English first
      editions of White-Jacket print "coiled," not "soiled."

110   WILLIAMS, STANLEY T.   "Book Reviews."   American Literature, 21
      (November), 367-368.
         Review of 1948.B9. The history of the Billy Budd manu-
      scripts attains a culmination in Freeman's edition, which clari-
      fies Melville's creative process in climax and decline. There
      will probably be other professional studies of Billy Budd, but
      they must begin here, and probably cannot go much further. The
      real sanity in Freeman's achievement lies in his analysis of the
      psychological implications of the characters of Billy, Claggart,
      and Vere. His tests for psychological attitudes are judicious
      and should bring to a halt much inferential nonsense fed us
      recently about Melville himself.

111   THORP, WILLARD.   "Freudian Eyes on Melville."   New York Herald
      Tribune Book Review (6 November), p. 27.
         Review of 1949.A1. Chase's study frequently forgets
      Melville's stories because he is bemused by the fashionable
      psychoanalytic myth that every work of art is "the product of a
      mind disburdening itself of its own potential insanity." Chase
      is no such judicious applier of psychological concepts to
      Melville's work as Murray [in 1949.B14] but writes as if
      Melville's library had been well stocked with the writings of
      Freud, Rank, Fraser, Boas, and Malinowski. The distortions in
      the book can be grouped in three categories: the incessant myth-
      making; the consequent failure to recognize Melville's constant
      recourse to theological concepts and terms; and the idea
      (Chases's dominant thesis) that Melville foresaw the failure of
      American progressive liberalism and that his books, in conse-
      quence, can help to "ransom liberalism from the ruinous sell-
      outs, failures and defeats of the '30s." Yet some of Chases's
      best pages explore Melville's understanding of America, his
      knowledge and use of American folklore, and the resemblances in
      Moby-Dick between some of its characters and American folk
      heroes. There are many other valuable insights: Chase has
      probably plucked out the interior secret of "The Bell-Tower" and
      certainly demonstrated why Benjamin Franklin, John Paul Jones,
      and Ethan Allen turn up in Israel Potter.

112   BEVERLEY, GORDON.   "Herman Melville's Confidence."   [Letter
      to the Editor.] London Times Literary Supplement, No. 2493
      (11 November), p. 733.
         The Confidence-Man is not a mere panorama of fraud by
      hypocritical impostors nor an incomplete essay in misanthropy.
      Far from being unfinished, the book is "so well planned and
      complete a whole that it cannot be understood until the very
      end, when everything falls into place. It is then to be noticed

that both the first and last chapters are concerned with the Bible. The first exposes the neglect by the world of I Corinthians, 13. The last effectually shows that the spiritual wisdom of the Bible, or doubtless of I Corinthians, 13, in particular, must be read and followed in its own pure light undimmed by that of the reeking wisdom of the world. Then and then only will perfect 'confidence,' both in the Universe and in Man, be found." "Something may follow of this Masquerade," if we draw this splendid picture of true confidence in our imagination and hold it there.

113   TOMLINSON, H.M. "London As Melville Saw It." <u>John O'London's Weekly</u>, 58 (11 November), 669.
      Review of 1948.B21. Everywhere and in everything the journal betrays the acute observation of a humane man.

114   VINCENT, HOWARD P. "Two Studies of Herman Melville." New York <u>Times Book Review</u> (13 November), p. 9.
      Review of 1949.A1–2. Chase's book is a work of boldness, subtlety, and originality, which will annoy the conventional, delight the more progressive, and be of great profit to both kinds of readers. Chase's criticism of <u>Moby-Dick</u> and <u>Pierre</u> is remarkably fine; but his most useful criticism is that of Melville's minor works, particularly <u>Israel Potter</u>, <u>Redburn</u>, and the poems. Chase makes the first intelligent appraisal of <u>The Confidence-Man</u>, convincingly demonstrating, despite his errors of fact and misinterpretation of the conclusion, the artistic unity of the work, and properly describing it as the product of a great moral intelligence. Chase demonstrates that when one is dealing with a great author the mythological and symbolical approach is the most rewarding for both writer and reader. Biographically, Stone adds nothing to our knowledge, makes puzzling omissions, and is ignorant of many new facts about Melville. His criticism is generally intelligent, especially when dealing with the more familiar novels, but is neither original nor more than useful when discussing the lesser works. He would not have concluded that <u>The Confidence-Man</u> is unfinished if he had closely studied the book's structure. Stone ably unifies the findings of others; but one wishes he had caught some of Melville's boldness.

115   FIEDLER, LESLIE A. "Out of the Whale." <u>Nation</u>, 169 (19 November), 494–496.
      Review of 1949.A3 and the Grove Press edition of <u>The Confidence-Man</u>. Most critical writing about Melville's work does not measure up to his intelligence. Behind Vincent's book there lurks the same embarrassing overenthusiasm that keeps so many responses to Melville down on the soggy level of "appreciation." Vincent "is not content with the simple sniffing out of sources; he promises to show us <u>how</u> Melville transmuted the crude material he found in whaling books into great art; and this he does not do, merely placing side by side the words of the cetologists and the words of the novelist, demonstrating what we had known to begin with, that much indifferent matter is mysteriously transmuted in creating a work of art." Chase's ambitious and

sensitivity reading of The Confidence-Man [in 1949.B118] is
marred only by being basically wrong. Fiedler has always read
the book as a study of how a Christ, who came into Melville's
world, would soon discover the impossibility of persuading men to
have "confidence"--the degraded word for "faith"--in the masquerades of humility, the pale sufferer, or the oppressed Negro; and
would learn to put on the guise of a flamboyant and successful
operator to bamboozle men into belief. The Confidence Man is not
a villain: "If he can be accused of fraud at all, it is only in
his contention that trust and generosity somehow pay; that is, as
Jesus himself might be considered a fraud to the modern for whom
God is dead. Melville himself, and here is the clue to the primary ambiguity of the book, was just not sure." At any rate The
Confidence-Man in a new edition is a greater contribution to an
understanding of Melville than Vincent's book.

116   HALSBAND, ROBERT. "Belles-Lettres Notes." Saturday Review of
      Literature, 32 (19 November), 23.
           Review of 1949.A4. The book has the commendable qualities
      of being compact, systematic, and literate. Wright's analysis is
      not merely textual, for she proceeds from her evidence to discuss
      with sensitivity and acuteness the total effect of the Bible on
      Melville's romances.

117   REDMAN, BEN RAY. "New Editions." Saturday Review of Litera-
      ture, 32 (26 November), 28.
           Review of Grove Press edition of The Confidence-Man. The
      book has been too little read since its first appearance and has
      been generally underestimated by those who have read it. The
      flame of genius was still burning high, if not steadily, in The
      Confidence-Man, a philosophical extravaganza, alive with
      Melville's unique humor, eloquent with his resounding rhetoric,
      and peopled by the originals and eccentricities of a great
      satirist, a great caricaturist, whose line is as individual as
      Rowlandson's or Daumier's. The book is perhaps unfinished, but
      Melville said in it what he set out to say and succeeded as
      conspicuously as he failed in Pierre. The book need not baffle,
      and no biographical interpretation is required. It is enough to
      follow the ceaseless struggle in it between suspicion and con-
      fidence, greed and fear, to understand Melville's view of human-
      ity, circa 1856, and to delight intellectually in the manner of
      its presentation.

118   CHASE, RICHARD. "Melville's Confidence Man." Kenyon Review,
      11 (Winter), 122-140.
           Usually considered a work of chaotic pessimism, The
      Confidence-Man is "one of the subtlest of all satires on the
      American spirit, a buoyant book despite the cunning with which
      it examines the national temperament. It is, furthermore, a
      respectably complete and well-rounded book." Melville's work
      would have been less complete without The Confidence-Man, "in
      which he was able to display a mature satirical intelligence in
      a style unique among his writings for its leaness, nimbleness,
      and jaunty vigor." At the center of the complex figure of the

confidence man is the Yankee peddler; the confidence man is also
"another version of the false hero whom we often meet in
Melville's books, the Promethean-Orphean figure who seems to be
the bringer of life and civilization to his people but who is not
what he seems." The main components of the confidence man's
character are the Yankee peddler, Brother Jonathan, Uncle Sam,
Orpheus, Christ. "Taken together, they embody virtues which
would ensure the success of the American venture. . . . All this
Melville implies by attributing to the confidence man the opposite characteristics of these figures." Above all, "the significant thing about the confidence man is that he is not a man; the
perpetually shifty mask never quickens into the features of a
human being. His supreme act of confidence is his refusal to
accept the full implications and responsibilities of manhood.
That is always what horrifies Melville: the human reality which
remains masked and will not declare itself." Rather than a dis-
organized fragment, which it is often said to be, The Confidence-
Man "is carefully planned. It has the unity of any episodic
book, the unity of the pervading themes. It has the dramatic
unity of a dialectical development of ideas. It is unified by
the character of the confidence man." The Confidence-Man "is
Melville's second-best achievement. More than any of his writings, it establishes his claim to moral intelligence; it is an
intellectual act of the greatest authority and force." The confidence man "represents all that was wrong with the liberalism of
Melville's day: its commercialism, its superficiality, its
philistinism, its spurious optimism, its glad-handed self-
congratulation, its wishful vagueness, its fondness for uplifting
rhetoric, its betrayal of all tragic or exalted human and natural
values, its easy belief in automatic progress." [Preliminary
version of chapter 6 in 1949.A1.]

119   LASH, KENNETH. "Captain Ahab and King Lear." New Mexico
      Quarterly Review, 19 (Winter), 438–445.
          Similarities and differences between Ahab and Lear. Both
      were rulers, both were damned, both were driven mad by awareness,
      both were given the motive for madness in the spectacle of evil's
      outrage and conquest of good, both were spiritually great. Lear
      is the perfect Aristotelian hero; but, unlike Lear, Ahab does not
      arouse pity in us. Lear is more than man, for he has something
      of the woman in him. Ahab is more the symbol, for he has some-
      thing of the god in him. Both are the rarest of all literary
      creations--the truly original character.

120   SEALTS, MERTON M., JR. "Melville's Reading: A Check-List of
      Books Owned and Borrowed." Harvard Library Bulletin, 3
      (Winter), 119–130.
          Continuation of 1948.B65. Continued in 1949.B43.

121   CAHOON, HERBERT. "Herman Melville and W.H. Hudson." American
       Notes & Queries, 8 (December), 131-132.
              Draws attention to Hudson's discussion of "The Whitness of
       the Whale" (Moby-Dick, chapter 42) in 1893.B5 and his reference
       to the chapter in 1909.B2. Morley Roberts briefly discusses
       Hudson's enthusiasm for Moby-Dick in 1924.B14; otherwise there
       seems to be no mention of Melville in various works on Hudson,
       and Hudson is not mentioned in the basic works on Melville. His
       affinity for Moby-Dick and his sensitive disagreement with
       Melville's ideas have both gone unnoticed.

122   [HILLWAY, TYRUS]. "Billy Budd as an Opera." Melville Society
       Newsletter, 4 [5] (December), n.p.
              Charles Anderson reports attending the premiere in Venice,
       Italy, on 8 September, of an opera called Billy Budd, based on
       Melville's novel. With libretto written by Salvatore Quasimodo
       (published in Milan, 1949) and music by Giorgio Federico Ghedini,
       the opera followed Melville's text rather faithfully.

123   M[ILLER], P[ERRY]. "Short Notices." New England Quarterly,
       22 (December), 558.
              Review of 1949.B9. Leyda "has evidently worked scrupu-
       lously on the text, correcting the obvious deficiencies of The
       Piazza Tales. His introduction and notes, without displaying
       any particular insight into the meaning of the tales, provide
       the reader with all the necessary data as to dates and circum-
       stances of publication."

124   MATHEWS, J. CHESLEY. "Melville and Dante." PMLA, 64
       (December), 1238.
              Response to 1949.B45. Cites three additional passages in
       Pierre reminiscent of Dante. [See 1950.B47 for reply.]

125   SEALTS, MERTON M., JR. "A Note on the Melville Canon."
       Melville Society Newsletter, 4 [5] (December), n.p.
              "Cruelty to Seamen," an article in Yankee Doodle, 2
       (21 August 1847), 193, is reminiscent of Melville's humanitarian
       point of view on the same subject in parts of Omoo, in his
       Literary World review of Etchings of a Whaling Cruise and
       Sailor's Life and Sailor's Yarns, and in his remarks on naval
       discipline in White-Jacket. Because the article was occasioned
       by an item in the New York Herald of 8 August 1847, when Melville
       was absent from New York on honeymoon, "it seems highly unlikely
       that even a possible glimpse of the Herald in Canada, at
       Lansingburgh, or at Boston would have moved him to compose
       'Cruelty to Seamen' and dispatch it to Yankee Doodle between
       August 8 and August 21."

126   WILLIAMS, MENTOR L. "Park Benjamin on Melville's 'Mardi.'"
       American Notes & Queries, 8 (December), 132-134.
              Reprints 1849.B51, attributing it to Park Benjamin, with
       brief commentary.

127   SUTCLIFFE, DENHAM. "Melville's Symbols." Christian Science
       Monitor (1 December), p. 13.
           Review of 1949.A1. Chase's critical technique makes
       ambiguous Ahab more comprehensible, offers a new and less lauda-
       tory estimate of Billy Budd, sharpens awareness at a hundred
       points of Melville's artistry, good and bad. Yet few readers
       will have patience to follow Chase's "hunting the letter." Many
       passages are simply bewildering: Chase spins too tenuous a
       thread of speculation.

128   WADE, MASON. "Books." Commonweal, 51 (2 December), 251-252.
           Review of 1949.A1-2. In view of the ever-rising flood of
       Melville scholarship, Stone has performed a useful service by
       surveying Melville's life and work for the general reader and by
       providing an interpretation based on the latest special studies.
       An admirable introduction for those unfamiliar with the subject,
       which also offers an interpretation that specialists may find
       challenging. Chase's more specialized study is less rewarding
       for all its delvings on deeper levels. Chase strains rather
       desperately to relate Melville's problems to those of the pres-
       ent, while using Melville to belabor the old progressive-
       liberalism on which he has declared war. Though he censures the
       academic fallacy of making an artist into a would-be philosopher,
       he falls himself into the fallacy of making the artist a politi-
       cal thinker. In his primary concern with Melville's images,
       symbols, ideas and moral attitudes, Chase carries his Freudian
       hunt for hidden meanings to lengths that would have dismayed the
       most pedantic medieval commentator. The intellectual acrobatics
       are often dazzling, always relentless, but seldom rewarding, for
       the text tends to be lost in the commentary, and the intricate
       problem of Melville the man is further confused rather than
       clarified.

129   ARVIN, NEWTON. "Melville: A Catholic View." Nation, 169
       (10 December), 574.
           Review of 1949.A2. As a Catholic, Stone stands in a posi-
       tion of some intellectual detachment from Melville's work and is
       not at its mercy philosophically, as some of Melville's other
       expounders have been; he is under no compulsion to elevate Moby-
       Dick, or Pierre, or The Confidence-Man to the status of a scrip-
       ture. He properly resists the temptation to read into Melville's
       later work a bias toward Catholic theology: Melville was and
       remained to the end a heretic; as time went on a Manichean dual-
       ism became the characteristic cast of his most serious thought.
       Stone is somewhat disappointing on Moby-Dick but writes inter-
       estingly about Mardi, White-Jacket, and Pierre; his sense of
       literary distinctions as much as his intellectual detachment
       saves him from overvaluing The Confidence-Man so extremely as
       Chase has recently done. [See 1949.A1, B118.] Stone is least
       satisfactory on the poems: what he says about their imperfec-
       tions is true enough, but their positive qualities, especially
       the extraordinary novelistic qualities of Clarel, are more re-
       markable than he allows. Stone has failed to take advantage of
       some recent significant biographical discoveries and is too

little interested in the complex relations between a man's life
and his work. His book is chiefly valuable for the distance it
maintains from its subject and for the purely critical discriminations it succeeds in making.

130   MACFALL, RUSSELL. "Melville: the Biografers' 1949 Man of
      Distinction." Chicago Sunday Tribune Magazine of Books
      (25 December), p. 8.
         Review of 1949.A1-2. Melville's critical vogue is now at
fever heat in this country. Chase's study "is one which restores
balance to Melville, and in a sense to American criticism, because it is difficult to find fault with his unsparing arraign-
ment of the 'liberal' critics and their political allies,
satirized so brilliantly in Melville's 'The Confidence Man,'
which by some gift of prescience exposes the utter intellectual
and spiritual frivolity of the Henry Wallace type." Although
published in the "Great Writers of the World" series, Stone's
book contains little argument or critical enthusiasm to justify
its subject's appearance in such a series. While he is convinced
of Melville's great gifts and achievements as an artist, Stone
seems to be laboring subconsciously under a feeling that if
Melville had only been a good Catholic he would not have written
all those nasty books. He is so occupied with the metaphysics
of Melville's supposed Calvinism that he has no time or energy to
point out those heroic elements in the novels that are Melville's
claim to a place among the great novelists.

1950 A BOOKS

1   ARVIN, NEWTON. Herman Melville. New York: William Sloane
    Associates, 312 pp. Reprint. New York: The Viking Press,
    1957; Westport, Conn.: The Greenwood Press, 1973.
       Biographical and critical. Arvin stresses Melville's
emotional insecurity, neurotic anxieties, and suffering stemming from the death of his father, whom he idealized, and his
"intense and contrarious relationship" with his mother, who
"could not or would not shower upon him the affection he craved."
Arvin pays particular attention to Melville's literary affilia-
tions and style in his commentaries on the works. In his long
central chapter on Moby-Dick, "a symbolist prose romance," he
analyzes the book's four basic "movements," its style, and its
four planes of significance: the literal (which reveals
Melville's passion for actuality); the oneiric or psychological
(where Moby Dick is "the archetypal Parent"); the moral (where
Ishmael affirms "human solidarity as a priceless good"); and the
mythic (where Moby Dick is "an Animal God," a "deity that represents not transcendent purpose and conscious design but mana;
energy; power"). The works following Moby-Dick, composed during
years of sickness, psychoneurotic miseries, and psychoneurotic
fatigue, leave "an inescapable effect of anticlimax," Arvin
finds. Pierre is "four-fifths claptrap, and sickly claptrap to
boot," despite its great theme and great insights into the
psychological subterranean. After Pierre, only once, in

"Bartleby," does Melville "achieve a clear and strong perfection
of fictional form; elsewhere, only in parts of 'The Encantadas'
and a few scenes in Israel Potter does he make on us an impression of great and unencumbered power." "Benito Cereno" has been
unduly celebrated: the story is an artistic miscarriage, with
moments of undeniable power. The Confidence-Man is not a great
allegorical satire because it is not a living narrative. From
Battle-Pieces to Weeds and Wildings "one follows the progress of
a great redintegration" in Melville, "a great though never a
perfect recovery of wholeness and well-being." Indexed. Reviewed in 1950.B41, B59, B67-69, B71-72, B77-78, B84, B91-92,
B96-97, B103, B105, B120; 1951.B27, B36, B42, B46, B54, B103.

2   HILLWAY, TYRUS. Melville and the Whale. Stonington, Conn.:
     Stonington Publishing Co., 12 pp. Reprint. Folcroft, Pa.:
     Folcroft Library Editions, 1971.
         Melville's use of his whaling sources [cf. 1949.A3]. While
Melville makes a great pretense at weighing pros and cons regarding certain disputed matters in relation to the whale, he usually
resolves these points through the use of data provided by Beale
or one of his other sources. Sometimes, however, he appears to
exercise some independence of judgment, as in his conclusion that
the whale has dual vision (a conclusion verified by recent research). One of Melville's inaccuracies is his exaggeration of
the sperm whale's dimensions. He appears to have used skeletal
dimensions in Beale and increased them by nearly 50 percent.
Influenced by Beale and perhaps by the vividness of his own
memories, Melville believed the sperm whale to be the largest of
living creatures, whereas now that distinction would be given to
the blue whale, a virtual stranger to naturalists of the mid-
nineteenth century. But to Beale, whose book on the sperm whale
still remains one of the best extant authorities, Melville was
indebted for the accuracy of most of his information on cetology.

3   PERCIVAL, M.O. A Reading of MOBY-DICK. Chicago: The Univer-
     sity of Chicago Press, 136 pp. Reprint. New York: Octagon
     Books, 1967.
         Running commentary on Moby-Dick, in which Ahab is likened
to the Kierkegaardian sufferer, who, feeling himself singled out
"to be the sport and jest of some malevolent deity," experiences
first despair and ultimately becomes either demonic or religious.
Moby Dick represents "the paradox of good and evil being ultimately one." Ishmael can accept this paradox and has a minimum
of faith "that good is somehow more real than evil" and so is
saved; while Ahab, for whom good and evil are in violent opposition, sees only evil in the whale, becomes demonic, and is
destroyed. Reviewed in 1950.B83, B91, B99, B119; 1951.B29, B74.

4   POMMER, HENRY F. Milton and Melville. Pittsburgh: Univer-
     sity of Pittsburgh Press, 172 pp. Reprint. New York: Cooper
     Square Publishers, 1970.
         After a brief survey of Milton's popularity among Ameri-
cans, including Melville's family, during the first half of the
nineteenth century, Pommer examines Melville's affinities with

Milton. Melville, he believes, would have enjoyed Milton's
attacks on priestcraft. Both men held a creed of individualism
and toleration; both had a minute knowledge of the Bible; both
were concerned with the freedom of the will and with the origins,
workings, and powers of evil; both were concerned with the common
man; and both recognized that "to produce a mighty book, you must
choose a mighty theme." Pommer next examines Melville's use of
Milton's life, prose, and minor poems, finding that his "knowledge of Milton provided one method by which he could shift from a
less richly to a more richly connotative style." Subsequent
chapters trace Milton's influence on Melville's vocabulary and
sentence structure; the poetic and epic influences of Paradise
Lost on Moby-Dick; Melville's use of persons and places from
Paradise Lost in prose works, Battle-Pieces, and Clarel; and the
influence of Milton's Satan on Melville, particularly in his
portrayal of Jackson (in Redburn), Ahab (in Moby-Dick), and
Claggart (in Billy Budd). Indexed. Reviewed in 1951.B64, B96,
B108.

1950 B SHORTER WRITINGS

1   ALTICK, RICHARD D. The Scholar Adventurers. New York: The
    Macmillan Co., p. 247.
        Discusses a passage in Hawthorne's notebook entry for
    1 August 1851 inked out by his wife and restored by use of infra-
    red light: "and if truth must be told, we smoked cigars even
    within the sacred precincts of the sitting room." Biographers
    have always assumed that the relations between Melville and
    Hawthorne were rather stiff. They "might have talked loftily and
    long of time and eternity, but the evidence hitherto available
    has not suggested that they were on easy personal terms. The
    fact that they dared to smoke their cigars in Mrs. Hawthorne's
    holy of holies, however, throws a new light on their relation-
    ship. They may have been philosophical conversationalists, but
    it is a closer bond that unites partners in domestic crime."

2   A[NDERSON], C[HARLES] R. "Melville, Herman," in Collier's
    Encyclopedia. New York: P.F. Collier & Son, pp. 380–381.
        Biographical and critical sketch. The early eclipse of
    Melville's brilliantly promising career has usually been ex-
    plained as the result of his disgust with a public that preferred
    his lighter work to his more serious efforts, or as the result of
    the more practical disappointment he felt as his income decreased.
    "But Melville was also handicapped by his failure to develop a
    theory of the craft of fiction adequate to sustain him when he
    was floundering in problems of form. He was limited, too, by the
    lack of a creative imagination sufficient to extend his expe-
    rience of life beyond the record of his own adventures and the
    stimulus of his reading, material that he had well-nigh exhausted
    with his first six books."

3   ANON.   "Melville, Herman," in The Columbia Encyclopedia.
      2d ed.   Ed. William Bridgwater and Elizabeth J. Sherwood.
      Morningside Heights, N.Y.: Columbia University Press,
      pp. 1257-1258.
          New entry [see 1935.B1]; more detailed biographical sketch.
      Puzzled by the symbolism and bitterness in Moby-Dick, Melville's
      readers ignored the ambiguous Pierre.   Clarel and Billy Budd re-
      flect the serenity of Melville's later life.

4   AUDEN, W.H.   The Enchafèd Flood: or The Romantic Iconography
      of the Sea.   New York: Random House, pp. 93-154, passim.
      Reprint.   Charlottesville: The University Press of Virginia,
      1979.
          An "attempt to understand the nature of Romanticism through
      an examination of its treatment of a single theme, the sea."
      Moby-Dick is used to illustrate romantic images of the sea and
      the desert, the oasis-island, and the "mechanized desert"; the
      "polemical situation of romanticism," romantic aesthetic theory,
      and the romantic use of symbols.   Moby-Dick and Billy Budd are
      discussed in relation to four types of hero Auden distinguishes:
      the aesthetic, the ethical, the religious, and the romantic.
      Reviewed in 1950.B55-58, B81, B86, B100; 1951.B34, B39, B53.
      Reprinted in part in Vincent (1969), pp. 146-151.

5   BLUNDEN, EDMUND.   "Herman Melville," in Chaucer to "B.V." With
      an Additional Paper on Herman Melville.   Tokyo: Kenkyusha,
      pp. 249-261.
          Biographical sketch and brief commentary on Moby-Dick.
      "Even now, when American writing is so multifarious and so
      capricious, the highest and best track that it takes is Mel-
      villian.   The immense view and the unifying isolated idea are
      still likely to be attempted in prose or verse by American
      authors.   The power is there, the accumulative and the self-
      devoting power which must be working if a 'Moby Dick' is to be
      envisaged and written at all.   No doubt there are false shows of
      energy too, as there are in the theatre or in the political or
      commercial world; but on the whole we shall grant that it is in
      America that new writers arise with tremendous general strength
      and range.   The trouble now may be what Melville did not feel or
      need to fear,--an insufficient metaphysical awareness."

6   BROWN, E.K.   Rhythm in the Novel.   Toronto: University of
      Toronto Press, p. 52.
          Cites the white whale and coffins in Moby-Dick as examples
      of the expanding symbol, a device "for rendering an emotion, an
      idea, that by its largeness or its subtlety cannot become wholly
      explicit.   The fixed symbol is almost entirely repetition; the
      expanding symbol is repetition balanced by variation, and that
      variation is in progressively deepening disclosure."

7   CHARVAT, WILLIAM. "Literary Economics and Literary History,"
    in English Institute Essays 1949. Ed. Alan S. Downer. New
    York: Columbia University Press, pp. 73-91.
       The effect of economic pressures on art forms and writers,
    including Melville. The superb balance of physical and imagina-
    tive adventure in Moby-Dick is partly traceable to the contempo-
    rary reader's preferring Typee and Omoo to Mardi. The nineteenth-
    century American artist was sometimes at his best when creative
    and social pressures were in equilibrium: it was the artist in
    balance with society who produced Tales of the Grotesque and
    Arabesque, English Traits, and Moby-Dick.

8   CHASE, RICHARD. "Introduction," in Selected Tales and Poems
    by Herman Melville. Ed. Richard Chase. New York: Holt,
    Rinehart and Winston, pp. v-xix.
       Relates "Benito Cereno," "Bartleby," "Jimmy Rose," and "The
    Fiddler" to Melville's personal circumstances in the 1850s.
    Melville's "tales give the impression that the author is often
    drawing upon personal experience and stating personal problems,
    that, in one way or another, he is seeking to establish fictional
    representations of himself, of the differing sides of his own
    temperament, of the personal situation in which he finds himself."
    One of Melville's greatest characters, the confidence man, appears
    in "The Lightning-Rod Man" in the guise of the salesman, while
    the narrator's wife in "I and My Chimney" is similarly possessed
    of the spirit of confidence. "The Paradise of Bachelors and the
    Tartarus of Maids" displays Melville's concern with sexual prob-
    lems, in particular with the mechanical quality of sexual expe-
    rience, which "must somehow be leavened or humanized by the
    humane ease, creative humor, and grace which are known to the
    bachelor existence," while "the bachelor life is incomplete with-
    out a knowledge of the inescapable suffering of sexual expe-
    rience." In "The Bell-Tower" Melville "is speaking of the
    emasculation of man, and perhaps of man's culture, which man
    imposes upon himself when he exchanges Prometheus for a machine--
    when . . . he reduces the creative magnitude and eventfulness of
    human experience to the narrow and rigid form of techniques."
    "The Encantadas" sketches continually return to a single ques-
    tion: "at how low a level, in point of vitality, can existence
    still go on?" In Billy Budd Melville "is saying that the 'hor-
    rible vulturism' of the world, of which he had written in Moby
    Dick, is a basic principle of things. Society, law, adulthood,
    worldly accomplishment can sustain themselves only by feeding on
    youthful innocence and generosity." Neither "nature nor society
    is totally destructive of what is admirable in human life. By
    some genial, liberating grace, innocence and beauty are empowered
    to renew themselves in the very teeth of destruction. And so we
    are enabled to feel that Billy Budd, though not quite successful
    as tragic drama [Billy is not quite adequately conceived, in some
    ways strikes us as not quite believable] remains immensely moving
    as a drama of pathos and myth. In this respect, its kinship is
    with the late plays of Shakespeare and with the New Testament, in
    its affirmation that out of the death inflicted by nature and
    society there issues new life." Melville's poetic art is seldom

flawless, though it is nearly so in a few pieces like "The Portent," "The Maldive Shark," and "Shiloh." Yet Melville is a far greater poet than Longfellow (though inferior in the superficial techniques of richness of his mind and the energy and forthrightness of his verse. A profound mind is at work in these poems, and a mind in vigorous motion. This can be said of only one other American poet of the time, Emily Dickinson."

9   DRUMMOND, ANDREW L. The Churches in English Fiction: A Literary and Historical Study, From the Regency to the Present Time, of British and American Fiction. Leicester: Edgar Backus, p. 310.
       Cites Father Mapple as an unconventional Methodist Evangelist, modeled on "Father" Taylor of New Bedford; Mapple's sermon is "the most wonderful sermon on Jonah ever delivered."

10   FADIMAN, CLIFTON. "Introduction," in Moby-Dick. Harper's Modern Classics. New York: Harper and Brothers, pp. iii–xii.
       Expanded, revised version of 1943.B24; adds biographical sketch. [See also 1955.B7.]

11   GIBBINGS, ROBERT. "Introduction," in Typee. London: The Folio Society, n.p.
       Much of Melville's account of life in the Marquesas was accurate, although at times he misinterpreted and embroidered. One aspect of life in the Typee valley he failed to understand was the amount of work performed in such a society.

12   HART, JAMES D. The Popular Book: A History of America's Literary Taste. New York: Oxford University Press, pp. 91–92, 98.
       Notes that a book like Moby-Dick inevitably would not have a wide public during the "feminine fifties," and "though four editions of Typee were sold in three years, the women over a long period required fifty pirated editions of the Reveries of a Bachelor, in addition to the million copies sold by the authorized publisher."

13   HOLDER, GLENN. "To the Reader," in Moby Dick, adapted by Glenn Holder. Ed. Erwin H. Schubert. New York: Globe Book Co., pp. v–viii.
       To enable the secondary school reader "to grasp more easily the story and its lesson in living," the adapter "has trimmed out or simplified the more difficult parts, simplified the vocabulary, sentence structure, and punctuation, and added footnotes, which deal principally with terms used in connection with the sea and whaling."

14   HOWARD, LEON. "Americanization of the European Heritage," in
      The American Writer and the European Tradition. Ed. Margaret
      Denny and William H. Gilman. Minneapolis: University of
      Minnesota Press, pp. 78-89.
         Sees the attempt to take European literary material and
      test it by the tenor of their own lives--to change it into some-
      thing that made sense in terms of their own experience--as the
      distinctive American characteristic, which can be found in such
      writers as Emerson, Thoreau, Hawthorne, Melville, Poe, and Whit-
      man. As Melville "grew in mind and in knowledge and as the range
      of his intellectual theorizing increased, he became involved in a
      conflict between the romantic will to believe and the realistic
      demand to be shown. It was this conflict--actually between a
      heritage of European philosophy and a characteristically American
      attitude of mind--that moved him to his most powerful expression
      in prose" (Moby-Dick).

15   HOWARD, LEON. "Introduction," in Moby Dick. New York: The
      Modern Library, pp. v-xvi.
         Account of Melville's life and the "two ways" to read Moby-
      Dick intensively. "One is to consider it as an extraordinary
      example of literary art and examine the success with which its
      author has blended its incongruous elements into a unified
      whole." The other "is to consider it as the expression of an
      alert, vigorous, and well-informed mind which was peculiarly
      sensitive to the major intellectual problems of its own time."

16   LAWSON, JOHN HOWARD. "The Hidden Heritage: A Rediscovery of
      the Ideas and Forces That Link the Thought of Our Time with
      the Culture of the Past. New York: The Citadel Press,
      pp. 427-431.
         Melville's "tragedy is the perennial tragedy of the intel-
      lectual: unable to achieve an integrated life devoted to rational
      social aims, he decided that social integration is neither possi-
      ble nor desirable. But his despair made him a victim of the power
      he hated. The society that called him back from his wanderings to
      earn his bread in bitterness wanted to enslave the mind as well
      as the body." "Benito Cereno" exhibits the tragic decline of his
      talent: "the tragedy is all the more poignant because the author
      is unconscious of the servitude to which he has submitted. . . .
      Melville changed Delano's tale in order to make it more effec-
      tive--as propaganda for slavery." Mumford's high estimate of the
      story [in 1929.A1] typifies "the disregard of social issues and
      the special callousness toward Negro slavery which characterizes
      American criticism." From an aesthetic point of view, "the story
      is cheap melodrama, a distortion of human and moral values; few
      heroes in literature are as absurd as the delicate Don Benito."

17   LEISY, ERNEST E. The American Historical Novel. Norman:
      University of Oklahoma Press, p. 96.
         Brief synopsis of Israel Potter. "The story has possibil-
      ities, as shown in Israel's meeting the King and in the interlude
      with Franklin, but Melville seems not to have been in a mood to
      develop them."

18 LEVIN, HARRY. "Some European Views of Contemporary American Literature," in The American Writer and the European Tradition. Ed. Margaret Denny and William H. Gilman. Minneapolis: University of Minnesota Press, pp. 169, 178, 183.
Brief references to Melville. America is "strengthened by a hybrid strain, the cross-fertilization of many different cultures. What is commonly regarded as peculiarly American is blatant and standardized: Ford, Luce, Metro-Goldwyn-Mayer. What is most original is most traditional: Melville."

19 MILLETT, FRED B. Reading Fiction: A Method of Analysis with Selections for Study. New York: Harper & Brothers, pp. 24–25, 29–30, 52–53.
Moby-Dick used to illustrate aspects of point of view, plot, and characterization in fiction.

20 MILLS, GORDON H. "The Castaway in Moby-Dick." Studies in English, 29, 231–248.
Pip's role in arousing Ahab's "humanities" and in Ahab's failure to achieve catharsis. Cowper's "The Castaway" considered as a possible influence.

21 PAUL, SHERMAN. "Introduction," in Moby-Dick. Everyman's Library. New York: E.P. Dutton and Co.; London: J.M. Dent and Sons, pp. vii–xvi.
Biographical and critical. Develops contrasts between Ishmael and Ahab. Submission and endurance are the lesson Ishmael learned by pursuing the white whale. Unrepentant Ahab "is not reborn from the belly of the whale, but Ishmael, purged of his own destructive forces by Ahab's death, is reburn to the possibility of belief." Moby-Dick is "an attempt to give the turmoils of its author a cosmic and universal validity," a myth of the self and the world, the self searching for "the peace of understanding, for self-hood and self-possession."

22 ROUTH, H.V. "The Nineteenth Century and After." The Years Work in English Studies, 1948, 29 (1950), 261.
Freemen [1948.B9] claims that Billy Budd is a second White-Jacket and the culmination of the art, emotion, and thought so vividly developed in Moby-Dick. The reader may not agree.

23 SCHUBERT, ERWIN H. "To the Teacher," in Moby Dick, adapted by Glenn Holder. Ed. Erwin H. Schubert. New York: Globe Book Co., pp. ix–x.
"Like many of the other great novels of the world, Moby Dick became an outlet for the author who poured into it vituperative venom conditioned by his personal life. Perhaps this shadowy symbolism lends to the greatness of the novel; however, the interpretation of this highly subjective part of Moby Dick is for literary critics and research scholars. Consequently, an adaptation of this work for the American reader became a necessity." The Holder adaptation "retains all the story and the qualities that style the Melville masterpiece. Some of the symbolism of Melville has been kept; the terror and the ominous

forebodings of doom have been retained; but the greatest whaling-sea story in the world has been graphically delineated in language modern American can comprehend. . . . The vocabulary in this school edition is such that students of the seventh grade and beyond can understand; always the student has been kept in mind. However, none of the elements that make the story of Ahab's search for revenge on the greatest living creature in the world the great book that Herman Melville's Moby Dick is, has been sacrificed."

24   SMITH, HENRY NASH. Virgin Land: The American West as Symbol and Myth. Cambridge, Mass.: Harvard University Press, pp. 76–80, 208–210.
       To Melville the Wild West, like nature in general, came to seem in the highest degree ambiguous, as we see in "The Whiteness of the Whale," chapter 42 of Moby-Dick. Ungar, in Clarel, expresses many of the ideas of Dew and Fitzhugh.

25   THARP, LOUISE HALL. The Peabody Sisters of Salem. Boston: Little, Brown and Co., pp. 196–197.
       Melville's visits to the Hawthornes in the spring of 1851. "In Melville, Hawthorne found the first friend of his own trade who was really congenial."

26   THORP, WILLARD. "American Writers as Critics of Nineteenth-Century Society," in The American Writer and the European Tradition. Ed. Margaret Denny and William H. Gilman. Minneapolis: University of Minnesota Press, pp. 100–103.
       Brief survey of Melville's social thought from Typee to Billy Budd. Except for Whitman, Melville was the most ardent democrat of the writers of the midcentury. He was wary of patrician Democrats like Cooper who believed that leadership should be in the hands of the natural aristocracy, by virtue of their education and desire to serve the state. Yet almost from the beginning Melville entertained doubts about equalitarianism, which Whitman experienced twenty years later in Democratic Vistas; for all his reverence before the godliness in man, he recognized the depravity in human beings and the consequent fallibility of an extreme democracy. In The Confidence-Man, where the mutual trust that holds a society together has turned to greed and suspicion, Melville reached the low point in his thinking about society. In Billy Budd he "struck a balance and found the point at which he could come to rest." There he is saying "that the society we live in is and always will be a world at war. There must be discipline and order to hold off the enemy from without and hold down the enemy within. Occasionally all that is fine and innocent . . . will suffer injustice under the discipline which keeps the ship in fighting trim. But man never forgets the myth of his lost innocence or his intuitions of the higher justice of which it is a part. There can be no order without sacrifice, but the sacrifice haunts the imaginations of men so that they perpetually remember how costly in human life is the stability of society."

27　TOMLINSON, H.M. <u>The Face of the Earth, with Some Hints for</u>
<u>Those About to Travel</u>. Indianapolis: The Bobbs-Merrill Co.,
pp. 114-118.
Reprints 1926.B13.

28　TRILLING, LIONEL. "Contemporary American Literature in Its
Relation to Ideas," in <u>The American Writer and the European</u>
<u>Tradition</u>. Ed. Margaret Denny and William H. Gilman.
Minneapolis: University of Minnesota Press, p. 150.
　　Notes that the men of the great period of American literature in the nineteenth century were not religious men, citing
Hawthorne and Melville as examples. They lived at a time when
religion was in decline and they were not drawn to support it;
but from religion they inherited a body of pieties and issues
"which engaged their hearts and their minds to the very bottom."

29　WILEY, LULU RUMSEY. <u>The Sources and Influence of the Novels</u>
<u>of Charles Brockden Brown</u>. New York: Vantage Press,
pp. 239-243.
　　Claims that Brown's novels influenced <u>Redburn</u> and <u>Pierre</u>.

30　WILLIAMS, STANLEY T. "Cosmopolitanism in American Literature
Before 1880," in <u>The American Writer and the European Tradi-</u>
<u>tion</u>. Ed. Margaret Denny and William H. Gilman. Minneapolis:
University of Minnesota Press, p. 53.
　　Sees books 17 and 18 of <u>Pierre</u> as a memorable picture of
the artist's plight in America and as part of a recurrent theme
among American writers--that for the artist America was impossible.

31　WILSON, CARROLL A. "Herman Melville, 1819-1891," in <u>Thirteen</u>
<u>Author Collections of the Nineteenth Century and Five Cen-</u>
<u>turies of Familiar Quotations</u>. Vol. 1. Ed. Jean C.S. Wilson
and David A. Randall. New York: privately printed for Charles
Scribner's Sons, pp. 307-316.
　　Describes Melville items in Wilson's collection: first
editions and association copies, including a copy of <u>White-Jacket</u>
with pencilled notes by Harrison Robertson, Melville's shipmate
on the <u>United States</u>; a manuscript draft of the <u>Omoo</u> "Round
Robin"; a manuscript draft of the poem "Camoens (Before)"; four
letters by Melville, to Richard Bentley, 20 July 1851 [<u>Letters</u>,
pp. 133-135], to William H. Barry, 12 February 1859 [<u>Letters</u>,
p. 194], to G.W. Curtis, 15 September 1857 [<u>Letters</u>, pp. 188-189],
and to Havelock Ellis, 10 August 1890 [<u>Letters</u>, p. 296]; and two
books from Melville's library, <u>Old Wine in New Bottles</u> by
Augustus Kinsley Garner, M.D., and <u>Poems</u> [7th edition] by
Emerson.

32　WILSON, EDMUND. <u>Classics and Commercials: A Literary Chron-</u>
<u>icle of the Forties</u>. New York: Farrar, Strauss and Co.,
pp. 175-176, 216, 229, 423-430.
Reprints 1944.B23, B25, B28, 1947.B72.

33   ALLMON, CHARLES. "Shores and Sails in the South Seas."
      National Geographic Magazine, 97 (January), 80, 91, 93, 97,
      104.
           Brief references to Typee in account of visit to the Typee
      valley. Photographs.

34   DAUNER, LOUISE. "The 'Case' of Tobias Pearson: Hawthorne and
      the Ambiguities." American Literature, 21 (January), 464-472.
           Finds similar irony and ambiguity in "The Gentle Boy" and
      Pierre. "Like Pierre, Tobias acts according to a simplest Chris-
      tian ethic, in an impulse of pure generosity and loving-kindness.
      And like Pierre, the very pillars of the Christian temple,
      ironically symbolized here by the persecuting Puritans, shatter
      about him and crush him in the ruins."

35   KAPLAN, SIDNEY. "'Omoo': Melville's and Boucicault's."
      American Notes and Queries, 8 (January), 150-151.
           Except for the similarity of titles, there seems to be
      little or no connection between Melville's Omoo and D.D.
      Boucicault's play Omoo; or The Sea of Ice (1864).

36   KAZIN, ALFRED. "On Melville as Scripture." Partisan Review,
      17 (January), 67-75.
           Review of 1949.A1. Of all the recent studies of Melville,
      the most brilliant and the most frustrating. "For while it is
      most clearly, and passionately, concerned with the moral signifi-
      cance of Melville's symbolism, and is surely the most affirmative
      statement ever made of Melville's distinction as a thinker, its
      conception of his art is static and even provincial." There are
      moving insights and a power of hauntingly exact definition; but
      Chase's subsidiary aim--to present Melville as a supreme example,
      or moral imagination, for the "New Liberalism"--is baffling. His
      critical method, especially on the works after Moby-Dick, seems
      astonishingly immature and full of the most reckless guesses and
      assumptions. Chase's personifications (The True Prometheus, The
      Handsome Sailor, etc.) "are applied with such finality to the
      American scene, move so autonomously across Melville's works, and
      are obviously so much more stimulating" to Chase's mind "than the
      concrete artistic experiences from which they have been taken,
      that Melville as man and practicing artist gets lost from sight."
      Strictures on the New Liberalism and the New Liberal, on the
      approach to literature through myth and folklore, and on readings
      and judgments by Chase. Reprinted in 1955.B16.

37   THORP, WILLARD. "Book Reviews." American Literature, 21
      (January), 508-509.
           Review of 1949.B14. Whatever objections one may have to
      some of Murray's hypotheses, we have at last a theory of the book
      that reconciles its many discordant elements. Few works by
      American writers have been so admirably edited. One of the
      excellencies of Murray's introduction is his demonstration of the
      way in which Melville, not by prescience, but out of his reading
      and experience, could create a hero who is evidently a psychia-
      trist's delight.

38   G[ARRISON], W.E. "Books." Christian Century, 67 (11 January), 51.
     Review of 1949.A1. Chase's study is the most complete and the best that has come to this reviewer's attention. If the note Melville sounded was a corrective for the overoptimism of his time, it may be no less a corrective for the pessimism that characterizes many of the writers and thinkers of ours.

39   DOUGHTY, HOWARD, JR. "Melville--a Fresh Reading." Nation, 170 (28 January), 90.
     Review of 1949.A1. As a critic, Chase "is largely concerned with shaping Melville to a preconceived pattern of what he considers to be psychically beneficial for us in our present crisis of spirit. To the unregenerate reader at least, the relevance of this scheme to what Melville actually wrote seems at times far-fetched indeed." It leads Chase "to expurgate--for the supposed good of our souls--much that is imaginatively effective in Melville, while minor aspects of his work are given an emphasis out of all proportion to their real value." Yet Chase's method yields points of genuine critical interest. His reading of Melville in the light of the search of the son for the father--certainly one of Melville's central themes--deepens our sense of the psychic tensions and stresses from which the work sprang and gives an impressively coherent import to the complex of symbols through which this inner drama projected itself as literature. Chase also develops interestingly Rourke's hints on Melville's use of American folklore. [See 1931.B19.] For all its overelaborate apparatus and its weird distortions of emphasis, the book communicates to some degree the excitement, legitimate or illegitimate, of D.H. Lawrence's pioneering act of intuition. [See 1923.B3-4.]

40   APPLEGATE, JAMES. "Brief Mention." Modern Language Notes, 65 (February), 143.
     Review of 1948.B24. "The specialist will find Professor Oliver's critical notes not full enough for definitive annotation, and the general reader will find many entries unnecessarily detailed and peripheral. Yet both will find brought together much interesting material that is otherwise scattered in journals, as well as useful and satisfactorily thorough amplification of the personal, local, and literary allusions in the stories." Oliver makes helpful suggestions toward interpretation, but it is regrettable that he did not do so in less fragmentary fashion by means of brief critical essays.

41   HART, H.W. "New Books Appraised." Library Journal, 75 (15 February), 313.
     Review of 1950.A1. For the serious reader, a balanced and acute work of literary criticism, and a valuable addition to the Melville bibliography.

42   ANDERSON, CHARLES. "Melville Portraits." <u>Hopkins Review</u>, 3
      (Spring), 37-39.
         Review of 1949.A1-2. Stone's is a modest book that makes
no pretensions to being a scholarly contribution to knowledge.
Stone has made rather full use of the large body of recent research and criticism, and though the special student will find
nothing here that is new, the beginner will find it a convenient
handbook or introduction to further study. Stone's lack of any
discernable critical principles makes it impossible to classify
his treatment of Melville's works as criticism. It must rather
be described as commentary, sensible enough on the whole but un-
distinguished. Chase's study "is the most fascinating of all the
books that have been written about Melville, but not the most
convincing; boldly original in its approach, but doctrinaire and
somewhat erratic in its execution; widely informed in mythology,
but inadequately informed in most other fields--notably in American literature and history." Though few readers will be convinced by it in extenso, it is full of suggestive illumination
for the student interested in Melville's hidden meanings. It is
also a rich book, opening out on many levels. Its examination
of American folklore ingredients in <u>Moby-Dick</u> is especially convincing. One "can only wish that in these less tenuous matters
the author's knowledge had been profounder so that his explication could have carried the elaboration and conviction of sound
scholarship." In spite of these reservations, one can conclude
that Chase has given us a brilliant and provocative book on
Melville.

43   ARVIN, NEWTON. "Melville's <u>Mardi</u>." <u>American Quarterly</u>, 2
      (Spring), 71-81.
         Discusses the "familiar literary modes" influencing the
"several manners" in which Melville wrote in <u>Mardi</u>; the partial
feeling of Polynesian legend and myth with which the narrative
is invested; the book's four inadequately integrated "centers,"
emotional, intellectual, social, and political; the relation of
the quest for Yillah to Melville's sexual guilt and anxiety; and
Melville's reconciliation of political and social pessimism with
democratic humanism. Incorporated in chapter 3 of 1950.A1.

44   GLIXON, NIEL. "Figure, Carpet, and Whole Cloth." <u>Kenyon
      Review</u>, 12 (Spring), 349-352.
         Review of 1949.A1. The first two chapters constitute one
of the few masterly and original critiques of American literature
we have had. That the principal figures, themes, and symbols
Chase describes, and the values he assigns them, are really in
Melville's work seems undeniable. "Most of us have needed the
aid rendered by a Melville study of exactly this type, combining
a penetrating knowledge of myth with literary acuity and moral
insistence. And in the study of <u>Moby-Dick</u> Chase has shown in
unprecedented fashion how far American folklore determined
Melville's characters and diction." Nevertheless, the book has
serious limitations. Chase fanatically applies his leading
themes to book after book; he superbly elucidates ancillary matters and consistently muffs the central points; and errors result

from his need to see Melville as a mirror of Chase. Chase "is
still a little gooey with Freudianism" and still a little
embarrassed by religious ideas. But these are limitations to
the best book on Melville we have, and one of the best books on
American culture.

45　　HALL, JAMES B. "Moby Dick: Parable of a Dying System."
　　　Western Review, 14 (Spring), 223–226.
　　　　　Moby-Dick as industrial saga, the Pequod as archetype of
capitalistic enterprise. The book illustrates the disintegrative
effects of the whaling machine on men. "The death of the Pequod
is the ultimate destiny of a culture which holds values that are
contradictory to human welfare." This "level of meaning . . . is
a real preoccupation with the future of America, the future of a
people involved in exploitation of raw materials and a constantly
expanding frontier, and the future of Men, generally, who live by
such assumptions."

46　　FOSTER, RICHARD. "Moby Dick: Symbol and Tragedy." Yeoman
　　　[Oberlin College] (March), 20–22.
　　　　　The truth or meaning of Moby-Dick "transcends any abstract
ideological statement and finds its real existence in the problems and passions of the characters themselves, and in the echoes
of the reader's own life experience as they are generated by the
story's impact."

47　　GIOVANNINI, G. "Melville and Dante." PMLA, 65 (March), 329.
　　　　　Reply to 1949.B124. The references to Dante that Mathews
cites appear in Giovannini's notes in 1949.B45. Another striking
parallel between Pierre and the Inferno is noted by Murray
(p. 489) in 1949.B14.

48　　HAMALIAN, LEO. "Melville's Art." Explicator, 8 (March),
　　　item 40.
　　　　　Explication of the poem "Art." Melville "defines art as
the response to the challenge to create; the artist creates the
challenge by his struggle to synthesize certain antithetical
forces."

49　　[HILLWAY, TYRUS]. "Melville's First Whaling Voyage?"
　　　Melville Society Newsletter, 6 (March), n.p.
　　　　　The New York Herald-Tribune and other newspapers report
Samuel T. Sukel's recent discovery of an essay on whaling written
by "a sturdy but well-educated young man of Massachusetts who had
been on a whaling voyage," in a young people's magazine of 1835,
the essay containing cetological information and figures of
speech strongly resembling passages in Moby-Dick and not found,
Sukel believes, in any of Melville's known sources. Hillway is
skeptical of Sukel's theory that Melville undertook a whaling
voyage at the age of twelve and wrote the essay for the magazine,
later using some of the same materials in Moby-Dick, because
Melville was not a "young man of Massachusetts" but a New Yorker;
the facts of his life are sufficiently well known to make such

an early whaling voyage improbable; all the literary and scientific sources of Moby-Dick have not necessarily been identified;
and the essay itself may have been one of Melville's sources.

50   VINCENT, HOWARD P. "Book Reviews." New England Quarterly, 23
     (March), 109-112.
          Review of 1949.A1, A4. Summarizes Wright's findings and
     approves of her judgments--an important subject has been well
     handled. The brilliance of Chase's book is its most obvious
     characteristic; the book proliferates with aperçus. What Chase
     says about the greater and better-known works is exciting and
     useful; he is even better on the short stories and sketches, for
     there he has attacked problems that most critics have neglected.
     Stories like "The Bell-Tower" and "The Lightning-Rod Man" fall
     into place at last into a coherent and intelligible pattern of
     Melville's developing art and mind. Even in his wrongness Chase
     is excellent, for what he says provokes one to exploration; he
     attempts so much that he often fails, but his failures are fine
     ones.

51   WAGENKNECHT, EDWARD. "Our Contemporary, Herman Melville."
     College English, 11 (March), 301-308.
          General commentary on most of the major works. "Contempo-
     rary study of Melville has . . . been greatly handicapped by lack
     of adequate biographical materials and at times by an equal lack
     of good judgment. It is time to state frankly that the reckless
     guesswork in which certain writers . . . have indulged concerning
     such matters as the character of Melville's parents and the
     writer's own friendship with Hawthorne come perilously close to
     criminal libel." Disillusioned moderns have often used Melville
     as a vehicle for the expression of their own disappointment in
     life. Readers of Melville's critics should always distinguish
     between criticism and autobiography. Expanded in 1952.B28.

52   WILLIAMS, MENTOR L. "Two Hawaiian-Americans Visit Herman
     Melville." New England Quarterly, 23 (March), 97-99.
          Account of visit to Melville by Titus M. Coan and John
     Thomas Gulick, 20 April 1859, with quotation from Gulick's
     journal.

53   ANON. "Hall of Fame Gets List." New York Times (2 March).
          Announces Melville's nomination to Hall of Fame.

54   MANSFIELD, LUTHER S. "Reviews." Modern Language Notes, 65
     (April), 285-286.
          Review of 1948.B21. "Melville let no image, no hint of
     drama or philosophical thought escape. Places, pictures, build-
     ings visited as a tourist, merely listed here, often serve as
     extended metaphors in Moby-Dick and other works--the Thames
     Tunnel, Nelson's Victory, the Hotel de Cluny, Ehrenbreitstein.
     Thus the Journal gives hints of Melville's creative processes.
     Many of the brief portraits . . . are brilliant and revealing of
     both the subject and the observer." In admirably chosen excerpts
     from Melville's letters, stories, and novels, Metcalf gives just

enough bait to lure readers into speculation about why Melville went where he did, met the people he did, and what literary use he made of his experiences.

55   GRAY, JAMES. "Age of Misgiving." <u>Saturday Review of Literature</u>, 33 (15 April), 40–42.

     Review of 1950.B4. Auden's performance is enormously stimulating to follow, but still not quite a satisfying way of coming at critical attitudes on the printed page. "The helterskelter rounding-up of such spirits as Wordsworth and Freud, Blake and Baudelaire makes a fine, rousing clamor in the seminar, but even when doom and blank misgiving are its themes criticism should not take quite so whimsical a way toward its goal."

56   WILSON, EDMUND. "Books." <u>New Yorker</u>, 26 (15 April), 106, 109.

     Review of 1950.B4. The defect of Auden's method is that he is always elaborating rules and making out lists of categories into which his concrete examples turn out only imperfectly to fit. But his insight is particularly valuable on <u>Moby-Dick</u>. He offers an illuminating discussion of the respective relations of the various members of the crew to Ahab's hunt and of the significance of the various ships encountered by the <u>Pequod</u>. Auden also makes some very shrewd points about the egoistic psychology of the romantic.

57   DAICHES, DAVID. "The Sea and the City." <u>New Republic</u>, 122, (17 April), 27.

     Review of 1950.B4. An interesting and ingenious book. Its value "lies less in its generalizations, suggestive and often illuminating though these are, than in the detailed illustrations, which are discussed with an almost irresponsible zest. The examination of the characters of <u>Moby Dick</u>, which occupies a large part of the book, is brilliantly done and makes other attempts to read the novel as a simple allegory look silly (Auden is fully aware of the difference between symbolism and allegory)."

58   GREENBERG, MARTIN. "Auden as Critic." <u>Nation</u>, 170 (29 April), 407–408.

     Review of 1950.B4. Auden has rather tamely submitted to the conventional notion of a classical or neoclassical thesis and a romantic antithesis or reaction. He does not deepen our knowledge of romanticism but extends what we already know to embrance another subject matter, the sea. His "iconographic" method creates an impression of pseudo-scholarship, which is aggravated by the show of logical and scientific rigor in the book's numbered paragraphs, catalogues, diagrams, and propensity to labor the obvious. Auden is best when farthest off his subject, as when he erects each of the three mates of the <u>Pequod</u> "into one of those wonderful moral-psychological types of the kind we come upon so often in his poetry."

59   VINCENT, HOWARD P.   "'Moby-Dick' Myth."   <u>Saturday Review of
     Literature</u>, 33 (29 April), 21, 36.
         Review of 1950.A1. The best general book on Melville ever
     published. The counterpoint of biographical record and of liter-
     ary achievement is brought off with great skill so that Melville's
     life illuminates his art, his art illuminates his life. The
     literary criticism is superb; the analysis of <u>Moby-Dick</u> is ir-
     reproachable. There will be disagreements with Arvin's judgments
     of the later works, but even in rebuttal one must respect the
     cogency and shrewdness of his arguments. His long study of
     Melville's poetry is original and interesting.

60   CHASE, RICHARD. "Reviews." <u>Modern Language Notes</u>, 65 (May),
     358-359.
         Review of 1949.B14. In considering a novel like <u>Pierre</u>,
     the psychologist's point of view is enormously valuable, and
     Murray gives the most cogent account of Pierre's troubles so far.
     Not everyone, however, will find Murray's scholarship unassail-
     able. One cannot agree, for instance that "the pervading temper
     of <u>Pierre</u> is that of German Romanticism"; the temper is partly
     German, but there is also the temper of Shakespeare, of the
     Bible (especially the prophetic books and gospels), of Hawthorne,
     and of Melville himself, an American original. Moreover, Murray
     the psychologist, looking for motives beneath ideas and for the
     self-symbolization and self-analysis of the author, forgets to
     look at <u>Pierre</u> the work of art.

61   HOFFMAN, DAN G.   "Melville's 'Story of China Aster.'"
     <u>American Literature</u>, 22 (May), 137-149.
         In this seemingly independent story, Melville restates the
     chief theme of the entire novel. It is also the climax of two
     subthemes that give the latter half of the book its unity. It
     recapitulates and concludes the dialectic on borrowing money
     through pretensions of friendship, the eventual subject of all
     discourse since chapter 28; and it demonstrates Mark Winsome's
     philosophy. But its essentiality lies "in its explication of the
     conflict between the two opposing forces which dominate the book:
     the Promethean-creative-civilizing impulse versus its opposite,
     the surrender of moral judgments and the perversion of the Pro-
     methean spirit to private ends at the expense of mankind." [Cf.
     Chase, 1949.A1, B118.]

62   LEWIS, R.W.B. "Melville on Homer." <u>American Literature</u>, 22
     (May), 166-176.
         Melville's markings in Chapman's translations of Homer form
     patterns. "The <u>Iliad</u>, under Melville's inspection, emerges as
     a tragedy: a dark portrait of a world at war, a world in which
     lonely, grieving men are caught up in vast, indefinable forces
     and move without hope to meet the violence and death that awaits
     them, under the rule of implacable divinities." The "impact of
     Melville on the <u>Odyssey</u> led it to take the form of a <u>Bildungs-
     roman</u> in which the relation between the characters and the
     sequence of the events stands for growth of insight into the
     heart of reality."

63　　PROCTER, PAGE S., JR.　"A Source for the Flogging Incident in
　　　White-Jacket."　American Literature, 22 (May), 176–177.
　　　　　　The incident in which Captain Claret unjustly sentences
　　White Jacket to flogging, so that he considers rushing Claret
　　overboard in a combined act of murder and suicide may derive from
　　William Leggett's "Brought to the Gangway," "the strongest liter-
　　ary indictment of the tyranny of naval officers between Roderick
　　Random and White-Jacket."　Leggett's story was published in the
　　New York Mirror, 19 April 1834, and in Leggett's Naval Stories
　　(New York, 1834).

64　　SCHIFFMAN, JOSEPH.　"Melville's Final Stage, Irony:　A Re-
　　　Examination of Billy Budd Criticism."　American Literature, 22
　　　(May), 128–136.
　　　　　　"Most critics, by mistaking form for content, have missed
　　the main importance of Billy Budd.　Actually, Melville's latest
　　tale shows no radical change in his thought.　Change lies in his
　　style.　Billy Budd is a tale of irony, penned by a writer who
　　preferred allegory and satire to straight narrative, and who,
　　late in life, turned to irony for his final attack upon evil."
　　Reprinted in Springer, pp. 23–31; reprinted in part in Vincent
　　(1971), pp. 98–100.

65　　SEALTS, MERTON M., JR.　"Did Melville Write 'October
　　　Mountain'?"　American Literature, 22 (May), 178–182.
　　　　　　Marshalls evidence that Melville did not write a sketch
　　titled "October Mountain," first mentioned by J.E.A. Smith in
　　1876.B2.　"As references to such a piece by other writers derive
　　from Smith's original error, and as Mrs. Melville herself re-
　　jected Arthur Stedman's mention of 'October Mountain' [in
　　1892.B5], it seems reasonably certain that Melville never com-
　　posed a story, sketch, or poem of that title."　In referring to
　　"October Mountain," Smith may have had in mind "Cock-A-Doodle-
　　Doo!"

66　　WILLIAMS, MENTOR L.　"Some Notices and Reviews of Melville's
　　　Novels in American Religious Periodicals, 1846–1849."　Ameri-
　　　can Literature, 22 (May), 119–127.
　　　　　　Discusses and quotes from 1846.B70, B73, B92; 1847.B20;
　　1848.B14; 1849.B96, B144.　"As one would expect, religious
　　opinion about Melville's views on the missionaries follows the
　　lines of cleavage that marked the essential differences of the
　　denominations on the subject of foreign missions.　The orthodox
　　evangelical churches had a heavy stake in missionary enterprise
　　and complained bitterly against all criticism of the missionary
　　activity.　The liberal churches, particularly the Unitarian,
　　recommended more attention to home missionary endeavors.　The
　　Catholic church, ever on the alert for a chance to attack their
　　Protestant enemies . . . welcomed all accounts of the perversion
　　and failure of Protestant missions."　Ranging "from the vitupera-
　　tive to the mildly skeptical," the reviews in the religious
　　press "show that Melville's course as a novelist was being
　　closely watched by the keepers of America's conscience--and by
　　the watchdogs of its morals."

67   KAZIN, ALFRED. "The Burning Human Values in Melville." New
     York Times Book Review (7 May), pp. 6, 22.
          Review of 1950.A1. The wisest and most balanced single
     piece of writing on Melville, marked by a thoroughly convincing
     analysis of his creative power and its limitations and by a
     wonderfully right feeling for the burning human values involved
     at every point of Melville's struggle with his own nature. Arvin
     seizes from Melville unexpected distinctions that are supports to
     our own struggle for survival in this period; he extracts from
     each rise and ebb of Melville's mind an appropriate psychological
     moral for our generation. He displays integrity of taste and
     ripe good sense about minor works like Pierre and The Confidence-
     Man, which are now admired largely for ideological reasons. His
     analysis of Ahab's relation to Moby Dick is the deepest note
     struck in the book, and one so closely and convincingly tied up
     with the analysis of Melville's childhood that it shows again how
     much more can be said about Moby-Dick, so long as we think of
     Melville as a man and not as a god.

68   ANON. "Herman Melville. By Newton Arvin." Newsweek, 35
     (15 May), 99.
          Review of 1950.A1. Extravagant praise of Melville in the
     recent works of Chase [1949.A1] and Vincent [1949.A3] has pro-
     duced a reaction against him. Arvin's biography restores balance
     and perspective to Melville's life and work, combining criticism
     and biography with a sure judgment. While Arvin's book offers
     little new material on Melville's career, it reinterprets what is
     known with unfailing imaginative insight. The best existing
     biography of Melville.

69   ENGLE, PAUL. "New Close-up of Melville as a Personality."
     Chicago Sunday Tribune Magazine of Books (28 May), p. 3.
          Review of 1950.A1. Contains more of "that possessed man"
     Melville than any other book, for Arvin has searched for the
     wild, essential part of the man, has found it, and expressed it
     with eloquence and firmness. His chapter on "The Whale" is an
     example of the best modern critical writing. Arvin "is also
     finely useful in his apprehensions of the tension in Melville's
     relations with his family, especially his mother, and of the
     probable pattern which that brought to his marriage."

70   BERLIND, BRUCE. "Notes on Melville's Shorter Poems." Hopkins
     Review, 3 (Summer), 24–35.
          Melville accomplished little as a poet. Unlike Hardy, he
     came to poetry late in his career and was unable to disentangle
     his techniques in verse from the techniques of his earlier work.
     His "poems are continuously trying to attain a movement of sym-
     bolic significance which their formal limitations at the outset
     forbid. His mind naturally searched for the deepest meaning in
     his subjects in terms of process, and this search was usually
     defeated by the largeness of the subject and the small number of
     lines in which he attempted to treat it." "Misgivings" is the
     one short poem in which he achieved the kind of movement he was
     searching for. "If there is a larger number of successful poems

in the later volumes, it is partially because Melville curbed his
efforts toward symbolic significance but more because these poems
are for the most part less ambitious than the best of Battle-
Pieces. They reveal, moreover, in their use of language, a loss
of that masculine vigor which makes the earlier volume especially
remarkable for the time in which it appeared. They are successful, in short, on a lower level."

71   CLOUGH, WILSON O. "Book Reviews." Western Humanities Review,
      4 (Summer), 258-260.
          Review of 1949.A1; 1950.A1. Arvin's book comes as an
      excellent and sensible introduction to the subject, practically
      superseding any previous work on Melville for its usefulness to
      the student or general reader who wishes a reliable first view
      of the man in his major outlines. With his excursions into
      mythopoeia and politico-didacticism, Chase seems more provoca-
      tive, more daring, and less academic.

72   LEISY, ERNEST E. "Melville: Mariner, Mystic." Southwest
      Review, 35 (Summer), 223-224.
          Review of 1950.A1. A vivid and moving account of Mel-
      ville's development as a writer. The general outlines of our
      knowledge are not materially changed, but the emphasis is shifted
      in many places and the reasons for older as well as newer valua-
      tions are definitely supported. Whatever light psychiatry can
      shed on the Melville problem is used without bordering on the
      absurd. The best all-round introduction to Melville and his
      work.

73   SPANGLER, EUGENE R. "Harvest in a Barren Field: A Counter-
      comment." Western Review, 14 (Summer), 305-307.
          In thirty years of effort, literary criticism has failed to
      evaluate and illuminate Melville's novels and short stories as
      art. There is hardly a greater need in American letters than for
      a carefully analytic body of criticism on Melville, and there is
      no greater tragedy than the caliber of criticism being published.
      Writing that purports to be criticism of Melville's art is by and
      large either an attempt at psychoanalysis of Melville the man (as
      in Chase [1949.A1] or Olson [1949.B87], or an attempt to wrench
      the diversity of Melville's work into a single-minded meaning or
      message (as in Hall [1950.B45]), with the consequent necessity
      for misinterpretation and the overlooking as "inconsequential" of
      a large segment of the total work. Valuable historical work has
      been done, such as Anderson's [1939.A1], but useful criticism of
      Melville has been astonishingly rare.

74   WEEKS, DONALD. "Two Uses of Moby Dick. American Quarterly, 2
      (Summer), 155-164.
          The first use is aesthetic: to enlarge our sense of the
      possibilities of form and structure in the novel. At least three
      themes in Moby-Dick serve the artistic end of balancing the evil
      represented by Ahab: the first theme is the story of whaling;
      the second theme "is an aggregate of ideas of peace, patience,
      dignity, joy, and delight"; the third theme is fellowship. The

second use of the book is moral: to enlarge our sense of
responsibility. Ahab is a dictator; Ishmael becomes a passive
acceptor of his tyranny, and then a participator in his madness.

75   HILLWAY, TYRUS. "Melville as Critic of Science." <u>Modern
    Language Notes</u>, 65 (June), 411–414.
        Science appalled Melville by its eagerness to capture the
minds of men and its pretended ability to answer the final
philosophical questions. He ridiculed the apparent esotericism
and mysteriousness of science, which he interpreted as largely
humbug; denounced the coldness and inhumanity of the scientific
mind; mistrusted the overconfidence of the enthusiasts who
thought science would solve every human problem; saw the analytical methods of the scientists resulting in the destruction
of beauty; and deplored the struggle between science and reli-
gious faith. Illustrations from <u>Omoo</u>, <u>Mardi</u>, <u>Redburn</u>, <u>White-
Jacket</u>, <u>Moby-Dick</u>, "The Happy Failure," "The Bell-Tower," "The
Tartarus of Maids," <u>Clarel</u>, and <u>Billy Budd</u>.

76   [HILLWAY, TYRUS]. "<u>Moby-Dick</u>: A Play." <u>Melville Society
    Newsletter</u>, 6 (June), n.p.
        Notes that dramatic versions of <u>Moby-Dick</u> have been pre-
sented on all major American radio networks in the past few
years. In 1947 the B.B.C. broadcast Henry Reed's dramatic version [see 1947.B13]; and in the summer of 1947 <u>Moby-Dick</u> appeared
on the stage at the Straight Wharf Theatre, Nantucket, in a
dramatic version by R.D. Wilson.

77   THORP, WILLARD. "Bold, Fresh Appraisal of Melville." New
    York <u>Herald Tribune Book Review</u> (11 June), p. 8.
        Review of 1950.A1. A very considerable achievement. The
high point of this skillfully organized biography is the long
critical section on <u>Moby-Dick</u>, which is more acute than anything
thus far written about it. The portrait of Melville that emerges
is full and bold in outline, yet, because Arvin relies heavily
on the psychoanalytical approach, he leaves the impression at
times that we know more about Melville than we do. The approach
does not leave enough play for Melville's passionate sincerity
in his search for truth, for his humor, vitality, and moral persistence.

78   REYNOLDS, HORACE. "More on Melville." <u>Christian Science
    Monitor</u> (15 June).
        Review of 1950.A1. Arvin is always in firm control of his
materials, and his writing is admirably homogeneous, neatly dis-
solving biography in criticism and criticism in biography. He
has studied Melville's books with care and insight, and he well
exposes both the struggle that was Melville's life and the greatness of the novel in which it found sublimated expression. But
in a book where the proportion of fact to theory is so small one
wonders and resists. How can Arvin repeatedly state as fact what
went on in Melville's mind?

79   GLICKSBERG, CHARLES I. "Melville and the Negro Problem."
      <u>Phylon</u>, 11 (3d Quarter), 207–215.
        Captain Delano in "Benito Cereno" is intended as a satiri-
cal portrait, a composite reflection of the righteous steretyped
attitudes prevalent at the time. "From the tone of the tale,
from the cumulative internal evidence, the inference must be
drawn that Melville did not attempt to blacken the blacks and
whitewash the whites. [<u>See</u> 1948.B22.] Far from arousing feelings of hatred against the Negro, the incarnate image of evil, he
presents a complex, artistically balanced story, which arouses
mixed emotion. Though we sympathize with the plight of Don
Benito, we admire the steadfast courage and indomitable spirit of
Babo, a born leader, just as we admire the capacity for self-rule
and the heroic resolution of the Negroes on board." Both <u>Moby-</u>
<u>Dick</u> and "Benito Cereno" reveal that Melville, "while no fire-
and-brimstone reformer, had definite and enlightened views on the
Negro problem, though as a novelist he wove these into the fabric
of his fiction so that they did not stand forth conspicuously as
preachment but as integral elements in the artistic structure."

80   LUTWACK, LEONARD. "Herman Melville and <u>Atlantic Monthly</u>
      Critics." <u>Huntington Library Quarterly</u>, 13 (August), 414–416.
        Reprints 1885.B4 in part. In 1890 Horace Elisha Scudder,
editor of the <u>Atlantic</u>, suggested that George Parsons Lathrop
write an article on Melville; Lathrop agreed, but Scudder then
decided to drop the project while Melville was still alive.
Prints relevant extracts from Scudder's and Lathrop's correspondence. Attributes notice of <u>Typee</u> and <u>Omoo</u> in the <u>Atlantic</u>,
70 (December 1892), 851, to Scudder.

81   SPEARS, MONROE K. "Reviews." <u>Poetry</u>, 76 (August), 291–294.
        Review of 1950.B4. Includes a "brilliant analysis" of
<u>Moby-Dick</u> and <u>Billy Budd</u> in terms of Auden's concepts.

82   HANSEN, HARRY. "This Vanishing Age Loses One of Its Literary
      Giants." Chicago <u>Sunday Tribune Magazine of Books</u> (6 August).
        Article on the death of Carl Van Doren, who "used to be
mildly amused because he had touched off the rediscovery" of
Melville. Van Doren recommended Melville to Weaver [<u>see</u>
1921.A1] as the subject for a thesis at Columbia.

83   ENGLE, PAUL. "If You Care for Melville--'Moby Dick' is
      Interpreted." Chicago <u>Sunday Tribune Magazine of Books</u>
      (13 August), p. 5.
        Review of 1950.A3. Percival gives many subtle illumina-
tions and establishes a sound basis for viewing the book not only
as a wonderful story of whaling but as a coherent account of
legendary characters acting out what really amounts to a moral
myth--all without straining the credulity of the reader. It is
a pity that the book was not given more shape, because an ordering of the attitudes Percival offers would have strengthened
their impact.

84   WADE, MASON. "Books." Commonweal, 52 (25 August), 492-493.
          Review of 1950.A1. In addition to an enriched account of
Melville's early life, particularly in the South Seas, Arvin
offers some penetrating analyses of Melville's rhetoric and of
other aspects of his literary method. But these fresh and
valuable contributions are overshadowed by the mass of psychological analysis. Arvin evidently felt the need to digest and
present in absorbed form all the recent pseudo-psychiatric
theorizing about Melville. He has avoided the excesses of
younger and more intemperate Melville enthusiasts, but the book
is top-heavy with psychiatric theories for its primary function
as a biographical and critical introduction to Melville's work.

85   BAIRD, JAMES R. "The Noble Polynesian." Pacific Spectator, 4
          (Autumn), 452-465.
          Surveys writers from Melville onward who have viewed
Polynesia in primitivist terms. Melville was the first to employ
the Polynesian as the symbol of unadulterated good opposed to the
evil of modern civilization. He "remained long enough in the
Marquesas and in Tahiti to set up within himself the ideal, the
proof, imagined or actual, that somewhere in this world there
exists a state of man which approximates, at least, God's original plan. The ideal never leaves him." The Polynesian as the
symbol of ultimate good in a world of evil is recurrent from
Typee to Billy Budd.

86   CHASE, RICHARD. "Another Harpoon." Kenyon Review, 12
          (Autumn), 717-718, 720-721.
          Review of 1950.B4. It is true that Melville may in one
sense be regarded as a theologian manqué, and Auden has done a
great deal on this assumption to clarify the meaning, for example, of the nine ships encountered by the Pequod in Moby-Dick.
But "his book as a whole would have been more persuasive if he
had made a work as exciting but as relatively mindless as Childe
Harold central to his argument instead of Moby-Dick and Billy
Budd." Auden "writes in a post-political era and in a post-
political frame of mind. Melville did not. If Ishmael was
seeking for the meaning of self in relation to God, he was also
seeking for the 'new nation' promised him by the Old Testament."
When someone finally succeeds in writing with full understanding
about Billy Budd, he will take seriously the explicitly political
cast of Melville's opening words. Auden is right in saying that
the partial artistic failure of Billy Budd may issue from the
identification of the hero with Christ. This is not all Melville
was attempting, however. In Billy Budd the central question is:
"What are the conditions under which the city of man can exist?"

87   HAUN, EUGENE. "Patriarch, Parent, and Prototype." Sewanee
          Review, 58 (Autumn), 708-716.
          Review of 1949.A1, A3-4. Vincent shows quite clearly that
Melville was conversant with whaling literature, but he frequently assumes that Melville borrowed information that his
immediate knowledge must have supplied. The result is a tendency
to view Moby-Dick as a "documentary" about whaling, yet Vincent

apparently feels in duty bound to regard the novel as a great
allegory; the tensions between what he believes and what he feels
he ought to believe are sometimes painfully apparent. The one
whaling document Vincent has failed to provide is the original
manuscript of the "whaling voyage" he claims Melville set out to
write; and his whole thesis is predicated on two short quotations
from Melville's letters, neither of which is conclusive. Chase
does not prove that Melville was a liberal-progressive, but he
proves that he himself is, in twentieth-century terms--a political bias coloring his cultural interpretation--which is completely deranged by the intrusion of a second interpretation, the
psychiatric, all written in prose complicated in style, polyglot
in vocabulary, and consequently inefficient in communication.
Wright's study is less pretentious than either of the other two
and more rewarding than both; her work is not so widely diverted
by prejudice nor so heavily diluted by speculation. Wright is at
her best in her discussion of Melville's imagery in relation to
its biblical sources, at her weakest on themes and plots. All
three commentators have consistently ignored one of the most
pregnant analogues in literature: chapter 41 of the Book of Job
is devoted to a metaphor in which God in his more terrifying
aspects is set forth as Leviathan; the result is a portrait of
Moby Dick himself. The transaction between author and source is
still a creative secret, possibly not known even to the author
himself; about the psychological process of the transaction the
scholar can only speculate.

88   LUEDERS, EDWARD G. "The Melville-Hawthorne Relationship in
       Pierre and The Blithedale Romance." Western Humanities
       Review, 4 (Autumn), 323–334.
          Similarities and differences between Pierre and The
       Blithedale Romance. In each novel the author makes a conscious
       subjective presentation of himself. Moreover, the "relationship
       of Coverdale and Hollingsworth, of Plinlimmon and Pierre is the
       relationship of Hawthorne and Melville all over again. It is
       the successful, compromising, rational intellect versus the
       emotional, ideal-seeking failure. Each relationship is, on the
       surface, free of animosity or hostility, yet the differences set
       the men apart and plague their consciences." Each author, "while
       writing his exegesis of the fundamental impasse reached in their
       relationship, recognized imperfections in his own makeup as well
       as those which were displayed by his companion. The novels,
       therefore, insofar as they may have been inspired by the period
       of intimacy in the Berkshires, are turned both inward and outward
       in an attempt to resolve the contrasts between their authors."

89   SLOCHOWER, HARRY. "Freudian Motifs in Moby Dick." Complex, 3
       (Fall), 16–25.
          On one level of Melville's "associations," Moby Dick stands
       for the feared and desired object harboring the secret of the
       sexes and of parental creation. The book's metaphors, imagery,
       and thought associations reveal Ahab's feelings of guilt,
       impotence, homoeroticism, and isolation.

90   SLOCHOWER, HARRY. "Moby Dick: The Myth of Democratic
      Expectancy." American Quarterly, 2 (Fall), 259–269.
         Finds in Moby-Dick "a continuation of the American myth of
      expectancy and an expression of disenchantment with it." Moby-
      Dick is also "the first major American literary myth sounding the
      central motifs of creation and quest. Its distinctive American
      quality lies in its uncertain attitude toward creation." Re-
      printed in 1960.A6.

91   CHASE, RICHARD. "Herman Melville." Yale Review, 40
      (September), 186–188.
         Review of 1950.A1, A3. Notes finely perceptive parts and
      questions a number of judgments in Arvin's book, which exhibits
      all the qualities that make him so valuable a critic--patient in-
      telligence, scrupulous care, wide culture, freedom from cant. The
      reader may feel that if the treatment of the early years occa-
      sionally pays too much tribute to caution and factuality, the
      treatment of the middle and later years occasionally pays too
      little. Arvin's unusual severity with all of Melville's prose
      between Moby-Dick and Billy Budd is salutary in at least two
      ways: it points up and preserves the unexampled supiority of
      Moby-Dick and warns us against the indiscriminate praise often
      accorded to the short prose pieces merely because Melville wrote
      them. As a short-story writer, Melville is certainly a good deal
      surpassed by such masters of the form as Hawthorne, James, and
      Chekhov. But Arvin's treatment of The Confidence-Man is not
      criticism at all. The naturalism, characterization, and drama
      of The Confidence-Man subsist at a different level from the
      literal--the level of myths and ideas in dialectic interplay,
      the level of meaning that Arvin has correctly discerned in
      Clarel; it is one of the world's great black books, and Arvin's
      purview simply does not accommodate its possibilities. Percival's
      reading of Moby-Dick is eloquent and sensitive, but somewhat
      marred by the inevitable diffuseness of the "comparative religion"
      approach. The most complete statement of the novel's religious
      meanings Chase has seen.

92   HAYFORD, HARRISON. "Herman Melville." Nineteenth-Century
      Fiction, 5 (September), 163–167.
         Review of 1950.A1. Arvin's clear and subtle study is the
      best general book that has been written about Melville, its value
      lying less in original biographical interpretation or new criti-
      cal judgments than in its own literary competence and in the
      balance and clarity with which it manages its complex materials.
      With remarkable flexibility, Arvin explores the psychological,
      philosophical, moral, and mythical implications of the works, but
      he evaluates each in the end by its primary qualities of language
      and form, as a piece of literary art. His most constructive
      criticism is his discussion of the poems and Clarel. Biographi-
      cally his study is less satisfactory: he does not make full or
      accurate use of the many new facts about Melville's life and
      literary career and does not find them relevant to an under-
      standing of the works. Aside from situations in the works,
      notably Pierre and Clarel, there is meager evidence for his

theory concerning Melville's relations with his mother, wife, and friends. The biographical approach to Melville employed by Arvin "was initiated by Weaver and confirmed by Mumford, in the primary period of Freudian impact and when very little research had been done on Melville's life and literary methods and milieu; and it has unfortunately held sway too singly. Scholars have published fractional investigations, but to date nobody has tried the experiment of constructing a picture of Melville beginning with the multitude of available objective data outside his writings and working inward from these data. His works and his actions are still interpreted as proceeding from an omnipotent neurosis. This or some inward, subjectively arrived-at theory of his motivation takes honorific precedence as the primary determinant of everything he wrote or did, over any ascertainable exterior circumstances. Such circumstances are evidently thought to be always secondary and somehow ineffective, except as they confirm deeper causes, because they are merely material and accidental. To mention them is apparently to lack imagination and insight." Nevertheless, the lesson of so fine a study as Arvin's "is that subjective biography of this sort has gone about as far as it ever can with Melville, and any further understanding is most likely to come by way of the wholly untried approach from exterior to interior. Such a biography, confronting and not dismissing objective circumstances, can be truly imaginative."

93   [HILLWAY, TYRUS]. "Naming the Pequod." <u>Melville Society Newsletter</u>, 6 (September), n.p.
     Melville undoubtedly knew something of New London, Connecticut, the ancestral home of the Pequot, or Pequod, Indians and prominent whaling port. If he was recollecting the <u>Acushnet</u>, presumably named after the Acushnet Indians, when he wrote about the <u>Pequod</u>, "he could hardly have chosen a name for her more appropriate than one which would recall the harbor from which sailed the second largest South Seas whaling fleet of his day."

94   HOFFMAN, DAN G. "Melville in the American Grain." <u>Southern Folklore Quarterly</u>, 14 (September), 185–191.
     Review of 1949.A1 and the Grove Press edition of <u>The Confidence-Man</u>. Chase's book should establish once and for all the extent of Melville's involvement with American culture, and thus modify the standing judgment of him as a creative spirit who rejected as well as was rejected by the popular culture of his country. Melville's intensity, symbols, and criticism of American culture, derive from his involvement in American life; his understanding of that culture was achieved by imaginative participation in the main currents of popular myth-making, rhetoric, anecdotal humor, and gullible optimism that in the nineteenth century helped to define the American national character. Chase amply demonstrates the influence of popular culture on <u>Moby-Dick</u>. With the aid of folklore he interprets and recovers for the modern reader two almost forgotten but fascinating books: <u>Israel Potter</u> and <u>The Confidence-Man</u>. He also defines an element of Melville's greatness that other critics, who missed his

dependence on native folklore, have underestimated or ignored: comedy. A parallel to Moby-Dick in the popular literature and folklore of the time, which Chase does not mention, is T.B. Thorpe's "The Big Bear of Arkansas." There are more extensive parallels to the Confidence Man in native myth than Chase cites—such as Simon Suggs, Johnny Appleseed, Mike Fink, and Davy Crockett. The Confidence-Man is a work no student of American culture can afford to ignore, and Chase's book is an invaluable guide to its themes and to all of Melville's work.

95   MORPURGO, J.E. "Herman Melville and England." Month
      [London], NS 4 (September), 180-186.
         American authors before Melville's generation must be judged by Europe's standards and in comparison with European writers. After Melville's generation, America's serious writers use a philosophical and sociological idiom that is foreign to Europe. Melville is the outstanding exemplar of mature Americanism that still used a language and a mode of thought convenient to European readers. An American and an international writer, Melville is "also and especially an American and an English writer. His spirit, his imagery, much even of his language he derived from the English heritage—above all from Shakespeare and from the Authorized Version—but he added to it something far older, something that is shared by England and America, and that explains . . . the very real closeness of English and American ideologies. He added a sense of space." Melville "found America's Frontier where it was also England's Frontier—on the seas. Melville knew that the sea is more than a physical challenge. It is, to Englishmen and American alike, a spiritual force."

96   PAUL, SHERMAN. "Book Reviews." New England Quarterly, 23
      (September), 405-407.
         Review of 1949.A2; 1950.A1. Although sympathetic and somewhat detached from the particularities of American religious experience, Stone's study has the critical suggestiveness inevitable in a discussion of the religious perplexities of Melville and his age from the viewpoint of "the one valid religion." But it jumps quickly into a pedestrian, almost wholly descriptive account of the monographic facts of Melville's life and work. Stone's close reliance on earlier commentators weakens the total interpretative impact; one gets little sense of the course of Melville's spiritual and artistic development. Arvin's study is more penetrating and many-sided, giving Melville the dimensions of an understood context. Arvin is especially able in relating the man and his work to the period, to expression in America and on the Continent. He keeps the fine line in the interplay of biography and books. Arvin gives a proportioned reevaluation of the books, and he succeeds especially in sharpening the picture of the man.

97   RAHV, PHILIP. "Melville and His Critics." <u>Partisan Review</u>,
     17 (September–October), 732–735.
       Review of 1950.A1. The finest critical biography of an
American author we have had in a long time. Arvin "treats text
and context with equal authority, combining in a masterly way the
traditional resources of literary criticism with a flexible and
entirely apposite use of the insights provided by the newer
psychological disciplines. The result is a critical interpretation so just and clear that it may well become the classic study
of Melville." Recent myth-happy critics have blown up the genuine mythic element in Melville to vast proporitons, interposing
a talmudic elaboration of mythology between the reader and the
reality of Melville, while traditionalist critics have eliminated
the contradictions in him. Yet these contradictions, at once
"creative and frustrating, agonisingly personal yet deeply expressive of national and universal culture," are "at the very
core of Melville's modernity and the symbolic fate of his
genius." Arvin, in his present phase freer perhaps of confining
allegiances than most critics, is able to lay hold of the contradictions and to disclose their psychodynamic meaning without any
squeamishness of failure in sympathy. He demonstrates anew the
relevance of the biographical mode to the job of criticism when
it is properly used and not made an end in itself. Reprinted in
1957.B26.

98   SCHIFFMAN, JOSEPH. "Critical Problems in Melville's 'Benito
      Cereno.'" <u>Modern Language Quarterly</u>, 11 (September), 317–324.
       Rejects "a customary misinterpretation"--that Babo is evil.
Babo's malignity is not motiveless: he was leading a rebellion
of slaves in their fight for freedom, and all his acts of cruelty
were dictated by this purpose. Throughout Melville's books,
there is warm understanding and sympathy shown for the Negro, and
it is in keeping with Melville's philosophy that Babo as a human
being would desire freedom. Melville did not intend "Benito
Cereno" as an abolitionist tract. But in selecting a theme of
slave rebellion and in treating Babo and his fellow slaves as
able, disciplined people as capable of evil as the white man, he
treated the Negro as an individual. Both subject and treatment
were conditioned by the 1850s, and both subject and treatment
marked advances for American literature. Babo emerges the moral
victor in the story.

99   R., D. "Belles-Lettres." <u>Saturday Review</u>, 33 (2 September),
     33–34.
       Review of 1950.A3. Brief synopsis. In presenting his
findings, Percival has rendered Melville a service.

100   FITTS, DUDLEY. "O Felix Culpa." New York <u>Times Book Review</u>
      (10 September), p. 35.
       Review of 1950.B4. The discussion of symbolism in Melville
is brief but memorable. The Ishmael-Don Quixote analysis is
endlessly provocative.

101   LEASE, BENJAMIN. "Melville's 'Gally,' 'Gallow.'" American
      Speech, 25 (October), 186.
          The interesting lexical--and thoroughly Melvillean--note
      on "gally" or "gallow" appears only in the British edition of
      The Whale (1851); American editions of Moby-Dick invariably omit
      it [from chapter 87]. "The OED traces gally from Lear to
      nineteenth-century whaling parlance but fails to mention its most
      illustrious literary occurrence."

102   LEYDA, JAY. "An Albany Journal by Gansevoort Melville."
      Boston Public Library Quarterly, 2 (October), 327-347.
          Prints journal kept by Herman's brother Gansevoort during
      the first three months of 1834, which contains brief mention of
      Herman. Leyda's introduction suggests the influence of John
      Gibson Lockhart's novel Reginald Dalton and Byron's The Bride of
      Abydos on "Fragments from a Writing Desk" and finds in Lockhart's
      book "an artistic ancestor of the character and situation" of
      Pierre Glendinning, a guitar-strumming heroine, a betrayed Lucy,
      and a reference to "Enceladus, jaculator audax."

103   F[AUSSET], H[UGH] I'A. "Great Americans." Manchester
      Guardian (20 October), p. 4.
          Review of 1950.A1. Arvin has risen finely to his subject.
      Melville presents a fascinating problem and is almost an arche-
      typal figure of modern man, torn between conscious rationality
      and the deeper impulses of the unconscious. But first and fore-
      most he was a great writer. Arvin explores revealingly Mel-
      ville's psychology and the spiritual conflict inherent in his
      life and works, but not at the expense of the writer whose cre-
      ative language and feeling for composition he so well appre-
      ciates.

104   BUSH, DOUGLAS. "American Writers Come Back from the Wars."
      New Republic, 123 (30 October), 22.
          Parenthetical reference in discussion of critical trends:
      "I have suggested elsewhere a new and really convincing theory
      of Moby Dick: the White Whale as a prophetic representation of
      the Spirit of Literature turning and rending the fanatical, one-
      legged exponents of symbolism."

105   COWLEY, MALCOLM. "Mythology and Melville." New Republic,
      123 (30 October), 24-26.
          Review of 1949.A1; 1950.A1. Arvin's book is remarkable
      because it is good--perceptive, reasonable, balanced, and per-
      suasive in its judgments. Arvin has mastered an art that is
      essential to sound criticism: the art of making qualifications
      that seem to weaken his direct statements, but really strengthen
      them by bringing them closer to the complicated truth. Another
      critical art he has mastered is that of rising to the level of
      his subject without overleaping it; his very long chapter "The
      Whale" is not only the best he has written but stands high among
      the achievements of recent criticism. His book will serve for a
      long time as the best general introduction to Melville's work.
      Chase's book is remarkable because there is no other book of our

time, and perhaps no other in the long history of critical writing, that seizes on a method and rides it so far into the clouds.
There is at least a germ or possibility of truth in almost everything he says, but unlike Arvin he has never learned to qualify
his statements. One weakness of his method is revealed by his
continual misuse of the copulative "is": thus, Bulkington, a
very minor character in Moby-Dick "is"--not "suggests" or "carries with him a hint of being," but flatly is--"the titanic body
of America." Misuse of the copulative gives a radically false
impression of the symbolic method Melville sometimes followed:
symbols are not equivalents or identities of the values symbolized; they are real persons or objects that suggest those
values among others. A still greater weakness of Chase's mythological or mystagogic criticism is that it encourages him to
misjudge the artistic quality of the works he is discussing, by
tempting him to believe that the greatest novels are those that
suggest the greatest wealth of allegorical meanings.

106   BRASWELL, WILLIAM. "Book Reviews." American Literature, 22
       (November), 359-360.
            Review of 1949.A4. Wright's book provides helpful insights
       into Melville's spiritual life, but it is most valuable for its
       illumination of his imagination at work transforming biblical
       phrase, character, and thought into some of his most original and
       most telling effects. It aids an understanding of how Melville
       developed his varied style, added an extra dimension to scenes,
       achieved magnitude in character, and gave a sense of vastness and
       terror to the universe. A sound and important contribution to
       Melville scholarship.

107   BRASWELL, WILLIAM. "The Early Love Scenes in Melville's
       Pierre." American Literature, 22 (November), 283-289.
            Instead of showing a sudden and inexplicable loss of taste,
       or the debilitating influence of cheap, sentimental fiction [see
       1929.A1; 1949.B14], Melville's style in the early scenes in
       Pierre reveals a satirical purpose. In his highly mannered pre-
       sentation of the fantastically idyllic love affair, Melville
       mocks the cloistered innocence of his own early spiritual life.
       Passages that have been criticized as insipidly sentimental are
       rather mock-romantic, and there is more irony in the opening
       chapters than has generally been recognized. Reprinted in part
       in Willett, pp. 20-23; reprinted in Higgins and Parker,
       pp. 210-216.

108   THORP, WILLARD. "Book Reviews." American Literature, 22
       (November), 355-356.
            Review of 1949.A3. Vincent has explored exhaustively the
       major whaling sources and ferreted out many sly shortcuts
       Melville took in search of useful whaling lore. This is source-
       hunting at its best, "for the quarry is nothing less than half
       the humor, sublimity, poetry, and metaphysics of Moby-Dick."
       Vincent's method of following the text of Moby-Dick has draw-
       backs. Since the materials Melville extracted from his major
       sources are widely scattered in the novel, Vincent is not able

to give a very clear total impression, in one place, of the particular impact on Melville's imagination of Beale or Scoresby or Bennett; and, since Vincent cannot stray too far from the chapters under consideration, his illuminating commentaries on theme, characterization, and symbols have to be related, in general, to the content of these particular chapters. Yet by this method we get a sense of Melville's struggle to concretize his theme, of what mighty effort was required to achieve the "trying-out" of Moby-Dick, paragraph by paragraph. Only a few of the book's illustrations have been published previously in connection with Melville scholarship; all of them are helpful to a better understanding of Moby-Dick.

109   THORP, WILLARD. "Book Reviews." American Literature, 22
       (November), 356–357.
         Review of 1949.A2. Stone's scholarship is, in the main, reliable and up to date. The special merit of the work derives from his Roman Catholic point of view; it is useful to have Melville's work and personality tested by Catholic dogma. What Stone finds of greatest interest in Melville's stories and novels is largely determined by the extent to which they exemplify his thesis; the works most useful to him are Mardi, Moby-Dick, Pierre, Clarel, and Billy Budd. In his excellently reasoned criticism of Billy Budd, Stone makes his best contribution, though not everyone will agree with his conclusions.

110   THORP, WILLARD. "Book Reviews." American Literature, 22
       (November), 357–358.
         Review of 1949.A1. Chase has gone too far with his mytho-logical approach. Murray "has shown how much of Melville's un-conscious life was transformed into the symbols and myths of Pierre. [See 1949.B14.] But how much further can one confi-dently go? Is it ture that the nameless foreboding which the narrator of Typee feels is specifically 'the fear of castra-tion'? If the lightning-rod in 'The Lightning-Rod Man' is a 'phallus-icon,' then what becomes of the theological implications of the story? Is the real theme of Billy Budd 'castration and cannibalism, the ritual murder and eating of the Host'?" Chase's "progressive" is a straw-man, bearing no relation to the great progressives of American history, to a La Follette or a Norris; but in trying to accentuate Melville's liberalism, Chase produces some of the best critical passages in his book. The section on The Confidence-Man is excellent, as are the observations on Israel Potter, the Civil War poems, and Clarel. But the best sections deal with the extent to which American folk life of the 1830s and 1840s influenced the language and tone of Moby-Dick. The greatest virtue of Chase's book is that just when you are about to toss out his newest cryptic mythological discovery, you come on brilliant critical observations.

111   SPILLER, ROBERT E.   "Melville: Our First Tragic Poet."
      Saturday Review of Literature, 33 (25 November), 24–25.
         Mainly on Moby-Dick. The central issue of will versus
      fate--Ahab versus the Whale--fans out into a network of symbols
      within symbols; the book improvises its own form and builds its
      own unity--part epic, part tragic drama, part comic commentary.
      Melville was our first and only tragic poet before the twentieth
      century, for Poe and Hawthorne never quite achieved the necessary
      intensity. Critical scholarship has mounted to make Melville the
      most thoroughly studied of all American authors.

112   FRYE, NORTHROP.   "The Four Forms of Prose Fiction."   Hudson
      Review, 2 (Winter), 583, 593.
         Classifies Moby-Dick as a "romance-anatomy." The "romantic
      theme of the wild hunt expands into an encyclopedic anatomy of
      the whale." Reprinted in 1957.B10.

113   HYMAN, STANLEY EDGAR.   "Two Views of the American Writer.
      1. The Deflowering of New England." Hudson Review, 2
      (Winter), 605–606.
         Review of 1949.A4. An example of superior scholarship.
      Wright's readings are often sharp and perceptive; her study of
      Bible relationships is generally on a high level. The chief
      flaws of Wright's book are a slighting of the short stories, some
      of which are far more significant than she recognizes to any dis-
      cussion of the novels, and a general assumption that the Bible is
      a volume of Semitic history (although her work cries out for the
      recognition that it is a body of myth).

114   LEWIS, R.W.B.   "Two Views of the American Writer. 2. The
      Shock of Repetition." Hudson Review, 2 (Winter), 612–619.
         Review of 1949.A1–3. Vincent's is the most unequivocally
      satisfactory of the three works. Vincent has definitely per-
      formed a service and nearly written a book of independent value.
      "That it cannot entirely stand alone is due partly to the limited
      objective; partly to a style which though amiable, mellow, and
      never intrusive descends occasionally into classroom chattiness,
      whereas precision--though not rigidity--is imperative in dealing
      with Melville; and finally to Mr. Vincent's decision not to take
      a few steps further back into the recesses of Melville's mind and
      reading or further forward to the shape and direction of the
      finished product." In the framework of Stone's convictions,
      "Melville appears as an American romantic who carried Calvinism's
      dark and submissive irrationalism forward into the desperate
      antitheses of satanic voluntarism." The noble rebel, according
      to Stone, "has adopted the hopeless and intrinsically contradic-
      tory and so self-destructive stand of the creature who resents
      the creation; and Melville's heroes, from Taji and Ahab to Pierre
      and Bartleby, are, like their author, intent upon the Narcissis-
      tic enterprise of self-drowning." Stone thus comes by way of
      theology to the interpretation arrived at by Murray in his valu-
      able psychopathological analysis of Pierre. [See 1949.B14.]
      Stone admires Melville, "but he keeps a fastidious distance away
      from him; and this produces an air throughout in general and

particular matters, of smooth and sustained distortion. The
terms of discussion are inevitably selective as well as prejudi-
cial," and Stone "even falls into the unrewarding practice of
lecturing Melville for not having been wiser or other than he
was." Chase's conception of the anagogic significance of recurring elements in Melville's works is in many respects extraordinarily fruitful; he includes an excellent and detailed account
of frontier humor; and his book is packed with perceptions. But
his matter is unordered; in his interpretations the literal level
is lopped off and forgotten, and the symbol itself becomes the
experience. There ought to be a distinction and thus a relation
between sex, psychology, history, poetics, political theory, and
philosophy; in Chase's book each can become another with be-
wildering speed. Yet Chase alone of the most recent writers on
Melville has attempted to bring to bear on his subject the complex experience of the past century, and to use the example of
Melville to interpret that experience for us. Chase "illustrates
again the danger of sovereignty: in this case, the sovereignty
of the present decade, and of the currently fashionable sciences.
If, as a writer, he had absorbed more of the entire tradition:
and if, as a critic of American literature, he had absorbed more
of what little is valid in scholarship and criticism: he might
have written the book we have been waiting for."

115   SEALTS, MERTON M., JR. "Melville's Reading: A Check-List of
      Books Owned and Borrowed." Harvard Library Bulletin, 4
      (Winter), 98-109.
           Continuation of 1949.B89, concluding the checklist. [See
      1952.B50 for a supplementary list.]

116   WOODS, JOHN. "Melville Has Green Eyes." Kenyon Review, 12
      (Winter), 84-85.
           Poem.

117   HAMILTON, CHARLES. "More About the Pequod." Melville Society
      Newsletter, 6 (December), n.p.
           Melville almost certainly knew the pamphlet Narrative of
      the Life and Adventures of Paul Cuffe, a Pequot Indian: During
      Thirty Years Spent at Sea, and in Travelling in Foreign Lands by
      Paul Cuffe, and perhaps even knew Cuffe himself. An acquaintance
      with either may have imprinted the name Pequod in his mind. It
      is also just barely possible that Cuffe served as prototype for
      one of Melville's aboriginal harpooners--perhaps even Queequeg.

118   MURRAY, HENRY A. "Book Reviews." New England Quarterly, 23
      (December), 527-530.
           Review of 1949.A3. The most informative, enlightened, and
      spirited account we have of Melville's use of literary sources,
      the definitive final word on the whaling sections of Moby-Dick.
      Vincent's most illuminating procedure is that of printing paral-
      lel passages from whaling authors and from Moby-Dick, showing how
      "the suffusing and transmuting power of America's greatest imag-
      ination succeeded in changing inert matter-of-fact into vital
      symbols." Vincent's interpretations of the main theme of Moby-

<u>Dick</u> are communicated casually, unsystematically, without sup-
porting evidence, and cannot be stretched to fit Melville's own
statements or the course and consequences of the novel's action.
Vincent is consciously or unconsciously disinclined to apperceive
that revenge is the central motive, preferring the theme of "The
Pursuit of an Ultimate Value," and thereby veiling the wickedness
of Melville's "wicked" book.

119   PAUL, SHERMAN. "Book Reviews." <u>New England Quarterly</u>, 23
       (December), 530–533.
         Review of 1950.A3. Percival's reading of <u>Moby-Dick</u> might
be more accurately described as a reading of Ahab's despair. He
is concerned almost entirely with the psychology of anxiety and
sees in Ahab a case study that bears out the commentary he supplies from Kierkegaard and Jung. For Percival, "the chapter on
the whiteness of the whale provides the key to <u>Moby-Dick</u>. And
perhaps it does. But one gets a little uneasy when the exegesis
becomes too tight and the strands of meaning are tied off too
neatly in the interest of this moral. Then, <u>Moby-Dick</u> becomes
an allegory, as Mr. Percival prefers to read it, and as Melville,
because of his effort to evoke symbolic resonances in the chapter
on the whiteness of the whale, did not."

120   ZABEL, MORTON DAUEN. "Melville: 1950." <u>Nation</u>, 171
       (23 December), 679–680.
         Review of 1950.A1. Not only the best literary biography of
1950 but one of the most valuable critical studies of the decade.
Arvin "succeeds in realizing the hazardous opportunity Melville
affords his critic--that of bringing into focus one of the radical forces in the American genius and of defining, in the face of
a forbidding amount of conjecture, the whole impulse--demonic,
prophetic, visionary--in the native imagination which Melville
beyond any other writer typifies." The chapter on <u>Moby-Dick</u>, the
critical center of the book, may miss some of the historical,
scientific, and symbolic elements that have been defined by
specialists, but it is difficult to see how it could be improved
upon as an account of the personal reference and the art that the
work embodies. By placing it at the peak of Melville's imaginative powers but in no position of secure vision, Arvin has given
<u>Moby-Dick</u> perhaps the most searching and inclusive interpretation
it has yet received and made it a clue to Melville's basic pre-
dicament. Arvin has seen how intricate and how elusive is the
connection between experience and imaginative creation; how little a purely documentary method serves the serious purposes of
literary biography.

<u>1951 A BOOKS</u>

1   BIRSS, JOHN H., GORDON ROPER, and STUART C. SHERMAN. <u>Annual
       Melville Bibliography, 1951</u>. Providence, R.I.: Providence
       Public Library.
         Checklist. Mimeographed.

2   GILMAN, WILLIAM H. <u>Melville's Early Life and REDBURN</u>. New
    York: New York University Press; Geoffrey Cumberlege, Oxford
    University Press; 378 pp. Reprint. New York: Russell &
    Russell, 1972.
      Detailed study of Melville's life from 1819 to 1841, "using
both old and unexplored sources and depending almost entirely
upon objective evidence," designed "to test the validity of
<u>Redburn</u> as autobiography and to find better grounds for discuss-
ing its rank as art." Exploring the relation of <u>Redburn</u> to
Melville's experiences and to forecastle traditions and the work
of literary predecessors, Gilman finds a large amount of invention in the book. Previously considered "autobiography with
elements of romance," <u>Redburn</u> is more correctly to be considered
"romance with elements of autobiography." Although it "seems
undeniable that Melville's own poverty and disappointments
account in large measure for those features in Redburn's story,"
to "insist that Redburn's emotions were Melville's neglects the
fact that Melville was older and more experienced than Redburn
and that many of the fictional hero's passionate outbursts arose
from incidents which did not occur." In the book's structure and
narrative technique, Gilman finds an artistic awareness of the
value of variety, contrast, and climax: each main division is
periodically spiced with dramatic incidents and concludes with a
scene of major disillusion or disappointment. Yet <u>Redburn</u> has
several minor flaws and a "ruinous defect," a "disrupting shift
in the angle of vision." Melville employs the young Redburn's
point of view with great success for almost all of the first half
of the book, but after the guidebook incident his technique fails.
Much of the description of Liverpool is unenlivened by the intensity of a boy's feelings, and this lapse is followed by a
persistent decline into the editorial manner. The portrayal of
Redburn, nonetheless, shows impressive development in Melville's
insight into psychological processes; though Ahab and Pierre are
much deeper characters than Redburn, the earlier book adumbrates
the psychological penetration of the later ones in its acute
revelation of human motives. In Redburn's artfully constructed
ramblings, Melville reproduces the natural digressiveness of a
youthful mind, mirroring not only a young boy's ideas but also
their movement, creating a psychological realism that takes us
into the inner nature of the hero. The book's editorial sections, though fatal to unity, contain some of the most sardonic
asides and impassioned strictures on social evils in the whole
body of Melville's work, his principal target the appalling
dearth of real brotherhood, human sensitivity, and charity in the
Christian world of the mid-nineteenth century. At the time he
wrote <u>Redburn</u>, Melville was probably in the position of the
Christian rebel who adheres to the basic doctrines of Christianity but who freely explores some of the problems it implies. The
Christian ethical beliefs that appear throughout the book form a
logical framework for Melville's active humanitarianism. In its
own genre, the nautical reminiscence, <u>Redburn</u> is preeminent, and
many single chapters or groups of chapters are superior to things
outside the genre. In its tender and varied depiction of the
woes of a disappointed adolescent, it is second only to such

works of its time as <u>David Copperfield</u>. Its scenes of physical
realism are masterpieces of their kind; its style is compact,
direct, and limpid; its sense of sin, evil, and tragedy is
balanced by a sense of humor and of comedy. Lacking the poetry
and symbolism of <u>Moby-Dick</u>, <u>Pierre</u>, and <u>Billy Budd</u>, <u>Redburn</u> still
offers a host of pictures from life invested with human sympathy,
moral earnestness, and vigorous creative power. "Appendix A"
reprints for the first time the texts of "the most significant"
of the eight letters of the Philo Logos controversy printed in
the <u>Albany Microscope</u>, 1838. "Appendix B" reproduces "for the
first time the full and correct text" of "Fragments from a Writing Desk. No. 2" (discussed at length in the text). "Appendix C"
notes parallels between Jackson and Ahab, and Appendix D traces
the reputation of <u>Redburn</u> from 1849 to 1950. Genealogical
charts of the Melville and Gansevoort families appear on the
endpapers. Indexed. Reviewed in 1951.B77, B95, B99, B106, B112,
B117; 1952.B56, B60, B72, B113; 1953.B32, B37, B39.

3   HOWARD, LEON. <u>Herman Melville: A Biography</u>. Berkeley and
    Los Angeles: University of California Press, 354 pp.
      Undertaken as "a coöperative venture" with Leyda's
<u>Melville Log</u> [1951.A4], Howard's biography provides a "formal
narrative," while the <u>Log</u> provides the source material and the
documentation. Howard's major aim is "to place the basic facts
of Melville's life in their proper physical, historical, intellectual, and literary contexts and to draw from them the inferences necessary for a coherent and human narrative." Concerned
with "the writing of Melville's books as a series of important
events in his life," Howard pays particular attention to "the
actual motives" affecting their composition, to "the observable
evidence of their growth," and to the methods by which Melville
put them together, including, notably, his use of literary
sources. The consistent approach is to consider the books as
"significant indications" of what was in Melville's mind at the
time he wrote "and to assume that their substance was derived
partly from a memory of his own experiences, partly from reading,
and partly from an invention which combined his real and vicari-
ous or imaginative experiences in an effort to tell as good a
tale as he could make sound plausible." The intent is "to understand the author of <u>Moby Dick</u> and other books as a human being
living in nineteenth-century America." Indexed. Reviewed in
1951.B93, B95, B99, B101, B106; 1952.B39, B58, B67, B81, B93,
B98; 1953.B37, B39, B76; 1954.B19.

4   LEYDA, JAY. <u>The Melville Log: A Documentary Life of Herman
    Melville, 1819–1891</u>. 2 Vols. New York: Harcourt, Brace and
    Co. 899 pp. Reprint. New York: Gordian Press, 1969.
      Chronologically arranged documents, including extracts from
letters, diaries, journals, ships' logs, books, contracts,
royalty statements, and reviews, relating to Melville's life and
works. In his "Introduction," Leyda writes: "I have tried to
hold to one main aim: to give each reader the opportunity to be
his own biographer of Herman Melville, by providing him with the
largest possible quantity of materials to build his own approach

to this complex figure. The only way I knew to do this was to put together everything that could be known about this life, to bring the reader close to Melville's progress through as many of his days as could be restored, so that the reader may watch him as he works, sees, reacts, worries--to make those seventy-two years, from 1819 to 1891, and a portion of the America they were lived in, in Henry James's word, visitable. This approach forbade an emphasis on any part of his life to the exclusion of any other part, and forbade the neglect of material that seemed, in itself, of small importance." The introduction also speculatively dates occasions on which Melville destroyed correspondence, unpublished manuscripts, and original drafts, and records the "bonfires" after his death in which relatives destroyed correspondence and other biographically significant records. At the end of volume 2, "The Endless Pursuit" lists trails Leyda did not follow in collecting material for the Log, "waiting jobs" for the Melville biographer. Indexed. Reviewed in 1951.B98, B99, B100, B101, B106, B109, B110, B115; 1952.B40, B53, B58, B67, B72, B98; 1953.B34, B39, B76. [See also 1953.B37.] Reprint edition has new supplement.

5   MASON, RONALD. The Spirit Above the Dust: A Study of Herman Melville. London: John Lehmann, 269 pp. Reprint. New York: Paul P. Appel, 1972.
        Written primarily for English readers. Analysis of the prose works and poems, with particular attention to Melville's evolving symbols and to his constant search "for the rediscovery of that innocence in the human soul of which contact with worldly experience has deprived it." Innocence, "at every stage of its universal progress to tragedy," was Melville's constant and central theme. Thus in "the tale of the progressive disintegration of Innocence" embodied in the sequence of his novels, the tragedy of Ishmael is "the tragedy of Innocence overwhelmed by Experience, while the tragedy of Pierre is rather the far more piteous tragedy of Innocence in rebellion against Experience." Clarel, "a contemplative recapitulation of all Melville's imaginative life," points forward "to a potential but untried faith"; Billy Budd "is proof that Melville had tested it and absorbed it into his vision." Here he records his final "conviction of the ultimate victory of innocence, in all the conflicts which experience can wish upon it." Indexed. Reviewed in 1951.B112, B117; 1952.B38, B75, B106; 1953.B55. Reprint has a foreword by Howard P. Vincent.

1951 B SHORTER WRITINGS

1   ATKINSON, BROOKS. "Foreword," in Billy Budd: A Play in Three Acts, by Louis O. Coxe and Robert Chapman. Princeton, N.J.: Princeton University Press, n.p.
        Reprints 1951.B33 in part.

2   AUDEN, W.H. The Enchaf èd Flood or The Romantic Iconography of the Sea. London: Faber & Faber.
        English edition of 1950.B4.

3   CHASE, RICHARD. "An Approach to Melville," in <u>Literary</u>
    <u>Opinion in America</u>. Ed. Morton Dauwer Zabel. New York:
    Harper & Row, pp. 588–596.
        Reprint of 1947.B39.

4   COXE, LOUIS O. and ROBERT CHAPMAN. <u>Billy Budd: A Play in</u>
    <u>Three Acts</u>. Princeton, N.J.: Princeton University Press.
        Dramatic adaptation of <u>Billy Budd</u>.

5   DEEGAN, DOROTHY YOST. <u>The Stereotype of the Single Woman in</u>
    <u>American Novels: A Social Study with Implications for the</u>
    <u>Education of Women</u>. New York: Columbia University, King's
    Crown Press, p. 133.
        In <u>Pierre</u> Isabel, "whose lot is one of misfortune from the
    moment of her illegitimate birth, finds herself the victim in an
    incestuous relationship with her half brother. . . . Isabel, of
    course, is only the passive partner, and as such is hardly more
    than any other woman controlled by conditions she can neither
    comprehend nor remedy, but the couple become so distraught by
    their sense of guilt that self-inflicted death seems the only
    solution. Though the circumstances differed, one may note that
    suicide, for Isabel as well as for Hawthorne's Zenobia, was the
    only way of escape in that day for women (in fiction, at least)
    who dared to deviate from the conventional pattern of thought and
    action."

6   FORSTER, E.M. "Letter from E.M. Forster." <u>Griffin</u>, 1
    (No. 1), 4–6.
        Problems in writing the libretto, with Eric Crozier, for
    Benjamin Britten's opera <u>Billy Budd</u>. [See 1951.B7.] "Melville's
    story has the quality of a Greek myth: It is so basic and so
    fertile that it can be retold or dramatized in various ways. . . .
    Each adapter has his own problems. Ours has been how to make
    Billy, rather than Vere, the hero. Melville must have intended
    this; he called the story Billy Budd, and unless there is strong
    evidence to the contrary one may assume that an author calls his
    story after the chief character. It is what I assume here. . . .
    But I also think that Melville got muddled and that, particularly
    in the trial scene his respect for authority and discipline de-
    flected him. How odiously Vere comes out in the trial scene!
    At first he stays in the witness-box, as he should, then he
    constitutes himself both counsel for the prosecution and judge,
    and never stops lecturing the court until the boy is sentenced to
    death. . . . His unseemly harangue arises, I think, from
    Melville's wavering attitude towards an impeccable commander, a
    superior philosopher, and a British aristocrat. Every now and
    then he doused Billy's light and felt that Vere, being well-
    educated and just, must shine like a star. . . . Billy's primacy
    granted, he must not be pathetic, and he must not be emascu-
    lated. . . . Claggart is less of a problem. Melville's hint of
    'natural depravity' has to be followed. Claggart gets no kick
    out of evil as Iago did, he is not an arch-devil, though Vere and
    Billy may mistake him for one, and if he utters a credo it must

be on different lines from Iago's in 'Otello.' He seems at
moments to be the 'Man of Sorrows.'" Forster and Crozier "have
ventured to tidy up Vere."

7   FORSTER, E.M. and ERIC CROZIER. Billy Budd: Opera in Four
     Acts. London and New York: Boosey & Hawkes, 64 pp.
       Libretto for Benjamin Britten's opera adapted from
Melville's story.

8   HEFLIN, WILSON L. "Melville and Nantucket." Proceedings of
     the Nantucket Historical Association, pp. 22-30.
       Melville's acquaintance with Nantucket whaling men and
whaling ships. His brief acquaintance with Nantucket Island came
too late (July 1852) to exert any influence on Moby-Dick. But
when "he came to write Moby-Dick, Melville could not have forgotten that his paternal grandfather . . . had modestly contributed to the making of Nantucket history. Melville had rich
memories, too, from his whaling years in the Pacific Ocean, of
Nantucket shipmates, of Nantucket craft with which he met at sea,
and of a Nantucket ship in which he made his final cruise in
search of the great sperm whale. Finally, he had at his writing
desk Nantucket books from which he could borrow facts and ideas
for his narrative." Reprinted in 1953.A3.

9   HOWLAND, CHESTER. "There Was a Moby Dick!" in Thar She Blows!
     New York: Wilfred Funk, pp. 292-301.
       Amos Smalley, harpooner aboard the New Bedford bark
Platina, harpooned and killed an all-white sperm whale on the
"Western Grounds" of the North Atlantic in 1902.

10   KNIGHT, GRANT C. The Critical Period in American Literature.
     Chapel Hill: University of North Carolina Press, pp. 6-7, 33.
       Sees Melville as "epical in despair," but "nevertheless
romantic in his picturing of idyllic Polynesian civilization and
in the agony with which he wrestled the angel of doubt." Lists
Melville among the romantics who died during the 1880s and 1890s,
thereby contributing to "the withering of American romanticism."

11   LEYDA, JAY. "An Introduction" and "Notes on Sources, &c.," in
     The Complete Stories of Herman Melville. Ed. Jay Leyda.
     London: Eyre and Spottiswoode, pp. ix-xxxiv, 455-472.
       English edition of 1949.B9.

12   MEAD, DAVID. Yankee Eloquence in the Middle West: The Ohio
     Lyceum 1850-1870. East Lansing: Michigan State College
     Press, pp. 74-77.
       Partial summaries of reviews of Melville's lectures in
1858.B8, B13, B21-22, B24, B26. The abundance of newspaper descriptions of Melville's appearance indicates that Ohio journalists were more interested in the man than in his lecture; and it
seems from the reviews that Melville's moderate success before
Ohio's lyceums was attributable to his somewhat notorious reputation as an author rather than to his subject matter or his eloquence.

13   MICHENER, JAMES A. <u>Return to Paradise</u>. New York: Random
House, p. 61.
      Melville included in list of English and American writers
on Polynesia. "It is provocative to remember that the greatest
American novel was conceived in these waters, for without
Melville's stay in Tahiti and the Marquesas there would never
have been a <u>Moby Dick</u>."

14   MILLER, F. DEWOLFE. "Melville, Whitman, and the Forty
Immortals," in <u>English Studies in Honor of James Southall</u>
<u>Wilson</u>. Vol. 4. University of Virginia Studies. Charlottes-
ville: University of Virginia Press, pp. 23–33.
      In 1884, the New York <u>Critic</u> conducted a poll to determine
which forty living American writers its readers thought destined
for literary immortality. Melville did not receive a single
vote. By 1890, nine of the "forty immortals" had died. The
<u>Critic</u> asked the thirty-one survivors to elect nine replacements.
Again Melville did not receive a single vote. The almost absolute indifference to Melville in America at the time of his death
has not been exaggerated.

15   NATHAN, GEORGE JEAN. "<u>Billy Budd</u>," in <u>The Theatre Book of the</u>
<u>Year, 1950–1951: A Record and an Interpretation</u>. New York:
Alfred A. Knopf, pp. 219–221.
      Commentary on the Coxe and Chapman play. [<u>See</u> 1951.B4.]
"Whether accidentally or by design, the basic elements of the
novel have been employed aforetime in quite a number of plays
and films, and hence, even in this greatly superior allegorical
dramatic treatment of them, miss some of their theatrical effect
because of the repetition. The theme, of course, is markedly
different, but the characters and dramatic machinery through
which it is percolated have come to have a familiar appearance,
which operates in the superficial minds of the non-critical to
the play's disadvantage." Though "ably designed and composed for
two of its acts, the third, in the first two of its three scenes,
surrenders drama to extended and largely static talk involving
the ethics of the ship's captain's decision as to Budd's fate.
Preachment takes the place of action, and it is just here that
the play, previously so compelling, goes afield to its temporary
loss of grip."

16   PAYNE, ROBERT. <u>The Wanton Nymph: A Study of Pride</u>. London:
William Heinemann, pp. 285–288.
      Identifies Melville's "pride" with the pride of Ahab and
Prometheus.

17   POWELL, LAWRENCE CLARK. "My Melville," in <u>Islands of Books</u>.
Los Angeles: The Zamorano Club, pp. 68–74.
      Slightly extended version of 1949.B37.

18   QUINN, ARTHUR HOBSON. "The Romance of History and the
     Frontier," in The Literature of the American People: An
     Historical and Critical Survey. Ed. Arthur Hobson Quinn.
     New York: Appleton-Century-Crofts, pp. 243-247.
        Revised version of 1936.B15, with essentially the same
     judgments. "Benito Cereno" is Melville's best fiction next to
     Moby-Dick, though the long deposition at the end prevents Mel-
     ville from bringing the story to an effective climax. Clarel,
     "written in a jog-trot measure which might just as well have been
     prose," shows that Melville was not a poet. Reprinted in part in
     Doubloon, pp. 238-239.

19   SCHEVILL, JAMES. "The Entrance of Herman Melville Into Hell,"
     in The American Fantasies. Agana, Guam: Bern Porter Books,
     p. 6.
        Poem.

20   SHAW, GEORGE BERNARD. "Preface," in Salt and His Circle, by
     Stephen Winsten. London: Hutchinson & Co., pp. 9, 11, 14.
        Shaw and Salt "agreed about Herman Merivale's Moby Dick,
     another of his [Salt's] pets."

21   WARNER, REX. "Introduction," in Billy Budd and Other Stories.
     The Chiltern Library. London: John Lehmann, pp. vii-xi.
        Introduction to "Bartleby," "The Encantadas," "The Paradise
     of Bachelors," "The Tartarus of Maids," "The Lightning-Rod Man,"
     "Benito Cereno," "The Piazza," and Billy Budd, Foretopman. Ad-
     mirers of Moby-Dick will find in the short stories and Billy Budd
     the same mystical profundity, the same energy and eagerness.
     They will find new qualities, too--in some of the stories a
     gentler humanity, in Billy Budd an extraordinary economy and
     precision. In Billy Budd the "ways of God are in no obvious
     sense justified, but, after the clash of good and evil, the
     dignity of man is upheld. This tragic story is a fitting and a
     glorious last word."

22   WINSTEN, STEPHEN. Salt and His Circle. London: Hutchinson &
     Co., pp. 82, 83, 189.
        Watts-Dunton talks to George Bernard Shaw and Salt about
     Meredith and Melville on the way to visit Swinburne, "taking it
     for granted that they had never heard of them, though Salt was
     a friend of both." In his eighties, Salt finds "an unfailing
     refuge" in old favorites like Shelley, Melville, and Thoreau.

23   FOSTER, ELIZABETH S. "Another Note on Melville and Geology."
     American Literature, 22 (January), 479-487.
        Reply to 1949.B53. Hillway's claims are overconfident and
     misleading. Other books will serve as well, and often better,
     as sources for the passages in question. Melville's actual
     knowledge of geology has been somewhat misrepresented and his
     relations with geology distorted. In the 1840s Melville read, if
     not the real thing, then derivatives of Lyell and Owen and prob-
     ably Darwin--contemporary scientists of the first rank. His

"knowledge of a most portentous chapter of geology was, for a
nonscientist, remarkably accurate, specific, and up-to-date."

24   HARDING, WALTER. "A Note on the Title 'Moby-Dick.'"
     American Literature, 22 (January), 500–501.
          In The Underground Railroad in Massachusetts (Worcester,
     Mass., 1936), Wilbur H. Siebert relates that Captain Austin
     Bearse brought the first fugitive slave from Albany, New York, to
     Boston in his yacht Moby Dick during the summer 1847. The activ-
     ities of Bearse and his ship could easily have reached Melville's
     notice and may have later influenced the title of his book.
     [See 1951.B47.]

25   HEFLIN, WILSON L. "A Man-of-War Button Divides Two Cousins."
     Boston Public Library Quarterly, 3 (January), 51–60.
          Chapter 59 in White-Jacket ("A Man-of-war Button divides
     two Brothers") is founded on Melville's own experience: his
     cousin Stanwix Gansevoort was a midshipman on the storeship Erie,
     while Melville was an ordinary seaman on the frigate United
     States, when both ships were in Callao Bay for nearly a week in
     February 1844.

26   PHOCAS, FRANCES CAPPON. "Herman Melville's Moby Dick." Book
     Bulletin of the Chicago Public Library, 33 (January), 3–5.
          Biographical sketch and brief summaries of several inter-
     pretations of Moby-Dick since the 1920s. There are almost as
     many interpretations of Moby-Dick as there are critics.

27   SEALTS, MERTON M., JR. "Book Reviews." American Literature,
     22 (January), 518–520.
          Review of 1950.A1. An understanding portrait of the artist
     and a temperate evaluation of his total achievement, with a
     brilliant chapter devoted to Moby-Dick. Arvin's handling of
     various lesser works is rich in critical insights though not
     always as rewarding as his centripetal emphasis on Moby-Dick
     itself. Some readers will quibble over the verdicts passed on
     individual works, particularly on those written after 1851;
     others will object to Arvin's penchant for psychologizing;
     specialists will bring to light minor biographical and biblio-
     graphical slips. "But of the dozen or so book-length studies of
     the man and his works produced to date this is nevertheless the
     one to be most unreservedly recommended to the general reader for
     its careful synthesis of available information, its freedom from
     partial vision and overpreoccupation with minutiae, and for its
     penetrating concentration on essentials and its largeness of
     spirit."

28   WATTERS, R.E. "The Meanings of the White Whale." University
     of Toronto Quarterly, 20 (January), 155–168.
          The meaning of the white whale, like the meaning of the
     doubloon, depends on the subject, on the one who does the look-
     ing--whether Ahab or member of the Pequod's crew or reader.
     There are therefore innumerable meanings for the white whale.
     For Melville, the more nearly omniscient the observer, the more
     true and valuable his interpretation. Reprinted in 1960.A6.

29   WRIGHT, NATHALIA. "Book Reviews." <u>American Literature</u>, 22
     (January), 520-521.
          Review of 1950.A3. Percival's "interpretation of the world
     of Melville in the language of Blake, Boehme, St. Augustine,
     Kierkegaard, the author of the <u>Bhagavad Gita</u>, and other mystics
     is inevitably unsatisfactory. That Melville's world was never,
     like theirs, entirely interior is at least as important a fact
     about it as that it was never exclusively external, and his
     arrival at symbolism from romanticism before naturalism bridged
     the gap for such myth-makers as Joyce and Mann must to the
     twentieth century be his most significant achievement." Perci-
     val's impressionistic allusions fail to explicate the deeper
     meanings of Melville or of themselves.

30   HAYFORD, HARRISON. "Reviews." <u>Modern Language Notes</u>, 66
     (February), 129-131.
          Review of 1949.A1. Chase's diverse purposes, methods, and
     critical weapons lead him to original insights and bold reinter-
     pretations--and to confusion and distortion. Most troublesome is
     the message-hunting: Chase is sure beforehand what message he is
     going to find because he takes one with him on the search and
     brings back only what matches it, supplying forced parallels,
     wrenched from their original application, taken out of context,
     or abstracted from their obvious meaning. He too often lets the
     preconceived message determine his readings. One is also
     troubled by his casualness about facts: his allegorizing both
     literature and life, his way of ignoring or misinterpreting the
     primary surface of works, his unconcern with Melville's actual
     biography. He blurs the distinction between raw materials and
     perfected art, between "dream" and what is recognized and con-
     fronted, between unconscious and conscious meanings.

31   ATKINSON, BROOKS. "At the Theatre." New York <u>Times</u>
     (12 February).
          Review of production of <u>Billy Budd</u>. [See 1951.B4.] It is
     going to be hard to avoid thinking about the malign implications
     of Melville's sea yarn now that Coxe and Chapman have made their
     horrifyingly candid drama out of it. They have written an
     extraordinarily skillful play. The fateful reasoning in the last
     act is hard to follow--it wrestles with so many abstract ideas
     and upsets so thoroughly most human assumptions. But there is a
     strong mind (Melville's) burrowing into Billy Budd's awful fate--
     a sympathetic mind that has no faith in men and is even skeptical
     of the goodness of God. On the surface <u>Billy Budd</u> is as pictur-
     esque as <u>Mister Roberts</u>; but after the scene is set a mind takes
     possession of it and proceeds to knock against some of the most
     tormenting problems of the universe.

32   GIBBS, WOLCOTT. "A Classic and a Casualty." <u>New Yorker</u>, 27
     (17 February), 70.
          Review of production of <u>Billy Budd</u>. [See 1951.B4.] Coxe
     and Chapman "have achieved a strange mixture of straight melo-
     drama and complex ethical discussion. Never having read the
     original (for me, as for too many people, Melville begins and

ends with 'Moby Dick'), I can't say how much the work at the
Biltmore resembles the novelette, but I'm afraid that what they
have written is a singularly shapeless, exasperating, and incredible play."

33   ATKINSON, BROOKS. "Melville's Sea Epic." New York Times
      (18 February), section 2, p. 1.
          Review of production of Billy Budd. [See 1951.B4.] Since
      the production of Uniform of Flesh, Coxe and Chapman have tight-
      ened the story and sharpened the writing. A theatergoer has an
      instinctive feeling that the play has caught the original spirit
      of Melville's work. Melville was convinced that absolute good
      and absolute evil must destroy each other--a thought most of us
      would like to reject. But there is no way of rationalizing the
      theme away by attacking the workmanship of the drama: although
      a dramatization of a novel, Billy Budd is a fully wrought play
      in its own right. [Reprinted in part in 1951.B1.]

34   ANON. "Romantic Meditations." London Times Literary Supple-
      ment, No. 2560 (23 February), p. 114.
          Review of 1950.B4. Notes that Auden's study includes
      "precise inquiries" into the characters of Moby-Dick and the
      things they represent.

35   MARSHALL, MARGARET. "Drama." Nation, 172 (24 February), 189.
          Review of production of Billy Budd. [See 1951.B4.] The
      dramatization "is consistently interesting and often moving,
      excellently acted, and very well mounted. The resolution is not
      convincing--for respectable reasons--and the whole third act is
      weak; but the play exercises the mind and engages the emotions
      on a mature level--which is mighty refreshing." The court mar-
      tial session and the conversation between the captain and Billy
      are crucial to the credibility of Billy's last words, and these
      two scenes fail to carry the conviction that Melville was able
      to impart. There is another reason why the resolution is not
      quite believable: "In the air of 1951 this situation of 1798 is
      superficially so near to being topical that the spectator tends
      to lose sight of the deeper and timeless significance of the story
      as the struggle between good and evil and to demand, 150 years
      after the French Revolution, a kindlier and quite possible con-
      temporary solution."

36   HARCOURT, JOHN B. "Reviews." American Quarterly, 3 (Spring),
      85-86.
          Review of 1950.A1. "Arvin has pulled Melville together
      and made sense out of his successes and his failures and their
      projection into the fantasy-world of art. If we reject his
      psychiatric speculations, we are left with a Melville of fasci-
      nating but unrelated fragments; and unless we can reconstruct
      the pattern along other lines, Arvin's interpretation stands as
      the most successful yet achieved." Other techniques of
      twentieth-century criticism--examination of ambiguity, symbolism,
      and archetypal patterns--are everywhere apparent and put to good
      use. Arvin's book has established itself as the best single

volume on Melville and perhaps as a point of departure for much subsequent criticism.

37   [HILLWAY, TYRUS]. "Billy Budd." Melville Society Newsletter, 7 (March), n.p.
     Notes opening of the Coxe and Chapman adaptation of Billy Budd [see 1951.B4] at the Biltmore Theater, New York, on 10 February 1951, after trial runs in Philadelphia and New Haven.

38   KERR, WALTER. "The Stage." Commonweal, 53 (2 March), 518.
     Review of performance of Billy Budd. [See 1951.B4.] Coxe and Chapman have failed to give the material theatrical tension. What is needed is some sense of doubt about the outcome. The dramatists have been so anxious to preserve the philosophical point and tone of Melville's allegory that they have not bothered to write a play. Both Billy and Claggart are hypothetical notions rather than persons, and the problem of giving them any human warmth or redeeming complexity would probably have proved insurmountable to better dramatists.

39   RAINE, KATHLEEN. "The Sea and the City." New Statesman and Nation [London], 41 (3 March), 252-253.
     Review of 1950.B4. Altogether an illuminating book, full of flashes of suggestion, of tentative yet penetrating answers, thrown out incidentally in Auden's pursuit of questions that lie still deeper. The book leaves the reader with the disturbing sense of more unsaid than said, and yet what it does say is remarkable.

40   SHUMLIN, HERMAN. "A Personal Statement." New York Times (5 March).
     Personal ad taken out after the decision had been made to extend the run of Billy Budd [see 1951.B4] at the Biltmore Theatre. Billy Budd "is an exciting play, a moving play, a stimulating and a beautifully acted and staged play."

41   ZOLOTOW, SAM. "'Billy Budd' Wins 2-Week Extension." New York Times, (5 March).
     Reports that Billy Budd [see 1951.B4], scheduled to close after its twenty-fifth performance, has won "a last minute reprieve" at the Biltmore Theatre for at least two more weeks.

42   DOBRÉE, BONAMY. "Melville--and More Melville." Spectator [London], 186 (9 March), 316, 318.
     Review of 1949.B9, 1950.A1. Arvin has given an admirable example of how to use the instrument of "depth" psychology; perhaps he insists upon it a little too much, but he never descends to jargon or assumes that brash air of confident omniscience, which in some writers, negates what value their work may have. But Arvin "is not primarily a psychologist; he is first and foremost an appraiser of literature, subtle, sensitive and able to analyse his pleasures. His book is beautifully balanced, with enough of the Life to illuminate the Works, and the works

themselves discussed with a just proportion of attention to the
various aspects of creative writing, the relation of fact to
symbol, the use made of the writings of others in combination
with personal experience, the invention of words and verbal forms
to strike fresh sparks." It is a book for writers and for
readers. Leyda provides excellent notes and an extremely interesting introduction to his collection. It is only in "Bartleby,"
perhaps, that the symbol and word become fused in obedience to
the intuition, for most of the stories exhibit a certain fatigue,
as in "Benito Cereno," which begins with such creative sureness
and ends so flatly, even boringly; while in "The Tartarus of
Maids" the symbol remains a piece of meaningless naturalism which
seems merely to state the dry bones of the intuition and fail to
give them significance. Yet every story or sketch has some
phrase or passage of magic, some moment where the deep sense of
life that was Melville's finds creative expression.

43　　BROWN, JOHN MASON. "Hurry! Hurry!" Saturday Review of
　　　Literature, 34 (17 March), 31-33.
　　　　　Review of production of Billy Budd. [See 1951.B4.] "Those
who did not see Billy Budd did their bit to discourage the
theatre from doing its best. They turned their backs on courage
and distinction. They helped the cause of cheapness and mediocrity, of the third-rate and the silly. . . . Worst of all, they
denied themselves an engrossing adventure." The result of the
expansion of "Baby Budd, Sailor" into Billy Budd, Foretopman [see
1948.B9], "though fragmentary, is beyond forgetting. It is distinguished by the same vividness of phrase, characterization, and
narrative, the same sense of being as at home with the soul as
with the sea, the same gift for prose which sings a song commonly
beyond the reach of prose, and the identical altitude of meditation which glorify Moby Dick." Its "subject refuses to be ship-
bound. It is a fable of Good and Evil and of the hatred which
goodness itself can create. It is an inquiry into the cold,
impersonal forces of authority as they ignore and obliterate the
individual who finds himself at odds with them. It is an incident at sea turned, as it were, into a morality play which deals
with the compromises exacted by organized society and the in-
justices carried out in its interest and name." The excitements
of Billy Budd, Foretopman "are sprung so surely from the fascination of Melville's digressions, his philosophical or descriptive passages, the power of his storytelling, and the sheer
melody of his prose" that Brown thought it would resist dramatization: but Coxe and Chapman succeeded in turning it into an
enthralling play. Reprinted in 1952.B5.

44　　HATCH, ROBERT. "Theatre: Reprieve for Billy." New Republic,
　　　124 (19 March), 23.
　　　　　Reports that Billy Budd [see 1951.B4] has been "granted a
two-week extension of its unseemly short run." The adaptation
has faults: the text at times becomes too wordy; the development
of character is sometimes stifled by the flow of eloquence; and
"in an effort to make sure their text would 'play,' the playwrights have gone too far in clothing Melville's austere argument

in warm particularity. Melville was discussing absolutes--good as such and evil as such, and authority in the abstract--while the play concerns an innocent boy, a wicked man and a sadly troubled captain." But, whatever its faults, the play is a demonstration of disciplined imagination vigorously carried out.

45   ANON. "'Billy Budd' Refuses to Fold." Life, 30 (26 March), 87.
       Reports that the Coxe and Chapman adaptation of Billy Budd is continuing to run on Broadway after its scheduled last performance. In the play Claggart and Budd "destroy each other and thus prove Melville's thesis that absolute good and evil cannot exist in a world of compromise." Prints photograph of a scene from the play.

46   MARSDEN, WALTER. "Stories from the Deeps." John O'London's Weekly, 60 (30 March), 181.
       Review of 1949.B9, 1950.A1. "The Encantadas," "Benito Cereno," and "Bartleby" are the most powerful pieces in Leyda's collection, yet several of the others would have made a lesser man's reputation. Arvin's is an informative, comprehensive, and stimulating study that increases our understanding of the man and the artist. Perhaps Arvin's best achievement is his account of Melville's later years and how, after all, Melville ended his literary work with serenity.

47   KAPLAN, SIDNEY. "The Moby Dick in the Service of the Underground Railroad." Phylon, 12 (2d Quarter), 173-176.
       Six months after the publication of Moby-Dick, the schooner Moby Dick, Captain Austin Bearse, master, began service for the Boston Committee of Vigilance as a major link in the underground railroad. Wilbur H. Siebert's statement in The Underground Railroad in Massachusetts that the Moby Dick brought the first fugitive slave to Boston in 1847 is based on a misreading of Austin Bearse's Reminiscences of Fugitive-Slave Labor Days in Boston (Boston, 1880). [See 1951.B24.] Richard Henry Dana, Jr., who was an active member of the Boston Committee of Vigilance at this time may have been responsible for the naming of the schooner.

48   ANON. "Billy Budd." Theatre Arts, 35 (April), 18.
       Review of production of Billy Budd. [See 1951.B4.] "The principal defect is a familiar one: the moral and intelligent content of Melville's novel is reduced to sketchiness by the stage, where the audience has not the time to ponder metaphysical niceties; on the other hand, those ideas are just tyrannical enough to reduce the characters to less than human stature, and to force the play into a theatrically anticlimactic last act. Caught between erratic melodrama and thumbnail debate, the playgoer is trapped by tedium. From the moment Billy Budd appears, his tragic downfall is properly inevitable, but there is little grandness to the unfolding of the design. The sense of tragedy is lost, because the authors have presented it in a dramatic vacuum. Nor are any of the big moments any the more effective

for being rendered in a flabby iambic pentameter, neither prose
nor poetry, which invites the brain to slumber."

49   BABCOCK, C. MERTON. "Melville's Backwoods Seamen." Western
     Folklore, 10 (April), 126–133.
        Examples of allusions in Moby-Dick by which Melville iden-
     tifies the temper of the whaling industry with the temper of the
     advancing western frontier; and examples of folk traditions
     employed in the book (superstitions of seafaring folk, practical
     lore, folk customs, folk art, tall talk, and tall tales). A
     survey of the folk elements in Moby-Dick shows a close affinity
     between the types of traditions among whalemen and the types of
     traditions among other American frontier peoples.

50   SEGAL, DAVID. Letter to the Drama Editor. New York Times
     (1 April).
        The Coxe and Chapman adaptation of Billy Budd [see
     1951.B4] "affords a rallying point for those of us who deplore
     the galloping commercialism of the Broadway theatre." The play
     provided one of Segal's "most moving and exciting evenings in
     the theatre."

51   ATKINSON, BROOKS. "About 'Billy Budd.'" New York Times
     (15 April), section 2, p. 1.
        Reports that New York critics cast eight votes for the Coxe
     and Chapman adaptation of Billy Budd [see 1951.B4], two fewer
     than for Darkness at Noon, winner of the critics' award. (No
     other play received more than three votes.) The crusading
     enthusiasm for the play is a sign of the spiritual vitality that
     is always lurking beneath the normal cynicism of Broadway. Some
     people who admire the play as a work of art feel nevertheless
     that the philosophy and the action have not been perfectly
     blended; but in general it is a powerful drama with vivid charac-
     ters and the pungent flavor of a rousing sea tale. There ought
     to be no confusion on this point: "The verdict of the court-
     martial is monstrously wrong. Although it adheres to the letter
     of the law, it is evil and vicious. It can be explained but it
     cannot be justified. Even Melville recognized it, not only as
     wrong, but as abnormal, for he intimates in the novel that the
     captain may have been mentally unbalanced at the time; and that
     if the captain had been in full possession of his powers he would
     not have pushed Billy into an immediate court-martial but would
     have held him for an impartial trial later before the admiral
     of the fleet." Coxe and Chapman "have eliminated Melville's
     tentative suggestion of mental unbalance. They represent the
     captain as a rationalizing intellectual who . . . confuses a
     simple matter brilliantly and thus provokes disaster. The cap-
     tain destroys not only Billy but himself, all his associates and
     the morale of the ship by venerating knowledge above morality.
     The conclusion would be unbelievable if Melville had not known
     that something of the same grisly sort occurred in the American
     brig-at-war, Somers, in 1842." Coxe and Chapman have made a
     trenchant drama out of Melville's rather clumsily written novel.

52   BEYER, WILLIAM H.   "The State of the Theatre: The Waning
     Season." School and Society, 73 (21 April), 248-249.
          Review of production of Billy Budd. [See 1951.B4.] In
     substance, the play "is a powerful indictment illustrating man's
     perpetual inhumanity to man and of the institution framed to give
     complete authority to tyranny, having man serve law, rather than
     law serve man. The forces of pure good and consummate evil are
     sharply drawn, and the tensions, not only between the two men
     symbolizing the two forces, but among those who are the very warp
     and woof of the fabric of 18th-century naval authority, provoke
     an arresting and fearful conflict. The universal quality of the
     theme underlying the drama lifts it out of routine melodrama into
     the realm of genuine tragedy and gives 'Billy Budd' its distinc-
     tion."

53   FORSTER, E.M. "The Unbuilt City." Listener [London], 45
     (26 April), 673.
          Review of 1950.B4. "Melville is being profoundly explored
     today, especially in the United States, and like all ploughed-up
     authors his surface has got rather bumpy. Fortunately Auden is
     a poet who understands what poems feel like as well as what they
     mean, and who does not rely too much upon incest and castration.
     The sea guides him. . . . Real and symbolic voyages coincide and
     by the end of the discussion we have a clearer vision of Ahab's
     tragedy."

54   CUNLIFFE, MARCUS. "American Classics." New Statesman and
     Nation [London], 41 (28 April), 484, 486.
          Review of 1950.A1. Arvin's book is first rate. Beauti-
     fully balanced between biography and criticism, it presents a
     complete and exciting picture of Melville, what he was trying to
     say, and why. The chapter on The Whale is masterly. Arvin,
     while warmly aware of Melville's greatness, is an admirer and not
     an infatuate. He admits the weaknesses even in Moby-Dick. It
     would be hard to overpraise Arvin's achievement.

55   BRASWELL, WILLIAM. "Melville's Opinion of Pierre." American
     Literature, 23 (May), 246-250.
          Melville's letter of 16 April 1852 to Richard Bentley
     [Letters, pp. 149-151] does not express his sincere estimate of
     Pierre. When one considers his knowledge of mid-nineteenth-
     century taste and his own as a novelist, it seems impossible that
     he could have believed Pierre "very much more calculated for
     popularity" than such books as Redburn and White-Jacket. He
     could not have been ignorant that Pierre lacked qualities admired
     by the general reader and could not possibly have conceived of
     Pierre as a regular romance--a genre for which he expresses con-
     tempt in Pierre itself. Instead of considering Melville obtuse
     enough to believe that Pierre would appeal to a wide audience, it
     seems more reasonable to think of him as a man who, in a dis-
     traught and complex state of mind, found perverse satisfaction
     in writing the book to please himself though he knew it would not
     please the public. There is also little reason for crediting
     Melville's statement that he planned to write more such books and

expected to make money from them; and his sincerity in suggesting that anonymous or pseudonymous publication might help the sale of the book is equally questionable. Why did Melville write such a letter? Though it may be impossible to arrive at a completely satisfactory answer, one important clue may be found in the sardonic humor manifested in his presenting the public so strange, wild, and terrifying a book as Pierre in the guise of a romance with a gay beginning.

56   FENTON, CHARLES A. "'The Bell-Tower': Melville and Technology." American Literature, 23 (May), 219-232.
    In "The Bell-Tower," Melville discusses "the technological man" of the American 1850s and "the desperate necessity for some decent and orderly relationship between him and his God, and . . . between him and his fellows." According to the story's implicit social commentary, there "is a mutual responsibility between the mechanician and his patrons, and between the mechanician and his employees." Patrons, employees, and the entire populace in "The Bell-Tower" participate in Bannadonna's crime.

57   ATKINSON, BROOKS. "Don't Hang Billy." New York Times (6 May), section 2, p. 1.
    Response to a number of people who have replied, in "long, closely reasoned letters" to 1951.B51, defending Vere's execution of Billy. Interpretation of Melville's thought "need not extend to the point where Melville is charged with endorsing what he reports. . . . We can revere the simple honesty of an old man who is leaving his last will and testament without assuming that he also approved of the frightful things he knew about. . . . Billy's 'God bless Captain Vere!' may indicate that Melville was leaving an imperfect world without rancor or bitterness. But it certainly does not mean that the destruction of goodness by inflexible law is a fine thing, or that Melville was purged and elated by hanging from the mastyard an ideal boy. Melville was not that inhuman."

58   ANON. "Outer Circle Names 'Billy Budd' Best Play." New York Times (27 May).
    Reports that Coxe and Chapman's Billy Budd [see 1951.B4] was chosen best play of the season by The Outer Circle, a group of correspondents and critics employed by out-of-town newspapers. Prints note by Melville's granddaughter Eleanor Melville Metcalf explaining how the manuscript of Billy Budd survived, to be read at the award-giving party.

59   MILLS, GORDON H. "American First Editions at TxU: VII. Herman Melville (1819-1891)." Library Chronicle of the University of Texas, 4 (Summer), 89-92.
    Reports that the University of Texas Library owns copies of all of the first American editions of the fourteen books Melville published in his lifetime, except for Clarel; three English first editions (Typee, The Whale, and The Confidence-Man); and the revised edition (1846) of Typee. "The collection of Melville books in TxU is now so good that there is reason to hope it may become outstanding."

60   PEARSON, NORMAN HOLMES. "Billy Budd: 'The King's Yarn.'"
     American Quarterly, 3 (Summer), 99–114.
          In Billy Budd Melville was trying "to give in as univer-
     salized a way as possible . . . another redaction of the myth
     which had concerned Milton" in the trilogy of his three major
     works, Paradise Lost, Paradise Regained, and Samson Agonistes--
     the myth of man's fall from innocence and redemption. The rela-
     tionship between Billy, Claggart, and Vere is dependent upon both
     Milton's poetry and the Bible. Billy has resemblances with both
     prelapsarian Adam and Christ, Claggart with Satan. Vere is post-
     lapsarian man who is redeemed. Reprinted in Springer, pp. 36–52.

61   CAHOON, HERBERT. "Herman Melville: A Check List of Books and
     Manuscripts in the Collections of The New York Public Library."
     Bulletin of the New York Public Library, 55 (June), 263–275.
          A checklist of collected and selected editions and indi-
     vidual works, including first editions, in the New York Public
     Library. [Continued in 1951.B72.]

62   CAMPBELL, HARRY MODEAN. "The Hanging Scene in Melville's
     Billy Budd, Foretopman." Modern Language Notes, 66 (June),
     378–381.
          Billy Budd records not Melville's "acceptance," as many
     critics have argued, but Melville's belief that in a universe
     like ours not even a Christlike innocence is any protection
     against universal doom. The overwhelming evidence for Melville's
     ironical pessimism lies in the hanging scene, where the text
     brings us to the "ironical realization" that Billy's "ascension"
     is only to the yard-end.

63   HILLWAY, TYRUS. "Melville as Amateur Zoologist." Modern
     Language Quarterly, 12 (June), 159–164.
          Errors in Melville's descriptions of southern Pacific sea
     life in Mardi. "Though he was later, in Moby-Dick, to show a
     surprising mastery of cetological information, in the trial
     period of Mardi he seems to have relied upon reading restricted
     to semiscientific works like those of [Frederick D.] Bennett and
     other travel writers as well as upon his own experiences and
     sailors' tales for his zoological facts. Thus he fell into in-
     evitable errors and inaccuracies. Like most of his contempo-
     raries, he seems not at this point to have been aware of the real
     nature of the scientific movement which was developing during the
     nineteenth century.

64   HOWARD, LEON. "'Milton and Melville.'" Nineteenth-Century
     Fiction, 6 (June), 76.
          Review of 1950.A4. The redaction of a doctoral disserta-
     tion that has the virtue of thoroughness and the fault of exces-
     sive self-consciousness in methodology and defensive pleading.
     Pommer is forced to strain the signs of direct relationship in
     order to justify his study. That Milton stands next to the Bible
     and Shakespeare in importance of literary influence on Melville
     remains doubtful, despite Pommer's conclusions.

65   LEASE, BENJAMIN. "Melville and the Booksellers." Melville
      Society Newsletter, 7 (June), n.p.
         Quotes prices obtained for first American editions of
      Melville's books in 1894, 1897, 1901, 1906, and 1914.

66   MABBOTT, THOMAS O. "Melville's A RAIL ROAD CUTTING NEAR
      ALEXANDRIA IN 1855." Explicator, 9 (June), item 55.
         The usual form of Sesostres, in line 6, is Sesostris.
      Miriam, in line 9, was the sister of Moses. Melville seems to
      have an idea her name was connected with the spice myrrh, for he
      first wrote her name with two r's. His joke is harmlessly in-
      correct. Melville seems to have wanted to say that the modern
      industrial invasion of Egypt lessened the dignity of that land,
      previously upheld by the most ancient traditions. "Watts his
      name," in line 8, refers to James Watts, inventor of the modern
      steam engine.

67   SHROEDER, JOHN W. "Sources and Symbols for Melville's
      Confidence-Man." PMLA, 66 (June), 363-380.
         Finds sources for The Confidence-Man in Hawthorne's "The
      Celestial Railroad," Bunyan's Pilgrim's Progress, and the Revela-
      tion of St. John. The world of The Confidence-Man "is a great
      Vanity Fair, situated on an allegorical steamboat which, pre-
      sumably sailing for New Orleans (on the symbolic level, for the
      New Jerusalem of nineteenth-century optimism and liberal theol-
      ogy), is inclining its course dangerously toward the pits of the
      Black Rapids Coal Company. Aboard the vessel we have pilgrimag-
      ing mankind." Snake and Indian imagery, among other clues, re-
      veal the diabolic nature of the shape-shifting confidence man,
      who is "inordinately active" amidst these pilgrims. The con-
      fidence he demands "is confidence that the world has no dark
      side; that the boat is unerringly and necessarily bound for the
      Celestial City." The penalty for giving this confidence is
      damnation. In the last chapter, the confidence man "has
      triumphed; he leads mankind, through an extinct universe, to his
      lightless kingdom. . . . [T]he steamboat, filled with those who
      have confidence in herbs and easy-chairs, nature and boys, coal
      companies and Indian charities, counterfeit detectors and
      chamber-stools, has taken a direct course for the pit." The
      Indian-hater is the world's only remedy against the confidence
      man; there is no distortion in his vision of spiritual reality.
      The Confidence-Man is complete within the limits it proposes to
      itself, complete in the same sense that Pilgrim's Progress and
      "The Celestial Railroad" are complete. Among Melville's writings
      other than Moby-Dick, it stands as a hale and well-proportioned
      giant. [See 1952.B122 for reply.] Reprinted in Norton The
      Confidence-Man, pp. 298-316.

68   STOLL, ELMER E. "Symbolism in Moby-Dick." Journal of the
      History of Ideas, 12 (June), 440-465.
         A protest against the excesses, vagaries, and far-fetched
      interpretations in criticism of Moby-Dick, the result of "the
      prevalent taste for symbolism." Moby-Dick is "the story of a
      man's lifelong revenge upon a whale for thwarting him in his

money-making designs upon its blubber." It is a good story, even a great one, but not one of really ecumenical or perennial importance. It is not by any means to be accounted an immortal masterpiece. As a whole the story is well constructed, but it suffers from two considerable defects: padding and sensationalism. Melville is a good writer, and in narrative at times a powerful one; but he is very uneven, uncertain.

69   WRIGHT, NATHALIA. "The Head and the Heart in Melville's *Mardi*." *PMLA*, 66 (June), 351–362.
      Mardi is the most important single work by Melville for the study of one of his most important themes: his search for the "full-developed man." The "pattern of the Mardian quest for this mean is a continual oscillation between two extremes: the life of the head, laid on a mountain or rock, realized in the projection of the ego, accomplished through acquisitiveness, symbolized by thieves and predatory creatures; and the life of the heart, laid in a valley or glen, devoted to sociability, expressed through the senses, symbolized by females and amphibians."

70   PAUL, SHERMAN. "Hawthorne's Ahab." *Notes and Queries*, 196 (9 June), 255–257.
      Similarities between Ethan Brand and Ahab, the literary counterparts of their author's unencumbered egos. Spiritual kin, both are demonic, both commit the unpardonable sin of intellect, both are immured in isolation, both are self-immolating. Mutual interest in such demonism probably made the strength of the friendship between Hawthorne and Melville.

71   ANON. "Melville Collection Donated to Library." New York *Times* (24 June), p. 36.
      Notes that Melville's granddaughter Mrs. Abeel D. Osborne has recently donated to the New York Public Library more than seventy volumes from Melville's library, including works by Balzac, Ruskin, Tennyson, and Disraeli, annotated in Melville's handwriting.

72   CAHOON, HERBERT. "Herman Melville: A Check List of Books and Manuscripts in the Collections of The New York Public Library." *Bulletin of the New York Public Library*, 55 (July), 325–338.
      Continued from 1951.B61. A checklist of individual works, including first editions; books containing contributions by Melville; periodical contributions; manuscripts and letters; and association copies.

73   HAYFORD, HARRISON. "The Sailor Poet of *White-Jacket*." *Boston Public Library Quarterly*, 3 (July), 221–228.
      Identifies Nord in *White-Jacket* as Oliver Russ, "who used the purser's name Edward Norton"; and "Lemsford the poet" as Ephraim Curtiss Hine, a minor sailor-poet. Both Russ and Hine were shipmates of Melville's aboard the *United States*.

74   ROPER, GORDON. "The Making and the Meaning of Moby-Dick."
      University of Toronto Quarterly, 20 (July), 434–436.
          Review of 1949.A3; 1950.A3. Vincent shows convincingly
      for the first time that Melville wrote two Moby-Dicks. He
      demonstrates how skillfully Melville transmuted his sources into
      the powerful prose and searching symbolism of Moby-Dick, but the
      final value of his book lies in the vigor of his able pursuit of
      the meaning of the Great White Whale. Percival assumes that the
      greatness of Moby-Dick is in its inspired bodying forth in fic-
      tional action of the most profound metaphysical truths. His
      interpretation sacrifices some of the elements of richness in the
      book, but gives clarity of insight into other elements and ought
      to send the reader back to his Moby-Dick again.

75   SUTTON, WALTER. "Melville's 'Pleasure Party' and the Art of
      Concealment." Philological Quarterly, 30 (July), 316–327.
          Apparent inconsistencies in the central character's point
      of view can be resolved by consideration of the poem's dominant
      images and allusions, notably to Platonic myth and the legend of
      Sappho's leap. The poem then "appears not merely as a considera-
      tion of the effects of frustration in love upon the personality
      of a man or woman, but rather as a concern for the effect upon an
      individual, as artist, of a frustrated bisexual love so con-
      fusedly oriented as to prevent the adjustment and fulfillment
      which the poet feels necessary to sustained creative effort.
      Knowing Melville's characteristic method of indirection and his
      reading in classical philosophy and mythology, one can be sure
      that the ambiguousness of Urania's sexual nature is an inten-
      tional effect and that Melville was fully aware of the bisexual
      implications of his allusions to Platonic myth and to the legend
      of Sappho's leap."

76   STARRETT, VINCENT. "Books Alive." Chicago Sunday Tribune
      Magazine of Books (29 July).
          Notes the centenary of Moby-Dick and the many different
      interpretations of the book by critics. Melville is now one of
      the towering figures in our literature, and the mounting number
      of biographical and critical studies suggests the growth of a
      new American industry.

77   TAYLOR, ROBERT S. "New Books Appraised." Library Journal, 76
      (August), 1214.
          Review of 1951.A2. A welcome well-written addition to
      Melvilliana, the first book-length treatment of Melville's youth,
      using sources heretofore unused.

78   CROZIER, ERIC. "The British Navy in 1797." Tempo [London],
      21 (Autumn), 11.
          Though sometimes bookish, Melville's account of naval life
      in 1797 is vivid and exact, for he had gathered its details from
      seamen who had "helped to win a coronet for Nelson at the Nile,
      and the naval crown of crowns for him at Trafalgar." Whether or
      not Billy, Claggart, and Vere in fact existed, they exist im-
      mortally in Melville's tragic story against a background of exact
      observation and realism.

79   GROSS, JOHN J. "The Rehearsal of Ishmael: Melville's
     'Redburn.'" Virginia Quarterly Review, 27 (Autumn), 581–600.
         Redburn marks a considerable advance over Mardi in the
mastery and control of style, in mature understanding of character, and in the effective use of symbol. But it contains serious
violations of point of view and tedious and digressive chapters,
evidence of hasty composition. When the ship reaches Liverpool,
one is forced to accept a new and more mature focus with the
emphasis shifting to social commentary as Melville steps forth
as narrator and speaks through a new Redburn, who brings to his
judgments upon man's inhumanity to man a much greater emotional
and experiential maturity than that implicit in the "boy" who had
shipped from New York. Redburn, moreover, remains too entirely
a victim ever to be realized dramatically in the course of the
novel; as a symbol of innocence he is too little the positive
force necessary for an effective agent in the struggle against
the evil of social and human depravity. Yet we recognize in
Redburn the principal elements of Moby-Dick clearly enunciated
for the first time. Redburn is an undeveloped Ishmael, innocent
and therefore sinless at the beginning, but losing his innocence
and consequently becoming aware of sin.

80   MASON, RONALD. "Herman Melville and 'Billy Budd.'" Tempo
     [London], 21 (Autumn), 6–8.
         It is impossible to value Billy Budd at its true worth
without studying it in the light of Melville's private despairs.
It records Melville's ultimate conviction that Good, by being
reconciled with Evil, can vanquish it altogether—dramatizes the
victory of Innocence over the deadly Experience that had appeared
to destroy it. Melville had traveled a long road from the convinced nihilism of Moby-Dick to the sublime acceptance of Billy
Budd. To understand Billy Budd properly we must first follow
Melville through the tortuous dogmas and debates of Clarel. In
the light of Billy Budd Melville's earlier work derives new illumination and perspective; and, although Billy Budd has neither
the stature nor the profundity of Moby-Dick, it is no longer possible to appreciate the one without the other. Billy Budd's
prime importance is in its expression of the serenity that accompanies the acceptance by a great tragic artist of a reconciliation
by which tragedy is at last transcended.

81   ROPER, GORDON. "Melville's Moby-Dick, 1851–1951." Dalhousie
     Review, 31 (Autumn), 167–179.
         Surveys the critical and scholarly response to Moby-Dick
from date of publication to centenary. The most significant
aspect of the rise in Melville's reputation is the change in the
judgment of the profundity of thought and the fineness of artistry
in his work. Matthiessen's [1941.A1] is still the most suggestive
analysis and synthesis of what Melville created in Moby-Dick.
"Much has been done; much remains to be done. We still lack a
comprehensive formal analysis of the fusion of content and form
in the book; we still have overlooked much of Melville's skillful
counterpointing of themes and orchestration of feeling; we still
tend to treat the book as a sea from which we can draw out just

the fish we find interesting. What has been written about the book are but soundings." Although British and American publishers published only the two original editions and four reprints in the nineteenth century, twelve more editions were published between 1900 and 1922, and British and American publishers alone have published over one hundred editions since 1922.

82   ANON. "Current Books." Nineteenth-Century Fiction, 6 (September), 151–152.
     Review of 1951.B4. A reader of the script will understand at once why the recent Broadway production was such a resounding critical success. Coxe and Chapman "have made the most of the opportunities which Melville's story afforded them to emphasize the morality theme of the conflict between good and evil. To this end the inquiry extends into the nature of justice, and particularly into the relationship between freedom and authority. These are pertinent questions at the moment, but the fundamental problem posed here transcends mere timeliness. Probing the heart of the most vital of all speculations, the relation between man and God, Melville rises above the local and the temporal to provide a commentary that urges resignation to the divine will."

83   BELL, MILLICENT. "Pierre Bayle and Moby Dick." PMLA, 66 (September), 626–648.
     The influence of Bayle's Dictionnaire historique et critique on Moby-Dick. Correlations "at times specific, at times philosophic, at times even stylistic" between Melville and Bayle "establish the depth of Melville's interest in the Dictionary and suggest the thoroughness with which he assimilated what he found there." Reprinted in part in Recognition, pp. 285–298.

84   BLOOM, EDWARD A. "The Allegorical Principle." ELH: A Journal of English Literary History, 18 (September), 188.
     Readers who see in Moby-Dick only an engrossing adventure story on the primary level of meaning have failed to take cognizance of Melville's complex and conscious union of the moral intellect and the aesthetic imagination. Melville's anxiety in chapter 44, "The Affidavit," that the story of the white whale might be construed as something other than a literal story is surely ironic.

85   HABER, TOM BURNS. "A Note on Melville's 'Benito Cereno.'" Nineteenth-Century Fiction, 6 (September), 146–147.
     Don Benito inflicts the razor cut on Babo's cheek after the shaving scene. Babo demonstrates at a moment of supreme provocation something that his civilized antagonist could not muster: restraint. [See 1952.B83 for reply.]

86 [HILLWAY, TYRUS]. "Bibliographical Notes." Melville Society
Newsletter, 7 (September), n.p.
The Report of the Committee on Trends in Research in American Literature, 1940-1950, by the American Literature Group of
the Modern Language Association, shows that Melville elicited
more scholarship during the decade than any other American
author. The committee counted 159 articles, 26 books, 30 theses,
25 research projects, and 3 MLA papers on Melville.

87 MABBOTT, THOMAS. "Melville Explicator." Melville Society
Newsletter, 7 (September), n.p.
Explains that the Hotel de Cluny was erected on ruins of
baths called les Thermes de Julien, the name referring to Emperor
Julian. [See Moby-Dick, chapter 41.] Suggests that the "block"
referred to in the first sentence of chapter 13 of Moby-Dick is
one used for showing a wig, though Melville may be punning on the
meaning "a bargain"; and that the "sea candies and macaroni" of
chapter 56 "are marine invertebrates which look like candies from
translucency and glitter, and worm-like creatures which remind
one of spaghetti."

88 NICHOL, JOHN W. "Melville and the Midwest." PMLA, 66
(September), 613-625.
Internal evidence from Melville's work used to reconstruct
his trip to and from Galena, Illinois, in 1840, "and to indicate
the extensive use of western imagery throughout his writing,
imagery which very possibly was suggested from personal observation." He probably traveled to Galena via the Erie Canal and the
Great Lakes, taking a stagecoach from Chicago to Galena, and
probably returned to Albany by way of the Mississippi-Ohio River
water highway.

89 STAFFORD, JOHN. "Henry Norman Hudson and the Whig Use of
Shakespeare." PMLA, 66 (September), 649-661.
The literary criticism of Hudson and his allies helps to
explain the reaction of Whitman, Melville, and other American
writers to Shakespeare and the lessons of the past. Melville's
remarks on Shakespeare in "Hawthorne and His Mosses" may reflect
his reaction to the conservatives' use of Shakespeare. Melville
sounds like a young American opponent of Hudson and G.W. Peck
when he defends the propriety of comparing Hawthorne to Shakespeare.

90 NEWBY, P.H. "The Sea and the Savage." Listener [London], 46
(20 September), 458.
On James Fenimore Cooper. What Cooper wrote about the
basic problems encountered by all American writers in the preface
to The Spy was later repeated by Hawthorne and Melville.

91 BABCOCK, MERTON C. "The Language of Melville's 'Isolatoes.'"
Western Folklore, 10 (October), 285-289.
Examples of "sea words and sayings" used by Melville. The
"colorfully metaphorical, albeit crude and uncouth, language of

seaways reached the high-water mark of literary significance" in
Moby-Dick.

92   SALE, ARTHUR. "Captain Vere's Reasons." Cambridge Journal, 5
      (October 1951–September 1952), 3–18.
          Analysis of Vere's reasoning and conduct in Billy Budd.
      Unfavorable to Vere. Vere and Claggart are more complementary
      than opposite.

93   SUTCLIFFE, DENHAM. "Probing Eye Turned on Melville."
      Christian Science Monitor (12 October).
          Review of 1951.A3. A book of sane and sound scholarship,
      appealing always to the demonstrable fact. Perhaps Howard's best
      accomplishment is that he admits one to a new understanding of
      the degree to which the books were shaped by Melville's reading,
      and that he relates so clearly the devious course of their compo-
      sition. All the work lacks "is a sense of Herman Melville as a
      man. In a way, the book tells more than one wants to know, for
      it adheres to the facts with a remorseless completeness. In
      another way, it tells too little. In a laudable effort to strip
      away the theoretical interpretations of the man it all but ex-
      plains him away. For the man who inspired those interpretations
      is not without his mystery."

94   LONGSTRETH, T. MORRIS. "Centenary of a White Whale."
      Christian Science Monitor (18 October).
          Biographical sketch; laudatory comments on Moby-Dick.
      Moby-Dick illustrations by Gene Langley.

95   WAGENKNECHT, EDWARD. "Sanity Now in Melville Scholarship."
      Chicago Sunday Tribune Magazine of Books (21 October), p. 2.
          Review of 1951.A2-3. Ever since the beginning of the
      Melville revival after World War I, Melville has been the special
      darling of the literary crackpot. It is the distinction of these
      two books that they have restored Melville scholarship to nor-
      malcy. Gilman subjects Redburn to such a searching critical
      examination as few American novels have endured; every page is
      both sound and exhilarating. Both writers set forth what is
      known about Melville, not what they have imagined; but neither
      thinks that important scholarship can exist without imagination.
      Howard speculates freely upon occasion, but he speculates sensi-
      bly and legitimately, and he tells his reader when he is specu-
      lating.

96   SPILLER, ROBERT E. "Book Reviews." American Literature, 23
      (November), 384–385.
          Review of 1950.A4. Pommer's book is far more important
      than its own subject matter: it attempts to develop a methodol-
      ogy for problems of literary influence. By showing at the start
      that Milton was in the thought stream of Melville's contempo-
      raries and associates, Pommer lays the foundations of his study
      on the broadest possible base; but he is never careless in his
      own thinking. If pedantic readers object to any of his conclu-
      sions, they will usually find that Pommer has been there ahead

of them with the same objection. For Pommer is apparently a pedant in the best sense—he never stretches nor distorts his facts knowingly, but he is not afraid of speculation, which he labels carefully as speculation.

97   ANON. "Princeton to Note Novel's Centenary." New York Times
       (11 November), p. 114.
       Reports that an exhibition of rare books and manuscripts has been arranged by Princeton University's Firestone Library to mark the hundredth anniversary of the publication of Moby-Dick, including first editions and original manuscripts from private collections of Melville scholars to supplement items from the university's collections.

98   COWLEY, MALCOLM. "An Indispensable Guide to a Fuller Under-
       standing of Herman Melville." New York Herald Tribune Book
       Review (11 November), p. 7.
       Review of 1951.A4. For more than a decade Melville has been the victim of interpretations and misinterpretations that have been weaving themselves into a Melville legend. Now we are at last given the sort of book about him that only national heroes receive. There have been too many comments on Melville; what we need now is exactly what Leyda has given us: the facts from which to compose our own picture of the man and his work. Some notions suggested by all the documents Leyda has collected, in their interrelationship are: (1) Melville was preeminently a family man, living surrounded by relatives; (2) his marriage was more successful than we would gather from reading some of the recent biographies; (3) Melville's central difficulty was pro-fessional, not sexual—the problem he never solved and finally abandoned as impossible of solution was that of finding a public prepared to read what he wanted to write; (4) the documents sug-gest a new interpretation of his estrangement from Hawthorne—that it was Melville, rather than Hawthorne, who allowed the friendship to lapse, just as he stopped seeing another friend, Evert Duyckinck; in his exhausted and dispirited state Melville was withdrawing into himself. The record shows that for the rest of his life Melville had no friends outside his own family.

99   VINCENT, HOWARD P. "The Man Melville Sheds His Myth." New
       York Times Book Review (11 November), pp. 1, 25.
       Review of 1951.A2-4. Especially during the past decade, "the White Whale has crashed head-on into the modern conscious-ness affecting the reader of comic strips as well as the long-haired critic of the little magazines." Four centennial con-ferences this year on Moby-Dick suggest a vogue enjoyed by no other American book, a vogue affecting also French, Italian, German and English readers. Part of the Melville myth was that everything in the novels must have autobiographical authority, must be literally true. This belief has relieved scholars of the tedious digging among documents for contemporary evidence, with the exception of Anderson [see 1939.A1] and the present three biographers. With Gilman's study, the myth immediately begins to disappear; its scholarly soundness and critical shrewdness

contrast strikingly with the shallow persiflage of some recent
Melville criticism. The myth vanishes completely with Howard's
biography: Howard "presents a portrait of Melville which is
human and comprehensible, one consonant with the Eaton portrait
rather than with the Romantic sterotypes, long overworked, of the
wanderer Ishmael, the vulture-torn Prometheus, the cynic
Diogenes." The biography is enriched by Howard's wide knowledge
of American civilization and his uncanny skill in placing two
details together to make a third. With the publication of
Leyda's findings--the most profitable in the history of Melville
scholarship--each student may construct his own biography of
Melville. With Howard's and Leyda's biographies, Melville is no
longer myth; he has become a human being, but in no way made
little--rather he is enlarged. These three books are what might
be termed "exterior" biographies: "that is, resisting the seduc-
tions of amateur psychologizing, they do not make their primary
goal the search for the 'mind' of Melville, nor do they crudely
read his life from his fiction. If their approach seems ultra-
cautious compared with the carefree flights of the impression-
ists, that is itself a tribute." Years from now "some brave man
may write a biography of Melville in which are blended the exterior facts with the interior facts, or insights."

100   ANON. "Notes on Melville." Newsweek, 38 (12 November), 110,
       112.
       Review of 1951.A4. Leyda's Log does not essentially change
the prevailing picture of Melville's life, which still seems
mysterious and haunting, but his life now seems infinitely more
tense, closer to the present, with its mysteries darker. The
Log builds such a picture of the times that readers without
knowledge of Melville's career and novels can follow it; and it
contains so much new material that even Melville scholars will
find it enlightening. The usual picture of Melville's later
years is that he lived in the dull bureaucratic monotony of his
customs job, forgotten by the literary world. The evidence Leyda
offers confirms this, but it also suggests that Melville's dull
routine involved great tragedy. The sequence of disasters after
the suicide of his son Malcolm (the deaths of his brothers and
sister and other son, Stanwix) gives the end of the book something of the air of the final scene in Hamlet, all the stranger
for being coupled with polite expressions of esteem from readers
who had thought Melville was dead. Leyda's patient accumulation
of detail in this instance is surely one of the finest pieces of
scholarly research ever devoted to an American writer, and it is
unforgettable. Leyda is one of the most extravagant of the new
critics of Melville, and his previous writing has been almost
unreadable in its excessive praise and exhaustive attempts to
wring symbolic significance from the simplest of Melville's
details. His attempt to make the recorded facts of Melville's
life speak for themselves is unquestionably more valuable than
another volume of the "new criticism" would have been.

101   CAHOON, HERBERT. "New Books Appraised." <u>Library Journal</u>, 76
      (15 November), 1931.
          Review of 1951.A3-4. Perhaps the most important and sig-
      nificant studies yet made of Melville's life. Publication of
      these two brilliant studies is a noble tribute to Melville and
      his literary reputation.

102   WISHART, DR. CHARLES F. "Birthday of a Whale." Wooster
      (Ohio) <u>Daily Record</u> (29 November).
          Notes the hundredth anniversary of publication of <u>Moby-Dick</u>
      and its status now, along with <u>The Scarlet Letter</u> and <u>Huckleberry
      Finn</u>, as "an outstanding classic American novel." Confesses
      never to have read <u>Moby-Dick</u> and claims acquaintance only with
      Melville's shorter stories and chiefly with one unforgettable
      poem, "The Martyr"--a "song of vengeance" that Melville "frankly
      states is intended to picture the popular feeling in April, 1865.
      Perhaps a frustrated and embittered man could best dramatize that
      feeling. At any rate it was this spirit of revenge which wrecked
      the humane plans of Abraham Lincoln, strengthened the hands of
      the bitter-end radicals in Congress, and subjected the South to
      ten years of horrible oppression and misrule."

103   LEWIS, R.W.B. "Yes and the Devil." <u>Hudson Review</u>, 3
      (Winter), 619-626.
          Review of 1950.A1. While leaving nothing out, Arvin exer-
      cises a critical method which permits every fact and every opin-
      ion to find its own place and assume its own significance; the
      result is a fresh organic whole in which the various parts of
      moments of the critical and biographical discussion serve to
      interanimate each other. Arvin's is the first Melville in whom
      we can believe as the author of <u>Moby-Dick</u>. His treatment of the
      early years and the first novels is uncommonly suggestive, since
      Arvin quietly underlines the way in which Melville began where
      the idealists left off: taking his start amid the idealist
      enthusiasm, Melville grew into full intellectual adulthood, to
      the point of a new and vital awareness of the relation, if not
      between man and God, between the human and the larger than human,
      though this original organic connection with the idealists did
      not prevent Melville later from writing about "the blackness of
      darkness." The unique and enduring value of Arvin's analysis of
      <u>Moby-Dick</u> is that he both disentangles and then orders the
      psychological-ethical and metaphysical levels, while not forget-
      ting that they are fused in the poem and are integral to a single
      rich poetic effect. Arvin makes a new use of the ancient four-
      fold method of exegesis, handsomely adapted to the nineteenth-
      century doctrine of correspondence as well as to the later reve-
      lations of psychiatry. Arvin's interpretation of the doubloon in
      <u>Moby-Dick</u> as the symbol of a necessary doubleness of vision is
      questionable, along with his odd undervaluation of "Benito
      Cereno"; the whale, seeing perhaps too liberally on both opposite
      sides, is smitten (Ishmael observes) with "a fatal perplexity of
      volition."

104   SNYDER, OLIVER. "A Note on 'Billy Budd.'" Accent, 11
       (Winter), 58-60.
          Agrees with Chase that "the real theme of Billy Budd is
       castration and cannibalism, the ritual murder and the eating of
       the Host," but finds a prior level of meaning, the political.
       "Like the maturing working class which they symbolize, both
       Claggart and Billy functioned efficiently in their jobs, but deep
       within Claggart was the ache for innocence, and within Billy, the
       stutter (castration, self-sacrifice, etc.). Man is more than a
       sailor (that is, man is more than an economic being), Melville
       seems to be saying, and must exist in this world which is Cain's
       City. Billy succeeds well in Eden and childhood, which is
       symbolized by the blissful period aboard the ship, Rights of Man
       (the natural rights are inherent in the state of nature). But
       the way of the world is Cain's law, force and law. And the work-
       ing class and Billy must come of age and take their place in the
       world as mature men." Billy has to confront his other, evil
       self, Claggart, while the conservative aristocratic law (Vere)
       judges. At the confrontation, Billy's intellect is bound by his
       very ignorance and his resulting lack of knowledge is the neces-
       sary evil concomitant. By striking Claggart on the forehead--
       trying to crush his apparent enemy, the mind (knowledge)--Billy
       both reveals and gives way to his limitations and ignorance,
       breaking the only laws ("measured forms") that can hold evil, the
       unconscious dark side of man (Claggart) in bounds. Too good, too
       innocent, and too dangerous to live in this world, the child man
       must be sacrificed to the new man who will be resurrected from
       him.

105   BABCOCK, C. MERTON. "Archaisms in Moby Dick. Word Study, 27
       (December), 7-8.
          Gives fourteen examples of archaisms in Moby-Dick, with
       definitions. The obsolete meanings of the cited words are now
       more antiquated, and presumably less familiar, than when Melville
       defined them in such rare and unusual contexts. His use of
       archaisms may have been part of his method of creating what he
       called an "indefinite, infinite background," or perhaps the words
       were nothing more than survivals in dialect of earlier current
       usages.

106   FEIDELSON, CHARLES. "Melville Chronicled." Yale Review, 41
       (December), 297-300.
          Review of 1951.A2-4. The three works are all directed
       against the intuitional, or high-flying, school of Melville stud-
       ies: their very simplicity or approach comes as a welcome change.
       It is questionable whether every reader can properly be expected
       to be his own biographer of Melville, as Leyda intends, and it is
       doubtful that a mere accumulation of data, especially when much
       of it is rather dreary stuff, is the best way to achieve the
       sense of immediacy Leyda hopes for. But every future biographer
       of Melville, in his own effort to evoke the immediate image of
       the man, will be indebted to Leyda's collection. Divided between
       his desire to woo the general reader and to put the Melville

scholar on a more solid footing, Leyda will satisfy neither and
has diminished the scholarly usefulness of the Log (seldom, for
instance, giving the complete text of a document). The book is
impressive for its scrupulous objectivity and for the enormous
industry that went into its making; but unless our interests are
merely anecdotal, this welter of disconnected and often trivial
data would seem to demand an even greater exercise of imagination
than any for which earlier biographers can be reproached. As a
simple chronicle of Melville's doings, Howard's biography will
not be superseded for many years. The deficiency in his account
lies in the distance between the external facts on which he
mainly depends and the complicated being who moves through the
language of the novels and poems; his Melville tends to become a
rather commonplace figure with an odd habit of shutting himself
up in his room and writing passionate books. Howard is also
inclined to lose the meaning of the novels in his scrutiny of the
conditions under which they were composed. While earlier biographers made the error of treating their images of Melville as
objective facts of Melville's life, the new school is in danger
of reducing Melville to the simplistic terms of an external
chronicle. What is most appealing about Gilman's study is its
avoidance of any such tendency. If his distinctions between fact
and fancy do not lead him into the central issues of Melville's
art, Gilman does bring into focus an important difference between
the art of invention and the art of recollection. The value of
this kind of study lies in bringing pressure to bear on the
speculative interpreter--in complicating, not simplifying, the
Melville problem.

107   MURRAY, HENRY A. "In Nomine Diaboli." New England Quarterly,
      24 (December), 435-452.
         Ahab is an embodiment of Lucifer or Satan, "the spitting
      image of Milton's hero, but portrayed with deeper and subtler
      psychological insight." Fedallah "represents the cool, heart-
      less, cunning, calculating, intellectual Devil of the Medieval
      myth-makers, in contrast to the stricken, passionate, indignant,
      and often eloquent rebel angel of Paradise Lost, whose rôle is
      played by Ahab." Through Fedallah, Queequeg, Tashtego, and
      Daggoo, Ahab "has summoned the various religions of the East to
      combat the one dominant religion of the West." In other terms,
      Ahab and his followers, Starbuck excepted, "represent the horde
      of primitive drives, values, beliefs, and practices which the
      Hebraic-Christian religionists rejected and excluded, and by
      threats, punishments, and inquisitions, forced into the uncon-
      scious mind of Western man." In psychological concepts, "Ahab is
      captain of the culturally repressed dispositions of human nature,
      that part of personality which psychoanalysts have termed the
      'Id.'" The White Whale is "none other than the internal institu-
      tion which is responsible for these repressions, namely the
      Freudian Superego." Because of "his whiteness, his mighty bulk
      and beauty, and because of one instinctive act that happened to
      dismember his assailant," Moby Dick "has received the projection
      of Captain Ahab's Presbyterian conscience, and so may be said to
      embody the Old Testament Calvinistic conception of an affrighting

Deity and his strict commandments, the derivative puritan ethic
of nineteenth-century America and the society that defended this
ethic. Also, and most specifically, he symbolizes the zealous
parents whose righteous sermonizings and corrections drove the
prohibitions in so hard that a serious young man could hardly
reach outside the barrier, except possibly far away among some
tolerant, gracious Polynesian peoples. The emphasis should be
placed on that unconscious (and hence inscrutable) wall of inhi-
bition which imprisoned the puritan's thrusting passions." Melville's "target in Moby-Dick was the upper middle-class culture
of his time." The "simplest psychological formula for Melville's
dramatic epic is this: an insurgent Id in mortal conflict with
an oppressive cultural Superego. Starbuck . . . stands for the
rational realistic Ego which is overpowered by the fanatical
compulsiveness of the Id and dispossessed of its normally regu-
lating functions." Ahab-Melville's "aggression was directed
against the object that once harmed Eros with apparent malice and
was still thwarting it with presentiments of further retalia-
tions." Melville, "in the person of Ahab, assailed Calvinism in
the Whale because it blocked the advance of a conscience benef-
icent to evolutionary love." Nonetheless, Melville makes a great
spectacle of Ahab's wickedness, and he could feel "spotless as
the lamb" after writing Moby-Dick, because "he had seen to it
that the huge threat to the social system, immanent in Ahab's
two cardinal defects--egotistic self-inflation and unleashed
wrath--was, at the end, fatefully exterminated." Reprinted in
1952.B118; 1953.A3; 1960.A6; Chase (1962), pp. 62-74; Vincent
(1969), pp. 52-66.

108   PAUL, SHERMAN. "Book Reviews." New England Quarterly, 24
      (December), 550-552.
          Review of 1950.A4. Too much space is taken up with the
attempt to demonstrate that Melville was a reader and that Milton
was pervasive in the climate of opinion. Certain of Pommer's
parallels are the hints we are looking for in order to understand
the kind of imagination Melville had, and they confirm Melville's
remarkable retentivity for certain kinds of things. Pommer,
however, does not show in what sense Milton became a part of
Melville. The section on the influence of Satan documents fully
the influence we most quickly perceive to be Miltonic; but if
Pommer had amplified the romantic utilization of Satan--the
usurpation of the satanic by the Byronic ego--he would not have
attributed to Melville a Miltonic psychology and he would have
prepared a surer ground for the widest aim of his study: to
show the influence of Milton in America. That influence, to
judge by Pommer's conclusions, was small, even for Melville; yet
Milton's theme of the fall of man and the loss of paradise was
not only influential as theology, it was most influential because
it revealed an archetypal pattern imprinted on the experience of
Melville's generation. Melville may have responded more deeply
to Milton's evocation of evil, but all felt the sense of loss.
Milton's influence on this generation was his example to those
seeking the vocation of literature. For Melville, whose measure

of a poet was his capacity to seek truth and proclaim it,
Milton, like Shakespeare and Solomon, was a worthy peer.

109   CHASE, RICHARD. "The Real Melville?" Nation, 173
      (1 December), 478–479.
            Review of 1951.A4. The burden of reviewers' praise of the
      Log has been that here at last is the "real" Melville and we need
      never again be concerned with the "mythical" Melville who has
      hitherto been presented by "over-imaginative biographers." From
      all appearances, "we are now fairly launched in a period of lit-
      erary Know-Nothingism, during which the criticism of American
      literature seems likely to lose whatever zest and enlightenment
      it has recently had." Melville criticism, since Arvin's admira-
      ble book [1950.Al], "has appeared eager to content itself with
      any kind of approach which does not involve judgments or ideas,
      and in general there has been no period in the last forty years
      when so many critics . . . have succumbed to a morose and pru-
      dential anti-intellectualism and have grown resentful and sus-
      picious of any writer who makes a judgment or is interested in
      ideas or who, writing about any of our lesser or greater literary
      artists of the past, implies that his subject had, or ought to
      have had, a mind, an imagination, and an imaginative sense of
      what his own life meant." In Melville criticism, we seem to be
      in a period in which Arvin's book will be thought fundamentally
      as indefensibly wild, "Freudian," and intellectual as Olson's
      [1947.Al] is usually said to be. Future critics and biographers
      may find some pages of the Log useful in evolving coherent con-
      ceptions of Melville.

110   SUTCLIFFE, DENHAM. "Melville to Your Taste." Christian
      Science Monitor (6 December).
            Review of 1951.A4. "With these volumes on his desk, the
      least scholarly reader will be able to check the interpretations
      of the formal biographers. . . . Leyda is doubtless right in
      thinking this the first work of its kind in American letters.   It
      deserves applause as a monumental piece of scholarship; it
      deserves use as an almost inexhaustible storehouse of knowledge
      about Melville."

111   ANON. "An Opera Text." London Times Literary Supplement,
      No. 2601 (7 December), 785.
            The libretto by E.M. Forster and Eric Crozier for Benjamin
      Britten's opera Billy Budd [see 1951.B6-7] not only makes appo-
      site use of English idiom but also shows how great are the pos-
      sibilities of a literary form that has scarcely been explored by
      good writers anywhere.

112   COHEN, J.M. "The Whiteness of the Whale." Spectator
      [London], 187 (7 December), 794, 796.
            Review of 1951.A2, A5. To read Moby-Dick in the light of
      Mason's theories is seriously to misread it. "For just as its
      secondary meanings, if they exist, were hidden from the author,
      so they will work most effectively on his reader if he accepts
      the book for what it purports to be--a sea-story with overtones

and discursions drawing on a wide field of reading--and lets it affect him as it will." It is still more essential to forget Mason's theories about <u>Billy Budd</u> before reading the book, "for the parallel between that simple sailor and Jesus Christ, even if it was present in the background of Melville's mind, cannot be taken seriously by anyone conscious of the difference between the Gospels and even the most inspired work of fiction." Mason's is a serious and painstaking book, marred by a persistent cloudiness of language. Gilman's ploddingly pursues some minor details of Melville's life and finds that <u>Redburn</u> is what Melville intended it to be, a work of fiction. In contrast to Mason's possibilities and probabilities, this is a reassuringly sober conclusion and one, apparently, that will set several previous scholars right.

113   COWLEY, MALCOLM. "Notes on the Literary Stock Exchange."
      <u>New Republic</u>, 125 (10 December), 14–16.
      Cites the rediscovery of Melville in support of the dictum that the "longer and more completely an author is neglected, the greater his eventual fame is likely to be--that is, if he belongs to the small band of genuine authors." Reports in a "market letter" on the course of literary values during the first two weeks of November 1951: "Among the American classics Melville continued to be the most active and once again ended the period with a net gain, but for the first time there was indication of short selling. Market insiders were saying that the Melville backers had become overextended and that a reaction was certain to follow." Revised version in 1954.B5.

114   KELSEY, W.K. "The Commentator." Detroit <u>News</u> (16 December).
      Notes the discrepancy between Melville's reference to the day's date as 16 December 1851 in chapter 85 of <u>Moby-Dick</u> and the book's publication in October 1851 in England and in November 1851 in the United States. Asks why, if it was a typographical error, Melville and the Harpers' proofreader failed to catch it and why it was never discovered and changed in the many subsequent editions. Reports that none of the contemporary reviews of <u>Moby-Dick</u> found in Melville's style that which it so greatly resembles--the style of Shakespeare in <u>Hamlet</u> and <u>King Lear</u>--and cites Shakespearean elements, setting out two passages (from chapters 106 and 37) as blank verse.

115   WAGENKNECHT, EDWARD. "More About Melville's Time." Chicago
      <u>Sunday Tribune Magazine of Books</u> (16 December), p. 3.
      Review of 1951.A4. "In view of what some of us have been saying about the paucity of biografical materials existing in Melville's case, it is satisfying, and a little amusing, to see how much there really is." For Melville scholars a priceless book.

116   DAHLBERG, EDWARD. "Laurels for Borrowers." Freeman, 2
      (17 December), 187–190.
          Sets passages from Arvin [1950.A1] against passages from
      Olson [1947.A2] and Lawrence [1923.B4] to show that Arvin has
      drawn on both writers without acknowledgment. Instead of erudi-
      tion and human wisdom, we now have books like Arvin's on Melville.

117   CUNLIFFE, MARCUS. "Diving into Melville." New Statesman and
      Nation [London], NS 42 (22 December), 738.
          Review of 1951.A2, A5. On the evidence of these excellent
      studies, Melville merits our serious attention; it is time we got
      to know him better. In comparing Melville's early life with its
      fictional parallel Redburn, Gilman shows in fascinating detail
      that the two are by no means the same thing; he has done a valu-
      able, scholarly job. Mason's book is perhaps not quite as good
      as Arvin's superb biography [1950.A1], but it was not rendered
      unnecessary by Arvin's, for it differs somewhat in its approach
      and conclusions. Mason views Melville without any prejudice save
      that of affection; the result is a study that is fresh, sensi-
      tive, and coherent. His book does not "offer any startlingly new
      picture of Melville. Its general theme, that of Melville's in-
      tellectual voyaging from uncertainty to despair, thence to
      despondency, to resignation and eventually to tranquillity, has
      been established by others. The value of the book lies in its
      close, acute comment and in the clarity with which the main
      theme is developed and codified."

1952 A BOOKS

1   DAVIS, MERRELL R. Melville's MARDI: A Chartless Voyage. New
     Haven: Yale University Press, 240 pp. Reprint. Hamden,
     Conn.: Archon Books, 1967.
         Davis's three-part study "is concerned with the literary
     and biographical background, the genesis, writing, and meaning"
     of Mardi. It attempts "to assemble for the first time all the
     available material for a study of the inception and growth of the
     book and for a detailed analysis of it as an independent literary
     production." Part 1 presents "in considerable detail" Melville's
     literary and personal life from his return from the South Pacific
     in 1844 to the end of 1847. "Through such detail the true pic-
     ture emerges of the young writer who began a third book excited
     by the prospects of authorship and interested in securing a place
     for himself in the publishing world." Part 2 presents the his-
     tory of the growth of Mardi during 1847–1848. From Melville's
     own statements about his aims and methods and from evidence in
     the book itself, Davis indicates "the various stages in its com-
     position and the methods Melville used as his plans changed."
     Part 3 gives an analysis of the published book, paying "particu-
     lar attention to the formulas which guide the narrative movement
     of the story and to the elements of that story which in them-
     selves make up the book."
         The literary voyage Melville made in Mardi "was a chartless
     voyage. It began with factual narration, proceeded after

alterations and repairs through the world of poetry and romance,
and finally entered the world of mind. Through his method of
revision and development by addition and elaboration (a method
already discovered in writing Typee and Omoo) he was able to make
a tentative investigation of such a world and to supplement what
he had already written with the chapters on politics which were
written last." The book he finally published "grew in stature
beyond his own expectations for it, and exhibited a solution to
many artistic problems faced for the first time." But, since
"the Narrator's quest through Mardi is a literary device to bind
together the book's varied and disparate ingredients and at the
same time to give coherence of meaning to the narrative, the
attempt to find a perfectly consistent allegory in the book is
fruitless." Melville "was not primarily concerned with the
representation of a precise meaning for the Narrator's quest."
In the appendices Davis prints twelve letters from Melville to
John Murray [Letters, pp. 37–41; 43–44; 44–47; 50–51; 52–55;
58–59; 65–67; 67–68; 69–72; 72–73; 75–76; 293]; letters from
Gansevoort Melville and Allan Melville to John Murray; and five
letters from Melville to Richard Bentley [Letters, pp. 81–82;
85–87; 87–89; 109–110; 149–151]. Indexed. Reviewed in 1952.B94,
B96–97, B109–110, B121; 1953.B36, B39; 1954.B46.

2   THOMPSON, LAWRANCE. Melville's Quarrel With God. Princeton:
     Princeton University Press, 475 pp.
        Thompson's primary concern is Melville's "artistic devices
of deception and hoodwinking" used "to conceal the nature of his
religious thought." In his youth, according to Thompson, Melville inherited the dogma of Calvin "in a quite undiluted form."
He "did not completely rebel against his Calvinistic heritage"
until after he had published Typee and Omoo. "Increasingly em-
bittered by a conjunction of unfortunate experiences, immediately
during and after the writing of Mardi," he "arrived at a highly
ironic conclusion: believing more firmly than ever in the God of
John Calvin, he began to resent and hate the attributes of God,
particularly the seemingly tyrannical harshness and cruelty and
malice of God." Instead of losing faith in his Calvinistic God,
Melville made a "scapegoat" out of him, blaming him for having
caused so many human beings to rebel. In this sense he became an
"inverted mystic." Still influenced "by the Calvinistic dogma
that God did indeed try to exact from mankind a rigid letter-of-
the-law obedience, and that Adam's fall was indeed the first
indication of the unjust ruthlessness of God's punishment,
Melville came to view God as the source from whom all evils flow,
in short, the 'Original Sinner,' divinely depraved." His "inverted mysticism became a fixed idea, an obsession, which persisted during most of his life."
        Melville's "spiritual idiom" controlled and determined his
artistic idiom. The tensions of his "peculiar and inverted
religious beliefs" prompted him to give them outlet in literary
expression, yet he hesitated to express himself frankly, knowing
that "his contemporary reading public was too deeply committed to
Christian beliefs in the goodness of God to tolerate any open
assertions as to the malice and evil of God." He therefore
ingeniously arranged to pretend in his narratives "that no matter
how much he indulged in occasional religious doubts and

questionings, his ultimate goal was to praise and honor the orthodox Christian viewpoint," devising a form of "artistic triple talk," layers of meaning designed for three kinds of readers: the "superficial skimmer of pages," the devout Christian, and the skeptical, more perceptive reader. Melville's art "dramatizes, more vividly than anything else, a kind of arrested development. Spellbound by his own disillusionments, he became stranded in the narcissistic shallows and miseries of those disillusionments." His "artistic limitation would seem to rest in part on the apparent necessity of his projecting his own personal Hamletism into symbolic actions," before "he had achieved a sufficiently mature perspective to give him and us a sense of adequate detachment." Analysis of the prose works (except for the tales) in these terms. Indexed. Reviewed in 1952.B61, B63-65, B71-72, B77, B86, B97-98, B104, B106, B116; 1953.B35, B38-40, B46, B53, B58-59, B76; 1954.B46; 1957.B7.

1952 B SHORTER WRITINGS

1   ANON. "Biographical Note: Herman Melville, 1819-1891," in Moby-Dick. Vol. 48 of Great Books of the Western World. Ed. Robert Maynard Hutchins. Chicago and London: Encyclopaedia Britannica Inc., pp. v-vi.
        Biographical sketch.

2   BAILEY, MATILDA and ULLIN W. LEAVELL, eds. The World of America. The Mastery of Reading. New York: American Book Co., p. 443.
        Designed for use in the eleventh grade. Biographical sketch ("Herman Melville"). Prints "Shiloh, A Requiem."

3   BEWLEY, MARIUS. "Hawthorne and Henry James," in The Complex Fate. London: Chatto and Windus, pp. 1-3.
        "Cooper, Hawthorne, Melville, and James form a line in American writing based on a finely critical consciousness of the national society. They all dealt with the American scene, but this is not the basis of their resemblance, which lies rather in their sense of the dangers and deficiencies which they saw encircling the possibilities they believed the country possessed. The tensions between their faith and their fears created the best art America has ever produced. They form a tradition, not by virtue of their relation with each other, but because, each in his own fashion, they were seriously concerned with the new nation in a way that European novelists are rarely, or never, concerned with theirs. They felt that the possibilities of creative achievement were intrinsically involved with the new patterns of life which were forming in America, and they feared with all their hearts, though not always consciously, the concomitant losses that inevitably came with the gains." Melville is a greater artist than Cooper "but overestimated today as seriously as Cooper suffers in the opposite direction."

4　　BROOKS, CLEANTH, JOHN THIBAUT PURSER, and ROBERT PENN WARREN,
　　　eds. An Approach to Literature. 3d ed. New York: Appleton-
　　　Century-Crofts, pp. 344–345.
　　　　　Comments and questions on "Commemorative of a Naval
Victory."

5　　BROWN, JOHN MASON. "Hanged from the Yardarm," in As They
　　　Appear. New York: McGraw-Hill Book Co., pp. 186–192.
　　　　　Reprints 1951.B43.

6　　CRANE, HART. The Letters of Hart Crane 1916–1932. Ed. Brom
　　　Weber. New York: Hermitage House, pp. 86, 235, 252, 258–260,
　　　331, 404–405.
　　　　　Letters mentioning Melville. Letter of 19 June 1926 to
Waldo Frank: "I read Moby Dick between gasps down in Cayman--my
third time--and found it more superb than ever. How much that
man makes you love him!" Letter of 20 March 1932 to Solomon
Grunberg: "A way, way back you asked me a question about what I
thought of Moby Dick. It has passages, I admit, of seeming
innuendo that seem to block the action. But on third or fourth
reading I've found that some of those very passages are much to
be valued in themselves--minor and subsidiary forms that augment
the final climacteric quite a bit. No work as tremendous and
tragic as Moby Dick can be expected to build up its ultimate
tension and impact without manipulating our time sense to a great
extent. Even the suspense of the usual mystery story utilizes
that device. In Moby Dick the whale is a metaphysical image of
the Universe, and every detail of his habits and anatomy has its
importance in swelling his proportions to the cosmic rôle he
plays."

7　　CURRENT-GARCÍA, EUGENE and WALTON R. PATRICK. "The Short
　　　Story in America," in American Short Stories, 1820 to the
　　　Present. Chicago: Scott, Foresman and Co., p. xxiv.
　　　　　The Piazza Tales was virtually the only collection of short
pieces of the 1850s fit to put beside those of Hawthorne and
Poe--though Melville had not as yet mastered the technique of the
short story, so that not more than two or three of the stories
bear comparison with Hawthorne's best work. "Bartleby" (printed
in this collection) may be interpreted as Melville's "symbolic
response to the commercialization of art in America at the fag
end of its romantic period."

8　　EDITORS OF THE MODERN LIBRARY. "Note," in Selected Writings
　　　of Herman Melville. New York: The Modern Library,
　　　pp. vii–viii.
　　　　　Biographical details and notes on the texts. (The plates
of Leyda's edition [1949.B9] were used for the stories.)

9   ELLIOTT, HARRISON. "A Century Ago An Eminent Author Looked
     Upon Paper and Papermaking." Paper Maker, 21 (No. 2), 55–58.
        Summarizes "The Tartarus of Maids" and cites evidence that
     as early as 1847 improvements in the operatives' working condi-
     tions were contemplated at Carson's mill, a visit to which pro-
     vided the theme of the story. "Melville's censure of the machine
     was hardly justified. It stepped up production, and had it not
     been for the advent of the machine, he would have had to pay much
     more for a grade of paper on which he did his voluminous writ-
     ings, and from which the printers set the type. The remorseless
     feeding of the paper machine was not the tedious and monotonous
     job he depicted it. It was employment requiring intelligence,
     responsibility, and ingenuity. The machine tender in a small
     mill was a versatile and all-around man whose functions were much
     less monotonous than the back-breaking labors of the vatman with
     his hand mold, however creative the vatman's work in forming each
     sheet separately as a personalized effort." The "finest Bath"
     Melville wrote on to Sophia Hawthorne [8 January 1852, Letters,
     p. 145] was a fine writing paper made in Bath, England. A high-
     grade writing paper is still produced and advertised as such in
     British paper-trade journals as "Bath Vellum."

10   FOGLE, RICHARD HARTER. "The Monk and the Bachelor:
     Melville's 'Benito Cereno.'" Tulane Studies in English, 3
     (1952), 155–178.
        Detailed analysis of "Benito Cereno," which after Moby-Dick
     is Melville's most fully achieved piece of writing. It is con-
     ceived as the realization of mystery, the effective presentment
     of overwhelming complexity. Cereno is one of Melville's monks,
     seeing too well that the world is evil and forced to retire from
     it. Delano is a good specimen of Melville's bachelor, who shuts
     his eyes to evil and pain and believes that men can be happy at
     the slight expense of a little commonsense and foresight. Re-
     printed in 1960.A2 and Chase (1962), pp. 116–124.

11   HANLEY, JAMES. "Introduction," in Moby-Dick. MacDonald
     Illustrated Classics, No. 21. London: MacDonald, pp. xv-
     xxvi.
        Biographical sketch and commentary on the book's power and
     "intervening tides of turgidity."

12   HART-DAVIS, RUPERT. Hugh Walpole: A Biography. New York:
     The Macmillan Co., pp. 187, 363–364.
        In a journal entry for 10 August 1919, Walpole records a
     conversation with Joseph Conrad, in which Conrad scoffed at
     Typee. In the fall of 1935 Walpole's great experience was the
     discovery of Melville. "He had read Moby Dick long ago, but only
     now did he attempt the other novels, and their impact was
     tremendous. With the assistance of Jean Hersholt he succeeded
     in buying first editions of almost all of them, he read them
     again and again, and fell so deeply under Melville's enchantment
     that 'it is as though he has been living in the house.'" Walpole
     writes in his journal: "Typee shines in my mind like the sun
     shining through the water in one of his own wonderful waterfalls.

It is his uniqueness that makes him so important. Two lines of
Lear, one sentence of Sancho Panza's, Mr. Collins's letter to
Elizabeth Bennet, Hawthorne's picture of the 'Seven Gables'--
these and such as these are all that is wanted. So with the
opening of Moby Dick, Franklin in Israel Potter, the escape in
Typee."

13   INGLIS, REWEY BELLE, et al. "Herman Melville," in Adventures
      in American Literature. Mercury Edition. Ed. Rewey Belle
      Inglis et al. New York: Harcourt, Brace and Co., pp. 531–533.
          Slightly revised version of 1947.B6. Prints extracts from
      chapters 28 and 36 of Moby-Dick, with discussion questions.

14   LEYDA, JAY. "Introduction," "Biographical," "Notes on Manu-
      scripts and Textual Sources," and "A Bibliographic Note," in
      The Portable Melville. Ed. Jay Leyda. New York: The Viking
      Press, pp. xi–xxii, 3–9, 743–745, 745–746.
          Melville was "an artist who depended for coherence and
      connection on actual experience rather than on forms, the designs
      offered by art." For that reason this collection "has by-passed
      the departments and strung the work selected along the thread of
      the life that produced it. Connecting comment is employed only
      when Melville's own explanation is missing." Reviewed in
      1952.B45–48, B58; 1953.B76.

15   LOCKE, LOUIS G., JOHN PENDY KIRBY, and M.E. PORTER, eds.
      Literature of Western Civilization. Vol. 2. New York: The
      Ronald Press Co., pp. 414–415.
          Biographical headnote ("Herman Melville, 1819–1891") to
      "Bartleby."

16   LYND, ROBERT. "The Learned Sailorman," in Books and Writers.
      London: J.M. Dent & Sons Ltd., pp. 142–146.
          Review of 1946.B2. Appreciation of Moby-Dick, which is
      more Ishmael's story than Ahab's, though Ahab's story gives the
      book its unity. The book rises most assuredly to greatness not
      in the soliloquies but in its descriptions of the ocean and the
      figures, human and other, that frequent it. Belgion is right:
      most of us are excited by Moby-Dick not as an allegory or philo-
      sophical work of any kind but as a story of a voyage, partly
      fiction, partly autobiography, and partly science, transmuted
      into art by a terrific imagination.

17   MANSFIELD, LUTHER S. and HOWARD P. VINCENT. "Introduction,"
      "Explanatory Notes," and "Textual Notes," in Moby-Dick. Ed.
      Luther S. Mansfield and Howard P. Vincent. New York:
      Hendricks House, pp. ix–xxxiii, 569–832, 833–838.
          The "Introduction" gives an account of the composition,
      publication, and contemporary reception of Moby-Dick and of
      subsequent commentary on the book. The "Explanatory Notes"--"in
      some sense a biography of Melville's mind during the years of
      Moby-Dick's composition--afford the interested critic a chance
      to study the borrowing techniques of a genius." Reviewed in
      1952.B44–46, B60, B69, B105–106; 1953.B43, B76; 1954.B24–25.

18   MASEFIELD, JOHN. So Long to Learn. New York: The Macmillan
     Co., p. 56.
         Passage on Masefield's Conway days: "I read and read,
     whatever I could find to read: mostly prose, borrowed from my
     ship-mates, and much of this of a nautical trend, the novels of
     Captain Marryat, Captain Glascock, Captain Chamier, W. Clark
     Russell, and some of Herman Melville. These I came to know
     pretty well."

19   MATTHIESSEN, F.O. "Melville as Poet," in The Responsibil-
     ities of the Critic: Essays and Reviews by F.O. Matthiessen.
     Selected by John Rackliffe. New York: Oxford University
     Press, pp. 77-80.
         Reprints 1944.B8.

20   MOSIER, RICHARD D. The American Temper: Patterns of Our
     Intellectual Heritage. Berkeley and Los Angeles: University
     of California Press, pp. 168-169.
         The "realism of Melville is the realism of tragedy, which
     through its symbols presages the death of every finite thought
     and the coming into birth of each infinite one. Melville was
     conscious that the demonic mystery of the White Whale lay behind
     a sea of phenomena. His indeed was the kind of consciousness to
     which each new fact in nature's lexicon was a symbol of the vast
     reservoir of fact with which nature both embodies and betrays our
     ideals."

21   PLOMER, WILLIAM. "Introduction," in White Jacket. The
     Chiltern Library. London: John Lehmann, pp. v-x.
         White-Jacket's merit as a work of art is not vitiated by
     its propagandistic purpose--on the contrary, it succeeds both as
     art and propaganda. It is an amazing gallery of characters.
     Even if idealized, Jack Chase is a central figure in the
     Melvillean mythology.

22   PLOMER, WILLIAM. "Introduction," in White Jacket. New York:
     Grove Press, pp. v-x.
         Reprints 1952.B21.

23   POOLEY, ROBERT C., et al. "The Paper Mill in Devil's
     Dungeon," in The United States in Literature. Ed. Robert C.
     Pooley et al. Chicago: Scott, Foresman and Co., pp. 141-146.
         Prints "The Tartarus of Maids" followed by questions on the
     "Author's Impressions" and brief commentary on Melville's detes-
     tation of the paper mill.

24   RICE, HOWARD C., JR., ALEXANDER D. WAINWRIGHT, JULIE HUDSON,
     and ALEXANDER P. CLARK. "Moby-Dick by Herman Melville: A
     Century of an American Classic, 1851-1951." Princeton Univer-
     sity Library Chronicle, 13 (Winter), 63-118.
         Catalogue of an exhibition celebrating the centennial of
     the publication of Moby-Dick held at Princeton University
     Library, 15 October-15 December 1951.

25   SCHERMAN, DAVID E. and ROSEMARIE REDLICH. Literary America: A Chronicle of American Writers from 1607-1952 with 173 Photographs of the American Scene that Inspired Them. New York: Dodd, Mead & Co., pp. 71-73.

    Black and white photographs of the Seaman's Bethel, New Bedford, and the entrance to Nantucket Harbor, with brief account of their relation to Moby-Dick.

26   STAFFORD, JOHN. The Literary Criticism of "Young America": A Study in the Relationship of Politics and Literature, 1837-1850. Berkeley: University of California Press, passim.

    The literary theory of the Duyckinck circle; the group's role in promoting rising American authors like Simms, Hawthorne, Emerson, Poe, and Melville.

27   VANCE, THOMAS H. "The Symbolist Tradition in American Fiction: From E.A. Poe to Henry James." Sprache und Literatur Englands und Amerikas, 1 (1952), 125-150.

    The symbolist tradition in American fiction is grounded in the condition of the imaginative life in America. "In Faulkner, as in Hawthorne or Melville, the imaginative life is one of solitude and separateness. It sees the things that are most real not as public and manifest, but as private and secret. It is filled with the sense that social forms and outward pressures, important as they may be, have less reality than the world of compulsions, desires, fears and dreams within us." Moby-Dick remains the supreme achievement of symbolism in American literature. The "essential symbolism of the book as a whole, as well as of its most effective scenes taken separately, is implicit rather than explicit. It grows out of a rich sense of metaphor, of the immanence of the spiritual in the concrete, rather than out of a deliberate theory or program." The "central symbolic action of the book," Ahab's compulsive mission of vengeance, "cannot be neatly analyzed. It is not a rational construction, but a richly developed metaphor, which includes apparent contradictions within itself."

28   WAGENKNECHT, EDWARD. "The Ambiguities of Herman Melville," in Cavalcade of the American Novel. New York: Henry Holt and Co., pp. 58-81.

    Expanded version of 1950.B51, drawing extensively on previous scholarship.

29   WEST, RAY B., JR. The Short Story in America, 1900-1950. Chicago: Henry Regnery Co., passim.

    Brief references to Melville as a writer of short stories.

30   WINTERS, YVOR. "To Herman Melville in 1951," in Collected Poems. Denver: Alan Swallow, p. 137.

    Two-line poem: "Saint Herman, grant me this: that I may be / Saved from the worms who have infested thee."

31   WHITE, ERIC WALTER. "Billy Budd." Adelphi, 28 (1st Quarter),
     492-498.
         On the libretto by E.M. Forster and Eric Crozier [see
     1951.B7] and the opera by Benjamin Britten. Notes differences
     but finds the libretto "conscientiously faithful to the spirit
     of Melville's story."

32   ADAMS, R.P. "Romanticism and the American Renaissance."
     American Literature, 23 (January), 419-432.
         Examining Moby-Dick, Walden, and "Song of Myself" in the
     light of a theory of romanticism proposed by Morse Peckham,
     Adams finds that in Moby-Dick and Walden "the pattern of symbolic
     death and rebirth is used to express a revolt against static
     mechanism in favor of dynamic organicism."

33   CANFIELD, FRANCIS X. "Moby Dick and the Book of Job."
     Catholic World, 174 (January), 254-260.
         Moby-Dick is Melville's dramatic representation of a theme
     of the Book of Job, the attempt to fathom the ways of Divinity.
     The white whale is the symbol of the inscrutable--the mystery of
     creation and the complex entity of Truth, including the whole
     mystery of good and evil. Ahab, like Job, attempts to unravel
     the inscrutable, thereby defying God. Job repents; Ahab does
     not. Consummate pride is the mainspring of Ahab's quest.

34   FITZGERALD, D. and P.M. FITZGERALD. "Billy Budd: The Novel
     by Herman Melville." World Review [London], NS 35 (January),
     9-12.
         Melville's near rebellion in White-Jacket (chapter 67)
     gradually turned into the mystical acceptance of punishment in
     Billy Budd. Behind all Melville's work (he invented almost
     single-handed the kind of symbolic tough-adventure stories that
     everyone tries to write today) "is the resolute effort to worst
     the huge question of good and evil." He came to express himself
     in Catharist or Zoroastrian terms--in a contrast of blackness and
     whiteness, or light and darkness: Claggart and Billy are the
     last two representatives of this dualism. He developed an idea
     of a mysterious reconciling agency, fixed and absolute, beyond
     our worldly conception, where the irritations of his own life,
     pain, insanity, oppression, injustice would be naturally re-
     solved into their proper place. In contrast with this distant
     region, glimpsed by Billy and Vere as a "white sail" on the
     horizon, everything in human existence is shifting and contra-
     dictory. He developed an obsession with the story of the
     crucifixion, evident in White-Jacket and Moby-Dick, which reaches
     its climax at Billy's execution. But Billy Budd is not only the
     story of Calvary transposed to a man-of-war: there is some sug-
     gestion that Billy's physical flaw brings punishment on itself;
     Vere is representative of Divine Justice, yet "he is also in a
     close relationship to Billy, fatherly perhaps, but with a faintly
     unwholesome tinge"; and Billy's innocence is Christlike but it is
     also the innocence of a healthy animal. Forster and Crozier
     [see 1951.B7] have preserved the atmosphere of Melville's book

faithfully, though the libretto lacks an effective ending. It
was well worth doing, since Melville is a first-class subject for
opera.

35   PLANISCIG, LEO. "Fasolato's Satan and Melville." Art News,
      50 (January), 21, 56.
          Melville refers to Agostino Fasolato's celebrated late
      Baroque marble group Fall of the Angels in his 1 April 1857
      Journal entry [see 1935.B14 and 1955.B14] and in his lecture
      "Statuary in Rome" [see 1957.A1].

36   STUART, CHARLES. "Billy Budd: The Score by Benjamin
      Britten." World Review [London], NS 35 (January), 12–14.
          "Allowance made for the occasional flawed page or episode,
      this is Britten's strongest and loveliest score so far."

37   GANNETT, LEWIS. "Books and Things." New York Herald
      (1 January), p. 19.
          Sales figures for Melville's books and details of
      Melville's earnings, drawn from 1951.A4.

38   ANON. "Herman Melville." London Times Literary Supplement,
      No. 2605 (4 January), p. 10.
          Review of 1951.A5. On "one's willingness to face a re-
      assessment that regards spiritual conflict rather than artistic
      achievement depends appreciation of this new study. For, al-
      though some of the poems and stories, and Billy Budd . . . stand
      in their own right, it is hard to believe in the real greatness
      of anything Melville wrote besides Moby-Dick. . . . The progress
      of an artist's spirit is a very real subject for study; but when
      the progress is so often unmatched by the books that reveal it the
      study is robbed of a good deal of its force. . . . On the other
      hand, it is fascinating to see analysed the often ill-matched
      balance between a writer's art and his spirit."

39   WHITRIDGE, ARNOLD. "Exploding Some Myths." Saturday Review
      of Literature, 35 (5 January), 13–14.
          Review of 1951.A3. Howard explodes various myths about
      Melville--that he was a tormented soul, a Byronic hero at war
      with the universe, domestically unhappy, a forgotten man at his
      death. Although Howard does not explicitly deny Parrington's
      dictum that there is no tragedy in American letters comparable
      to the tragedy of Melville [see 1927.B12], his biography cer-
      tainly does not support it. The difference between this biog-
      raphy and most of its predecessors is that every opinion is
      buttressed with facts. Howard has resisted the temptation to
      reconstruct Melville's life out of his books. His approach is
      welcome in view of the frightening structure of symbolism and
      psychology that other critics and biographers have erected
      between Melville and his readers.

40   SUKEL, SAMUEL T.   "Logbook of Herman Melville's Stormy
     Voyage."   Berkshire Evening Eagle (12 January).
        Review of 1951.A4. Although the Log does not profess to
be the final definitive work on Melville's life, it is most certainly the cornerstone of the one to be written in the future.
The book reviews impede the chronological sequence of the biographical entries, and it might have been better to segregate
them into a separate section. During his researches, Leyda found
"an appalling apathy" in Pittsfield toward Melville and his work.

41   BELL, MILLICENT.   "Melville and Hawthorne at the Grave of St.
     John (A Debt to Pierre Bayle)."   Modern Language Notes, 67
     (February), 116–118.
        Melville's reference to the stirring sod over the grave of
St. John in Moby-Dick, chapter 111, probably came from Pierre
Bayle's Dictionnaire Historique et Critique in English transla-
tion. (Hawthorne clearly drew on Bayle in his article on "St.
John's Grave" in The American Magazine of Useful and Entertaining
Knowledge.)

42   SEALTS, MERTON M., JR.   "Melville's 'NeoPlatonical Originals.'"
     Modern Language Notes, 67 (February), 80–86.
        Melville's satirical treatment, in Mardi, of unintelligible
passages in Proclus (in Thomas Taylor's translation) and his
later thrust, in The Confidence-Man, chapter 36, at the "oracular
gibberish" of both Proclus and Emerson indicate his hostility to
certain characteristics of transcendentalism, ancient and modern.

43   VOGELBACK, ARTHUR L.   "Shakespeare and Melville's Benito
     Cereno."   Modern Language Notes, 67 (February), 113–116.
        Similarities between Babo and Iago. Melville made changes
in his source [see 1928.B26] to make Babo, rather than Mure, the
leader in the revolt and a creature of undiluted evil. It seems
not improbable that Melville was struck by the similarity of the
Negro's name to that of Iago. It is in the traits with which
Melville endows Babo that we see the latter's unmistakable kinship to Iago.

44   BRADLEY, VAN ALLEN.   "'Moby-Dick' Gets a New Boost from No. 1
     Chicago Admirer."   Chicago Daily News (13 February).
        Review of 1952.B17. No other American book has been so
extensively annotated. The chief virtue of Mansfield's and
Vincent's labors is that here, in one volume, is just about
everything the critics have had to say, plus a great wealth of
background information. "Most interpreters agree that Melville,
in writing his story, was designing a vast allegory of man's fate
that has far greater significance than appears on the surface of
the simple tale. Their speculations differ widely, but they
generally agree that the evil white whale symbolizes the terrible
natural forces of the universe and that the doomed Capt. Ahab
represents mankind." Despite this new mountain of notes, the
mystery of Melville's meaning--if he had an esoteric meaning--
still remains.

45   POORE, CHARLES. "Books of the Times." New York <u>Times</u>
     (16 February), p. 11.
          Review of 1952.B14, B17. The Mansfield-Vincent edition
     brings together an immense collection of scholarly and enter-
     taining Melville lore with the greatest degree of usefulness and
     the most commendable minimum of clutter. It "is as unostenta-
     tious a way of bringing out what is really a wonderfully wide-
     ranging and penetrating study of Melville as you can hope to
     discover." Leyda's <u>Portable Melville</u> is the anthological tour
     de force of the season.

46   WAGENKNECHT, EDWARD. "Two Additions to the Great Melville
     Lore." Chicago <u>Sunday Tribune Magazine of Books</u>
     (17 February), p. 8.
          Review of 1952.B14, B17. More than 250 pages of notes in
     the Mansfield-Vincent edition, creating a kind of summary of
     Melville scholarship, make <u>Moby-Dick</u> the most elaborately anno-
     tated of all American novels. When the editors remark that "no
     other is great enough to submit to such treatment," they may
     simply show that their knowledge of other American writers does
     not match their knowledge of Melville. Nevertheless, this is
     <u>the</u> edition of <u>Moby-Dick</u>, making for the present--and perhaps
     permanently--all others unnecessary. Leyda's is one of the most
     expertly edited volumes in "The Viking Portable Library."
     Through his selections and commentary he achieves a coherent,
     progressive account of Melville's life and aesthetic development.

47   WHICHER, GEORGE F. "Reprints, New Editions." New York <u>Herald
     Tribune Book Review</u> (17 February), p. 16.
          Review of 1952.B14. Leyda has centered attention on the
     man behind the book rather than on the books themselves as suc-
     cessive artistic monuments. His selections give the skeleton of
     the novelist, deftly articulated by Leyda's unobstrusive
     "continuity." Leyda's care to secure reliable texts is beyond
     praise. If he has not fully succeeded in the all but impossible
     task of reducing Melville to a microcosm, he has at least com-
     posed an accessory volume that lovers of Melville will eagerly
     welcome.

48   G[ARRISON], W.E. "Books in Brief." <u>Christian Century</u>, 69
     (20 February), 222.
          Review of 1952.B14. A grand selection from the works of
     one of the greatest American writers; but all the rest of
     Melville is supplementary to <u>Moby-Dick</u>.

49   BREIT, HARVEY, C.L.R. JAMES, and LYMAN BRYSON. "Herman
     Melville: <u>Moby-Dick</u>." <u>Invitation to Learning</u>, 2 (Spring),
     41-47.
          Transcript of radio conversation between Breit, James, and
     Bryson about <u>Moby-Dick</u> in the CBS "Invitation to Learning"
     series.

50   SEALTS, MERTON M., JR. "Melville's Reading: A Supplemental
     List of Books Owned and Borrowed." Harvard Library Bulletin,
     6 (Spring), 239–247.
          Supplement to 1948.B44, B65; 1949.B43, B89, B120;
     1950.B115. Revised and reprinted in Sealts (1966).

51   WEST, RAY B., JR. "The Unity of Billy Budd." Hudson Review,
     5 (Spring), 120–127.
          Contrary to current critical opinion, Billy Budd is a uni-
     fied work--not marred by digressions and irrelevancies, but a
     triumph of architectonic structure. It is not a tragedy but a
     satiric-allegory--its subject the renewal of myth. Reprinted in
     Stafford, pp. 119–125; reprinted in part in Vincent (1971),
     pp. 95–97.

52   WILLIAMS, STANLEY T. "Spanish Influences in American Fiction:
     Melville and Others." New Mexico Quarterly, 22 (Spring),
     5–14.
          In Melville's mind the Spaniard stood for both an illus-
     trious, if decadent, civilization and also for a form of Chris-
     tianity for which he felt alternately attraction and repulsion.
     Benito Cereno represents the proud but crippled civilization of
     Spain and is associated with the decline of the Catholic church.
     Reprinted, with slight changes and added notes, in 1955.B30.

53   ANON. "Current Books." Nineteenth-Century Fiction 6 (March),
     293.
          Review of 1951.A4. An accomplishment of patient, selfless
     scholarship that is almost beyond praise. Of principal interest
     and reward has been the search through Melville family papers
     and through the archives of descendants of Melville's friends.
     It is clear that virtually nothing of the slightest importance
     has been overlooked. "This is the raw material of biography, of
     course, and some may object that what we have printed here is
     simply a scholar's undigested notes. But Melvillians, quite
     properly, will settle for nothing but the whole truth, from which
     each reader may construct his own biography. The publishers are
     to be congratulated for their fortitude in issuing such a book in
     parlous times, but they are to be censured for the fiendishly
     awkward arrangement of the documentation."

54   [HILLWAY, TYRUS]. "Addition to the Melville Log." Melville
     Society Newsletter, 8 (March), n.p.
          Melville's marriage was recorded in the New England His-
     torical and Genealogical Register, 1 (October 1847), 380, in a
     list of prominent marriages.

55   HORSFORD, HOWARD C. "Evidence of Melville's Plans for a
     Sequel to The Confidence-Man." American Literature, 24
     (March), 85–89.
          Jottings in Melville's journals of his trip to Europe and
     the Near East during the winter of 1856-1857 suggest that he may
     have planned a sequel to The Confidence-Man. Reprinted in
     Norton The Confidence-Man, pp. 356–360.

56   HOWARD, LEON. "'Melville's Early Life and Redburn.'"
      Nineteenth-Century Fiction, 6 (March), 291–292.
          Review of 1951.A2. Gilman's notes provide complete docu-
      mentation for the extraordinarily large number of new facts that
      are brought together in his study, and a comprehensive index
      makes it as usable for reference purposes as it is readable for
      its inherent interest to students of Melville or of early
      nineteenth-century American life and culture. Among the numerous
      recent books on Melville, Gilman's shares with Leyda's Log
      [1951.A4] "the distinction of being one of the few that might be
      called indispensable. A fine example of accurate and imaginative
      scholarship, it fits together the circumstantial details of
      Melville's early life so completely that no room is left for the
      fanciful interpretations of his youth which have, in turn, led to
      even more fanciful misinterpretations of his books. The result
      of an application of these details to a study of Redburn itself
      is a demonstration that the book is a much more imaginative work
      of art than one would suppose from the accounts given of it by
      many effusive critics who have been too preoccupied by their own
      inventiveness to discover and appreciate Melville's."

57   WRIGHT, NATHALIA. "A Note on Melville's Use of Spenser:
      Hautia and the Bower of Bliss." American Literature, 24
      (March), 83–85.
          Parallels between Taji's meeting with Hautia in Mardi
      (chapters 192–193) and Sir Guyon's visit to Acrasia's Bower of
      Bliss in Spenser's The Faerie Queene, book 2, canto xii.

58   HOSKINS, KATHERINE. "The Continuing Pursuit of Herman
      Melville." New Republic, 126 (3 March), 18–19.
          Review of 1951.A3–4; 1952.B14. The Portable Melville is
      not only much fuller than the Modern Library's Selected Writings
      of Herman Melville but much better devised, providing a survey
      of Melville that, with its extensive bibliography, is altogether
      as satisfactory as such a book can be. Probably no one could
      form much idea of Melville's life from Leyda's Log alone (though
      he pretends that with it in hand each reader can be his own
      biographer), but as a reference and compendium of Melvilleana it
      is of the greatest value and interest. Perhaps the most reward-
      ing single item is the complete text of Melville's 17[?] Novem-
      ber 1851 letter to Hawthorne; no second-hand account can do
      justice to the caliber of the love that it expresses for
      Hawthorne, seemingly the kind of love that, according to
      Montaigne, occurs about once in three hundred years—a coup de
      foudre that few are of the stature to experience. In its great
      happiness, the letter is a moving reminder of how brief was the
      period in which, though himself drawn to a heroic scale, Mel-
      ville could create and live in a climate of unfearful freedoms.
      If for Howard's intention "to understand" Melville "as a human
      being living in nineteenth century America" we substitute "to
      present" Melville, then we must admit that his work is vastly
      successful: Howard recreates in terrifying detail the society
      in which Melville seems to have lived. "Howard does not evoke
      a very different Melville from the one we have been accustomed

to; he merely makes him harder to get at. To a far greater
extent than the more intuitive biographers, it is he who brings
home to us the inexorable domesticity, the crowding trivia of
Melville's life, who lays him out helpless as Gulliver in
Lilliput. It is Howard who underlines the schizophrenic
solution that most societies ask of their gifted members and that
our own so fiercely exacts." But we shall continue to have
recourse to Arvin [1950.A1] and Sedgwick [1944.A1]. "For their
books are the kind that kindle us to meditate on a great writer
and on the mysteries of creation. And that . . . is the function
of biography. Insistence on externals as constituting the important life of an artist seems false primarily because it is a
denial of that blackjacking of the self experienced by every man
who produces a work of art and which prevents him thereafter
from standing forsquare to the world, from regarding the world's
work as more than his left-handed concern. However ambidexterous
he may be, it is a cruelty and a cheapening to treat him as a man
of letters, an ordinary citizen who writes books."

59 MARTIN, PETE. "He Finds Fortunes in Forgotten Corners."
    Saturday Evening Post, 224 (22 March), 111.
        David Randall tells of his discovery of Melville's anno-
    tated copy of Beale's Natural History of the Sperm Whale in a
    bale of books being sold for paper pulp.

60 SAWYER, ROLAND. "Centennial Edition of 'Moby Dick.'"
    Christian Science Monitor (27 March), p. 15.
        Review of 1951.A2; 1952.B17. Mansfield's and Vincent's
    explanatory notes could scarcely be more complete or shed more
    light on Melville's choice of words, references, and stagings.
    Much of their material is of interest primarily to the teacher
    and specialist, but there are treasures for everyone. As a
    result of Gilman's thorough research, Redburn becomes something
    more than a journal. Gilman has established that Melville's
    creative artistry was not confined to the single book for which
    he is remembered; whether Redburn "will emerge from the archives,
    where it has reposed for a century, because of this book is
    problematical."

61 VINCENT, HOWARD P. "The Real Melville?" New York Times Book
    Review, (30 March), p. 6.
        Review of 1952.A2. Thompson's book will upset Melville
    readers more than any book about his mind and art published in
    many years. It is built on a single thesis forced on Melville's
    pluralistic mind. Melville attacked Christian institutions and
    had his moments of uncertainty and doubt, of actual antagonism,
    but he had these moments along with others of an opposite nature,
    moments as real in their way as the doubt and anger. "What is
    one to do with the completely Christian statements, found in his
    letters, which may be set against the viewpoint charged to him
    now? . . . The cunning campaign of deception argued for Melville
    is completely out of character with the forthright man" revealed
    in such a book as Leyda's Log. But Thompson offers more than a

startling thesis ingeniously argued: he provides fine studies of
the influence of writers like Bayle, Milton, Montaigne, Camoens,
and Carlyle on Melville's art and thought. He also gives excellent analyses of important, if neglected, poems. The book's final failure may be attributed to the supersubtlety of its author,
who perceives a bear where there is but a bush. Whether one
likes it or not, the conclusions of <u>Moby-Dick</u> and <u>Billy Budd</u> are
in the deepest sense of the word religious.

62   KAPLAN, SIDNEY. "Can A Whale Sink A Ship? The Utica <u>Daily</u>
      <u>Gazette</u> vs the New Bedford <u>Whalemen's Shipping List</u>." <u>New</u>
      <u>York History</u>, 33 (April), 159–163.
        Account of the sinking of the New Bedford whaleship <u>Ann</u>
<u>Alexander</u> by a whale in August 1851; a skeptical response to the
story in the Utica <u>Daily Gazette</u>; and a reply in the New Bedford
<u>Whalemen's Shipping List</u> by the editor, Benjamin Lindsey.

63   CAHOON, HERBERT. "New Books Appraised." <u>Library Journal</u>, 77
      (1 April), 595.
        Review of 1952.A2. A detailed and thorough study of an
aspect of Melville's work that has generally escaped the attention of his numerous biographers and commentators. Thompson's
analyses are fascinating to any student of Melville and show a
splendid knowledge of Melville's work and artistry. The reader
may quarrel with some of Thompson's findings but will find the
book a stimulating contribution to American criticism.

64   WAGENKNECHT, EDWARD. "Melville's Ironic Triple-Talk: His
      Quarrel with God." Chicago <u>Tribune</u> (13 April).
        Review of 1952.A2. Thompson is ingenious and persuasive;
at the very least he has illuminated Melville's irony. Sometimes
he seems to distinguish insufficiently between Calvinism and
Christianity--or even religion--and in his first chapter he seems
without warrant to assume that humanism is necessarily anti-
Christian. Gilman, Howard, and Leyda [1951.A2, 1951.A3, and
1951.A4] have recently done much to place Melville study on a
sound basis of ascertainable fact. With Thompson we are back in
the quagmires of subjectivity.

65   GARRISON, W.E. "Grudge Against God." <u>Christian Century</u>, 69
      (23 April), 497.
        Review of 1952.A2. There are occasional points at which
Thompson seems to discover sinister meanings that are not there
(as in his reading of Father Mapple's sermon), but on the whole
the interpretation is convincing. It exhibits Melville as
vividly illustrating "the common tendency to build a cosmic
philosophy on a limited base of personal experience. His thinking was arrested at the point of his early disillusionment.
Thereafter he spent his life generalizing upon this and constructing artistic expressions of it with fictional invention,
satire and symbol."

66   BABCOCK, C. MERTON. "The Vocabulary of Moby Dick." American
      Speech, 28 (May), 91-101.
          Lists of Melville's contributions to the English and Ameri-
      can languages. Supplies "contextual evidence from Moby Dick for
      specific Melville usages which antedate the earliest cited evi-
      dence in the historical dictionaries"; and furnishes "historical
      evidence for expressions either not listed in the dictionaries
      or not supported by contextual references." One hundred and
      fifty items listed.

67   BRASWELL, WILLIAM. "Book Reviews." American Literature, 24
      (May), 245-247.
          Review of 1951.A3-4. Both, in their own right, are notable
      achievements. Leyda's book should prove especially welcome to
      readers who, puzzled and dismayed by what they found in earlier
      biographies, have wished for as complete a compilation as possi-
      ble of material about Melville's life so that they might con-
      struct their own biography. The Melville readers become
      acquainted with in these pages will probably be rather different
      from the man they had in mind before; here, minus the legends,
      is the man as he acted, as he appeared, and so far as the non-
      fictional documents reveal, as he thought. Howard's book "pre-
      sents a well-sustained narrative of Melville's experiences, both
      exciting and prosaic. . . . Sometimes the scene is so thick with
      relatives that one wonders how Melville accomplished as much as
      he did; yet, on the other hand, one realizes that in various ways
      he was quite dependent on them, as copyists, as agents with pub-
      lishers, as lenders and donors of financial aid, and the like.
      There is much about Melvile and his wife, but there are no sur-
      mises about the marital relationship such as one finds in Newton
      Arvin's biography." The biography is greatly enriched by
      Howard's recreation of "the nineteenth-century world in which
      Melville sailed before the mast, wrote Moby-Dick, and drank
      brandy"; the intellectual, social, and literary milieu that
      helped shape him is likewise made real. One is bound to be im-
      pressed by Howard's enlightening comments on the effects of Mel-
      ville's reading on his various works--some of the best concern
      Moby-Dick--and by the careful scrutiny of Melville's craftman-
      ship. Much of the criticism is incisive, and all of it is pro-
      vocative, though the criticism in itself will probably not
      receive such wholehearted approbation as is sure to be accorded
      the more general features of the biography.

68   FIESS, EDWARD. "Melville as a Reader and Student of Byron."
      American Literature, 24 (May), 186-194.
          A study of Melville's markings and annotations in his
      sixteen-volume set of Byron's Life and Works.

69   G[OHDES], C[LARENCE]. "Brief Mention." American Literature,
      24 (May), 275.
          Notice of 1952.B17. Far and away the best edition of
      Moby-Dick.

70   KAPLAN, SIDNEY. "Herman Melville and the Whaling Enderbys." American Literature, 24 (May), 224–230.

     Benjamin Lindsey, editor of the New Bedford Whalemen's Shipping List, used Omoo "to bolster an attack on a project of Charles Enderby of London designed to rejuvenate the British whale fishery. Although the citation makes clear that Omoo was well received in professional whaling circles, there is little doubt that Lindsey exploited the book in a manner that Melville could hardly have intended or approved." Chapters 100 and 101 of Moby-Dick ("The Pequod Meets the Samuel Enderby of London" and "The Decanter") indicate that Melville never intended the captain and crew of the Lucy Ann (in Omoo) to be typical of British whalemen.

71   STONE, GEOFFREY. "Three Levels of Melville." Commonweal, 56 (16 May), 152–154.

     Review of 1952.A2. Thompson "has written as ingenious an exegesis of Melvillian allegory as has been done since William S. Gleim . . . demonstrated that Moby Dick was an exercise in crypto-Swedenborgianism. [See 1938.A1.] What makes it all the more distressing is that he is right a good part of the time." But "so fascinated is he with his key to Melville's meaning that he insists on opening all sorts of doors that simply aren't there." To his praise, however, he "has avoided the genetic fallacy and allowed that a man's theological concerns are not to be explained only on another level of experience--infantile resentments, un-recognized sexual frustrations, maladjustment to some social circumstance." Although quite properly admitting that Melville was nothing exceptional as a philosopher, Thompson has stressed a fact that the more recent searchers after the facts of Mel-ville's life sometimes overlook: "that Melville was a meta-physical novelist who sought dramatic expression for mind's mountains and cliffs of fall."

72   CHASE, RICHARD. "His Own Hero." Saturday Review, 35 (31 May), 13–14.

     Review of 1951.A2, A4; 1952.A2. Writers about Melville fall into one of two categories, producing either factual books that never get beyond the facts or books interesting for their ingenuity or speculative or polemical point of view that are not convincing. Despite moving passages, Leyda's Log is, fundamen-tally, merely an exhaustive piece of scholarship of the drabbest and critically most noncommittal sort; this is its substantial value and limitation. Many readers will be oppressed with the feeling that Gilman is going through laborious motions a good deal in excess of what the subject demands: it is obvious to any perceptive reader of Redburn that the book is part auto-biography and part romance; Gilman's biography of Melville to 1841 is undistinguished. The more Thompson extends his argument, the more he unwittingly demonstrates the untenability of his view of Melville and the more he irritates the reader with his rigid and monolithic exposition. Why Melville should have gone to such lengths to hide his message is never made clear. Thompson's difficulty is that he will never allow Melville to say anything with simple, heartfelt sincerity.

73   CASPER, LEONARD. "The Case Against Captain Vere."
      Perspective, 5 (Summer), 146-152.
         Marshalls evidence that Melville does not endorse Vere,
      though Vere is treated with some sympathy and much understanding.
      Billy Budd is no testament of acceptance. [See 1933.B26.] Re-
      printed in part in Stafford (1961), pp. 153-155.

74   FIEDLER, LESLIE A. "Italian Pilgrimage: The Discovery of
      America." Kenyon Review, 14 (Summer), 374.
         Among postwar Italian intellectuals, Faulkner is the best
      living American writer; Melville the greatest of the classics.

75   FITZPATRICK, KATHLEEN. "A Century of Moby-Dick." Meanjin
      [University of Melbourne], 11 (Summer), 374-381.
         Mainly a review of 1951.A5. Questions a number of Mason's
      critical judgments and objects that it hardly appears from his
      study how unsophisticated a writer Melville was, and at times
      how incompetent. Mason "has many useful and interesting things
      to say about Melville's work, and his study of Mardi is probably
      the best that has yet been made. But to some extent the song of
      the siren symbols has deflected his aim." He fails to tell us
      about Melville's style, "that utterance at once eclectic and
      individual which, when all is said and done, is Melville's unique
      quality."

76   HILLWAY, TYRUS. "Billy Budd: Melville's Human Sacrifice."
      Pacific Spectator, 6 (Summer), 342-347.
         Billy Budd presents neither Melville's acceptance of the
      world nor his ironical censure of it. The death of Billy is
      heroic tragedy. Billy knowingly accepts the role of sacrificial
      victim, and his heroism arises chiefly from his understanding of
      the sacrifice demanded of him and from his willingness to undergo
      the suffering required by his role. He can "accept his fate
      willingly only because the welfare of his fellows claimed it.
      Regarded in this light, his act of devotion and completely volun-
      tary sacrifice loses the aspect of punishment and becomes instead
      the most noble gesture of which any man is capable." Billy is
      "the token victim, standing in the place of all men, demanded by
      the world's law." He is hanged not so much for his personal
      crime "as by way of partial atonement for the evil in humanity."

77   McGREAL, IAN. "'In Nomine Diaboli!'" Southwest Review, 37
      (Summer), xii, xiv-xv, 254-255.
         Review of 1952.A2. Thompson supports his interpretation
      of Moby-Dick by a capable analysis, but no careful working out of
      implications from scattered phrases is necessary: the theory
      reveals the book, clarifying the allegorical depth of each scene,
      with results so persuasive that had Thompson done nothing but
      present his theory, a rereading of Moby-Dick would have settled
      the issue in his favor. Thompson also shows how the course of
      Melville's growing disillusionment is evident in his other novels
      as well. The result is an exciting, responsible work of scholar-
      ship.

78   ZINK, KARL E. "Herman Melville and the Forms." Accent, 12
      (Summer), 131–139.
          Billy Budd is Melville's tragic allegory of nineteenth-
      century American society. "The lesson is not that Billy learns
      to accept the necessary harshness of the forms, but that in their
      high impersonality there is a dangerous lack of discrimination--
      dangerous to the individual and to the social structure itself.
      For in justifying Billy's death, the structure deprived itself
      symbolically of the force for good. And part of the lesson is
      that men tolerate this inherent evil of the structure passively,
      uncritically. Moral integrity is often, unhappily, endangered
      by or sacrificed to the impersonal dicta of the forms." Billy
      Budd is ironic social criticism, not acceptance. Reprinted in
      Gordon, pp. 713–718.

79   BREWER, D.S. "Wanderer, Lines 50–57." Modern Language Notes,
      67 (June), 398–399.
          Attempts to clarify a passage in the Old English poem The
      Wanderer by reference to lines in "John Marr." There is "a
      remarkably close similarity" between the older poem and Mel-
      ville's "in their connection with the sea, their sense of loss,
      their bitter-sweet memory of past comradeship. (Melville, with
      his whaler's acquaintance with the oar, is a particularly happy
      example of one whose experience of the sea must have been very
      close to that of a sailor a thousand years earlier.)" Granted
      the essential similarity between the two poems, it is reasonable
      to suppose that a disputed image in The Wanderer is the same as
      one Melville uses in "John Marr." [See 1953.B45 for reply.]

80   BURNAM, TOM. "Tennyson's 'Ringing Grooves' and Captain Ahab's
      Grooved Soul." Modern Language Notes, 67 (June), 423–424.
          In Locksley Hall, Tennyson writes of the "ringing grooves
      of change" down which "the great world" is to "spin forever."
      Melville seems to have been under much the same impression that
      train wheels run in a groove (the source of Tennyson's image):
      Ahab says, "The path to my fixed course is laid with iron rails,
      whereon my soul is grooved to run"; and in "The Bell-Tower"
      Melville "repeats Tennyson's error exactly": Bannadonna's
      arrangement for advancing the automaton into position to strike
      the bell is to slide the figure "along a grooved way, like a
      railway."

81   HAYFORD, HARRISON. "Leon Howard's 'Herman Melville.'"
      Nineteenth-Century Fiction, 7 (June), 61–67.
          Review of 1951.A3. Howard's "is the first book that has
      attempted to present an objective interpretation of Melville's
      whole life based on an exhaustive recovery of the contemporary
      records. It does more than any other book to give us an under-
      standing of Melville as a human being in specific personal,
      family, social, and literary circumstances. Other books about
      Melville are missing one or another of the essential elements
      that make this one original: its objectivity, its completeness,
      its primarily and consistently biographical approach, or its full
      use of contemporary records." Leyda's Log [1951.A4] provides

source material for the biography, but Howard's own intellectual
and imaginative contribution is very great. The Melville who
emerges here is not the Melville we have known: he "is a
Melville of human proportions, whose quarrel day-to-day was less
with gods and the world in general than with the conomic exigencies of supporting a family by writing books that would both pay
and allow him to follow the bent of his own speculations."
Howard's conception might be called a realistic one: "Melville
is not defined in static terms of a dominant psychological or
moral syndrome which shaped all his actions but is revealed in
terms of his dealings with various situations as he went along.
These are interpreted on the level of our ordinary consciousness
and common-sense understanding of experience, in a closely artic-
ulated narrative that has the effect of bringing Melville into
normal focal distance. Paradoxically, this gives us a much
greater feeling of understanding him and of getting an inside
story than do the reductive generalizations in terms of which his
life has usually been schematized." The richness of the book's
narrative weave is due not merely to facts supplied by the Log
but comes as much from elements supplied by Howard himself: the
historical and literary materials, by which he re-creates the
situations in which the given facts make sense. The book's most
illuminating contribution "is its sustained analysis of Melville's successive works in terms of the motives, materials, and
ideas that went into their making and of the way in which what
they are reveals Melville's shifting purposes under the pressure
of intervening and usually conflicting influences." To some
readers, it will seem that the psychological patterns they have
discerned in Melville's personality and works are not so entirely
speculative as Howard feels. Their most restrained judgment may
be that in his effort to correct their simplications he has over-
compensated by disregarding even those broad patterns that most
other students agree are there. In any case, this is likely to
be the standard biography of Melville for some time to come.

82   [HILLWAY, TYRUS]. "Ahab's Leg." Melville Society Newsletter,
     8 (June), n.p.
         Unless Ahab was left-handed the leg he lost was the right
one. If he had lost his left leg, it would hardly have been possible for him to brace himself properly against the thigh thwart,
used by the boat-steerer or harpooner for bracing his left knee
while throwing the harpoon. [See also 1956.B82.]

83   PAFFORD, WARD and FLOYD C. WATKINS. "'Benito Cereno': A Note
     in Rebuttal." Nineteenth-Century Fiction, 7 (June), 68-71.
         Refutes 1951.B85. There is nothing in Melville's source to
indicate that Benito had the courage to challenge the Negro
against the odds to be faced in the cuddy, and Melville's Benito
is even weaker than the original. Babo's deliberate self-injury
"is typical of his ruthless deception and of his disregard of
life and pain. It heightens the contrasts between the three
races presented: the hardy, democratic American; the decadent,
aristocratic Spaniard; and the inhumanly cruel and subtle
savage." To interpret Babo's wound as having been inflicted by

his "master" would detract seriously from the effectiveness of
Benito's desperate leap into Delano's boat, "which must come as
a thing completely unexpected by Delano, by Babo, and by the
reader. At no point before Benito's impulsive act does Melville
permit any suggestion that the Spanish master is capable of such
a move." Examination of the artful way in which Melville has
woven the shaving scene into the fabric of his narrative--as a
diversion created by Babo when Delano comes too close to ferret-
ing out the truth for Babo's comfort--reveals how perfectly fitting it is to interpret Babo's injury as self-inflicted.

84   WRIGHT, NATHALIA. "Form as Function in Melville." PMLA, 67
      (June), 330–340.
            Melville belongs, with Emerson, Thoreau, and Whitman among
      the American literary discoverers of the principle of organic
      form. The principle of form as organic and functional is enun-
      ciated in all Melville's major works and is also embodied in
      them.

85   WRIGHT, NATHALIA. "Mosses From An Old Manse and Moby-Dick:
      The Shock of Discovery." Modern Language Notes, 67 (June),
      387–392.
            Mosses From An Old Manse influenced Melville's use of fire
      imagery in Moby-Dick and his portrayal of Ahab as the intellec-
      tual as black magician, like Faust. Reprinted in Vincent (1969),
      pp. 110–115.

86   FERGUSON, DELANCEY. "Three Layers of Meaning in All of
      Melville's Work." New York Herald Tribune Book Review
      (22 June), p. 6.
            Review of 1952.A2. Thompson so thoroughly documents his
      case that it will not be easy to confute him. He is admirably
      objective in presenting his thesis and turns a revealing light
      into the murkier depths of Melville's books.

87   THOMSON, VIRGIL. "The Trouble with 'Billy Budd.'" New York
      Herald Tribune (22 June), section 4, p. 6.
            Review of the London production of Benjamin Britten's opera
      Billy Budd at the Théâtre des Champs-Élysées, Paris. The opera
      is a noble work of music not wholly successful on the stage. The
      librettists, E.M. Forster and Eric Crozier, and the composer
      "have omitted Melville's rather grand moral conception" and "have
      not replaced it by any equally impressive general idea." Homo-
      sexuality, "never quite overt in the novel, becomes the whole
      theme of the opera's pathos. In spite of the plot's many melo-
      dramatic occasions, the work is thus essentially sentimental."
      The musical treatment is varied and vigorous, but the drama "does
      not move forward with any anxiety, any suspense. It mostly just
      feels very sorry about the sad fate of its hero." Many individ-
      ual scenes have a real dramatic animation, but the overall
      dramatic impact is weak, and, for all its detailed excellencies
      dramatic and musical, Billy Budd became "an interminable, an un-
      conscionable bore."

88   STEWART, RANDALL. "Melville and Hawthorne." South Atlantic
     Quarterly, 51 (July), 436-446.
          Discusses Melville's friendship with Hawthorne and
     Hawthorne's possible influence on Melville's use of allegory and
     concern with "blackness." Reprinted in 1953.A3.

89   THOMPSON, FRANCIS J. "Mangan in America, 1850-1860: Mitchel,
     Maryland and Melville." Dublin Magazine, NS 27 (July-
     September), 35, 40-41.
          Sees the influence of James Clarence Mangan in a number of
     Melville's poems.

90   WILDER, THORNTON. "Toward an American Language." Atlantic,
     190 (July), 34-37.
          Analyzes New World elements in the language of a passage
     describing the appearance of the white whale in Moby-Dick,
     chapter 133. The first eleven pages of Moby-Dick "are the worst
     kind of English English"--the English of the contemporary New
     York literary cliques. Under the mounting emotion of composi-
     tion, Melville's "Americanism" erupted in spite of himself.

91   HOLT, ELLIS J. "The Meaning of Moby Dick." [Letter to the
     Editor.] Christian Century, 69 (16 July), 829.
          Reply to 1952.B65. Moby-Dick portrays the microcosm of a
     whaler's crew reacting to the incomprehensible amoral reality of
     the white whale. "Ahab was driven to harpoon the whale, bringing
     it under his control at all costs. His spiritual successors in
     the ship of the church are still trying to harpoon the whale of
     social disorder, seeking to bring in the Kingdom by the violence
     of social martyrdom. Starbuck much preferred to let the white
     whale go his way, and rather to fill the hold with rich oil so as
     to go home to enjoy his wife and family. His attempted defiance
     of Ahab is still being re-enacted by substantial laymen and
     affluent preachers who are calling into question the social
     action committees of their churches. Stubbs piously concluded
     that in any event it was all predestined. His views likewise one
     can still hear among those who sit at the captain's table in the
     World Council of Churches. Little Pip even went mad." In the
     crew of the Pequod one senses the whole gamut of the reaction of
     men to their "white whales."

92   WILSON, GILBERT. "Moby Dick and the Atom." Bulletin of the
     Atomic Scientists, 8 (August), 195-197.
          The White Whale as symbol bears disturbing resemblance in
     our time to the atomic bomb--or rather to the power within the
     atom. If we approach the tremendous force in the atom with
     hostile and destructive intentions as Ahab approached the White
     Whale, perhaps we too are doomed. Moby-Dick's "arresting
     prophecy of doom, and at the same time its reaffirmation of man's
     transcendent spirit in his struggle against natural force, might
     serve as a revealing reflection of the world predicament today.
     Possibly no tragedy in world literature quite succeeds as power-
     fully or as clearly in pointing up the mortal errors of domina-
     tion and destruction."

93   ANON. "Portrait of Melville." London <u>Times Literary Supple-</u>
      <u>ment</u>, No. 2635 (1 August), p. 499.
            Review of 1951.A3. The portrait "is of an honest, lonely,
      troubled writer whose tragedy was to be ruined by speculation.
      That was the flaw in his character, that he could not settle in
      one cockpit of the imagination." Howard's "picture is without
      the bold strokes of the biographer who likes a flourish of
      guesswork; he prefers to work on a smaller, truer scale, and does
      it convincingly. . . . One thing that emerges is Melville's
      adaptability. Perhaps it was this—the fact that he could live
      with the county as well as the foc'sle, could write a clerk's
      fist for 19 years after a life of free-lancing—that became, on a
      different level, the indecision that was his artistic downfall."

94   HOUPT, C. THEODORE. ". . . Shaping Power of the Imagination."
      <u>Christian Science Monitor</u> (21 August), p. 13.
            Review of 1952.A1. Davis's study is in the tradition of
      John Livingston Lowes' <u>The Road to Xanadu</u>. It is now apparent
      that <u>Mardi</u> deserves an independent study, because it reveals a
      good deal about Melville's compositional method, which was in the
      process of development. One of the surprising aspects of Davis's
      study is that <u>Mardi</u> owed as much to Melville's extensive reading
      as to his experience.

95   CARY, JOYCE. "The Sources of Tension in America." <u>Saturday</u>
      <u>Review</u>, 35 (23 August), 6–7, 35.
            Finds a "sense of the individual soul in battle with fate,
      with the powers of evil" haunting all American letters. Poe,
      Melville, James, Dreiser, Lewis, Hemingway, Faulkner, all from
      their different points of view, ask, "What shall a man do to be
      saved?" or in Melville's (as in Fitzgerald's) case, "What shall a
      man do not to be damned?"

96   THORP, WILLARD. "The Evolution of 'Mardi.'" New York <u>Herald</u>
      <u>Tribune Book Review</u> (31 August).
            Review of 1952.A1. Finds Davis's use of Melville's letters
      to John Murray, printed in their entirety for the first time, the
      most interesting of his many contributions to a clearer under-
      standing of "this cloudy book."

97   STEWART, RANDALL. "Two Approaches to Melville." <u>Virginia</u>
      <u>Quarterly Review</u>, 28 (Autumn), 606–609.
            Review of 1952.A1-2. The two books illustrate the extremes
      of scholarly objectivity on the one hand and critical virtuosity
      on the other. Thompson's book is a rather formidable demonstra-
      tion. The thesis obviously has a good deal to recommend it:
      Melville is undoubtedly a master in the arts of equivocation,
      ambiguity, and irony. But it is difficult to believe that he was
      habitually a deliberate hoodwinker and deceiver. Reducing Mel-
      ville's symphony to the monotone of a sneer seems an oversimpli-
      fication and impoverishment of his rich orchestration. Thompson's
      critical ingenuity lessens Melville's stature as man and author.
      Melville's moods were many; he speculated freely and imaginatively
      about things of this world and the next; more perhaps than any

other modern writer, he approached the myriad-mindedness and
variety of Shakespeare. Is not, therefore, some violence done by
an analysis that equates the complete works to a single thesis,
or attitude, or purpose? Moreover, Melville's works are fictional, imaginative, and essentially dramatic; it is dangerous,
therefore, to identify Melville with any of his fictional characters, or to suppose that he endorses a particular character or
act in his fictions. Davis's concise, factual, severely academic
monograph gives the most detailed and authoritative account to be
found anywhere of Melville's life from 1844 to 1847 and a careful
history of the writing of Mardi. Davis brings to bear on his
survey of the book's action a wide knowledge of the literary and
traditional sources Melville drew upon. The concluding chapter
of interpretation is remarkable, in these times, for its
sobriety. Along with a number of other Melville studies,
similarly restricted in scope, that have been going forward at
Yale, the book constitutes a solid, enduring contribution to our
knowledge of Melville and his work.

98   WALCUTT, CHARLES CHILD. "Book Reviews." Arizona Quarterly, 8
      (Autumn), 254-263.
          Review of 1951.A3-4; 1952.A2. The extent, the patience,
the ingenuity, and the success of Leyda's researches justify the
word fantastic. A career that had turned into a myth of frustration and bitterness is now brought back into the realm of fact
with enormous detail and accuracy. The extent of Leyda's findings, however, cannot entirely conceal their limitations: lot
after lot of Melville documents have been burned by Melville and
his relatives. It is surprising, in view of the scarcity of
letters that reveal what Melville was thinking, that Leyda should
have omitted considerable portions of Melville's letters to
Nathaniel Hawthorne and Evert Duyckinck. Howard has performed a
very great service in producing a book free from myth and unfounded legend. He creates and maintains the illusion of an
active personality without doing violence to truth, filling page
after page with plausible inferences based on the scantest
factual evidence. Howard's analyses of the composition of Moby-
Dick and of Melville's attitude toward Ahab are questionable,
however. Thompson's absorbing and challenging study is worth all
the rest of the Melville interpretation that has been published:
his case is tremendously convincing. In the light of Thompson's
detailed explication, it becomes impossible to suppose that the
furious rebellion of Moby-Dick could have been turned into the
utterly abject acceptance of authority that we find in Billy Budd
if we do not read that work as a sustained irony and satire on
God's "justice." This book will settle the Billy Budd controversy.

99   WILLIAMS, STANLEY T. "Who Reads An American Book?" Virginia
      Quarterly Review, 28 (Autumn), 523, 530.
          Contemporary European attitudes to American literature.
One Cambridge don has remarked that Melville succeeds in doing
more successfully in The Confidence-Man what Voltaire was trying
to do in Candide. The "different levels of meaning in Melville

or Faulkner delight European students; these they recognize as akin to techniques and esthetic patterns in their own writers. . . . Connected with this phase of European interest, it is also true that some few saddened spirits find in the pessimism of Melville or the tensions of Faulkner complements of the nihilism or existentialism of Kafka or Sartre, on which European minds have fed so long."

100   WRIGHT, NATHALIA. "The Confidence Men of Melville and Cooper: An American Indictment." American Quarterly, 4 (Fall), 266-268.
    The Confidence-Man was written in a tradition almost as old as American literature: the analysis and criticism of national character. The structure of Cooper's Homeward Bound, the most celebrated novel in this tradition, is also a voyage, and it contains the confidence man Steadfast Dodge, who may have influenced the final embodiment, in Frank Goodman, of Melville's slowly growing conception. The core of both Cooper's and Melville's novels is an attack on the twin American concepts that a democracy is a rule of the majority and that the majority is always right. Both authors pled passionately for the correction of that delinquency to which a democracy is inherently inclined-- personal irresponsibility.

101   BABCOCK, C. MERTON. "Melville's World's Language." Southern Folklore Quarterly, 16 (September), 177-182.
    Examples of the "folk language" Melville used (proverbs, tall talk, localisms) "as a means of dramatizing his democratic theme" in his tales of the sea.

102   DICHMANN, MARY E. "Absolutism in Melville's Pierre." PMLA, 67 (September), 702-715.
    The philosophical basis of Pierre is the concept of the oneness of time and human experience, "of the simultaneity of past, present, and future and of all human history." The book's "imaginal" patterns--season imagery, darkness-in-light and light- in-darkness imagery--reinforce the related concept that "good and evil are inseparable, since they are merely obverse sides of the same absolute." Reprinted in part in Willett, pp. 24-26.

103   [HILLWAY, TYRUS]. Melville Society Newsletter, 8 (September), n.p.
    Details of gifts to the Melville collection at the Berk- shire Athenaeum in Pittsfield and of plans for establishing a Herman Melville Memorial Room there.

104   MARX, LEO. "'Melville's Quarrel With God.'" Nineteenth- Century Fiction, 7 (September), 138-140.
    Review of 1952.A2. Thompson's argument is pressed relent- lessly from the introduction through the body of the book, which consists of a close and often brilliant reading of the major texts. The result is a bold, imaginative, and irresponsibly crotchety study. No one has succeeded so well in demonstrating the pervasiveness of the spiritual conflict reflected in

Melville's work. By bearing down on passage after passage
Thompson reveals that the tension between the will to believe and
the necessity of doubt makes itself felt in virtually every line.
But in the presence of this recurrent conflict of meaning,
Thompson somehow became convinced that he could determine what
Melville really intended. Although this study will help every
reader see many things he had not seen before, it is impossible
to credit the conception of Melville or his work that Thompson
provides. "How is it possible to reconcile the fantastic degree
of subtle contrivance attributed to Melville with what we know of
the headlong impetuosity with which he so often wrote? Why, in
nineteenth-century America, was it necessary for Melville to re-
sort to such calculated deception? The paradox is that we can
hardly expect to find answers to such questions in the novels."
Thompson's hypothesis is one that can be substantiated only by
historical, biographical, and even psychoanalytical data, but his
book deals almost exclusively with Melville's writings. It is
irresponsible chiefly because it pretends to do what cannot be
done: it is a study of Melville's motives.

105   PAUL, SHERMAN. "Book Reviews." New England Quarterly, 25
      (September), 423–424.
         Review of 1952.B17. Raises the question of editorial pro-
priety, troubled by the volume's size and by its mingling of
extended interpretation with the notes. "The confusion of fact
and criticism gives the criticism a bulwark it might not have
otherwise. And a critical approach through the notes results in
many interpretative fragments, but no total view: a kind of
scholar's paradise, perhaps, but a critic's hell--and a reader's
purgatory." This "attempt at critical security" probably "follows from the recent general retreat from the interpretation of
Melville to the fortress of external facts. Facts are important
and are the basis of criticism, but they are not a substitute for
insight." The "externalists," such as Vincent [1949.A3] and
Howard [1951.A3], have been unable to resist minor critical
forays; they are drawn to the water's edge but are afraid to
plunge and accept the inevitable but rewarding failure of the
critic's job of work. This is the major flaw of the edition: a
mistake in critical strategy, an attempt to establish by bulk
alone the merits of Moby-Dick.

106   OLSON, CHARLES. "Materials and Weights of Herman Melville."
      New Republic, 127 (8 September), 20–21.
         Review of 1951.A5; 1952.A2, B17. The intelligence and
limpidity of Mason's book measures the soddenness of the
scholarship of the new edition of Moby-Dick and the perverseness
of thinking in Thompson's book. The very badness of the two
American books necessitates that attention be called to the
exceptional work on Melville by Jay Leyda, Harrison Hayford,
Henry A. Murray, F. Barron Freeman, Merton Sealts, Nathalia
Wright, and Walter Bezanson. Continued in 1952.B107. Reprinted
in Olson (1965), pp. 109–112.

107   OLSON, CHARLES. "Materials and Weights of Herman Melville, II." New Republic, 127 (15 September), 17-18, 21.
          Continued from 1952.B106. Melville's importance, greater than ever, lies in (1) his approach to physicality, his ability to go inside a thing and know not only its essence but its dimension; (2) his address to character as necessary human force; and (3) his application of intelligence to all phenomena as the ordering agent. One of the losses of all the criticism and scholarship surveyed in 1952.B106, including the three new books, is that the totality of Melville's effort is not dealt with as one. By his impeccable and continuous inquiries into what ways ideality no longer fit modern reality in a form proper to its content, he drove further than any of his predecessors toward forcing totality of effort to yield some principle out of itself. Reprinted in Olson (1965), pp.112-116.

108   BABCOCK, C. MERTON. "Melville's Proverbs of the Sea." Western Folklore, 11 (October), 254-265.
          Lists of Melville's "proverbs, proverbial sayings, and sententia, which deal strictly with the sea or the life of seamen." Melville's "method with respect to proverbs is somewhat evolutionary: from direct quotation to conscious paraphrase and imitation, to allusive echoes and verbal synthesis."

109   DUFFY, CHARLES. "The Meaning of 'Mardi.'" New York Times Book Review (5 October), p. 42.
          Notice of 1952.A1. Brief synopsis.

110   F[AUSSET], H[UGH] I'A. "Mardi." Manchester Guardian (7 October), p. 4.
          Review of 1952.A1. A most scholarly study. Brief synopsis.

111   DAHL, CURTIS. "Moby Dick and Reviews of The Cruise of The Cachalot." Modern Language Notes, 67 (November), 471-472.
          Only two London reviews in 1899 mention Melville in connection with Frank T. Bullen's work. [See 1899.B7, B13.] Melville may have been better known at the time in England than in America but evidently he was not widely known.

112   FRAIBERG, LOUIS. "The Westminster Review and American Literature, 1824-1885." American Literature, 24 (November), 314, 323, 325.
          For no known reason, some major works of important American writers were not reviewed in the Westminster Review, including The Scarlet Letter, The House of the Seven Gables, and Moby-Dick. "These and other writings, like the poems of Poe and Bryant, were brought into later discussions in such a way that the familiarity of the reviewers with them was evident, but they did not receive critical notice from the Westminster when they first appeared." Brief references to the treatment of Melville in 1852.B18 and 1857.B42.

113 THORP, WILLARD. "Book Reviews." <u>American Literature</u>, 24
     (November), 391–393.
          Review of 1951.A2. Gilman brings to light a multitude of
     new facts, and his detailed criticism of <u>Redburn</u> is based solidly
     on the biographical facts already adduced. He puts his scholar-
     ship to work with excellent results. "<u>Redburn</u> can tell us a
     great deal about Melville's mind and art, because it does in fact
     contain much of the young Melville but even more because it was
     taken off the top of his mind at high speed and in order to make
     money. He put into it art enough to make it an attractive story.
     How superior that necessary modicum of art proved to be can best
     be seen when <u>Redburn</u> is compared with the many sea tales contem-
     porary with it."

114 WHIPPLE, A.B.C. "Three-Month Ordeal in Open Boats." <u>Life</u>, 33
     (10 November), 144–146, 149–150, 152, 154, 156.
          Account of the crew's ordeal after the <u>Essex</u> was sunk by a
     whale in 1820. Refers to Melville's use of the sinking as the
     basis for the climax of <u>Moby-Dick</u> and to his meeting with Captain
     Pollard in Nantucket in 1852.

115 FOLLAND, HAROLD F. "Book Reviews." <u>Western Humanities Review</u>,
     7 (Winter), 74–75.
          Review of 1951.B4. Coxe and Chapman's play closed after a
     short run on Broadway, but the play has not died. It has been
     published in a compact handy form; it has been turned into an
     opera by Benjamin Britten; and lately it has begun a career in
     the nonprofessional theaters sponsored by universities and civic
     groups. There a play so honest, so well made, and so powerful in
     its emotional impact should prosper, despite the difficulty of
     casting Billy, Claggart, and Vere. The novel, like the play,
     treats a theme of profound concern in the present day—the dis-
     parity between man and his systems, between justice and law, and
     between the motives and the results of men's actions. Coxe and
     Chapman have achieved the incarnation of Melville's undramatic,
     even unnovelistic novel with tact, ingenuity and force, and
     without violating its spirit.

116 HILLWAY, TYRUS. "Book Reviews." <u>Western Humanities Review</u>,
     7 (Winter), 72–73.
          Review of 1952.A2. An interesting and thought-provoking
     essay, making of Melville a kind of nineteenth-century existen-
     tialist. Anyone who has spent even a small amount of time con-
     sidering Melville's religious and philosophical beliefs will find
     it profitable reading. But once one accepts the premise that
     Melville did not mean what he said in his writings, almost any
     interpretation becomes possible; and if a scholar also grants
     himself the right of selecting the statements that he regards as
     truly expressive of Melville's thought, of rejecting those he
     thinks extraneous, and of ignoring all facts that do not fit his
     thesis, scholarship can become a delightful exercise of the
     imagination. Thompson's main argument for his interpretation of
     Melville boils down to the fact that he <u>feels</u> it to be true.
     Thompson ignores the outspokenness of many of Melville's critical

ideas, while accusing him of hiding his real thoughts under a
veil of symbols. He fails to see that Melville's thoughts about
God and nature largely reflect a rebellion against the optimism
of the romantic, pre-Darwinian era. Even the nonconformist
Melville would have seen the utter futility of a quarrel with
God.

117   JARRELL, RANDALL. "Walt Whitman: He Had His Nerve." Kenyon
      Review, 14 (Winter), 63.
        "Whitman, Dickinson, and Melville seem to me the best poets
of the 19th Century here in America. Melville's poetry has been
grotesquely underestimated, but of course it is only in the last
four or five years that it has been much read; in the long run,
in spite of the awkwardness and amateurishness of so much of it,
it will surely be thought well of. (In the short run it will
probably be thought entirely too well of. Melville is a great
poet only in the prose of Moby Dick.)"

118   MURRAY, HENRY A. "In Nomine Diaboli." Princeton University
      Library Chronicle, 13 (Winter), 47–62.
        Slightly abbreviated version of 1951.B107, as delivered at
Princeton University on the centennial of the American publication of Moby-Dick, 14 November 1951.

119   QUINN, PATRICK F. "Poe's Imaginary Voyage." Hudson Review, 4
      (Winter), 579–585.
        Finds an extraordinary degree of similarity between Moby-
Dick and Arthur Gordon Pym. Notes similar incidents, similarities between Ishmael and Pym, and similarities between Queequeg
and Peters. Through "a corresponding pattern of narrator-and-
comrade" both works dramatize the theme of death and rebirth.
Moby-Dick's theme of the deceptiveness of nature's appearances
lies implicit at the heart of Pym. Melville often states
directly the kind of thing Poe leaves inferential and latent; the
two works illustrate the differences between the use of conscious
and unconscious symbols. Both Melville and Poe were fascinated
by whiteness: it is virtually impossible to read "The Whiteness
of the Whale" without feeling persuaded that Melville was following Poe's lead in the last pages of Pym. If Melville "did not
long and seriously study the essential drift" of Pym, the similarities between the two books must be accounted one of the
most extraordinary accidents in literature.

120   HIGGINS, PAUL LAMBOURNE. "Religious Values in Melville."
      Pastor, 16 (December), 36–37.
        In the last analysis, Melville "believed in the authority
of God, although he could not understand the ways of the Divine.
Melville would trust in the Great Ruler and would try to obey
Him, even though he could not approve of some of the commands."
Melville "persisted in believing that man could improve, and
while he held man's laws in contempt, he trusted always in the
law of love. Although unorthodox in many respects, the essence
of Melville's religious faith is expressed in his devotion to the
way and spirit of Jesus."

121   PAUL, SHERMAN. "Book Reviews." New England Quarterly, 25
       (December), 555–557.
           Review of 1952.Al. Davis is a superb detective: he not
only tracks down the sources of names, incidents, and symbolisms
large and small in Mardi, but gives convincing data of the unfolding of the book. Everything but the "something unmanageable"
in Melville himself is here, for it is Davis's intention to
verify, to make the facts tell the story, and only in the small-
est way to interpret. Because of these self-imposed restric-
tions, (and within them Davis's book has its excellences), the
extensive materials Davis provides toward a fuller interpretation
of Mardi will have to await the critic who includes in his aim
the relation of Mardi to the rest of Melville's work and who
starts with a more complex view of literary creation. To elim-
inate the author as a creative personality is patent reduction;
to deny that Mardi was the allegory of Melville's inner life is
one thing, but to assert--by the implication of method--that his
choice of symbols and themes is fortuitous is another. One must
account for the deeper tensions of the book, those of faith and
doubt, of purity and sensuality, the tone of disillusionment,
the militancy and energy. The books Melville read at this time
were more than sources: they were instruments of liberation.
In spite of the valuable delving, the questions we ask about
this difficult book are not answered by Davis's study. His pages
of analysis make Melville's "new departure" a continuation of the
travel writer's methods--they do not account for Melville's
development, his new social, philosophical, literary, and personal interests. Mardi is an unusual departure: a new "style"
bespeaking a new man.

122   PEARCE, ROY HARVEY. "Melville's Indian-Hater: A Note on the
       Meaning of The Confidence-Man." PMLA, 67 (December), 942–948.
           Reply to 1951.B67, arguing that "there is nothing but dis-
tortion in the Indian-hater's vision of spiritual reality, that
the price he pays for resisting the confidence-man is exactly as
high as the price he would pay for surrendering to him. For the
Indian-hater can see nothing but the dark side of life. In that
darkness he loses sight of his human self. The issue of blind
confidence and blind hatred is in the end identical. But, in the
Melville of The Confidence-Man, there seems to be no way to avoid
either one or the other"--the "blackness is complete." Comparison of Moredock's story with its original in James Hall's
Sketches of History, Life, and Manners, in the West.

1953 A BOOKS

  1   FEIDELSON, CHARLES, JR. Symbolism and American Literature.
       Chicago: The University of Chicago Press, pp. 27–36, 162–212,
       passim.
           Rather than "their devotion to the possibilities of
democracy," the more likely "vital common denominator" among the
five writers Matthiessen studied in 1941.Al is "their attitude
toward their medium," their "devotion to the possibilities of

symbolism." Emerson, Melville, Hawthorne, Poe, and Whitman
"inherited the basic problem of romanticism: the vindication of
imaginative thought in a world grown abstract and material. . . .
Considered as pure romantics, they are minor disciples of European masters. Their symbolistic method is their title to literary independence. Whether romantic or symbolistic, they wrote
no masterpieces; the relative immaturity of the American literary
tradition cannot be denied. But as symbolists they look forward
to one of the most sophisticated movements in literary history;
however inexpert, they broaden the possibilities of literature."
Each was preoccupied with a kind of archetypal figure--"the figure of Man Seeing, the mind engaged in a crucial act of knowledge." Beyond their obvious differences of literary theory and
practice, they "were committed to a common theory and practice of
perception, which entered into both the form and the content of
their work. Their movement was not obscurantist [as Winters
maintains in 1938.B23] but honest, an ingenuous attempt to explore a common intellectual situation." Emerson and Melville
"were the polar figures of the American symbolist movement."
Between them "they ran the gamut of possibilities created by the
symbolistic point of view." Emerson "was the theorist and advocate, Melville the practicing poet." Melville "assumed the
ambient idea that Emerson made explicit."
    Analyses of Melville's prose works stress Melville's symbol-
istic practice and complex modernity. Extended comparison between Pierre ("the best vantage point for a general view of
Melville's work") and Gide's Les Faux-monnayeurs. "The preoccupations of Les Faux-monnayeurs were Melville's standing
questions, and they led him to attempt in Pierre a similar tour
de force. As in Gide's novel, every character, including the
author, is a counterfeiter; man's life is a construct; the artist
is the archetypal man." Indexed. Reviewed in 1953.B61, B69;
1954.B32-33.

2   HILLWAY, TYRUS, comp. Doctoral Dissertations on Herman
     Melville: A Chronological Summary (1933-1952). Greeley,
     Colorado: The Melville Society, 39 pp.
         An annotated checklist of Melville dissertations.

3   HILLWAY, TYRUS and LUTHER S. MANSFIELD, eds. MOBY-DICK
     Centennial Essays. Dallas: Southern Methodist University
     Press, 182 pp.
         A collection of essays read at centennial celebrations of
     the publication of Moby-Dick. [See 1953.B4, B9, B11-12, B17,
     B19-20, B25, B29 for annotations of individual essays.] Reviewed
     in 1954.B29, B55; 1955.B48.

4   JAMES, C.L.R. Mariners, Renegades and Castaways: The Story
     of Herman Melville and the World We Live In. New York:
     C.L.R. James, 203 pp. Reprint. Detroit: Berwick Editions,
     1978; London: Allison & Busby, 1985.
         Devoted mainly to Moby-Dick, but includes survey of the
     other works. In his earlier books, Melville moves steadily
     "towards that rarest of achievements--the creation of a character

[Ahab] which will sum up a whole epoch of human history." Ahab is the "embodiment of the totalitarian type," a leader comparable to Hitler and Stalin; the crew of the Pequod are the workers in his totalitarian state. Ishmael is the weak "modern young intellectual" who wavers constantly between totalitarianism and the workers. By the time he wrote "The Encantadas," Melville had "come finally to the conclusion that modern civilization is doomed."

5   METCALF, ELEANOR MELVILLE. Herman Melville: Cycle and
     Epicycle. Cambridge, Mass.: Harvard University Press,
     311 pp. Reprint. Westport, Conn.: The Greenwood Press,
     1970.
         Mainly a collection of letters and diary entries by
Melville, his relatives, friends, and acquaintances. Much of
the family correspondence here was previously unpublished. The
documents, chronologically ordered, illuminate Melville's family
relations and friendships--"the intimate social scene" in which
he lived and moved. Passages of narrative and commentary by
Metcalf (Melville's granddaughter) include family reminiscences
of Melville and "legends and anecdotes alive in the family into
the twentieth century" but mostly unpublished. Indexed. Reviewed in 1953.B72-75; 1954.B31, B34, B36, B38-39.

6   [TREEMAN, ELIZABETH]. Corrigenda for Melville's Billy Budd.
     Cambridge, Mass.: Harvard University Press, 14 pp.
         Pamphlet "records certain errors in the printed transcrip-
tion of the text of the novel Billy Budd [1948.B9] that came to
light upon a careful reëxamination of the manuscript. It does
not contain corrections to the notes."

1953 B SHORTER WRITINGS

1   ANDERSON, SHERWOOD. Letters of Sherwood Anderson. Ed. Howard
     Mumford Jones and Walter B. Rideout. Boston: Little, Brown
     and Co., p. 241.
         Letter of 10 February 1931 to Charles Bockler: "I used to
look with horror, for example, upon the fate of Melville. There
were years of his life when he was an old man, as I will presently be, and when he had nothing. He had to live a strange life
of obscurity in a little hole, as did also the painter Albert
Ryder." [Complete Melville reference.]

2   ANON. "Moby Dick," in Plot Outlines of 100 Famous Novels.
     Ed. Roland A. Goodman. Garden City, N.Y.: Doubleday & Co.,
     pp. 251-256.
         Synopsis of Moby-Dick, with one-paragraph biographical
headnote.

3   AUSTIN, JAMES C. Fields of THE ATLANTIC MONTHLY: Letters to
     an Editor, 1861-1870. San Marino, Ca.: The Huntington
     Library, pp. 154, 364-365.
         Although Whitman was neglected, Melville was almost com-
pletely ignored by the Atlantic. He was the only one of the

major writers of the North (excluding Emily Dickinson, who did
not publish) who was not represented in the magazine, though he
was once invited to contribute and consented. [See 1907.B9.]
The only mention of Melville during the first twenty-five years
of the Atlantic was Howell's review of Battle-Pieces. [See
1867.B3.]

4   BEZANSON, WALTER E. "Moby-Dick: Work of Art," in MOBY-DICK
     Centennial Essays. Ed. Tyrus Hillway and Luther S. Mansfield.
     Dallas: Southern Methodist University Press, pp. 30–58.
       An examination of Moby-Dick as a work of art in terms of
its matter, dynamic, and structure. The book's matter, whaling,
is subjected to the purposes of art through a dynamic and a
structure. The central dynamic is neither Ahab nor the White
Whale but Ishmael, who is the real center of meaning and the
defining force of the novel. There are two Ishmaels: forecastle
Ishmael and narrator Ishmael. Forecastle Ishmael is simply one
of the characters of the novel, though a major one. Narrator
Ishmael is the essential sensibility in terms of which all
characters and events of the fiction are conceived and evaluated.
The prime experience for the reader is this unfolding sensibility. Complex in temperament, narrator Ishmael has above all an
inexhaustible sense of wonder. The first level of the book's
structure consists of several levels of rhetoric--the expository,
the poetic, the idiomatic, and the composite (a blending of these
three). Beneath the rhetoric is a play of symbolic forms; the
persistent tendency in the book is for facts, events, and images
to become symbols. The symbolism is not static but is in motion;
it is in process of creation for both narrator and reader. Dream
sense is an important mood in Moby-Dick, and dream form is an
incipient structural device. Other structural elements include
the book's individual chapters (many of them in drama or sermon
form), chapter sequences, and chapter clusters. Relations between any one chapter and another chapter or chapters tend to be
multiple and shifting--like the symbols, the chapters are "in
process." Two sets of events occur along the simple linear form
of the voyage: whale killings and ship meetings. Each killing
provokes either a chapter sequence or a chapter cluster of
cetological lore; except for the first and last, the killings are
not so much narrative events as structural occasions for ordering
the whaling essays and sermons. The ship meetings provide a
psychograph of Ahab's monomania, but any single systematic treatment of all the ships does violence to some of them and to their
rich amplitude of meanings. There are elaborate relationships
among the book's parts, but there is no overreaching formal pattern. In the literature of the nineteenth century Moby-Dick is
the single most ambitious projection of the concept of organic
form. Reprinted (minus the first one and a half paragraphs) in
Norton Moby-Dick, pp. 651–671.

5   BROOKS, VAN WYCK. <u>The Writer in America</u>. New York: E.P.
    Dutton & Co., p. 20, passim.
        "What makes literature great, of course, is the quality of
    its subject-matter,--the permanent important and interest inher-
    ing in this,--together with as much formal virtue as the writer
    is able to compass, though in this he may be, at moments, sadly
    deficient. Melville was deficient in this more than half the
    time and Mark Twain at least seven-eighths, and even the greatest
    works of each, <u>Moby-Dick</u> and <u>Huckleberry Finn</u>, were gravely de-
    fective in their structure."

6   CARPENTER, FREDERIC IVES. <u>Emerson Handbook</u>. New York:
    Hendricks House, pp. 231-233.
        "Even more than Hawthorne, Melville stood in ideal opposi-
    tion to Emerson, for Melville expressed most clearly in the
    American nineteenth century that 'modern' pessimism which most
    distrusts Emerson's optimism. Moreover, Melville came under
    Emerson's influence later than did Hawthorne, and reacted more
    emphatically, more specifically, and more articulately." The
    "most famous and significant satire upon Emerson's Transcendental
    philosophy" is probably that contained in <u>Pierre</u>, and embodied in
    the character of Plinlimmon. The "whole idea" of Plinlimmon's
    pamphlet is the conflict between transcendental idealism and
    realistic common sense. Melville preferred the latter. In <u>The
    Confidence-Man</u> he drew fictional caricatures of Emerson and
    Thoreau, as Winsome and Egbert, which declared the "humbug" of
    these "confidence-men" and the actual evil effects of their false
    idealism. In his short stories "Cock-A-Doodle-Doo!" and
    "Bartleby," he satirized Emerson's self-reliance by the process
    of reductio ad absurdum [cf. Oliver, 1946.B30 and 1948.B57].
    Melville's marginal comments on Emerson's essays [<u>see</u> 1937.B38]
    "emphasize the fact that for Melville, as also for Hawthorne,
    Emerson had first defined those fundamental problems and ideal
    conflicts which the two novelists then embodied fictionally in
    their plots and characters."

7   d. R., H. "Herman Melville," in <u>Moby Dick</u>. London: Collins,
    pp. 5-7.
        Biographical sketch.

8   DIXSON, ROBERT J. "Preface," in <u>Moby Dick</u>, simplified and
    adapted by Robert J. Dixson. American Classics. New York:
    Regents Publishing Co., n.p.
        The story is presented in a vocabulary range of one
    thousand words, without many of the long descriptive passages of
    the original treating of whales and the whaling industry.

9   HEFLIN, WILSON L. "Melville and Nantucket," in <u>MOBY-DICK
    Centennial Essays</u>. Ed. Tyrus Hillway and Luther S. Mansfield.
    Dallas: Southern Methodist University Press, pp. 165-179.
        Reprint of 1951.B8.

10   HEISER, M.F. "The Decline of Neoclassicism, 1801-1848," in
     Transitions in American Literary History. Ed. Harry Hayden
     Clark. Durham, N.C.: Duke University Press, pp. 97, 105,
     123.
          As America approached the end of the period 1801-1848, "the
     clash between ideals of primitivism and progress is increasingly
     marked. Primitivism is no longer related to a classical golden
     age, but is either escape into a medieval past (the Scott vogue),
     sentimental and ineffectual lament for the vanishing American
     Indian (after the fashion of The Last of the Mohicans), praise of
     the wildness of nature (e.g., Walden), or search for Utopia
     (Melville and Charles W. Webber). The idea of progress becomes
     by this time social progress and 'manifest destiny' (the march
     of mind and the progress of public improvement)." De Tocqueville
     in Democracy in America anticipates Whitman by twenty years and
     "predicts the psychological probings and gropings of the
     Transcendentalists, of Poe, and of Hawthorne and Melville."
     Unique in English letters, Emerson, Thoreau, Hawthorne, Poe,
     Melville, and Whitman exemplify the individualism of the age:
     concerned as they ultimately were with the nature of society, all
     of them were first concerned with the individual.

11   HETHERINGTON, HUGH W. "Early reviews of Moby-Dick," in
     MOBY-DICK Centennial Essays. Ed. Tyrus Hillway and Luther S.
     Mansfield. Dallas: Southern Methodist University Press,
     pp. 89-122.
          A study of the contemporary reception of Moby-Dick "based
     on a far more extensive examination of magazines and particularly
     newspapers than has been made by Potter, McCloskey, or other
     scholars." Potter [1940.B34] is more judicious than McCloskey
     [1946.B16], who is unsound. Sections on "British Reviews in
     1851," "American Reviews in 1851.," "Reviews in January and
     February, 1852," and "The Delayed Reaction." "Although the
     'immediate reactions' were so varied that it is possible, by
     biased selection of quotations, to build up a case for either a
     welcome or a rejection, as has been done, the 'delayed reaction'
     was clearly adverse." The "unfriendly 'delayed reaction' had
     already begun to set in as early as January, 1852, during which
     month two Americans asserted dogmatically that Melville's writ-
     ings had been getting progressively worse. The peak of the early
     fame of Moby-Dick had come in the first part of December, 1851."
     Melville might well have been more affected by the particularly
     corrosive censure in the "immediate reaction" than by the praise.
     It is implicit in Pierre that he believed Moby-Dick had failed.
     Reprinted in 1960.A6.

12　HILLWAY, TYRUS. "A Preface to Moby-Dick," in MOBY-DICK
　　Centennial Essays. Ed. Tyrus Hillway and Luther S. Mansfield.
　　Dallas: Southern Methodist University Press, pp. 22-29.
　　　　The great question Moby-Dick raises is: What have the gods
　　to do with man? Whatever the correct answer may be, Ahab's was
　　the wrong one. To rebel against one's destiny, to defy God,
　　leads only to tragedy.

13　HILLWAY, TYRUS and LUTHER S. MANSFIELD. "Introduction," in
　　MOBY-DICK Centennial Essays. Ed. Tyrus Hillway and Luther S.
　　Mansfield. Dallas: Southern Methodist University Press,
　　pp. vii-xiv.
　　　　Summary of the most important centennial celebrations of
　　the publication of Moby-Dick and brief synopses of the essays in
　　the collection. [See 1953.A1.]

14　HOLMES, OLIVER WENDELL and HAROLD J. LASKI. Holmes-Laski
　　Letters: The Correspondence of Mr. Justice Holmes and Harold
　　J. Laski, 1916-1935. 2 Vols. Cambridge, Mass.: Harvard
　　University Press, 1: pp. 323-324, 327, 328, 331, 539;
　　2: pp. 997, 1000, 1079, 1091, 1146-1147, 1170, 1172, 1299.
　　　　Appreciative comments by both men on Moby-Dick. In 1921
　　Holmes discovers Melville: "He used to live within 3/4 of mile
　　of us at Pittsfield and don't I wish that small boy as I was I
　　had tried to get hold of the (if my memory is right) rather gruff
　　taciturn man that I saw in my father's study." Laski in 1927
　　quotes H.G. Wells's opinion (given in conversation over dinner)
　　that "Herman Melville was easily the biggest of all the Americans
　　as Dostoievski of the Russians" and in 1929 quotes Wells as say-
　　ing (also over dinner, with Laski and Arnold Bennett) "that he
　　was convinced that few Americans had ever equalled Hawthorne in
　　style, and that as the years went on, he put him even higher,
　　though he thought Moby Dick the greatest single work an American
　　had done." In 1929 Holmes writes disparagingly of Mumford's
　　"tone and attitude" in 1929.A1.

15　KAZIN, ALFRED, LAWRANCE THOMPSON, and LYMAN BRYSON. "Moby-
　　Dick." Invitation to Learning, 11 (1953), 205-211.
　　　　Transcript of radio conversation between Kazin, Thompson,
　　and Bryson about Moby-Dick in the CBS Invitation to Learning
　　series. Reprinted in Crothers, pp. 224-231.

16　KERN, ALEXANDER. "The Rise of Transcendentalism, 1815-1860,"
　　in Transitions in American Literary History. Ed. Harry Hayden
　　Clark. Durham, N.C.: Duke University Press, p. 248.
　　　　Notes that American transcendentalism affected Hawthorne
　　and Melville, "if negatively."

17　LEISY, ERNEST E. "Fatalism in Moby-Dick," in MOBY-DICK
　　Centennial Essays. Ed. Tyrus Hillway and Luther S. Mansfield.
　　Dallas: Southern Methodist University Press, pp. 76-88.
　　　　Moby-Dick portrays the futility of human effort in the war
　　against Fate and the brute energy of the universe. It portrays
　　too the increased suffering that the growth of knowledge brings

man. At the same time, Melville "sees that though the evil in
the universe cannot be conquered, neither can it conquer as long
as man preserves his integrity by fighting that evil. To that
extent at least he let Ahab retain his dignity and nobility of
soul even though his quest was a failure."

18   LUDWIG, JACK BARRY and W. RICHARD POIRIER. "Instructor's
     Manual," for Stories British and American. Boston: Houghton
     Mifflin Co., pp. 6-8.
         Analysis emphasizes "Bartleby's" structure and shifting
     tonality. "Bartleby" is "essentially a study in eccentricty, of
     people who are off the center of things."

19   MILLER, PERRY. "Melville and Transcendentalism," in MOBY-DICK
     Centennial Essays. Ed. Tyrus Hillway and Luther S. Mansfield.
     Dallas: Southern Methodist University Press, pp. 123-152.
         Longer version of 1953.B66.

20   MURRAY, HENRY A. "In Nomine Diaboli," in MOBY-DICK Centennial
     Essays. Ed. Tyrus Hillway and Luther S. Mansfield. Dallas:
     Southern Methodist University Press, pp. 3-21.
         Reprint of 1951.B107.

21   ORIANS, G. HARRISON. "The Rise of Romanticism, 1805-1855," in
     Transitions in American Literary History. Ed. Harry Hayden
     Clark. Durham, N.C.: Duke University Press, p. 171.
         Finds that, though "Melville speaks of going to sea as a
     substitute for ball and pistol, American romanticists did not,
     at least not for long, accept either pessimism or despair or
     profligacy as a consistent mood."

22   RITTER, DECKARD. "Envoi: An Exercise in Herman-Eutics, or
     Contraverse to End all Controversy." CEA Critic, 15
     (November), 3.
         Poem.

23   ROURKE, CONSTANCE. American Humor: A Study of the National
     Character. Doubleday Anchor Books. Garden City, N.Y.:
     Doubleday & Co., pp. 154-162.
         Reprint of 1931.B19.

24   SIMMS, WILLIAM GILMORE. The Letters of William Gilmore Simms.
     Vol. 2. Ed. Mary C. Simms Oliphant and T.C. Duncan Eaves.
     Columbia: University of South Carolina Press, pp. 158,
     189-190, 273.
         In letters of 27 March 1846, 1 October 1846, and 25 February
     1847 to Evert A. Duyckinck, Simms notes that he has "recieved
     [sic] but not yet read" Typee; wishes "to have a copy of the new
     ed. of Typee--containing the sequel"; and notes that he has never
     received "the second part" of Typee.

25   SMITH, HENRY NASH. "The Image of Society in Moby-Dick," in
      MOBY-DICK Centennial Essays. Ed. Tyrus Hillway and Luther S.
      Mansfield. Dallas: Southern Methodist University Press,
      pp. 59–75.
          By explicit assertions and indirect propositions conveyed
      by symbols (particularly sharks), Moby-Dick posits that organized
      society is intrinsically evil. There is no evidence in the book
      "that society can be redeemed, or that institutions once regarded
      as wicked are later discovered to be otherwise. Melville's pro-
      cedure is rather to single out certain experiences within the
      larger field of social relationships which can be affirmed and
      from which durable values can be derived. If society is evil,
      some human relationships are nevertheless good. These can be
      designated by the general name of brotherhood or community, and
      Ishmael's love for Queequeg is the most obvious example of a
      redeeming force brought to bear upon him in the course of
      action. . . . Men can be saved although society is damned.
      From his intense personal relationship with Queequeg, Ishmael
      eventually broadens his capacity for comradeship to include the
      crew as a whole." The august dignity of "man, in the ideal,"
      celebrated in chapter 26, is the central affirmation of the
      novel. Alienation "is the central theme of the book as a whole.
      This view makes Ishmael rather than Ahab the 'hero,' and rele-
      gates the quest of the White Whale to a subordinate position in
      the basic structure of the narrative. Ahab, from this standpoint,
      can be taken as an exemplification of any of a number of wrong
      and dangerous attitudes. . . ." For Melville, American society
      of the mid-nineteenth century "represented not the benign present
      and hopeful future proclaimed by official spokesmen, but an
      environment threatening the individual with a disintegration of
      personality which he could avoid only by the half-miraculous
      achievement of a sense of community, of brotherhood, unattainable
      within the official culture." Reprinted in Tuten, pp. 35–51, and
      Gilmore, pp. 27–41.

26   SPARK, MURIEL. John Masefield. London: Peter Nevill, p. 41.
          "Herman Melville's The Green Hand [sic] he [Masefield] had
      read but it 'was not much use to me'--a phrase which suggests
      that already he was reading as a writer reads, with a view to
      using the book for his own development. He read other works by
      Melville, and enjoyed parts of Moby Dick. Surprisingly, he does
      not seem to have been an enthusiast for Melville at this time
      [his late teens], though he was keenly interested in all sea
      literature."

27   STACKPOLE, EDUOARD A. The Sea-Hunters: The New England
      Whalemen During Two Centuries, 1635–1835. Philadelphia:
      J.B. Lippincott Co., 335–337.
          Prints extracts from Melville's annotations in his copy of
      Owen Chase's Narrative. Notes that Chase was not the master of
      the Charles Carroll, which the Acushnet spoke in 1841; the master
      was Captain Thomas Andrews.

28 STEIN, WILLIAM BYSSHE. Hawthorne's Faust: A Study of the
    Devil Archetype. Gainesville: University of Florida Press,
    pp. 32–33.
        Melville's observations in "Hawthorne and His Mosses" on
    "the gloom that shadowed the most joyful of Hawthorne's tales"
    imply his "spiritual and imaginative kinship with Hawthorne.
    Without having met the latter, he nevertheless sensed his crea-
    tive mission. In effect, he believed that Hawthorne's apparent
    preoccupation with the darkest aspects of Calvinistic dogma
    disclosed not especially a theological bias but rather a con-
    sciousness of man's necessity to somehow overpower his predispo-
    sitions toward evil."

29 STEWART, RANDALL. "Melville and Hawthorne," in MOBY-DICK
    Centennial Essays. Ed. Tyrus Hillway and Luther S. Mansfield.
    Dallas: Southern Methodist University Press, pp. 153–164.
        Reprint of 1952.B88.

30 STOVALL, FLOYD. "The Decline of Romantic Idealism, 1855–
    1871," in Transitions in American Literary History. Ed.
    Harry Hayden Clark. Durham, N.C.: Duke University Press,
    p. 324.
        When he wrote The Confidence-Man, Melville was in a mood of
    bitter cynicism. The steps by which he was able to regain some
    of his confidence in himself and in humanity through fresh
    philosophical inquiry are obscurely indicated in Clarel. "Unlike
    Hawthorne, Melville found it impossible to devote himself whole-
    heartedly to writing except in the positive mood, and since his
    method was largely subjective, his failure to establish a right
    relation between the self and the universe was a major obstacle
    to his continued success in literature."

31 SULLIVAN, J.N. "Introduction," in Moby Dick. London:
    Collins, pp. 13–16.
        Reprints greater part of 1923.B27.

32 THOMPSON, MARJORIE. "The Nineteenth Century and After." The
    Year's Work in English Studies, 1951, 32 (1953), 269.
        Review of 1951.A2. Gilman's study "is a balanced, heavily
    detailed piece of scholarship which confirms the general view
    that though Melville may not have directly transcribed personal
    experience, he needed it as the basis of his work, which is
    rightly defined as 'heightened journalism.'"

33 T[HORP] W[ILLARD]. "Melville, Herman," in Encyclopaedia
    Britannica. Vol. 15. Chicago: Encyclopaedia Britannica,
    Inc., pp. 231–231B.
        Biographical and critical survey. Yearly reprintings
    through 1974.

34 ANDERSON, CHARLES. "Reviews." Modern Language Notes, 68
    (January), 62–64.
        Review of 1951.A4. Whether Leyda's method be considered a
    new high in scholarly objectivity or a side-stepping of the

scholar's final responsibility to interpret his findings,
Melville specialists will welcome it as an indispensable tool and
all students of American literature will find it a valuable reference book. A sizable portion of it is new, the results of
indefatigable searching by Leyda, who has proved himself the most
zealous and sharp-eyed of Melville sleuths. For the peak of
Melville's career, the years just before and after Moby-Dick, the
Log makes rewarding reading indeed--largely because of the ingenious arrangement, which brings out new relations among documents most of which have long been known. The virtues of the Log
are its thoroughness and accuracy; after such perseverance and
resourcefulness, it is unlikely that significant additions will
be made to our factual knowledge of Melville's life. Yet the
picture is strangely unsatisfying--only glimpses of a rare mind
and personality, even less of an imagination powerful enough to
create the White Whale--limitations of method rather than of
author. Moreover, many small matters call for explanation or
interpretation, but the method of the Log excludes these aids.
A large number of marked passages are quoted from books Melville
probably read, but no proof is given that he made the markings,
when they were made, or what they really signify. A large number
of passages from Melville's own fictions are placed in the
chronological record with the inevitable suggestion that they are
genuine autobiography, unless the reader happens to catch and
remember the single-line disclaimer in the Introduction. But
these are not too serious defects in a large-scale enterprise of
this sort, in which one finds so much that is admirable, reliable,
and useful.

35   GILMAN, WILLIAM H. "Book Reviews." American Literature, 24
      (January), 558-561.
          Review of 1952.A2. Since so much of Thompson's book
      depends on a knowledge of Melville's life, especially on the
      early years and religious training, his apparent ignorance of the
      discoveries of Leyda [1951.A4] and Howard [1951.A3] does not help
      his case much. "Even so, he knew that at the very time Melville
      was, by his account, a God-hater, he could write 'thank God' in
      his journal for news that his family was all well, and tell
      Hawthorne that the two of them helped form 'a chain of God's
      posts round the world.'" More consideration of the facts of
      Melville's life might have forced Thompson to account for many
      other challenges to his thesis. His methods of interpretation
      create even greater obstacles, though he has made illuminating
      commentaries and unearthed a new vein in Melville's art. To
      defend his thesis he is forced to resort continually to special
      pleading, slanting, and mere ingeniousness. "Characteristically,
      he interprets a given passage in the light of 'the larger con-
      text.' But since this 'larger context' is composed of his read-
      ing of hundreds of separate passages, plus external evidence, and
      since most of these readings seem forced, or tendentious, or
      dependent upon remote or accidental resemblances, the appeal to
      the 'larger context' has a steadily decreasing validity." Per-
      haps the most irritating of Thompson's expository methods is the
      regular habit of italicizing words or phrases from Melville's

texts, not because there seems to be any logical or rhetorical reason for stressing them, but because the unnatural emphasis favors his exegesis. Throughout Thompson has attempted to prove that there is no real ambiguity even in darkest Melville, that Melville was perfectly certain of what he believed--that God was evil and nothing but evil, and that no other reading of Melville is possible for those who pretend to know anything about him. One may grant that Thompson may be right, and still protest that his indiscriminate methods make him a most vulnerable champion of his own cause.

36   HOWARD, LEON. "Book Reviews." American Literature, 24
      (January), 557–558.
          Review of 1952.A1. Davis's book "is perhaps the most succinct, comprehensive, and intelligent study of a single prose work in the history of American literary scholarship--a volume which not only reveals the literary processes of a major author at an important transition point in his creative life but might also serve as a model of thoroughness and coherent method for other scholars interested in the rich harvest of human and critical understanding that can be cultivated by intensive literary research." Davis has provided a realistic log of Melville's "chartless voyage" and a valuable account of the "significant growth" Melville went through while making it. Davis's success in obtaining eighteen previously unknown letters from Herman, Gansevoort, and Allan Melville to the English publisher John Murray adds greatly to the solidity of his study. The publication of these letters, with five others from Melville to Richard Bentley, makes the volume a valuable reference work for Melville scholars generally.

37   MURRAY, HENRY A. "Reviews." Modern Language Notes, 68
      (January), 60–62.
          Review of 1951.A2-3. First questions Leyda's aim in 1951.A4 to give each reader the opportunity to be his own biographer: "What does this last imply? That the People should decide? That, since thirty years of long-haired thinking has resulted in nothing but a 'bog' with a 'thick growth of wild guesses,' the trained and devoted scholar should stop thinking and confine himself to the task of garnering as many documents as possible? That, given the scholar's data, the untrained and undevoted reader is capable of arriving at a better conception of Melville's personality than is the scholar himself, and, therefore, the more difficult and important task of interpretation should be left to him? That every reader wants to make his own interpretation and the scholar should not interfere by publishing his? That the goal is ten thousand private biographies, all of them suppressed because their publication could only serve to deepen the bog and thicken the growth of wild guesses? That the only way we Melvillians can avoid trouble is to take flight into facts and become quiz kids?"
          Howard's biography contains a much larger hoard of knowledge pertinent to the circumstances of Melville's life than has ever been packed between two covers. Thanks to Howard's

"unwearied devotion to time and place, stretches of the record which have long been vacant are now studded, if not with eventful incidents, at least with something or other. Most conspicuous among the studs are the recurrent reports of Melville's finances. Detailed enough to satisfy any income tax inspector, these figures come in handy whenever the author feels called upon to account for one of Herman's seasons of 'over-ruling morbidness,' or even a surge of creativity. Implicit here is an economic theory of Melville's personality and writings." Besides "these bona fide facts the reader is proffered a disconcerting run of unwarranted inferences masquerading as facts—too many poor guesses . . . for a book which boasts of its close adherence to the documents." Tepid, practical, and prosaic feelings and thoughts "are blandly ascribed to Melville—that open and closed volcano—at climactic points in his career." There is "a thick growth of guesses" in the book—"the Log has not protected us from these—but they are tame, not wild. Instead of projecting uncommon things into Melville's uncommon mind," Howard "has projected the most commonplace." By this device, "as well as by overlooking the significance of many facts, omitting others, disregarding the pith of Melville's works, side-tracking his ceaseless quest and quarrel, and focussing attention on a string of irrelevant side issues," Howard "has succeeded in shielding himself and his reader from the experience that is Melville. His representation of a mediocrity without depth, subtlety, or humor gets in the way, stands between the reader and the mind that created Mardi, Moby-Dick, and Pierre. This could fairly be called the dayalization of genius, Melville's most dreaded fate."

Gilman seems to share Leyda's and Howard's common distrust of the imagination, but his inaccurate criticism of Weaver and others is less sneerful than Howard's, he lets you know when he is guessing, and his guesses do not turn the young Melville into his antithesis, though they do rob him of some of his more engaging qualities. The book is a forthright, perfectly documented, wholly dependable account of Melville's first twenty-one years, containing a great deal of new material, much of it unearthed by Gilman himself. "In contrast to the early biographers who perceived each successive situation as Melville perceived it in his own imagination," Gilman "is disposed to look at things more objectively, from the viewpoint, say, of all the nice and moral members of the Melville family, taken as a whole. As a result, Herman gets less sympathy as a person vis-a-vis the others than he has previously been accorded." Gilman does an excellent job separating fact from fiction in Redburn and concludes with a judicious appraisal of the book, his best chapter.

38   WRIGHT, NATHALIA. "Book Reviews." South Atlantic Quarterly, 52 (January), 155–156.
     Review of 1952.A2. The book's thesis is implausible because it slights biographical fact, assumes that Melville and his characters are one, and rests entirely upon Thompson's subjective reading of the novels. According to Thompson, Melville revolted from the Calvinism inculcated by his parents, but the family papers reveal neither Allan nor Maria Melville to be concerned by

religious doctrine and Allan to be more inclined toward a
Unitarian moralism and benevolence than toward Calvinism.
Thompson often takes Melville's allusions to authors in his
novels as evidence that he had read widely in their writings
despite numerous proofs that he customarily gleaned much knowledge from a few secondary sources; on such evidence he is cred-
ited with aligning himself consciously with the traditions of
literary deception, Renaissance humanism, and the Satanic School.
To say that Melville's intent each time was "to tell a story
which would illuminate, obliquely, his personal declaration of
independence not only from the tyranny of Christian dogma but
also from the sovereign tyranny of God Almighty" is to ignore the
dissimilar literary traditions of Mardi, Redburn, Moby-Dick,
Pierre, the short stories, and the poems. Thompson's approach
also excludes Melville's naturalism, his technical experiments,
and his politics; like most genuine critics, Melville had a
quarrel with men and nations also, to which his quarrel with God
is fast linked. His irony, on the one hand less consistent than
Thompson represents it, is on the other a far more general
vehicle for his thought.

39   BAKER, CARLOS. "Melville: Fact and Interpretation."
      American Quarterly, 5 (Spring), 77–82.
         Review of 1951.A2–4; 1952.A1–2. Though the Log makes dis-
appointing reading, Leyda has worked with great intelligence and
critical discernment. Future elaborations are unlikely to alter
in any fundamental sense its sturdy groundwork of physical facts.
Material in Howard's biography supplementary to the Log consists
largely in the determination of causal relationships, in the
drawing of inferences, and in the seriatim critical discussion of
Melville's works. Since Howard has dispensed with documentation,
anyone wishing to discover the grounds of an inference has the
inconvenience of having to turn to the Log. Otherwise, the
biography is "judicious, well-organized, and capably if just a
shade monotonously written. It reads like an orderly continuum
without glistening crests or dark troughs. Staying commendably
close to the physical facts, it is rarely bold or startling in
what is done with them. Melville scholars, accustomed to some of
the headier exotic fruits, will not need to be reminded that such
a hardtack and salt-horse book has long been a desideratum in
Melville scholarship. But they may not be totally satisfied with
a work which takes so little account of the spiritual facts."
Thompson's book is valuable for its "many-angled interpretation
of the warp and woof (especially the warp) of Melville's esthetic
and metaphysic"; and even where we doubt one of his details or
elaborations, we have to admit a cumulative force in his arguments. Davis provides the biographical and factual background
of Mardi and offers a thorough and often enlightening analysis
of the book. Gilman shows that Redburn, though hardly so ambitious as Mardi, was "more packed with art and artifice, of
biography transmuted and transcended, than has commonly been
supposed. Like Davis's, his book is a solid contribution in a
limited area of endeavor."

40   BERNARDIN, CHARLES W.   "Book Reviews."   Thought, 28 (Spring),
      132-133.
      Review of 1952.A2. Thompson's interpretation of Melville's
life and work fails to take into account the general decline of
Protestant orthodoxy in America during the middle of the nineteenth century. Like Holmes, Dickinson, and Emerson, Melville
was representative of his milieu in experiencing occasional
doubts about Presbyterianism, but his faith in basic Christianity
remained unassailed. "In stressing the purely negative facets of
Melville's religious views, Thompson oversimplifies a highly complex spiritual struggle and he does not do justice to the positive aspects of Melville's faith. To achieve his intended effect,
Thompson selects and stresses the facts that favor his thesis and
subordinates or omits evidence to the contrary. If Melville
thought so little of Christianity why did he bother to visit the
Holy Land? And why does Thompson dispose so hastily of Clarel,
the poem in which Melville formulates his religious views?" As
literary criticism, Thompson's book is injudiciously daring.
Many of the satiric interpretations he wrenches from Melville's
text can in no wise be proved; he finds hidden meanings in words
Melville uses quite innocently. The virtues of the book lie in
its provocativeness and its awareness of literary sources and
parallels in continental literature. It calls attention to the
possibility of satire in Melville's novels, and it shows how much
Melville was indebted to his reading of Rabelais, Montaigne, and
Bayle. In general, however, it is a disappointing critical performance, and the student of Melville will find Howard [1951.A3]
and Leyda [1951.A4] more trustworthy guides to Melville's life
and meaning.

41   GEIGER, DON. "Demonism in 'Moby Dick': A Study of Twelve
      Chapters." Perspective, 6 (Spring), 111-124.
      Chapters 55-66 are especially important in "establishing
the monstrous character of reality" and "incidentally reveal
Melville's interest in the means of knowing reality (an increasingly intense pre-occupation as the story develops) and his doubt
that even the best of man's means can ever fully discover it."
The "first three chapters, showing the monstrosity of the true
nature of reality, suggest that, though ultimately unknowable, it
is least vaguely discerned by those to whom it is both most revealing and most dangerous--to those who have some direct experience of it. The nine chapters that follow attribute the same
character to the entire range of the subject-object aspects of
reality: that is, to the world surrounding man, to his means of
dealing with it (scientific-technological and social-political),
and to his own soul."

42   GLICK, WENDELL. "Expediency and Absolute Morality in Billy
      Budd." PMLA, 68 (March), 103-110.
      Melville agreed with Vere that justice to the individual is
not the ultimate loyalty in a complex culture; the stability of
the culture has the higher claim, and when the two conflict,
justice to the individual must be abrogated to keep the order of
society intact. The ultimate allegiance of the individual is not

to an absolute moral code but to the utilitarian principle of
social expediency. But social stability based upon expediency is
paid for not only by the sacrifice of Billy Budds and the suffering of Captain Veres but also by a general, blighting, human
mediocrity. In making social expediency an ethic superior to
absolute morality, Melville found himself pushed close to a
weltanschauung that would admit slight, if any, possibility of
personal greatness. Nelson served as his necessary example of
heroic expediency: the act that on the surface seemed sheer
"bravado" (exposure of his own person in battle at Trafalgar)
still inspired posterity to deeds of greatness. Reprinted in
Stafford (1961), pp. 104–111, and Springer, pp. 53–61.

43   HOWARD, LEON. "'Moby-Dick.'" Nineteenth-Century Fiction, 7
      (March), 303–304.
          Review of 1952.B17. A copious, valuable, and puzzling
book. Such a collection of miscellaneous information related to
Melville and more or less relevant to the text of Moby-Dick
should be of real use to scholars and of genuine interest to
enthusiastic readers. Mansfield and Vincent have made an elaborate and almost exhaustive investigation of sources and analogues
and have drawn extensively, if not always wisely, on recent
Melville scholarship. There is a general lack of judiciousness
in the commentary: considerably less peripheral commentary and
a few additional notes on matters central to an understanding of
the book and its background would have been welcome. Cooper's
influence is more evident than one would gather from reading the
notes, and the parallels between Coleridge's diagnosis of Hamlet
and Melville's of Ahab are clearer and more important than many of
the literary analogies discussed at length. More attention to
Melville's humor would also have been welcome. Typographical
errors in the notes, extraordinary inconsistency in the form of
bibliographical references, and the abbreviation of periodical
names make the trustworthiness of the volume questionable.
Howard has observed no particular errors in the text, but such
carelessness in the notes leaves him still inclined to trust
Arvin's Rinehart edition as the most carefully prepared modern
text of Moby-Dick.

44   MOORMAN, CHARLES. "Melville's Pierre and the Fortunate Fall."
      American Literature, 25 (March), 13–30.
          Since a critic can only come to grips with the meaning of
Pierre by dealing "with the novel as a consistent pattern of
imagery existing on a level below the narrative," Moorman
attempts to show through an examination of its imagery that
Pierre "is not a hodgepodge of irresponsible language and meaningless ambiguities, but that it is Melville's considered and
systematic reworking of the myth of the Fall of Man and its
attendant tradition of felix culpa. While the story deals only
with the fall of Pierre, "the imagery which accompanies the
action contains symbols which are generally associated with the
story of the Fall as contained in Genesis and the other Fall
myths." Melville's "use of the imagery of the Fall of Man defines the structure, action, and theme of the novel." [See

1955.B32 for reply to Moorman and 1956.B29 for Moorman's response.] Reprinted in Willett, pp. 30–44.

45   OWEN, W.J.B. "Correspondence." Modern Language Notes, 68 (March), 214–216.
      Reply to 1952.B79. Disputes similarities between The Wanderer and "John Marr," finding no evidence that the former was written by a sailor and seeing only the vaguest kind of parallel, namely that both poets deal with men separated from friends.

46   BEZANSON, WALTER E. "Reviews." Modern Language Notes, 68 (April), 266–268.
      Review of 1952.A2. Thompson's critical method "becomes the examination of passage after passage from the work at hand to find when Melville agrees with his fictional narrator and when he doesn't. The method even at its best is a delicate one, and at its worst encourages critical irresponsibility." Thompson's "almost savage wielding of his weapon after a while numbs the reader into insensibility. All the crucial passages inevitably turn out to have a third level of meaning that is 'covert' or 'sinister' or 'sarcastic' or 'sneering.' . . . The proof? Either reference back to the premise that Melville was violently heretical or a specious appeal to what is called 'the larger context.'" Since Thompson is often more interested in an argued thesis than in the sensitive reading of a given passage for whatever it may contain, the book as a whole is a failure. The study has its uses, however. Many of the specific insights are provocative and the reading of Billy Budd, in spite of excesses of tone, seriously and successfully challenges the "testament of acceptance" thesis. Melville scholars will need to consult the book for its provocative use of analogues and contrasting passages from several writers, especially from Carlyle, Milton, and the Bible. But for the general student of literature the book is a mantrap. "He will find here a harshly written, thesis-ridden, argument which on the whole is graceless and obsessive. Melville's quarrel with authority was a complex affair, and to strip his profoundly symbolic writings down to theological allegories which ignore that Melville was also son to his father, seamen under many captains, and citizen in a democracy that hated kings and tyrants, is indeed reductive."

47   KLIGERMAN, CHARLES. "The Psychology of Herman Melville." Psychoanalytic Review, 40 (April), 125–143.
      An attempt "to illuminate some of the conflicts [hostile feelings to his mother, oral-cannibalistic tendencies, passive homosexual attitude toward men] which motivated Melville and which ultimately led to the emotional crisis which sapped his creative strength in the hour of his artistic triumph." Strengthened by his relationship with Hawthorne, (the Good Father), Melville in Moby-Dick attacked the hated Bad Mother. To Melville "the whale represented the mother, or more specifically the maternal breast—the largest breast in the whole world." Pierre is "an act of expiation for the murderous attack in Moby-Dick— the beginning of Melville's long period of self-immolation."

48   BRIGHAM, CHARLES S. "A B Mail Box." Antiquarian Bookman, 11
      (2 May), 1512.
            From 1845 to 1847 Josiah A. Fraetas published four novels,
      The Cruiser, Fatal Legacy, Master of Langford, Ethan Allen, and
      The Buckskin, under the pseudonym Melville. In the "Preface" to
      Guildford; Or, Tried by His Peers (New York, 1849), Fraetas
      states that since he now finds that his nom de plume is the real
      name of the author of Typee, he plans hereafter to write under
      his own name.

49   VINAL, HAROLD. "Once When the Sea." Saturday Review, 36
      (30 May), 31.
            Poem, with two stanzas relating to Moby-Dick.

50   CARPENTER, FREDERIC I. "Melville: The World in a Man-of-
      War." University of Kansas City Review, 19 (Summer), 257-264.
            Throughout his life Melville denied the real possibility of
      the democratic dream, even while reaffirming its desirability.
      In the ideal realm of values, he always praised democratic
      freedom and criticized authoritarian compulsion. But in the
      world of actuality, Melville increasingly counseled the accep-
      tance of authoritarian laws and the resignation of personal
      rights. In Moby-Dick his disbelief in the possibility of
      actually realizing the American dream found perfect expression.
      The tragedy of Moby-Dick is the tragedy of a weak and romantic
      democracy, in which the crew of the Pequod abdicate their demo-
      cratic rights and the freedom of their free wills and voluntarily
      submit themselves to a deluded leader. In Billy Budd Melville
      finally rejected the democratic principle of active independence
      and the Protestant belief that disobedience to human law may be
      obedience to God's law. Reprinted in 1955.B4.

51   [HILLWAY, TYRUS]. "Hemingway on Melville." Melville Society
      Newsletter, 9 (Summer), n.p.
            Reprints Melville reference in 1935.B8.

52   [HILLWAY, TYRUS]. "On Encyclopedias." Melville Society
      Newsletter, 9 (Summer), n.p.
            Notes frequent complaints in recent years about the in-
      accuracies in the Melville biographies in the standard encyclo-
      pedias. "In spite of much new information which is constantly
      being turned up, these presumably careful compendiums of accurate
      knowledge continue to include year after year statements about
      Melville's life and works which are no longer regarded as true."
      The Encyclopedia Americana seems to be the first encyclopedia to
      announce a complete revision of its Melville biography, allotting
      a full column to Melville instead of half. "Efforts to persuade
      the editors of other standard reference works to accomplish a
      similar revision of the Melville materials have thus far proved
      unavailing."

53   WANN, LOUIS. "Melville's Quarrel with God." Personalist, 34
      (Summer), 290–293.
      Review of 1952.A2. A very provocative study and in some
ways a very provoking one. The alternative that Thompson himself
suggests--"that Melville never did quarrel with God; that he
merely quarreled with the Calvinists for having created such an
outrageous concept of God"--will seem to many nearer the truth.
"Melville failed to take the final step, the step which all truly
great writers have taken--Shakespeare, Dante, Goethe--and to
realize that, whatever we want to call it (God, Nature, the
Scheme of Things, or whatnot), Man's blind fighting against it
gets him nothing but destruction. We may well sympathize with
Melville's hatred of Calvinism, but Calvinism was Man's device
and carried the seeds of its own destruction."

54   ADERMAN, RALPH M. "When Herman Melville Lectured Here."
      Historical Messenger [Milwaukee County Historical Society],
      9 (June), 3–5.
      Notes the divided opinion of Milwaukee newspapers on
Melville's lecture on the South Seas on 25 February 1859, with
brief synopses of 1859.B22-24. "The stimulator of the Daily
Wisconsin's unusual interest in Melville was the editor and owner
of the paper, William E. Cramer, an Albany, N.Y. journalist who
had come to Milwaukee in the spring of 1847, and had known
Melville in Albany, and had entertained him warmly. Melville, in
turn, had presented Cramer with an autographed copy of his first
novel, 'Typee.'" Melville's "only visit to Milwaukee added but
little to his purse and nothing to his reputation as a serious
literary figure."

55   PAUL, SHERMAN. "Book Reviews." New England Quarterly, 26
      (June), 276–278.
      Review of 1951.A5. The closest parallel in American
scholarship to Mason's is Sedgwick's [1944.A1], a study of the
soul's voyage. Mason's is the same voyage in terms of the
imagination. The interpretations waver with specific books, but
the conclusions of both show Melville's essential victory over
the nihilism of his middle and later years, that reliance on
faith that Mason finds in Clarel and Sedgwick in Billy Budd. It
is the "quest of meaning in the calculus of symbol" that Mason
finds fascinating in Melville: "the use of the imagination to
project problems and attempt solutions, the exploratory symbolism
provoked by man's quest for certainty, not the allegory of moral
certitude." Mason's analyses are hardly superfine, yet the book
is good because it makes foreground what should be foreground:
Melville's long pre-occupation with the conflict of innocence
and experience. Most of the chapters, however, illuminate only
the larger symbols and the stages of spiritual crisis. The best
chapters treat crisis books like Mardi and Clarel. Mason mutes
the resonances of Moby-Dick and oversimplifies; there seems to be
a similar wrenching of detail in his study of Melville's indebtedness to Hawthorne, in his emphasis on Plinlimmon, and in his
treatment of Melville's Americanism. Mason might have

strengthened his interpretation if he had seen the fall from innocence as a peculiarly American as well as universal myth.

56   HOFFMANN, CHARLES G. "The Shorter Fiction of Herman Melville." South Atlantic Quarterly, 52 (July), 414–430.
     Melville's artistic development in his shorter fiction of the 1850s. "Through suggestive imagery, a tighter control over language and structure, and the discipline of a limiting form, he attempted to achieve, and in a large degree did achieve balance between content and technique, theme and artistic expression, structure and form. . . . Through the discipline of short prose fiction Melville learned to control language and symbol so as to form a structural whole out of his narrative material. He learned to rely more on the inherent emotional and intellectual content of the narrative for his images than on literary sources. . . . He learned the value of an inclosed action structurally unified. He learned to isolate his symbols and make them an integral part of the narrative instead of piling them on to a structure that could not hold all of them." Analysis of "Bartleby," "Cock-A-Doodle-Doo!" "The Encantadas," "Poor Man's Pudding and Rich Man's Crumbs," "The Paradise of Bachelors and the Tartarus of Maids," "The Lightning-Rod Man," and "Benito Cereno." Reprinted in part in Rountree, pp. 63–69.

57   MOLYNEUX, WILLIAM. "Less Than Meets The Eye." Theatre Arts, 37 (August), 69–72.
     On the television set design for the American première of Benjamin Britten's Billy Budd, by the set designer.

58   ROPER, GORDON. "Book Reviews." Modern Philology, 51 (August), 70–72.
     Review of 1952.A2. Thompson seems to have constructed his method on three major premises—about Melville's religious development, his parental relations, and his attitude toward his readers. The three premises are original, but the grounds for making them are not discussed adequately. On the larger issue of Melville's quarrel with God, the book at least succeeds admirably in convincing one of Melville's quarrel with Carlyle—his vigorous "Everlasting Nay" to Carlyle's "Everlasting Aye." But further than that many Melville readers may decline to go. One may agree that Melville's tendency to assault God and his contemporary reading public manifests itself at certain points in certain of his books and be grateful to Thompson for providing new insights for us; but many "will not agree that it must be taken as the true reading—the key to the understanding of Melville's meaning and art. Surely, Melville's vision was more profoundly ambiguous than it is here made out to be, and his achievement greater than that of a gifted but spoiled boy deriding his elders?"

59   BEWLEY, MARIUS. "A Truce of God for Melville." Sewanee
      Review, 61 (Autumn), 682-700.
           Review of 1952.A2. Thompson's analysis is an impressive
      and in some ways a valuable performance. But more than any
      other recent book of Melville criticism, it requires much energy
      to separate what is good in it from a disastrously misleading
      emphasis. The Melville we have at the end of this book is a
      dull and tedious monomaniac, the parish free-thinker too dis-
      creet, or timid, or cowardly to speak up till the local clergyman
      leaves the room. Thompson's constant assumption that there were
      dangerous inquisitors from whom Melville had to hide his "sinis-
      ter" meaning is puzzling, and to treat his novels as if they were
      esoteric rituals for a somewhat questionable secret society is to
      deprive them of their claim to be taken seriously as works of
      art. Unless we make constant adjustments of Thompson's argument
      to a larger vision of Melville than he tolerates, we end up with
      a Moby-Dick that is not worth the time he asks us to give it: an
      irascible diatribe against God and the universe in the weary old
      tradition of romantic diabolism. The giant squid, rather than
      Leviathan, was surely meant by Melville as his symbol of evil.
      Leviathan symbolizes an image of God outside a specific theology.
      It represents, as the influence of Dante's Paradiso on "The
      Grand Armada" helps us determine, "a religious intuition of life
      itself in some of its most positive and basic affirmations. At
      the same time, it is essentially a tragic intuition--and
      Leviathan is a suffering God. If the image is not strictly
      Christian, it is filled with Christian overtones, and they lend
      Leviathan a large part of his power and evocativeness." Despite
      such reservations, Thompson performs a decided service in calling
      attention to the moral and emotional seediness that seems to
      invest Moby-Dick whenever Ahab is puffed up into a great hero.
      Yet even if Thompson is right in converting The Confidence-Man
      into a blasphemous but veiled attack on God, he ought to pay at
      least some lip service to Melville's quarrel with America, the
      greatest interest of the book.

60   BOND, WILLIAM H. "Melville and Two Years Before the Mast."
      Harvard Library Bulletin, 7 (Autumn), 362-365.
           The first instance of flogging in White-Jacket (chapter 33)
      contains more than a hint of the flogging scene depicted by Dana
      (chapter 15). In an addition to the account of the flogging in
      the 1869 edition of Two Years Before the Mast, Melville found the
      cue he needed to bring about the catastrophe in Billy Budd. Just
      as Captain Claret's blasphemy in White-Jacket resembles Captain
      Thompson's during the flogging of John the Swede, so does Billy
      Budd's stammer resemble Sam's in precipitating their several
      crises.

61   BURKE, KENNETH. "The Dialectics of Imagery." Kenyon Review,
      15 (Autumn), 625-632.
           Review of 1953.A1. When Feidelson's book "rounds the
      circle by the discovery that symbolism, as he defines it, cul-
      minates in Melville's 'radical nihilism,' has he not brought
      language to the point where, in confronting its own forms, it

confronts the negative? . . . A symbolist like Melville, who
claims to be symbolically peering into another realm, and whose
peerings encounter the forms of symbolism itself, might properly
be expected to find things coming to a focus in the discovery of
'nothing.' But beyond that, there would be room for the analysis
of linguistic negativity as such."

62   [HILLWAY, TYRUS]. "Another Literary Melville." Melville
      Society Newsletter, 9 (Autumn), n.p.
         Summarizes 1953.B48.

63   [HILLWAY, TYRUS]. "Notes." Melville Society Newsletter, 9
      (Autumn), n.p.
         Notes ceremonies held in Albany and Lansingburgh on
      26 June 1953 dedicating markers at the two houses formerly occu-
      pied by the Melville family. William H. Gilman spoke at both
      ceremonies, describing Melville's life in the area and its prob-
      able influence on his art and thought. Melville's grandnieces,
      Miss Agnes Morewood of Pittsfield and Miss Helen Gansevoort
      Morewood of New York City, were among the spectators.

64   [HILLWAY, TYRUS]. "Notes." Melville Society Newsletter, 9
      (Autumn), n.p.
         "On the opening night of Captain Ahab, Tyrus Hillway's play
      based upon Moby-Dick, which was presented August 3-15 at the
      Straight Wharf Theater in Nantucket, actor Russell Gold's arti-
      ficial leg became unscrewed and fell apart, leaving him in a
      somewhat awkward position. Equal to the occasion, he shouted
      for a harpoon and used it as a crutch during the remainder of
      the performance. The demands of the part (Ahab) proved so
      strenuous that Gold lost his voice temporarily, so that for two
      nights the play had to be called off, until he could recover
      it."

65   [HILLWAY, TYRUS]. "Notes." Melville Society Newsletter, 9
      (Autumn), n.p.
         Announces that Willard Thorp has recently completed a new
      biography of Melville for the next printing of the Encyclopaedia
      Britannica. The present article is only two hundred words long
      and has a number of errors on important points. The Thorp ver-
      sion will consist of approximately three thousand words. [See
      1953.B33.]

66   MILLER, PERRY. "Melville and Transcendentalism." Virginia
      Quarterly Review, 29 (Autumn), 556-575.
         From the beginning of his career, Melville was schooled in
      the romantic conventions of Scott and Cooper. Like theirs, his
      romances proclaim a victory of nature over culture, simplicity
      over complexity, country over city. Yet Melville, "unlike
      Cooper, employed the pattern of the romance to explode the
      romantic thesis. The inner history of his mind, from 1846 to
      1852, seems to be a mounting loathing of his own premises, until
      at last [in Pierre] he is flagrantly abusing those very devices
      by which other romancers attained proper endings." Yet in

Moby-Dick and Pierre his terms are still those of the romance.
The fundamental premises of Scott, Cooper, Byron, Rousseau,
Goethe--and transcendentalism--are those that lead Ahab and
Pierre to destruction, but they are never declared by Melville
to be false. For all his criticism of Emerson and transcendentalism, Melville "never got free of the incubus of Emerson."
Moby-Dick and Pierre are not Christian works. "In the two books
there is compassion, but there is no intercession, and no for-
giveness. The fundamental terms are not God and Man, but man in
nature. In the vulgar use of the word they are 'tragic,' but in
the proper meaning they reject tragedy. They are, to the end,
implacably, defiantly, unrepentantly, Transcendental." Longer
version printed in 1953.A3. Reprinted in part in Willett,
pp. 45-46.

67   LEYDA, JAY. "The Engine Melvill: Two American Processionals
     of 1832." Boston Public Library Quarterly, 5 (October),
     206-212.
        The Boston Rapid Fire Association honored Major Thomas
Melvill, Melville's grandfather, in 1832, naming its new engine
after him.

68   MARX, LEO. "Melville's Parable of the Walls." Sewanee Review,
     61 (October-December), 602-627.
        "Bartleby" is "about a writer who forsakes conventional
modes because of an irresistible preoccupation with the most baffling philosophical questions. This shift of Bartleby's attention is the symbolic equivalent of Melville's own shift of interest between Typee and Moby Dick." The story does not by any
means proclaim the desirability of this change. It was written
in a time of deep hopelessness, and it reflects Melville's doubts
about the value of his recent work. He may have taken his
extraordinary pains to mask its meaning because it reveals so
much of his situation. Only the reader who comes to the story
after an immersion in the other novels can be expected to see how
much is being said here. Whatever Melville's motive may have
been, it is a grave defect of the parable that we must go back to
Typee and Moby-Dick and Pierre for the clues to its meaning.
Reprinted in part in Stallman and Waldhorn, pp. 359-362; reprinted in Browne and Light, pp. 290-309, and Inge, pp. 84-106.

69   CHASE, RICHARD. "Book Reviews." American Literature, 25
     (November), 378-380.
        Review of 1953.A1. Another "essay in the history-of-ideas
approach to literature, with its characteristic habit of reading
novelists and poets from the point of view of their scientific,
philosophic, and epistemological preoccupations." On a historical view, Feidelson "finds it easier to understand Hawthorne,
Poe, Emerson, Whitman, and Melville in their relation to Puritanism and to 'modern' literature than in their relation to European
Romanticism." His "unique contribution, however, is his wedding
of the history of ideas with the 'new criticism,' so that we have
in his book a very welcome novelty: namely, that his interest in
epistemology does not lead him away from works of literature, or

merely alongside them, but leads him instead directly into fundamental questions of language, metaphor, and artistic structure.
He thus escapes, up to a point at least, the extraordinary ab-
stractness of so much of the critical and scholarly study of
American literature." His formulations produce some illuminating
and essentially sound readings, especially of Emerson and Melville. They also vindicate, at least as a working idea, the view
that mid-nineteenth century American writing is a "major phase"
of "modern literature." Feidelson is even able to make good use
of extensive comparison of Pierre with Gide's Counterfeiters. On
theoretical grounds his method is open to the charge of vastly
overestimating the scope of what can profitably be discussed as
aspects of "language." And although he "is right to look for the
distinctive quality of the American literature he discusses in a
realm which is neither 'romantic' nor 'realistic' nor a combination of the two, his 'symbolistic' approach cannot be grounded
deeply enough or shown to appertain extensively enough in the
major literary works to convince us that it does not remain
unduly special." His reading of the works is actually rather
thin; his rigorous critical discriminations, his large competence,
appear to leave him a little dispirited, and he mistakenly finds
that the American authors "wrote no masterpieces."

70   JERMAN, BERNARD R. "'With Real Admiration': More Correspon-
      dence between Melville and Bentley." American Literature, 25
      (November), 307-313.
          Prints Melville's letter of 19 June 1847[?] to Richard
      Bentley [Letters, pp. 63-64] and five letters from Bentley to
      Melville, written between 1849 and 1852. [See 1948.B58.]

71   STONE, EDWARD. "Melville's Pip and Coleridge's Servant Girl."
      American Literature, 25 (November), 358-360.
          In chapter 110 ("Queequeg in His Coffin") of Moby-Dick,
      Starbuck remembers hearing "that in violent fevers, men, all
      ignorance, have talked in ancient tongues; and that when the
      mystery is probed, it turns out always that in their wholly for-
      gotten childhood those ancient tongues had been really spoken in
      their hearing by some lofty scholars." The passage derives from
      "the detailed German case study" that Coleridge discusses in
      Biographia Literaria, volume 1, part 2. The "very first words
      with which Melville invests Starbuck's recollection ["I have
      heard"] are identical with those of Hamlet when the Mouse Trap--
      also a question of the liberation of repressed knowledge--first
      occurs to him. Here Melville was investing a seemingly casual
      mental interjection with a Shakespearean rhetoric that is con-
      sistent with the tone of Pip's clown-like utterances both before
      and after Starbuck's 'aside.'" A "Coleridge anecdote woven with
      Shakespearean threads into the fabric of a Nantucket sailor's
      thoughts--truly a remarkable instance of the intricate artistry
      that went into the creation of a brief paragraph in the greatest
      of Melville's literary 'botches.'"

72   CAHOON, HERBERT. "New Books Appraised." Library Journal, 78
     (1 November), 1930.
          Review of 1953.A5. A splendid biographical record.
     Metcalf's connecting commentaries and prefaces to the letters are
     frequently a source of valuable information.

73   ARVIN, NEWTON. "Those Close to Melville." New York Times
     Book Review, (8 November), p. 6.
          Review of 1953.A5. Biographically speaking, Melville has
     been so fully treated in recent years, especially by 1951.A3-4,
     that there is really only one book left, of this sort, that one
     could very much wish to see appear just now--and Metcalf's is
     that book. She has performed her task with the greatest tact,
     modesty, and discretion; the result is to give the reader a
     lively sense, not so much of Melville's inner world, of his
     solitude, of the abysses he approached, as of the other pole--
     his existence as a son, a cousin, a nephew, a father, and a
     friend. Most of the letters included are not publshed for the
     first time, but many of them are published in complete or nearly
     complete versions instead of, as hitherto, in excerpts. Metcalf
     has too strong a sense of Melville's greatness to suppress any of
     the details of the less engaging Melville--including the morose,
     suffering, imperious, and sometimes inconsiderate older man; and
     it is one reason, among several, why her book has the strong
     authenticity it does have.

74   STARRETT, VINCENT. "Books Alive." Chicago Sunday Tribune
     Magazine of Books (8 November).
          Review of 1953.A5. An "absolutely delightful book of let-
     ters in which the great white whale of our literature comes alive
     as perhaps in no other book." A book of sprightly literary
     gossip.

75   WAGENKNECHT, EDWARD. "Flashes in Total Darkness--Light on
     Herman Melville." Chicago Sunday Tribune Magazine of Books
     (15 November), p. 2.
          Review of 1953.A5. In its general arrangement Metcalf's
     book resembles Leyda's Log [195].A4], but because she does not
     spread her net so wide she can cover family material more
     thoroughly, though the materials are not confined to the family.
     With "all his greatness, Melville was, as Hawthorne knew, a
     self-tormentor. His letters in this book are fascinating in the
     extreme, like a series of blinding flashes in total darkness.
     Again and again they go to the heart of the matter, but they
     tantalize more than they satisfy."

76   CHASE, RICHARD. "Melville Without Method." Perspectives USA,
     2 (Winter), 172-177.
          Review of 1951.A3-4; 1952.A2, B14, B17. The authors and
     editors of these books all make the by now classic academic
     assumption that there are two kinds of Melville critics: first,
     the "sound," "convincing," and "objective" scholar-critics who
     place Melville as solidly as possible within the context of the
     facts known about him; second, the "unsound" critics, who may be

"provocative" but who remain "subjective" and, instead of writing about Melville and his works as observable facts, "indulge" in self-projection or irrelevant myth-spinning. Chase proposes instead that two traditions of interpretation are already well established: first "there are those writers (sometimes the fact-observing scholar, sometimes the visionary interpreter) who, whatever their interest in Melville, are not really interested in his works, in his art, his politics, his morals, his imaginative idea of himself and of the culture he lived in"; and second, "there are those who are." The current Melville scholars are totally oblivious of the "cultural" tradition of Melville criticism, those books that try to make explicit the political, moral, and mythic assumptions of the society Melville lived in and try to discern how Melville's art both transformed and was conditioned by the native culture. Mansfield and Vincent's long appendix creates an image of Melville as Scholar and inevitably suggests that Melville wrote Moby-Dick by sticking together passages from Carlyle and whaling authorities. Leyda's and Howard's idea of objectivity is to reduce Melville and his works to the mere unselective flux of the ten thousand or so facts about them now known to scholarship. In the interstices of Howard's implacable register of statistics, we catch glimpses of Melville as philosopher, a now classic image among scholars of Melville as a sort of puzzled sophomore. Thompson is so pursuant of this image that he has written his book for the purpose of maintaining that Melville is to be understood in the light of a single idea. The trouble is that we are uncertain about the proper "approach" to Melville. He must be regarded as a man whose fundamental and determining attitudes were derived from the preliterary and sometimes from the preconscious assumptions of his culture and as a writer whose mind evolved very complex and wonderful images of America and of himself as an American.

77　　FISKE, JOHN C. "Herman Melville in Soviet Criticism." Comparative Literature, 5 (Winter), 30–39.
　　　　Summary and analysis of three short commentaries on Melville and one longer, sixteen-page article in a History of American Literature (Soviet Academy of Sciences, 1947), "by far the longest and most thorough study" of Melville "that has yet been made in the Soviet Union." Marxist in orientation, the latter attempts "to place Melville in a broad literary and philosophical as well as socioeconomic background." Melville is still unknown to most citizens of the Soviet Union. The Melville revival in the United States seems to have evoked only the slightest interest among the Soviet intelligentsia. Only Typee has been translated into Russian.

78　　GRANGER, BRUCE INGHAM. "The Gams in Moby Dick." Western Humanities Review, 8 (Winter 1953–1954), 41–47.
　　　　The meetings with other ships at sea, four of them gams, lend greater coherence and a more varied rhythm to Moby-Dick, the tragic drama, than any other single dramatic device.

79   [HILLWAY, TYRUS]. "Notes." <u>Melville Society Newsletter</u>, 9 (Winter), n.p.
     Notes radio dramatization of <u>Moby-Dick</u> on the NBC Star Playhouse on 8 November 1953. Frederic March played Ahab.

80   HYMAN, STANLEY EDGAR. "Melville the Scrivener." <u>New Mexico Quarterly</u>, 23 (Winter), 381–415.
     Considers aspects of Melville's life and works, with strictures on recent books on Melville. Basic questions about Melville, from his view of the absolute to his sexual leanings, are unanswerable. Melville, like Shakespeare, is ultimately unknowable.

81   BABCOCK, C. MERTON. "Melville's 'Moby Dictionary.'" <u>Word Study</u>, 29 (December), 7–8.
     Melville's accuracy and precision in the definition and employment of whaling terms assures him a rightful place among significant contributors to the American language. Cites dictionaries, including the <u>Oxford English Dictionary</u> and <u>Dictionary of American English</u>, that make use of Melville's definitions of specific whaling terms and representative words for which Melville's usage constitutes the earliest or only historical evidence recorded.

1954 A BOOKS--NONE

1954 B SHORTER WRITINGS

1   ALLEN, WALTER. <u>The English Novel: A Short Critical History</u>. London: Phoenix House, p. 188.
     The fictional characters that have the closest relationship to Heathcliff and Catherine Earnshaw in <u>Wuthering Heights</u> are some of Dostoevski's and Melville's.

2   ANON. "Herman Melville," in <u>The Great Decade in American Writing 1850-1860: Emerson, Hawthorne, Melville, Thoreau, Whitman</u>. New York: The American Academy of Arts and Letters and The National Institute of Arts and Letters, pp. 12-15.
     Catalogue for exhibition (3-30 December), listing twenty-two items by or relating to Melville, including Melville manuscripts and first editions.

3   BLACKMUR, R.P. "The Craft of Herman Melville: A Putative Statement," in <u>The Achievement of American Criticism: Representative Selections from Three Hundred Years of American Criticism</u>. Ed. Clarence Arthur Brown. New York: The Ronald Press Co., pp. 638-653.
     Reprint of 1940.B2.

4   BROWN, CLARENCE ARTHUR. "The Aesthetics of Romanticism," in <u>The Achievement of American Criticism: Representative Selections from Three Hundred Years of American Criticism</u>. New York: The Ronald Press Co., pp. 166-170.

Melville came to believe, no less than Emerson, that "Nature is the symbol of spirit." His "conception of the relation between spirit and matter, and of the function of the imagination in relation to them and to art, precluded for Melville, as it did for Hawthorne, any satisfaction with fiction which strove merely to reproduce the surface details of life with a literal realism. It meant that if art were to retain its organic expression the method of fiction would be allegorical and symbolic, the use of natural fact as spiritual symbol." Stemming partially from Hawthorne and resembling Hawthorne's prefaces, Melville's own defense of his idealization, his heightening of reality, occurs in The Confidence-Man (chapters 14, 33, and 44). He seems to have placed comparatively little emphasis on the classic principles of unity and order that form a central aspect of Poe's theory, feeling that symmetry of form is often impossible to attain and that the demand for consistency of character in fiction is far from being true to the higher reality that fiction attempts to portray. His comments on "originality" of character are particularly illuminating in view of his own propensity for the creation of characters of such magnitude as Ahab and Pierre. A judicial standard is implied in "Hawthorne and His Mosses": great literature must reveal a ripeness, a maturity of thought and style; it must reveal the originality of a "deeply thinking mind" to which must be added "a boundless sympathy" and an "omnipresent love." The essay displays a remarkably perceptive judgment of Hawthorne and a nationalism that, though enthusiastic, is not provincial.

5   COWLEY, MALCOLM. The Literary Situation. New York: The
     Viking Press, pp. 14-15, 124-131.
          "Perhaps the principal creative work of the last three
     decades in this country . . . has been the critical rediscovery
     and reinterpretation of Melville's Moby-Dick and its promotion,
     step by step, to the position of national epic." Prints revised
     version of 1951.B113.

6   CUNLIFFE, MARCUS. "Melville and Whitman," in The Literature
     of the United States. Harmondsworth, Middlesex: Penguin
     Books, pp. 115-128.
          Critical survey. "Hawthorne feels that all excess is to be
     deplored; Melville, with a more generous sense of human poten-
     tiality, insists that virtues and vices alike depend upon a
     certain excess."

7   EBY, E.H. "Myth, Freud and Existentialism." Interim, 4
     (Nos. 1 and 2), 93-95.
          Review of 1949.A1. Chase "has mixed a fabulous cocktail
     principally made up of one part anthropology, two parts Freud,
     some extract of Existentialism and a dash of Melville bitters.
     . . . Unfortunately the Melville flavor is all but lost in
     the other ingredients." Chase's errors of fact are mere fly-
     specks compared to his greater and more serious distortions of
     Melville's meanings. Out of the plenty of Melville's creation
     his interpretation picks and chooses to make a pattern of its

own devising. At least half of Melville is left out, and that
the most explicit part. Thus, Chase ignores the explicit criticism of Western civilization in Typee, Mardi, Redburn, and White-
Jacket in favor of far-fetched speculations about other elements
to the same end. Even worse, he neglects almost the whole of
Melville's religious-philosophical thinking. The main reason
for this distortion comes from Chase's two instrumentalities for
interpretation--his Freudian and mythic approaches, which make
possible an interpretation not only of Melville but of almost
any writer, and resemble cheating at solitaire. Chase "has begun
with a method he hopes will evaluate literary merit but ends
beyond the boundaries of literature in the land of Cuckoo."

8   FOGLE, RICHARD HARTER. "Melville's Bartleby: Absolutism,
     Predestination, and Free Will." Tulane Studies in English, 4
     (1954), 125-135.
         "Bartleby" is a story of absolutism, predestination, and
free will in which predestination predominates. The narrator-
god plays the role of fate but does not deprive Bartleby of his
free will. Bartleby insists upon his destiny--absolutism is the
mainspring of his character and the cause of his spiritual isolation, his great affliction. But his free will has been perverted before the story opens; apparently freely offered an
opportunity to choose, he will choose nothing--and seems predestined not to. Reprinted in 1960.A2.

9   FOSTER, ELIZABETH S. "Preface," "Introduction," "Explanatory
     Notes," "Textual Notes," and "Appendix: Surviving Manu-
     scripts," in The Confidence-Man. Ed. Elizabeth S. Foster.
     New York: Hendricks House, pp. v-vi, xiii-xcv, 287-365,
     367-371, 373-392.
         In addition to reviewing the circumstances of Melville's
life and literary career around the time of the composition and
publication of The Confidence-Man and surveying its British and
American reception and twentieth-century commentary up to 1953,
the six-part "Introduction" evaluates and interprets the book in
considerable detail. Foster holds that The Confidence-Man "is
well worth recovering now from the dust of neglect and the murk
of obscurity" and that the time for such recovery is propitious:
the book is more accessible to readers now because "cryptic,
triple-tiered, all but private styles" employed by Joyce and
other twentieth-century writers "have taught us to read poly-
phonic literature without much in the way of a key." According
to Foster, the first half of the book "satirizes credulity and
the second half points out the evil consequences of too much
distrust," while Melville also satirizes the dearth of charity
among Christians, greed, gullibility, the invasion of all areas
of Western (particularly American) life, "even religion and
philanthropy, by the 'Wall Street spirit,' the hope of millennial
enlightenment from a free press, laissez-faire." But the book is
fundamentally a philosophical satire on optimism, a modern
Candide: through the activities of the Confidence Man, Melville
satirizes "cheating optimisms" injurious to man's humanity,
whether it be Shaftesburyan optimism, utilitarian optimism, the

nature cult of the eighteenth and nineteenth centuries, modernist
Christianity, or any ideology that assumes that "the universe is
benevolent and human nature good." The book's most obvious
theme, however, is the failure of Christians to be Christian.
Under a pretense of Christianity, the supernatural and diabolic
Confidence Man destroys, in his April Fool's Day sport, the roots
of faith and brotherly love. The book's last chapter is a pes-
simistic apocalypse in which the Confidence Man extinguishes the
light of Christian faith in the world. Unlike a number of
earlier commentators, however, Foster finds that Melville "stops
short of Timonism" in The Confidence-Man, which embodies "a sort
of last-ditch humanism," not misanthropy. Melville's attitude
is that one "cannot trust God; one cannot trust nature; but one
must cling to some faith in man, for the alternative is too
frightful." The Confidence-Man, "in appearance without form or
pattern or progression, is in reality as formal as a fugue,
richly patterned, a progression from the ideal to the presently
real, from Christian charity and brotherhood to Emersonian
individualism and the extinction of Christianity, from arguments
for the necessity for skepticism to the one argument for the
necessity for charity—the intolerable heartlessness and inhumanity of Winsome-Egbert's world of complacent egoists."
Foster pays particular attention to the account of Indian-hating,
which she views as the "rooftree" in the book's framework—"the
culminating argument for skepticism and the forecast of a world
without charity"—and to Winsome and Egbert, whom she identifies
with the metaphysics and ethics respectively of Emerson's philosophy, the satiric portraits embodying the faults of his mind
and thought. In her "Explanatory Notes," Foster rejects Oliver's
identification of Egbert with Thoreau. [See 1946.B30.]

The characters in The Confidence-Man are brilliantly
realized, according to Foster, "as vivid to the eye as Hogarth
could have made them," individual in gesture, voice, word, and
deed; but, "since this is an allegory, their deepest inner
reality, unlike the inner reality of characters in a dramatic
novel, is moral and representative rather than moral-
psychological and individual." The book's "pruned, deft,
subtle style" has unwavering distinction. In her analysis of
early drafts of chapter 14 in the "Appendix," Foster finds that
in his revisions Melville moved always in the direction of
"understatement, underemphasis, litotes, and complexity that
looks like simplicity" away from "the loose structure, open
clarity, and directness of his earliest versions," so that many
of his ideas grow less and less obvious. But the charm of The
Confidence-Man is its irony. "Much of the subtle air of false-
ness that Melville has contrived to throw over his hero, which is
one of the marvels of craftsmanship in this book, derives from
ironic implication and equivocation. Irony is the very stuff of
a world in which deceit masquerades as faith, misanthropy as
universal brotherhood, and cynicism as philanthropy; the misan-
thropic Pitch is the true lover of his fellow men. What are in
their appearance only petty swindles, paltry cheats, are in their

reality the nullification of every large hope of humanity.
Reviewed in 1955.B42, B45. Reprinted in part in Norton The
Confidence-Man, pp. 321-323, 333-339.

10   KOERNER, JAMES D. "The Wake of the White Whale." Kansas
     Magazine, 4 (1954), 42-50.
          1921.Al, 1929.Al, 1932.B45, 1941.Al, 1949.A3, 1951.A4, and
     1952.Bl7 constitute the more worthwhile Melville scholarship.
     1949.Al and 1952.A2 are part of the "scholarly junkyard" of
     Melville criticism. Moby-Dick is the relatively simple and very
     ancient story of man's search for the meaning of life. Ahab is
     symbolic of man's universal fear and hatred of the apparent
     malevolence and inscrutability of the universe. The moral impli-
     cations of Moby-Dick, like those of most great works, are pretty
     much what the individual reader wants to make them. On the basis
     of the book we are led to certain conclusions: (1) Melville's
     was not a philosophically sophisticated mind, but one that saw
     the universe and man in terms of relatively simple problems;
     (2) one of these was the apparent irreconcilability of evil with
     a benevolent Creator; and (3) Moby-Dick is the story of one man's
     (not necessarily Melville's) struggle, at once heroic and shame-
     ful, to make that reconciliation and arrive at understanding
     through assaulting the White Whale, which personifies the whole
     mysterious universe.

11   LEARY, LEWIS. "Melville, Herman (1819-91)," in Articles on
     American Literature, 1900-1950. Durham, N.C.: Duke Univer-
     sity Press, pp. 204-211.
          Unannotated listing of articles on Melville from 1900 to
     1950; arranged alphabetically by name of author.

12   McCORQUODALE, MARJORIE KIMBALL. "Melville's Pierre as
     Hawthorne." University of Texas Studies in English, 33 (1954),
     97-102.
          Similarities between Hawthorne, his family, and problems
     and Pierre, his family, and problems suggest that Hawthorne was
     the inspiration for Pierre and that Hawthorne's life, personality,
     and experience contributed important elements to the book. The
     publication of Pierre, "its contents perhaps unavoidably apparent
     to Hawthorne as a replica of his own experience or ancestry" (a
     charge of incest was made against an ancestor of Hawthorne in
     1681), may have been responsible for the break in the relation-
     ship between Melville and Hawthorne.

13   MARIE THERESA, SISTER, et al., eds. Adventures in American
     Literature. Cardinal Newman Edition. New York: Harcourt
     Brace and Co., pp. 531-533, 541-546.
          Reprints Melville material in 1952.B13, except for an un-
     attributed illustration of Ahab (p. 545) in place of a Rockwell
     Kent illustration of Ahab.

14   MAUGHAM, W. SOMERSET. "Herman Melville and Moby Dick," in
     Ten Novels and Their Authors. London: William Heinemann
     Ltd., pp. 178–203.
          Revised, slightly extended version of 1948.B20.

15   MILLER, PERRY. "The Location of American Religious Freedom,"
     in Religion and Freedom of Thought. Garden City, N.Y.:
     Doubleday & Co., pp. 9–23.
          Finds similar attitude toward nature in William Starbuck
     Mayo's Kaloolah (1849) and in Moby-Dick. Both Mayo and Melville
     "managed to say, through the indirections in which they were
     obliged to hide themselves, through romantic fictions, that
     freedom of the mind is not to be found in a sniveling church
     which humiliates a man by advertising his sins, but in the
     sublimity of Nature, even though that sublimity slay him."
     Reprinted in Miller (1967), pp. 150–152.

16   PAUL, SHERMAN. "Introduction," in Moby-Dick. Everyman's
     Library. London: J.M. Dent & Sons; New York: E.P. Dutton
     & Co., pp. v–xii.
          Moby-Dick belongs to one of the preeminent forms of the
     nineteenth-century imagination, the imaginary voyage, having more
     affinities with Coleridge's "The Ancient Mariner" and Poe's The
     Narrative of Arthur Gordon Pym than with the novel. Whatever
     actualities it depicts have the higher purpose of symbolizing the
     world of mind—its ultimate concern is "spiritual," the nature
     and destiny of men. Its voyage takes place on psychological,
     sociopolitical, and mythical levels. Psychologically, Moby-Dick
     is an analysis of human motivation and need. Sociopolitically,
     Melville explores the problem that democracy set his age—the
     relation of the great man to the multitide. Mythically, Moby-
     Dick evokes the archetypal hunt of the old sagas and epics. To
     seek the knowledge of heaven is a human sacrifice, the book
     shows. Ishmael is saved because he learns the lesson of human
     solidarity and the lesson taught by Father Mapple's sermon; he
     earns his rebirth from the sea by understanding the malevolence
     of Ahab's heartless will.

17   ROBERTSON, R.B. Of Whales and Men. New York: Alfred A.
     Knopf, pp. vii, 5–9.
          References to Moby-Dick: "it is difficult for any literate
     person who has been a-whaling to write of his experiences without
     constantly quoting and referring to the masterpiece of whaling
     literature, Moby Dick. For even in these mechanized days, when
     one is with the whalers, one finds that daily, even hourly, the
     thoughts turn to some phrase or incident in Melville's classic;
     and, while there is much that is different from the whaling of
     a hundred years ago, much is still the same, and little is so
     greatly changed that constant comparisons cannot be made between
     modern whaling and whalemen, and the events and men that Mel-
     ville described."

18   STEWART, RANDALL and DOROTHY BETHURUM. "Introduction," in
     Classic American Fiction. Book 2 of Living Masterpieces of
     American Literature. Ed. Randall Stewart and Dorothy
     Bethurum. Chicago: Scott, Foresman and Co., pp. 177-183.
         Introduction to "Benito Cereno," with sections on
     "Melville's Modern Reputation," "Melville's Affinity to
     Hawthorne," "Benito Cereno," and "Life and Works." [See also
     1956.B3.]

19   THOMPSON, MARJORIE. "The Nineteenth Century and After." The
     Year's Work in English Studies, 1952, 33 (1954), 262-264.
         Review of 1951.A3; 1952.A1-2. Howard's biography, "some-
     what flat and desultory in the beginning, gathers depth and
     impetus as it proceeds, finally rendering a full account of
     Melville the man and the probable mental background of his
     books." The "portrait of the man is merged into sensitive and
     modest analyses of his work, able in the presentation of both
     content and style." Thompson shows clearly how Melville's
     spiritual idiom shaped his artistic idiom. His book might have
     been shorter, but the theme is stimulating, and constantly before
     us. Davis's pleasant, readable, and careful study draws con-
     vincing evidence from what Melville was reading at the time. All
     these studies make great use of Sealts's recent work on Melville's
     reading.

20   WHIPPLE, A.B.C. "The Whaleman Novelist," in Yankee Whalers in
     the South Seas. Garden City, N.Y.: Doubleday & Co.,
     pp. 40-54.
         Account of Melville's whaling years and his literary use of
     them, emphasizing his knowledge and use of Owen Chase's Narrative
     of the Essex.

21   CONNOLLY, THOMAS E. "A Note on Name-Symbolism in Melville."
     American Literature, 25 (January), 489-490.
         The name "Bonito Sereno" in Amasa Delano's original narra-
     tive [see 1928.B26] can be translated as "the handsome, shameless
     fellow." Such a description "is perfectly in keeping with the
     character of the Spanish captain as it is there presented. . . .
     For the purposes of his story, in which the Spaniard is the
     representative of pure goodness as opposed to Babo's pure evil,
     Melville had to suppress these unfavorable traits of character,
     and in so doing rechristened his hero Benito Cereno or 'Blessed
     Serenity.'" The name existed in both spellings in the original,
     however, and obviously one spelling had to be selected. Perhaps
     Melville saw the possible meanings in the two names; perhaps not.

22   DAVIDSON, FRANK. "Melville, Thoreau, and 'The Apple-Tree
     Table.'" American Literature, 25 (January), 479-488.
         In his use of the story of an insect hatching from a
     table, Melville was indebted to the closing paragraphs of
     Thoreau's Walden as well as to A History of the County of
     Berkshire, Massachusetts (cited by Leyda in 1949.B9). The story
     "may reflect symbolically" Melville's "irresolution and hesitance
     in accepting a religious faith. The story, one may conjecture,

really represents his taking stock in 1856 of his speculations on Calvinism, the liberalization of Calvinistic thought, the inter-mingling of good and evil, paganism, nature and spirit, and the immortality of man."

23   GEIGER, DON. "Melville's Black God: Contrary Evidence in 'The Town-Ho's Story.'" <u>American Literature</u>, 25 (January), 464–471.
     The God of the <u>Town-Ho</u> episode is a barely distorted caricature of the orthodox Calvinist God, meting out a special, Calvinist version of Christian justice, more marked by wrath and punishment than by love. Yet the God of this episode, however barbarous in His methods, punishes a human crime and so is, in human eyes, a just God, however harsh. When Ahab attempts to right a wrong perpetrated by the nature of the universe, God defends His own malicious actions. This is, as Thompson [1952.A2] suggests, a tyrannous God: a ruler who refuses redress to His subjects for the evil consequences of the bad laws He has Himself legislated. "This is Melville's ultimate image of the Calvinist God of the Puritan. However just He may occasionally be, He is without love or mercy, or even common fairness." Reprinted in 1960.A6.

24   GILMAN, WILLIAM H. "Reviews." <u>Modern Language Notes</u>, 69 (January), 63–65.
     Review of 1952.B17. A vast amount of information, most of it available nowhere else, is assembled in the volume, which as one instrument for understanding Melville's mind and creative methods, for teaching, and for research, is of great value. But misprints in Mansfield and Vincent's notes create unfortunate doubts about the volume's reliability. On the whole the notes are good and necessary, but unfruitful speculation, tenuous logic, apparent determination to find sources at any cost, and even wild guesses mark far too many of them. The possibility that Melville drew much of his information from common knowledge or experience is generally overlooked.

25   HUTCHINSON, WILLIAM H. "A Definitive Edition of <u>Moby-Dick</u>." <u>American Literature</u>, 25 (January), 472–478.
     Review of 1952.B17. Prints list of 108 "Compositors' Errors" and 20 "Emendations Not Noted" in the Mansfield-Vincent edition, based on a collation with the first American edition. If we are willing to make allowance for compositors' errors and some editorial oversight, we have a definitive edition. Neither the scholar nor the serious critic can afford to ignore the "Explanatory Notes," which, indexed and cross-referenced, have a value they would not have if dispersed among a number of articles in a number of books and journals.

26   STEWART, GEORGE R.   "The Two Moby-Dicks."   American Literature,
     25 (January), 417-448.
          Primarily on the basis of internal evidence, such as shifts
     in conception and function of characters, style, Shakespearean
     influence, and atmosphere, argues that Moby-Dick is tripartite:
     (1) chapters 1 through 15 represent an original story, very
     slightly revised; (2) chapters 16 through 22 represent the orig-
     inal story, with a certain amount of highly important revision,
     splicing on Melville's new conception; (3) chapter 23 through
     the "Epilogue" represents the story as it was written after
     Melville reconceived it, but may preserve certain passages of the
     original stury, doubtless somewhat revised.

27   YAGGY, ELINOR.   "Shakespeare and Melville's Pierre."   Boston
     Public Library Quarterly, 6 (January), 43-51.
          Borrowings, direct and indirect, establish Romeo and
     Juliet, rather than Hamlet "and the incest theme," as the
     "primary organic influence on Pierre."

28   YOUNG, JAMES DEAN.   "The Nine Gams of the Pequod."   American
     Literature, 25 (January), 449-463.
          "All nine gams of the Pequod are important relations to the
     world.   Each gam deals to some degree with the problem of com-
     munication and the problem of alternative; each is a focal point
     in the action and part of the matrix for the narrative. . . .
     The series of gams is a stable reference for understanding the
     structure and action of the narrative; no other group of chapters
     forms such an integrated series."   Reprinted in 1960.A6.

29   CLOUGH, WILSON O.   "Book Reviews."   Western Humanities Review,
     8 (Spring), 157-159.
          Review of 1953.A3.   A worthwhile addition to Melville lit-
     erature.   All the essays are of interest and some of them genuine
     contributions: those by Murray and Bezanson are outstanding.   A
     consensus of sorts, proving Melville from every angle a rebel,
     appears in the essays.

30   [HILLWAY, TYRUS].   "Notes."   Melville Society Newsletter, 10
     (Spring), n.p.
          Notes NBC radio dramatization of "Bartleby" on Sir Laurence
     Olivier's "Theatre Royal" on 14 February 1954.

31   LEISY, ERNEST E.   "Melville as Family Man."   Southwest Review,
     39 (Spring), 184.
          Review of 1953.A5.   Melville "received from his family more
     sympathy than understanding, and altogether too much worry."
     Metcalf's "book is excellent for what one may read between the
     lines."

32   O'CONNOR, WILLIAM VAN. "Reviews." American Quarterly, 6 (Spring), 86-88.

Review of 1953.A1. Feidelson makes excellent use of the relation between the theoretical observations and the creative practice of his five writers, and many of his brief analyses--notably of Whitman and Melville--are very astute. But the writers are closer to the romantics than he wants to admit.

33   HOWARD, LEON. "'Symbolism and American Literature.'" Nineteenth-Century Fiction, 8 (March), 318-320.

Review of 1953.A1. Despite "the fact that most critical discussions of literature from a new angle have the value of offering new insights and new grounds for appreciation, Feidelson's "is a curiously barren book. None of the major authors under consideration seems to grow in meaning or value under . . . Feidelson's scrutiny. Instead, they shrink." The reason for this barrenness may perhaps be found in Feidelson's unsatisfactory definition of a "symbol"; or perhaps the barrenness is the result of his apparent lack of familiarity with English literature--a lack that enables him to attribute to his American authors a unique quality they do not really possess.

34   ROPER, GORDON. "Herman Melville: Cycle and Epicycle." Canadian Forum, 33 (March), 282-283.

Review of 1953.A5. The rapid postwar reconstruction of Melville's biography has been aided incalculably by Metcalf. Her "book orders between two covers the most important sources of our information about Melville, apart from his own books. . . . Taken altogether, these letters from Melville, his wife, and his numerous relatives and friends show the tragedy of a profound spirit produced by and yet caught in a large, tight, orthodox family in a rapidly changing America. They reveal that much of the struggle of Melville's protagonists was a projection of his own life."

35   ROPER, LAURA WOOD. "'Mr. Law' and Putnam's Monthly Magazine: A Note on a Phase in the Career of Frederick Law Olmsted." American Literature, 26 (March), 88-93.

Frederick Law Olmsted became a partner in the publishing firm Dix & Edwards in April 1855 and was editor of its principal periodical Putnam's Monthly from April 1855 to February 1856, subordinate to George William Curtis and Charles A. Dana (whose connection with the magazine was kept a secret). Curtis protested strongly against Olmsted's introduction of some of Webster's spelling innovations into the magazine, particularly in the September and October 1855 issues. [See spelling in "Benito Cereno," Putnam's Monthly, 6 (October, November, December 1855), 353-367, 459-473, 633-644.]

36   F[AUSSET], H[UGH] I'A. "Melville." Manchester Guardian
     (26 March), p. 6.
         Review of 1953.A5. Although Melville voyaged alone in
     pursuit of truth spiritually, he was, as Metcalf's book shows,
     a warm-hearted and companionable man. The book "is primarily a
     family album and reveals what his nearest and dearest saw or
     failed to see in him and how they helped or hindered."

37   CLIVE, GEOFFREY. "'The Teleological Suspension of the
     Ethical' in Nineteenth-Century Literature." Journal of
     Religion, 34 (April), 75–87.
         In Billy Budd Vere and Billy "represent concrete embodi-
     ments of the ethical and religious ways of being in the truth as
     Kierkegaard differentiates the two. Both act in accordance with
     their respective knowledge of the good; but, whereas the Captain
     is unwilling to deviate from the highest ethics of conformity,
     Budd, almost unconsciously it appears, takes a stand above the
     law. Nowhere else in American literature is there a more con-
     vincing exploration of the question raised by Kierkegaard in Fear
     and Trembling." [Reprinted in 1960.B6.]

38   ANON. "Melville Mysteries." London Times Literary Supple-
     ment, No. 2724 (16 April), p. 250.
         Review of 1953.A5. Metcalf "leaves the numerous mysteries,
     the lost lives of the novelist and poet, untouched," when she
     "might have tried to solve" them.

39   ANDERSON, CHARLES. "Book Reviews." American Literature, 26
     (May), 262–264.
         Review of 1953.A5. The most detailed picture we have of
     Melville's outward life in the setting of a large circle of
     relatives and friends. The value of the book lies in the cumu-
     lative effect of the various documents, brought together in an
     orderly chronicle for the first time. The fullest part of the
     record is also the most interesting part, the six years between
     Typee and Pierre. After the decade of active authorship is over
     interest falls off sharply; there is little to reward the student
     of literature in the dull records of the later years, beyond the
     pathos and irony of a great author torn between two lives. Poe
     and Whitman suffered in greater degree from poverty, lack of
     recognition, and tortured personalities, "but having no solici-
     tous and hovering clan to save them, or smother them, they
     struggled on through to the end. Melville withdrew into a moody
     silence, neither achieving his highest literary fulfillment nor
     finding his being in the bosom of the family." In abandoning
     authorship in midcareer, did Melville "yield to family pressures,
     implied and overt, from within himself as well as from those
     nearest and dearest, solicitous but not really sympathetic?"
     And "to what extent did these same conflicting forces constitute
     the psychic pressures that drove him to seek definition in lit-
     erary expression in the first place?"

40   COLLINS, CARVEL. "Melville's Mardi." Explicator, 12 (May),
     item 42.
          An examination of several Pacific Island languages,
     Marquesan, Samoan, Tahitian, Maori, Mangarevan, and Hawaiian,
     suggests that Melville based many of the seemingly meaningless
     names in Mardi, including those of major characters, on Pacific
     Island words whose meanings relate to the allegorical meanings of
     the novel. Examples given.

41   CREEGER, GEORGE R. "Melville Explicator." Melville Society
     Newsletter, 10 (Summer), n.p.
          Proposes emendation of sentence in Moby-Dick, chapter 121,
     "Shake yourself; you're Aquarius, or the water-bearer, Flask;
     might fill pitchers at your coat collar"--which "seems to make
     very poor sense"--to "Shake yourself; your Aquarius, or the
     water-bearer, Flask, might fill pitchers at your coat collar,"
     which "makes eminently good sense." [See 1954.B50 for reply.]

42   GAVIN, HELENA. "The Watches of Ishmael." Melville Society
     Newsletter, 10 (Summer), n.p.
          Poem inspired by Moby-Dick.

43   BEZANSON, WALTER E. "Melville's Clarel: The Complex
     Passion." ELH, 21 (June), 146-159.
          Interpretive summary, intended to reveal the "main archi-
     tectural outlines," the "primary design" of the poem. The phrase
     "complex passion" signifies "the total historical, theological,
     and psychological dilemma which permeates the poem."

44   BEZANSON, WALTER E. "Melville's Reading of Arnold's Poetry."
     PMLA, 69 (June), 365-391.
          Analysis of Melville's marginalia in his copies of Arnold's
     Poems (1856) and New Poems (1867), made in 1862 and 1871
     respectively--"clusters of marginalia relating to poets and
     poetry, and to themes of death, resignation, and asceticism" and
     notably recording "the profound impact" of two major poems,
     "Empedocles on Etna" and "Stanzas from the Grande Chartreuse."
     "It seems clear that Melville read the poems for aesthetic expe-
     rience, for orientation towards his own future poetry, and for
     support and subtilization of his own attitudes towards expe-
     rience. Melville responded with vigor and taste to sharp images,
     eloquent phrases, successful narrative passages, skillful allu-
     sions, and total poetic effects. . . . Consciously or not he was
     soaking up prosodic patterns, moods, vocabulary, imagery, and
     themes for his own writing. During the decade in which he read
     Arnold's poetry Melville was making fundamental decisions about
     the structure and themes of Clarel. Arnold helped him toward
     conceptualization."

45   LEYDA, JAY. "Another Friendly Critic for Melville." New
     England Quarterly, 27 (June), 243-249.
          Quotes from reviews and mentions of Melville in the
     Springfield Republican from 1847 to 1891. Attributes 1849.B81,

B127; 1850.B57; 1851.B46; 1852.B51; 1856.B37; 1857.B33 to J.G.
Holland, and 1866.B3 to F.B. Sanborn.

46   GORDON, D.J. "Reviews." Review of English Studies, NS 5
      (July), 326-328.
         Review of 1952.A1-2. Thompson's method and his success or
failure depend on his reading of Melville's ironies. He is far
too ingenious here; by the time he has finished with Melville's
"triple talk" he has arrived at a point where nothing can possibly mean what it seems to mean and everything can mean just
what Thompson wants it to mean. Yet account will have to be
taken of the many things in the book, particularly of Thompson's
perception of certain symbolic organizations. Davis admirably
succeeds in placing Mardi in the history of Melville's development, and he is not blind to its grave deficiencies.

47   CONDON, RICHARD A. "The Broken Conduit: A Study of Aliena-
      tion in American Literature." Pacific Spectator, 8 (Autumn),
      326-332.
         Puritan writers, Hawthorne and Melville, and modern writers
"have the same kind of hero--the man with the good (that is,
guilty) conscience, the man with the wound that isolates and
alienates him, yet gives him his significance and his grandeur.

48   [HILLWAY, TYRUS]. Melville Society Newsletter, 10 (Autumn),
      n.p.
         Notes that CBS television's educational series "Camera 3"
presented a six-week series of half-hour sequences based on
Moby-Dick, which began on 16 October 1954.

49   [HILLWAY, TYRUS]. "Motion Picture News." Melville Society
      Newsletter, 10 (Autumn), n.p.
         The "new John Huston production of Moby-Dick bids fair to
be the best publicized motion picture since Gone with the Wind.
Comments and photographs have been appearing in magazines and
newspapers throughout the English-speaking world. . . . The
picture is being spoken of as 'the real Melville' on the basis
of Huston's repeated comment to the effect that he is trying to
produce a film story which will be exactly like the story Melville
wrote." On 21 November 1954 Ed Sullivan interviewed Huston and
Gregory Peck (Ahab) on his television program "Toast of the
Town." Peck stated that as a young man he had played the part of
Ahab in "a truly splendid production of the story on the legitimate stage at the Pasadena Playhouse."

50   ROSENBERRY, EDWARD H. "Melville Explicator." Melville
      Society Newsletter, 10 (Autumn), n.p.
         Reply to 1954.B41. "Stubb is merely playfully equating
Flask with Aquarius as the water runs off him in the storm.
Calling Flask a water-bearer is a standard Melvillian pun. All
that is needed to make perfect grammatical sense is the omitted
subject in the last part of the sentence: '[one] might fill
pitchers at your coat collar.'"

51   FIREBAUGH, JOSEPH J.   "Humorist as Rebel: The Melville of
      Typee." Nineteenth-Century Fiction, 9 (September), 108-120.
          Analysis of Melville's humor in Typee, with emphasis on
      his use of ironic incongruity. "A pervasive tolerant
      geniality . . . is the special contribution of Melville's humor.
      It suffuses his treatment both of savage custom and civilized
      foible. When he is genuinely angry, the humor sometimes becomes
      savagely ironic: the rebel in Melville sometimes conquers the
      humanist and the humorist. But in the main his richly tolerant
      humor is the palliative of his rebellion." Reprinted in part in
      Rountree, pp. 55-61.

52   BABCOCK, C. MERTON.   "Herman Melville's Whaling Vocabulary."
      American Speech, 29 (October), 161-174.
          Supplies "contextual evidence from Melville's published
      works for specific whaling usages which antedate the earliest
      cited evidence in the historical dictionaries (OED, DAE, DA)"
      and "historical-lexical evidence for whaling expressions either
      not listed in the dictionaries or not supported by contextual
      evidence."

53   O'CONNOR, W.V.   "The Novel and the 'Truth' about America."
      English Studies, 35 (October), 207-209.
          Hawthorne, Melville, and James cited as major nineteenth-
      century novelists who "delivered themselves of critical comments
      which make clear their understanding of fiction as nature, or
      reality, idealized or transformed"--as in chapter 33 of The
      Confidence-Man. Should Israel Potter be read as a trustworthy
      account of a soldier-hero in the American Revolution? "The novel
      is based on a chapbook autobiography, but anyone reading a few
      chapters into the novel recognizes that this is a picaresque
      tale." Potter "is the wanderer (Israel) and he is the common
      man (Potter's field)--and, Melville says in his fierce irony,
      his reward is what the hero can expect. Certainly this is not
      history; it is Melville's bitter view of things at a stage in his
      career when the current was running strongly against him, carry-
      ing him, like Israel Potter, toward inevitable defeat. . . .
      Anyone reading Israel Potter as a good document of the American
      Revolution and the reward of heroes would, of course, have an
      apparitional sense of historical fact." Reprinted in 1960.B28.

54   BOWEN, MERLIN.   "Redburn and the Angle of Vision." Modern
      Philology, 52 (November), 100-109.
          Melville places the controlling center of consciousness in
      Redburn not in young Redburn but in the mature Redburn, the
      retrospective narrator--as truly independent a fictional charac-
      ter as Conrad's Marlow. Redburn, to a considerable extent, falls
      apart in the middle, but the break cannot be attributed to any
      serious departure from the established point of view (as
      Matthiessen [1941.A1], Gilman [1951.A2], and Gross [1951.B79]
      maintain). It must rather be charged to Melville's failure, in
      the latter half of the book, to hold clearly to his evident
      design to use Harry Bolton as the principal dramatic means for
      the discovery that completes young Redburn's education--"the

discovery that the sufferings attending his own initiation have been neither accidental nor exceptional but in strict accordance with the ever repeated pattern of life." The detailed pattern of parallels between young Redburn and Harry contributes very little to the forward movement of the narrative. The incidents of the homeward voyage--unlike those of the passage out--are not shown as effecting a series of progressive changes in anyone's character.

55   VINCENT, HOWARD P. "Book Reviews." American Literature, 26 (November), 444–445.
          Review of 1953.A3. The "most memorable essays and those most stimulating to fruitful speculation are those by Murray, Bezanson, Smith, and Miller. . . . In fact, the excellence of the entire volume justifies the existence of a Melville Society as something more than a cult."

56   BERGLER, EDMUND. "A Note on Herman Melville." American Imago, 11 (Winter), 385–397.
          Masochism was the key to Melville's personal and literary life (including his attachment to Hawthorne, which was not homosexual but masochistic). Typee and Omoo, "the vehicles of his initial literary alibi," embodied "an autarchic defense" against masochism. When this "first inner defense" collapsed during a period of increased internal conflict, "a stronger defense was instituted, and in Moby-Dick masochism is no longer fought with the weapon of autarchy, but through identification with Captain Ahab, who carries on a furious and unrelenting battle against the devouring white whale, symbolizing the 'bad' mother. The substitute defense also proves too weak, and is followed by the 'rescue attempt' via Oedipal admission, as presented in Pierre. Finally (helped along by Melville's unconscious misuse of critical and popular rejection), everything collapses; the literary escape is 'out,' and camouflaged writing block sets in, to last until Melville's death." Final acceptance of masochistic submission in Billy Budd is wisdom's last word in Melville.

57   [HILLWAY, TYRUS]. "Evening Meeting." Melville Society Newsletter, 10 (Winter), n.p.
          Account of "the final half-hour sequence of the brilliant TV production of Moby-Dick by 'Camera 3' (the last of six programs)," shown at an evening meeting of the Melville Society on 27 December 1954 in New York City. Robert Herridge's production "without question was powerful, complex, and rich--a real contribution to Melville literature."

58   [HILLWAY, TYRUS]. "Morning Meeting." Melville Society Newsletter, 10 (Winter), n.p.
          Synopses of talks given by Wilson Heflin and H.L. Shapiro at the annual meeting of the Melville Society on 27 December 1954 in New York City, concerning aspects of Melville's career aboard the Acushnet and in the Marquesas Islands.

59   KAPLAN, SIDNEY. "A Transcendentalist Reader." Melville
     Society Newsletter, 10 (Winter), n.p.
          Notes reference to Typee in Marx Edgeworth Lazarus's
     Comparative Psychology and Universal Analogy (p. 127) and
     reference to Omoo in Lazarus's The Human Trinity: or Three
     Aspects of Life: the Passional, the Intellectual, the Practical
     Sphere (pp. 116–117).

60   ROCKWELL, FREDERICK S. "DeQuincey and the Ending of 'Moby-
     Dick.'" Nineteenth-Century Fiction, 9 (December), 161–168.
          Passages in DeQuincey's "The English Mail-Coach" and
     Suspiria de Profundis may have prompted images and ideas in the
     last three chapters of Moby-Dick.

61   YATES, NORRIS. "A Traveller's Comments on Melville's Typee."
     Modern Language Notes, 69 (December), 581–583.
          Reprints remarks on Typee in 1856.B5, with commentary.
     "Grs. X." appears to have been E.K. Drayton, ship's doctor on
     the U.S.S. St. Mary's.

1955 A BOOKS

1   ROSENBERRY, EDWARD H. Melville and the Comic Spirit.
     Cambridge, Mass.: Harvard University Press, 211 pp. Reprint.
     New York: Octagon Books, 1970.
          It was as a "comic writer" that Melville won his early
     fame, but in the twentieth century his humor has been generally
     missed or ignored. Rosenberry traces the growth of Melville's
     comic artistry from Typee to The Confidence-Man through "four
     theoretical and somewhat arbitrary phases": (1) the jocular-
     hedonic, "instantly translatable into the simple idea of
     fun . . . joking in the most light-hearted vein merely for the
     shared pleasure involved," an "unreflecting expression of the
     native play-spirit of the individual and his folk tradition";
     (2) the imaginative-critical, "more literary in its origins, more
     sophisticated in its tone, more ulterior in its motives," the
     writer's interest having "passed beyond laughter--usually without
     sacrificing it--to the more serious business of casting balances
     and judging values"; (3) the philosophical-psychological, con-
     cerned with "the ambiguous nature of values themselves, the
     interrelations of comedy and tragedy, and the bearing of both
     problems on the life of man," a "stage which represents the
     artist's search for a balanced view of himself and his world";
     (4) the dramatic-structural, which "fuses the disparate elements
     of comedy and tragedy into a balanced work of art." Typee and
     Omoo represent the first phase; Redburn and White-Jacket combine
     phases one and two; Mardi combines phases one, two and three; and
     Moby-Dick combines all four phases. After Moby-Dick, Melville's
     great comic talent declined in scope if not in vigor; thereafter
     perhaps only "Bartleby," in "its brief and muted way," displays
     the full range of his comic genius. During his decline, his
     "principal absorption, a philosophical-psychological one, was the
     grimly amusing problem of ambiguities, particularly the ambiguity

of comedy itself and the dilemma in which it involves the artist between the dark and bright views of life. In the imaginative-critical vein, he turned his invention and wit to primarily satiric purposes in a war of ideas that reached its stunning climax in The Confidence-Man. And finally he made a partial return toward the purely playful laughter of his earliest books, a tendency culminating in a remarkable valedictory burst of native humor coloring all the work of 1856." In discussing the works, Rosenberry focuses chiefly on humorous techniques (such as exaggeration, stylistic ingenuity, puns, and comic conceits), characters, and satire, frequently relating Melville's humor to American folk and frontier humor and, in Mardi, Moby-Dick, and The Confidence-Man, showing its indebtedness to his reading. Indexed. Reviewed in 1955.B56, B73-74; 1956.B46, B85; 1957.B5, B29.

1955 B SHORTER WRITINGS

1   ADAMS, HAZARD. Blake and Yeats: The Contrary Vision. Ithaca, N.Y.: Cornell University Press, pp. 133-134.
     Ahab typifies the modern consciousness--adrift on a wide sea, seeking completion of self in the distortion called nature's "vegetable glass"; for him there is no resolution of the subject-object problem, no escape from himself. In Moby-Dick only Ishmael escapes through the vortex to some understanding. The Pre-Raphaelites and other nineteenth-century poets searched constantly for the vortex of vision achieved by Ishmael.

2   AUDEN, W.H. "The Anglo-American Difference." Anchor Review, No. 1. Garden City, N.Y.: Doubleday & Co., p. 212.
     At the end of Huckleberry Finn, Huck leaves Jim behind like an old shoe, just as in Moby-Dick Ishmael becomes a blood brother of Queequeg and then forgets all about him. The daydream of the lifelong comrade in adventure often appears in American literature, but no American seriously expects such a dream to come true.

3   BLACKMUR, R.P. "The Craft of Herman Melville: A Putative Statement," in The Lion and the Honeycomb: Essays in Solicitude and Critique. New York: Harcourt, Brace and Co., pp. 124-144.
     Reprint of 1940.B2; reprinted in 1960.B3 and Chase (1962), pp. 75-90.

4   CARPENTER, FREDERIC I. "Melville and the Men-of-War," in American Literature and the Dream. New York: Philosophical Library, pp. 73-82.
     Reprints 1953.B50, with minor revision.

5   CLARK, HARRY H. "Changing Attitudes in Early American Literary Criticism, 1800-1840," in The Development of American Literary Criticism. Ed. Floyd Stovall. Chapel Hill: University of North Carolina Press, 38-39, 72.
     The favorable reviews of Typee and Omoo cited as evidence of an "increase in critical hedonism." Melville, Lowell, Emerson,

and Whitman are "associated with Coleridge's idea that the fullness of the innate organic form is one with the perfection of the
outward form" in arguing "that the parts of a work of art are
interrelated and consonant with the whole in a manner analogous
to the way in which the branches and roots of a tree are interrelated, interdependent, and consonant with its organic life."

6　CREALOCK, W.I.B. <u>Cloud of Islands: By Sail to the South
Seas</u>. New York: Hastings House, pp. 39, 148, 149-150.
　　Account of voyage to the Galapagos and Marquesas Islands
and Tahiti. Brief references to Melville. Photographs of the
Galapagos and Marquesas Islands, including Typee valley.

7　FADIMAN, CLIFTON. "Moby Dick," in <u>Party of One: The Selected
Writings of Clifton Fadiman</u>. Cleveland and New York: The
World Publishing Co., pp. 136-144.
　　Reprints 1943.B7, with minor omission.

8　FICK, REVEREND LEONARD J. <u>The Light Beyond: A Study of
Hawthorne's Theology</u>. Westminster, Md.: The Newman Press,
pp. 45-46, 52-55.
　　"Not the objective fact . . . but a too acute realization
of the fact that the ideal exists and that it is beyond realization, at least in this life, makes for the tragedy that befalls
Ahab and Pierre and Aylmer. . . . Aylmer is the true Melvillian
tragic hero: an intellectual aristocrat who becomes conscious
of the cleavage between what is and what ought to be, tries to
mend it, and fails. Hawthorne, equally with Melville, held that
the tragedy of Aylmer was ascribable, not to the existence of the
cleavage, but to Aylmer's awareness of the cleavage coupled with
his efforts to remedy it." Melville, however, "posited a tragic
aristocracy: only the chosen few can be truly tragic, and
tragedy, for him, is synonymous with grandeur. Hawthorne
posited a tragic democracy: all men, though not all in equal
measure, are tragic figures in the sense that the dichotomy is
present in them all. And though they may not be aware of it, the
duality in them is productive of consequences which have an objective reality. In other words, Hawthorne, unlike Melville,
did not stress the awareness of the ideal. The tragedy is
heightened when that awareness is present; but even without the
awareness, the tragedy is still there, though in this latter
case it might perhaps be more accurately termed frustration."
Both Hawthorne and Melville explore the depths of the human
heart; but not until <u>Billy Budd</u> did Melville discover, like
Hawthorne, the "eternal beauty" beneath the darkness and gloom.

9　FIEDLER, LESLIE. "Come Back to the Raft Ag'in, Huck Honey!"
in <u>An End to Innocence</u>. Boston: Beacon Press, pp. 142-151.
　　Reprint of 1948.B55.

10   FOGLE, RICHARD H. "Organic Form in American Criticism, 1840–
      1870," in The Development of American Literary Criticism. Ed.
      Floyd Stovall. Chapel Hill: University of North Carolina
      Press, pp. 102–106.
            The crucial problem in Melville is an unresolved conflict
      between his concept of form and his concept of organic expansiv-
      ism. He clearly enunciated the full and ideal theory of organic
      form achieved by the reconciliation of opposites only once—in
      "Art."

11   FORBES, ALLAN. Whale Ships and Whaling Scenes, as Portrayed
      by Benjamin Russell. Boston: Second Bank-State Street Trust
      Co., pp. 36–39.
            Claims that it was customary for the congregation of the
      New Bedford Seaman's Bethel to sing the hymn in chapter 9, "The
      Sermon," in Moby-Dick and that Melville visited the bethel before
      sailing on his whaling voyage to the South Seas in the Pequod.

*12   GETTMANN, ROYAL A. and BRUCE HARKNESS. "Billy Budd, Foretop-
      man," in Teacher's Manual for "A Book of Short Stories." New
      York: Rinehart and Co., pp. 71–74.
            Cited in Beebe, Hayford, and Roper, p. 328.

13   HART, JAMES, D. and CLARENCE GOHDES, eds. America's Litera-
      ture. New York: Henry Holt and Co., pp. 512–514.
            Biographical and critical sketch ["Herman Melville (1819–
      1891)"]—headnote to extracts from Typee (chapter 18), White-
      Jacket (chapter 92), Moby-Dick (chapters 7–9), Pierre (Book 14),
      and selections from Battle-Pieces and Clarel.

14   HORSFORD, HOWARD C. "Preface," "Introduction," and
      "Chronology of the Trip," in Journal of a Visit to Europe and
      the Levant, October 11, 1856–May 6, 1857, by Herman Melville.
      Ed. Howard C. Horsford. Princeton: Princeton University
      Press, pp. vii–ix, 3–49, 51–53.
            "Introduction" comments on Melville's habits and interests
      as a traveler; the nature, style, and literary quality of the
      journal entries; their biographical, psychological, and philo-
      sophical significance; Melville's revisions in the journal; and
      his use of material from the journal in his lectures and in his
      poetry, particularly in Clarel. The journal shows "how certain
      ideas and symbolic values, evident enough in the short stories
      and novels of the last years, continued to obsess" Melville's
      thinking. It gives, too, "unquestionable evidence of the per-
      sistence of the mood in which The Confidence-Man had been writ-
      ten, of the doubt and skepticism which had increasingly obsessed
      him since 1850, not only for the period of the nearly eight
      months in 1856–1857 which the journal covers, but for that
      length of time, probably another fifteen years, during which he
      continually reread and revised it." The text of the journal is
      accompanied by textual and explanatory notes. Indexed. Reviewed
      in 1955.B57; 1956.B39.

15   HOWARD, LEON, LOUIS B. WRIGHT, and CARL BODE, eds. <u>American</u>
<u>Heritage: An Anthology and Interpretive Survey of Our Liter-</u>
<u>ature</u>. Boston: D.C. Heath and Co., pp. 724–727.
     Biographical and critical survey ("The New Explorers").
Prints chapters 158, 161, and 162 from <u>Mardi</u>; chapters 60–63
from <u>White-Jacket</u>; chapters 41 and 42 from <u>Moby-Dick</u>; book 14,
chapters 2 and 3 from <u>Pierre</u>; Sketch First and Sketch Eighth from
"The Encantadas," and selections from <u>Battle-Pieces</u>, <u>Clarel</u>, <u>John</u>
<u>Marr</u>, and <u>Timoleon</u>.

16   KAZIN, ALFRED. "On Melville as Scripture," in <u>The Inmost</u>
<u>Leaf: A Selection of Essays</u>. New York: Harcourt, Brace ar
Co., pp. 197–207.
     Reprint of 1950.B36.

17   LEWIS, R.W.B. "Melville: The Apotheosis of Adam," in <u>The</u>
<u>American Adam: Innocence, Tragedy, and Tradition in the</u>
<u>Nineteenth Century</u>. Chicago: University of Chicago Press,
pp. 127–155.
     Melville, the one novelist in nineteenth-century America
gifted with a genuinely myth-making imagination, was able to
elevate the "anecdote" of the fortunate "fall" to the status of
myth and so gave it a permanent place among the resources of our
literature. Melville took the loss of innocence and the world's
betrayal of hope as the supreme challenge to understanding and
to art. In novel after novel he dispatched hero after hero, Adam
after Adam, sending them forth, full of hopeful expectancy, only
to tell how, in every case, they fell among cannibals. At the
end of his career he "found a new conviction about the saving
strength of the Adamic personality. When this conviction became
articulate in <u>Billy Budd</u>, the American hero as Adam became the
hero as Christ and entered, once and for all, into the dimension
of myth." The last three paragraphs of "The Try-Works," chapter 96 in <u>Moby-Dick</u>, serve as a guide to Melville's treatment of
innocence and evil in <u>Typee</u>, <u>Redburn</u>, and <u>Moby-Dick</u>. <u>Moby-Dick</u>
"is an elaborate pattern of countercommentaries, the supreme
instance of the dialectical novel—a novel of tension without
resolution. Ishmael's meditation, which transfigures the anger
and sees beyond the sickness and the evil, is only one major
voice in the dramatic conversation; and not until <u>Billy Budd</u>
does this voice become transcendent and victorious." <u>Billy Budd</u>
is unmistakably the product of aged serenity; Melville has unmistakably gotten beyond his anger or discovered the key to it.
If Melville celebrates the fall of the Adamic hero, he also celebrates the one who fell, "and the qualities and attitudes which
insure the tragedy are reaffirmed in their indestructible worth
even in the moment of defeat. Melville exposed anew the danger
of innocence and its inevitable tragedy; but in the tragedy he
rediscovered a heightened value in the innocence." Incorporates
1950.B62. Reprinted in Goldberg and Goldberg, pp. 321–341; reprinted in part in Norton <u>Moby-Dick</u>, pp. 676–677. Reviewed in
1957.B61, B70, B87.

18   MARSHALL, THOMAS F. "Herman Melville: The Transcendental
      Traveller," in Three Voices of the American Tradition: Edgar
      Allan Poe, Herman Melville, Ernest Hemingway. Athens, Greece
      [U.S. Embassy], pp. 31–45.
          Biographical survey, with commentary on "Benito Cereno,"
      Billy Budd, and Moby-Dick. Although Melville was never an actual
      member of the transcendentalist group, he was strongly affected
      by it. Never a reformer, and never sure of himself, he was,
      nevertheless, always observing and commenting on life as he had
      seen it, applying always a mystical and transcendental yardstick.
      "Benito Cereno" is perhaps the best of Melville's shorter fiction
      both in its coherence and its wealth of reference. In no other
      story was he able to maintain the necessary relationships of
      setting, character, situation, and plot so well. If Billy Budd
      just misses greatness, it is because Billy's mindless innocence
      is not quite the stuff for tragedy. The conflict between
      Melville's observation of life and the orthodox formulas he had
      been taught produced Ahab. In revealing Ahab's hatred of evil,
      Melville shows that men, in hating evil passionately, eventually
      become what they hate.

19   MAUGHAM, W. SOMERSET. "Herman Melville and Moby Dick," in
      The Art of Fiction: An Introduction to Ten Novels and Their
      Authors. Garden City, N.Y.: Doubleday & Co., pp. 189–213.
          Reprints 1954.B14.

20   MUMFORD, LEWIS. "Moby Dick," in The Human Prospect. Boston:
      Beacon Press, pp. 31–49.
          Reprints part of chapter 7 in 1929.A1.

21   ROSENTHAL, M.L. and A.J.M. SMITH. Exploring Poetry. New
      York: The Macmillan Co., pp. 372–375.
          Analysis of "Billy in the Darbies" in Billy Budd as an
      example of dramatic monologue.

22   SANTAYANA, GEORGE. The Letters of George Santayana. Ed.
      Daniel Cory. New York: Charles Scribner's Sons, pp. 225,
      229, 325.
          In letter of 22 May 1927 to Van Wyck Brooks: "when you
      speak of the older worthies [in 1927.B4], you seem to me to
      exaggerate, not so much their importance, as their distinction:
      wasn't this Melville (I have never read him) the most terrible
      ranter? What you quote of him doesn't tempt me to repair the
      holes in my education." In letter of 21 December 1927 to Logan
      Pearsall Smith: "it is hopeless, so late in life, to fill up the
      lacunae in one's education. I tried the other day to read Moby
      Dick, but in spite of much skipping, I have got stuck in the
      middle. Is it such a masterpiece as they say?" In letter of
      12 December 1938 to Mrs. C.H. Toy: "It [Anthology of American
      Literature, eds. Benét and Pearson, (1938.B10)] is modern, and
      therefore, to me, instructive, and it may actually lead me to
      reconcile myself with some authors that I could never stomach,
      Melville for instance."

23　　SPILLER, ROBERT E.　"Romantic Crisis:　Melville, Whitman," in
　　　The Cycle of American Literature:　An Essay in Historical
　　　Criticism.　New York:　The Macmillan Co., pp. 89–99.
　　　　　Biographical and critical survey.

24　　STOCKTON, ERIC W.　"A Commentary on Melville's 'The Lightning-
　　　Rod Man.'"　Papers of the Michigan Academy of Science, Arts,
　　　and Letters, 40 (1955), 321–328.
　　　　　"The Lightning-Rod," in which the salesman is Satan, is
　　an affirmation of New Testament Christianity.　The story grad-
　　ually reveals the narrator to represent humanity with its in-
　　stincts of charity and hospitality, and with traits of sturdy
　　individualism and self-respect, as contrasted with false, satanic
　　pride.　The salesman stands for false, hidebound, unbenevolent
　　Christianity in opposition to Christ's loving, nondogmatic
　　Gospel, represented by the cottager.　Melville's own position is
　　that of a fatalistic theist, a nonsectarian with confidence in
　　both God and man.　The failure of "The Lightning-Rod Man," like
　　that of Pierre, is one of language:　the tale is too slight to
　　bear the linguistic burden imposed upon it.

25　　STOVALL, FLOYD.　"Introduction," in The Development of Ameri-
　　　can Literary Criticism.　Ed. Floyd Stovall.　Chapel Hill:
　　　University of North Carolina Press, pp. 7–8.
　　　　　A "genuinely national point of view in literature" devel-
　　oped in New York City in the 1850s.　"Melville was less radically
　　the nationalist than Whitman, and yet he was not less certain
　　that America must and will produce its own literature and that it
　　will not . . . appear 'in the costume of Queen Elizabeth's day.'
　　His own creative work owed something to his reading, and what he
　　owed shows up more obviously than it would have done if he had
　　taken the time, as Whitman did, to digest his reading and make it
　　a part of his own mind.　It may be that Whitman and Melville are
　　freer from the past because their minds were not at an early age
　　subjected to the discipline of Greek, Latin, and the English
　　classics.　By the time they came under the influence of the great
　　masters of literature their individualities had become firmly
　　integrated with their own time and place.　Besides, . . . they
　　belonged to New York City, which even then had no provincial
　　character distinct from the character of America as a whole."
　　The "contemporaries of Whitman and Melville did not recognize
　　them as symbols of American cultural nationalism because but few
　　of them had a clear notion of what American culture was or was to
　　be.　Most literate Americans in 1850 or 1860 believed Longfellow,
　　Holmes, and Lowell to be the architects of American literary
　　culture. . . ."

26　　TARG, WILLIAM.　"Moby-Dick:　The Great American Novel," in
　　　Bouillabaisse for Bibliophiles.　Ed. William Targ.　Cleveland:
　　　The World Publishing Co., pp. 299–307.
　　　　　Introduction to Moby-Dick, with notes on the first American
　　edition.　"Depending on condition, color of binding, advertise-
　　ments and end papers--and the prevailing market climate--Moby-
　　Dick ranges in value from about two hundred to a thousand dollars.

27   TINDALL, WILLIAM YORK. The Literary Symbol. New York:
      Columbia University Press, pp. 21-27.
           Examines the approaches of various critics to the symbolism
      of Moby-Dick and considers "clues" Melville gives for interpreta-
      tion of the book.

*28   TOMITA, AKIRA. "How to Read Moby-Dick." Rikkyo Review of
      Arts and Letters [Tokyo], 16 (1955), 1-16, 53-55.
           Cited in Beebe, Hayford, and Roper, p. 341.

29   UNTERMEYER, LOUIS. "Herman Melville," in Makers of the Modern
      World. New York: Simon and Schuster, pp. 47-59.
           Biographical and critical survey, with brief synopses and
      evaluations of most of the major works and a brief account of
      "the Melville renaissance."

30   WILLIAMS, STANLEY T. The Spanish Background of American
      Literature. Vol. 1. New Haven: Yale University Press,
      pp. 224-227, 394-96.
           Reprints 1952.B52, with slight changes and with notes
      added.

31   WILSON, EDMUND. The Shock of Recognition: The Development of
      Literature in the United States Recorded by the Men Who Made
      It. 2d ed. New York: The Modern Library, pp. 185-186.
           Reprints note on "Hawthorne and His Mosses" from 1943.B18.

32   KISSANE, JAMES. "Imagery, Myth, and Melville's Pierre."
      American Literature, 26 (January), 564-572.
           Disputes the reading of Pierre in 1934.B44 and finds in-
      herent limitations in the growing tendency to approach fiction
      through imagery and myth, which it represents. Though Pierre
      draws its imagery in part from the Fall of Man, the novel does
      not therefore necessarily constitute a systematic reworking of
      that myth. Moorman substitutes for meaning that which is acces-
      sory to meaning, referring the novel to an external design in-
      stead of attempting to discover the internal controls and the
      way in which they employ that design in the artistic whole.
      Despite the importance of symbol, the basic structure of Pierre
      is essentially dramatic, and it is toward the tracing out of
      plot, in its most inclusive sense, that all elements are arranged.
      Moorman's method of discovering whole by scrutiny of part cannot
      cope with a dynamic structure in which parts are modified by
      changes that the totality describes. Many of Moorman's key
      interpretations, such as the "Isabel-life-fertility, Lucy-death-
      sterility dichotomy," are also questionable. [See 1956.B29 for
      reply.]

33   SHERBO, ARTHUR. "Melville's 'Portuguese Catholic Priest.'"
      American Literature, 26 (January), 563-564.
           The "Portuguese Catholic priest" Melville cites in "Jonah
      Historically Regarded," chapter 83 of Moby-Dick, was probably
      Father Jerome Lobo, author of A Voyage to Abysinnia (a work
      translated into English in 1735 by Samuel Johnson), described on

the title page of the English translation as a "Portuguese
Jesuit"; but the idea of Jonah's going around the Cape of Good
Hope came from the sixth dissertation Abbé Joachim Legrand
appended to Lobo's history of Abysinnia. The trip around the
Cape of Good Hope is not, however, advanced "as a signal magni-
fication of the general miracle" in Lobo-Legrand.

34   WILLIAMSON, EDWARD. "Brief Mention." Modern Language Notes,
      70 (January), 74-75.
          Review of Melville o le ambiguità, by Gabriele Baldini
      [Milan, 1952]. An effective contribution to Melville scholarship.
      "The book's limitation is clear: it is essentially a study of
      Moby-Dick, Pierre, 'Bartleby' and Billy Budd. The other works are
      treated only in relation to these four, without regard to their
      autonomy. . . . The five chapters on Moby Dick are the heart of
      the study, but the one on Pierre seems exceptionally felicitous.
      The chapter on Billy Budd suffers from the notion that the work
      rests upon an utter acceptance of a Christian universe. No such
      false monism mars the consideration of Moby-Dick. Baldini has
      recognized that behind the work there is no precise system of
      thought, that in Melville a puritan theology placed in crisis by
      philosophic doubts and external events is laced with traits of
      rationalism and fatalism. He has equally recognized that the
      novel does not function as a coherent system of symbols, but is a
      plotted narrative which flashes off intuitions of univeral value."
      A safe guide to Melville's chief works for Italians, which merits
      consideration by American scholars.

35   ELISOFON, ELIOT. "Voyages to Paradise: A Camera in South
      Seas Seeks Famous Scenes in Literature." Life, 38
      (24 January), 60-61, 74.
          Photographs, by Elisofon, inspired by passages in Moby-Dick
      and Typee.

36   COOK, CHARLES H., JR. "Ahab's 'Intolerable Allegory.'"
      Boston University Studies in English, 1 (Spring-Summer),
      45-52.
          Melville's admonition against scouting at the white whale
      as a fable or an allegory is for the most part rightly understood
      as Melville's (or Ishmael's) protest that white whales are
      realities, not imaginary sea monsters. It may also be the key
      to the main theme of the novel and to the tragic flaw in Ahab's
      character. "Aware of the human temptation to project simple,
      personal meanings upon things which are formless or incompre-
      hensible, Melville may be giving us the tragedy of a man who
      yields his whole soul to this temptation, who inflates his own
      private hurt into the hurt of all mankind, and who allegorizes
      the inflictor of this hurt as the dwelling place of all human
      evil." To Ishmael, by contrast, the whale is "a symbol of in-
      finitely multiple significance beyond the full comprehension of
      any man." The wisest course for critics would probably be to
      follow Melville's example and refrain from applying any specific
      abstract term to the mystery symbolized by the white whale. Re-
      printed in 1960.A6.

37　[HILLWAY, TYRUS].　"Huston's Moby Dick."　Melville Society
　　Newsletter, 11 (Spring), n.p.
　　　　The John Huston movie Moby-Dick, starring Gregory Peck, has
　received more advance publicity than almost any film of recent
　years.　"Newspaper columnists and radio and television commen-
　tators followed nearly every step in the filming of the picture
　with avid interest and reported its progress to enchanted
　audiences."　Publicity photographs show that there will be some
　technical errors in the movie.　Gil Wilson, who has made three
　hundred drawings based on Moby-Dick will visit schools and col-
　leges throughout the United States to discuss the book and show
　color slides of his work.

38　[HILLWAY, TYRUS].　"Notes."　Melville Society Newsletter, 11
　　(Spring), n.p.
　　　　Notes that Pond's Theater presented Billy Budd on the ABC
　television network on 10 March 1955.

39　WILLSON, LAWRENCE.　"Yet Another Note on Moby-Dick.　Dalhousie
　　Review, 35 (Spring), 5–15.
　　　　Moby-Dick is Melville's Paradise Lost, his attempt to
　justify God's ways to man.　Melville distrusted the bland assump-
　tions of his time that man has an independent spirit and is mas-
　ter of his fate.　The tragedy of Moby-Dick belongs wholly to
　Ahab, whose vanity is man's greatest vanity:　his imagination of
　himself as a creature of power.　Ahab "is the extraordinary man,
　stricken by the knowledge of sin and impelled by his will,
　governed by the necessity of fate, into participation in
　sin. . . .　He is the noble soul who suffers but who learns
　from his suffering, not the lesson of humility . . . but the
　lesson of rebellion."

40　MILLER, JAMES E.　"Hawthorne and Melville:　The Unpardonable
　　Sin."　PMLA, 70 (March), 91–114.
　　　　"Ahab's character is . . . the key to Moby Dick, and the
　key to Ahab's character is the unpardonable sin.　Ahab follows
　the same fatal byway taken by Ethan Brand, Chillingworth, Aylmer,
　Rappaccini, and the rest."　His pride, "together with his posi-
　tion of command, naturally isolates him, cuts him off from the
　common human feelings that bind the crew together.　He violates
　the soul of his crew by imposing his powerful will on theirs, by
　implicating them in his diabolical schemes.　And, as happened
　with all of Hawthorne's great transgressors, Ahab finds himself,
　finally, in league with the devil, dedicated to evil, at war with
　God, attempting to take over God's role in the universe."

41　HARVEY, EVELYN.　"Moby-Dick."　Collier's, 135 (4 March),
　　70–73.
　　　　Account of the making of the movie directed by John Huston.
　Photographs of scenes from the movie.

42   ANON. "The Misanthrope." Time, 65 (7 March), 114, 116, 118.
       Review of 1954.B9. The Confidence-Man remains the least
known work of America's greatest novelist. What it needs, and
ably gets in Foster's introduction, is a key to its structure
and a path through its symbols. The book is a satiric picaresque
allegory that indicts not only man's inhumanity to man, but, as
Melville saw it, God's as well. Melville offers a scathing,
nihilistic critique of every reigning belief of nineteenth-
century America but will not stop until he can debunk the goodness and glory of God. As a novel, The Confidence-Man is a near
miss, one of those pregnant and provocative failures that prove
more rewarding to read than a whole litter of lesser writers'
tidy but empty triumphs.

43   McELDERRY, B.R., JR. "Three Earlier Treatments of the Billy
      Budd Theme." American Literature, 27 (May), 251–257.
       Two of Douglas Jerrold's popular plays, Black-eyed Susan
(1829) and The Mutiny at the Nore (1830) and Marryat's novel The
King's Own (1830) have elements parallel to the main action of
Billy Budd. Each "tells a story of a sailor who attacks a
superior officer under the severest provocation, is sentenced to
death through inflexible naval discipline, and in preparing to
die forgives his enemies." Billy Budd "has usually been discussed as if it were unique in theme, a strange, unprecedented
story. Future discussion must take into account the fact that
Billy Budd himself is distilled from a well-established type,
the nautical hero for whom duty, no matter how unfair or un-
reasonable it may appear, is nevertheless the voice of God." His
"God bless Captain Vere!" is "the traditional ritual of the condemned man forgiving the official who is duty bound to order his
death. Melville's achievement was to make real and convincing
an attitude and a speech which for centuries has been a staple
of popular accounts of executions." Reprinted in part in
Springer, p. 69.

44   WATKINS, FLOYD C. "A Note on Melville's 'Three Twin Sons.'"
      American Speech, 30 (May), 152.
       The "three twin sons" in chapter 53 of Redburn are
triplets. The most recent illustration of the dialectal usage
of twin for triplet in the Oxford English Dictionary is from
1646. Yet Melville and his publishers must have expected many
readers to understand this usage: no explanation is given.

45   KORG, JACOB. "Selected New Books." Nation, 180 (28 May),
      468.
       Review of 1954.B9. Foster's introduction and notes bring
a neglected masterpiece to life by revealing the subtle irony
that makes an apparently aimless narrative about a Mississippi
steamer into a taut satirical allegory of the spirit.

46   CHITTICK, V.L.O. "The Way Back to Melville: Sea-Chart of a
      Literary Revival." Southwest Review, 40 (Summer), 238-248.
          Surveys Melville's reputation in the 1880s and 1890s and
      claims Archibald MacMechan as "the rediscoverer of Melville,"
      citing his essay on Moby-Dick [1899.B12] as "the earliest appre-
      ciation of Melville's masterpiece, by as much as a full decade,"
      the findings of which "have since been confirmed over and over."
      By far "the most interesting fact" about MacMechan's "endorsement
      of Melville's style is the degree to which in recording it he
      anticipated the present-day taste for native folk-flavor in
      writing, as reflected in the now current opinions of scholars and
      critics." Details of MacMechan's career; reprints his corre-
      spondence with Melville. [See Log, pp. 817-819.]

47   [HILLWAY, TYRUS]. Melville Society Newsletter, 11 (Summer),
      n.p.
          Notes that Jerry Winters' half-hour film Herman Melville's
      Moby Dick opened at the Paris Theatre, New York City on 23 May
      1955. The film (in color) is based on more than two hundred
      drawings by Gil Wilson. Thomas Mitchell is the narrator; the
      original musical score was composed by Richard Mohaupt.

48   JONES, JOSEPH. "Reviews of Books." Southwest Review, 40
      (Summer), x-xi, 271-272.
          Review of 1953.A3. Of the nine essays, Bezanson's is the
      most useful to the general reader; a closely packed and most
      luminous piece of exposition that makes clear the matter,
      dynamic, and structure of the novel with uncommon success.
      Brief summaries of the other essays.

49   KAPLAN, SIDNEY. "Addition to Melville Log." Melville Society
      Newsletter, 11 (Summer), n.p.
          Notes item in the Boston Daily Times, 21 November 1850,
      reporting Melville's purchase of a Berkshire farm, "where he
      intends to raise pigs, poultry, turnips, babies, and other
      vegetables."

50   MASON, RONALD. "Orson Welles as Ahab." Melville Society
      Newsletter, 11 (Summer), n.p.
          Review of a blank verse adaptation of Moby-Dick, written
      and produced by Orson Welles, that ran for three and a half weeks
      in the summer, at the Duke of York's Theatre, London, with Welles
      playing Captain Ahab, Father Mapple, and a theater manager. The
      production "proved strangely impressive," a "remarkable feat of
      imaginative representation." The "inescapable factor in the
      evening's experience was the astonishingly Shakespearean quality
      of the language." Though "we knew (academically) all about
      Melville's debt to Shakespeare, to hear it and experience it on
      a kind of Shakespearean stage made it at last no academic point
      but a blazing certainty--that in Melville we have the unique
      spectacle of a man who could write like Shakespeare without dis-
      gracing either Shakespeare or himself."

51　　STEIN, WILLIAM BYSSHE. "The Moral Axis of 'Benito Cereno.'"
　　　Accent, 15 (Summer), 221–233.
　　　　　Changes of an additions to the original narrative in
　　　"Benito Cereno" [see 1928.B26] stem from Melville's treatment of
　　　the idea of Christian salvation, in which he uses the redeemer
　　　myth to determine the symbolic roles of his main characters.
　　　Benito plays the role of the mock Christian host or false Christ.
　　　Delano's role is that of an initiant in the ritual presentation
　　　of the host. In the Passion enacted before Delano, Melville
　　　stages a mock presentation of the host, a parody on the sacrament
　　　of the Eucharist. Delano's spiritual response to this ceremonial
　　　performance is a travesty of faith. Both he and Benito exhibit
　　　physical and moral cowardice. Both are "oblivious to the message
　　　of the cross that a God of mercies comforts the individual in
　　　every situation so that he may be enabled to comfort others in
　　　need of succor." In this story the redeeming power of the
　　　Christian Savior is dead in man. The death of Benito, more
　　　spiritual than physical, impugns the vital function of the
　　　Catholic church in human affairs. At the end, the rootlessness
　　　of Protestant iconoclasm is indicted through Delano.

52　　VOGEL, DAN. "Note: 'The Coming Storm.'" Melville Society
　　　Newsletter, 11 (Summer), n.p.
　　　　　The artist who painted the picture called The Coming Storm,
　　　which inspired Melville's poem of the same title, was Sandford
　　　(or Sanford) Robinson Gifford (identified in Melville's note
　　　heading the poem as S.R. Gifford) and not Robert Swain Gifford,
　　　as claimed in the Collected Poems [1947.B19], p. 456, and in the
　　　Log, p. 674.

53　　FOGLE, RICHARD H. "The Unity of Melville's 'The Encantadas.'"
　　　Nineteenth-Century Fiction, 10 (June), 34–52.
　　　　　"The unity of these sketches is comprised in their master
　　　theme of the Fall, which is explicitly stated, and in their in-
　　　direct assertion of the fact of complexity. . . . The world is
　　　one, and all is relationship, but the relationship is too vast
　　　and too difficult for the eye to unravel it. These themes con-
　　　trol the method of organization, which uses seeing as a concrete
　　　metaphor for knowing. Much can be seen and known, and much can
　　　be inferred, but not everything. The most perfect human per-
　　　spective cannot attain to full unity of vision." Reprinted in
　　　1960.A2.

54　　MILLHAUSER, MILTON. "The Form of Moby-Dick." Journal of
　　　Aesthetics & Art Criticism, 13 (June), 527–532.
　　　　　In form Moby-Dick is a tragedy, "though a tragedy dras-
　　　tically modified by adaptation to the vehicle of the prose
　　　novel." Reprinted in Rountree, pp. 76–80.

55　　INGLIS, BRIAN. "Contemporary Arts: Theatre." Spectator
　　　[London], 194 (24 June), 800.
　　　　　Review of Orson Welles' adaptation of Moby-Dick at the
　　　Duke of York's Theatre. The play's "rehearsal formula" enables

Welles "to play not Ahab, but an actor-manager trying to play
Ahab; to create an allegory of an actor-manager in search of his
soul, success in the part having the same symbolic significance
for him as the destruction of the white whale had for Ahab." But
Welles's Ahab "is like a corn-fed Middle-West senator, up for a
filibuster"; his hatred of nature's inscrutable malice is not
obsession, but merely obstinacy.

56   CAHOON, HERBERT. "New Books Appraised." Library Journal, 80
     (August), 1687.
          Review of 1955.A1. Entertaining and instructive, success-
     fully avoiding the temptations to find humor where there is none.

57   ANON. "Melville in Decline." London Times Literary Supple-
     ment, No. 2788 (5 August), p. 446.
          Review of 1955.B14. A piece of careful editing; not the
     least notable of an already ample body of scholarly work on which
     future scholars can draw. As a travel book the Journal has lit-
     tle value; though now and again a phrase bites, this is Melville
     in decline. The reader's interest is almost wholly confined to
     Melville's wounded spirit, a melancholy fascination.

58   CAMERON, KENNETH WALTER. "More Grist for Melville's Moby-
     Dick." Emerson Society Quarterly, 1 (4th Quarter), 7-8.
          Newspaper clipping, "Trials and Dangers of the Whale
     Fishery," taken "from a Concord scrap book dating back to the
     1830's and 1840's, illustrates the genre of article on socio-
     logical aspects of the whaling industry popular with church
     papers in Melville's day. All these Melville assumed as part of
     his donnée and utilized creatively in Moby-Dick."

59   BARRETT, LAURENCE. "The Differences in Melville's Poetry."
     PMLA, 70 (September), 606-623.
          The differences in Melville's poetry—unique devices of
     technique—are both difficulties and virtues. They all arise
     from the history of the symbols he developed in his prose works,
     beginning with Typee. The first difference is his employment of
     a highly personal symbolism developed from metaphor, a symbolism
     that often goes unrecognized because it makes sense as ordinary,
     often trite, poetic idiom. Only with detailed study of the
     genesis of each of these symbols in his prose works will we
     realize how rich in profound meanings they were for Melville and
     how rich they can become for those who know him well. The second
     difference is his use of metaphors and images to mean something
     other than what we expect them to mean. The third difference
     lies in Melville's use of poetic form, which he seems to have
     come to consider a virtue in writing, but one still to be vio-
     lated for the sake of true expression. In his poems in Mardi
     he had disregarded the significance of form; some of the
     importance of form he had discovered in Greek architecture as
     he returned home from the Holy Land through the Aegean in 1857.
     The differences in Melville's poetry not only give it a virtue
     in itself but cast a revealing light on his previous prose works,
     in which his highly personal symbols were taking shape, and on

<u>Billy Budd</u>, which is an assertion of order and form--its theme is that measured form makes it possible for man to live with ambiguities. "Through the writing of poetry Melville had discovered that the measure of verse is in itself creative. He had discovered that form for man acting and for poet writing--both being the same thing--is life-giving and makes real and undeniable those truths felt by the heart but ambiguous to the head. He had found that forms, measured forms, are the resolution of the dissociation of sensibility and that in them alone lies the answer to the inability to believe or to be content in unbelief."

60   MORISON, SAMUEL ELIOT. "The Sea in Literature." <u>Atlantic</u>, 196 (September), 70-71.
      Ranks Melville with Conrad as the best of the nineteenth-century sea novelists, though there "has never been anything like <u>Moby Dick</u> in all sea literature, and there is not likely to be."

61   PARKE, JOHN. "Seven <u>Moby-Dicks</u>." <u>New England Quarterly</u>, 28 (September), 319-338.
      Analyzes the "many-layered theme" of <u>Moby-Dick</u>, focusing mainly on Ahab: the physical adventure; the spiritual adventure of hazardous voyaging; the interaction of husbandmen and nature; the pride and retribution; the nemesis of self-mutilation through the exalting of will at the expense of instinct; the confrontation of chaos; and the chaos of evil, idealism, and madness in the individual. Reprinted in 1960.A6, and Tuten, pp. 15-34.

62   ROPER, GORDON. "Before <u>Moby Dick</u>." <u>University of Chicago Magazine</u>, 48 (October), 4-9.
      The "dramatic story of Toby's reappearance." Reprints 1846.B74, B79, B83.

63   BATTENFELD, DAVID H. "The Source for the Hymn in <u>Moby-Dick</u>." <u>American Literature</u>, 27 (November), 393-396.
      The source for the hymn in chapter 9 is the rhymed version of the first part of Psalm 18 as found in <u>The Psalms and Hymns . . . of the Reformed Protestant Dutch Church in North America</u> (Philadelphia, 1854), pp. 34-35. "The Psalm, however, speaks only of a very generalized situation; Melville's problem therefore was to alter it to fit the specific reference to the story of Jonah." Prints the original and Melville's version side by side and comments on the skill in Melville's changes.

64   CAMPBELL, HARRY MOEDEAN. "The Hanging Scene in Melville's <u>Billy Budd</u>: A Reply to Mr. Giovannini." <u>Modern Language Notes</u>, 70 (November), 497-500.
      Reply to 1955.B65, finding contradictory elements in Giovannini's arguments and citing aspects of <u>Billy Budd</u> supporting an ironical reading of the hanging scene that Giovannini overlooks.

65   GIOVANNINI, G.   "The Hanging Scene in Melville's Billy Budd."
     Modern Language Notes, 70 (November), 491-497.
        Reply to recent scholarship, particularly 1950.B64 and
     1951.B62, which finds irony in the hanging scene.   While the
     religious symbolism in chapter 26 sharply outlines the brutal
     injustice of the handing of Christlike innocence, at the same
     time it should be seen as confirming Vere's judgment that at the
     last Assizes Billy will be saved.   A token of Divine acquittal
     and salvation occurs in the hanging scene: the execution is
     described as marvelous, with the powerful ironic implication that
     it is an execution in name only--the empty gesture of suspending
     a body already dead.   The subtle ridicule of the surgeon in
     chapter 27 supports the idea that Billy dies a painless and
     providential death at the moment before the suspension.   [See
     1955.B64 for reply.]

66   GRDSELOFF, DOROTHEE.   "A Note on the Origin of Fedallah in
     Moby-Dick."   American Literature, 27 (November), 396-403.
        Rejects Mansfield and Vincent's suggestion concerning the
     origin of Fedallah in 1952.B17 and suggests that Melville drew on
     published accounts of the Ismailiya movement for the character of
     Fedallah.   Fedallah would then mean "one who sacrifices himself
     for God" and would symbolize the "destroying angel" sent by God
     to bring about the "assassination" of Ahab, the heretic.   In
     accomplishing his mission, Fedallah offers up his life and thus
     becomes a feda, a "sacrifice" or "ransom."

*67   RICHIE, DONALD.   "Herman Melville."   Study of Current English
     [Tokyo], 10 (November), 33-40.
        Cited in Beebe, Hayford, and Roper, p. 321.

68   BARBAROW, GEORGE.   "Leyda's Melville--A Reconsideration."
     Hudson Review, 7 (Winter), 585-593.
        "Leyda's method [in 1951.A4] imposes a task upon the
     reader: the valuation of particular pieces of evidence, taken
     in conjunction with others.   It goes further than his announced
     intention ('. . . to give each reader the opportunity to be his
     own biographer') and requires that reader to be a critic, not
     only of the Log, but also of the materials that go to make it
     up.   Leyda does not summarize the evidence, he presents it,
     making changes mostly by elision. . . .   It is by contrasts,
     strikingly appropriate to its subject, that the Log proceeds, and
     in them it finds its justification.   The significance of any one
     piece of evidence is found in its difference from those before
     and those after; no detail is absolutely trivial, . . . it is
     only more or less trivial than its fellows, or . . . more or
     less tremendous.   And the Log, feeding on evidence of all sorts,
     exploiting vivid contrasts and discrepancies, one part illuminat-
     ing others and itself being lighted, also gains strength from
     the comparison between what is in its pages and what is not.   The
     rules forbid commentary and more than minimal open guesswork by
     the editor; conversely, they require the reader to make measure-
     ments and estimates concerning holes in the chain of informa-
     tion."   Leyda does not attempt to fill the holes; instead he
     increases them by cutting almost every document.   This deliberate

cutting holds the reader in a state of constant realization that
not everything is here, that there are gaps, as there are in the
original mass of material. The cutting tends to increase awareness of the extent of the lost material, and it emphasizes what
most biography blandly skips or smoothes over: the difficulty of
being certain about a famous man who lived in another age. Nom-
inally chronological, Leyda's arrangement contains deliberately
"misplaced" material. The Log "has turned out to be more than it
was planned to be (a 'simple chronology of events recorded'),
partly because of the useful and wholly defensible expedients of
shaping, cutting, and 'misplacement,' and partly because such
manipulation here brilliantly demonstrates the potential strength
that artifically arranged source materials may have. . . .
Leyda's Melville already appears to be on a sufficiently high
level to be set beside another radical departure undertaken in an
altogether different society and century: Boswell's Johnson."

69　KENDALL, LYLE H., JR. "Ahab's Hat." Melville Society
　　Newsletter, 11 (Winter), n.p.
　　　　Having lost his slouch hat in chapter 130, Ahab appears
only two chapters later wearing the same hat or a similar one.
In drawing attention to Ahab's slouch hat, Melville was perhaps
intending to force a comparison between Ahab and Father Mapple's
Jonah, who "with slouched hat and guilty eye," skulks from his
God (chapter 9). Yet Jonah is not much like Ahab, and Melville
had no intention of creating a latter-day Jonah but rather he
probably wanted to demonstrate men's eternal unwillingness to act
according to the divine plan.

70　O'CONNOR, WILLIAM VAN. "Melville on the Nature of Hope."
　　University of Kansas City Review, 22 (Winter), 123–130.
　　　　Discussion of Pierre, "Cock-A-Doodle-Doo!" "Jimmy Rose,"
"Benito Cereno," and The Confidence-Man. As an American,
Melville "was profoundly interested in the nature of hope as a
human phenomenon."

71　PETRULLO, HELEN B. "The Neurotic Hero of Typee." American
　　Imago, 12 (Winter), 317–323.
　　　　In terms of Otto Rank's concept of birth trauma, the
neurotic hero of Typee regresses to the womb (Typee valley),
where his alternating despair and passive happiness and alternating sympathy for savage and civilized man reflects the "primal
ambivalence of the psychical."

72　HETHERINGTON, HUGH W. "A Tribute to the Late Hiram Melville."
　　Modern Language Quarterly, 16 (December), 325–331.
　　　　Summarizes twenty-five newspaper and magazine items that
"during the last four months of 1891 marked Melville's passing."
The misnomer in the title of 1891.B24 is symptomatic of the state
of knowledge about Melville at the time of his death. Except in
1891.B23, which championed Moby-Dick, Melville was important, if
important at all, because he was the author of Typee.

73   THOMPSON, LAWRANCE. "The Kinship of Mirth and Sorrow." New
     York <u>Times Book Review</u> (25 December), p. 4.
          Review of 1955.A1. Rosenberry's book adds to previous
     scholarship and contains some valuable insights, but does not
     satisfactorily probe and illuminate the difficult problem of the
     deeper relationships between the comic and the tragic in
     Melville's major work.

74   ANON. "A Study of Melville's Comedy." London <u>Times Literary
     Supplement</u>, No. 2809 (30 December), p. 794.
          Review of 1955.A1. Rosenberry's ventures into abstract
     theory, with their inevitable supporting quotations from
     Meredith and Max Eastman, are fortunately brief; the bulk of his
     study is made up of well chosen quotations and a thoroughly
     sensible commentary on Melville and his critics. Rosenberry is
     most interesting when he begins to stretch the conventional con-
     ception of comedy--as one must with a writer like Melville--so
     that it will cover the tortured ambiguities of romantic irony.
     When he raises the larger question of Melville's whole character
     as a writer, Rosenberry's modest critical resources limit his
     usefulness. Until we stop dodging the "immense deal of
     flummery" in Melville or glossing it blandly over, we shall not
     be able to distinguish and describe the greatness his remarkable
     and extravagant perception made possible.

1956 A BOOKS

1   BAIRD, JAMES. <u>Ishmael</u>. Baltimore: The Johns Hopkins Press,
    445 pp. Reprint. New York: Harper and Brothers, 1960.
         A study of "the nature of modern primitivism," influenced
    by the works of Suzanne Langer, Paul Tillich, and Carl Jung. In
    this study, "the mode of feeling which exchanges for traditional
    Christian symbols a new symbolic idiom referring to Oriental
    cultures of both Oceania and Asia is admitted as genuine primi-
    tivism" or "existential primitivism"; most of the authors in-
    volved traveled in the Orient and "derived from direct physical
    experience a medium of feeling to inform the symbols which their
    art presents." In "existential primitivism the journey to the
    Orient is the quest for the material of new symbols to serve the
    need of the Protestant mind," a need created by cultural fail-
    ure--"the loss of a regnant and commanding authority in religious
    symbolism." Melville is viewed as "a supreme example of the
    artistic creator engaged in the act of making new symbols to
    replace the 'lost' symbols of Protestant Christianity" and is
    studied in relation to "the authors of primitivism who were his
    contemporaries and successors [such as Becke, Loti, Stevenson,
    Gauguin, Leconte de Lisle, Rimbaud], with whom he belongs in a
    community of allegiance to a system." After examining expe-
    riences in Melville's Pacific voyages, which became "symbolisti-
    cally authoritative" in his works, Baird studies Melville's major
    Oceanic and Oriental symbols or "avatars"; his images from the

Urwelt, the world before civilization; and his images of cities
(emblems of cultural failure). Indexed. Reviewed in 1956.B57,
B62, B73; 1957.B38, B44, B47, B51, B53, B67, B76; 1958.B20, B52.

2   GOULD, JEAN. Young Mariner Melville. New York: Dodd, Mead
      & Co., 280 pp.
       Biography of Melville for young readers. Reviewed in
1956.B79–80, B87.

1956 B SHORTER WRITINGS

1   BRADLEY, SCULLEY, RICHMOND CROOM BEATTY, and E. HUDSON LONG,
      eds. The American Tradition in Literature. Vol. 1. New
      York: W.W. Norton & Co., pp. 706–709.
       Headnote ("Herman Melville, 1819–1891") to Billy Budd.
Biographical and critical sketch.

2   BROOKS, VAN WYCK and OTTO L. BETTMANN. "The Times of Melville
      and Whitman," in Our Literary Heritage: A Pictorial History
      of the Writer in America. New York: E.P. Dutton & Co.,
      pp. 110–114.
       Biographical and critical sketch. Melville was an instance
of the well-known fact that when artists take to theorizing it is
often because their creative power is gone. The opaqueness of
The Confidence-Man, a laborious satire, resulted from his obvious
inability to draw characters any longer that were vivid enough to
support the burden of thought.

3   BUTLER, JOHN F. "Melville: 'Benito Cereno,'" in Exercises in
      Literary Understanding. Chicago: Scott, Foresman and Co.,
      pp. 22–25.
       Instructor's manual for 1954.B18. Questions and comments
related to point of view in "Benito Cereno."

4   CADY, EDWIN HARRISON, FREDERICK J. HOFFMAN, and ROY HARVEY
      PEARCE. "Herman Melville, 1819–1891" and "Notes on Reading
      Moby-Dick," in The Growth of American Literature: A Critical
      and Historical Survey. Ed. Edwin Harrison Cady, Frederick J.
      Hoffman, and Roy Harvey Pearce. New York: The American Book
      Co., pp. 599–603, 603–606.
       Brief comments on most of the major works. Commentary on
Moby-Dick emphasizes Ishmael's role as narrator, Ahab's attitude
toward the natural world and toward his crew and his whaling
society as the moral center of the novel, and Moby Dick as the
central symbol in the novel. Prints selection of Melville's
poems, his letter of 16[?] April[?] 1851 to Hawthorne (Letters,
pp. 123–125], and "Benito Cereno."

5   CUNLIFFE, MARCUS. "American Literature." The Year's Work in
      English Studies, 1954, 35 (1956), 232–233.
       Review of 1953.A5 and several articles on Melville pub-
lished in 1954. Metcalf's fascinating compilation puts Melville
"into his family circle. Through their eyes, he is a baffling
figure, irritable, excitable, and unreliable." Stewart's article

on the two Moby-Dicks [1954.B26] is an ingenious and important essay. Whether or not one agrees with the minor details of Stewart's thesis, his main argument seems brilliantly convincing.

6   EDEL, LEON. "Introduction," in Henry James: The American
      Essays. New York: Vintage Books, pp. vii–viii.
          Notes gaps in James's treatment of American authors.
"Above all, we experience a deep sense of frustration when we come upon the solitary mention of Herman Melville, a mere name thrown into an enumeration that includes Ik Marvel, in which the novelist recalls his boyhood readings in Putnam's Magazine. [See 1898.B5.] It is here that we inevitably experience the deepest regret: for our literature would cherish a Henry James essay on the author of Moby-Dick. . . . [I]n spite of their dissimilarity, James and Melville alone, among the writers of their day, had glimpsed faraway places and distant horizons and had understood that there were things that could not be measured by an American yardstick. Melville was a cosmopolitan of the spirit; James, more fortunate in his career, was a cosmopolitan of fact. Melville discovered among the Polynesians certain fundamental truths that James discovered among the Europeans. It was inevitable that they would not be understood by their contemporaries, to whom the Atlantic and Pacific seaboards were boundaries enough for a continent just being opened up."

7   GABRIEL, RALPH HENRY. "Melville, Critic of Mid-Nineteenth-
      Century Beliefs," in The Course of American Democratic
      Thought. 2d ed. New York: The Ronald Press Co., pp. 70–79.
          Essentially a new chapter. [See 1940.B6.] In an age of
humanitarian reform that believed increasingly in the moral progress of civilization, Melville did not think that mankind was advancing toward any moral utopia. His suggestion in Mardi that the fate of the Republic might be that of Rome "must be read in the light of the rampant materialism of which the rush to gain wealth in California was momentarily the most conspicuous manifestation" and "must also be read against the background of the power in national councils of the representatives of the section whose economy was built on slavery and who were determined at all costs to preserve the peculiar institution." Melville may have got the first suggestion for what became the symbol basic to his art and thought from the crow's nest of the Acushnet. For the lookout, the horizon circumscribed a circle with no beginning and no end, each sector, each pair of opposite sides being united to and part of all the rest; beyond the horizon lay the unknown, within the circle the malignant sea. Melville was convinced that truth lay partly in the unseen, unknown universe beyond the limits of pedestrian reason. The theme of dualities in unities runs through most of his writings: his "method was to state problems through juxtaposing opposites with the understanding that the opposites were somehow, as part of the same circle, one." If the method did not lead on to attempts to provide systematic answers to the questions raised, it emphasized the complexity of problems of life and conduct. Melville's experience with life impressed on him first of all a sense of the

mysteries of life and of the universe. He was close to the
ethical preoccupations of the age, but for him the search for the
fundamental law ended in mystery. Melville "made no important
impression on the thought of nineteenth-century America. He
rejected the optimistic belief in progress. He insisted that
evil is permanent. Philosophies of security seemed to him illusions. He believed hazard to be the primary condition of life.
He found reality ultimately lost in mystery and seemed almost to
have made acceptance of and wonder at mystery his religion. Even
so, his basic outlook was positive, not negative. He was no
nihilist or futilitarian."

8   GODLEY, JOHN (LORD KILBRAKEN). Living Like a Lord. Boston:
     Houghton Mifflin Co., The Riverside Press, pp. 186-224.
         Account of the author's screenwriting for John Huston's
Moby Dick and of his reading and screen test for the role of
Ishmael in the movie.

9   HEILMAN, ROBERT B. Magic in the Web: Action & Language in
     OTHELLO. Lexington: University of Kentucky Press, pp. 37,
     43, 113, 116, 247-248.
         Similarities between Iago and Claggart, and a difference.
In Iago "Shakespeare has included what Melville has excluded from
the narrower and more schematic Claggart--the dimension of
vulgarity--and he has thus strengthened the impression of the
potency and resourcefulness of the evil agent, whose universality
permits him to operate simultaneously on different levels,
through a flair for sotto voce scheming and an appetite for
clangor."

10   HUGO, HOWARD E. "American Romanticism--Poe, Whitman,
     Hawthorne, and Melville," in World Masterpieces. Vol. 2.
     Ed. Maynard Mack et al. New York: W.W. Norton & Co.,
     pp. 1378-1392.
         Brief comments on Moby-Dick and "Bartleby." The
Confidence-Man, "which bitterly emphasizes the cash nexus as the
sole trust between men, depicts what Bartleby resents in modern
society." Prints "Bartleby" (pp. 1660-1691).

11   KAZIN, ALFRED. "Introduction" and "A Note on the Text," in
     Moby-Dick. Riverside Editions, No. A9. Boston: Houghton
     Mifflin Co., pp . v-xiv, xv.
         The "Introduction" stresses the roles of Ishmael and Ahab
and Melville's portrayal of the struggle between man and nature.
The emphasis on Ishmael's personal vision gives us a new kind of
book. "It is a book which is neither a saga, though it deals in
large natural forces, nor a classical epic, for we feel too
strongly the individual who wrote it. It is a book that is at
once primitive, fatalistic, and merciless, like the very oldest
books, and yet peculiarly personal, like so many twentieth-
century novels, in its significant emphasis on the subjective
individual consciousness." Ishmael suffers from doubt and
uncertainty far more than from homelessness--this agony of disbelief is is homelessness. He is modern man cut off from the

certainty that was once his inner world. While both Ishmael and
Ahab are thinkers, Ishmael has identified his own state with
man's utter unimportance in nature; Ahab, by contrast, actively
seeks the whale in order to assert man's supremacy. Ahab is a
hero of thought who is trying to reassert man's place in nature.
In the struggle between man's effort to find meaning in nature,
and the indifference of nature itself, Melville sees the whale's
view of things far more than he does Ahab's; he speaks for the
whirlwind, for the watery waste, for the sharks. It is this that
gives Moby-Dick its awful and crushing power. Reprinted in
1956.B78; 1959.B19; 1960.A6; Kazin (1961), pp. 112–113; Kazin
(1962), pp. 29–46; Chase (1962), pp. 39–48.

12   KÜHNELT, HARRO H. "The Reception of Herman Melville's Works
      in Germany and Austria." Innsbrucker Beiträge zur Kultur-
      wissenschaft, 4 (No. 2), 111–121.
         Survey of the German and Austrian reception of Melville's
books in the nineteenth and twentieth centuries. Bibliography of
German translations of Melville's works and of books and articles
on Melville in German.

13   LACY, PATRICIA. "The Agatha Theme in Melville's Stories."
      University of Texas Studies in English, 35 (1956), 96–105.
         Melville's interest in Agatha's patience emerges in three
of his stories: Bartleby, Merrymusk, and Hunilla are members of
one family. Bartleby tries to evade necessity by withdrawing from
society. Merrymusk tries to evade necessity by relying on his
own self-sufficiency. Both policies of isolation meet with
tragedy. In Hunilla patience appears in its pure form--as
strength, a natural pride that can subdue the torments of nature
and regulate reaction to circumstance, though it cannot change
the course of fate. The eighth sketch of "The Encantadas" may be
considered the "essential plank in the bridge between the un-
controlled and incomplete philosophical assertion of evil resulting from misdirected good in Pierre and the beautifully controlled acceptance of necessity and of good evolving in evil
circumstances" in Billy Budd.

14   LEVIN, HARRY. Symbolism and Fiction. Charlottesville:
      University of Virginia Press, passim.
         Discusses the problem of the relation between the literal
and symbolic meanings of a literary work and the possibility of
developing criteria and technical means for determining the
relevance, if not the truth, of any given interpretation. Moby-
Dick used as an example. Reprinted in 1957.B21.

15   MILLER, PERRY. The Raven and the Whale: The War of Words and
      Wits in the Era of Poe and Melville. New York: Harcourt,
      Brace and Co., passim. Reprint. Westport, Conn.: The
      Greenwood Press, 1973.
         Examines the influence, both favorable and unfavorable, of
contemporary literary rivalries on Melville's works and their

reception, focusing particularly on Melville's association with
Evert Duyckinck and the Young America movement. Reviewed in
1956.B50, B58, B73; 1957.B55, B69.

16   MILNE, GORDON. George William Curtis & The Genteel Tradition.
      Bloomington: Indiana University Press, pp. 68-69.
          "Bartleby," "The Encantadas," "The Lightning-Rod Man,"
      "The Bell-Tower," "Benito Cereno," and "I and My Chimney" were
      all published in Putnam's Monthly "with Curtis's endorsement upon
      them." Quotes Curtis's remarks on the stories.

17   MONTAGUE, GENE B. "Melville's Battle-Pieces." Studies in
      English, 35 (1956), 106-115.
          Examples of faults in the poems and examples of successful
      passages. Many of the poems are marred by difficulties with
      imagery, lack of unity, faulty diction, tortured rhyme, and
      metrical ingenuousness. The more glaring structural deficiencies
      are often the result of Melville's inability or unwillingness to
      create and maintain a definite image. Battle-Pieces "as a sus-
      tained experiment in a new medium introduces an empirical justi-
      fication of Melville's established beliefs. Submerged in
      violence, Melville had clung to an objectivity which enabled
      him to draw from the war the proof of his fundamental principles,
      principles here based on an understanding of the demands of
      practical necessity and on sympathy for its victims."

18   MYERS, HENRY ALONZO. "Captain Ahab's Discovery: The Tragic
      Meaning of Moby Dick," in Tragedy: A View of Life. Ithaca,
      N.Y.: Cornell University Press, pp. 57-77.
          Reprint of 1942.B11.

19   POULET, GEORGES. "Melville," in Studies in Human Time.
      Trans. Elliott Coleman. Baltimore: The Johns Hopkins Press,
      pp. 337-341.
          Posits ways in which Melvillean characters try to escape a
      sense of predestination. "Just as for Poe, consciousness for
      Melville is never so complete as when it is consciousness not
      only of existence, but also of the ineluctable end of existence.
      The human being recognizes himself in the foreknowledge of a
      future catastrophe which has nevertheless been resolved upon for
      a long time. He recognizes himself to be predestined." It "is
      the greatness of Melville not to have been willing to accept this
      situation [of predestination]. He protests, he appeals a deci-
      sion that he nevertheless knows to be irrevocable. Like Kierke-
      gaard, he is the Job of temporality."

20   PRAZ, MARIO. The Hero in Eclipse in Victorian Fiction.
      London and New York: Oxford University Press, p. 449.
          Shelley, Dickens, and Melville were all captivated by the
      "so-called portrait" of Beatrice Cenci. "Melville, in fact, was
      to be truly haunted by it, as can be seen in the last two books
      of his novel Pierre, and in certain lines of Clarel, where he
      discovers upon the lips of the so-called Beatrice a trembling as

of lustful pleasure in pain, a quiver of algolagnia. To such an
extent were the Romantics able to clothe with their dark imaginings even the most innocent and positively stupid facial expressions."

21   RUDD, MARGARET. Organiz'd Innocence: The Story of Blake's
     Prophetic Books. London: Routledge & Kegan Paul, p. 214.
        Compares Albion in Jerusalem to Hamlet, Ahab, and the hero
     of James's The Beast in the Jungle. Like them he "is so much the
     artist of roundabout self-suicide, that he wills to destroy not
     only himself but all that could conceivably give him pleasure,"
     hating "the low, enjoying power" in himself and in others.

22   SCHRAMM, WILBUR, et al. "Our Greatest Novelist of the Sea--
     Herman Melville (1819-1891)," in Adventures for Americans.
     Ed. Wilbur Schramm et al. Reading Development Program. New
     York: Harcourt Brace and Co., pp. 84-85.
        Biographical sketch, headnote to chapter 135 of Moby-Dick.
     Photographs and captions from John Huston's movie production.

23   TINDALL, WILLIAM YORK. "The Ceremony of Innocence," in Great
     Moral Dilemmas in Literature, Past and Present. Ed. R.M.
     MacIver. New York: Institute for Religious and Social
     Studies, pp. 73-81.
        However different it looks, Billy Budd is not altogether
     different in kind from Moby-Dick, "another structure of digres-
     sion, discourse, action, and image." Billy Budd is "not an essay
     on a moral issue but a form for embodying the feeling and idea of
     thinking about a moral issue, the experience of facing, of choos-
     ing, of being uneasy about one's choice, of trying to know. Not
     a conclusion like a sermon, Billy Budd is a vision of confronting
     what confronts us, of man thinking things out with all the
     attendant confusions and uncertainties. Disorder is a form for
     this and the apparently formless book a formal triumph. To do
     what it does it has to be a fusion of tight-loose, shapeless-
     shaped, irrelevant-precise, suggestive-discursive--a mixture of
     myth, fact, and allusion that has values beyond reference. The
     discursive parts represent our attempts at thinking, while the
     action, images, and allusions represent what we cannot think but
     must approximate. Arrangement of these discordant elements forms
     a picture of a process." It follows that the center of this form
     is neither Vere nor Billy but rather the teller of the story or
     Melville himself, who presents man's feeling in the face of any
     great dilemma. "The effect of this form is moral in the sense
     of enlarging our awareness of human conditions or relationships
     and of improving our sensitivity. In such a form Kierkegaard's
     esthetic, moral, and divine become a single thing." Reprinted
     in Gordon, pp. 719-723; Stafford (1961), pp. 125-131; Springer,
     pp. 70-77; Vincent (1971), pp. 34-40.

24   VIERECK, PETER. Conservatism: From John Adams to Churchill.
      Princeton, N.J.: D. Van Nostrand Co., pp. 102–103.
          Cooper, Hawthorne, Poe, Melville, Henry James, and Faulkner
      cited as examples of "cultural conservatives" in their anti-
      optimism and qualms about external reforms.

25   WALCUTT, CHARLES CHILD. American Literary Naturalism, A
      Divided Stream. Minneapolis: University of Minnesota Press,
      pp. 290–291.
          "The prophetic visions of Shelley, the despair of Manfred,
      the frantic defiance of Ahab, however bitter, magnify a vision
      of man to the superhuman. . . . Man's vision of good and evil
      measures his greatness, for in these romantic terms man thinks
      Himself against the universe. The effect is not very different
      whether like Ahab he defies God, like Hardy denounces him, or
      like Zola and Norris identifies himself, emotionally, with the
      social and natural cataclysm that he portrays in the naturalistic
      novel. The force and scope of such novels express their meanings
      with a roar that drowns out the statements of abstract theory
      that appear in them."

26   WILLIAMS, STANLEY T. "Melville," in Eight American Authors:
      A Review of Research and Criticism. Ed. Floyd Stovall. New
      York: Modern Language Association, pp. 207–270.
          Bibliographical essay on Melville scholarship and criticism
      since the 1920s, with some discussion of earlier writings. Sec-
      tions include "Bibliography and Manuscripts," "Editions, Reprints,
      Selections, Letters, Journals," "Biographies," and "Criticism."

27   WOLFE, THOMAS. The Letters of Thomas Wolfe. Ed. Elizabeth
      Nowell. New York: Charles Scribner's Sons, p. 254.
          Letter to A.S. Frere-Reeves, August 1930: "As to 'Moby
      Dick,' I read that magnificent work for the first time about six
      months ago in America in order to understand something about this
      man Melville that I had been imitating."

28   CAMERON, KENNETH WALTER. "Billy Budd and 'An Execution at
      Sea.'" Emerson Society Quarterly, No. 2 (1st Quarter),
      pp. 13–15.
          "An Execution at Sea. A Sketch," published in The
      Knickerbocker, 8 (March 1836), pp. 285–288, and reprinted in
      other periodicals soon afterwards, may have offered Melville
      suggestions while he was at work on Billy Budd. "The Claggart
      type of character is mentioned in the first paragraph. The
      sketch contains a court-martial. No fear is manifested in the
      man executed. The commodore is described as 'just and firm.'
      There is no movement in the figure at the yardarm. . . .'"

29   MOORMAN, CHARLES. "Melville's Pierre in the City." American
      Literature, 27 (January), 571–577.
          Reply to 1955.B32. Briefly defends the applicability of
      the myth approach to Pierre, arguing that in this work the myth
      is the "process." In response to Kissane's contention that he
      is unable to account for the conclusion of Pierre, Moorman argues

that the second section (books 13–36) deals with Pierre as Fallen
Man. With the departure of Pierre and Isabel for the City,
Melville for the most part abandons the Fall imagery of the first
half of the novel, concentrating instead on Pierre's inability to
cope with the world outside Eden, a world of terrifying ambiguity. In undermining Pierre's every action by examining its
ambiguity, he is denying the validity of a "fortunate fall" in
modern life. For Melville, the Fall can be "fortunate" only in
myth and in the nonpedestrian world of art and symbol. Reprinted
in part in Willett, pp. 55–59.

30 WEIDMAN, JEROME. "Moby Dick: An Appreciation." Holiday, 19
    (February), 50–51, 80, 82, 84, 87–89.
       Mainly plot summary; prints chapter 135.

31 BEACH, JOSEPH WARREN. "Hart Crane and Moby Dick." Western
    Review, (Spring), 183–196.
       Crane's "Voyages" owe much in imagery and phrasing to Moby-
    Dick. The "poetic genius of Crane is brought into higher relief
    by noting how his imagination transformed and glorified the hints
    taken from Melville's brilliant but often meretricious prose."

32 DICKINSON, LEON T. "The 'Speksnyder' in Moby-Dick." Melville
    Society Newsletter, 12 (Spring), n.p.
       The word "speksynder" in chapter 33 of Moby-Dick represents
    a misspelling. The correct form of this Dutch compound is
    speksnyder or speksnijder. If Melville knew the Dutch components,
    as he suggests ("Literally this word means Fat-Cutter"), the
    wrong form in the chapter title and text could be the error of
    his copyist or printer. More likely, however, he was repeating
    the error of one of his chief sources, William Scoresby's An
    Account of the Arctic Regions.

33 GROSS, JOHN J. "Melville, Dostoevsky, and the People."
    Pacific Spectator, 10 (Spring), 160–170.
       Compares Melville's and Dostoevski's attempts to resolve
    the modern conflict between the individual and his community--to
    reconcile the individual will and consciousness with meaningful
    community. Not until he wrote Billy Budd "did Melville achieve
    the sense of a Christ-suffused universe which characterizes the
    answer of Dostoevsky to the problems of a world of ambiguously
    diffused good and evil."

34 [HILLWAY, TYRUS]. "Notes." Melville Society Newsletter, 12
    (Spring), n.p.
       The American Tradition in Literature, vol. 1, [See
    1956.B1] is advertised as containing "the only truly accurate
    edition available anywhere" of Billy Budd.

35 [HILLWAY, TYRUS]. "Notes." Melville Society Newsletter, 12
    (Spring), n.p.
       John Huston, whose film of Moby-Dick was recently completed
    at a cost of some four million dollars, is reported to have de-
    cided at age twenty-one, on first reading the book, that he would
    some day make it into a movie.

36   LARRABEE, STEPHEN A. "Some Translations of Melville."
      Melville Society Newsletter, 12 (Spring), n.p.
          Details of German, Finnish, Swedish, Italian, Serbian,
      Croatian, and Norwegian translations of works by Melville.

37   W[EST], R[AY] B. "An Age of Comedy." Western Review, 20
      (Spring), 178, 254.
          The modern age is predominantly an age of comedy.
      Melville's Ahab represents the last glimmer of the tragic spirit.
      Henry James composed a comedy of manners. "[N]o such American as
      Ahab ever did or ever could exist outside the pages of Moby Dick;
      James's Christopher Newman, Isabel Archer, Lambert Strether, and
      even Milly Theale are recognizable portraits in America's compli-
      cated gallery. They are, indeed, distortions, but their reality
      is undeniable; they are spectators from society who come on stage
      in a way in which Ahab could never be made to appear. Ahab is
      the general American raised to the height of particularity;
      James's Americans are the particular generalized."

38   WOODRESS, JAMES. "American History in the Novel, 1585-1900:
      The Revolution and Early National Periods, 1775-1815."
      Midwest Journal, 8 (Spring-Fall), 386.
          Recommends Israel Potter as a good readable historical
      novel of antebellum vintage, which credibly projects John Paul
      Jones and Benjamin Franklin against a backdrop of intrigue in
      England and France.

39   GILMAN, WILLIAM H. "Book Reviews." American Literature, 28
      (March), 82-93.
          Review of 1955.B14. The manuscripts of the journal are
      probably among the most difficult of modern times. They are also
      among the most interesting, not only for their direct illumina-
      tion of Melville's mind under stress but also for the editorial
      problems they pose. Horsford's most meticulous text will become
      the standard scholarly edition, to which everyone must go who
      wants to know what Melville really confided to his private note-
      books on his journey to Europe and the Levant in 1856-1857. The
      introduction furnishes a thoughtful biographical background,
      which works in new facts uncovered in the study of the journals.
      Thanks to the explanatory notes, the cryptic quality of the jour-
      nal is substantially reduced. The improvements over Weaver's
      haphazard methods are extensive, not the least of them being the
      recovery of Melville's real words. Altogether, the detailed
      improvements over Weaver must run into the hundreds. Most of
      this review is devoted to weaknesses in Horsford's edition--to
      lists of errors and questionable readings in the text and ques-
      tionable editorial practices. But the merits of the book "out-
      number any defects a hundred to one." [See also 1957.B40, B42.]

40   MARX, LEO. "The Machine in the Garden." New England
     Quarterly, 29 (March), 27–42.
         Similarities between Hawthorne's "Ethan Brand" and "The
     Try-Works," chapter 96 in Moby-Dick. In the latter, fire is
     again a means of production, rendering the whale's fat, and also
     the source of alienation. Like Ethan, Ishmael momentarily suc-
     cumbs to the enchantment of fire, and so nearly fulfills Ahab's
     destructive destiny. If the voyage merely reinforces Ahab's
     worship of the power of fire, it provokes in Ishmael a reaffirma-
     tion of the Garden. His rediscovery of a pastoral accommodation
     to the mystery of growth and fertility is vital to his salvation.
     The close identity of the great democratic God and the God of the
     Garden was a central fact of Melville's apocalyptic insight.

41   D'AZEVEDO, WARREN. "Revolt on the San Dominick." Phylon, 17
     (2d Quarter), 129–140.
         Melville'a artistry in "Benito Cereno" substantially
     altered not only the tone of the original narrative [see
     1928.B26] but its entire content and theme. "Within the general
     outlines of a slaveship revolt, provided by Delano's earlier
     account, Melville has managed a profound analysis of the effects
     of slavery and oppression upon the relationships of men. If the
     Spanish captain symbolizes anything. It is the tortured con-
     science of those European whites who rationalized the existence
     of slavery as a necessary or unavoidable evil. If Babo is a
     'personification' of anything [see 1928.B26], it is of the un-
     yielding determination of men to be free. But it is in giving
     us a view of the events and persons through the eyes of the
     American captain, Delano, that Melville wielded his most master-
     ful device and succeeded in refining the intricate theme of his
     tale. . . . With immense skill and irony Delano is made the
     spokesman of the stock evaluations concerning the Negro people
     which were in general usage among the typical Northern whites of
     his day." The strain of humanism in Delano's "intellectual
     make-up, with its preponderant element of paternalism, defines
     him most typically. Being narrow and complacent, his 'humanism'
     actually prevents him from understanding clearly what he sees.
     His ready classification of people, his stock categories for
     behavior and appearances, lead him and the average white reader
     (more or less similarly afflicted) deeper into the enigma rather
     than out of it." Nowhere can the reader detect any condescension
     toward the Negro characters, except in the thoughts of Delano.
     By the end of the story they are intelligent and determined human
     beings fighting their way out of slavery. "Babo stands out as
     one of the great Negro figures created by white authors in Ameri-
     can fiction. Melville wisely did not presume, as did many writ-
     ers, to know a Negro slave's innermost mind or the complex
     structure of his personality. He shows us Babo, instead, through
     the eyes and accounts of the other characters. We learn about
     him by what he does. He is the awesomely brilliant leader of a
     revolt under appalling conditions. He has masterminded a plan
     so exacting that it almost succeeds. He is only sinister to the
     degree that the reader identifies with the characters and
     prejudices of Delano or Cereno. His motive is to free himself

and his companions from slavery and to return to 'any negro country.' His performance in victory and defeat is heroic. . . . His
keen intelligence, Atufal's magnificent dignity, and the compact
unity of all the Negroes on the ship, leaves an impression on the
reader achieved by few white writers even to this day." The theme
of the story, the psychological impact of slavery and revolt upon
Delano and particularly Cereno, is one that had no precedent in
Melville's time, nor has this fact been adequately recognized
since.

42   OSBOURN, R.V. "The White Whale and the Absolute." Essays in
      Criticism, 6 (April), 160–170.
          Examines symbolic passages, notably chapters 1 ("Loomings"),
      23 ("The Lee Shore"), and 42 ("The Whiteness of the Whale"), for
      their philosophical meanings.

43   BEACH, JOSEPH WARREN. "Book Reviews." American Literature,
      28 (May), 250–252.
          Review of Die Typischen Erzählsituationem im Roman, by
      Franz Stanzel (Wien-Stuttgart, 1955). A penetrating and masterly
      account of narrative techniques, though at times Stanzel "seems
      to think the authors of such brilliant books can do no wrong.
      Above all, this impresses one in the case of Moby-Dick, whose
      complicated and often incongruous procedures all impress him as
      marvels of unerring artistry."

*44   HARADA, KEIICHI. "The Theme of Incest in The Sound and the
      Fury and in Pierre." American Literary Review [Tokyo], 14
      (May), 1–7.
          Cited in Beebe, Hayford, and Roper, p. 343.

45   JEFFREY, LLOYD N. "A Concordance to the Biblical Allusions in
      Moby Dick." Bulletin of Bibliography, 21 (May–August),
      223–229.
          Concerned "only with actual echoes of biblical phraseology"
      in Moby-Dick, the concordance "ignores the biblical allegories in
      the novel, except in so far as allegory is sometimes inherent in
      the allusions themselves." It lists only references to the
      books of the King James Bible and the Apocrypha, so does not
      include "indirect biblical allusions or references to non-
      biblical religious writings, ritual, and liturgy." Keyed to
      the Constable and Modern Library editions.

46   MANSFIELD, LUTHER S. "Book Reviews." American Literature, 28
      (May), 239–240.
          Review of 1955.A1. Convinced by Rosenberry's shrewd ob-
      servation and analysis that there is a much larger element of
      the comic than commonly assumed in Melville's books; but takes
      exception to his "virtual assertion that all is comedy up through
      1856, or at least somehow ought to have been comedy, was intended
      to be comedy, so that any artistic failure in Melville's work over
      something like a decade is failure in comprehension of the comic
      spirit or failure in giving form to this comprehension." In
      spite of the brilliance of specific insights, Rosenberry's basic

thesis is as far-fetched and unscholarly as the one developed by
Thompson in 1952.A2. Both books are often penetrating, but cannot be taken on the whole as anything more than provocative. In
Rosenberry's book whatever is not literal becomes comedy, and
poetry is thus lost. Although Rosenberry defines Melville's
ideal as a marriage of the comic and the tragic visions, he
hardly allows the tragic an independent status. Humor here
sometimes seems merely a synonym for a sense of proportion or
artistic control.

47   STERN, MILTON R. "A New Harpoon for the Great White Whale."
      Clearing House, 30 (May), 564-565.
            Suggestions for using John Huston's movie in teaching Moby-
      Dick. The movie is so untrue to the book that the very contrast
      provides insight for the student.

48   STERN, MILTON R. "The Whale and the Minnow: Moby Dick and
      the Movies." College English, 17 (May), 470-473.
            The movie, directed by John Huston, "is a suspenseful
      adventure film, a salty, wet western. But as a rewriting of
      Melville's book, the script loses thematic profundity and unity."
      The movie, nonetheless, can be a valuable aid to "teaching the
      novel."

49   WARD, J.A. "The Function of the Cetological Chapters in
      Moby-Dick." American Literature, 28 (May), 164-183.
            The cetological chapters add variety to the story and pro-
      vide the reader with a necessary body of information. They also
      serve thematic and aesthetic purposes. The intense study of the
      whale is a search for total knowledge. Through his transcenden-
      tal perception of the natural fact of the whale, Melville
      attempts to realize in all its implications and manifestations
      the profound truth of reality itself. "In Ahab's illusory views
      of reality, in the transcendentalist in the masthead, in the
      gathering around the doubloon, and in Ishmael at the tryworks,
      we see the danger of the unrestrained imagination that loses its
      grasp on objective reality; in the cetological chapters, the
      quasi-scientist Ishmael demonstrates the futility of his empiri-
      cal approach to reality." Melville's symbolism, perhaps most
      masterfully handled in "The Whiteness of the Whale" but inter-
      woven throughout the texture of the entire novel, "gives perhaps
      a vaguer and less logical knowledge than does science, but the
      truth that the symbol evokes is, at least in terms of the novel,
      both penetrative to and consistent with the essential truth of
      nature because the symbol and the thing symbolized are insepara-
      ble. Melville's symbolism is a truer knowledge than that of the
      transcendentalist or of Ishmael at the tryworks because it does
      not superimpose meaning on concrete reality, but draws out the
      truth latent in reality."

50   POORE, CHARLES. "Books of the Times." New York <u>Times</u>
        (9 May).
            Review of 1956.B15. "It is often hard to see the great
      trees of Poe and Melville in this book's thickets of ambuscades.
      Yet they stand secure; not many others who took part in the
      blisteringly unkind remarks that passed back and forth rival
      them in the long run."

51   [HILLWAY, TYRUS]. <u>Melville Society Newsletter</u>, 12 (Summer),
        n.p.
            Notes that the Dell Publishing Co. has recently issued in
      its "Movie Classic" series a comic book (No. 717) based on the
      movie <u>Moby Dick</u> and containing photographs of Gregory Peck as
      Ahab.

52   [HILLWAY, TYRUS]. <u>Melville Society Newsletter</u>, 12 (Summer),
        n.p.
            Reports that Gil Wilson has donated to the Melville Society
      two of his original paintings, titled <u>Ahab</u> and <u>Queequeg</u>, and is
      also presenting to the society a full set of colored slides made
      from his illustrations of <u>Moby-Dick</u>.

53   [HILLWAY, TYRUS]. <u>Melville Society Newsletter</u>, 12 (Summer),
        n.p.
            Reports that Frankie Lane sings a "ballad" about Moby Dick
      the White Whale on a recent recording.

54   [HILLWAY, TYRUS[. <u>Melville Society Newsletter</u>, 12 (Summer),
        n.p.
            Notes that the world premiere of John Huston's movie <u>Moby
      Dick</u>, starring Gregory Peck and a rubber whale, will be held at
      New Bedford, Massachusetts, on 27 June 1956.

55   OLIVER, EGBERT S. "Herman Melville's Lightning Rod Man."
        <u>Philadelphia Forum</u>, 35 (June), 4-5, 17.
            In "The Lightning-Rod Man" Melville may have been challeng-
      ing one of the defenders of orthodox Calvinism, the Reverend Mr.
      John Todd, minister of the First Christ Church (Congregational)
      of Pittsfield, Massachusetts. Reprinted in Oliver (1965),
      pp. 71-77.

56   SALE, ARTHUR. "The Glass Ship: A Recurrent Image in
        Melville." <u>Modern Language Quarterly</u>, 17 (June), 118-127.
            The image of the glass ship recurs in various forms--as
      sealed microcosm or enclosure--in Melville's works, reflecting a
      continuous development in his attitude toward life and death.

57   CAHOON, HERBERT. "Too Late for Last Issue." <u>Library Journal</u>,
        81 (15 June), 1616.
            Review of 1956.A1. A thorough, capable examination of the
      influence of the Orient and the South Seas on Western literature
      and a rewarding, careful delineation of interacting influences
      among the authors studied.

58   ALLEN, GAY WILSON. "The Flowering of New York." Saturday
     Review of Literature, 39 (23 June), 23–24.
          Review of 1956.B15. "Although it is well known that
     Melville and Whitman were New Yorkers, and Poe, too, during the
     last years of his brief triumph and pathetic failures, it re-
     mained for a Harvard professor to discover the importance of the
     society in which these men lived and worked, a society which both
     nurtured and flawed their art. . . . [E]ven the numerous
     Melville biographers have inadequately treated the city of his
     nativity, and the Poe biographers have paid still less attention
     to New York in the 1840s."

59   ANON. "White Whale and Woeful Sea." Life, 40 (25 June),
     50–53.
          Color photographs from John Huston's movie Moby Dick. Of
     the three movies of the book, Huston's is far and away the best,
     the only one to come out true Melville. It has all of the book's
     high adventure and some of its mystic overtones.

60   MORISON, SAMUEL ELIOT. "How to Read 'Moby Dick.'" Life, 40
     (25 June), 57–58, 61–62, 67–68.
          A guide for the first-time reader of Moby-Dick, recommend-
     ing chapters to skip and chapters which are "must" reading.

61   HUTCHENS, JOHN K. "Field Report on Mr. Melville's New One."
     New York Herald Tribune Book Review (22 July), p. 2.
          Fictional account of the puzzlement of Melville's contempo-
     raries over Moby-Dick.

62   QUINN, PATRICK F. "The Ishmael Complex." Commonweal, 64
     (3 August), 444–448.
          Review of 1956.A1. By placing Melville in the line of
     modern Ishmaels--self-exiled from civilization, revitalized by
     their experience of primitive life--Baird opens up in a most
     suggestive way the problem of explaining his imaginative vir-
     tuosity, making Melville the more comprehensible and illuminating
     their work through his. Many books and authors are compared and
     discussed in Ishmael, but the best pages are appropriately those
     on Moby-Dick. Baird's demonstration of his theory illuminates
     virtually everything Melville wrote, whether major or minor, in
     prose or in verse.

63   BOHN, WILLIAM E. "Melville's Neglected Masterpiece." New
     Leader, 39 (6 August), 5.
          Brief appreciation of the "greatest work of the literary
     imagination produced on this continent," which "has lain
     neglected and forgotten except for praise and analysis in recent
     years by a select circle of the intelligentsia." Applauds
     Morison's recent article [1956.B60] but would by no means
     encourage the reader to skip chapters 7–9, which are both amusing
     and deeply significant of what is to follow.

64   BARRETT, CLIFTON WALLER. "Contemporary Collectors X: The
      Barrett Collection." Book Collector, 5 (Autumn), 226.
         Details of Melville first editions in the Barrett collec-
      tion, including presentation copies.

65   BEATTY, LILLIAN. "Typee and Blithedale: Rejected Ideal
      Communities." College English, 37 (Autumn), 367–378.
         Finds fundamental reasons why Melville and Hawthorne "did
      not stay in their idealized states of society": (1) both be-
      lieved that man must not alienate himself from society to achieve
      the ideal (and so disagreed with much of transcendentalism, which
      exalted and isolated the individual); (2) both had the Calvin-
      ists' deep sense of evil and thought it folly to try to reform an
      evil world; (3) both believed that intellect should not be glori-
      fied at the expense of the heart.

66   GROSS, JOHN J. "The Writer in America: A Search for
      Community." Queen's Quarterly, 63 (Autumn), 375–391.
         Melville's difficulties in reconciling individualism with
      his need as an artist for a vital relationship with society.
      "With no well-developed tradition of the novel behind him, and
      with abstract concepts of the nature of man and the state,
      products of the Enlightenment, as his only source of American
      political and social tradition, he was forced to create his own
      pattern of man in society, which in turn was derived from arche-
      typal mythical formulations of man and God. A great part of
      Melville's problem as artist was that of attempting a reconcilia-
      tion of the essentially optimistic, non-tragic concept of man
      fostered by American political thought with those recurring pat-
      terns of myth which demonstrate the tragic struggle of man in
      the sacred and profane literature of all the world. As Mel-
      ville's career developed, the contradictions became increasingly
      irreconcilable, and the tragic darkness of Melville's personal
      life deepened." The conflict "we discover in both Hawthorne and
      Melville is that both were struggling to be born, to emerge as
      sentient beings into the only kind of reality that has any mean-
      ing: that reality in which the creative individual seeks to
      recognize his place in nature and his vital relationship to man
      in a social order which counts him a significant unit."

67   [HILLWAY, TYRUS]. "Honorary Members." Melville Society
      Newsletter, 12 (Autumn), n.p.
         Notes that two eminent South American scholars, Dr. Jorge
      Luis Borges and Don Manuel Mujica Lainez, have been elected to
      honorary membership of the Melville Society, upon nomination by
      Luther S. Mansfield.

68   [HILLWAY, TYRUS]. "Notes." Melville Society Newsletter, 12
      (Autumn), n.p.
         Notes a new comic strip version Moby-Dick, divided into
      twenty-eight episodes, appearing in several American newspapers
      in the "Dickie Dare" series by Coulton Waugh.

69   KAPLAN, SIDNEY. "Notes." <u>Melville Society Newsletter</u>, 12
     (Autumn), n.p.
          Reprints 1851.B49.

70   KNOX, G.A. "Communication and Communion in Melville."
     <u>Renascence</u>, 9 (Autumn), 26-31.
          Breakdowns in communication in "Benito Cereno," <u>Billy Budd</u>,
     and particularly in "Bartleby," examined from a Christian per-
     spective. In "Bartleby," communion "is thwarted partly because
     the narrator opens himself only through a charity-supper, à la
     dole, kind of gesture, instead of an all-out faith in <u>Agape</u>."
     Bartleby, "and what he represents spiritually, is the dead let-
     ter, an ineffectual incarnation of the Word, rejected and un-
     realized.

71   STONE, EDWARD. "<u>Moby Dick</u> and Shakespeare." <u>Shakespeare
     Quarterly</u>, 7 (Autumn), 445-448.
          Takes issue with Stewart's claim in 1954.B26 that (1) chap-
     ters 1-15 ("UMD") of <u>Moby-Dick</u> are almost completely free from
     Shakespearean influence, and (2) the reference to "a Scandinavian
     sea-king, or a poetical Pagan Roman" in chapter 16 alludes to
     Hamlet and Brutus (or some other character from Shakespeare's
     Roman plays). Cites echoes of Shakespeare in chapters 1-15;
     argues that "in UMD there was much less reason for borrowing
     (except generally for very incidental effects), because UMD is
     fundamentally a spry, Rabelaisian story closer in spirit to the
     low-life novel of the eighteenth century than to high tragedy;
     whereas when he moved on to the weightier reflections with which
     the later chapters of <u>Moby Dick</u> abound, the 'bold and nervous
     lofty language' of Shakespeare was more appropriate, and by
     nature so striking as to overtower his actually rather frequent
     borrowings in UMD."

72   WINTERS, YVOR. "Problems for the Modern Critic of Litera-
     ture." <u>Hudson Review</u>, 9 (Autumn), 345-346.
          While both "Benito Cereno" and <u>Billy Budd</u> employ the method
     of "undisguised exposition" with great effect, the method is used
     more sparingly but more expertly in the former. <u>Billy Budd</u>
     appears to be the unfinished draft of a great work. "Benito
     Cereno" is the most successfully written of Melville's works and
     deserves careful study for its methods and for the kinds of prose
     it contains.

73   FEIDELSON, CHARLES, JR. "Culture, Religion, and Imagination."
     <u>Yale Review</u>, NS 46 (September), 122-126.
          Review of 1956.A1, B15. Where Miller's subject is the
     contact of literature with the perennial "befuddlement" of mun-
     dane controversy, Baird's is the power of literature to transcend
     the fragmentation of culture, to revalue it, and thereby to
     manifest the spiritual nature of art. Despite Miller's adroit-
     ness and knowledge, one "cannot escape the feeling that Lewis
     Clark and Evert Duyckinck and their followers were very small
     men . . . that personal antagonisms and confused apprehensions
     are not the channel through which a viable literary self-

consciousness primarily develops--above all, that these people had little to teach Melville which he did not already know in a much more fundamental and productive way." Miller's "picture of Melville as a kind of yokel drinking deep of metropolitan sophistication is overdrawn. Surely Melville's method and theme began to take form long before he entered the Duyckinck circle, notably on ships and South Sea islands, and he was rejected by his time because of a pattern of experience related only tangentially to the fumblings of the New York literati." Ishmael has a complexity of argument, a range of allusion and an intellectual care, that give it real distinction. Baird has made a brave attempt to describe the imaginative level on which art and cultural history are intermeshed. But his tone often seems too positive and the argument unduly tendentious for a work based on so widely synthetic, and therefore so tentative, a theory. To establish the distinctive character of "primitivistic" symbolism, Baird dwells with almost scholastic rigidity on categories that for one reason or another fail to make the grade; in the end Melville turns out to be the only purebred specimen of his race. A less rigidly applied scheme would have made for a fuller sense of the historical movement in which Melville belongs: nothing is gained and much is lost by ruling out his entire American context, and an opportunity seems to be missed when Baird ignores the interplay between Melville's primitivism and his anti-primitivism.

74   GIFFORD, GEORGE E., JR. "Melville in Baltimore." Maryland Historical Magazine, 51 (September), 245–246.
      Reprints 1859.B11, B16.

75   HARADA, KEIICHI. "Melville and Puritanism." Studies in English Literature [Tokyo], 32 (October), 1–20.
      Melville's "homely images," his emphasis on the mystical "heart," his life-long search for "the secret of the soul," his "symbolical mind," and his tragic vision reveal his Puritan heritage.

76   KAPLAN, SIDNEY. "Herman Melville and the American National Sin: The Meaning of 'Benito Cereno.'" Journal of Negro History, 41 (October), 311–338.
      Survey of Melville's depiction of the Negro and his problems from Typee to Moby-Dick. In one view it may be seen as an ascending development, beginning conventionally with old Baltimore and Billy Loon and reaching a peak in the heroic symbolic figures of Daggoo and Pip. From another standpoint, looked at as a composite, it is variously tinted with the "corresponding coloring" of its times--with minstrel stereotypes, comic patronization, chauvinist lapses, mystic defeatism. Yet, though he was never an abolitionist, Melville uttered from time to time the most powerfully democratic words of his age on the dignity of the Negro as a part of American life. Scattered through the writings of his first years is "a goodly company" of truthfully portrayed Negroes that is unique prior to Leaves of Grass. Summary of previous criticism of "Benito Cereno." Continued in 1957.B43.

77   PITT, A. STUART. "Moody Ahab and his Heaven-Insulting
     Purpose." Historic Nantucket, 4 (October), 23-27.
          Ahab is guilty of sinful arrogance, he "has gazed so long
     into the hell fires of speculation that he has maddened himself,"
     and his fate "is that of him who dares to meddle with things
     inscrutable."

78   KAZIN, ALFRED. "Ishmael and Ahab." Atlantic, 198 (November),
     81-85.
          Reprints 1956.B11, with minor omissions.

79   H, E.B. "High Adventures in Earlier Times." Chicago Sunday
     Tribune Magazine of Books (11 November).
          Review of 1956.A2. Recommends Gould's book without reser-
     vation. Its full measure of knowledge about Melville can only
     add to the enjoyment of reading his books.

80   ANON. "Significant, Exciting Biographies for Young and Old."
     New York Herald Tribune Books (18 November), p. 12.
          Review of 1956.A2. A splendid biography, an adventure
     story, and a perceptive study of the experiences and feelings
     Melville was later to put into Moby-Dick, Typee, and his other
     works. A valuable book for young people.

81   BIRDSALL, RICHARD D. "Berkshire's Golden Age." American
     Quarterly, 8 (Winter), 329, 342-355.
          Account of Melville's Berkshire years. Melville eventually
     came to feel an attachment for the land in Berkshire surpassing
     any personal attachment there, except for his past friendship
     with Hawthorne. Neither Catherine Sedgwick nor Oliver Wendell
     Holmes nor Samuel Ward ever knew the Berkshire countryside so
     intimately or expressed that knowledge so eloquently as Melville.

82   HEFLIN, WILSON. "Ahab's Leg." Melville Society Newsletter,
     12 (Winter), n.p.
          Quotes from Moby-Dick, chapter 50, which refers to Ahab's
     exact shaping of the "clumsy cleat" in his whaleboat, to support
     the notion that Ahab's right leg was the ivory one (not the left
     one as in the recent movie). Tyrus Hillway adds that in every
     whaleboat he has examined the "clumsy cleat" or "thigh thwart"
     had its depression for the knee placed somewhat left of center,
     a fact that would indicate it was intended to support the har-
     pooner's left leg. [See also 1952.B82.]

83   [HILLWAY, TYRUS]. "Motion Picture and Opera." Melville
     Society Newsletter, 12 (Winter), n.p.
          Reports that Gil Wilson, who has spent the last six months
     of 1956 on a nationwide tour publicizing John Huston's movie
     Moby Dick, has prepared the libretto of an opera, The White
     Whale, for which he hopes to secure a musical score by Dmitri
     Shostakovich. "An invitation extended to the great Russian
     composer has brought a cordial reply, indicating that

Shostakovich is deeply interested in the idea of international cooperation among artists. At the moment, however, he is busily engaged in writing a new symphony for Sweden."

84 [HILLWAY, TYRUS]. "Notes." Melville Society Newsletter, 12 (Winter), n.p.
Notes broadcast of radio version of "Bartleby," titled "The Strange Mr. Bartleby," on the "Favorite Story" program of the ABC network, 25 November 1956. William Conrad was narrator of the story.

85 LEISY, ERNEST E. "Howling Cheese?" Southwest Review, 41 (Winter) 110–111.
Review of 1955.A1. By stressing Melville's sense of humor, Rosenberry's book serves as a corrective of the prevailing view that Melville had an essentially tragic view of life. Rosenberry's conclusion that "the abandonment of comedy meant the abandonment of Melville's true milieu" is overstatement, yet his book is a useful balance in Melville criticism.

86 WEST, RAY B., JR. "Primitivism in Melville." Prairie Schooner, 30 (Winter), 369–385.
One of Melville's most constant subjects was the relation of primitive virtue to modern life. "What were the values and the limitations of primitive innocence? What advantages or disadvantages could be offered by a cultivated Christian society? The answers are implicit in Moby Dick: innocence and evil are closely allied; the tragic hero is vulnerable, in part at least, because he attempts to return to his primitive origins, to see the world singly in terms of instinct and action. In Billy Budd, the problem is turned about: primitive innocence [in Billy] is a regenerative force to quicken the existence and fulfill the forms of a dying society." The seeds of Billy's existence were planted in Typee valley; they developed through all the works that preceded Billy Budd into a final statement of Melville's moral and aesthetic creed. Clarel and Billy Budd are so related in terms of theme that one can draw upon the statements of the poem to elucidate the meanings of the allegorical terms of the novel.

87 SIMPSON, ELAINE. "Jr. Books Appraised." Library Journal, 81 (15 December), 3000.
Review of 1956.A2. The reader of Gould's book gets a feeling for Melville's restlessness and craving for adventure. Book report material for junior high or perhaps even some tenth grade students as an introduction to Melville. Popularity of the movie Moby Dick might influence demand for the book.

1957 A BOOKS

1   SEALTS, MERTON M., JR. <u>Melville as Lecturer</u>. Cambridge,
    Mass.: Harvard University Press, 202 pp. Reprint. Folcroft,
    Pa.: Folcroft Library Editions, 1973.
        Part 1 examines the structure and content of Melville's
    lectures, relates their themes to the prose of the 1850s and to
    the later poetry, traces the course of Melville's three seasons
    as a lecturer, and summarizes and analyses the reviews of the
    lectures. The underlying assumptions of "Statues in Rome" and
    "The South Seas" are strikingly similar. Along with Melville's
    characteristic sympathy for paganism, ancient or modern, is found
    his correlative skepticism about Christianized civilization and
    its supposed "daily progress" toward "intellectual and moral per-
    fection." The two lectures are extensions of his previous social
    criticism; in the years to come he was to hold the same funda-
    mental ideas and attitudes. Notably in <u>Clarel</u> and in <u>Billy Budd</u>
    he once again examined the contrasting values brought into ques-
    tion in the lectures. For the proper study of these later works,
    the journal of 1856-1857 and the lectures of 1857-1860 are the
    indispensable introductions. "Traveling" also demonstrates the
    essential unity of Melville's throught through its recollections
    of his earlier writings and foreshadowing of passages in his
    later work. "Statues in Rome" met with "widely different
    responses in different areas and cities, pleased some listeners
    by what repelled others, and received mixed and even contradic-
    tory reviews from the press"; eastern notices of "The South
    Seas," with one exception, were "uniformly favorable," but those
    in Illinois and Wisconsin were "decidedly mixed." Melville gave
    his lecture on "Traveling" only three times. The state of the
    Lyceum movement in the late 1850s was not auspicious for Mel-
    ville: "Light entertainment and perhaps some utilitarian in-
    struction, but less culture and nothing controversial--these were
    the watchwords of the day" when he "followed Curtis and Holmes to
    the platform." Audiences of 1857 and 1858 would still turn out
    for a glimpse of the author of <u>Typee</u> and <u>Omoo</u>, "but in none of
    his programs did they find sufficient reward either to rejuvenate
    his reputation or to keep him permanently in demand as a
    speaker."
        Part 2 supplies annotated texts of the lectures recon-
    structed from the reviews. An appendix provides a facsimile of
    "Melville's Notebook of Lecture Engagements" and a transcription
    of "Melville's Memoranda of Travel Expenses 1857-58." Indexed.
    Reviewed in 1957.B84; 1958.B33, B48, B56, B58, B69, B81;
    1959.B33, B53.

2   STERN, MILTON R. <u>The Fine Hammered Steel of Herman Melville</u>.
    Urbana: University of Illinois Press, 297 pp.
        Central to Melville's work is his "naturalism," which is
    opposed in many respects to transcendental idealism, and the
    character of the quester, "the individual who makes a philosophi-
    cal voyage, which is symbolized by a physical journey." The
    "totality of the books presents man's search for an informing
    ideal that is more than physical causation. Idealists all, the

characters search for a causality that is more than something
merely external to man's moral sphere." The quest is always
futile: "heroic or pathetic, noble or ludicrous, Melville's
idealists are all finally fools," though they are not always
portrayed unsympathetically. Unlike the transcendentalists,
Melville subordinated ideal to the facts of material history.
He "utilizes the plight of the very pronounced individuals in his
books to achieve a constant formula: idealistic vision results
in personal vision; personal vision results in separation of self
and community; separation results in monomania; monomania results
in a sterilizing and frantic quest for the attainment of vision
according to the dictates of self; the quest results in oblitera-
tion of self and in murder." For Melville, "true identity lies
not in Emerson's suprahistorical self-reliance, but, paradoxically, in a highly individuated identification of self with history." Melville "demands in his naturalism a seer who feels the
compulsion to widen or define the boundaries of action through
historical knowledge rather than through the speculations of
cosmic idealism." Melville stands "at the head of a tradition
that extends (with basic modifications) through Twain, Dreiser,
Hemingway, and Faulkner, in distinction to the transcendental
continuum." Analysis of Typee, Mardi, Pierre, and Billy Budd.
If Melville is to be identified with any of his characters, it
must be with Captain Vere, his one real hero, rather than with
anyone else except Ishmael. Indexed. Reviewed in 1958.B33,
B38, B55, B57-58; 1959.B32, B35, B47; 1960.B43, B87.

1957 B SHORTER WRITINGS

1 BLUESTONE, GEORGE. Novels into Film. Baltimore: The Johns
    Hopkins Press, p. 206.
       In John Huston's movie version of Moby-Dick, the mythic
   element is absent from the sinking of the Pequod because the
   cinema is incapable of rendering it.

2 CHASE, RICHARD. "The Broken Circuit: Romance and the Ameri-
    can Novel." Anchor Review, No. 2. Garden City, N.Y.:
    Doubleday & Co., pp. 205-220.
       Distinctions between the "great tradition" of the English
   novel and the American novel. Hawthorne and Melville mentioned
   passim. Based on chapter 1 in 1957.B4.

3 CHASE, RICHARD H. "Cesare Pavese and the American Novel."
    Studi Americani, 3 (1957), 349, 356, 358-359.
       Pavese sought and found in Melville, particularly in Moby-
   Dick, "some reflection of his own intuitive grasp of the nature
   of story-writing; and thus was able to clarify this intuition
   into some intellectual system of the world as it is." Melville
   provided him with the symbolic expression of those forces he
   himself intuited as behind the apparent world and contributed to
   his understanding of man's loneliness before events.

4   CHASE, RICHARD. "Melville and <u>Moby-Dick</u>," in <u>The American</u>
      <u>Novel and Its Tradition</u>. Garden City, N.Y.: Doubleday & Co.,
      pp. 89-115.
           Melville's imagination originates in his powerful sense of
      the irrationality and contradictoriness of experience. By the
      time he had finished <u>Mardi</u> and <u>White-Jacket</u>, he had gotten hold
      of such truth as was to come to him--the truth "that man lives
      in an insolubly dualistic world, that his profoundest awareness
      does not transcend the perception of his paradoxical situation,
      caught as he is between apparently eternal and autonomous oppo-
      sites such as good and evil, heaven and hell, God and Satan, head
      and heart, spirit and matter." With the exception of some of his
      poems, not until <u>Billy Budd</u>, which dramatizes the conservative
      idea that society must follow a middle way of expediency and
      compromise, does Melville seem to give us a sense of ambiguities
      resolved and irreconcilables reconciled.
           If Ahab is akin to Shakespeare's heroes, he is more so to
      such Hawthorne characters as Chillingworth, yet in taking the
      view that a work of art is not a completed object but an imper-
      fect form that should be left only potentially complete, Melville
      is much closer to Whitman than to Hawthorne. <u>Moby-Dick</u> is a
      hybrid, an epic romance--in one sense a symbolist poem--with
      novelistic, melodramatic, comic, lyrical, and folk elements. It
      is a book about the alienation from life that results from an
      excessive or neurotic self-dependence. The "moral action of
      <u>Moby-Dick</u> is not strictly tragic or Christian. It is an action
      conceived as taking place in a universe of extreme contradic-
      tions. There is death and there is life. Death--spiritual,
      emotional, physical--is the price of self-reliance when it is
      pushed to the point of solipsism where the world has no existence
      apart from the all-sufficient self. Life is to be clung to, if
      only precariously and for the moment, by natural piety and the
      ability to share with others the common vicissitudes of the
      human situation." Melville's mind is comparatively narrow and
      abstract. In this, as in its discoveries of language, appro-
      priation of new subject matters, and opening out ˌof new aesthetic
      experience, <u>Moby-Dick</u> is at once the most startling and the most
      characteristic product of the American imagination. Reviewed in
      1958.B35, B61-63; 1960.B24. Reprinted in Browne and Light,
      pp. 260-272.

5   CUNLIFFE, MARCUS. "American Literature." <u>The Year's Work in</u>
      <u>English Studies, 1955</u>, 36 (1957), 231-232.
           Rosenberry [1955.A1] "develops his theme with an appro-
      priate dexterity and geniality, and he supplies a useful cor-
      rective to Melville scholarship. But it leads him to extend his
      definition of 'comedy' to alarming limits." Foster, who makes
      out an impressive case for serious study of <u>The Confidence-Man</u>
      [1954.B9], provides an opportunity to test his thesis. Horsford
      [1955.B14] has performed a valuable editorial labor, though it
      is possible to query a few of his readings and one or two of his
      editorial principles [<u>see</u> Gilman, 1956.B39].

6   DAVIS, DAVID BRION. <u>Homicide in American Fiction, 1798–1860:</u>
    <u>A Study in Social Values</u>. Ithaca, N.Y.: Cornell University
    Press, pp. 111–112, 214.
       <u>Moby-Dick</u> is the highest point in the American literary
    study of monomania. "It is simple enough to say that Moby-Dick
    represents a father, or God, or Nature, or the Unknowable, but
    Ahab's voyage was not an intellectual quest. The whale was not
    a man nor an idea, but a feeling. Killing the whale was not a
    matter of subduing Nature or of revenge against a castrating
    father. It was the attempted assertion of a wounded self at
    bay." In "the figure of the hesitating mate [Starbuck],
    Melville stated what many other writers at least implied:
    revenge and murder were not determined by reason. Men might
    justify their vengeance with very good reasons, but the origins
    of violence were nonintellectual."

7   DICKINSON, LEON T. <u>English Studies</u>, 38 (Nos. 1–6), 184–187.
       Review of 1952.A2. In spite of Thompson's erudition and
    ingenuity, he gives a misleading interpretation of Melville. To
    represent Melville as one who had settled the religious problem
    for himself with assurance and finality, and whose basic literary
    strategy was to make dupes of his readers is to distort the
    truth, because it rules out ambiguity as the central character-
    istic of Melville's world view. Melville was torn by doubt. At
    times he entertained views of God as hostile as those Thompson
    ascribes to him, but they were not held without misgiving nor
    without challenge by the orthodoxies of his youth. It is the
    tension created by these antithetical forces that vitalizes his
    work.

8   FADIMAN, CLIFTON. "Herman Melville," in <u>Jubilee: One</u>
    <u>Hundred Years of the ATLANTIC</u>. Boston: Little, Brown and
    Co., pp. 309–314.
       Slightly shortened version of 1943.B24.

9   FRIEDRICH, GERHARD. "Postscript to 'Moby Dick,'" in <u>The Map</u>
    <u>Within the Mind</u>. New York: Exposition Press, p. 27.
       Reprints sonnet in 1949.B38.

10 FRYE, NORTHROP. <u>Anatomy of Criticism: Four Essays</u>.
    Princeton: Princeton University Press, pp. 303–314.
       Reprints 1950.B112.

11 GAREY, DORIS B. "Lyric and Dramatic Authors" and "Symbol,"
    in <u>Putting Words in Their Places</u>. Chicago: Scott, Foresman
    and Co., pp. 216–217, 312–314.
       Melville cited as one of those writers who "impress us as
    very distinct types of personalities, with special insights into
    some aspects of human experience and perhaps conspicuous blind-
    ness to other aspects. When we read them, we are always con-
    scious of looking at life through a particular pair of eyes."
    Other writers, such as Shakespeare, "give us the impression of
    somehow escaping the confines of a particular personality and

flowing into a great variety of other personalities." Insofar
as we "role-play" in reading Moby-Dick, "we find ourselves enter-
ing into the role of Melville himself as one powerful and complex
type of human personality—not into the roles of his various
characters as such. In reading Macbeth . . . we are likely to
role-play the central character himself and to forget 'Shakespeare' altogether." Moby Dick is perhaps a symbol for all the
mysterious "evil" in the universe; he may symbolize a diabolical
conception of divinity—a kind of God that man is led to defy.
We cannot be quite sure.

12   GRAHAM, PHILIP. "The Riddle of Melville's Mardi." University
     of Texas Studies in English, 36 (1957), 93-99.
          Melville's "private" outline for Mardi must have been
     "Part 1 (Chaps. I-LXII, to the arrival at Odo), Man's past, his
     development during the prehistoric age; Part II (Chaps. LXIII-
     LXXXII, to the arrival at Serenia), Man's present state, as he
     has recorded it in his institutions; Part III (Chaps. LXXXIII to
     the end), Man's future. The over-all theme is the quest begun
     by Man before the dawn of history, continued through the recorded
     centuries to the present, with the promise that it will continue
     into the future." The "assumption that Melville was working in
     terms of time—past, present, and future—in relation to Man's
     development establishes a harmonious pattern that makes room for
     many of the hitherto puzzling incidents of Mardi. Such an
     assumption provides the book with a unified theme, the develop-
     ment of Man, which now becomes applicable to all its parts."

13   HILLWAY, TYRUS. "Melville, Herman," in Encyclopedia
     Americana. Vol. 18. New York: Americana Corporation,
     p. 611.
          Biographical sketch.

14   HILLWAY, TYRUS. "Moby-Dick," in The Encyclopedia Americana.
     Vol. 19. New York: Americana Corporation, pp. 281-282.
          Moby-Dick is made up of three elements: a fairly full and
     accurate account of American whaling customs in the 1840s and the
     natural history of the sperm whale; an exciting narrative depict-
     ing the hunt for a particular white whale; and a philosophical
     commentary upon human life and fate, which has been variously
     interpreted. "Whatever he symbolizes, Ahab's final failure re-
     veals the tragedy of unconquerable pride. So rich in symbolism
     is the style of the book that every reader can interpret the
     underlying philosophy according to his own prejudices."

15   HILLWAY, TYRUS. "Omoo," in The Encyclopedia Americana.
     Vol. 20. New York: Americana Corporation, pp. 731-732.
          While written primarily for entertainment, Omoo exhibits
     much of Melville's habit of shrewd observation and candid com-
     ment. It is probably closer to reality than Typee and also
     somewhat more mature in its point of view.

16   HILLWAY, TYRUS. "<u>Typee</u>," in <u>The Encyclopedia Americana</u>.
      Vol. 27. New York: Americana Corporation, p. 238.
           Brief summary of the book and its contemporary reception.
      <u>Typee</u> "contains both fact and fiction, considerable ethnological
      information derived from other books, and fanciful descriptions
      of an idyllic but primitive way of life. . . . While the work
      has real anthropological value, modern readers enjoy it chiefly
      for its fascinating narrative and its Rousseauesque descriptions
      of primitive life."

17   LARRABEE, STEPHEN. <u>Hellas Observed: The American Experience
      of Greece, 1775–1865</u>. New York: New York University Press,
      pp. 273–282.
           Summarizes Melville's responses to aspects of Greece in
      <u>Journal of a Visit to Europe and the Levant</u>, "The Archipelago,"
      "The Apparition," "The Parthenon," "Greek Masonry," and book 3 of
      <u>Clarel</u>.

18   LEARY, LEWIS. "Introduction," in <u>His Fifty Years of Exile
      (Israel Potter)</u>. New York: Sagamore Press, pp. vii–xii.
           <u>Israel Potter</u> is an important statement of Melville's
      increasingly critical attitude toward the boisterous young coun-
      try that had so little time for the books he cared most to write.
      It contains some of his most ironic comments on what he describes
      as "the primeval savageness which ever slumbers in human kind."
      It asks the question: "Is civilization a thing distinct, or is
      it an advanced stage of barbarism?" To suggest an answer, he put
      together a tale of adventure in which there is no villain except
      mankind, restless, jealous, ambitious, and dominated by the
      slogan "God helps them that help themselves." Like Carlyle and
      Emerson, Melville searched the foreground of history for great
      figures who might be considered heroes or representative men,
      responsible for the attitudes of his time. He discovered four
      and drew their portraits with perceptive fidelity: Israel, the
      forgotten man, representing thousands of honest, ineffectual
      anonymous men; Benjamin Franklin, representing the level that
      civilization in the United States had reached; John Paul Jones,
      representing what it was in danger of becoming; and Ethan Allen,
      representing what with intelligent craft and strength it might
      develop into.

19   LESSER, SIMON O. <u>Fiction and the Unconscious</u>. Boston:
      Beacon Press, pp. 66, 92, 118, 120, 182.
           <u>Billy Budd</u> cited as the kind of fiction in which the under-
      lying issues are "unusually anxiety-laden" and in which "obtru-
      sive discussion of moral issues seems to be employed quite
      clearly as a façade, designed--how 'deliberately' we cannot say--
      to distract our conscious attention from the work's latent mean-
      ing." <u>Billy Budd</u> incarnates the attitude in which the "ego
      withholds nothing and it asks for nothing, neither for extenua-
      tion of punishment nor even for forgiveness. The superego
      voluntarily gives the ego something it evidently values even more
      than these, understanding and the assurance of continued love."
      Although the relationship between Billy and Vere and the sentence

passed upon Billy "have definite sexual significance, at the deepest level <u>Billy Budd</u> is a legend of reconciliation between an erring son and a stern but loving father figure. No less instinctively than he had recoiled from Claggart's hostile assault, Billy submits to his sentence because he feels that Captain Vere has decreed it in love." Murray's paper on <u>Moby-Dick</u> [1951.B107] encompasses at the same time that it extends most of the more valuable insights of earlier exegeses. "Ahab, in one sense, is not even the whole id. Just as an enraged child may injure himself, he has completed the white whale's work and uprooted Eros from his soul. From one point of view Ahab is aggression run wild, a cancerous growth. But, though in the wrong way, Ahab is attacking the most deadly enemies of happiness and creative fulfillment, and he is seeking to avenge a real and horrible injury." [Cf. Mumford, 1929.A1, and Arvin, 1950.A1.]

20   LEVIN, HARRY. "<u>Don Quixote</u> and <u>Moby-Dick</u>," in <u>Contexts of Criticism</u>. Cambridge, Mass.: Harvard University Press, pp. 97–109.
      Reprints 1947.B8, with minor revision and minus notes.

21   LEVIN, HARRY. "Symbolism and Fiction," in <u>Contexts of Criticism</u>. Cambridge, Mass.: Harvard University Press, pp. 190–207.
      Reprints 1956.B14.

22   McCORMICK, JOHN. <u>Catastrophe and Imagination: An Interpretation of the Recent English and American Novel</u>. London and New York: Longmans, Green and Co., pp. 271–272.
      The "split between satire and allegory" in Melville's mind provided a source of literary energy and also accounts for resounding failures. His frequent failures in structure must be attributed to this split. Like Hawthorne's, his greatest work was allegorical, and like Hawthorne, too, he was uneasily aware of the limitations for a novelist in the method of allegory.

*23 MERCHANT, NORRIS. "The Artist and Society in Melville." <u>Views</u>, 4 (1957), 56–57.
      Cited in Ricks and Adams, p. 264.

24   POCHMANN, HENRY A. "Herman Melville (1819–1891)," in <u>German Culture in America: Philosophical and Literary Influences, 1600–1900</u>. Madison: University of Wisconsin Press, 436–440, 756–760.
      Melville's knowledge of German authors and, in particular, of Kant. "It was inevitable that sooner or later Melville's questions respecting God, immortality, and freedom would lead to the crucial one underlying all problems affecting the Ideas of the Reason, namely, the epistemological one which Kant had considered in his two Critiques. Melville saw that all answers must remain tentative until the validity of the Reason itself is established." The "influence of Kant on Melville is not one of clear-cut concepts or precise propositions, but rather one of Melville's understanding and applying the main or broad

conclusions of the Kantian criticism. His interpretation of
Kant, as voiced by Babbalanja, Taji, Ahab, and Pierre, is that
Kant had marked the boundaries of 'the Empire of Human Knowledge.' Rightly or wrongly interpreted, Kant furnished Melville
with the backbone upon which to build his anatomy of despair."

25   RAHV, PHILIP. "Introduction: The Native Bias," in Literature
      in America: The National Literature in the Light of the
      National Experience. New York: Meridian Books, pp. 13, 17.
          The new voice of D.H. Lawrence heard in the old American
      classics originated in the psychic shift that occurred in the
      movement to the Western hemisphere. Melville was heroic in
      trying to do justice to this displacement, as Lawrence called it,
      but soon suffered a breakdown because he could not sustain the
      pitch of intensity at which he expended himself. There were no
      real novelists in America until the 1880s and 1890s, only pre-
      novelists and romancers, as conspicuously attested by Pierre,
      the one work in which Melville undertook to possess himself of
      the forms of realism developed by his European contemporaries and
      in which he failed dismally.

26   RAHV, PHILIP. "Melville and His Critics," in Image and Idea.
      Norfolk, Conn.: New Directions, pp. 182–187.
          Reprint of 1950.B97.

27   STEGNER, WALLACE and MARY STEGNER. "Introduction," in Great
      American Short Stories. Ed. Wallace Stegner and Mary Stegner.
      New York: Dell Publishing Co., pp. 15–16.
          Melville was "not influential upon the short story habits
      of his own or any other generation." But "Bartleby" provides "a
      solid bridge" between Hawthorne and James.

28   STEWART, RANDALL. "The Vision of Evil in Hawthorne and
      Melville," in The Tragic Vision and the Christian Faith.
      Ed. Nathan A. Scott, Jr. New York: Association Press,
      238–263.
          If Emerson and Whitman are romantics who deny the Fall of
      man, Hawthorne and Melville are "Counter-Romantics"—both were
      orthodox Christians, at least to the extent that they believed
      in Original Sin. Ahab (who is basically similar to Hawthorne's
      Ethan Brand) illustrates man's powers and their misuse: he is
      romantic individualism carried to the last absurd degree. His
      defiance is a manifestation of Original Sin. Paradoxically,
      man's great heroisms and his great crimes spring from the same
      source. In Billy Budd, Billy's stutter is a symbol of Original
      Sin. The story is "a brilliant and moving statement of the
      ultimate Christian wisdom of resignation to God's overruling
      Providence." Revised version in 1958.B22.

29   THOMPSON, MARJORIE. "Reviews." <u>Review of English Studies</u>,
     NS 8, 328–330.
         Review of 1955.A1. With a welcome change of emphasis,
     Rosenberry's book brings out the comic element in Melville's
     genius. Sometimes Rosenberry's original four categories are lost
     sight of in the wealth of examples, so that one has to grope for
     them, and sometimes retrace one's steps, especially in the second
     half of the book; but valuable definitions and interpretations
     can be extracted from the mass of data, despite the need for more
     pointers. The conclusion seems to be that Melville's comedy,
     like all comedy, is a question of values, but his particular
     achievement was the juxtaposition and fusion of these values with
     tragic ones. The most satisfying section of the book is the
     analysis of <u>Moby-Dick</u>. The narrower satire of the later work is
     freshly treated, though the material tends to overwhelm the
     thesis.

30   THOMPSON, W.R. "'The Paradise of Bachelors and the Tartarus
     of Maids': A Reinterpretation." <u>American Quarterly</u>, 9
     (Spring), 34–45.
         The two sketches need equal attention if we are to recog-
     nize this work for what it is, namely the definitive--because
     explicit--expression of Melville's feelings concerning the linked
     civilizations of America and Europe. "The Paradise of Bachelors"
     presents a secularized society that is an emasculated shadow of
     its former self. "The Tartarus of Maids" constitutes Melville's
     most direct indictment of industrialism and his recognition of
     the direction toward which his country was inclining. America
     in its efforts to substitute matter for spirit is a false
     Prometheus. The maids as victims exemplify the harsh disregard
     for human values that characterize the American scene. Both
     civilizations are morally weak. "The Old World suffers from
     inertia; the New World is spiritually stunted. Europe possesses
     spiritual values but is too decrepit to translate them into
     action; America, physically strong and vigorous, rejects all that
     lies beyond its material ken."

31   THURBER, JAMES. <u>The Years With Ross</u>. Boston: Little, Brown
     and Co., p. 77.
         "Ross was unembarrassed by his ignorance of the great
     novels of any country, and one of the indestructible items of
     Rossiana tells how he stuck his head into the checking department
     of the magazine one day to ask, 'Is Moby Dick the whale or the
     man?'"

32   T[RILLING], L[IONEL]. "<u>Moby Dick</u>," in <u>American Panorama:</u>
     <u>Essays by Fifteen American Critics on 350 Books Past and</u>
     <u>Present Which Portray the U.S.A. in its Many Aspects</u>. Ed.
     Eric Larrabee. New York: New York University Press, p. 229.
         <u>Moby-Dick</u> is a story of adventure and should be read as
     one--an awareness of its complex meanings should not be allowed
     to obscure the pleasure of its sheer excitement of quest and
     chase. It is also natural history, a first-rate account of the
     habits of whales; and it is a superb description of the whaling

industry. But its greatness derives from its symbolic representation of man's existence. Most critics agree that Moby Dick
represents the evil of the universe. Whether Ahab's fanatic
desire to destroy him is to be praised or blamed, or both, has
been a matter for debate, and each reader will, and should,
settle the question in his own manner.

33   V[AN] D[OREN], M[ARK]. "Selected Writings of Herman
       Melville," in American Panorama: Essays by Fifteen American
       Critics on 350 Books Past and Present Which Portray the U.S.A.
       in its Many Aspects. Ed. Eric Larrabee. New York: New York
       University Press, p. 230.
           Brief comments on Typee; Billy Budd (one of the most inter-
       esting tales ever to probe the recesses of man's morality); and
       the miscellaneous shorter tales, which tend to bewilder by their
       radical variety.

34   WIMSATT, WILLIAM K., JR. and CLEANTH BROOKS. Literary
       Criticism: A Short History. New York: Alfred A. Knopf,
       pp. 587–588.
           Even more than Emerson, Melville was shaken by a sense of
       crisis in epistemology. "The heroes of Melville's novels are
       all concerned with the problem of knowledge. Each of them asks
       whether we can truly know anything, or whether we are not
       actually caught in a quicksand of our own dreams and imaginative
       projections, a quicksand into which our struggles to reach
       objective truth can only mire us deeper."

35   WOLFE, DON M. The Image of Man in America. Dallas: Southern
       Methodist University Press, pp. 357–359.
           Sees Hemingway's naive image of man as remote from "the
       great tradition" of Hawthorne, Melville, and Dostoevski. "One
       cannot imagine Melville reading Hemingway except with recurrent
       gasps of pain. Though he did not pass through the shocking war
       experiences of Hemingway, Melville was a man hardened by life
       before the mast, accustomed to the sight of incredible cruelties
       and contrasts, such as the flogging of old Ushant in White
       Jacket. The naïveté of Hemingway lies in his inability to por-
       tray a human being of the stature and complexity of Ahab, White
       Jacket, or Lord Jim." To "compare the invincible courage of the
       old man [in The Old Man and the Sea] with the complex heart of
       Captain Ahab is to see in one image Hemingway's limitations as a
       searcher for the nature of man. Ahab also has a fierce courage,
       but Melville places it in perspective, picturing the frenzied
       captain in revealing action among his men, showing us the great
       depths of Ahab's mind, depths in which courage is an element of
       manhood subordinate to his search for life's central meaning."
       Like Hemingway, "Faulkner has also failed, though to a lesser
       degree, in tracing the polarities of human conduct [the wavering
       between cruelty and tenderness, hate and love, and the many
       shadings of these emotions] in the great tradition of Mark Twain,
       Hawthorne, and Melville."

36   WOODRESS, JAMES. "Melville, Herman," in Dissertations in
     American Literature, 1891-1955. Durham, N.C.: Duke Univer-
     sity Press, 31-33.
        Checklist of dissertations on Melville.

37   WRIGHT, LYLE H. "Melville, Herman," in American Fiction,
     1851-1875: A Contribution Toward A Bibliography. San Marino,
     Ca.: The Huntington Library, pp. 228-229.
        Bibliographical entries for The Confidence-Man, Israel
     Potter, Moby-Dick, The Piazza Tales, and Pierre, with selective
     list of libraries owning copies of the editions noted.

38   C[AMERON], K[ENNETH] W[ALTER]. Emerson Society Quarterly,
     No. 6 (1st Quarter), 45.
        Review of 1956.A1. Mainly synopsis. An illuminating and
     challenging book. For Cameron, the "book of the decade."

39   COSTELLOE, M. JOSEPH. "A Whaler's Delight." Queen's Work, 49
     (January), 8-9.
        Review of John Huston's movie Moby Dick. Despite the
     film's many merits and the valiant attempts to remain faithful
     to the spirit of the original, it is somewhat disappointing in
     comparison with the original. The movie really fails in Gregory
     Peck's portrayal of Ahab. Peck has too much of "Honest Abe"
     about him to be able to portray the captain of the Pequod.

40   GILMAN, WILLIAM H. "Melville's Journal of a Voyage to Europe
     and the Levant: A Reply to a Rejoinder." American Literature,
     28 (January), 523-524.
        Reply to 1957.B42. Gilman states the points at which he
     agrees or disagrees with Horsford's rejoinder to 1956.B39.
     Others may make helpful suggestions concerning a handful of prob-
     lematical readings, but Horsford's work is unlikely ever to be
     superseded as the definitive edition of this journal.

41   GOLLIN, RICHARD and RITA GOLLIN. "Justice in an Earlier
     Treatment of the Billy Budd 'Theme.'" American Literature, 28
     (January), 513-515.
        Of the three earlier treatments of the Billy Budd theme
     McElderry cites, in 1955.B43, "Douglas Jerrold's melodrama Black-
     Ey'd Susan (1829) strikes closest to Melville's central concern,
     and contains the most significant structural and verbal paral-
     lels. The play seems to be the source of features usually
     attributed to Melville's unaided imagination [as in 1940.B37 and
     1948.B9]. In Black-Ey'd Susan as in Billy Budd, but not in any
     other parallel yet suggested, a morally innocent sailor is con-
     demned to hang for inadvertently striking his superior, an act
     technically chargeable as mutiny. His judges are forced to up-
     hold the legal code, submitting a higher moral justice to its
     necessary tyranny. The reader is not urged to deplore specific
     legal abuses, as in other Billy Budd parallels, but is rather
     asked to recognize that man cannot attain absolute justice."

42   HORSFORD, HOWARD C. "Melville's <u>Journal of a Voyage to Europe</u>
      <u>and the Levant</u>: A Rejoinder to a Review." <u>American Litera-</u>
      <u>ture</u>, 28 (January), 520–523.
            Rejoinder to 1956.B39. Objects to a few of Gilman's read-
      ings, expresses doubt over others, and concurs with the rest.
      [<u>See</u> 1957.B40 for Gilman's reply.]

43   KAPLAN, SIDNEY. "Herman Melville and the American National
      Sin: The Meaning of 'Benito Cereno.'" <u>Journal of Negro</u>
      <u>History</u>, 42 (January), 11–37.
            Continuation of 1956.B76. The image of Melville as subtle
      abolitionist [<u>see</u> 1950.B79] is a construction of generous wish.
      The final truth Delano learns is that Babo is the embodiment of
      "malign evil," Cereno of goodness maligned. Babo is the baboon,
      ringleader of the Negroes, who are primitives, beasts. The
      imagery connected with Babo and the other Negroes is strictly
      from the bestiary. There are moments of undeniable power in
      "Benito Cereno," but, looked at objectively, the tale seems a
      plummetlike drop from the unconditionally democratic peaks of
      <u>White-Jacket</u> and <u>Moby-Dick</u>--an "artistic sublimation" of notions
      of black primitivism dear to slavery's apologists, a sublimation
      of all that was sleazy, patronizing, backward, and fearful in
      Melville's works that preceded it. Reprinted in part in Runden,
      pp. 167–178, and Gross and Hardy, pp. 135–162.

44   MILLER, PERRY. "Book Reviews." <u>American Literature</u>, 28
      (January), 534–537.
            Review of 1956.A1. One more of those tormented works in
      which a young writer of deep sensitivity projects his passionate
      convictions about life, modern art, and the existential predica-
      ment upon the helpless surrogate known as Herman Melville, con-
      verting him into a quarry of symbols. There is enough of an
      apocalyptic method in Baird's madness to come up with exciting
      insights into Melville's imagery that have eluded even the horde
      of preceding symbolizers. But Baird has used Melville too
      glibly, and so does him the injustice of not recognizing how
      fully heroic, how much more aware of the ramifying implications
      of this posing of the primitive against the civilized, he
      really--and quite simply--was. Melville was a noble, angry,
      exasperated man, but we do him no justice when we turn him into
      so egregious an exception to his time and place that we must
      invent an esoteric vocabulary to obfuscate the real issues of
      his life and art. Whenever Baird approaches a hard or tricky
      point in his reasoning, he abandons the effort to state it him-
      self and falls back on lengthy quotation from Susanne Langer,
      Paul Tillich, Spengler, and especially Jung.

45   ANON. "World's Most Translated Authors (1948–1955)." New
      York <u>Unesco Courier</u>, 10 (February), 8.
            Notes 105 translations of Melville's works in this period
      (347 of Jack London's).

46   KAHN, SHOLOM J.   "Herman Melville in Jerusalem: Excerpts from
     a Journal." Commentary, 23 (February), 167-172.
         Excerpts from Melville's Journal of a Visit to Europe and
the Levant [1955.B14], with brief introduction. Melville's
hurriedly jotted notes and phrases have many of the vivid qualities of his genius. Melville seems to have written Clarel over
a period of some ten years in the great anguish of soul fore-
shadowed in his Journal.

47   PEARCE, ROY HARVEY.   "Reviews." Modern Language Notes, 72
     (February), 141-145.
         Review of 1956.A1. A powerful book and a dedicated one,
its analytical skill suffused with a sense of mission, so that
readers are enlightened and moved even when they are not convinced. We are convinced at the end that a large portion of the
world that Melville made had its origins as much in Polynesia and
the Orient as in his own creativity. But Baird seems convinced
that this is Melville's whole world or primary world—and here it
is somewhat difficult to follow him. He begins with two assumptions he never permits himself to question:(1) that the crisis
of our culture is that of a failure of Christian sacramentalism,
that we suffer from a disintegrative "ego-sickness of the self"
and need a sense of divine community in which the self can find
a new identity; and (2) that Jung has led the way to this
realization, that his psychology furnishes the best means to
moving from critical analysis to the philosophy of religion.
Baird misunderstands, moreover, in his early pages, primitivistic
writers who are not of his kind. There is something static in
his view of Melville—little or no sense of the movement and
growth that are so important a part of Moby-Dick in particular,
a narrative in which something happens to Ishmael, in which he
happens and retrospectively views himself as happening. A
Jungian view of Ishmael's adventure as a heroic rebirth cannot
take its novelistic quality into account. We wonder how it would
be if Baird had approached Moby-Dick as "an enlightened Freudian,
with a concern for the prime experiential quality of the novel,
with a concern for its narrative as something worked through,
with an eye on the Ishmael who is creating a novel in order to
create himself, with a counter-Jungian assumption as to the
potential sufficiency of the ego." Such an approach would have
the virtue of coming at Moby-Dick as a whole, which Baird does
not do, and it would give Melville, as artist, an independent
status that Baird's autotypography of his work does not allow
him. Ishmael is like all books that would change our minds, one
that readers must use with caution, lest it use them.

48   CHITTICK, V.L.O.   "Haliburton Postscript I: Ringtailed
     Yankee." Dalhousie Review, 37 (Spring), 19-20.
         Finds Chases's claim [in 1949.A1] that Melville derived
inspiration for his extravagant style from Haliburton's version
of the comic Yankee "quite unsupported."

49   DALE, T.R. "Melville and Aristotle: The Conclusion of Moby-
      Dick as a Classical Tragedy." Boston University Studies in
      English, 3 (Spring), 45-50.
          The last four chapters of Moby-Dick "constitute a drama in
      narrative form which conforms in all but a few respects to
      Aristotle's principles as presented in the Poetics and which
      exhibits marked similarities to features of Sophocles' trage-
      dies." If Melville "discovered for himself unaided the chief
      structural principles employed by Sophocles and enunciated by
      Aristotle, the chapters constitute a remarkable vindication of
      both Aristotle's Poetics and Melville's dramatic perceptions."
      If he "read a few of Sophocles' plays in translation the wonder
      is hardly less--though of a different kind: that he should learn
      so much from Sophocles, apply it so well, and yet say little or
      nothing about it."

50   KLICKOVIC, SAVA. "Enemies (In Memory of Herman Melville)."
      Melville Society Newsletter, 13 (Spring), n.p.
          Poem.

51   PEARSON, NORMAN HOLMES. "Sacraments and the South Seas."
      Sewanee Review, 65 (Spring), 294-299.
          Review of 1956.A1. A religious document as well as an
      essay in literary history; a thoughtful examination of the nature
      of modern primitivism as an escape from the plight of modern man
      in an ambience of decay. "Yet the situation of Western culture
      cannot with any real validity be simply equated with that of
      Protestant Christianity, nor Protestant Christianity with Chris-
      tianity in a non-denominational sense." Baird "sometimes seems
      causatively to be talking about the decline of the West, some-
      times about the withering of Christianity, and sometimes about
      Protestantism in all its ambiguity. The result is his question-
      able privilege of citing an observation or protest against a
      single manifestation (for example, the curse of the cities) as
      though it were definitive for the whole." Similarly he roams
      "within an at best nebulous definition of the Orient, so that he
      can include not only Oceania, China, and Japan, but also Islam
      and India which constituted the earlier familiar European concept
      of the 'East' as 'Near East.'" That "Melville should have con-
      tinued to find resources in the memories of his earliest voyages
      is no more necessarily surprising than the nostalgia for the
      green countryside where one spent one's youth. What is a little
      disturbing . . . is that Baird should not examine the echoes from
      other and later memories (vicarious experience through reading)
      which must be taken account of, inventoried, and balanced with
      those of Oceania. Shakespeare, Byron, and Milton furnish compo-
      nents of Melville's complex of symbols; so do the Bible, the
      mysteries of Zoroastrianism and Persian Sufism. They are not
      Oceanic. So strongly is their impact felt upon Melville's writ-
      ing, that Baird's book performs a valuable service in demonstrat-
      ing that a certain primitivism, ab origine, was nevertheless a
      component part of the whole literary span. That this primitivism
      was, however, . . . the dominant force for any but the earliest

of his [Melville's] novels remains unproved, simply because Baird
has in general chosen to select and arrange in terms of a projected creed."

52   YAMAYA, SABURO.   "The Stone Image of Melville's Pierre."
     Studies in English Literature [Tokyo], 34 (Spring), 31–57.
        Reads Pierre in the light of passages in Bayle's Dictionary
     citing Brahmin and Buddhist views that to become holy and perfect
     a man must become like "a stone." Stone imagery reveals that by
     the end of the book Pierre finally attains "the saintly, holy
     status of man." Pierre "may be said to be a story of an innocent
     young man maturing through the agony and woe inflicted by this
     world into a stone or a man of perfect holiness."

53   CARPENTER, FREDERIC I.   "Book Reviews." New England
     Quarterly, 30 (March), 113–116.
        Review of 1956.A1. An important book, big in every sense—
     in size, in imaginative scope, and in variety of illustrative
     detail—proposing and developing a major new idea. A book at
     once impressive and bewildering, challenging and disturbing,
     conceiving and describing both "Orientalism" and "primitivism" in
     new ways, and using an essentially new tool of scholarship—the
     symbolic analysis developed by Suzanne Langer and other philoso-
     phers. The very virtues of Ishmael—its originality of subject
     and of method, and its largeness of scope—involve corresponding
     faults. If Baird uses the new methods of symbolic analysis, he
     sometimes ignores the old methods of historical scholarship and
     traditional logic. By limiting both his attention and his sympa-
     thetic understanding to those who have described the East at
     first hand, he has produced an original—but also a narrow and
     somewhat distorted—interpretation of the major cultural phenom-
     enon of modern times. The narrowness is more unfortunate in that
     it is unnecessary: what Baird disparagingly calls "the Orient as
     idea"—in oversimplified terms the idea that "good and evil are
     relative"—is essentially the same as what he praises as "the
     Orient as experience." The important difference between the
     "academic" Orientalists and Melville is not that they failed to
     experience the Orient at first hand, but that they treated it in
     terms of philosophic and poetic mysticism, rather than in terms
     of symbolic action and tragedy. Baird's "Ishmaels" are neither
     so unique nor so isolated as he supposes.

54   DAY, A. GROVE.   "Hawaiian Echoes in Melville's Mardi." Modern
     Language Quarterly, 18 (March), 3–8.
        Allusions to the Hawaiian Islands and Hawaiian customs in
     Mardi, which are surprisingly frequent "if we consider that the
     setting of this novel presents a fictional and allegorical micro-
     cosm, and that none of the action takes place in the Hawaiian
     archipelago." Melville may have drawn on Charles S. Stewart's
     Journal of a Residence in the Sandwich Islands for his Hawaiian
     material, in addition to Ellis's Polynesian Researches. [See
     1937.B25.]

55   THORP, WILLARD. "Book Reviews." <u>American Literature</u>, 29
     (March), 97–98.
          Review of 1956.B15. The book gives sharpened focus to a
     number of literary works: with Miller's assistance we can now
     view "The Literati of New York," <u>Typee</u>, <u>Moby-Dick</u>, <u>Pierre</u>, <u>A</u>
     <u>Fable for Critics</u>, and other lesser works, and the reviews they
     received, as they looked to the partisans in the two camps. The
     record shows that scarcely a review was written in these fifteen
     years without partisan bias; failure to review was often a parti-
     san act as well. Miller also has a number of gleanings that the
     biographers of Poe and Melville had failed to gather, and his
     discussion of the "Young America in Literature" chapter in <u>Pierre</u>
     adds to our knowledge of the relationship between Melville and
     Evert Duyckinck (though the satire may not have offended
     Duyckinck as much as Miller imagines).

56   CRAMER, MAURICE B. "<u>Billy Budd</u> and <u>Billy Budd</u>." <u>Journal of</u>
     <u>General Education</u>, 10 (April), 78–91.
          Text of lecture comparing <u>Billy Budd</u> and the Coxe and
     Chapman play [<u>see</u> 1951.B4] to illustrate formal differences
     between novels and plays.

57   PITZ, HENRY C. "A Painter of Themes--Gil Wilson." <u>American</u>
     <u>Artist</u>, 21 (April), 30–35.
          Discusses Wilson's <u>Moby-Dick</u> paintings and drawings;
     reproduces eleven of them.

58   BRASWELL, WILLIAM. "Melville's <u>Billy Budd</u> as 'An Inside
     Narrative.'" <u>American Literature</u>, 29 (May), 133–146.
          As an inside narrative, <u>Billy Budd</u> reveals Melville telling
     his own story as objectively as he could. In Billy he presents
     the dominant tendencies of his young manhood; in Vere he presents
     in essence the later Melville. "The crucial point in Melville's
     development came when he realized the necessity for curbing the
     wild, rebellious spirit manifested in <u>Moby-Dick</u> and <u>Pierre</u>. The
     fact that the rebelliousness was inspired, in part at least, by
     the highest idealism was no justification for its being tolerated,
     especially since it threatened to destroy his whole being." The
     passing years brought about a change in Melville's attitude
     toward the teachings of Plinlimmon's pamphlet, which are satirized
     in <u>Pierre</u>. In writing <u>Billy Budd</u>, he was sympathetic toward not
     only the Christlike Billy but also toward the philosophical Vere.
     Reprinted in Stafford, pp. 91–103.

59   STEIN, WILLIAM BYSSHE. "Melville's Poetry: Its Symbols of
     Individuation." <u>Literature and Psychology</u>, 7 (May), 21–26.
          Poems in <u>John Marr and Other Sailors</u>--verbal representa-
     tions of intimations of personal disaster that threatened
     Melville inwardly and outwardly--reveal what can only be defined
     as a search for psychic balance. Melville "exorcises the hideous
     demons of his imagination by transforming them into the embodi-
     ments of art, through sublimation achieving a transfiguration of
     fear and insecurity by a denial of the Fates without."

60   WHEELER, OTIS. "Humor in Moby-Dick: Two Problems."
     American Literature, 29 (May), 203-206.
        The two problems are Ishmael's apparently contradictory
statements about the value of laughter and sorrow, respectively,
in chapters 5 and 96, and the shifting of the humorous burden of
the book from Ishmael and Queequeg in the early chapters to Stubb
and Flask after the voyage begins. Both can be explained in
terms of Stewart's thesis of "two Moby-Dicks" [1954.B26]. Partly
by reason of the experiences he undergoes but chiefly by reason
of the necessities of the reconceived novel, Ishmael changes from
a good-humored and predominantly light-hearted protagonist to a
philosophical observer. His contradictory statements, taken with
the uncertain point of view and the shifting concept of Ishmael's
character, may indicate only an imperfect joining of the novels,
resulting from the pressure under which Melville was forced to
work during the winter and spring of 1850-1851, when he was re-
writing the book. Queequeg's original humorous function is precluded by the change in Ishmael, and he fades into the background.

61   ANON. "Adam in America." London Times Literary Supplement,
     No. 2879 (3 May), pp. 265-267.
        Review of 1955.B17. Recapitulates the Adamic figures in
Melville's works.

62   BRUMM, URSULA. "The Figure of Christ in American Literature."
     Partisan Review, 24 (Summer), pp. 405-406, 411-413.
        Notes the "presence of and analogies to Christ" in Moby-
Dick, Pierre, and Billy Budd. Billy Budd "is really the prototype of the Puritan tragic hero: the innocent man encountering
evil 'for which the creator alone is responsible'--because he is
the all-sufficient God of Calvinism. Billy Budd is wholly without that share in human failing which for the Greek hero is a
requirement of his tragic consummation. This is also mainly
true of Pierre. . . . Not only the evil men but also the good
are really the adversaries of the truly innocent; this is a note
already sounded in Billy Budd." It "is outraged and implacable
innocence, converted into cruelty, which creates the perverted
Christ figures of American literature, like the Quaker Nick of
the Woods . . . or the violated Ahab, who baptizes in nomine
diaboli, pursuing evil with a self-destructive, holy madness."

63   CHASE, RICHARD. "The Fate of the Avant-Garde." Partisan
     Review, 24 (Summer), 368.
        In "Hawthorne and His Mosses" Melville is "pleading for
what we should call an avant-garde movement."

64   [HILLWAY, TYRUS]. "Melville First Editions." Melville
     Society Newsletter, 13 (Summer), n.p.
        A standard price list compiled by the editor of the
newsletter, representing prices paid for Melville first editions
within the last five years: Battle-Pieces, $15-20; The
Confidence-Man, $15; Israel Potter, $5-10; Mardi, 2 vols., $20;
Moby-Dick, $150-250; Omoo, $15; The Piazza Tales, $10-20; Pierre,
$15-20; Redburn, $20-25; Typee, 2 vols., $150; Typee, $50;

Typee (London), $15.; White-Jacket, $20; The Whale, 3 vols.
(London), $250; Works, 16 vols. (London, 1922–24), $75.

65   [HILLWAY, TYRUS]. "Queequeg's Mark." Melville Society
      Newsletter, 13 (Summer), n.p.
         Query: what was the "queer round figure" Queequeg used as
his mark in chapter 18 of Moby-Dick, and what, if anything, may
it symbolize? [See 1957.B72.]

66   KAPLAN, SIDNEY. "Explication." Melville Society Newsletter,
      13 (Summer), n.p.
         In the subtitle of Billy Budd, Melville is saying that
"this is no yarn, no salty tale, no 'mere' external narrative,
but 'the inside story' of what really happened. Of course, the
really is the Budd that blooms a variety of flowers. Note how
little of the outside sea is present in Billy Budd (symbolically
or otherwise)--unlike Moby-Dick or Benito Cereno."

67   THORP, WILLARD. "Book Reviews." Western Humanities Review,
      11 (Summer), 287–288.
         Review of 1956.A1. Questions Baird's contention that one
finds in Melville's writing six major symbolic forms that are
manifestations of God, just as six avatars of Vishnu represent
six incarnations of the Hindu Preserver upon the earth. "Why
these six which fit so patly as Hinduistic incarnations? It is
the exclusiveness of the argument which gives one pause. Where
is the rest of Melville as we know him--his turn to Stoicism
after the failure of Pierre and his preoccupation with the problems of the artist in this same period; the strangely healing
effect of his concern for the nation in the time of civil war
and the consequent explorations he made in Battle-Pieces of the
meaning of history?" Baird has shown in great detail--his important contribution--"how the images impressed on Melville's
imagination during his months in the South Seas stayed fresh all
his life and were an immense and continuous resource in his
writing. But must these images, which became autotypes after a
time, invariably be read as Oriental?"

68   SMALLEY, AMOS. "I Killed 'Moby Dick.'" Reader's Digest,
      70 (June), 172–174, 176–178, 180.
         Smalley harpooned and killed a white sperm whale in the
Western Grounds south of the Azores in the summer of 1902.

69   BEARD, JAMES F., JR. "Book Reviews." Pennsylvania Magazine,
      81 (July), 333–334.
         Review of 1956.B15. A delightfully orchestrated, many-
faceted study of Knickerbocker letters in the 1840s and 1850s,
almost Melvillean in conception. Miller rediscovers a fascinating galaxy of minor literary worthies, scrutinizes shrewdly the
impact of cultural forces in the shaping of Melville's art, and
evolves a composite portrait of an era which--he wants to sug-
gest--is significantly analogous to our own. "On a philosophic
level, The Raven and the Whale is concerned with the inter-
relationships between American cultural forces and imaginative

creation. Confusion within a culture may, we are shown, confuse
the greatest artist because he must, almost of necessity, accept
as the terms of his problem the structures his society propounds
to him. If he accepts these structures, he violates his own
integrity. If he accepts them and then rebels, as Melville
rebelled, he almost surely forfeits the audience on which successful artistic communication depends. The process is older
than Melville in American literary history, and it is still
being repeated."

70   THORP, WILLARD. "Book Reviews." <u>Modern Philology</u>, 55
      (August), 70-72.
           Review of 1955.B17. A significant addition to the growing
      number of works that do not merely describe the stages of the
      maturing of American literature between 1820 and 1860 but attempt
      to explain why it grew as it did and what in the end character-
      ized it as distinctively American. The most valuable of the many
      striking concepts Lewis develops is his explanation of the
      typicalness of the heroes of American fiction—lonely men, some-
      times orphaned, outside society and detached from it. In the
      enduring fables of the American Adam, the narrative theme becomes
      that of the solitary hero and his moral engagement with the alien
      tribe. Lewis juggles, however, to produce a palpable Adam on the
      <u>Pequod</u>: when the act is over, we do not know whether we have
      seen Ahab or Ishmael in the role.

71   BEWLEY, MARIUS. "The Cage and the Prairie: Two Notes on
      Symbolism." <u>Hudson Review</u>, 10 (Autumn), 403-405.
           There was "a sufficiently reciprocal relation" between
      Melville "and the extramental world to permit a significant
      symbolic relation between nature and the moods of his mind. But
      symbolist theory has made great strides toward abolishing the
      possibility of such reciprocity. . . . It is able to show us, as
      the ultimate vision, the self-subsistent, self-sufficient Symbol,
      out of relation with anything but its own eternally evolving
      being." This extreme theory of symbolism, exemplified by
      Feidelson in 1953.A1, "denies to the artist the role of inter-
      preting in his art the world in which he lives: or, at any rate,
      the world of his religious, political, and social experience and
      belief. It is pointless to argue with such a theory, for in a
      world where the ground of the symbol is only itself and language
      is autonomous the credentials of any opposing argument are auto-
      matically open to question."

72   [HILLWAY, TYRUS]. "Notes." <u>Melville Society Newsletter</u>, 13
      (Autumn), n.p.
           "Several members have suggested that Queequeg's mark [<u>Moby-
      Dick</u>, chapter 18] may well have been a cross drawn roughly in the
      shape of a figure eight lying on its side. The figure, with one
      loop somewhat larger than the other and with the smaller loop
      flattened at the end, vaguely resembles a whale. Symbolically,
      it could have represented a whale." [<u>See</u> 1957.B65.]

*73   KASEGAWA, KOH. "Moby-Dick: A Tragedy of Madness." Thought
       Currents in English Literature [Tokyo], 30 (Autumn), 63–88.
         Cited in Beebe, Hayford, and Roper, p. 338.

74   NEWMAN, ROBERT G. "An Early Berkshire Appraisal of Moby-
       Dick." American Quarterly, 9 (Fall), 365–366.
         Reprints 1851.B84 in part. Wonders if the editor, A.J.
Aikens, in casually referring to Melville's Moby-Dick, assumed
that his readers knew all about the author or if, like so many
Pittsfield citizens of the time, he was entirely unaware of the
writer's nearby presence and merely copying "filler" from other
newspapers.

75   PECEK, LOUIS G. "Additions to Melville Log." Melville
       Society Newsletter, 13 (Autumn), n.p.
         Quotes from 1855.B14 and 1856.B36.

76   BRUNIUS, TEDDY. "Reviews." The Journal of Aesthetics & Art
       Criticism, 16 (September), 139–140.
         Review of 1956.A1. An excellent collection of essays on
primitivism in literature; particularly Baird's interpretations
of Melville's books are elucidating. There are weaknesses,
however. A "symbol which is used by a primitivist is to be
interpreted according to the situation in which it was used. The
meaning of the symbol will be changed if it will be used in a
situation other than the original. If the interpreter is un-
familiar with the artist's or poet's use of the symbol, then the
interpretation will be rather arbitrary. Baird is very careful
in reconstructing the symbolism of Melville in relation to
Melville's situation. However, he compares this symbolism with
other primitivists' symbolisms. These comparisons are not always
based on a careful reconstruction." Gauguin's primitivism, for
example, is interpreted in a very superficial way and without
taking into account the fine, readily available, source material.
If Baird's comparisons between Melville and Gaugin are to be
taken seriously, he needs to show what Melville and Gauguin had
in common—but he does not engage in this sort of discussion.

77   DOBBYN, DERMOT. "The Birthplace of 'Moby Dick.'" Catholic
       World, 185 (September), 431–435.
         The "birthplace" is the Bible's Third Book of Kings.
Parallels between the story of King Achab and that of Ahab. The
desire of both "was to be free, to be their own masters. Their
consuming pride would not let them submit by one iota to the
demands of God. By doing just the opposite of what is good and
God's law, they thought they would be free. The captain and the
king never learned that freedom resides in doing God's will.
Instead they became slaves, bound to do that which was contrary
to God's wish, bound to sin. At every crossroad they were forced
to choose a hell-bent avenue and avoid the one which would lead
back to God."

78 McDERMOTT, JOHN FRANCIS. "The Spirit of the Times Reviews
Moby-Dick." New England Quarterly, 30 (September), 392–395.
Reprints most of 1851.B80.

79 SEALTS, MERTON M., JR. "The Ghost of Major Melvill." New
England Quarterly, 30 (September), 291–306.
   To Melville, Uncle Thomas Melvill "seemed another
'isolato,' another Ishmael driven into the wilderness, sometimes
presenting himself in the altered guise of a John Marr, a Jimmy
Rose, or a Jack Gentian. All of these roles, moreover, are semi-
autobiographical characterizations as well, through which
Melville himself, in Lewis Mumford's phrase, 'plays with his
possible fate' as man or as author. The aging veteran outliving
his best days, unable to come to terms with an unsympathetic
environment, yet unalterable within 'however it might fare
without'--such was the recurrent character-type suggested to
Melville the writer by the example of his uncle's personality
and career, with which he tended to identify his own." The unfavorable view of the French Revolution in Billy Budd may also
have been influenced by Melville's memories of Major Melvill.
Reprinted in Sealts (1982), pp. 68–77.

80 CAWELTI, JOHN G. "Some Notes on the Structure of The
Confidence-Man." American Literature, 29 (November),
278–288.
   A "structural analysis that appears to illuminate some of
the novel's important themes and the way in which the author
relates them." The "three philosophical interludes [chapters 14,
33, and 44] are of utmost significance to the novel as a whole:
they provide a frame of ambiguity within which the enigmatic
action of the narrative takes place; and they furnish the key to
the structural representation of a dark reality that is, by
definition, past finding out. That key is what we might call the
incomplete reversal: something is presented, a character, an
incident, an idea, anything which might give the reader some clue
to the interpretation of the represented reality; then a counter
incident or idea appears, powerful enough to destroy the usefulness of the first clue, but insufficient to provide a foundation
for a new interpretation of what has been presented. We are left
in the air with no way of resolving two mutually exclusive possi-
bilties." The Confidence-Man is structured around incomplete
reversals at every level--reversals of roles, reversals of ideas,
reversals of the reader's expectations and interpretations. The
first scene, the appearance of the mute, and the Charlie Noble-
Frank Goodman episode demonstrate how carefully Melville has
employed reversal throughout The Confidence-Man. Several idea
reversals take place in the Noble-Goodman scene, the most important centering on the antitheses of confidence-suspicion,
isolation-sociability, love-hate, and philanthropy-misanthropy.
"In Melville's world the philanthropist is bound to be surly and
isolated from other men, for his love of his fellows makes his
expectations too high. Being cut off from society, however, he
is cut off from life. On the other hand, the misanthrope, hating
his fellows, can at least accept them and be sociable. . . . We
sense that Melville, himself, feels that he has passed through

the stage of surly philanthropy and has reached a kind of passive acceptance of things in the role of the genial misanthrope." The Confience-Man is "a serious, carefully planned attempt to present one man's vision of reality. As the vision sees ambiguity at the heart of things, so the basic structural principle is one that leaves the reader alone with an enigma." The confidence-man, enigmatic, ambiguous, inscrutable, and vaguely terrifying, is the paradigm of reality as Melville envisages it.

81   FREIMARCK, VINCENT. "Mainmast as Crucifix in Billy Budd." Modern Language Notes, 72 (November), 496–497.
    To Vere, "it would have been intolerably ironic to hang Billy from the foreyard [the usual place of execution], in the very area of his faithful and outstanding performance of his duties as foretopman. And to Melville, in this story in which many allusions to the Crucifixion have been noted, the cruciform aspect of the mainmast and the mainyard may well have been significant. . . . Further, Melville may have seen in the three masts of H.M.S. Indomitable an intimation of the crosses on Calvary."

82   JAFFÉ, DAVID. "Some Origins of Moby-Dick: New Finds in an Old Source." American Literature, 29 (November), 263–277.
    In Charles Wilkes, Narrative of the U.S. Exploring Expedition . . . 1838–1842, Melville found material for Queequeg's origin, background, appearance, characteristics, manners, beliefs, and customs as well as for most of the adventures and incidents in which he is involved. [See also 1959.B36; 1960.B45.]

83   NOONE, JOHN B., JR. "Billy Budd: Two Concepts of Nature." American Literature, 29 (November), 249–262.
    In Billy Budd, Billy is a Rousseauan primitive, while Claggart is the apotheosis of Rousseau's conception of "civilized" man. Vere is a Hobbesian rationalist. Rousseauan instinctualism, with its vision of primitive innocence, and Hobbesian rationalism, with its vision of a statically ordered society, are shown to be incapable of supplying man with a meaning that can withstand the realities of life as he lives it. Nelson represents an ideal synthesis of instinct and reason in an artificial society.

84   CAHOON, HERBERT. "New Books Appraised." Library Journal, 82 (15 November), 2926–2927.
    Review of 1957.A1. An important contribution to Melville studies.

85   HILLWAY, TYRUS. "Hollywood Hunts the White Whale." Colorado Quarterly, 5 (Winter), 298–305.
    Account of Hillway's role as advisor during the making of the movie Moby Dick, directed by John Huston. Cites flaws in the movie and infidelities to the text.

86   KENNEDY, RICHARD S. "Melville's Use of the Quest Theme in
      'Moby Dick.'" English Record, 8 (Winter), 2-7.
         Discussion of Ahab's quest for and conflict with the powers
of the universe, and Ishmael's quest for self-knowledge and for
answers to the riddle of his universe. Melville possibly intended to place the two quests in equilibrium but did not develop
Ishmael's quest carefully or fully. Nor did he adopt for Ishmael
the classic form of the night journey, a movement through confusion, languor, and despair toward a climactic event that forces
self-knowledge and reorientation. Thus the grandiose proportions
of Ahab dominate the book for us. At the end Moby-Dick leaves us
with all the sense of mingled indignation and pity that the death
of a heroic rebel will bring.

87   MALE, ROY R., JR. Review of The American Adam, by R.W.B.
      Lewis. Books Abroad, 31 (Winter), 82.
         The crucial problems entailed in the heart of Lewis's book
[1955.B17] can be summed up in one question: What kind of
psychological or moral change is possible for the solitary,
detached hero? Lewis cogently maintains that insofar as
Hawthorne and Melville solved this problem we had the first
fulfillment of a genuinely American fiction.

88   LAURENTINA, MOTHER MARIE. "The Humor in 'Moby Dick.'"
      Philippine Studies, 5 (December), 431-442.
         In Moby-Dick "the multiform humor is in the theme (the tall
tale) and in the technique (a folk epic), in the tone and in the
style, in the descriptions and in the characters, in the soliloquies and in the conversations, in the parenthetical expressions
and in the unexpected snappers, in the long digressions and even
in the footnotes." The humor is omnipresent and all-pervading
and "serves many ends: first, to provide relief against the
grim reality of the long, tenuous and strenuous whaling experience; secondly, to place the characters of this American epic
in their true perspective, for the typical American folk spirit
has always been humorous; thirdly, to keep the reader's interest
from lagging and to make the long book not only readable but
enjoyable; fourthly, to expose all there is of the ridiculous,
incongruous and absurd in man, specifically in the man who wants
to attain the stature of a demi-god."

1958 A BOOKS

1   FRIEDRICH, GERHARD. In Pursuit of MOBY-DICK: Melville's
     Image of Man. Wallingford, Pa.: Pendle Hill Pamphlets,
     32 pp.
        Views Moby-Dick in the light of Quakerism, emphasizing the
role of Quakers and their paradoxical behavior. Starbuck's lone
opposition to Ahab is of such enormous importance that Moby-Dick
"may be read as a battle of wits between the Quaker-minded chief
mate and the demoniac captain, with the entire world as the
prize, and Starbuck's--more conclusively than Ahab's--the major

self-divided tragedy." Through Ishmael, Melville reaffirms in
the broadest sense the age-old faith in the possibility of a
society of friends.

2   JARRARD, NORMAN, comp. Melville Studies: A Tentative
     Bibliography. Austin, Tex., 43 pp.
         Chronological checklist (1846-1958). Mimeographed.

3   LEVIN, HARRY. The Power of Blackness: Hawthorne, Poe,
     Melville. New York: Alfred A. Knopf, pp. 165-237, passim.
     Reprint. New York: Vintage Books, 1960; Athens: Ohio
     University Press, 1980.
         In Levin's two-chapter treatment of Melville, "The Avenging
Dream" traces "the thread of blackness" in his works. "The Jonah
Complex" focuses mainly on Moby-Dick, where blackness was
"counterbalanced" by whiteness "in such dazzling radiance that
its successor was bound to be an anticlimax." Melville exempli-
fies the Jonah complex, "the outlook of the reluctant prophet,
brought to recognize his responsibilities, forced to propound
unwelcome truths, and treated without honor by his compatriots
and contemporaries." Reviewed in 1958.B46, B49, B54, B61-63,
B70, B74; 1959.B60; 1960.B9, B24, B95.

1958 B SHORTER WRITINGS

1   AIKEN, CONRAD. The Collected Criticism of Conrad Aiken from
     1916 to the Present: A Reviewer's ABC. New York: Meridian
     Books, pp. 91-92.
         Without question the greatest book that has come out of
New England, and one of the very greatest works of prose fiction
ever written in any language, Moby-Dick "is also the final and
perfect finial to the Puritan's desperate three-century-long
struggle with the problem of evil." The white whale "is the
Puritan's central dream of delight and terror, the all-hating
and all-loving, all-creating and all-destroying implacable god,
whose magnetism none can escape, and who must be faced and fought
with on the frontier of awareness with the last shred of one's
moral courage and one's moral despair." Reprinted in Vincent
(1969), pp. 160-161.

2   ARNOLD, ARMIN. D.H. Lawrence and America. London: The
     Linden Press, pp. 28-29, 80-85.
         Details of Lawrence's reading of Melville, and earlier
versions of Lawrence's essays on Typee, Omoo, and Moby-Dick.
[See 1923.B3-4.]

3   BOOTH, BRADFORD A. "The Novel," in Contemporary Literary
     Scholarship: A Critical Review. Ed. Lewis Leary. New York:
     Appleton-Century-Crofts, p. 270.
         Tindall [1955.B27] "points out that all great novels are
to some extent symbolic, that Dickens, Meredith, Hardy, and
others developed symbols thematically in a way that anticipates
the richness and precision of the technique in the twentieth

century. The first novel to use symbols as extensively and as
integrally as they are used today was Moby Dick. Flaubert, not
knowing Melville, proceeded along the same lines independently in
Madame Bovary."

4   BROOKS, VAN WYCK. The Dream of Arcadia: American Writers and
      Artists in Italy, 1760–1915. New York: E.P. Dutton & Co.,
      pp. 135–136.
      In his lecture "Statuary in Rome," Melville compared the
Laocoön with the locomotive as symbols of two civilizations, the
ancient and the modern (though what lingered in his mind most of
all from the visit to Rome was the portrait of Beatrice Cenci,
described in Pierre, a portrait Hawthorne was obsessed with--vide
The Marble Faun). Melville "seems to have had in mind some such
comparison between the characters of two civilizations as Henry
Adams later suggested in comparing the Virgin and the Dynamo."

5   BROOKS, VAN WYCK. From a Writer's Notebook. New York: E.P.
      Dutton & Co., pp. 74, 101.
      "The infallible way to produce uniformity is to cultivate
individuality, which, in its proper growth, is always a by-
product. The great age of American genius, just before the
Civil War,--certainly not yet equalled in this respect by any
succeeding generation,--was an age of rigid social discipline.
Michelet said that he grew up like a blade of grass between two
paving-stones. So did Thoreau, Emerson and Hawthorne. So did
Emily Dickinson and Winslow Homer. It is true that Poe and
Melville encountered too much incomprehension. The last straw
breaks the camel's back, but at least a certain proportion of
the other straws serve to develop its muscles." In "one of his
letters, Melville praised what he called 'oldageifying youth in
books,' as one of the two great arts that were yet to be discovered, and he tried in Redburn to extract and reproduce the
antiquated style of an obsolete Liverpool guide-book. The
seventeenth-century flavour of many a page of Moby Dick was the
fruit of a taste as consciously cherished and developed as the
taste of certain American painters from William Page to Duveneck
for the so-called 'brown sauce' of the school of Munich. These
painters also wished to achieve the amber patina of age, the
sombre harmonious richness of so many old masters, attempting to
reach this normal effect of the gradual oxidation of the oil by
constantly using bitumen as an undertone and glaze. Melville
used literary bitumen in a similar fashion."

6   CUNLIFFE, MARCUS. "American Literature." The Year's Work in
      English Studies, 1956, 37 (1958), 246.
      Review of 1956.A1. Baird "inflates Melville once more to
larger-than-life proportions. . . . Incidental comments are
frequently acute; yet it is hard not to share the opinion of
other reviewers that this is a curious, congested chop suey of
a book."

7   FADIMAN, CLIFTON. "Introduction," in Typee. New York:
    Bantam Books, pp. xv–xxi.
       It is vain to try to detect the future creator of Moby-Dick
    in Typee. The style is circumlocutory, the movement uncertain,
    the humor arch or heavy. The best one can say for it as an
    adventure yarn (no faint praise) is that it should be ranged a
    few shelves below Robinson Crusoe. But Typee stands as a land-
    mark in the literature of primitive utopias, an eloquent if
    simple presentation of the case against the hypocrisies and
    coercions of civilization. Melville's perception of nobility in
    his savages sprang from the nobility in his own nature, his re-
    fusal, even at age twenty-one, to accept the shibboleths of civ-
    ilization as God-ordained. Reprinted in Fadiman (1962),
    pp. 178–184.

8   FAULKNER, WILLIAM. Writers at Work: The PARIS REVIEW
    Interviews. Ed. Malcolm Cowley. New York: The Viking Press,
    pp. 132, 136–137.
       Brief references to Melville and Moby-Dick. "Writers have
    always drawn, and always will draw, upon the allegories of moral
    consciousness, for the reason that the allegories are matchless--
    the three men in Moby Dick, who represent the trinity of con-
    science: knowing nothing, knowing but not caring, knowing and
    caring. The same trinity is represented in A Fable by the young
    Jewish pilot officer, . . . the old French Quartermaster
    General, . . . and the English battalion runner." The "books I
    read are the ones I knew and loved when I was a young man and
    to which I return as you do to old friends: the Old Testament,
    Dickens, Conrad, Cervantes--Don Quixote. . . . Flaubert,
    Balzac . . . Dostoevski, Tolstoi, Shakespeare. I read Melville
    occasionally. . . . I've read these books so often that I don't
    always begin at page one and read one to the end. I just read
    one scene, or about one character, just as you'd meet and talk
    to a friend for a few minutes. . . . Everybody talked about
    Freud when I lived in New Orleans, but I have never read him.
    Neither did Shakespeare. I doubt if Melville did either, and
    I'm sure Moby Dick didn't."

9   FIEDLER, LESLIE A. "American Literature," in Contemporary
    Literary Scholarship: A Critical Review. Ed. Lewis Leary.
    New York: Appleton-Century-Crofts, pp. 157–185.
       Survey of scholarship in American literature since the
    1920s. Notes "the astonishing richness, the maddening prolixity,
    the contradictory and confused nature" of the literature on
    Melville in general and Moby-Dick in particular. The "essential
    fact" to be recorded is that Melville, especially in Moby-Dick,
    "has come to seem not only for America but for the Western world
    of eminent importance. He is our age's darling; and this has
    meant not only a revision of the earlier estimates of him and
    his work, but a redefinition of the writers around him (Hawthorne
    attracted to his pole, Emerson thought of as opposite to him in
    temper and theme), indeed, of our literature as a whole."
    Melville has come to be regarded as essentially a symbolist

writer. Such a reading has led to a continuing revaluation of
the books around Moby-Dick, "an elevation in importance of works
especially amenable to symbolic analysis (the stories 'Benito
Cereno' and 'Bartleby, the Scrivener'--almost extravagantly Billy
Budd, even, in some cases, The Confidence Man) with the consequent deflation of the early romances like Typee and Omoo, still
excessively admired by D.H. Lawrence." Clarel still awaits a
satisfactory analysis. Brief comments on 1921.A1; 1926.A1;
1929.A1; 1946.B19; 1947.A2; 1949.A1, B14; 1950.A1, B4; 1951.A3-4;
1952.A2; 1954.B9.

10 FLOAN, HOWARD R. "Melville," in The South in Northern Eyes,
    1831-1861. Austin: University of Texas Press, pp. 131-147.
        Melville saw the dilemma of the South as an aspect of man's
    incapacity in an ugly, inhospitable world. Beginning with Mardi,
    he revealed an awareness of the most urgent social problem of his
    day and an ability to rise above regional prejudice in judging
    it. "Melville knew the injustice and inhumanity involved in the
    system of slavery. But unlike the New England writers of his day
    he was not led by this knowledge into distorting criticism of the
    Southerner, for he saw more deeply than they the full tragic
    truth which lay at the base of America's intersectional struggle."

11 FOGLE, RICHARD HARTER. "Billy Budd--Acceptance or Irony."
    Tulane Studies in English, 8 (1958), 107-113.
        Billy Budd is both tragic and ironic. Like Moby-Dick, it
    can be described as Melville's nineteenth-century version of
    classical tragedy. It is not ironic in the sense of a more or
    less complete reversal of the ostensible meaning, with an effect
    of painful mockery. It is ironic in that it often means more--
    not other--than it seems to say. Its ironies and ambiguities are
    Melville's acceptance of the limits of interpretation: they are
    intended neither to confuse nor mock. Reprinted in Gordon,
    pp. 758-761, and Vincent (1971), pp. 41-47.

12 GEHLMANN, JOHN and MARY RIVES BOWMAN. "Herman Melville," in
    Adventures in American Literature. Olympic Edition. Ed. John
    Gehlmann and Mary Rives Bowman. New York: Harcourt, Brace
    and Co., pp. 550-552.
        New biographical sketch and brief commentary on Moby-Dick
    [see 1954.B13], stressing the profundity of its symbolism. Same
    extracts from Moby-Dick.

13 HEWETT-THAYER, HARVEY W. "The Voice of New England; and
    Melville," in American Literature as Viewed in Germany, 1818-
    1861. University of North Carolina Studies in Comparative
    Literature, No. 22. Chapel Hill: University of North
    Carolina Press, pp. 38-39.
        A translation and adaptation of 1849.B59 appeared in the
    Magazin (June-July 1849). By contrast, the Blätter printed only
    a short notice of Typee.

14 HICKS, GRANVILLE. "A Re-Reading of Moby Dick, in Twelve
    Original Essays on Great American Novels. Ed. Charles
    Shapiro. Detroit: Wayne State University Press, pp. 44–68.
        Summary interspersed with interpretation and evaluation.

15 HOLDER, GLENN, et al., eds. Journeys in American Literature.
    An Anthology for Secondary Schools. New York: Globe Book
    Co., pp. 239–240.
        Biographical sketch ("Herman Melville, 1819–1891"). Prints
    adapted extracts from chapters 35 and 36 of Moby-Dick.

16 LAWRENCE, D.H. The Selected Letters of D.H. Lawrence. Ed.
    Diana Trilling. New York: Farrar, Straus and Cudahy, p. 141.
        Letter of 23 August 1916 to Amy Lowell: "Have you still
    got humming birds, as in Crèvecoeur? I like Crèvecoeur's
    'Letters of an American Farmer,' so much. And how splendid
    Hermann Melville's 'Moby Dick' is, & Dana's 'Two Years before
    the Mast.' But your classic American literature, I find to my
    surprise, is older than our English. The tree did not become
    new, which was transplanted. It only ran more swiftly into age,
    impersonal, nonhuman almost. But how good these books are! Is
    the English tree in America almost dead? By the literature, I
    think it is."

17 LEARY, LEWIS. "Studies in American Literature in the United
    States Since World War II." Jahrbuch für Amerikastudien, 3
    (1958), 226–228.
        Survey of Melville scholarship and criticism since 1945.
    "To one who is not professionally a Melvillean, such which passes
    for scholarship in this area seems haphazard and irresponsible.
    Solid factual material put together by men like Leyda, Gilman,
    Davis, Howard, and Willard Thorp . . . seems little to deter or
    greatly to influence the deep diving and high flying of other
    students, many of whom create Melville much in their own image.
    The spectacle is exciting, but the result seems to be that, while
    more is known of Melville, his daily life, his family, and his
    friendships, than ever before, he is only little better under-
    stood than when rediscovered in the 1920s. The fault seems to be
    not so much with Melville as with students who . . . bind them-
    selves too firmly within the fragile strands of his metaphysical
    reachings."

18 LYNN, KENNETH S. "Herman Melville," in The Comic Tradition
    in America. Ed. Kenneth S. Lynn. Garden City, N.Y.:
    Doubleday and Co.; London: Victor Gollancz, pp. 258–261,
    289–290.
        Headnotes to "Cock-A-Doodle-Doo!" and chapter 9 of Israel
    Potter. The gamecock of the wilderness is the most recurrent of
    all American symbols of pride, defiance, and unlimited assertion
    of the self. "Cock-A-Doodle-Doo!" gives evidence, in its refer-
    ence to Beneventano (whom Melville heard on Christmas Eve, 1847)
    that in Moby-Dick Melville drew not only on Shakespeare and epic
    poetry, but also on opera. The "alternation of recitative and

and aria in Italian opera was in some ways a better structural
model for Moby Dick than the drama. For the 'action' of the
Pequod's final cruise is not so much a dramatic development as it
is a sequence of spaced crises, almost all of which involve
Ahab--a sequence of recitatives, one might say, which are punctu-
ated by Ahab's arias. Ahab's great speeches are pure, sheeted
flames of emotion; occasionally startlingly close to the soliloquies of Shakespearean drama, they are more often like the
crowing of a haughty cock, or the singing of a Beneventano; they
have the operatic intensity of Lucia's mad song. . . . Melville
attempted to drive expression to some final reach of emotion
which can be attained only when the voice is lifted to an
operatic pitch--or shrieks with the archangelic fury of an
imperial bird."

19   MORRIS, WRIGHT. "The High Seas: Herman Melville," in The
      Territory Ahead. New York: Harcourt, Brace and Co.,
      pp. 67-77.
      Melville illustrates the tendency of American writers to
prefer the "raw material" of experience to imagination and to
turn in nostalgia away from the present and from society to the
past and solitude, to nature, the woods, the sea, the river.
"The isolation at sea, the prophetic blending of security and
flight, order and freedom, fact and fancy, symbolized the tension, and the metaphysical woods, at the core of Melville's mind.
His thinking began at the beginning, and he attempted to resolve
the unresolved problems, to hew the raw truth out of a world of
discordant facts. This metaphysical agony, generated by the
sea and such a fermenting mind as Shakespeare's, also nourished
and sustained his impulse to be annihilated."

20   O'CONNOR, WILLIAM VAN. "Modern Literary Criticism," in
      Contemporary Literary Scholarship: A Critical Review. Ed.
      Lewis Leary. New York: Appleton-Century-Crofts, pp. 230-231.
      Review of 1956.Al. The correctness of Baird's interpreta-
tions "probably should be left to Melville scholars and to those
who know a good deal about archetypes. Even the general reader,
however, can observe that Melville, like so many other American
writers, was in pursuit of innocence."

21   STERN, MILTON R. "Introduction," in TYPEE and BILLY BUDD.
      New York: E.P. Dutton & Co.; London: J.M. Dent & Sons,
      pp. vi-xxv.
      Melville was indebted to the transcendentalists for their
insistence on imaginative truth and for their new symbolism. But
in opposition to the transcendentalists he concluded that men
must fashion their morality according to human limitations and
actualities rather than according to supernatural and transcendent idealities. Melville's view of the cosmic idealist becomes
a picture of the man who commits the outrageously self-centered
blasphemy of judging all creation according to his own ideal, all
experience by a predetermining assumption. In Moby-Dick
Melville created the greatest single, sustained dramatization of
his case by showing that man murders life when he guides humanity

by his transcendent visions. In <u>Typee</u> he began his opposition to
romantic idealism by taking exception to the romantic concept of
primitive nature and primitive man. In <u>Billy Budd</u> he rested his
case with a final statement about the nature of human necessities. In <u>Typee</u> the "whole scheme of salvation is inverted. To
remain in Typee is to be lost in an impossible dream of non-
existent pure innocence and perfection. To escape from Typee is
to front distress and limitation, but by struggling with them,
to earn the true noble savagery of which man is capable. The
Fall from Grace is the Fall <u>into</u> Eden. The escape from Eden is
the capture of whatever grace man can find, not in his infini-
tude, but in his vulnerability." In <u>Billy Budd</u> "Vere has to make
a choice between the impossible values of ideal goodness, represented by Billy in all their mute, appealing beauty, and the
painful experience of historical necessity, occasioned by
Claggart in all their murderous ugliness. Inevitably he must
choose the latter in order to regulate it. He chooses the latter
knowing that he must reject the vision of transcendent ideality
in order to continue a proper government of the reality." The
"true atheism, against which Vere fights, is the denial of historical necessity in favor of absolute ideals. Yet Melville's
angry irony is directed at the fact that ideals must inform the
administration of necessities."

22   STEWART, RANDALL. <u>American Literature & Christian Doctrine</u>.
      Baton Rouge: Louisiana State University Press, pp. 50–51,
      73–78, 89–102, 106, 148–149.
            Revised version of 1957.B28. Hawthorne, Melville, and
      James are counterromantics "because they recognize Original Sin,
      because they show the conflict between good and evil, because
      they show man's struggle toward redemption, because they drama-
      tize the necessary role of suffering in the purification of the
      self. They do not apotheosize the self, as romantics like
      Emerson and Whitman do, but warn against its perversities, its
      obsessions, its insidious deceptions. They side with the ortho-
      dox, traditional Christian view of man and the world."

23   STONE, GEOFFREY. "Loyalty to the Heart," in <u>American Classics
      Reconsidered: A Christian Appraisal</u>. Ed. Harold C.
      Gardiner, S.J. New York: Charles Scribner's Sons,
      pp. 210–228.
            Discusses the "long conflict of head and heart in
      Melville's works" from a Roman Catholic perspective. "Had
      Melville known another God than the one he found in the pyramids,
      his loyalty to the heart surely would not have had so much rage
      and defiance in it, and his final renunciation of rage might well
      have shown more joy."

24   TILLYARD, E.M.W. "Melville: 'Moby Dick,'" in <u>The Epic
      Strain in the English Novel</u>. London: Chatto & Windus,
      pp. 119–120.
            On the surface, <u>Moby-Dick</u> "might well be the choric expres-
      sion of the world's multitude of men living dangerously and close
      to nature and unencumbered by women. It could even be maintained

that Ahab, among other things, symbolizes the canalisation of
energies and the isolation from the norm of human living that
such a life imposes as its penalty. Nonetheless he is apt to
his context: he may live apart from the rest of his ship's
crew; yet not more than that crew lives from the majority of man
who lead more stable and more variedly social lives. If he
exists apart, to hunt one whale in particular, the men he commands have a vocation as sharply severed from those of the gen-
erality as the miner's vocation underground." But Melville "has
not grasped and realised the choric potentiality. For one thing,
his technique of alternating whale-lore with action ends by grow-
ing monotonous and mechanical. The spinning out, acceptable up
to a point, lowers the pitch, weakens the intensity. We are not
convinced that the author is not inflating his theme, is not
giving it a bulk it cannot properly bear. Then the three ships's
officers are not memorable enough figures to bear a great weight
of meaning. For the book to create the epic effect it was
absolutely necessary that these major characters should cover
between them a large area of the human spirit, and that their
different temperaments should be clearly and cogently displayed.
Only so could the reader acquire the confidence that the author
is qualified to speak for men as well as for himself. It is true
that Starbuck makes a considerable impression and Stubb some.
But Flask makes none at all; he is a superfluity. We have only
to compare Melville's trio with the brothers Karamazov to see
their comparative poverty." Moby-Dick, "though a great book,
remains something of an oddity. It is individual, not choric.
It reflects the spirit of a great and strange man, but it does
not interpret the 'accepted unconscious metaphysic' of a group."

25   VILLIERS, ALAN. Give Me a Ship to Sail. London: Hodder &
     Stoughton, pp. 13-49.
        Difficulties in filming sea scenes in John Huston's movie
     Moby Dick. The choice of ship (a "miss-rigged and ill-balanced
     little brute, product of a non-maritime art department and a
     trawler yard at Hull") and the choice of the Irish sea were
     fatal. [See also 1959.B29.]

26   WAGNER, VERN. "Billy Budd as Moby Dick: An Alternate Read-
     ing," in Studies in Honor of John Wilcox. Ed. A. Dayle
     Wallace and Woodburn O. Ross. Detroit: Wayne State Univer-
     sity Press, pp. 157-174.
        Billy Budd is "cousin-german" to Moby Dick (the similarity
     between the two is "striking"); Claggart is in most respects an
     exaggerated version of Ahab.

*27 YAMAYA, SABURO. "The Inner Struggle in Melville's Pierre."
     Journal of Humanities [Hosei University], 3 (1958), 101-120.
        Cited in Ricks and Adams, p. 396.

28   LOWRY, THOMAS C.F. "Melville's Moby-Dick, XXXI." Explicator,
      16 (January), item 22.
          In Stubb's dream, Ahab turns into a pyramid when Stubb
      kicks him, and the "gross meaning" is unmistakable: Ahab is un-
      movable. The key to the old man whose "stern was stuck full of
      marlinspikes" is contained in the Acts of the Apostles, 9, v:
      "It is hard for thee to kick against the pricks." According to
      Lowry, just as Paul "up to this time had been rebelling against
      Christ, so Stubb has refused to own Ahab's preëminence. Just as
      Paul's vision accomplished his conversion, so Stubb's dream
      accomplishes his."

29   MACSHANE, FRANK. "Conrad on Melville." American Literature,
      29 (January), 463–464.
          In a letter of 15 January 1907 to Humphrey Milford, Conrad
      refused to write a preface for an edition of Moby-Dick that
      Oxford University Press intended to publish: "Years ago I looked
      into Typee and Omoo, but as I didn't find there what I am looking
      for when I open a book I did go no further. Lately I had in my
      hand Moby Dick. It struck me as a rather strained rhapsody with
      whaling for a subject and not a single sincere line in the
      3 vols of it."

30   PHILBRICK, THOMAS L. "Another Source for White-Jacket."
      American Literature, 29 (January), 431–439.
          Discusses Melville's use of William McNally's Evils and
      Abuses in the Naval and Merchant Service, Exposed. His "borrow-
      ings from McNally may be arranged in four categories: supporting
      material consisting of statistics and the citation of authority;
      general accounts of naval practices and customs; suggestions for
      the characterization of Bland, the master-at-arms; and the de-
      tails of the near mutiny which precedes the massacre of the
      beards."

31   ROUDIEZ, LEON S. "Strangers in Melville and Camus." French
      Review, 31 (January), 217–226.
          "Strangers" in Melville's works. Comparisons with Camus.

32   STEVENS, VIRGINIA. "Thomas Wolfe's America." Mainstream, 11
      (January), 24.
          "The criticisms that have been levelled at Wolfe's work are
      not unlike those suffered by Melville of whom it was said that he
      was excessive and inaccurate. . . . Like Melville too he was
      concerned with the immensely varied range of experience, as he
      also affirms Melville's feeling that the deepest need for
      rapaciously individualistic America was a radical affirmation
      of the heart."

33   ALLEN, GAY WILSON. "Pioneer of Naturalism." Saturday Review,
      41 (11 January), 18–19.
          Review of 1957.A1-2. Stern's book will be debated for a
      long time, but it makes an intelligent, and often illuminating
      contribution to the growing library of Melville studies. Sealts
      unexpectedly adds some details for the testing of Stern's

interpretation. (Melville's lecture on "Statues in Rome" revealed an unmistakable "affection for heathenism," according to one reviewer.) Sealts documents Melville's failure as lecturer and reveals the depth and seriousness of Melville's disapproval of his world.

34   BABCOCK, C. MERTON. "Explication: Zadockprattsville." Melville Society Newsletter, 14 (Spring), n.p.
      Zadock Pratt was a folk tale mountaineer of the Catskill region of New York, noted not only for his exploits but even more for his willingness to appreciate his own superior talents. "When one remembers that Zadockprattsville is the headquarters for Braggadocio Incorporated, he gets a slightly clearer picture of Melville's true valuation of the literary people of his day." [See Pierre, book 17, chapter 2, for an invitation for Pierre to lecture at Zadockprattsville.]

35   ELLIOTT, GEORGE P. "They're Dead But They Won't Lie Down." Hudson Review, 11 (Spring), 134.
      Review of 1957.B4. Chase's use of myth-criticism in his discussion of Moby-Dick is pertinent and just.

36   [HILLWAY, TYRUS]. "Melville in Japan." Melville Society Newsletter, 14 (Spring), n.p.
      Notes several translations of Melville's works into Japanese since the war and recent articles on Melville in Japanese periodicals.

37   [HILLWAY, TYRUS]. "Notes." Melville Society Newsletter, 14 (Spring), n.p.
      The Unesco Courier for February 1957 reports a total of 105 different translations of Melville's works into various foreign languages. (Translations of Jack London numbered 347.)

38   REDDING, SAUNDERS. "Brief Comments." American Scholar, 27 (Spring), 264, 266.
      Review of 1957.A2. Stern's thesis is not new (generally speaking, it is accepted by most present-day Melville scholars), but some of his formulations are--and they reveal some refreshing critical insights. Stern's prose carries without noticeable strain a rather heavy burden of scholarly paraphernalia.

39   SEALTS, MERTON M., JR. "Melville's Burgundy Club Sketches," Harvard Library Bulletin, 12 (Spring), 253-267.
      Analyzes and dates stages in the composition of the Burgundy Club sketches and discusses the "content" of the sketches, which, though "of no great significance in itself," helps "to suggest the nature of Melville's detachment from the American scene during intervals of his 'silent years' after the Civil War, when under the negative influence of an uncongenial environment his subject matter became increasingly retrospective, his characters developed the traits of friends of his past and turned into idealizations of values not found in his own life, and his settings remained distant in place and time from

nineteenth-century New York." For fully rounded interpretation
the sketches must be read in context with their companion poems
and with <u>Clarel</u> and <u>Billy Budd</u>. Reprinted in Sealts (1982),
pp. 78-90.

40   HENNESSY, HELEN. "The <u>Dial</u>: Its Poetry and Poetic Criti-
        cism." <u>New England Quarterly</u>, 31 (March), 70-72.
        Notes Melville's satire of the transcendentalist doctrine
of poetic inspiration and the transcendentalist worship of solitude in <u>Mardi</u>. It was unkind of Melville (in "Hawthorne and His
Mosses") to accuse the transcendentalists of literary flunkeyism
toward England. "Europe, far more than America, was wife to
their creating thought simply because they were products of
European ideas transplanted to another land. Loneliness is a
constant theme in the <u>Dial</u>, and the philosophic justification
given loneliness by the new German thought made the expression
of that isolation no less poignant."

41   MILLER, JAMES E., JR. "<u>Billy Budd</u>: The Catastrophe of
        Innocence." <u>Modern Language Notes</u>, 73 (March), 168-176.
        The portrait of Billy completes Melville's gallery of
Titanic "masked" Innocents—Taji, Ahab, Pierre, Mortmain—all of
whom suffer from some intricate disorder that renders them ultimately nonhuman. Billy is "the subtly masked man of innocence,
appearing in the cloak of Christ's purity to the world and to
himself while in reality harboring the savage impulse of the
barbarian, the child, the animal." Claggart is the deceitfully
masked man, deliberately misleading the world as to his true evil
nature. Vere is Melville's maskless man of forthrightness and
frankness, who by his balance of reason and emotion "recognizes
evil and its inevitability on earth, comes to honorable terms
with it, and endures, albeit with a heightened tragic vision."
Reprinted with some revision in Miller (1962), pp. 218-228.

42   STEIN, WILLIAM BYSSHE. "The Old Man and the Triple Goddess:
        Melville's "The Haglets.'" <u>ELH</u>, 25 (March), 43-59.
        Analysis of Melville's revision of "The Admiral of the
White" into "The Haglets." "Contradicting the major premise of
'The Admiral of the White' in its original version, Melville
celebrates the transfiguration of the malignant force of fate.
Without any reservations he accepts his role in nature, harmoniz-
ing his thought to the eternal cycle of birth, life, and death."
Fate "is no longer an inscrutable force of evil or a divine
retributive agency. Instead it is the sacred law of nature which
is administered through the intercession of the Great Mother in
her role of Triple Goddess, at once creator, preserver, and
destroyer."

43   TAGLIABUE, JOHN. "After Reading the Last Pages of <u>Moby-Dick</u>."
        <u>College English</u>, 19 (March), 241.
        Poem.

44 PETERS, ROBERT L. "Melville's Moby Dick." Explicator, 16
(April), item 44.
Bulkington should rightly be compared with, not contrasted
to, Ahab. Both men, with a consuming, Thoreaulike self-reliance,
strive to chart and to pursue "mortally intolerable truth."
Melville's analysis of Bulkington is like the early introduction
of a major symphonic theme or of a leitmotiv.

45 YATES, NORRIS. "An Instance of Parallel Imagery in Hawthorne,
Melville, and Frost." Philological Quarterly, 36 (April),
276-280.
An abandoned woodpile, stacked many years ago, is used in
The Blithedale Romance (chapter 24), in Israel Potter (chapter
26) and in Frost's "The Woodpile." "In The Blithedale Romance
the woodpile represents toil wasted in the pursuit of false
social as well as personal ideals; in Israel Potter it seems to
indicate a life arrested by the blows of fate rather than by a
warped personality or a mistaken good intent to reform the un-
reformable. Melville's theme in this, his blackest book, is that
a cosmic malignancy seems to be persecuting man with satanic
cunning. War, commercialism, and the unjust class structure of
English society, ostensibly the forces which crush Potter, are ·
only manifestations of this vast ill-will. In Hawthorne's novel,
however, man helps to make his bad fortune worse by ignoring the
evil already in his own heart, an evil that he might at least
fight if not conquer."

46 COXE, LOUIS O. "Questions to be Answered." Nation, 186
(12 April), 325-326.
Review of 1958.A3. Questions raised by Levin remain un-
answered: How "American" are these authors? how romantic? To
what extent is the "romance" (as opposed to the "novel") an
American predilection? To what extent European and modern? But
Levin has had the sense and judgment not to pursue symbols too
far or too hard; his method is descriptive and eminently sane.
What he tells us to look at is there. The final point, that of
the increasing rapprochement of American and English or European
literature, considered thematically, comes satisfyingly out of
Levin's careful establishment of the preoccupation with death,
evil, and decay as a dominating concern of Hawthorne, Poe, and
Melville. If there is nothing new here, there is nothing false,
prejudiced, or narrow.

47 PRITCHETT, V.S. "Without the Whale." New Statesman [London],
55 (19 April), 504-505.
Occasioned by publication of Grove Press editions of White-
Jacket, Pierre, and The Confidence-Man. Pierre has been rightly
condemned by the critics. Written under Hawthorne's influence,
it is totally unbelievable cardboard drama, although the idyllic
early chapters of autobiography are one more example of the
American genius for creating legend. In all that provokes dream
and myth, Melville is the richest exponent of the American nostalgia for the last golden age or for the heroic. His gift, even
in the briefest sketch of character, is for breaking through

appearance and for seeing the world as it rocks in the individual imagination. But the gift fails him in <u>Pierre</u>, which he wrote on one of those waves of hysterical exhaustion that are among the calamities of authorship. <u>The Confidence-Man</u> is another land failure: Melville was cut out for the great torments, not for the little moralistic punnings of this book; we feel his vital-ity, but compared with Mark Twain on this subject Melville is at a loss. <u>White-Jacket</u> belongs to his genius: leisurely, laugh-ing, spirited and thorough, Melville suns himself in an illusion-less observation of human nature at its happy lowest, but also in the active pride of protest; we have the impression throughout of a sensitive man in complete possession of himself. Melville hates brutality and injustice but doesn't whine like a sea-lawyer; he is sure of his moral ground; he revels in human ingenuity and argumentativeness--a quality that gives even his metaphysical speculations a certain laughing pleasure in ambiguity.

48   STARRETT, VINCENT. "Books Alive." Chicago <u>Tribune</u>
     (20 April).
          Notice of 1957.A1. Sealts brings together remarkably full texts of Melville's three lectures.

49   HICKS, GRANVILLE. "The Power of Blackness." <u>Saturday Review</u>,
     41 (26 April), 12, 32.
          Review of 1958.A3. Through the constant analysis of sym-bols, rigorous but never carried to extremes, Levin delves through stratum below stratum of meaning. Not much of what he says about Hawthorne, Poe, and Melville is absolutely fresh, but this is a very balanced discussion, which like any book that deals perceptively with the literature of the past bears strongly on present-day literary problems.

50   DURHAM, PHILIP. "Prelude to the Constable Edition of
     Melville." <u>Huntington Library Quarterly</u>, 21 (May), 285-289.
          Details of correspondence in the 1920s between Havelock Ellis and Raymond Weaver concerning Melville and of correspon-dence between Michael Sadleir and Weaver concerning the forth-coming Constable edition [1922-1924]. Weaver supplied Sadleir "with material useful to the project: texts unavailable in England or only in the British Museum, and bundles of magazine and typescript materials."

51   FIEDLER, LESLIE A. "From Redemption to Initiation." <u>New</u>
     <u>Leader</u>, 41 (26 May), 20-23.
          Relates Pip to "sentimental prototypes" of redeemer-children (encountering seducer-adults) in fiction. Even Melville is unwilling to portray the corruption of a child. Unlike the rest of the crew, Pip is unseduced by Ahab's quest and dies pure, the innocence of his vision only refined by his suffering.

52   FRENZ, HORST. "Books in English." Books Abroad, 32 (Summer),
     321.
          Review of 1956.A1. An original and highly philosophical
     study, which shows convincingly how a careful study of Eastern
     thought and culture may provide new insights into the work of
     Western artists.

53   [HILLWAY, TYRUS]. "Melville Bibliography." Melville Society
     Newsletter, 16 (Summer), n.p.
          Announces imminent completion of a multilithed bibliography
     prepared by the Melville Society's bibliography committee, Stuart
     C. Sherman, John H. Birss, and Gordon Roper. The bibliography
     lists, insofar as possible, every edition of Melville and every
     American book and article about Melville or his works that
     appeared from 1952 to 1957. [See 1959.A2.]

54   MILLER, JAMES E., JR. "America's Classic Authors." Prairie
     Schooner, 32 (Summer), 86–88.
          Review of 1947.A2 (reissued by Grove Press) and 1958.A3.
     Levin has succeeded admirably in doing what he set out to do: to
     analyze that "note of anguish" that reverberates so loudly in
     Hawthorne, Poe, and Melville. But if most of the time, in tracing
     out the image of blackness, Levin soars with intellectual intoxi-
     cation, he occasionally descends to the level of the mere cata-
     loguer. Olson's excellent if eccentric commentary on Melville
     does not always appear to be coherent but never fails to be in-
     teresting. Like Lawrence's criticism of American witers [see
     1923.B3–4], Olson's criticism invariably fascinates even though
     it seldom convinces. Probably Olson's most valuable contribution
     is his detective work in Melville's copies of Shakespeare and his
     discussion of King Lear's impact on Moby-Dick.

55   OLSON, CHARLES. "Equal, That Is, To The Real Itself."
     Chicago Review, 12 (Summer), 98–104.
          Review of 1957.A2. "The idea on which this book is based,
     naturalism, is useless to cope with Melville, either as a life
     lived in such a time or as an art, the first art of space to
     arise from the redefinition of the real [by the German mathe-
     matician Riemann], and in that respect free, for the first time
     since Homer, of the rigidities of the discrete." Reprinted in
     Olson (1965), pp. 117–122; Olson (1966), pp. 46–52.

56   PARK, B.A. Review of Melville as Lecturer, by Merton M.
     Sealts, Jr. Books Abroad, 32 (Summer), 325.
          Review of 1957.A1. "All that could be desired in an
     otherwise careful work is a more precise editorial technique:
     A limited apparatus criticus would be neither useless nor
     pedantic in the present case, and a list of the fifty-four news-
     paper sources should be given somewhere. . . . The three chap-
     ters on the biographical details of the tours are admirable, as
     are the three devoted to the interpretation of the lectures."

57 GEISMAR, MAXWELL. "Book Reviews." New England Quarterly, 31
    (June), 263–265.
        Review of 1957.A2. A solid and definitive study of
    Melville's naturalism, showing the essential difference of
    Melville's mind from that of the transcendentalist idealists, and
    in the process making clear that naturalism is, in the American
    context, a philosophic approach to the universe rather than a
    literary school. Yet the so-called naturalists of the 1900s,
    such as Norris and Dreiser, were also transcendentalist in their
    yearnings, while Melville's philosophical development was accom-
    panied by a deep inner conflict and by level on level of ambi-
    guity. Stern rather stubbornly denies the psychological and
    oedipal roots of this philosophical and spiritual struggle, tend-
    ing to make Melville into a good Social Democrat, rather than a
    fiery, complex, and tormented artist who may remind us of nothing
    so much as a transcendental Dostoevski. Stern is strongest in
    his close study and interpretation of Melville's ideological
    development, weakest in his rejection of the parallel psycholog-
    ical forces behind these ideas that Melville himself offered to
    the world in Pierre. Melville's unruly temperament, directly
    involved with oedipal and incestuous love, with recurrent symbols
    of mutilation and castration, led directly to the central drama
    of his work: the demonic and questing hero, the silent, blank or
    "white" universe against which the hero is splintered. By re-
    jecting the "economic" or biopsychic base of Melville's ideas,
    Stern puts himself squarely in that idealistic tradition against
    which his book is ostensibly directed. In Billy Budd Melville
    finally compromised both his psychoreligious conflict and his
    ideological extremes. The "middle-world" of Vere, the world of
    responsible social authority halfway between the Sermon on the
    Mount and the Articles of War, was the only sensible answer.
    "But beneath the classical serenity of Melville's beautiful
    fairy-tale, there were still rumblings of something more divine,
    something more diabolic, in the artist himself. The rebellious
    and possessed spirit, the broken son, paid in final but grudging
    homage to the wise, the 'good,' but perhaps the impossible father
    of western patriarchal society."

58 HOWARD, LEON. "Notes and Reviews." Nineteenth-Century
    Fiction, 13 (June), 73–75.
        Review of 1957.A1–2. Sealts has made an admirable addition
    to the relatively small collection of informative, essential
    books about Melville that are not likely to be superseded by the
    works of later scholars. The commentary accompanying the texts
    of the lectures is detailed and illuminating. Thoroughly docu-
    mented and indexed, the book is a fine example of careful scholar-
    ship that will be of permanent value to students of Melville and
    of popular culture in the United States on the eve of the Civil
    War. Summary of Stern's argument.

59   STERN, MILTON R.   "Some Techniques of Melville's Perception."
     PMLA, 73 (June), 251–259.
          Melville "adjusts the thematic progress of his details" by
     means of four basic techniques: reinforcement, contrast, the
     multiple view, and circular reflexion—techniques by no means
     peculiar to him. He uses common instruments whose thematic
     functions, rather than originality, define his position in Amer-
     ican literature. His greatness lay in his offering of new
     ideas: like the romantics who made him possible, he offered a
     new way to see. The functions of his techniques indicate that
     he used everything the romantics had to offer to come at a per-
     ception of the universe that is essentially closer to naturalism
     than to romantic, cosmic idealism. "Yet Melville remains mid-
     nineteenth-century because he does not conform to what we have
     conditioned ourselves to expect from literary naturalism. He
     does not test the validity of the meaning of his books with lists
     of social, economic, biological, and political facts; rather he
     tests his materials by the poetic superlogic of his symbolism,
     using to his ends the poetic mode of the romantic mind." Analy-
     sis of the four techniques and their antiidealistic, naturalistic
     function. Reprinted in 1960.A6.

60   KIRSCH, JAMES.   "The Enigma of Moby Dick.   Journal of Analyt-
     ical Psychology, 3 (July), 131–148.
          Jungian reading of Moby-Dick, examining "the relationship
     of the ego to the self" as it unfolds in the book.

61   MOORE, GEOFFREY.   "A Great American Literary Tradition?"
     Listener [London], 60 (24 July), 133.
          Review of 1957.B4 and 1958.A3. Chase's analyses of indi-
     vidual novels are sound but his treatment of his main theme is
     sketchy and his definitions are not always as sharp as they might
     be. There seem to be not one (as Chase maintains) but two tradi-
     tions in the American novel. On the basis of style, they may be
     called the "genteel" and the "vernacular"; on the basis of
     approach to subject matter, they may be called the "symbolic" or
     "poetic" and the "realistic." Chase ignores the realists, early
     and late, from Eggleston to Mailer. By contrast with Chase's
     rather hurried book, Levin's is thoroughly scholarly and
     detailed, charmingly and wisely written. As in the social
     sphere, America has been a testing ground for ideas and customs
     that have, in a modified form, radically affected Europe; so in
     literature American works in many instances prefigure similar
     experiments in Europe.

62   PRITCHETT, V.S.   "Novel and Romance."   New Statesman [London],
     56 (26 July), 119–120.
          Review of 1957.B4 and 1958.A3. Chase's book "leads to an
     illuminating interpretation of what American individuals have
     demanded or despaired of in one another; and we begin to under-
     stand, in a general way, why American novels appear to set inter-
     esting people in a poorly equipped society, to treat it perfunc-
     torily, and yet to extend the range of emotional experience
     available for the novelist." A "more consciously brilliant and

hard-driving critic with the allusive and obsessive bent," Levin is "more interesting for his incidental remarks than for the main argument that provokes them. He weighs his novelists down with far too much capacity for coherent thought. Melville, especially, requires a cooler mind."

63   FULLER, ROY. "Book Reviews." London Magazine, 5 (August), 58–60.

     Review of 1957.B4, 1958.A3, and the Grove Press edition of Pierre. The romance plays a far more important part in English fiction than Chase is willing to concede: there is a line that stems from Godwin, through Lytton, takes in much of Dickens and Wilkie Collins, is continued by Stevenson, and brought up to date by Graham Greene. Nor is it generally true to say that the English novel has no "highly skilled practitioners" as has the American—as Austen, Stevenson, Meredith, and Conrad show. The uneasiness one feels about the soundness of Chase's general notions is carried over into his discussion of particular works: he knows his material, he has read all the other critics, he makes his mild distinctions and discoveries—but his book is not very illuminating. One longs before the end for the more positive tools of a Marxist or Freudian; one longs, indeed, for a few simple value judgments. Levin has a simpler mind than Chase; his main theme is not dissimilar from Chase's: the defense of the romance, and his discussion, though naturally more detailed, is no more satisfying. He is an indefatigable and humorless symbol chaser and conducts a dizzy-making and finally pointless free-association method of analysis. Though Pierre is less pig-headedly unreadable than The Confidence-Man, it is a far more uneven book—in many passages scarcely acceptable to a modern reader. Its beginning can only be explained as a ghastly attempt by Melville to retrieve his literary fortunes by writing a popular book. Such a feat was by then quite beyond him, and with the change of scene from country to city, the tone is almost completely abandoned. The hard, bitter style and sentiments of The Confidence-Man begin to be heard, and the later book's terrifying, nonmoral, Kafkaesque world appears in the brilliant account of the travelers' arrival in the town.

64   LANSDALE, NELSON. "Literary Landmarks, USA." Saturday Review, 41 (30 August), 22.

     Details of the Melville collection in the Berkshire Athenaeum, the public library at Pittsfield, Massachusetts.

65   EHNMARK, ANDERS. "Rebels in American Literature." Western Review, 23 (Autumn), 54.

     Notes Melville's development of the theme of rebellion in The Confidence-Man and his description in "The Encantadas" of "a waste land, more terrible perhaps than any other in American literature."

66   HOLMAN, C. HUGH. "The Reconciliation of Ishmael: <u>Moby-Dick</u> and the Book of Job." <u>South Atlantic Quarterly</u>, 57 (Autumn), 477-490.
   The influence of the Book of Job on <u>Moby-Dick</u> is "pervasive and controlling, basic and thematic, the most informing single principle of the book's composition. The structure and fundamental unity of the novel, often considered to be non-existent, are explicable functions of Melville's use of the Book of Job." He found "in the pre-Christian drama of Job a philosophical order for his universe and a frame of belief and attitude adequate to order the actions of his fictional characters. The Book of Job presented him with Leviathan, a symbol thoroughly harmonious with a book about whaling; it presented him with a theme, the question of evil and suffering in the world; and it presented him with a theological frame for his fictional world." Narrator-hero Ishmael learns the lesson of acceptance of the mixed good and evil in all things, the prevalence of suffering in the world, the horror in which at times the universe seems formed. Like Job, Ishmael rebels against the order of the universe; a vast inscrutable symbol of incomprehensible reality looms before him, as before Job, in the form of a great whale; and, like Job, Ishmael learns (in contrast to Ahab) that, though wisdom is woe, man must learn to avoid the woe that is madness.

67   MATHEWS, J. CHESLEY. "Melville's Reading of Dante." <u>Furman Studies</u>, NS 6 (Fall), 1-8.
   Allusions to Dante and <u>The Inferno</u> in <u>Mardi</u>, <u>Redburn</u>, <u>White-Jacket</u>, "Hawthorne and His Mosses," <u>Israel Potter</u>, "The Tartarus of Maids," and <u>Clarel</u>. It was in <u>Pierre</u> that Melville revealed most about his reading of Dante and made most use of what he had read. If he ever read the <u>Purgatory</u> and <u>Paradise,</u> they seem to have made much less impression upon him than the <u>Inferno</u>. His appreciation even of the <u>Inferno</u> was somewhat limited. He seems to have been too much inclined to see in the <u>Inferno</u> the spirit of pessimism and revenge.

68   PHELPS, LELAND. "<u>Moby Dick</u> in Germany." <u>Comparative Literature</u>, 10 (Fall), 349-355.
   Survey of Melville's reputation in Germany. Neglect of <u>Moby-Dick</u> before 1946 was due to the "woefully inadequate" first translation (1927) and the poor reputation of the series in which it appeared. Its reputation as a great work of art is now firmly established.

69   WRIGHT, NATHALIA. "Reviews." <u>American Quarterly</u>, 10 (Fall), 381.
   Review of 1957.A1. This concise study of a brief episode in Melville's career illuminates to a remarkable extent the whole course of his thought and expression and of his relation to the society in which he lived. In "the relationship between what he said and how his often enthusiastic but hardly perspicacious audiences responded, part of his long retreat from popularity may be seen for what it all was: to some extent deliberate and inevitably part of his development as a thoughtful man and an artist."

70   FOGLE, RICHARD H. "Notes and Reviews." <u>Nineteenth-Century</u>
      <u>Fiction</u>, 13 (September), 167–170.
         Review of 1958.A3. Levin is quite good on his three
authors, whom he reads acutely; but his portraits of them are a
little lacking in vitality and complexity. His neat antithesis
between Hawthorne the home-seeker and Melville the voyager is a
bit too pat for the whole truth—especially for the truth of
Hawthorne, whose restlessness was consistent and noteworthy,
while Melville's nostalgia was not only for faraway places.
Levin is a good reader, with a sharp eye for telling points and
for new, yet convincing, relationships. Criticism of his book
must be aimed at his archetypal method, not at his acumen. Levin
grants Hawthorne, Poe, and Melville their right to be symbolists,
but gives too much weight to the facts that are symbolized and
not enough to the intrinsic worth of the symbols; he remakes
imaginative art into oblique autobiography, which is never as
good as autobiography or biography, direct and legitimate.
Levin explicates incisively and has ranged widely, so that he
allows plenty of opportunity for legitimate disagreement.

71   MILLER, PAUL W. "Sun and Fire in Melville's <u>Moby-Dick</u>."
      <u>Nineteenth-Century Fiction</u>, 13 (September), 139–144.
         Mythological and historical background of the sun and fire
symbolism in <u>Moby-Dick</u>. Melville attached to sun and fire at
least a measure of their conventional significance in mythology,
Zoroastrianism, and Judaism, but at times he revised or expanded
their usual meaning.

72   O'DANIEL, THERMAN B. "An Interpretation of the Relation of
      the Chapter Entitled 'The Symphony' to <u>Moby-Dick</u> as a Whole."
      <u>CLA Journal</u>, 2 (September), 55–57.
         In chapter 132, "The Symphony," Melville completes his
delineation of Ahab's character, making him a complete human
being, possessed of a variety of disturbing emotions and complicated passions, and so a fit subject for a great tragedy.
Second, the chapter emphasizes Starbuck's philosophy and puts
the final stamp on him: he believes in the two extremes of
afterlife, eternal salvation and eternal damnation, and in the
freedom of the will. Third, the chapter exhibits the fatalism of
the novel in its most intense form: there is no freedom of will
for Ahab, nor any for Starbuck, who only thinks there is.
Finally, the chapter is significant for its artistic perfection—
the consonance in everything in it. No where else in the book
does Melville so clearly show the relationship between human and
external nature.

73   ADLER, MORTIMER J. "The Meaning of Moby-Dick." Chicago <u>Sun-</u>
      <u>Times</u> (19 October), section 2, p. 2.
         The greatness of <u>Moby-Dick</u>, like that of <u>War and Peace</u>,
cannot be separated from its symbolic significance—what it tells
us about the condition of man at all times and everywhere. "It
brings us face to face with one of the greatest mysteries of
life—the mystery of good and evil which confronts us every time
we feel (with Hamlet) that the world is out of joint and we are

called upon to set it right. Our sense of what is fitting and
just doesn't jibe with the inexorable laws of the universe, the
blind decrees of Fate, or the inscrutable will of God. We become
rebellious and puff ourselves up to ask questions and act defiantly out of all proportion to our wisdom or our power. . . .
If the whale is the symbol of evil to Ahab, Ahab symbolizes the
mistake all of us make when our pride leads us to pit ourselves
against the whole world--or against God. We are saved from
tragedy only if we learn before it is too late that that way
lies madness or destruction."

74   ARVIN, NEWTON. "Book Reviews." American Literature, 30
     (November), 380-381.
         Review of 1958.A3. Though Levin's thesis--the dark wisdom
of our deeper minds, the symbolic character of our greatest fic-
tion--is acceptable without debate, there are very few scholarly
or critical writers who have developed that thesis in concrete
application to the writings of Hawthorne, Poe, and Melville with
the authority, the critical fineness, or the richness of literary
reference he has brought to his treatment. His chapter on Moby-
Dick succeeds in adding novelties of interpretation to a subject
that has notoriously not been undertreated.

75   HAYFORD, HARRISON. "Melville's Freudian Slip." American
     Literature, 30 (November), 366-368.
         On the official birth record of Stanwix Melville, the
maiden name of the mother was recorded not as Elizabeth Shaw
(Melville's wife) but as Maria G. Melville (Melville's mother).
[See Log, I, 430.] On the assumption that Melville himself
filled out the official form or reported the birth and supplied
the misinformation, Murray [1949.B14] and Arvin [1950.A1] use
the error to support evidence of a mother complex in Melville.
Information provided by the city clerk of Pittsfield accounts for
the error, however, on grounds other than a "Freudian slip" of
Melville's own pen. There are additional errors in the official
record: "the erroneous birthdate October 25 for October 22, and
the misspelling 'Stanwicks' for 'Stanwix,' which certainly cannot
be attributed to Melville, however wildly he spelled upon occasion. Finally, . . . the birth was reported not at the time of
its occurrence but at the beginning of the following year, 1852.
This fact negates the implied assumption that Melville's emotional distraction at the time of the birth contributed to a
slip of his pen."

76   WELSH, ALEXANDER. "A Melville Debt to Carlyle." Modern
     Language Notes, 73 (November), 489-491.
         The figure in Moby-Dick of sheep leaping over a vacuum
"because their leader originally leaped there when a stick was
held" (chapter 69, "The Funeral") is taken directly from
Carlyle's essay on "Boswell's Life of Johnson." The essay
appears in Carlyle's Critical and Miscellaneous Essays, Vol. 5
of The Modern British Essayists (Philadelphia: Carey and Hart,
1847-1849), the set tentatively identified by Sealts as the one
purchased by Melville in 1849 [Sealts (1966), p. 79, No. 359].

77   [HILLWAY, TYRUS]. "Notes." Melville Society Newsletter, 14
      (Winter), n.p.
          Notes that Dana Andrews and Jane Powell are costars in a
      Warner Brothers technicolor movie called Enchanted Island. "The
      plot follows Typee more closely than the previous movies based
      upon Melville's first novel, though Hollywood has added a few
      necessary embellishments. The hero, according to an attractive
      advertising brochure, is 'captured by cannibals' and becomes a
      'slave to the blue-eyed [sic] princess of the dreaded Typee
      headhunters . . . and to her savage code of love and taboos.'"

78   HONIG, EDWIN. "In Defense of Allegory." Kenyon Review, 20
      (Winter), 9–11.
          Melville's reply to Sophia Hawthorne in his letter of
      8 January 1852 [Letters, pp. 145–147] seems more than a polite
      acknowledgment of the latter's ingenious reading and praise of
      the novel. It is quite probable that Melville, at the instiga-
      tion of the Hawthornes, was coming round to a more receptive
      opinion of allegory and its possibilities as a literary instru-
      ment. The novels and tales of Melville, Poe, Hawthorne, and
      James, "like the narrative poems of Coleridge, seem often to
      hide behind the fanciful, even when they are most serious. Gen-
      erally in their work the qualities of elusiveness and under-
      statement, of mystification and wit, presented in an excrutiating
      tone of lightness that pretends to be a salutary suppression of
      the horrible and irrational, make for a growing tension that
      ultimately reveals the dead-seriousness behind the make-believe.
      These qualities, expressed in different ways by each of them,
      unite such writers on a common ground of symbolic intent; the
      same qualities also attract modern readers who see in them the
      essence of symbolic or allegorical art without necessarily dis-
      tinguishing between the two."

79   SEALTS, MERTON M. "Reviews." American Quarterly, 10
      (Winter), 504–505.
          Review of Die Funktion des Ich-Erzählers in Herman
      Melvilles Roman 'Moby Dick' by Hans Helmcke (Max Hueber, 1957).
      The book "will be of interest chiefly to students of the more
      technical aspects of fiction and to those concerned with
      Melville's aims and achievements as literary craftsman. . . .
      Helmcke's work, originally a dissertation, covers essentially
      the same ground as Barbara Morehead's 'Melville's Use of the
      Narrator in Moby-Dick' (University of Chicago, 1950). . . . Both
      studies hold Melville's shifts in point of view technically
      justifiable as well as artistically successful. Helmcke, stress-
      ing potentially disparate elements in the constituent parts of
      Moby-Dick, finds its peculiar narrative technique functioning as
      a structurally unifying force throughout the book. The presenta-
      tion of his case is logical and clear, although his system of
      analytical categorizing followed by broader synthesis involves
      considerable rehandling of material."

80   STONE, HARRY. "Dickens and Melville Go to Chapel."
     Dickensian, 54 (Winter), 50-52.
         Dickens's American Notes (1842) and Melville's Moby-Dick
     (chapters 7-9) both describe the identical seaman's chapel (the
     Seaman's Bethel in Boston) and seaman's preacher ("Father" Edward
     Thompson Taylor), and both recreate the preacher's sermon. "The
     similarities and differences in the two re-creations are strik-
     ing, although the differences result in part from the fact that
     Dickens was giving a matter-of-fact description of Father Taylor's
     Seaman's Bethel for a book of travels, while Melville was using
     the same material as a symbolic segment of a complicated work of
     fiction. Nevertheless, both authors portray the chapel, the
     preacher, the prayer, the hymn, the sermon, and the delivery,
     reproducing the rhythms, repetitions, nautical metaphors, and
     biblical references of Father Taylor's sermons.

81   LARRABEE, HAROLD A. "Book Reviews." New England Quarterly,
     31 (December), 547-548.
         Review of 1957.A1. In spite of increasingly sardonic per-
     sonal philosophy, so far removed from that of most of his
     "practical-minded" hearers, Melville's foreordained "failure" as
     a popular lecturer in the 1850s was far from complete. Some of
     his audiences warmed to him, and he to them. Nevertheless the
     lectures were (in Sealts's words) "the product of a mind grown
     alien to mid-century America," and the beginning of a decline in
     vigor and youth that Melville imputed to Christianized civiliza-
     tion in general.

82   LEITER, LOUIS. "Queequeg's Coffin." Nineteenth-Century
     Fiction, 13 (December), 249-254.
         Queequeg's coffin symbolizes the universe, man, his life,
     and his death. It is a symbol of the fate of man on this earth.
     Ishmael is saved because, unlike Ahab, he has reached a state
     not only of understanding man's role in the universe but also of
     accepting it. "Wedded" to Ishmael early in the novel, Queequeg
     points the way to sanity, not through corrosive philosophical
     questioning, nor through acceptance of religious dogma, but by
     what he is. Queequeg, dead, lives on in the form of the coffin,
     once more saving Ishmael from the wolfishness of sharks and
     self.

83   VOGEL, DAN. "The Dramatic Chapters in Moby Dick."
     Nineteenth-Century Fiction, 13 (December), 239-247.
         Analysis of the thirteen "stage-set, stage-directed chap-
     ters," in which Melville portrays "the battle of Ahab against
     types of mankind--the hero vs. lesser men."

84   ZINK, SIDNEY. "The Novel as a Medium of Modern Tragedy."
     Journal of Aesthetics & Art Criticism, 17 (December), 169-173.
         The modern man of disbelief may be of tragic magnitude both
     in his nature and in his suffering. But to present such a hero
     the artist requires special devices--those belonging not to the
     stage drama but to the novel. Some modern novelists, such as
     Dostoevski and Melville, have presented this hero of disbelief

with complete success: Raskolnikov, Ivan Karamazov, and Ahab are
not petty or merely pathetic. The modern hero of disbelief must
be a person of reflection, as well as of feeling and action. The
tragedy of Ivan and Ahab is grounded as basically in abstract
thought as in feeling. The novel has a vast advantage in depict-
ing such a figure. The specific value of the play--the bodily
presence of the actor--prevents its treating ideas with any
fullness.

1959 A BOOKS

1   JARRARD, NORMAN, comp. Melville Studies: A Tentative
    Bibliography. Melville Society Special Publication, No. 1.
    Austin, Tex.: The Melville Society, 49 pp.
      Expanded version of 1958.B2. Mimeographed.

2   SHERMAN, STUART B., JOHN BIRSS, and GORDON ROPER, comps.
    Melville Bibliography, 1952-1957. Providence, R.I.:
    Providence Public Library.
      Checklist. Mimeographed.

1959 B SHORTER WRITINGS

1   BABCOCK, C. MERTON. "Introduction" and "Bibliographical
    Note," in Typee. New York: Harper & Brothers, pp. vii-xiv.
      Biographical sketch to 1846 and brief commentary on Typee,
    which "deserves a place in the history of important American
    ideas for its fearless denunciation of America's special brand
    of ethnocentrism and the vacuous platitudes used to justify it."
    Its greatest importance, however, perhaps "lies in the fact that
    it furnishes a significant chapter in the spiritual autobiography
    of a man of genius." Reviewed in 1960.B39.

2   BETTS, WILLIAM W., JR. "Moby Dick: Melville's Faust."
    Lock Haven Review, 1 (1959), 31-44.
      In Moby-Dick Melville "consciously conceived his narrative
    in terms of the Faustian ritual." His conception of Ahab was
    influenced by the saga of Faust, and the whole design of the
    novel was influenced by Goethe's Faust especially.

3   BEWLEY, MARIUS. The Eccentric Design: Form in the Classic
    American Novel. New York: Columbia University Press,
    pp. 187-219.
      Moby-Dick is Melville's great attempt to create order in a
    universe in which a breakdown of the polarity between good and
    evil is threatened, the threat coming from Ahab, whose hatred of
    creation is the symptom, or perhaps the consequence, of the
    democrat's characteristic disillusionment with the universe and
    resentment of God's betrayal of the world. Ishmael represents
    Melville's resistance against his own powerful temptation to
    follow Ahab. The sanity and grace that shaped Moby-Dick vanished
    with Pierre. "With no metaphysical poles of good and evil, and
    no dialectical pattern on the pragmatic levels of life to guide
    them, Melville's heroes became incapable of development or pro-
    gression. They became the passive victims of their situation in

life, trapped in the endless unfolding of moral ambiguities whose total significance was to drain all possible meaning from life." As for the elder Adams, so for Melville--"the very texture of the American universe revealed the way it had been betrayed by God. Democracy existed only in ruthless competition, and God, who alone might have redeemed it, was unequal to the task: that, if anything, seems to be the meaning of the final chapter of The Confidence-Man." Incorporates 1953.B59 in slightly shortened and revised form. Reprinted in Chase (1962), pp. 91-115, and Browne and Light, pp. 273-290; reprinted in part in Vincent (1969), pp. 152-157.

4   BODE, CARL. The Anatomy of American Popular Culture, 1840-1861. Berkeley: University of California Press, pp. 225-229.
    Typee is the arch example of the South Sea island adventure, spiced with as much sex as Victorian publisher could permit. To a generation used to being muffled in heavy clothes, the idea of bathing naked, as Melville did with Fayaway and her friends, was a shocking, tantalizing thing. "Swimming itself constituted more of an exciting innovation than one might expect. It would not be until twenty years after Melville published Typee that American men and women would begin to enjoy their oceans, lakes, and rivers; and when they did it would be with three-quarters of their bodies covered by woolen bathing suits." Moreover, "the genial waters of the South Pacific were a perfect fertility symbol, regardless of whether the nineteenth-century readers of Typee consciously recognized the fact or not."

5   BRÉE, GERMAINE. Camus. New Jersey: Rutgers University Press, pp. 116, 191, 244-245.
    Moby-Dick exercised a powerful hold over Camus' imagination, and Billy Budd is not unrelated to L'Etranger. Among all novels, Moby-Dick is, according to Camus, the highest form of that particular form of art, la création absurde, as is Billy Budd, though to a lesser extent. As Camus interprets them in his essay on Melville (1953), Melville's works "are the record of an experience of the mind unequaled in intensity and are in part symbolic." They create great myths; the myth of man's endless "quest, pursuing and pursued on a limitless ocean." Moby-Dick is "one of the most disturbing myths ever invented concerning man's fight against evil and the terrible logic which ends by first setting the just man against creation and the creator, then setting him against himself and his fellow men." Billy Budd portrays "youth and beauty," killed "so that an order can be maintained." Melville surpasses Kafka as a creator "because in Kafka's work the reality described is summoned by the symbol, the fact is a consequence of the image, whereas, in Melville, the symbol is born of reality, the image, of perception."

6   CHARVAT, WILLIAM. <u>Literary Publishing in America, 1790-1850</u>.
    Philadelphia: University of Pennsylvania Press, pp. 23, 37,
    44, 60, 75, 83.
        Brief comments on the effects of mid-nineteenth-century
publishing practices and public taste on Melville.

7   CHARVAT, WILLIAM. "Melville and the Common Reader." <u>Studies
    in Bibliography</u>, 12 (1959), 41-57.
        Analyzes differences between Melville's early "common
readers" and his critics in their responses to his persona in
<u>Typee</u> and <u>Omoo</u>; and examines Melville's "two ways of writing,"
for the common reader and for the profound reader, in <u>Mardi</u>,
<u>Moby-Dick</u>, and <u>Pierre</u>, which he first conceived as popular books
and then drastically reconceived. "In the finished forms of all
three, the popular materials remain either as a base or a start-
ing point for the more private material which he imposed on
them." It is impossible to read books so composed in the way
many Melville critics try to do—"as structurally organic wholes
all the parts of which can be schematically related to all the
other parts. Melville's gift was not for unity, or integrated
structure, but for diversity and digression." <u>Mardi</u> and <u>Moby-
Dick</u> "are based on precisely those popular materials which pre-
dominate in his four successful travel works—loose, episodic,
anecdotal narrative; information; and informal, intimate commentary. These materials the readers liked and the critics
praised, even though they rejected the two books as wholes. What
he was 'most moved to write' he added, to <u>Mardi</u>, in the shape of
intellectual allegory; to <u>Moby Dick</u>, in the Ahab drama. And it
was the allegory and the drama which the public disliked. The
rejection, it appears, was due primarily to Melville's shift from
direct commentary to forms of [speculative] thinking which the
public found repulsive." Melville originally conceived <u>Pierre</u> as
a domestic thriller in which he would conceal profundities under
a surface of popular formulas, through which the reader looking
for mere diversion could not penetrate. He does not attempt to
train the reader in speculation in <u>Pierre</u> as he had done in
<u>Moby-Dick</u>; the reader "gets no guidance toward possibility."
Much of Melville's blundering may have been due to his having
radically reconceived and rewritten the book during the course of
compositon, adding a story of authorship, which ends in defeat,
to a tragedy of morals. It was in his magazine stories that
Melville practiced most successfully the deceptions he had intended in <u>Pierre</u>. "The Fiddler" suggests that Melville had
finally come to terms with himself as a writer, in his time and
in America. Reprinted in Charvat (1968), pp. 262-282.

8   CRUICKSHANK, JOHN. <u>Albert Camus and the Literature of Revolt</u>.
    London: Oxford University Press, pp. 16, 165.
        The original conception of <u>La Peste</u> owes a good deal to
Camus' reading of <u>Moby-Dick</u>, particularly its interpretation as
an allegory of man's fight against the radical evil of the universe. The interest of French critics in non-French authors
like Melville, Dostoevski, Kafka, and Faulkner is stimulated

and maintained by the discovery of certain central myths in their
work. These authors have also been the subject of essays along
the same lines by those very novelists in France--Malraux and
Camus--to whose own work the expression roman-mythe is most
frequently applied.

9 EDEL, LEON, et al., eds. Masters of American Literature.
   Vol. 1. Boston: Houghton Mifflin Co., The Riverside Press,
   pp. 724-730.
        Headnote ("Herman Melville, 1819-1891"), partly biographi-
   cal, emphasizing Melville's "skepticism." Prints "Hawthorne and
   His Mosses," "Benito Cereno," Billy Budd, selections from Battle-
   Pieces, John Marr, Timoleon, and Weeds and Wildings, and "Jonah's
   Song" from Moby-Dick.

10 FALK, ROBERT P. "Preface," in The Reinterpretation of American Literature. Ed. Norman Foerster. New York: Russell &
   Russell, p. xii.
        Refers to the rapid growth of the great "corporations" in
   criticism--Melville, James, Faulkner, Eliot--that has had the
   effect of limiting the function of full-length histories to the
   less critical functions of reference, definition, organization,
   and large-scale mapping of national trends.

11 FAULKNER, WILLIAM. Faulkner in the University: Class Con-
   ferences at the University of Virginia, 1957-1958. Ed.
   Frederick L. Gwynn and Joseph L. Blotner. Charlottesville:
   University of Virginia Press, pp. 15, 50, 56.
        Comments on Moby-Dick, which Faulkner regarded as probably
   the single greatest book in American literature, though it "was
   still an attempt that didn't quite come off, it was bigger than
   one human being could do."

12 FOGLE, RICHARD HARTER. "Melville and the Civil War." Tulane
   Studies in English, 9 (1959), 61-89.
        Analysis of Melville's artistry and attitudes in Battle-
   Pieces.

13 GIBSON, WILLIAM. "Introduction," in Moby Dick. Laurel
   Edition. The Sunrise Semester Library. New York: Dell
   Publishing Co., pp. 9-14.
        The book's two central symbols are "the blackness of
   darkness," standing for the mystery of iniquity, and the "dead
   blind wall," symbolizing the inscrutability of the divine power
   that created man.

14 GLASHEEN, ADALINE. "Out of My Census." Analyst [Northwestern
   University], No. 17, p. 10.
        Finds allusions to Billy Budd in Joyce's Finnegans Wake
   and a paragraph in which Joyce echoes and parodies Melville's
   description of Billy.

15 HARKNESS, BRUCE. "Bibliography and the Novelistic Fallacy." Studies in Bibliography, 12 (1959), 62–63.

Illustrates the nonchalance of scholars about the texts of novels, citing 1949.B109 and 1954.B25 among the examples.

16 HAYFORD, HARRISON, ed. The Somers Mutiny Affair. Englewood Cliffs, N.J.: Prentice-Hall, 224 pp.

Collection of documents relating to the Somers mutiny. [See 1940.B37.]

17 HONIG, EDWIN. Dark Conceit: The Making of Allegory. Evanston, Ill.: Northwestern University Press, pp. 140–145, passim.

Commentary on Ishmael's role ("to transform actions into ideas and ideas into actions") in Moby-Dick, which is treated passim as allegory. [See 1958.B78.] "The triumph of the allegorical method in Melville and Dante is that the vision of each is embodied and effected through the transmutation of the narrator's ideational role into a dramatic human role. In such a way the world is thoroughly remade without any violation of its physical and historical forms."

18 HOVEY, RICHARD B. John Jay Chapman: An American Mind. New York: Columbia University Press, p. 325.

In the early 1920s Chapman "discovered Melville and was so fascinated by Moby Dick that he could hardly put it down."

19 KAZIN, ALFRED. "Ishmael and Ahab," in American Critical Essays: Twentieth Century. Ed. Harold Beaver. London: Oxford University Press, pp. 332–347.

Reprints "Introduction" in 1956.B11.

20 LUDWIG, RICHARD M. "Herman Melville," in Bibliography Supplement to Literary History of the United States. Ed. Robert E. Spiller et al. New York: The Macmillan Co., pp. 164–168.

Lists items under headings "Collected Works," "Edited Texts," "Biography and Criticism," and "Bibliography" for the years 1948–1957, supplementing 1948.B30.

21 LYNN, KENNETH S. Mark Twain and Southwestern Humor. Boston: Little, Brown and Co., pp. 95, 101–102, 273.

In Delano in "Benito Cereno" Melville characterized the gullibility of the Northern innocent, with his willingness to be taken in by the masquerade of the contented slave. The gathering disquietude Melville creates in the minds of his readers brilliantly reproduces the uncertain psychological atmosphere of the plantation South, where the white master class could never be sure that the obsequiousness of the slave was not in some way a mockery. Reminiscent of "Benito Cereno," Twain's "George Harrison Story" differs in that it is as much concerned with the psychology of the Negro aggressor as of the white victim.

22   MARTIN, HAROLD C.   "The Development of Style in Nineteenth-
     Century American Fiction," in Style in Prose Fiction. English
     Institute Essays, 1958. New York: Columbia University Press,
     pp. 133, 136.
         Melville makes a particular virtue of melting jargon,
     dialect, elegant and low diction, apostrophe, rhapsody, and
     objurgation in the same great pot. The anagogical relations
     between earth and infinity that preoccupy Sylvester Judd's
     heroine in Margaret are implicit throughout Melville, the par-
     ticular expanding endlessly to the universal.

23   MILLER, JAMES E., JR.   "Moby Dick: The Grand Hooded Phantom."
     Annali Istituto Universitario Orientale (Sezione Germanica)
     [Napoli], 2 (1959), 141-165.
         Moby-Dick exhibits the thematic drama found in all
     Melville's earlier work, essentially unchanged; although the
     context is altered Melville's "statement" remains constant. A
     "basic discovery for Ishmael on his voyage is his own complicity
     and the need to acknowledge the universal brotherhood of cast-
     aways." His immersion in the sea symbolizes his final and total
     acceptance of man and the world in all their possibilities and
     imperfections--the knowledge that drove Ahab to his death.
     Ishmael divests himself of his mask of innocence, which he
     assumes when he isolates himself from humanity on the opening
     page of Moby-Dick. He is the single survivor "because he is the
     only man aboard the Pequod to achieve the balance of intellect
     and heart, knowledge and love, that renders human existence
     possible and probable." Ahab assumes a mask of innocence calcu-
     lated not only to deceive the world but, more importantly, him-
     self, unwilling to take up his burden of guilt in this imperfect
     world and so pushing his awareness of "complicity" into the dim
     recesses of his mind. Reprinted in revised form in Miller
     (1962), pp. 75-117.

24   MILLER, PERRY.   "Introduction," in The Golden Age of American
     Literature. Ed. Perry Miller. New York: George Braziller,
     pp. 20-25.
         Biographical and critical sketch. Having no other educa-
     tion, Melville took so seriously the precepts of his New York
     "Young America" instructors--that a stupendous American litera-
     ture should be proportionate to the vastness of the naked
     continent--that he blew them up into the giganticism of Moby-
     Dick. He thus not only insulted the cosmopolites, such as
     Longfellow and Holmes, but bewildered his friends, who, for all
     their imaginations of the American sublime, had never quite
     imagined anything so sublimely ferocious as Moby-Dick. For Poe,
     the romantic artificer, Hawthorne is to be judged by the
     standard of preconceived effect, to be praised for a natural
     cheerfulness that he sacrifices to the vice of allegory. For
     Melville, the world, including Poe, is deceived in supposing
     Hawthorne a sunny disposition, failing to comprehend the "black-
     ness" in his work, which resembles that in Shakespeare. Yet
     Emerson asks whether, measured by American standards of sincer-
     ity and public responsibility, even Shakespeare, being only an

entertainer, must not be rated somewhat superficial. "Bartleby" makes a double appeal, both for the inherent pathos of the story and for its evident connection with Melville's literary suicide. "Benito Cereno" clearly comes out of a condition of exhaustion, in too many respects following its original with slavish exactitude, though there are touches in it of the great Melville. Prints (pp. 315–419) "Benito Cereno," "Bartleby," and "Hawthorne and His Mosses."

25 O'BRIEN, BRIAN. Scrimshaw and Sudden Death: A Salty Tale of Whales and Men. New York: E.P. Dutton & Co., p. 173.
The whaleship Charles W. Morgan played the part of the Pequod in The Sea Beast, the 1926 movie adaptation of Moby-Dick.

26 SEWALL, RICHARD B. "Moby Dick," in The Vision of Tragedy. New Haven: Yale University Press, pp. 92–105.
Ishmael is far more than the chorus to Ahab as tragic hero—he is a constant link to the known and familiar, he is average, good-hearted humanity, the bridge between the world of Melville's readers and the tragic world of his imaginings. At the beginning of his story Ishmael is a shallow optimist; Melville leads him by slow degrees toward tragic truth. The book "neither justifies nor condemns Ahab. Tragedy is witness to the moral ambiguity of every action, and Melville is true to the witness of Job, Dr. Faustus, and Lear in conceiving of Ahab's action in just this light." Ahab is tragic man in finally coming to terms with existence, tragic hero to the extent that he transcends it and finds "greatness" in suffering. Reprinted in Norton Moby-Dick, pp. 692–702, and Gilmore, pp. 42–58.

27 VANČURA, ZDENĚK. "The Negro in the White Man's Ship." Acta Universitatis Carolinae--Philologica, No. 2 (1959), pp. 73–97.
Commentary on Prosper Mérimée's Tamango, Melville's "Benito Cereno," and Conrad's The Nigger of the Narcissus. It is strange that Delano should flourish, unmoved and untouched by the evil (slavery) that destroys Benito Cereno. If one acknowledges Melville's symbolic method, one might expect Delano to become in his own way the secret sharer of Benito's physical decline, for the United States too was torn with internal dissension on account of slavery and Negroes were supporting the foundations of the American social pyramid. The two men are not viewed from the same perspective, which results in a blurred effect. Only because Melville has equated the Negro with crime can Delano be made to shine as the paragon of humanity. He is not ridiculed for his short-sightedness but commended for it. The "truth" Benito professes to know and Delano comes to learn is merely the conventional teaching of racial inequality and white superiority. Babo's side of the story is never told nor even hinted at; his point of view does not come out, as he is seen "objectively" through the eyes of the whites. Thus Melville's technique allows him symbolically to deprive Babo of the last shreds of his humanity and condemn him to the nethermost hell. Benito's frame of reference is overstressed and misleading: it does not admit of correction by the other protagonists. The three

respective views--those of Benito, Delano, and Babo--were never clearly dissociated in Melville's mind, as they should have been. They do not connect in a balanced whole. They are each charged with symbolic meaning, though not with equal force and discern- ment; so the tale is vague and uncertain as to its deeper mean- ing, even though it achieves an admirable surface integration on the level of imagery and plot. Reprinted in 1959.B28.

28   VANČURA, ZDENĚK. "The Negro in the White Man's Ship." Prague Studies in English, 8 (1959), 73-97.
          Reprint of 1959.B27.

29   VILLIERS, ALAN. Give Me A Ship to Sail. New York: Charles Scribner's Sons, pp. 3-46.
          American edition of 1958.B25.

*30   ZIEGLER, ARTHUR. "Moby Dick," in From Homer to Joyce: A Study Guide to Thirty-Six Great Books.   Ed. J. Sherwood Weber. New York: Holt, pp. 210-217.
          Cited in Ricks and Adams, p. 398.

31   ANON. "Book Reviews." Emerson Society Quarterly, No. 14 (1st Quarter), p. 35.
          Review of paperback edition of 1951.A3. A useful and sig- nificant "life" as well as a caveat to the many theorists and lay psychoanalysts of Melville who confuse his finished novels with out-and-out autobiography or build great scaffoldings of interpretation upon inadequate foundations. Howard's "Preface" is a worthy critical document in its own right, indicating a respect for "fact," an interest in literature for its human qualities, and a primary concern with available evidence con- cerning the growth of Melville's literary tree. The volume in many respects complements and contrasts with Arvin's [1950.A1.].

32   ANON. "Book Reviews." Emerson Society Quarterly, No. 14 (1st Quarter), p. 38.
          Review of 1957.A2. An attractive and challenging study. In chapter 1, Stern sets forth the thesis he somewhat rigidly applies throughout his remaining chapters, excluding theses like those of Baird [1956.A1] or Freeman [1948.B9] or even Thompson [1952.A2] and precluding philosophical or religious development. Under this view, Melville loses stature, being deprived of normal ambivalence and creative complexity. Stern's definitions may be challenged: his interpretation of "idealists" is psychological rather than historical; Emerson and Thoreau can hardly be classified with Ahab and other Melvillean types. Stern's scheme lacks a tertium quid for contrast with his extremes.

33   ANON. "Book Reviews." Emerson Society Quarterly, No. 14 (1st Quarter), p. 43.
          Review of 1957.A1. Covers a critical turning point in Melville's career, which bears on the later period of Clarel

and <u>Billy Budd</u>. Carefully documented and indexed, the synthetic
texts of the lectures provide valuable links between Melville's
early and late periods.

34   CROWLEY, WILLIAM G. "Melville's Chimney." <u>Emerson Society
      Quarterly</u>, No. 14 (1st Quarter), pp. 2-6.
          "I and My Chimney" contains a "conscious statement" of
Melville's literary position in the 1850s. The chimney symbolizes his creative source; he is saying that he no longer plumbs
the deepest reaches of his talent. The tale also contains an
account of his mental-physical illness that resulted in an examination by Dr. O.W. Holmes; an attack on feminity; a classic
picture of the unhappy marriage--in some respects his own.

35   BAIRD, JAMES. "Reviews." <u>Modern Language Notes</u>, 74
      (January), 83-86.
          Review of 1957.A2. In Stern's closely fashioned chapters
the strength of an authentic critical judgment is steadily
apparent. But we have not yet heard on Melville "the voice of
supreme critical wisdom, perhaps that wisdom which we might
expect from some old Dante scholar who has encompassed all the
conflicts of the Renaissance between the vision of man in the
shadow of God and that of man abandoned to himself. We need this
voice to resolve the paradoxes in Melville. . . . For Melville,
the reality of existence had to be tested from as many different
angles as a lifetime can temporally allow. The best that one can
do is to select the angle of Melville that yields the largest
gain for the measurement of his art. There is always a critical
'leaving out,' because, unhappily for criticism, no art is subject to the disciplines of steady view and consistency which
govern critical intent." Stern has selected an angle of vision
that has its own insistent, if limited, justifications, but his
demonstrated thesis does not answer certain demanding questions
toward a comprehensive truth of Melville's art. One wishes
Stern had provided a chapter setting forth his own aesthetic, for
it is difficult to deal fairly with his view of Melville as dog-
matist until we understand his own speculation on the character
of art as expression. He praises Melville as a writer who
struggled to join "the artist and moral essayist or tractarian
system-builder"; but tractarianism in the work of Melville, as
in that of Tolstoy, is only one range, and often a limited one,
in the encompassment of an art.

36   ROSENBERRY, EDWARD H. "Queequeg's Coffin-Canoe: Made in
      Typee." <u>American Literature</u>, 30 (January), 529-530.
          A more likely original of Queequeg's coffin than the pas-
sage in Charles Wilkes's <u>Narrative of the U.S. Exploring Expedition . . . 1838-1842</u> cited in 1957.B82 is the passage in chapter
24 of <u>Typee</u>, in which Melville describes a pavilion housing an
effigy of a deceased warrior-chief seated in a canoe.

37   SATTERFIELD, JOHN. "Perth: An Organic Digression in Moby-
     Dick." Modern Language Notes, 74 (February), 106-107.
        If the forging of Ahab's harpoon in "The Forge" (chap-
     ter 113) is Homeric in inspiration [see 1950.B62], a smith of
     epic origin would be more fitting as its maker than one parodying
     Longfellow's [see 1947.B42]. Although Perth may have been the
     concrete, if fictional, counterpart of the Acushnet's real smith
     (as Anderson suggests in 1939.A1), and although Melville may have
     used him incidentally to blow condescending sparks toward Long-
     fellow, at the most meaningful symbolic level he seems to have
     been Melville's re-creation of Hephaestus.

38   CHAMBERLAIN, JOHN. "High School Pap." Wall Street Journal
     (11 February).
        The Globe Book Company's Moby-Dick [1950.B13], a typical
     cutdown "classic" for high school students, so far distorts the
     original that it becomes an entirely different book. The
     adaptor, Glenn Holder, produces an exciting tale, but in erasing
     the difficulty from Melville he has erased Melville, taking the
     bounce and wild humor out of Melville's language, unnecessarily
     simplifying it, and cutting most of the symbolism from the book.
     As Holder depicts Ahab, he is on the level of a child who strikes
     back at a chair because he has stubbed his toe against it.

39   WILSON, EDMUND. "Books." New Yorker, 34 (14 February),
     129-130, 133-134.
        Review of reprints of books by John S. Mosby. The mythical
     aspect of Mosby so seized upon Melville's imagination that he
     made it the subject of "The Scout Toward Aldie," which belongs
     with Melville's stories, especially with "Benito Cereno" and
     Billy Budd, though strangely, with all the attention recently
     paid to Melville, it has not been dealt with in connection with
     his other fiction. It is one of the most ambitious pieces
     Melville attempted in verse, and as a poet he is not quite up to
     it. His complicated stanza form, knotted and jolting style, and
     elliptical way of telling his story--which seem to derive from
     Browning--require a master to bring them off. But as a story
     the poem is tightly organized, well contrived, and effectively
     creates suspense. In the story we recognize Melville's familiar
     favorite theme: the pursuit or the persecution by one being of
     another, with an ambivalent relation between them that mingles
     repulsion and attraction but binds them inescapably together.
     Though the death of the young colonel is a tragedy and though
     Mosby plays the role of menace, the whole poem, in a way charac-
     teristic of Melville, involves a glorification of Mosby. We are
     made to feel that the colonel has a fatal rendezvous with the
     mysterious ranger, that he is drawn to his opponent by a kind of
     spell that is somehow a good deal more powerful than the attrac-
     tion exercised by his bride. So personal a product of Melville's
     imagination, the story has also historical significance in its
     insight into one aspect of the Civil War: a mutual fascination
     of each of the two camps with the other, the intimate essence of
     a conflict that, though fratricidal, was also incestuous. There

is even something of Ahab and Moby Dick implied in Grant's
pursuit of Lee in Grant's Personal Memoirs.

40   ARVIN, NEWTON. "The House of Pain: Emerson and the Tragic
      Sense." Hudson Review, 12 (Spring), 38–39, 42.
        Hawthorne and Melville, Eliot and Yeats all found Emerson
deficient in the tragic sense of life. Yet the young Emerson, in
his letters and journals, can sound strangely like the mature
Melville.

41   HOGAN, ROBERT. "The Amorous Whale: A Study in the Symbolism
      of D.H. Lawrence." Modern Fiction Studies, 5 (Spring), 39–46.
        Details in Lawrence's poem "Whales Weep Not!" and in
Kangaroo derive from "The Grand Armada," chapter 87 in Moby-Dick.
In Kangaroo "Whitmanism," the ache of amorous love and Christ's
love, is opposed by "the isolate, phallic being" derived from
Melville. Aaron's Rod and Kangaroo can be properly understood
only by the realization that their symbols have a vital structural importance and that the chief symbols in both novels were,
through a process of assimilation over a period of years, derived
ultimately from Lawrence's reading of Leaves of Grass and Moby-
Dick.

42   JOHNSON, JEANNE. "The White Jacket." Thoth, 1 (Spring),
      15–19.
        The narrator's jacket in White-Jacket symbolizes both "the
Ego" and "the hodge-podge of material goods and illusion that man
burdens himself with for security."

43   DAHL, CURTIS. "Moby Dick's Cousin Behemoth." American
      Literature, 31 (March), 21–29.
        Parallels between Moby-Dick and Cornelius Mathews'
Behemoth: A Legend of the Mound-Builders.

44   MILLER, JAMES E., JR. "The Confidence-Man: His Guises."
      PMLA, 74 (March), 102–111.
        Meaning in The Confidence-Man exists on three interlocking
levels--the realistic Western narrative, the symbolic American
satire, and the universal allegory. The common view is that the
book represents a new and fundamental turn in Melville's attitudes, an intense pessimism and misanthropy foreign to his
earlier and later work. But Melville had portrayed in all his
early novels the confidence man in many guises, such as the
missionary in the South Seas, and had always portrayed evil as a
prevalent and powerful force. The theme of the necessity of
coming to terms with evil, not through absolute (and suicidal)
observance of divine law but through modification and adaptation
of heavenly ethics to the exigencies and limitations of human
life runs through his novels from the first. The Confidence-Man
is the only one of Melville's works, however, that makes the
devil the protagonist, reducing him to comic proportions for the
leading role in a comedy. In this sense the book seems to be one
of his happiest utterances--he seems to have conceived evil from

a steadier perspective. In The Confidence-Man he "seems to have that control of his talent, that grasp of his material, and that assurance of his attitudes which emerge only from some cosmic-- and comic--vision." Shortened version in Miller (1962), pp. 170–192.

45   MILLER, JAMES E., JR. "Redburn and White Jacket: Initiation and Baptism." Nineteenth-Century Fiction, 13 (March), 272–293.
        Redburn and White-Jacket belong together in conception, spirit, and theme. They "form a single whole through the unified development of the protagonist and the pervasive single sensi- bility of the author. The two books tell one story of initiation into the evil of the world; observation, criticism, and sampling of that evil; and, finally, baptism into evil as the protagonist discovers and acknowledges to himself and the world his place in the sinful brotherhood of mankind." Redburn-White Jacket, "like Taji in Mardi, is confronted with the choice of retaining the mask of innocence and continuing and intensifying his isolation from mankind, or of discarding the mask and confessing his heri- tage of guilt and accepting the bonds of human brotherhood." Like Taji, he weighs the world and finds it wanting and yearns for the impossible ideal; unlike Taji, he settles for a Serenia of "sailors and sinners" where man, though idealizing Christ, makes allowances for humanity's imperfections, where individuals, though abhorring sin, save their souls by accepting their share of the world's burden of guilt. "By his choice, Redburn-White Jacket saves himself from the terrible fate of those tyrants of virtue yet to be created by Melville, Ahab and Pierre, who cannot in their pride come down from aloft." Reprinted, with minor omissions, in Miller (1962), pp. 54–74.

46   STEIN, WILLIAM BYSSHE. "Melville Roasts Thoreau's Cock." Modern Language Notes, 74 (March), 218–219.
        Agrees with Rosenberry [1955.A1] that "Cock-A-Doodle-Doo!" is a parody of the transcendentalists, but attempts to show that the story was inspired directly by Thoreau's essay "Walking" and that "we can take each instance of preposterous conduct in the story as a direct projection of an exaggeration of the principle of self-reliance in present time, the code of the essay's cockerel."

47   VINCENT, HOWARD P. "Book Reviews." American Literature, 31 (March), 84–86.
        Review of 1957.A2. The book might have been called Melville's Quarrel with Idealism: here Melville takes the un- welcome side of materialism against absolutism, of the hard phys- ical fact against the preconceived idealistic system. One almost visualizes Melville kicking an Arrowhead boulder to refute Berkeley. It is a good book, in which a point glancingly treated in earlier scholarship is now fully, perhaps overly demonstrated. But it is a one-sided book, made so, probably, by the scholastic need to support a thesis. Stern finds grist for his mill in every passage and in every symbol. Often he presses too hard.

All his adult life Melville the naturalist "played an undecided
deuce set" with Melville the idealist; he was a dualist, not a
monist, so that it is profoundly wrong to say that to him
"idealists are all finally fools."

48　　[HILLWAY, TYRUS]. "Notes." Melville Society Newsletter, 15
　　　　(Spring–Summer), n.p.
　　　　　　Notes outstanding performance of Billy Budd on CBS tele-
vision's Du Pont "Show of the Month" program on 25 May 1959.
Audrey Gellen and Jacqueline Babbin adapted for television the
Coxe and Chapman drama [see 1951.B4]. Starring in the broadcast
were James Donald (as Captain Vere), Don Murray (as Billy), Jason
Robards, Jr. (as Claggart), and Roddy McDowell. [See 1959.B55.]

49　　[HILLWAY, TYRUS]. "Notes." Melville Society Newsletter, 15
　　　　(Spring–Summer), n.p.
　　　　　　The number of Melville titles at prices under $3 has in-
creased from three in 1956 to twelve in 1959, according to Walter
Harding's latest checklist of inexpensive reprints of works by
important American authors. At least twenty-nine inexpensive
editions of Melville novels or tales are now being published.

50　　BABCOCK, C. MERTON. "Some Expressions from Herman Melville."
　　　　Publication of the American Dialect Society, No. 31 (April),
　　　　pp. 3–13.
　　　　　　Melville recorded a large number of folk expressions that
were part of the rising vocabulary of the time and gave his narratives a certain vigor and earthiness not possible with standard
English. The vernacular he employed is characterized by unin-
hibited inventiveness, youthful exuberance, defiance of propriety
and convention, and grandiloquence suggestive of frontier extravagances. Examples of vernacular expressions with definition
and quotation from Melville's works.

51　　RIFFATERRE, MICHAEL. "Criteria for Style Analysis." Word, 15
　　　　(April), 172–173.
　　　　　　Analysis of sentence ("And heaved and heaved, still un-
restingly heaved the black sea, as if its vast tides were a
conscience") in Moby-Dick, chapter 51.

52　　CARDWELL, GUY A. "Melville's Gray Story: Symbols and Meaning
　　　　in 'Benito Cereno.'" Bucknell Review, 8 (May), 154–167.
　　　　　　Focuses on "major unifying features," the "relationship
between structure and meaning," and "the moral intent of the
story." Most critics see Don Benito as pure good, Babo as pure
evil, and Delano as the genial, insensitive observer. But
Delano is not simply the obtuse observer—rather he is innocently
perceptive. With Delano as our guide we see that the world is
not neatly dichotomized, does not fall into a simple Manichean
dualism. Gray—a mixture of black and white—is the thematic
color of "Benito Cereno." Reprinted in part of Runden,
pp. 133–142.

53   GILMAN, WILLIAM H.   "Book Reviews." <u>American Literature</u>, 31
     (May), 203-204.
          Review of 1957.A1.   Sealts has now gone about as far as
     one can in re-creating the texts of Melville's lectures, handling
     the manifold problems with his usual meticulousness. Particu-
     larly rewarding is his evidence that differences between Eastern
     and Western audiences explain the greater and hitherto unsus-
     pected favor Melville won in the East. Relating the themes of
     the lectures to the prose of the 1850s and to the later poetry,
     Sealts further documents the conclusion that Melville, an alien
     to the late 1850s, was more at home in the past, among the
     ancients or among his own memories. He has also added to our
     knowledge of Melville's aesthetics by stressing his defense of
     "ideality," his denial of any "polar opposition" between the two
     kinds of representational art, realistic and idealized, and his
     preference for the second because it has more reality than real
     life. Sealts's handling of the texts raises some questions: at
     one point the language and thought seem to be purely the re-
     porter's; at other points Melville is made to sound incoherent
     or obscure. Anyone quoting Sealts's texts need to be very much
     on his guard. It would have been helpful if those sections that
     are not certainly Melville's were bracketed or queried. But
     Sealts's numerous cross-references to anecdotes, themes, and
     images common to the lectures and to other works of Melville do
     something to overcome one's doubts about the texts. Some of the
     hitherto unreproduced passages of the lectures seem relatively
     valuable. With these and other additions, future biographers or
     critics may be sure that they have about as much evidence as they
     are likely to have about Melville's public thought during the
     lecture period.

54   STANTON, ROBERT.   "<u>Typee</u> and Milton: Paradise Well Lost."
     <u>Modern Language Notes</u>, 74 (May), 407-411.
          Cites passages in <u>Typee</u> that echo specific scenes in
     <u>Paradise Lost</u>, as well as general similarities between Milton's
     pre-Fall Paradise and the Typee valley. Tommo's symbolic iden-
     tification with Satan reminds us that, however personally harm-
     less, he is a member of that corrupt and Satanic civilization
     that had spoiled so many Polynesian paradises. But his helpless-
     ness, illness, and desire to escape suggest also a more important
     theme: that modern man, in spite of his longing for a garden of
     innocence, would find such a place unbearable. Modern man and
     Paradise are mutually destructive.

55   SHANLEY, JOHN P.   "Distaff Writing Team." New York <u>Times</u>
     (24 May), p. 11.
          Details of television adaptation of <u>Billy Budd</u> by
     Jacqueline Babbin and Audrey Gellen for CBS's "Show of the
     Month," 25 May 1959. [<u>See</u> 1959.B48.]

56　　KNOX, GEORGE. "Lost Command: Benito Cereno Reconsidered."
　　　Personalist, 40 (Summer), 280–291.
　　　　　"Benito Cereno" makes the carefully developed statement
　　that "the precarious control of evil depends on our tenuous hold
　　on reality. . . . Our control of evil partially depends on our
　　fallible perceptions, and often, when we are motivated by humane
　　sentiments, we are apt to abdicate our precarious exercise of
　　command-reason and relinquish the wheel to darkness." Hints at
　　Manichaeism are only in the story to reinforce the major point:
　　man's own responsibility in controlling good and evil.

57　　AULT, NELSON A. "The Sea-Imagery in Herman Melville's
　　　Clarel." Research Studies [State College of Washington], 27
　　　(June), 115–127.
　　　　　"Disregarding inserted sea stories, references to lakes and
　　bodies of water actually encountered by the pilgrims on their
　　journey, and scores of passing allusions too slight to be of much
　　significance, well over a hundred images, tropes actually built
　　from impressions and memories of the sea, remain." In Moby-Dick,
　　working from the concrete and specific to the general and ab-
　　stract, Melville succeeded in producing a masterpiece, "one in
　　which the sea forms a basic factual ingredient." In Clarel,
　　"moving from the abstract to the concrete, using the sea as a
　　means of lending substance, through metaphor and analogy, to the
　　bare bones of abstract theorizing, he can produce no uniformly
　　excellent result." Central to Melville's creative imagination
　　lies the ocean, "physical sign of all that is ambiguous and
　　shifting, elusive and unknowable. His sense of craftsmanship
　　overpowered by the strength of his obsession, he turns again and
　　again to the sea to find life for his barren desert cantos."

58　　WITHIM, PHIL. "Billy Budd: Testament of Resistance." Modern
　　　Language Quarterly, 20 (June), 115–127.
　　　　　Accepts the view that Billy Budd was written in a basically
　　ironic style [see, for example, 1950.B64] and attempts to demon-
　　strate that the "testament of acceptance" theory [see, for
　　example, 1933.B26] is essentially self-contradictory. Focuses
　　mainly on Vere, who "far from being a wise man, balanced in his
　　judgments and fair in his attitudes, is discovered to be narrow,
　　literal, prejudiced, completely circumscribed by the needs of the
　　navy, less compassionate than his officers, and lastly, guilty of
　　that worst of naval sins, over-prudence." In "local context"
　　Billy Budd "suggests that it is wrong to submit to unjust law.
　　Those in power, such as Vere, should do all they can to resist
　　the evil inherent in any institution or government. All men are
　　flawed, but not all men are depraved; and we must not let those
　　institutions designed to control the evil destroy the good. In
　　a larger context, man should not resign himself to the presence
　　of evil but must always strive against it." Reprinted in
　　Stafford (1961), pp. 78–90.

59   MILLER, JAMES E., JR.   "The Many Masks of Mardi."   JEPG, 58
      (July), 400-413.
            In Mardi country after country wears a mask; the Yillah-
      seekers must look behind the mask to discover things as they are.
      Babalanja, the book's deepest diver and its one wholly unmasked
      man, is the best example in Melville of the terrible struggle
      entailed in the determination not to don a mask but to confront
      reality directly. Leaving Serenia, Mardi's maskless society,
      and continuing his suicidal quest for Yillah, Taji wears a double
      mask, turned toward the world but turned inward too, willfully
      denying his guilt and asserting his innocence. "Like Ahab and
      Pierre, Taji lacks the courage to peer closely into the darkness
      of his own deep soul. In attempting to gain all, Taji loses all.
      In seeking total innocence, he discovers total corruption. In a
      ruthless quest for heaven, he wins his way to hell." Reprinted,
      with some revision, in Miller (1962), pp. 36-53; reprinted in
      part in Rountree, pp. 63-69.

60   STERN, MILTON R.   "Book Reviews."   JEGP, 58 (July), 546-551.
            Review of 1958.A3. A suggestive and provocative scrutiny
      of the American preoccupation with darkness, treating Hawthorne,
      Poe, and Melville with lucidity, wit, and a steady control that
      bespeaks Levin's constant critical intelligence. Ultimately the
      success and importance of the book are disappointingly limited,
      however. The "impressive detailed applications that are made,
      with such deft and comprehensive brevity as to compel respect,
      result in a total body of cross reference that tends to flatten
      the authors into a common entity just as the archetypal method
      tends to flatten symbols into a common dimension." Levin can
      wonderfully display one general aspect of "the symbolic character
      of our greatest fiction" but little of the specific definitions
      and uses of "the dark wisdom of our deeper minds." His prefer-
      ence for "patterns created by images" (by which he seems to mean
      archetypes) to the large exclusion of "patterns created by words"
      (ideas, purposes, moral evaluations) leaves the reader's expecta-
      tions unsatisfied. "The over-all effect is of assertion vice
      demonstration. No one work is examined with satisfactory in-
      tensity or completion. Rather a great many works of the three
      authors are blended . . . into a running commentary which seems
      to try to statisticize American blackness more than it tries to
      explain it." Levin's method, moreover, has an unfortunate con-
      sequence in tone: everything is so easy, so sure. He never
      really defines his terms, but seems to take for granted a vague
      equation between romance and symbolic fiction and between
      "critical realism" and reportorial narrative. One objects to
      the easy assurance with which he builds around one undefined
      term and with which he dismisses the other.

61   BRATCHER, JAMES T.   "Moby Dick: A Riddle Propounded."
      Descant, 4 (Autumn), 34-39.
            "Rather than the demonstration that each man sees in the
      universe good and evil in proportion to his own, Moby Dick is by
      intent more probably the depiction--or decrial--of an age-old
      problem. Moby Dick is a riddle; it is a riddle in the sense

that it propounds questions for which it provides no answer.
Leading among these is: Why evil at all?"

62   MILLER, JAMES E., JR. "The Complex Figure in Melville's
      Carpet." Arizona Quarterly, 15 (Autumn), 197–210.
          Melville's whole work was an extended "drama of masks," a
"prolonged morality pageant" with a constant, unchanging vision.
From the beginning to the end, Melville asserted the necessity of
man to compromise with his ideals in order to come to terms with
the world's evil and his own. His masked characters all protest
their innocence and desire for good; most frequently they are
crusaders destroying the world in an attempt to set it right.
His maskless men stand naked and exposed before the world,
accepting with equanimity their share of the world's guilt.
Between the masked and the maskless are the wanderers and seek-
ers, the Omoos and the Ishmaels, who, in the progress of their
quest, must decide with what face to confront the world. Reprinted, with minor revision, in Miller (1962), pp. 3–17.

63   MILLER, JAMES E., JR. "Melville's Quest in Life and Art."
      South Atlantic Quarterly, 58 (Autumn), 587–602.
          Outlines Melville's biography, rejecting facile Freudian
interpretations, and reviews two "crucial relationships"--to his
wife (the "best guess" as to why he married her "seems to be that
he looked upon her with the obligation of an older brother to a
sister in possible danger of spinsterhood") and to Hawthorne.
"The recurring crises of his life, when both his physical and
mental health seemed in jeopardy, were probably most frequently
precipitated by an acute, if not overwhelming, sense of the
deficiency of his few close relationships among family and
friends. Whenever he set off on a search, from the time of his
first voyages during the early forties through the 1856/1857 tour
of the Holy Land, there seemed to lurk somewhere in his psyche
the desperate need for the close bonds of friendship."
Melville's first six novels--Typee through Moby-Dick--all have
in common their dramatization of Whitmanian "Calamus" relationships. Melville must have felt that in Moby-Dick he had exploited to the limits of meaning the intensely felt attachment
of "adhesiveness" or comradeship--afterwards he never portrayed
again precisely the same kind of companionship. These elements
in Melville's works, "and many more too," allow for a multitude
of conclusions about Melville's personality. His works should
be read as art, not as neurosis, as fiction, not as biography.
All of the themes he treats are testimony to the complexity of
his vision.

64   PHELPS, LELAND R. "The Reaction to Benito Cereno and Billy
      Budd in Germany." Symposium, 13 (Fall), 294–299.
          In the consensus of modern German critics, Melville is one
of the great figures of world literature, that reputation resting
primarily on Moby-Dick, "Benito Cereno," and Billy Budd. Some
German intellectuals have found in the latter two works (first
published in German translation in 1938) "significant symbols for
their own problematical existences during the critical period of

the Third Reich and for the position of the European intellectual
in general in the tumultuous modern world." "Benito Cereno"
became "a symbol for the individual's inability of self-
determination in the face of an overpowering and unavoidable
destructive force and Billy Budd became a symbol for the cruelty
of a state which ruthlessly levels the individual element."
Other critics are able to approach the works without political,
sociological, or intellectual biases. The artist's reaction to
Melville is best represented in Germany by Thomas Mann, who
"admired above all the poetic and manly artistry with which
Meville handled the theme of the assertion of the senselessness
of an archetypal evil."

65   PUTZEL, MAX. ["Addition to Melville Log."] Melville Society
      Newsletter, (Autumn), n.p.
         Cites review, by Alexander de Menil, of 1896 edition of
      Moby-Dick in the St. Louis Hesperian, 1 (Spring 1897), 497.

66   STALLMAN, R.W. "Melville's Encantadas." University of Kansas
      City Review, 26 (Autumn), 2-3.
         Poem.

67   ANON. "'Moby Dick' in Soviet." New York Times (20 Septem-
      ber), p. 32.
         Reports that Moby-Dick is to be published soon by the
      Leningrad branch of the Soviet Fiction Publishing House, which
      also plans to print editions of Stephen Crane, Richard Hildreth,
      Sinclair Lewis, and other American writers. Recent Leningrad
      publications include editions of Sherwood Anderson, Washington
      Irving, and O. Henry.

68   GROSS, JOHN J. "Melville's The Confidence-Man: The Problem
      of Source and Meaning." Neuphilologische Mitteilungen, 60
      (25 September), 299-310.
         A central problem of interpretation in The Confidence-Man
      is the meaning Melville attached to the man in cream colors.
      Rather than the confidence man in one of his guises, Melville
      "intends him to represent another of the Christ-figures seen in
      the works of this period who suffer mutely and alone in the
      absence of any true believing community of man." Joseph
      Glanvill's The Vanity of Dogmatizing was "very possibly" the
      source Melville used as the basis for The Confidence-Man.

69   MILLER, JAMES E., JR. "The Achievement of Melville."
      University of Kansas City Review, 26 (October), 59-67.
         Depicts the origin, evolution, and ultimate fate of
      Melville's major character types: the primitive, instinctive
      individuals; the over-intellectualized, obsessed rebel; the
      masked men, the pretenders (those who compromise their integrity
      and make a hypocritical adjustment to life's realities); the
      purely Satanic figures; and those who work out some kind of
      tolerable and frank reconciliation with life. The last category
      includes Melville's Young Seekers; a number of protagonists in
      the short stories; Melville's practical mystics (the vessels of

his insight into truth's paradox); and his admirable men of
action (who know and accept the world for what it is and assert
their rightful place in it). In direct confrontation of the
harsh facts of life--the universe is an incomprehensible and
inextricable tangle of good and evil, man inevitably becomes
involved with evil--Melville "worked out a solution which is the
bitter, because only, alternative to death"--a frank compromise
of the ideal and the practical, as proposed by Plinlimmon's
pamphlet. Reprinted, with minor omissions, in Miller (1962),
pp. 229-241.

70   WHICHER, STEPHEN E.   "Swedish Knowledge of American Litera-
      ture, 1920-1952:   A Supplementary Bibliography."   JEGP, 58
      (October), 671.
          Melville is the "only American author before 1900 to be
attracting much current attention in Sweden."

71   LUCID, ROBERT F.   "The Influence of Two Years Before the Mast
      on Herman Melville."   American Literature, 31 (November),
      243-256.
          Passages in Dana's Two Years Before the Mast influenced
passages in Redburn and White-Jacket.

72   GLICKSBERG, CHARLES I.   "The Numinous in Fiction."   Arizona
      Quarterly, 15 (Winter), 313.
          Looks forward to the appearance of a novelist who will
repudiate the dismal confusions and sophomoric nay-saying of the
novelists of "the beat generation" and, like Dostoevski,
Hawthorne, and Melville, "recapture the numinous vision in all
its intractable contradictions of ecstasy and terror, seeking to
reconcile faith and doubt, the inner and outer, spirit and flesh,
the diabolical and the divine, the sense of mystical blessedness
with existential dread."

73   JONES, BARTLETT C.   "American Frontier Humor in Melville's
      Typee."   New York Folklore Quarterly, 15 (Winter), 283-288.
          Examples of the tall tale, braggadocio, exaggerated lan-
guage, rustic figures of speech, understatement in the face of
danger, and discussion of visceral responses in Typee.   "These
devices must have been difficult for nineteenth century reviewers
to accept in a book purporting to state facts.   When frontier
humor clashed with sensibilities matured in European literary
traditions, the rapport between author and reader must have
suffered."

74   RIDGE, GEORGE ROSS and DAVY S. RIDGE.   "A Bird and a Motto:
      Source for 'Benito Cereno.'"   Mississippi Quarterly, 13
      (Winter), 22-29.
          Coleridge's "The Rime of the Ancient Mariner" is a major
source for "Benito Cereno"--as numerous striking parallels of
theme, thematic development, imagery, symbolism, and metaphysical
message help to show.

75   TILTON, ELEANOR M. "Melville's 'Rammon': A Text and Commen-
      tary." Harvard Library Bulletin, 13 (Winter), 50-91.
          Edits "Rammon" from the manuscript, with detailed descrip-
      tion of the manuscript, extensive notes, and interpretive commen-
      tary. The subject of "Rammon" is not "the problem of Evil" [see
      Vincent, 1947.B19]; the work is "a somewhat clumsy parable of
      Melville's uncertainty of belief and ambivalence of feeling"
      about immortality.

76   BLUEFARB, SAM. "The Sea--Mirror and Maker of Character in
      Fiction and Drama." English Journal, 48 (December), 501-510.
          Discusses the themes of "escape," "the sea as antagonist,"
      and "nostalgia" in Moby-Dick and in works by Joseph Conrad and
      Eugene O'Neill.

77   CARPENTER, FREDERIC I. "'The American Myth': Paradise (To
      Be) Regained." PMLA, 74 (December), 602.
          Cites Pierre Glendinning and Billy Budd as genuinely naive
      Adamic heroes, who "are unable to understand or to cope with
      worldly evil." Pierre and Billy are contrasted to such wisely
      innocent Adamic heroes as Adam and Maggie Verver in James's The
      Golden Bowl, who "learn both to understand and to cope with
      evil."

78   HAYFORD, HARRISON. "Melville's Usable or Visible Truth."
      Modern Language Notes, 74 (December), 702-705.
          No other phrase of Melville's was singled out more often in
      critical works of the 1940s than "the usable truth," which occurs
      in Melville's letter of 16 April 1851 to Hawthorne, as tran-
      scribed by Julian Hawthorne in 1884.B3. Lathrop in 1876.B1
      transcribes the phrase "whole truth." Neither "usable" nor
      "whole" fits the context of the passage, which calls for a word
      like "visible." Melville's misspelling "visable" occurs in three
      of his manuscripts, where it looks like "usable." Hayford's
      emendation, first suggested in his dissertation "Hawthorne and
      Melville: A Biographical and Critical Study" (Yale, 1945), was
      adopted by Leyda in 1951.A4 and 1952.B14 and by Metcalf in
      1953.A5; so the phrase "visible truth" appears in the quotations
      of recent critics, who do not appear to recognize that a textual
      change has taken place.

79   HAYFORD, HARRISON. "Poe in The Confidence-Man." Nineteenth-
      Century Fiction, 14 (December), 207-218.
          In portraying the "crazy beggar" in chapter 36 of The
      Confidence-Man, Melville used details of Edgar Allan Poe's phys-
      ical appearance, dress, and personal manner, and part of his
      psychology and history. Melville probably did not intend his
      portrait of Poe to be recognized--he habitually wrote from expe-
      rience, observation, and reading, rather than from pure inven-
      tion. The context calls for Winsome-Emerson first to reject an
      impractical brand of "transcendentalism" and then to endorse a
      commercially successful one. The fact that Emerson had not
      publicly rejected a disciple forestalled Melville's use of any
      actual follower of his; but Poe might have come to his mind as

"a crackbrained exponent of a rhapsodical apostleship, who had
gone begging and been despised as a madman and scoundrel." One
cannot assume Melville saw Poe only in the light in which he
presented some of his attributes here, since not all of whatever
he may have known or thought of him was to the purpose. One has
to be careful, too, in drawing any conclusion from the response
of either the Cosmopolitan or Winsome. Melville endorses not
only the Cosmopolitan's courtesy and at least manifest sympathy
but also Winsome's perception of the fellow's insanity and possible charlatanism. So far as we can deduce or disengage anything Melville is saying about Poe, there is a dismissal of his
pretensions to reason, there is some admiration for his pride and
quiet self-respect, and there is an austere pity for the man.
Melville was probably well aware of similarities to himself in
the picture. He had looked straight at his own situation and
seen it as one not far removed from that of this crackbrain.
Reprinted in Norton The Confidence-Man, pp. 344–353.

80   MILLER, JAMES E. "Melville's Search for Form." Bucknell
     Review, 8 (December), 260–276.
        Melville's works cannot be condemned as "novels" that
failed formally. [See 1938.B31.] It is now common critical
knowledge that the tradition of the novel is not the primary
force that shaped his intentions or imagination. He synthesized
several elements in our literary heritage, among which the novel
is of relatively minor importance, constructing his books out of
the classic literature of the past; out of a central cultural
tradition of epic, allegory, satire, philosophy; out of the
clash of ideas of his own time; out of the subliterary folk
culture of whaling ships and New England country towns. America
has rarely had a creative writer attempt such a variety of forms.
His entire literary career may be characterized as a vision in
search of embodiment, a theme in quest of a form. Reduced to its
lowest common denominator, his obsessive idea may be defined:
"the necessity of man to abide by the human terms of this world
as it is, not by the heavenly terms of another world as it might
be. All of Melville's books, though varied in their form,
dramatize the quest for this truth, or the catastrophe of ignoring it, or the glory of discovering it." Reprinted in part in
Miller (1962), pp. 242–252.

1960 A BOOKS

1   BOWEN, MERLIN. The Long Encounter: Self and Experience in
     the Writings of Herman Melville. Chicago: University of
     Chicago Press, 282 pp.
        Bowen examines "the part played by the concept of selfhood"
in Melville's works and attempts to show "how this persistent
concern helped to determine his subject matter, his imagery, his
view of character, the shape of his narratives, and his at times
equivocal attitude toward his material." The works are treated
as "dramatic representations of the encounter of the self and the
not-self, of the single human person and all that is set over

against him--the total reality of nature, mankind, and God. For
it was in terms of this conflict that the human experience, from
first to last, presented itself to Melville." At the center of
all his work is the pitting of the single individual against the
universe. The strategies the self adopts toward its adversary,
the not-self, are defiance (exemplified by Taji, Ahab, and
Pierre), submission (exemplified by Benito Cereno, Babbalanja,
Falsgrave, Plinlimmon, and Vere), and "armed neutrality"--the way
of wisdom: resistance without defiance and acceptance without
surrender (exemplified mainly by Ishmael and Clarel). Indexed.
Reviewed in 1960.B66, B73, B88, B92.

2   FOGLE, RICHARD HARTER. Melville's Shorter Tales. Norman:
    University of Oklahoma Press, 150 pp.
    Commentary on tales written between 1853 and 1856. The
purpose of the tales as of all Melville's fiction is to penetrate
as deeply as possible into metaphysical, theological, moral,
psychological, and social truths; to refute the shallow and conventional notions of his times; to provide a spacious and undi-
vided wisdom. Melville is fond of apologue and parable, but in
these tales he wishes to conceal his direct purposes "for artistic, personal, financial, and sometimes humorous reasons. Further, his state of mind at the time of writing is morbid, his
sensibility heightened to the point of disease, and it must go
veiled in public in sheer self-preservation." These concealments
are in conflict with Melville's other purposes of being free,
uncommitted, impartially able to record the visible truth. The
form of his tales "is determined by the direction and quality of
his thought, in which man as the seeker for knowledge is always
pitted against a finally inscrutable reality, and this conflict
is further complicated by the need for concealment. Since every
man sees reality differently, partially, and from his own point
of view, the tales are often ambiguous." The tales have either
the pattern of the quest, in which a seeker actively pursues
truth or the naturally converse situation of a man's being thrust
into circumstances that dismay and baffle but conclude by educat-
ing him. "The quest and its object are represented primarily in
visual terms, and thus the problem arises of point of view, alike
mental and physical." Melville had too little contact with his
social audience, and as a result his tone in the tales is usually
too violent, too tragic, too apocalyptic for his material.
    The tales are very uneven in quality. "When every quali-
fication has been made, Melville is still not a craftsman in the
ordinary meaning of the term. He remains a Romantic apostle of
the grand unfinished, the all-or-nothing man of the one stroke.
He is too heavy for the delicate fabric of the kind of tale he is
trying to write; what he really has to say is at odds with the
limits he has chosen to observe." "Benito Cereno" alone is a
complete artistic triumph. "To respect these tales at their full
value, one must have respected Melville to begin with. Yet at
worst they are transformed by Melville's brooding and contem-
plative intelligence, indefatigably exploring all facets and
perspectives, as it steadily searches for the full vision of his
object." Reprints 1952.B10; 1954.B8; 1955.B53. Indexed. Reviewed in 1960.B92.

3   HOUGH, HENRY BEETLE. <u>Melville in the South Pacific</u>. North
Star Books. Boston: Houghton Mifflin Co., 179 pp.
    A retelling of Melville's "true adventures in the South
Seas," based on <u>Typee</u> and <u>Omoo</u>.

4   MAYOUX, JEAN-JACQUES. <u>Melville</u>. Trans. John Ashberry. New
York: Grove Press; London: Evergreen Books, 190 pp.
    Partly biographical, seeing Melville as "peculiarly frigid"
in nature, with a "neurotic need for support and sympathy," and
partly general critical commentary. Many illustrations. Prints
extracts from chapters 165 and 168 in <u>Mardi</u> and from chapters 61
and 92 in <u>White-Jacket</u>; chapter 51 and <u>most</u> of chapter 133 in
<u>Moby-Dick</u>; "Sketch First" in "The Encantadas"; and most of
"Bartleby." Indexed. First published in Paris: Editions du
Seuil, 1958.

5   PHELPS, LELAND R. <u>A Preliminary Check-List of Foreign Lan-
guage Materials on the Life and Works of Herman Melville</u>.
Melville Society Special Publication No. 2. Evanston, Ill.:
The Melville Society, n.p.
    Checklist of foreign language books and articles on
Melville. Mimeographed.

6   STERN, MILTON R., ed. <u>Discussions of MOBY-DICK</u>. Boston:
D.C. Heath and Co.
    Reprints 1923.B3; 1945.B34; 1946.B19; 1948.B76; 1949.B56;
1950.B90; 1951.B28, B107; 1953.B11; 1954.B23, B28; 1955.B36, B61;
1956.B11; 1958.B59.

1960 B SHORTER WRITINGS

1   ARMOUR, RICHARD. "Herman Melville" and "<u>Moby Dick</u>," in <u>The
Classics Reclassified</u>. New York: McGraw-Hill Book Co.,
pp. 85–103.
    Humorous version of Melville's biography and <u>Moby-Dick</u>.

2   BEZANSON, WALTER E. "Preface," "Introduction," and
"Appendices," in <u>Clarel</u>. Ed. Walter E. Bezanson. New York:
Hendricks House, pp. i–ii, ix–cxvii, 525–652.
    The "Introduction" includes an account of the composition
of the poem; its relation to Melville's journey to the Levant in
1856–1857; his reading during his apprenticeship as a poet; his
literary sources for the poem, including his own <u>Journal</u> of 1851–
1857; the publication, reception, and twentieth-century criticism
of the poem; a reading of the poem that defines its "series of
large and powerful movements"; an analysis of its language,
prosody, formal structure, major images, and major characters;
and an account of Melville's "version of what was happening to
post-bellum America; and his view of the science-versus-religion
controversy." Rivalled by few works of Anglo-American literature
as a rendering of the spiritual exigencies of the late Victorian
era, <u>Clarel</u> "is an intricate documentation of a major crisis in
Western civilization—the apparent smash-up of revealed religion
in the age of Darwin"—an "in-close fictional study of what the

crisis meant to various representative men." Melville "did his
utmost to project more than his own spiritual dilemma. His
effort to cope with the major tensions of an age makes Clarel a
historical document almost of the first order."

After leaving Jerusalem, however, "where he phrased his
'problem' as a series of questions about faith, dogma, and
creeds, Clarel's concern shifts toward the study of personalities." He "goes increasingly from asking whose beliefs are right
to asking who is the right kind of man. Though he clings to his
original hope of finding an Answer, the search becomes in effect
an effort to judge why the others believe as they do, and what
their beliefs or doubts do to them. Although questions of belief
continue throughout the poem, even reaching a tone of insistence
in the final cantos, the inner movement, as defined by Clarel's
experience, is away from theology towards a kind of pragmatic
humanism, or speculative psychology. Thus character analysis
becomes itself a theme of the narrative." Only minor characters
of the poem are clear types--a major premise of the narrative is
that the individual life is invariably complex and buried. One
of the relevances of Clarel to our time is "the narrator's concern with the kind of threshold materials out of which modern
depth psychology has been constructed. Even minor acts relate
meaningfully to fundamental commitments and tensions within the
self. There is close attention to the symbolic role of gesture:
the meaning of a glance, a pause in speech, a facial flush, a
turning toward or away from, absence as well as presence. And
always, an effort to capture the special tone of the gesture."
At intervals in the poem come moments of sudden, unconscious,
self-revelation. The real interest in the poem's discussions
lies in the exchange of private tensions; they resemble modern
experiments in group dynamics. The "dominant psychological
thesis of Clarel is that individual lives are infinitely complex,
men do and think as they must, self-knowledge is hard won and
limited, and full understanding between man and man is more than
can be expected." The "loss of faith is the basic assumed fact
of the poem, and its largest problem is how to endure the overwhelming sense of a shattered vision." The "Appendices" include
a chronology of the pilgrimage, a "Critical Index" of thirty-two
characters of the poem, explanatory notes, and textual notes.

3   BLACKMUR, R.P. "The Craft of Herman Melville," in American
    Literary Essays. Ed. Lewis Leary. New York: Thomas Y.
    Crowell Co., pp. 102-115.
        Reprinted from 1955.B3.

4   BLACKMUR, R.P. "Introduction," in American Short Novels.
    Ed. R.P. Blackmur. New York: Thomas Y. Crowell, pp. 5-8.
        Introduction to Billy Budd. "Melville wrote Allegory in
    all the machinery of capital letters in the hope of finding--or
    creating--an absolute structure within which he could make a
    concert of the contrary powers of heaven and earth. Like
    Shakespeare, he had to make a concord out of discord, and espe-
    cially out of the shifting discords of good and evil. His story
    could never be content to be a story, or its own meaning, but was

compelled to assert a meaning which had not yet come to pass."
Though "there is a story--a series of connected events--the story
provides chiefly a frame for a series of meditations, and the
story in the end would not hang together without the meditations
which extract, which create, meaning from the series of events in
the words of the mind as they are fused in the words of the
senses." Rather than recording a final reconciliation with life,
society, and nature, in Billy Budd Melville "set loose one more
set of images in a continuing allegory of how it is that we seek
what we must shun."

5   CANADAY, NICHOLAS, JR. "A New Reading of Melville's 'Benito
    Cereno,'" in Studies in American Literature. Ed. Waldo McNeir
    and Leo B. Levy. Baton Rouge: Louisiana State University
    Press, pp. 49–57.
        The theme of authority is the tale's organizing principle.
    Melville demonstrates two things: (1) the result of Benito's
    status as a ship captain without the power to enforce his com-
    mands; (2) the misuse of power by usurping Negroes who rule
    without authority. Delano, combining both authority and power,
    illustrates the ease with which command can be exercised under
    normal conditions. Chaos and disorder are the inevitable results
    of authority functioning without power and of power exercised
    without authority. Although it is not possible to transfer
    authority by force, the authority of Benito and his officers was
    made ineffectual by their loss of power. Melville recognizes
    that once a captain's authority is overthrown it can only be
    replaced by the same agency that originally established it.
    Once the revolt was successful, only Spanish law could return
    the ship's government to order. The force represented by
    Delano could only destroy the power of the mutineers. It became
    the task of the courts to restore authority.

6   CLIVE, GEOFFREY. The Romantic Enlightenment. New York:
    Meridian Books, pp. 161–165.
        Reprints 1954.B37.

7   COOK, ALBERT. "Romance as Allegory: Melville and Kafka," in
    The Meaning of Fiction. Detroit: Wayne State University
    Press, pp. 242–247.
        The white whale in Moby-Dick is symbolic, not allegorical,
    but the symbolism is "allegory-like." The white whale "seems to
    stand for something single, however infinitely complex."

8   CREEGER, GEORGE R. "The Symbolism of Whiteness in Melville's
    Prose Fiction." Jahrbuch für Amerikastudien, 5 (1960),
    147–163.
        Examines the symbolism of whiteness in Melville's prose
    works from Typee to Billy Budd, defining the symbolic process as
    "the exploration of imagery for potential meaning."

9   CUNLIFFE, MARCUS. "American Literature." The Year's Work in
     English Studies, 1958, 39 (1960), 293-294.
          Includes review of 1958.A3. Levin's skillfully written and
     well-documented book approaches the same problem as Chase in
     1957.B4--the nature of the American "tradition" in literature--
     but Levin confines himself to Hawthorne, Poe, and Melville, and
     also relies less on theory and more on fact. "In seven penetrat-
     ing chapters Levin proves his point by sheer illustration, a
     method which is vitally needed in a field of study where theories
     are more plentiful than documentary evidence."

10   DAHLBERG, EDWARD. Can These Bones Live. New York: New
     Directions, pp. 43-46, 121-127, 129-133, passim.
          Reprints most of the Melville material in 1941.B8, with
     some revision.

11   DAVIS, MERRELL R. and WILLIAM H. GILMAN, eds. "Introduction,"
     "Check List of Unlocated Letters," and "Textual Notes," in The
     Letters of Herman Melville. New Haven: Yale University
     Press, pp. xv-xxviii, 309-319, 321-385.
          The "Introduction" includes a history of earlier publica-
     tion of letters by Melville, description of the types of letters
     in Melville's surviving correspondence, details of the tantaliz-
     ing "possibilities of Melville's lost correspondence," an account
     of the characteristics of Melville's hand, and an account of
     editorial procedures. This edition "is an attempt to collect all
     the available letters into one convenient edition with appro-
     priate commentary and careful transcription for each letter."
     Reviewed in 1960.B55, B64, B67-69, B73, B78, B83, B92, B96.

12   DILLISTONE, F.W. "The Angel Must Hang," in The Novelist and
     the Passion Story. New York: Sheed & Ward, pp. 45-68.
          Melville was not prepared to accept all of the dogmas of
     Calvinism without question, yet even when he was criticizing or
     opposing he was still moving within the framework of its general
     assumption. In Billy Budd he constructs a less rigid conception
     of the Divine Ruler than that of Calvinism--through Vere, who
     symbolizes the Lord and manifests the inward compassion that is
     the deepest truth of the Divine Being; a more profound represen-
     tation of human sin--through his analysis of the "mystery of
     iniquity" exemplified by Claggart; and a more realistic drama-
     tization of the act of redemption--through the character and the
     final willing surrender of Billy Budd, "an aesthetic representa-
     tion of the Christ-figure and of His perfect self-offering on
     behalf of mankind" (though Billy "bears many of the marks of
     Adam" in the first part of the story).

13   DURHAM, PHILIP and TAUNO F. MUSTANOJA. American Fiction in
     Finland: An Essay and Bibliography. Helsinki: Societé
     Néophilologique, p. 74.
          No one in Finland questions the classic quality of Moby-
     Dick, though it came late there. Its first translated edition,
     abridged, appeared in 1928. "With the exception of Moby Dick,
     none of Melville's works has been translated, nor is any of them

available in the bookstores in the original. <u>Moby Dick</u> can be purchased in English, but only in two British editions."

14   FADIMAN, CLIFTON. "Herman Melville (1819–1891): <u>Moby Dick</u>,"
      in <u>The Lifetime Reading Plan</u>. Cleveland and New York: The
      World Publishing Co., pp. 126–128.
         Biographical sketch and brief commentary on <u>Moby-Dick</u>,
      which can appeal to children as a thrilling sea story (with a
      little judicious skipping) and to grownups as a tempestuous work
      of art.

15   FIEDLER, LESLIE A. "Introducing Cesare Pavese," in <u>No! in</u>
      <u>Thunder: Essays on Myth and Literature</u>. Boston: Beacon
      Press, p. 138.
         "The assimilation of Melville to the Italian imagination,
      the long effort which has finally made a nineteenth-century
      American writer a living force in contemporary Italian fiction,
      was not begun by Pavese, but realized itself chiefly in his
      astonishingly successful translation of <u>Moby Dick</u> and in his
      various essays on Melville." [<u>See</u>, for example, 1960.B59.]

16   FIEDLER, LESLIE A. <u>Love and Death in the American Novel</u>.
      New York: Criterion Books, pp. 520–552, passim. Reprint.
      Cleveland and New York: Meridian Books, 1962. Rev. ed.
      New York: Stein and Day, 1966.
         <u>Moby-Dick</u> must be read not only as an account of a whale
      hunt, but also as a love story, perhaps the greatest love story
      in American fiction, love taking the peculiar American form of
      innocent homsexuality. The redemptive love of man and man is
      represented by the tie binding Ishmael to Queequeg, while the
      commitment to death is portrayed in the link joining Ahab to
      Fedallah, though the two relationships are disturbingly alike:
      both between males, one white and one colored. Queequeg and
      Fedallah represent the polar aspects of the id, beneficient and
      destructive. They "represent the basic conflict which lies at
      the heart of the book, the struggle between love and death.
      Queequeg stands for the redemptive baptism of water (or sperm),
      and around him the 'Western' or sentimental story which is one
      half of <u>Moby Dick</u> develops; while Fedallah stands for the
      destructive baptism of fire (or blood), and around him the gothic
      or Faustian romance which is its other half unfolds. But it is
      Queequeg who wins, though the two never meet face to face, Eros
      which triumphs over Thanatos." Though Ahab and Ishmael are
      opposites, they are also one—two halves of a single epic hero;
      only in their essential unity is the final unity of the book to
      be found. In <u>Moby-Dick</u> "the king-god-culture hero, who kills and
      is redeemed, is split into an active older brother and a passive
      younger, different sons of the same terrible father, who move, as
      it were, through separate works of art: the first through a
      belated horror tragedy, the latter through a nineteenth-century
      <u>Bildungsroman</u>." Yet even structurally their two actions become
      one. The tragic play is enclosed in a comic narrative frame.
      Ishmael, the protagonist of the frame story, "becomes the trapped
      spectator of the drama of Ahab's fall, experiencing the catharsis

of which Ahab is incapable. The heart, that is to say, witnessing the mad self-destruction of the head is itself purged and redeemed."

17   FOGLE, RICHARD HARTER. "Melville's Clarel: Doubt and Belief." Tulane Studies in English, 10 (1960), 101–116.
       Summary interspersed with interpretation.

18   GASSNER, JOHN. "Allegory: Coxe and Chapman's Billy Budd," in Theatre at the Crossroads: Plays and Playwrights of the Mid-Century American Stage. New York: Holt, Rinehart and Winston, pp. 139–141.
       The production of Coxe and Chapman's Billy Budd at the Biltmore Theatre, New York [in 1951; see 1951.B4], promised tragedy but provided only pathos.

19   HOWARD, LEON. "The Time of Tension," in Literature and the American Tradition. Garden City, N.Y.: Doubleday & Company, pp. 167–182.
       Survey of Melville's works. The mid-nineteenth century in America was a period of tension and conflict between the forces of empiricism and transcendentalism, skepticism and faith. Moby-Dick is a reflection of the prevailing attitude of mind—"a rational commitment to empiricism as a philosophy but with enough doubts and reservations to admit the possibility of intuition and inspiration and permit admiration for those bold spirits who, like Emerson and Thoreau in literature, would follow their own genius to whatever crazy lengths it might lead. Melville was the first American author to realize within himself his whole intellectual heritage and give it expression in the underlying pattern which controlled the composition of a single book. Moby Dick is the 'representative' American novel of its time, and it is a great novel because it brings a broad cultural heritage to focus within a single individual's capacity for realization and thus transmits it, with a new emotional power, to posterity."

20   JAFFÉ, ADRIAN H. and HERBERT WEISINGER. "Herman Melville," in The Laureate Fraternity: An Introduction to Literature. Ed. Adrian H. Jaffé and Herbert Weisinger. Evanston, Ill.: Row, Peterson and Co., pp. 142–143.
       Headnote to Billy Budd, Foretopman, which Melville wrote "probably as a sort of final testament" of his mature beliefs. "Man, says Melville, cannot do more in his capacity as man than to administer as best he can the laws of God, even when those laws seem to operate with cruel injustice. Any other course is to question the divine law, for divine law can be altered only by God and not by man."

21   JONES, JOSEPH, et al. American Literary Manuscripts. Austin: University of Texas Press, p. 252.
       Lists libraries with Melville manuscripts and special collections of material relating to Melville.

22   JUSTUS, JAMES. "Beyond Gothicism: Wuthering Heights and an
      American Tradition." Tennessee Studies in Literature, 5
      (1960), 29–30.
            Comparisons between Wuthering Heights and Moby-Dick, with
      Ahab seen as an American Heathcliff. Ahab's vengefulness grows
      into monomania when he refuses to recognize that the natural
      world exists apart from his subjective interpretation. Mel-
      ville's prose rhythm in the final paragraph of Moby-Dick suggests
      the removal of one irritant in the spiritual harmony of the uni-
      verse: not the whale but his pursuer.

23   KAPLAN, SIDNEY. "Introduction," "A Note on the Text," and
      "Melville's Revisions," in Battle-Pieces and Aspects of the
      War. Gainsville, Fla.: Scholars' Facsimiles & Reprints,
      pp. v–xix, xxi–xxiii, xxv–xxviii. Reprint. Amherst:
      University of Massachusetts Press, 1972.
            "Introduction" gives biographical background to Battle-
      Pieces with particular attention to Melville's reading between
      February and April 1862, which "reflects his grappling with the
      problems he was by then posing to himself--as prospective poet of
      the war." List of Melville's revisions before and after publica-
      tion of Battle-Pieces.

24   KETTLE, A.C. "Reviews." Review of English Studies, NS 11
      (1960), 114–117.
            Review of 1957.B4 and 1958.A3. Critical of Levin for see-
      ing as the dominant strain in Hawthorne and Melville that "power
      of blackness" that is admittedly an important and significant
      feature in the work of both writers, and for dragging in on equal
      terms Poe, a writer of incomparably lower stature, apparently to
      bolster up a theory that is schematic in its nature and dubious
      in its relevance. For all the talk of tradition in Chase's book,
      no coherent tradition of the American novel emerges. Chase's
      use of the word "romance" is not merely loose but positively
      unhelpful, for it is never quite clear whether the word is used
      to indicate a particular attitude to life on the part of the
      novelist or in a more technical sense as a contrast to the
      naturalistic method of presentation.

25   KRIEGER, MURRAY. The Tragic Vision: Variations on a Theme in
      Literary Interpretation. New York: Holt, Rinehart and
      Winston, pp. 195–209, 249–260. Reprint. Chicago: University
      of Chicago Press, 1960.
            Commentary on Pierre and Moby-Dick. The essential cause of
      Melville's difficulties in Pierre is his failure to hold con-
      sistently to the distinction between himself and Pierre: "As he
      yields uncritically to the absurdities of his hero, so we refuse
      any longer to yield to him." Melville fails to do what he did
      in Moby-Dick--"to transcend despair by giving it an aesthetically
      controlled voice." Pierre illustrates "the inescapable demoniz-
      ing consequence" of "Hegelian (or Emersonian) immanence claiming
      our too enthusiastic allegiance, which means our abandonment of
      everything less abstract, of all that touches us and warms our
      flesh." In considering Ishmael's role in Moby-Dick, Krieger

first shows "the grounds on which Ishmael may be seen as pointing
to a profound Christian affirmation that would take account of
Ahab's darker vision even as it swept beyond it in the direction
of divine grace"; he then indicates "the grounds on which
Ishmael's affirmation could be seen as more aesthetic than
thematic in its significance," and on which, "rather than resolving a Manichaean into a Christian vision," he can be seen to
superimpose "an inconclusive Manichaeism upon Ahab's exclusive
demonism."

26   McELDERRY, B.R., JR. "A Melville Note: The National Era
Review of White-Jacket." Melville Society Newsletter, 15
(Winter), n.p.
       Reprints 1850.B83. Notes the seafaring experience of Dr.
Gamaliel Bailey, the editor of The National Era and likely author
of the review, who on shipboard "no doubt saw essentially what
Melville was to see a few years later. The conscience which made
Bailey so able an abolitionist would have been similarly
aroused."

*27   MORDELL, ALBERT. "Frank T. Bullen and Herman Melville."
Today's Japan, 6 (1960), 77–83.
       Cited in Ricks and Adams, p. 274.

28   O'CONNOR, WILLIAM VAN. "The Novel and the 'Truth' about
America," in Studies in American Culture. Ed. Joseph J. Kwiat
and Mary C. Turpie. Minneapolis: University of Minnesota
Press, pp. 74–83.
       Reprint of 1954.B53.

29   OLSON, CHARLES. "Letter for Melville 1951," in The Distances.
New York: Grove Press; London: Evergreen Books, pp. 46–54.
       Poem, with prose introduction, condemning the Melville
Society's "One Hundredth Birthday Party" for Moby-Dick at
Williams College, 2–4 September 1951. Asks: "do you for a
moment think . . . that I would have anything to do with their
business other than to expose it for the promotion it is, than to
do my best to make clear who these creatures are who take on
themselves to celebrate a spotless book a wicked man once made,"
that "I find anywhere in my being any excuse for this abomina-
tion, for the false & dirty thing which it is--nothing more than
a bunch of commercial travellers from the several colleges? . . .
Can anything be clearer, as to how Melville is being used?"

30   POWELL, LAWRENCE CLARK. Books in My Baggage: Adventures in
Reading and Collecting. Cleveland and New York: The World
Publishing Co., pp. 50–53.
       Reprints 1954.B53, with some revision.

31   PRIESTLEY, J.B. Literature and Western Man. New York:
      Harper & Brothers, pp. 237-239.
          Brief critical survey, devoted mainly to Moby-Dick.
      Melville was "a morbid, ambiguous, unfinished character; one
      half of him a belated Elizabethan genius, the other half an
      untalented, cranky, pseudo-philosophic, mock-profound type."

32   RIDEOUT, WALTER B. "Instructor's Manual," for The Experience
      of Prose. Ed. Walter B. Rideout. New York: Thomas Y.
      Crowell Co., pp. 15-16.
          Interpretive note on "Benito Cereno"; draws attention to
      complexity and ambiguities in the story.

33   STEIN, WILLIAM BYSSHE. "Melville and the Creative Eros."
      Lock Haven Bulletin, 1 (1960), 13-26.
          In "After the Pleasure Party" Melville explores the rela-
      tions between the rational and intuitive faculties in creative
      endeavor. "The poem is a symbolic disclosure of a compulsive
      desire to write and the inability to do so. It describes how
      consciousness, in its intellectual orientation, frustrates the
      function of intuition. Melville envisages this condition as
      eros, the intuitive feminine source of inspiration, under the
      domination of logos, the masculine principle of reason. And it
      is for this reason that his Muse, Urania, is depicted as
      estranged from her natural womanhood. Thus the recurrent sexual
      imagery comments on the defeminization of his creative impulses."
      In the coda of the poem, Melville "gives sacral recognition to
      eros in her most instinctual manifestation. And with it
      Aphrodite Urania is restored to her ancient role. Now the poet's
      intuitions are in balance with the Protestant bias of his intel-
      lect. Significantly, out of this reconciliation blooms the late
      rose of the poetry of his old age."

34   STEINMETZ, LEE. "But God He Keeps the Middle Way," in The
      Poetry of the American Civil War. Ed. Lee Steinmetz.
      Lansing: Michigan State University Press, pp. 54-60.
          Apart from Whitman's Drum-Taps, Battle Pieces is the only
      book of 1860s war poetry that rises above its fellows. One
      reason for the superiority of some of Melville's war poems over
      those of most of his contemporaries lies in his habit (as in
      "Donelson" and "The Armies of the Wilderness") of juxtaposing
      passages varying greatly in tone, a technique that gives these
      poems a richer texture than was usual at the time. Battle-
      Pieces, like Drum-Taps, achieves a total cumulative effect
      through having an underlying theme. The somber view of human
      destiny implicit in Melville's novels echoes throughout the book.
      Melville consistently decries the unthinking emotional hysteria
      engendered by the war and stands opposed to the prevailing temper
      of his time, which held that the war was a holy war. "The Con-
      flict of Convictions" is one of the most artistic statements of
      the theme underlying much of Battle-Pieces.

35   STERN, MILTON R.   "Introduction," in Discussions of MOBY-DICK.
     Ed. Milton R. Stern.   Boston: D.C. Heath and Co., pp. vii–xi.
     Survey of Melville's reputation since 1846.

36   THORP, WILLARD.   "Herman Melville," in Literary History of the
     United States.   Rev. ed.   Ed. Robert E. Spiller et al.   New
     York: The Macmillan Co., pp. 441–471.
     Reprints 1948.B30.

37   THURSTON, JARVIS, O.B. EMERSON, CARL HARTMAN, and ELIZABETH V.
     WRIGHT, comps.   "Herman Melville," in Short Fiction Criticism:
     A Checklist of Interpretation since 1925 of Stories and
     Novelettes (American, British, Continental), 1800–1958.
     Denver: Alan Swallow, pp. 154–162.
     Checklist of criticism of Melville's short fiction since
1925.

38   WOODWARD, C. VANN.   The Burden of Southern History.   Baton
     Rouge: Louisiana State University Press, pp. 31, 110–117,
     134–139.
          One of the most curious phenomena in the intellectual his-
     tory of the post–Civil War period was that it remained for three
     Northern writers, Melville in Clarel, Henry Adams in Democracy,
     and Henry James in The Bostonians, to acknowledge the relevance
     of the Southern tradition and bring to bear that point of view
     in their critique of American society.   As a Confederate veteran
     and as a Southerner of Indian heritage, Ungar is an American who
     has suffered two rejections, two defeats, and a double estrange-
     ment from his native land.   Whether he speaks as a Southerner or
     as part Indian, his heritage of multiple grievances lends both
     motivation and authority to his bitter pronouncements upon con-
     temporary civilization.   In framing Ungar's reply to Rolfe in
     book 4, canto 21, Melville in all probability penned the blackest
     commentary on the future of his country ever written by an Ameri-
     can in the nineteenth century.   Melville, Adams, and James were
     all deeply concerned about what had overtaken heir own society
     since the Civil War, the mediocrity, the crassness, and the
     venality they saw around them.   The South or the Southern hero,
     past or present, was a useful foil for the unlovely present or
     the symbol of some irreparable loss.

39   BENTON, RICHARD P.   "Books."   College English, 21 (January),
     238.
          Review of 1959.B1.   Babcock's introduction is all right,
     though it speaks of Typee's being part of a larger unity that
     includes Mardi, Moby-Dick, and Pierre without showing just how it
     is.   We still need introductions that are not graceful essays
     but real teaching aids.

40   JEROME, JUDSON.   "Ishmael to Ahab."   College English, 21
     (January), 228–229.
          Poem.

41 REEVES, PASCHAL. "The 'Deaf Mute' Confidence Man: Melville's
    Imposter in Action." Modern Language Notes, 75 (January),
    18-20.
        The deaf-mute in chapter 1 may Be based on a confidence-man
who passed himself off as a deaf-and-dumb Herman Melville, author
of Typee and Omoo, in Fayetteville, North Carolina, in April
1850.

42 SCHLESS, HOWARD H. "Flaxman, Dante, and Melville's Pierre."
    Bulletin of the New York Public Library, 64 (February), 62-82.
        Examination of certain central images in Mardi, Moby-Dick,
and Pierre shows that Melville often had John Flaxman's illustrations of Dante before him and used direct descriptions of them
along with the text of the Divine Comedy. Though he used Hamlet
as a source for the theme of incest, Melville's primary frame of
reference in Pierre, both structurally and symbolically, was the
Divine Comedy as a whole and the Inferno in particular. By
direct quotation from or allusion to Dante at crucial moments of
narrative and psychological crisis, Melville "foreshadows or
resolves the action of the characters and brings into focus the
background in which they move."

43 THORP, WILLARD. "Book Reviews." Modern Philology, 57
    (February), 213-215.
        Review of 1957.A2. It is difficult to get a good grip on
Stern's book. Its thesis emerges fitfully, though in the end one
has a clear idea of what is new in his approach to Melville. One
encounters many excellent insights, but the prose is often
opaque, and Stern so delights in following out every possible
ray of every putative symbol that the argument is sometimes left
behind for pages. There was undoubtedly in Melville a strong
pull to this world, this time, this place. He was suspicious of
the cloudy abstractions of the transcendentalists. He sought new
experience avidly and loved the amiable life, with all its acces-
sories of conversation, drink, news of the newest thing. Stern
focuses a strong light on this side of Melville's nature, and it
was high time a scholar did; but in so doing he leaves in shadow
other aspects of the thought and belief of this paradoxical man.
He fails to touch on crucial questions. To what extent was
Melville himself a quester? Was he invariably unsympathetic with
the Grail-seeking of his questers? Are there no tragic implications in Melville's novels, despite the fact that they do not
present the reconciliations of classical tragedy? And to what
extent is Melville's lifelong fascination with the Christ-story
reflected in his writing? At least once, in Clarel, Melville
presented a character who saw the whole history of Christianity
as a tragic unfulfillment (Celio, in part 1, canto 13). There
may be futility there, but where is the fool?

44   ABEL, LIONEL. "Metatheater." Partisan Review, 27 (Spring),
      325-326.
          Billy Budd is not a tragedy because Melville does not
      accept as true at least one implacable value--ship discipline on
      a man-of-war. (One cannot create tragedy without accepting some
      implacable values as true.) Melville was only able to get to the
      externally tragic ending of his story by depriving Vere of the
      very kind of self-consciousness he has throughout led us to
      believe Vere possessed--deprived him of self-consciousness at a
      crucial moment to make him capable of representing an implacable
      value. Melville, if captain of the Indomitable, would not have
      sentenced Billy Budd to hang.

45   JAFFÉ, DAVID. "The Captain Who Sat for the Portrait of Ahab."
      Boston University Studies in English, 4 (Spring), 1-22.
          Ahab was probably modeled on Charles Wilkes, whose six-
      volume Narrative of the U.S. Exploring Expedition . . . 1838-1842
      Melville used as a model for Queequeg and Fedallah [see 1957.B82]
      as well as for elements of plot and atmosphere. The two men have
      the same basic traits: strong will, egotism, fierce independence
      and pride, defiance of authority, monomania, harshness, lack of
      humor, energy, intellect, humanitarianism, and conscientiousness.

46   LUTWACK, LEONARD. "Mixed and Uniform Prose Styles in the
      Novel." Journal of Aesthetics & Art Criticism, 18 (March),
      351, 356.
          Moby-Dick, "even more than Tom Jones, is a prime example of
      a novel with mixed styles growing out of unassimilated genres and
      the divided mind of the author who regarded his material as both
      common whale blubber and rare mythic poetry." Between Moby-Dick
      and Ulysses the novel was committed to a uniform plain style.
      Moby-Dick is the last specimen of the early mixed-style novel,
      and Ulysses begins the return of the contemporary novel to mixed
      styles. In the period between these two works, the novel
      attained a degree of stylistic stability that made possible the
      perfection of the genre in that time.

47   SEELYE, JOHN. "The Golden Navel: The Cabalism of Ahab's
      Doubloon." Nineteenth-Century Fiction, 14 (March), 350-355.
          Discusses the meaning and structural significance of the
      doubloon in terms of the symbols stamped upon it. Its signs
      recommend moderation or balance between extremes, Ishmael's
      position. Symbolically it is the golden navel, knotting all
      conflicting attitudes to the mast, to the center of the ship.

48   CAMERON, KENNETH WALTER. "Emerson and Melville Lecture in
      New Haven (1856-1857)." Emerson Society Quarterly, No. 19
      (2d Quarter), pp. 85-96.
          Reprints advertisements and items in the New Haven Journal
      and Courier, Daily Register, and Daily Palladium, in November and
      December 1857, announcing Melville's forthcoming lecture in New
      Haven on "Roman Statuary." [See 1857.B47, B60-61.]

49   CAMERON, KENNETH WALTER. "A Note on the Corpusants in <u>Moby-Dick</u>." <u>Emerson Society Quarterly</u>, No. 19 (2d Quarter), pp. 22-24.
　　　Reprints article on "Saint Elmo's Fire" from the <u>Penny Magazine</u>, 14 (22 March 1845), pp. 106-107, which Melville may have known. Chapter 119, "The Candles," in <u>Moby-Dick</u> will eventually deserve careful study for Melville's treatment of Saint Elmo's Fire.

50   HENDRICK, GEORGE. "Literary Comments in the Letters of Henry S. Salt to W.S. Kennedy." <u>Emerson Society Quarterly</u>, No. 19 (2d Quarter), pp. 25-29.
　　　In letters to Kennedy from 1921-1928, Salt comments on <u>Typee</u> and <u>Moby-Dick</u>, refers to Arthur Stedman's abandoned intention to write a biography of Melville, and comments adversely on Weaver's biography [1921.A1].

51   WEISSBUCH, TED N. "A Note on the Confidence-Man's Counterfeit Detector." <u>Emerson Society Quarterly</u>, No. 19 (2d Quarter), pp. 16-18.
　　　Prior to the National Bank Act of 1863, counterfeit detectors were issued semiweekly, weekly, semimonthly, and monthly and were as well known as the financial pages in today's newspapers. The counterfeit detector is another one of the evils of the age that Melville was satirizing in <u>The Confidence-Man</u>.

52   FUKUMA, KIN-ICHI. "'Billy Budd': The Testament of Acceptance?" <u>Kyushu American Literature</u> [Fukuota, Japan], No. 3 (May), pp. 9-14.
　　　Melville's resignation in <u>Billy Budd</u> is not quite "rapturous," as Arvin maintains in 1950.A1, "but the surrender profuse in humane tears."

53   WRIGHT, NATHALIA. "Pierre: Herman Melville's <u>Inferno</u>." <u>American Literature</u>, 32 (May), 167-181.
　　　Parallels between the structure and some of the scenes and action of <u>Pierre</u> and Dante's <u>Inferno</u> are so extensive that <u>Pierre</u> might be called another <u>Inferno</u>. The first part of <u>Pierre</u>, set at Saddle Meadows (books 1-13), corresponds roughly to cantos 1-8 of the <u>Inferno</u>, set in the Gloomy Wood and the first five circles of hell; the second part, set in the city (books 14-26), corresponds somewhat more closely, to cantos 9-34, set in the City of Dis and the last four circles. The influence of the <u>Inferno</u> extends to the theme and meaning of the novel. In <u>Pierre</u>, Melville came close to writing an anatomy of sin, as in <u>Moby-Dick</u> he wrote an anatomy of cetology. His hero proceeds systematically through most of the categories of sin recognized by the ancient and medieval worlds, from the least to the most offensive. Reprinted in part in Willett, pp. 74-78.

54   CECCHI, EMILIO. "Two Notes on Melville." ["Moby Dick"
     (1931) and "Israel Potter" (1945).] Sewanee Review, 68
     (Summer), 398–406.
         Moby-Dick is considered in relation to "the myths which
     lie at the origin of history" (Hercules fighting the Hydra and
     the lion, Theseus killing the Minotaur, Perseus slaying the sea
     monster), and is viewed as typically American in its literary
     form, yet having a tone of its own. The longer note on Israel
     Potter finds the book dissatisfying as a whole: the story fails
     to build up internal echoes. "Melville hated the society to
     which he belonged, a society which sprang from the very exploits
     whose history he was engaged in writing. This hate robbed his
     narrative of all warmth and light." Reprinted in Vincent (1969),
     pp. 138–145.

55   FERGUSON, DeLANCEY. "The Legacy of Letters." American
     Scholar, 29 (Summer), 414.
         Review of 1960.Bll. The majority of the letters are of
     almost monumental unimportance. Perhaps 10 percent of them con-
     tain some allusions to Melville's work or express some definite
     opinions; the rest are routine business letters or family reports
     on family affairs. It is cause for endless regret that
     Hawthorne's side of the correspondence with Melville was
     destroyed: the Hawthorne-Melville letters might have equalled
     the Howells-Clemens ones, for in each case two gifted men met on
     a basis of shared ideas and mutual respect. For the sake of the
     letters to Hawthorne, a gloriously comic letter to Dana describ-
     ing an interview with Edward Moxon, and the letters to James
     Billson, the volume is worth owning. But most of the letters to
     the relatives are mere padding.

56   LA VIOLETTE, WESLEY. "Moby-Dick--A Study in Symphonic Prose."
     Literary Criterion [India], 4 (Summer), 19–23.
         Moby-Dick has a "symphonic" form of three movements of
     poetic prose.

57   MILLER, JAMES E., JR. "Tape Recorders and Fugitives."
     Prairie Schooner, 34 (Summer), 95.
         Quotes Faulkner on Moby-Dick from 1959.Bll.

58   MONTALE, EUGENIO. "An Introduction to Billy Budd (1942)."
     Sewanee Review, 68 (Summer), 419–422.
         Melville's sense of darkness and damnation finds its full
     expression in the short but perfect Billy Budd. From this point
     of view, Billy Budd, supported and illuminated by the books that
     precede it, is the crowning gem of Melville's work. Melville's
     poetic testament is at the same time an epic and an adventure
     story, a Platonic dialogue, a critical essay tinged with a
     revolutionary spirit, and a play: a mystery play showing the
     supreme sacrifice, the Christian sacrifice of the Cross. By
     making Billy Budd a real man in a real period of turmoil and
     growth, by projecting him effortlessly into a seething cultural
     world, and by giving him two exceptional men as antagonists, two
     such typical intellectuals as Claggart and Vere, Melville raised

the story of Billy Budd not only to a moral but also to an artistic height that is rarely reached. Billy Budd is a great subject in the hands of a powerful poet who has concentrated into it all the phantasms, all the idols and the secrets of a lifetime. Reprinted in Vincent (1971), pp. 17–19.

59 PAVESE, CESARE. "The Literary Whaler." Sewanee Review, 68 (Summer), 407–418.
    Unlike "fastidious neo-barbarians" of today making their return to nature, Melville "lived first through real adventures, through the primitive state. He was first a barbarian and then, later, he entered the world of culture and thought, bringing with him the sanity and balance he had acquired in the life he had been leading." His ideal is Ishmael, "a sailor who can row half a day behind a whale with his illiterate companions, and then retire to a masthead to meditate on Plato." Melville was the brother of the many barbarous Americans who were among the least easily satisfied and most refined craftsmen of the century. He was "a true Greek. Reading European evasions of literature makes you feel more literary than ever; you feel tiny, cerebral, effeminate; reading Melville . . . you expand your lungs, you enlarge your brain, you feel more alive and more of a man." Melville's roots are in "the seventeenth century which includes a good half of the sixteenth century as well." In Moby-Dick "the Bible is to be felt at every step," not only in the characters' names but in "the constant presence of a spirit of Puritan awe and severity, turning what might have been a scientific tale of terror in the Poe tradition into a dark moral tragedy." The writers with whom "he can most justifiably be connected are Rabelais and the Elizabethans, in whom the same love of catalogues, of verbal profusion and of vivez joyeux are present." But "the current at which Melville drank most deeply" was Platonizing rationalism. Thomas Browne "was not only his teacher of style, but his spiritual father." Melville "is one of the doubting Thomases who are to be found precisely in the seventeenth century." Moby-Dick maintains a balance between its rational and transcendental elements. In Melville's failures—Mardi, Pierre, The Confidence-Man—"the rational element might be said to kill the transcendental." First published in Italian in La Cultura (January–March 1932). Reprinted in Recognition, pp. 194–203; reprinted in part in Vincent (1969), pp. 141–145.

60 SEIDENSTICKER, EDWARD. "Redskins in Japan." Kenyon Review, 22 (Summer), 380 , 384–385.
    Reports that Moby-Dick is more praised than admired in Japan, the result perhaps of problems in translating the book into Japanese.

61 SUTTON, WALTER. "Melville and the Great God Budd." Prairie Schooner, 34 (Summer), 128–133.
    The concepts of Buddhism, as interpreted by Schopenhauer, were particularly congenial to Melville during his last years. They help to explain some of the problems of motivation in Billy Budd and to provide a consistent reading of the work. Vere,

apprehending the truth that "we had better not be," sees his condemnation of Billy as less a punishment than a boon. Billy conquers his will to live, while Vere, who recognizes in Billy an ideal of renunciation toward which he aspires, lives in the agony of the will till his death scene. Central to Melville's controlling point of view in Billy Budd is the Buddhist idea of the illusory nature of human existence. Reprinted in Springer, pp. 83–89.

62 VITTORINI, ELIO. "An Outline of American Literature (1941)." Sewanee Review, 68 (Summer), 433–434.
    Of Poe, Hawthorne, and Melville, the latter was the most pessimistic. He did not really believe that man could raise the whole of himself and of his life to the level of absolute purity, always suspecting that some part of man would remain corrupt. His skepticism increased his bitterness; but he believed in the struggle, wanting to fight to the death for the purity he was unable to believe in. Only in the sea could Melville find complete certainty.

63 WOODRUFF, STUART C. "Melville and His Chimney." PMLA, 75 (June), 283–292.
    "I and My Chimney" is a thoroughgoing symbolic expression of Melville's basic epistemology. Critics (such as Sealts in 1941.B26, Sedgwick in 1944.A1, and Arvin in 1950.A1) are mistaken in taking the chimney as an emblem of the narrator or Melville himself. The chimney is an emblem of the empirical reality of time and its manifestation as history. One of the main themes of the story is the inevitable necessity and wisdom of living within a temporal, historical dimension, without, like the narrator's wife, trying to destroy or ignore the only existence we may have—the "sober, substantial fact" of the chimney itself. Through the wife Melville criticizes idealism and America's lack of an historical perspective and its unwillingness to face empirical realities that tended to refute the flattering but naive concept of the new Eden.

64 HICKS, GRANVILLE. "Correspondence of a Gentle Man." Saturday Review, 43 (18 June), 15.
    Review of 1960.B11. Surprisingly, Davis and Gilman have not located a single letter written between January 1841, when Melville set sail on the Acushnet, and October 1844, when he returned on the United States. We know Melville well enough to be sure that there were letters to his home, and it seems a pity they have all vanished, for there is much they could tell us about the way his imagination worked. The letters to Hawthorne stand apart from the remainder of the correspondence, their quality more startlingly apparent when we come upon them after reading dozens of formal business letters and pleasant little notes to relatives and friends. Melville sometimes revealed himself in letters to Evert Duyckinck, but it was only to Hawthorne that he disclosed the heights and depths of his being. The letters do not bear out the suggestion of some biographers that Melville became something of a recluse after the collapse

of his literary career. In these later years we see Melville as moderately sociable, affectionate in his relations with those who were close to him, outwardly cheerful; but he seems subdued, and the letters have an air of gentle resignation. Melville was not a man who as a rule put much of himself into his correspondence, but for that very reason the letters probably give us an accurate impression of him as he appeared to most of his contemporaries. For once, in the letters to Hawthorne, he took off the mask but soon resumed it, and few could have had glimpses behind it. Who would have guessed that the amiable old man of the later letters wrote <u>Billy Budd</u>?

65   ABEL, DARREL. "'Laurel Twined with Thorn': The Theme of Melville's <u>Timoleon</u>." <u>Personalist</u>, 41 (July), 330–340.
      <u>Timoleon</u> is unifed by its varied reiteration of the theme that preoccupied Melville's thoughts at the close of his career--that bold and original thinking alienates artists and intellectuals from their fellow men.

66   MOORE, HARRY T. "One of the Heroes is Ahab." New York <u>Times Book Review</u> (17 July), p. 4.
      Review of 1960.A1. Finds similarity between Bowen's view of Vere in <u>Billy Budd</u> and the central character in <u>The Confidence-Man</u> and Thompson's view in 1952.A2. Instead of putting Bartleby with Ahab, Bowen should perhaps have devised another category for passive resisters and inept heroes. Part of his difficulty springs from his laudable and often useful attempt to impose formulas on dynamically complex material. In trying to stir up greater appreciation of <u>Pierre</u> and <u>Clarel</u>, Bowen has further difficulty because he is working almost exclusively in thematic terms that cannot in themselves provide the basis for final evaluation of the works: the ideas ultimately have to be judged in terms of their expression. When this is done with <u>Pierre</u>, it comes out as crude in prose and melodramatic in incident, while <u>Clarel</u> reveals much of the commonplace in its imprisoning short lines, though it also contains some excellent poetry and is grandly conceived against the background of the Holy Land. Bowen's book is a valuable addition to Melville criticism, however; the first part in particular should both help the general reader and please the specialist.

67   THOMPSON, LAWRANCE. "In His Own Hand." New York <u>Times Book Review</u>, (17 July), p. 4.
      Review of 1960.B11. The work has been carried out with meticulous care and supplemented with excellent textual notes. It is not the editors' fault that many of these too few letters were written to publishers about relatively uninteresting technical arrangements and that none of the newly printed letters adds importantly to our knowledge of Melville. Our "primary concern is likely to be with letters that help to illuminate the only partially understood phases of that psyche which could permit Melville to be affable to friends and neighbors even while feeling a deeply anguished sense of physical and metaphysical isolation, not only from society in general but also from

certain individuals who were most closely related to him. Our
primary source of information on that score is provided, not by
his letters so much as by the sarcastic and satirical elements
in his prose narratives." A few exceptions: Melville's letters
to Hawthorne (the one man with whom Melville could share even his
metaphysical suspicions) and to the admiring English coterie of
his later years (Billson, Salt, Barrs), which ought to be enlightening to those who may still try to read the ambiguous
Billy Budd as Melville's final testament of acceptance. One
possible gap in this impeccable edition: the failure to include
as textual and supporting notes the best of Mrs. Melville's letters concerning her husband's mental health, written to Catherine
Gansevoort Lansing in 1877, just after Melville had finished
Clarel. Already available in print, those letters tell us more
about Melville's temperament at that time than all of his known
letters to his relatives.

68   LASK, THOMAS. "Books of the Times." New York Times
      (20 July), section 3, p. 27.
         Review of 1960.B11. Finds in Melville's letters a massive
reticence about anything that touched their author deeply and a
marmoreal formality of manner. Only in the letters to Hawthorne,
and to a lesser extent to Evert Duyckinck, do we see the man
behind the full-length beard. This is not to say that there is
nothing of interest in the rest of the correspondence--which is
revealing in many ways. But the Letters give us Melville as he
lived; the vital part of him lies elsewhere.

69   THORP, WILLARD. "Much Has Perished; These Have Survived."
      New York Herald Tribune Book Review (24 July), p. 6.
         Review of 1960.B11. To two men only did Melville let him-
self go in letters that are full of the excitement of self-
discovery--Nathaniel Hawthorne and Evert Duyckinck. Oddly
enough, the surviving letters make up a true representative
selection, with letters from Melville the family man and Melville
the author. The editorial skill of Davis and Gilman cannot be
praised too highly. The reader who wishes to go straight through
with the letters is not held up by long footnotes or arguments
about the text; yet everything is in the "Textual Notes" which
the Melville scholar needs. The text can be trusted concerning
what Melville wrote or intended to write. Only a few of the
forty-two previously unpublished letters are intrinsically
valuable, but each in its way helps to enlarge the picture.

70   DAHLBERG, EDWARD. "Moby-Dick--An Hamitic Dream." Literary
      Review, 4 (Autumn), 87-118.
         Dahlberg used to love Melville [see 1941.B8] but has
changed his mind. Melville's separation from the human race was
as deranged as Bartleby's. Moby-Dick, a verbose, tractarian
fable on whaling, is a book of monotonous and unrelenting gloom.
The malady common to both Ishmael and Ahab is unrelieved, warping
coldness. Melville seems to have taken his revenge against the
characters in his book as a reprisal for his own solitude--they
have private, mouldy hearts. In Moby-Dick water is less a

natural element than a biblical, allegorical substance. Of the
four powers of nature, Melville selected the one that grieved his
spirit the most. He had no understanding of heroic size in literature and tried to achieve the epic by hurling hoaxing, hot
phrases at the reader. Melville was as luckless with his metaphors as he was with his characters. The atrabilious Ahab is
only wicked in the sluttish, supine words with which Melville
depicts him. Moby-Dick is only the lees of other men's marine
law. Though he was a novelist, Melville had almost no knowledge
of people. Like Whitman, Poe, and Thoreau, he loathed the
female. Eros is the source of masculine life and wit, but in
Melville's work no woman is bedded, seduced, or gulled. Melville
composed amorous canticles to an oceanic brute; woman is a per-
fidious creature in Moby-Dick. It is inhuman literature. Melville's imagination was sodomitic; he abhorred nature; he was a
perverted Christian; and the tawdry writing in Moby-Dick is to
some extent willful self-hatred. Reprinted in Burnshaw,
pp. 183–213, and Dahlberg (1964), pp. 115–142.

71   HOWARD, LEON. "The Case of the Missing Whaler." Manuscripts,
      12 (Fall), 3–9.
         Account of the ultimately successful search, by Leon
Howard, Harrison Hayford, Wilson Heflin, and Jay Leyda, for the
document that proved that Melville was a member of the crew of
the whaler Charles and Henry from early November 1842 to early
May 1843.

72   PHILBRICK, THOMAS. "Melville's 'Best Authorities.'"
      Nineteenth-Century Fiction, 15 (September), 171–179.
         The many authorities cited in White Jacket have been taken
as evidence of Melville's wide knowledge of world naval history,
but the bulk of his information was drawn from three articles
published in two of the best known periodicals of his day, two
in the Edinburgh Review and one in the Democratic Review. That
Melville usually made little effort to improve or even alter the
plodding diction and syntax of his originals testifies to his
relative lack of interest in his role as expositor and propa-
gandist.

73   FORREY, ROBERT. "On Melville." Mainstream, 13 (October),
      63–65.
         Review of 1960.A1, B11. The Letters will be a valuable aid
to future Melville scholarship and will probably appeal mainly to
specialists. The notes attached to the letters are probably the
most valuable part of the book. Davis's and Gilman's own work
[1952.A1 and 1951.A2, respectively] and the Letters "are part of
the best Melville scholarship in this country. Along with Jay
Leyda's Melville Log, this school of Melville criticism has
avoided the Freudian approach. Instead of concentrating on
Melville's psyche, they have examined instead the actual events
which make up the life and age of Melville and brought this to
bear on their treatment of his writing. The chief limitation of
this school is its disinclination to do much with the wealth of
material they have painstakingly accumulated." On the other

hand, Bowen's "avowed purpose is to avoid making application of any of the historical and literary material on Melville that has been gathered by a generation of Melville scholars. Just what the advantages of such a scholarly blackout are one can not easily see."

74   KAPLAN, CHARLES. "Jack Burden: Modern Ishmael." College English, 22 (October), 19–24.
         Finds "remarkable parellelisms" between Moby-Dick and Robert Penn Warren's All the King's Men.

75   KASEGAWA, KOH. "Melville's Image of Solitude." Aoyama Journal of General Education, No. 1 (November), 157–199.
         Examines the theme of solitude or isolation in Melville, "paying special attention to his concept that man should attain to a state of spiritual perfection by looking away from the external life to the inner life of his soul."

76   POCHMANN, HENRY A. "Book Reviews." American Literature, 32 (November), 333–334.
         Review of Primitivismus und Naturalismus im Prosaschaffen Herman Melvilles, by Klaus Lanzinger (Insbruck, 1959). One of the soundest books on American literature that has come out of Germany in twenty-five or thirty years, certainly the best on Melville since Sundermann's Melvilles Gedankengut. [See 1938.B32, B42; 1939.B16, B18, B25; 1940.B19.] Even so, it provides incontestable evidence that literary scholarship in Germany has not yet regained its erstwhile status. The book has all the marks of having originated as a series of undergraduate lectures on Melville in general and then, having been revised in line with the special subject of its title, with the result that many pages are either tangential or entirely extraneous to the matter in hand. Aside from what he has to say about primitivism and naturalism, Lanzinger adds very little to what Anderson [1939.A1], Arvin [1950.A1], Howard [1951.A3], Leyda [1951.A4], Sedgwick [1944.A1], and Thorp [1938.B22] long ago put before us. The book takes into account special insights provided by Baird [1956.A1], Chase [1949.A1], Geist [1939.A2], Stern [1957.A2], Thompson [1952.A2], and Vincent [1949.A3]; but here again Lanzinger's observations are largely gratuitous because they are repetitious. Lanzinger's judgments appear sound without being startling. There is a regrettable overemphasis on the auto-biographical content of Melville's writings, with a corresponding minimizing of the influence on Melville of his reading. The strict definition Lanzinger fastens on naturalism may not be in accord with what practicing naturalists consider naturalism, but he is undoubtedly correct in concluding that Melville, despite his flirtations with primitivism and naturalism, vitalism and nihilism, remained basically a dualist and a humanist.

77   SHERMAN, STUART C. "Logbooks and Leviathans: An Account of
      the Nicholson Whaling Collection." <u>Polar Notes: Occasional
      Publication of the Stefansson Collection, Dartmouth College
      Library</u>, No. 2 (November), 24–31.
          Details of the whaling collection at the Providence, Rhode
      Island, Public Library, which in August 1960 included 611 manu-
      script logbooks and journals, 66 account books and outfitting
      records, 18 crew lists, and thousands of miscellaneous letters,
      diaries, and economic papers involved in the outfitting of ves-
      sels, the sale of oil, and the settlement of voyages. The col-
      lection has been used by scholars charting the course of
      Melville's whaling experience.

78   GLAZIER, LYLE. "American Originals." <u>American Quarterly</u>, 12
      (Winter), 520–522.
          Review of 1960.B11. The volume is "modestly but thoroughly
      annotated. Though there are few new letters, Melville scholars
      will welcome this authoritative and complete edition up to date."

79   STEIN, WILLIAM BYSSHE. "The Motif of the Wise Old Man in
      <u>Billy Budd</u>." <u>Western Humanities Review</u>, 14 (Winter), 99–101.
          The characterization of the ancient Dansker illuminates the
      betrayal of traditional morality in <u>Billy Budd</u>. Melville intends
      the reader to find both Vere and the Dansker guilty of a sin
      against common humanity, specifically disregard for the Eucharis-
      tic injunction of Christ: "A new commandment give I unto you,
      that ye love one another." The Dansker's frivolous insinuations
      constitute a betrayal of the archetypal role of the Wise Old Man:
      knowing Billy's lack of sophistication, he nevertheless persists
      in mocking his gullibility. His "guarded cynicism" implies an
      absence of faith in human virtue and his alienation from the
      Christian community of love and fellowship and from the basic
      teachings of the Savior, the ideal of brotherhood embodied in
      the "new commandment." While he remains faithful to the king in
      his obedience of the naval code, he betrays the King of all man-
      kind, as does Vere in his abject submission to the authority of
      a temporal monarch.

80   TANSELLE, G. THOMAS. "Herman Melville's Visit to Galena in
      1840." <u>Journal of the Illinois State Historical Society</u>, 53
      (Winter), 376–388.
          Details of the people and places Melville saw during his
      visit to his Uncle Thomas drawn from contemporary records.

81   WEATHERS, WILLIE T. "<u>Moby Dick</u> and the Nineteenth-Century
      Scene." <u>Texas Studies in Literature and Language</u>, 1 (Winter),
      477–501.
          The fictional events of <u>Moby-Dick</u> and the actual events of
      the period present a striking parallelism of fact and fiction.
      "The historical evidence supports belief that Bulkington, the
      Pequod's pilot as she leaves harbor, is meant for commentary on
      the tragic flaw in Ahab's leadership by recalling the rational
      idealist Thomas Jefferson; and that the characterization of the
      Pequod's irrational captain is indebted not only to the

Promethean rebels and reformers of myth and literature, but more immediately to the radical abolitionist and moral perfectionist, William Lloyd Garrison."

82   BERTHOFF, WARNER. "'Certain Phenomenal Men': The Example of Billy Budd." ELH, 27 (December), 334–351.
        Common to most discussion of Billy Budd is the assumption that the story is allegorical--a narrative representation of some universal truth or law or balance of contraries, a parable of Good and Evil, a reenactment of the Fall, a projected myth of a ritual killing that is also a resurrection. The story is full of quickening intimations as to the larger, perhaps universal, circumstance of human life, but its decisive narrative logic and cogency are to be found elsewhere--in Melville's effort to "define and denominate certain phenomenal men." In Billy Budd he undertakes to define not universal truth but certain specific and contingent examples of being and behavior. The decisive virtue in Melville's best writing is its insistent thrust toward an entire explicitness, an unstinting exactness. Like so many major Americans, he is an explainer, and his stories are very often most satisfying when most explanatory, contrary to Jamesian dogmas of dramatization. What Melville chiefly wants us to know in Billy Budd is the phenomenal quality of character, the magnanimity and greatness of soul in his two heroes, Billy and Vere. As the story moves to its close, we are shown how each in his own way has instructed the other--how the magnanimity possible to virtuous innocence has fulfilled itself and in turn given its mysterious blessing to the world-sustaining magnanimity of experienced and commissioned virtue. In Billy Budd we find a concentration and integrity of performance that match the best of Melville's earlier career. There is no indignation or outrage in the telling of Billy Budd--no quarrel with God or society or law or nature or any agency of human suffering. Rather there is a poise, a sureness of judgment, a compassionate objectivity, and most of all a readiness of apprehension possible only to an actual, measurable greatness of mind. Reprinted, with some revision, in Berthoff (1962), pp. 183–203, and Vincent (1971), pp. 67–81.

83   CATTON, BRUCE. "Deep-Diving Whale." American Heritage, 12 (December), 110–111.
        Notice of 1960.B11. Mostly quotations from the letters.

84   CLUBB, MERREL D., JR. "The Second Personal Pronoun in Moby-Dick." American Speech, 35 (December), 252–260.
        Among the many variations from the standard you form in Moby-Dick three patterns seem to develop: (1) both ye and thou forms appear to be used realistically in certain instances for purposes of characterization (as a rendering of Quaker usage); (2) Ishmael often switches from an ordinary indefinite you to an elevated indefinite thou form; (3) Ahab almost always uses singular thou forms, both realistically and metaphorically. Further, you, as it is used for straight narration and realistic

description, becomes symbolic of the common-sense view of the world, and _thou_ becomes symbolic of the philosophical view.

85   FINKELSTEIN, SIDNEY. "Six Ways of Looking at Reality." _Mainstream_, 13 (December), 32-33.
        Analysis of the "strong, direct and realistic description" of the Church of the Apostles in _Pierre_, book 19, chapter 1, and the passage's ironic questioning of industrial progress.

86   FOGLE, RICHARD HARTER. "_Billy Budd_: The Order of the Fall." _Nineteenth-Century Fiction_, 15 (December), 189-205.
        In opposition to various "heretical" readings of _Billy Budd_ as an exercise in irony [unspecified, but _see_, for example, 1950.B64], Fogle emphasizes "the large affirmative elements" of the work, "which make of it a celebration rather than a condemnation of reality and its mysterious Master." A story not of diminution but of magnification, not of Aristotelian comedy but of Aristotelian tragedy, _Billy Budd_ "contains ironies and ambiguities aplenty, but they are such as arise naturally from profound meditation upon a tragic theme of great magnitude." Vere resembles Melville, particularly in his conservative love of order. We can "confidently exculpate" Vere "from the guilt that inheres in the code he carries out because he so thoroughly understands its limitations, and so clearly distinguishes between its empirical measures and the absolute values of divine justice." Reprinted in part in Springer, pp. 81-82.

87   HOUGH, ROBERT L. "Books." _College English_, 22 (December), 207.
        Review of 1957.A2. Though Stern's view of Melville as an antiromantic in revolt against transcendentalism is not new, his book is a discerning summary of that position. Stern demonstrates Melville's ultimate attitude that nature and God are uncaring and completely amoral and that man operating within this framework must plan and impose "his own pattern of morality upon history by controlling his own fate." In Stern's view, Captain Vere becomes _the_ Melville hero because he uses his understanding of the universe to guide his actions even though he foresees the ultimate tragedy. Stern's analyses are perceptive and tightly organized though his prose is overwrought in places.

88   HOWARD, LEON. "Notes and Reviews." _Nineteenth-Century Fiction_, 15 (December), 262-265.
        Review of 1960.A1. Few critics who feel Melville's attraction can resist the temptation to read into his writings their own fears and fancies. Bowen is one of these few. Part 1 of his book is brilliantly successful: one gets a persuasive demonstration of the increasing depth of Melville's concern for the problem of self and its pervasive effect on every aspect of his imagination. In his discussion of Melville's tragic heroes Bowen is equally successful. Nowhere in print is there a better critical estimation of Ahab and Pierre and of their relationship to certain of Melville's other characters. But in the weakly

submissive characters (Nehemiah, Babbalanja, Starbuck, and especially Vere), Bowen loses touch with Melville's imagination and perhaps begins to substitute his own view of the world for Melville's. Surely Melville intended Billy to be the submissive character, not Vere, despite Vere's acceptance of the conventions Pierre defied. Bowen is right in denying that Billy Budd is Melville's "testament of acceptance," but wrong in considering it a study in compromise. He is even more wrong in presenting Ishmael and Clarel as representatives of "the way of wisdom" by which the self "accepts" the world in an attitude of "armed neutrality." Neither is well armed or very wise, and neither is required to face the challenge of Ahab's emotions or the social responsibility of Vere. Melville the artist is quietly transformed in the course of Bowen's book, losing the depth and intensity of imagination attributed to him at the beginning and becoming a manipulator of "strategies." The Tennysonian wisdom of the Epilogue to Clarel somehow becomes more profound than the questioning ambiguities of Pierre. Yet The Long Encounter is substantially the best critical essay on Melville, and probably a better will be written only by someone who is willing to follow Bowen's lead by delving into the questions and contradictions in Melville's mind without yielding to his impulse to resolve them.

89   JACKSON, MARGARET Y. "Melville's Use of a Real Slave Mutiny in 'Benito Cereno.'" CLA Journal, 4 (December), 79–93.
       Melville transformed a dull uniliterary narrative into a structurally perfect tale of terror by presenting the action rather than by narrating it, by avoiding a monotonous repetition of incidents, by withholding the surprise element (the mutiny) until the final scene, and by maintaining a unity of impression throughout. He also made slaves, the only ones in any way excusable for their actions, into the single force of evil and could not have been completely oblivious of the damaging consequences of his distortion of the truth at a time when the controversy over slavery was at its peak. Proslavery readers could read between the lines that Melville supported the institution of slavery in America. Melville's chief concern in "Benito Cereno" is not with the slavery question but with the problem of good and evil; he seized upon the Negro to represent the formidable force against which good could offer no substantial resistance.

90   KASEGAWA, KOH. "On the Symbolic Meanings of Blackness and Darkness in Melville." Thought Currents in English Literature [Tokyo], 33 (December), 75–103.
       The symbolic meanings are mental suffering, intellectual perplexity, and sin.

91   O'DANIEL, THERMAN B. "Herman Melville as a Writer of Journals." CLA Journal, 4 (December), 94–105.
       Account of the contents of Melville's three journals, Melville's circumstances at the time of their composition, and his use of them in his subsequent works.

92   ROSENBERRY, EDWARD H. "Awash in Melvilliana." New England
      Quarterly, 33 (December), 523-528.
         Review of 1960.A1-2, B11. The three volumes prove in vary-
      ing degrees useful and sensible, if less than final and indis-
      pensable. The most nearly final and indispensable is, by its
      very nature, the long-awaited collection of Melville's letters.
      Few of the previously unpublished letters, apart from Melville's
      first letter to Hawthorne, can boast much inherent interest. Far
      more significant is the establishment of a reliable text of what
      Melville wrote, even or especially in the case of letters re-
      printed in a score of places. Instances of pedantry occur in the
      maintenance or correction of Melville's spelling; but faced with
      the irregularities and frustrations of a Melville manuscript, few
      readers could find cause to complain seriously of the judgments
      of these wise and careful scholars. Most valuable of all their
      contributions are the notes, providing a wealth of background and
      commentary that may surely make some claim to being definitive,
      despite occasional documentary error. In a sense, the real
      importance of the book is not the letters--which have already
      been made to tell their story in Leyda's Log [1951.A4] and
      elsewhere--but the annotations, which enable even a reader long
      familiar with the best of the letters to reread with fresh under-
      standing and appreciation.
         Bowen's thesis is clear, stimulating, and essentially un-
      assailable. Bowen describes the confrontation of the self and
      the not-self in Melville's writings with thoroughness, insight,
      and judgment; that is the strength of his book. He does not
      assess their power to impel imaginative participation in the
      confrontation, and that is its weakness. His method illuminates
      the meaning of a book or poem but passes no judgment on how well
      it is written. Some of the quotations, particularly from Mardi
      and Pierre, are positively embarrassing to the lucid, unpreten-
      tious discussions they are called on to illustrate.
         An introductory chapter in Fogle's book generalizes on
      several relevant aspects of Melville's mind and art, but it lacks
      focus; the book as a whole has nothing in particular to say. No
      central thesis unites the chapters; no sustained consideration of
      genre lends peculiar point to the selection of material. But the
      reader in search of a helpful analysis of this or that story will
      find it in many cases. Fogle is best on "Benito Cereno," weakest
      on "Cock-A-Doodle-Doo!" of which his reading seems simply unin-
      formed. Where Fogle is well informed, he is sometimes, as in his
      discussion of "The Tartarus of Maids," unable to escape the
      duplication that constantly threatens so crowded a field as
      Melville criticism. Among the many, if miscellaneous, strengths
      of the book, is a clear recognition of Melville's faults as a
      storyteller: his lack of ease, his difficulty with narrative
      point of view, his frequent inappropriateness of tone. So
      obtrusive are these faults that it is hard for the critic who
      cannot fall back on praise of Moby-Dick to maintain the image of
      Melville's greatness. Fogle proposes that even the worst of the
      tales are "transformed" by Melville's searching intelligence, but
      he does not say what they are transformed into. He admits it is

not art, and the alternatives are not easy to name with the
standard critical vocabulary. These three books enforce the
conclusion that Melville's power lay mainly in his conceptions,
and his weakness mainly in his execution--his craft. It is clear
from the letters that for all his sensitivity and perspicacity
Melville had a defect of taste that betrayed him into strange
excesses, and an impatience with mechanical punctilio that
hindered his mastery of technique.

93   ROSENBERRY, EDWARD H. "Melville's Ship of Fools." PMLA, 75
     (December), 604-608.
        Both White-Jacket and the Ship of Fools tradition "may have
exerted a significant or even a definitive influence" on the
structure and meaning of The Confidence-Man.

94   STEIN, WILLIAM BYSSHE. "Melville's Comedy of Faith." ELH, 27
     (December), 315-333.
        "The Piazza" dramatizes the narrator's quest for spiritual
regeneration and his failure to pass crucial tests of self-
knowledge. In his reluctance to apply any kind of moral discrim-
ination to the ambiguities of human experience, he disqualifies
himself as a potential redeemer of the waste land of his age,
figuratively the region through which he journeys. Since "he
refuses to recognize his innate visionary and spiritual propensities, he becomes a fool of thought, a caricature of the
nineteenth-century mind in its optimistic rationalism. Alienated
from the vital sources of traditional morality and yet secretly
dissatisfied with the limitations of reason, he compulsively
resorts to fantasy in order to adjust himself to the imperfections of temporal existence." In this displacement of God with
wishful dreams, Melville isolates a characteristic of the igno-
minious comedy of faith in his times. The ordeal in fairy cot-
tage recapitulates the trial of the Grail Knight in the Marvelous
Castle. The initiation is designed to offer the hero a chance to
attain a new identity, a new awareness, that will elicit the
virtue of selflessness. He fails the test, preferring self-
deception to the self-knowledge that would guide him back to
Christian faith. "All of Melville's short stories deal with the
problem of faith, and each of them employs a reflecting sensibility that captures a different facet of the dissociation of
thought engendered by the nineteenth-century conflict between
morality and moralism, between traditional Christianity and
rational piety."

95   W[INTERICH], J[OHN] T. "With the Paperbacks." New York
     Herald Tribune Book Review (25 December), p. 32.
        Review of paperback edition of 1958.A3. Levin throughout
maintains an admirable perspective and nowhere loses his way
among the minutiae of scholarship.

96   ANON. "Diving Deep." London <u>Times Literary Supplement</u>,
      No. 3070 (30 December), p. 838.
          Review of 1960.B11. Another example of the thoroughness we
      have come to expect from the better American scholars. The anno-
      tation is always adequate and more often good, though on occasion
      unnecessarily full. The only grounds for complaint are an
      irritating finicalness in the textual notes and the annoying
      relegation to the back of all information about the sources of
      the texts. Melville's letters to his English publishers and
      those of the same years to the few friends he could address
      intimately, especially Evert Duyckinck, display something of the
      power he was showing in his books and are fine letters, anthology
      pieces of their kind. The significance of the letters to the
      Hawthornes, the most remarkable of all, can hardly be over-
      estimated, but the swift undercurrent of hysteria running through
      them makes them as painful as they are absorbing. After them
      comes the silence, broken only by domestic notes, which once or
      twice expand to show that the even tenor of Melville's days was
      more apparent than real. It is splendid to dive as Melville
      could; but to dive too deep is to be lost, to yourself as well as
      to the world, as the epistolary record of Melville's last thirty
      years so pitiably shows--years relieved only by the late inter-
      ruption of his young admirers.

Subject Index

Dwight, Timothy, <u>Travels in New England and New York</u>, 1940.B20

Eggleston, Edward, 1958.B61
Eliot, Thomas Stearns, 1941.B1; 1944.B38; 1959.B40
Ellis, Havelock, 1950.B31; 1958.B50
Ellis, William, <u>Polynesian Researches</u>, 1937.B25; 1957.B54
Elwes, Robert, 1936.B30
Emerson, Ralph Waldo, 1931.B5-6, B22, B39; 1932.B21; 1933.B17; 1934.B3; 1935.B16, B31; 1936.B6; 1937.B38; 1938.B23, B32, B42; 1939.B18, B37; 1941.A1, B1, B7, B29, B37, B41; 1942.B6, B10; 1943.B21; 1944.B9; 1945.B4, B21, B23; 1946.B13, B30; 1947.B32, B73; 1948.B4, B6, B17, B54; 1949.B13, B19, B37, B94; 1950.B14, B31; 1952.B26, B42, B84; 1953.A1, B6, B10, B66, B69; 1954.B4, B9; 1955.B5; 1957.A2, B18, B28, B34; 1958.B5, B9; 1959.B24, B32, B79; 1960.B19, B48
-The <u>Conduct of Life</u>, 1937.B38
-<u>Essays: First Series</u>, 1937.B38
-<u>Essays: Second Series</u>, 1937.B38
-<u>Nature</u>, 1931.B6
-<u>Poems</u>, 1950.B31
"Encantadas, The," 1931.B18, B31; 1932.B34-35; 1936.B2, B15; 1938.B23; 1940.B14-15; 1941.B20; 1948.B12, B31, B79; 1949.B2, B22, B58, B69, B99; 1950.A1; 1951.B21; 1953.A4, B56; 1955.B15, B53; 1956.B13; 1958.B65; 1960.A4
<u>Encyclopedia Americana</u>, 1953.B52; 1957.B13
<u>Encyclopaedia Britannica</u>, 1953.B65
Everett, Edward, 1948.B21
Evil, 1931.B1, B6, B19; 1932.B1, B16; 1933.B11, B22; 1934.B7, B10; 1935.B31; 1936.B31; 1937.B15, B20, B33, B38;
1938.B10, B23, B45; 1939.B25; 1940.B21, B32, B39; 1941.B22; 1945.B4; 1943.A1, B11; 1945.B35; 1946.B9, B13, B17, B24, B34; 1947.B5, B13, B16, B62, B64, B71; 1948.B1, B22-23, B59, B70, B81; 1949.B6, B24, B54, B61, B63, B65, B79, B96; 1950.A3-4, B64, B85; 1951.A2, B6, B21, B33, B44-45, B80, B104; 1952.B10, B33-34, B78; 1953.B6, B17, B25, B28, B35, B59; 1954.B9, B21-23; 1955.B17-18, B36, B40, B61; 1957.B4, B11, B32, B62; 1958.B1, B41, B45, B73; 1959.B3, B27, B45, B52, B56, B58, B61-62, B64, B69, B75, B77; 1960.B4, B51, B89

Farquhar, Sir Walter, 1932.B17; 1948.B21
Fasolato, Agostino, 1952.B35
Faulkner, William, 1931.B39; 1936.B6; 1944.B9; 1949.B25; 1952.B27, B95, B99; 1956.B24, B45; 1957.A2; 1959.B10-11; 1960.B57
Fayaway, 1937.B34; 1948.B11, B49; 1959.B4
Ferguson, Robert, <u>Artic Harpooner: A Voyage on the Schooner Abbie Bradford, 1878-1879</u>, 1939.B28
Field, D.D., <u>A History of Berkshire County, Mass.</u>, 1940.B20
Fielding, Henry, <u>Tom Jones</u>, 1960.B46
First editions, 1931.B8, B40; 1932.B8, B28; 1938.B37; 1939.B5; 1940.B13; 1941.B2; 1945.B15; 1947.B15, B20, B31, B55; 1948.B5; 1949.B28, B47; 1951.B61, B65, B72, B81; 1952.B12; 1954.B2; 1956.B64; 1957.B64; 1958.B53
Fitzgerald, Francis Scott, 1952.B95
Flaubert, Gustave, 1944.B28; 1958.B3, B8
-<u>Madame Bovary</u>, 1958.B3

Hawthorne, Nathaniel, 1931.A1,
  B2, B5-6, B10, B24, B34, B39;
  1932.B1, B7, B11-12, B20,
  B24, B36; 1933.B7; 1934.B1,
  B3, B19; 1935.B7, B23;
  1936.B3, B5-6, B9, B31, B35;
  1937.B2, B22; 1938.B4, B14,
  B22, B42; 1939.B18; 1940.B8,
  B33, B38; 1941.A1, B1, B4,
  B9-11, B29, B37, B39;
  1942.B25-26; 1943.B15, B18;
  1944.B3, B5, B9, B16, B23,
  B29; 1945.B27, B30; 1946.B1,
  B11-13, B33-34; 1947.B32,
  B53, B69-70, B73; 1948.B4,
  B6, B8, B17, B28, B47, B73-
  74; 1949.A3, B13-16, B21,
  B36-37, B52, B77, B94, B98;
  1950.B1, B14, B25, B28, B60,
  B88, B91, B111; 1951.B5, B70,
  B89-90, B98, B102; 1952.B3,
  B7, B12, B26-27, B41, B58,
  B85, B88, B98; 1953.A1, B6,
  B10, B14, B16, B28-30, B35,
  B55, B69, B75; 1954.B4, B6,
  B12, B18, B47, B53; 1955.B8,
  B31, B40; 1956.B4, B40, B65-
  66, B81; 1957.B2, B4, B22,
  B27-28, B35, B63, B87;
  1958.B4-5, B9, B22, B40, B45-
  47; B54, B67, B70, B74, B78;
  1959.B9, B24, B40, B60, B63,
  B72, B78; 1960.B9, B24, B55,
  B62, B64, B67-69, B96
-The Blithedale Romance,
  1936.B31; 1941.B9; 1950.B88;
  1951.B5; 1958.B45
-"Ethan Brand," 1931.B24;
  1932.B7; 1946.B12; 1951.B70;
  1955.B40; 1956.B40; 1957.B28
-The House of Seven Gables,
  1952.B12
-The Marble Faun, 1936.,B31;
  1958.B4
-Mosses From an Old Manse,
  1932.B3; 1940.B33; 1949.A3,
  1952.B85
-The Scarlet Letter, 1931.B6;
  1935.B7; 1936.B9, B35;
  1938.B42; 1941.B11; 1942.B25;
  1951.B102; 1957.B4

-A Wonder-Book for Girls and
  Boys, 1944.B29
Hawthorne, Sophia, 1931.B27-29;
  1945.B27; 1950.B1; 1952.B9;
  1958.B78
"Hawthorne and His Mosses,"
  1940.B8; 1942.B25-26;
  1943.B18; 1944.B5; 1948.B8;
  1949.B15; 1951.B89; 1953.B28;
  1954.B4; 1955.B31; 1957.B63;
  1958.B40; B67; 1959.B9, B24
Hazlitt, William, The Round
  Table, 1948.B50
Hearn, Lafcadio, 1949.B25
Hemingway, Ernest, 1931.B39;
  1935.B8; 1952.B95; 1953.B52;
  1957.A2, B35
-The Old Man and The Sea,
  1957.B35
Henry, O., 1959.B67
Herridge, Robert, 1954.B57
Hildreth, Richard, 1959.B67
History of the County of
  Berkshire, Massachusetts, A,
  1954.B22
Hobbes, Thomas, 1957.B83
Hogarth, William, 1954.B9
Holmes, Oliver Wendell, 1934.B1;
  1935.B16; 1937.B36; 1938.B4;
  1939.B8; B26; 1947.B68;
  1955.B25; 1956.B81; 1959.B24,
  B34
Homer, 1932.B9; 1949.B77;
  1950.B62; 1959.B37
-The Iliad, 1950.B62
-The Odyssey, 1950.B62
Homer, Winslow, 1958.B5
Homosexuality, 1947.B3; 1948.B14,
  B20; 1949.A1; 1950.B89;
  1951.B75; 1952.B87; 1953.B47
Hone, Philip, 1936.B7
Housman, A.E., 1938.B22
Howells, William Dean, 1931.B5,
  B11; 1935.B7; 1953.B3;
  1960.B55
Hudson, Henry Norman, 1951.B89
Hudson, W.H., 1934.B6
Humor, 1931.B19, B25; 1932.B6;
  1933.B2, B9; 1934.B12;
  1937.B1; B20, B26, B45, B50;
  1940.B10; 1941.B27; 1942.B10;
  1943.B24; 1945.B5; 1946.B2;

Monroe, Harriet, 1937.B12
Montaigne, Michel Eyquem de,
    1931.B17; 1952.B8, B61;
    1953.B40
Montgomery, Isaac, 1935.B18
Moore, Marianne, 1935.B3
Moore, Thomas, 1949.B14
Morality, 1931.B35; 1933.B22;
    1937.B22, B33; 1938.B23;
    1939.B25; 1940.B6,m B21;
    1943.B14; 1945.B22, B24, B26;
    1946.B19; 1947.B22, B39, B75;
    1948.B10, B14, B70; 1949.A1,
    B3, B14, B16, B55, B118,
    B128; 1950.B4, B16, B36, B58,
    B61, B67, B77, B92, B98,
    1951.B107; 1952.B78, B81,
    B87; 1953.B42, B55, B59, B76;
    1954.B9; 1956.B7, B23;
    1957.B30, B41; 1958.B1, B21,
    B47, B63; 1959.B35, B60;
    1960.A2, B58, B94
Morewood, Agnes (grandniece),
    1947.B70; 1953.B63
Morewood, Helen Gansevoort
    (grandniece), 1953.B63
Morrell, Lady Ottoline, 1932.B15
Morris, William, Sigurd the
    Volsung, 1934.B16, B22
Mosby, John S., 1959.B39
Moxon, Edward, 1960.B55
Mumford, Lewis, 1931.B24;
    1935.B11; 1937.B17; 1938.B22;
    1939.A1, B16; 1945.B14
Murray, Don, 1959.B48
Murray, Henry A., 1945.B14
Murray, John, 1932.B17, B48;
    1936.B32; 1944.B4; 1947.B74;
    1948.B58; 1952.A1, B96;
    1953.B36
Mysticism, 1931.B20, B38;
    1932.B22; 1933.B29; 1938.B3,
    B20; 1939.A1, B24, B32;
    1944.B14; 1946.B5; 1948.B7;
    1949.B74; 1950.B72; 1952.A2,
    B34; 1956.B75-76
Mythology, 1936.B35; 1938.A1;
    1943.B14, B24; 1944.B33;
    1945.B9; 1946.B31; 1947.A2,
    B39, B59; 1948.B43, B66;
    1949.A1, B14, B90, B105,
    B111; 1950.B36, B71, B90,

B92, B94, B97, B105, B110,
    B113; 1951.B6, B60, B75,
    B107; 1952.B21, B51;
    1953.B44, B76; 1954.B7, B16;
    1955.B17, B32; 1956.B29, B66;
    1958.B35, B71; 1959.B8;
    1960.B16, B82

Narrative technique, 1931B6;
    1932.B21, B42; 1935.B9;
    1937.B15; 1938.B31, B46;
    1940.B31; 1948.B22; 1949.B83;
    1950.B64; 1952.A1; 1953.B4,
    B56; 1954.B9, B54; 1955.B34;
    1958.B79; 1959.B17; 1960.B42
Naturalism, 1936.B18; 1944.B38;
    1949.B24; 1950.B91; 1951.B29,
    B42; 1953.B38; 1956.B25;
    1957.A2; 1958.B33, B55, B57,
    B59; 1959.B47; 1960.B76
New English Dictionary, 1941.B40
Newell, Charles Martin, Pêhe-
    Nû-e, The Tiger Whale of the
    Pacific, 1933.B23
Nichols, Thomas L., 1932.B37;
    1943.B13
-Forty Years of American Life,
    1932.B37
Nietzsche, Friedrich Wilhelm,
    1937.B9; 1938.B17; 1949.B14
-Thus Spoke Zarathustra, 1937.B9;
    1938.B17
Norris, Frank, 1956.B25; 1958.B57

O'Brien, Fitz-James, 1934.B17
Ochiltree, Henry, Redburn,
    1947.B25
"October Mountain," 1934.B23;
    1950.B65
Oedipus complex, 1949.A1, B14
Omoo, 1931.B18, B22, B37;
    1932.B16-17, B48; 1933.B4,
    B6, B24, B30; 1934.B6;
    1935.B29; 1936.B23; 1937.B6
    B16, B22, B35; 1938.B15, B17,
    B23-24, b30; 1939.A1, B9,
    B13, B21, B30; 1941.B40;
    1943.B5, B13; 1944.B4, B14;
    1946.B29; 1947.B2, B24, B40,
    B78; 1948.B5, B29, B34, B39,
    B58; 1950.B31, B35, B78, B80;
    1952.A2, B70; 1954.B56, B59;

(Religion)
B19, B21, B24, B31, B38;
1941.B25, B32; 1942.B22;
1943.A1, B15, B21, B23-24;
1944.B9, B15, B17, B26-27,
B38; 1945.B4, B14, B17-18,
B21, B26, B29, B32; 1946.B19,
B21; 1947.A2, B13, B65, B75;
1948.B9, B33; 1949.B2, B4,
B20, B39, B63, B94, B111;
1950.A3, B4, B28, B44, B66,
B75, B91, B96, B106; 1952.A2,
B33, B61, B64, B71, B116,
B120; 1953.B12, B35, B38,
B40, B58, B66; 1956.A1, B7,
B45, B66; 1957.B7, B51;
1958.B21, B73
Reynolds, J.N., "Mocha Dick,"
1932.B47; 1937.B43; 1939.B37
Rimbaud, Arthur, 1956.A1
Ringbolt, Captain, Sailor's Life
and Sailor's Yarns, 1938.B22
Robards, Jason, Jr., 1959.B48
Robertson, Harrison, 1950.B31
Romanticism, 1931.B2; 1932.B14,
B34; 1937.B18; 1938.B14;
1939.B25; 1942.B22; 1943.B14;
1947.B13, B37; 1950.B4, B14,
B56, B58, B60, B114; 1951.B2,
B10, B29, B34, B108; 1952.B7,
B32, B116; 1953.A1, B21, B66,
B69; 1954.B32; 1956.B20, B25;
1958.B46, B59
Roosevelt, Franklin Delano,
1937.B23
Rousseau, Jean-Jacques, 1953.B66;
1957.B83
Rowlandson, Thomas, 1949.B117
Ruskin, John, 1951.B71
Russ, Oliver, 1951.B73
Ryder, Albert, 1953.B1

Sadleir, Michael, 1958.B50
Sady, (Saadi), Gulistan, or Rose-
Garden, 1948.B50
Salt, Henry S., 1960.B67
Sappho, 1951.B75
Sartre, Jean Paul, 1952.B99
Satire, 1931.B37; 1932.B24;
1933.B31; 1935.B14; 1936.B2,
B22; 1937.B25; 1938.A1, B26;
1939.B26; 1940.B1; 1942.B12;

1945.B27; 1949.B4, B117-118,
B130; 1950.B107; 1952.B42,
B51, B65; 1953.B6, B40;
1954.B9; 1955.A1, B42, B45;
1956.B2; 1957.B22, B29;
1958.B40; 1959.B44, B80;
1960.B67
Saunders, Frederick, 1943.B13
Schopenhauer, Arthur, 1944.B15;
1948.B9; 1949.B77; 1960.B61
Scoresby, William, 1936.B34;
1948.B71; 1949.A3; 1950.B108;
1956.B32
-An Account of the Arctic
Regions, with a History and
Description of the Northern
Whale-Fishery, 1936.B34;
1948.B71; 1949.A3; 1956.B32
Scott, Michael, 1931.B30; 1934.B2
Scott, Sir Walter, 1934.B2;
1949.B14; 1953.B10, B66
The Sea Beast, 1933.B2
Sedgwick, Catherine, 1933.B7;
1938.B4; 1956.B81
Shakespeare, William, 1936.B21;
1939.B18; 1941.A1; 1945.B33;
1947.A2, B4, B13, B35, B41,
B44, B67, B73; 1948.B1, B20,
B33, B35; 1949.A3, B14, B77,
B105, B119; 1950.B8, B60,
B95; 1951.B64, B89; 1953.B80;
1954.B26; 1955.B50; 1956.B71;
1957.B4, B11, B51; 1958.B8,
B18-19, B54, 1959.B24
-Antony and Cleopatra, 1938.B45;
1947.A2
-Hamlet, 1933.B9; 1938.B23;
1940.B33; 1942.B10; 1949.B14;
1951.B100, B114; 1953.B43,
B71; 1954.B27; 1956.B71;
1958.B73; 1960.B42
-Julius Caesar, 1957.B71
-King Lear, 1933.B9; 1938.B45;
1939.A2; 1945.B33; 1947.A2;
1949.B119; 1950.B101;
1951.B114; 1952.B12;
1958.B54; 1959.B26
-Macbeth, 1938.B45; 1957.B11
-Othello, 1951.B6; 1952.B43;
1956.B9
-Richard II, 1931.B37

Author Index

Conner, Frederick William, 1949.B4
Connolly, Thomas E., 1954.B21
Connor, C.H., 1948.B68
Cook, Albert, 1949.B5; 1960.B7
Cook, Charles H., Jr., 1955.B36
Cook, Reginald L., 1948.B76
Costelloe, M. Joseph, 1957.B39
Couch, H.N., 1933.B21
Cowie, Alexander, 1948.B7; 1949.
  B23
Cowley, Malcolm, 1950.B105; 1951.
  B98, B113; 1954.B5
Coxe, Louis, O., 1951.B4; 1958.B46
Cramer, Maurice B., 1957.B56
Crane, Hart, 1952.B6
Crawford, Bartholow V., 1945.B3
Crealock, W.I.B., 1955.B6
Creeger, George R., 1954.B41;
  1960.B8
Croll, Morris W., 1938.B47
Cross, Tom Peete, 1931.B7
Crowley, William G., 1959.B34
Crozier, Eric, 1951.B7, B78
Cruickshank, John, 1959.B8
Cunliffe, Marcus, 1951.B54, B117;
  1954.B6; 1956.B5; 1957.B5;
  1958.B6; 1960.B9
Curl, Vega, 1931.A1
Current-García, Eugene, 1952.B7
Currie, Barton, 1936.B29
Curti, Merle, 1941.B19-20; 1943.B4

D

Dahl, Curtis, 1959.B43
Dahlberg, Edward, 1941.B8; 1951.
  B116; 1960.B10, B70
Daiches, David, 1949.B83; 1950.B57
Dakin, William John, 1934.B5
Dale, T.R., 1957.B49
Dauner, Louise, 1950.B34
Davidson, Carter, 1934.B14
Davidson, Donald, 1939.B3
Davidson, Frank, 1954.B22
Davis, David Brion, 1957.B6
Davis, Joe Lee, 1948.B8
Davis, Merrell R., 1941.B23, B44;
  1949.B67, B93; 1952.A1
Davis, Robert Gorham, 1949.B34
Day, A. Grove, 1957.B54
D'azevedo, Warren, 1956.B41

Deegan, Dorothy Yost, 1951.B5
Deferrari, Roy J., 1944.B2
Deutsch, Babette, 1941.B29
De Voto, Bernard, 1932.B6; 1943.B5
Dichmann, Mary E., 1952.B102
Dickinson, Leon T., 1956.B32;
  1957.B7
Dickinson, Thomas H., 1932.B7
Dillistone, F.W., 1960.B12
Dix, William S., 1948.B59
Dixon, Alec, 1937.B8
Dixson, Robert J., 1953.B8
Dobbyn, Dermot, 1957.B77
Dobree, Bonamy, 1951.B42
Dodge, Norman L., 1931.B30; 1932.
  B35; 1937.B23
Doughty, Howard, Jr., 1950.B39
d.R., H., 1953.B7
Driven, Leota S., 1933.B7
Drummond, Andrew L., 1950.B9
Duffus, R.L. 1949.B74
Duffy, Charles, 1941.B43; 1942.
  B20; 1952.B109
Dulles, Foster Rhea, 1932.B47;
  1933.B8
Dumble, Wilson R., 1938.B13
Duncan, Harry, 1948.B54
Durham, Philip, 1958.B50; 1960.B13

E

E.,T.T., 1943.B26
Eby, E.H., 1940.B25; 1945.B4;
  1948.B37; 1954.B7
Edel, Leon, 1956.B6; 1959.B9
Edgar, Pelham, 1933.B9
Editors of the Modern Library,
  1952.B8
Ehnmark, Anders, 1958.B65
Ekirch, Arthur Alphonse, 1944.B3
Elisofon, Eliot, 1955.B35
Elliott, George, P., 1958.B35
Elliott, Harrison, 1952.B9
Ellis, Milton, 1940.B4-5
Emerson, O.B., 1960.B37
Engle, Paul, 1950.B69, B83

F

Fadiman, Clifton, 1941.B30; 1943.
  B6-7, B24; 1950.B10; 1955.B7;

Glicksberg, Charles I., 1950.B79;
  1959.B72
Glixen, Niel, 1950.B44
Godley, John. See Kilbraken, Lord
Gohdes, Clarence L.F., 1931.B9;
  1937.B34; 1939.B16; 1942.B8;
  1944.B4, B11; 1952.B69
Gollin, Richard, 1957.B41
Gollin, Rita, 1957.B41
Goodspeed, Charles E., 1937.B11
Goodspeed, George T., 1948.B47
Godron, D.J., 1954.B46
Gorman, Herbert, 1939.B26
Gould, Jean, 1956.A2
Graham, Philip, 1957.B12
Granger, Bruce Ingham, 1953.B78
Gray, James, 1947.B50; 1950.B55
Grdseloff, Dorothee, 1955.B66
Greenberg, Martin, 1950.B58
Greenslt, Ferris, 1947.B34
Gregory, Horace, 1938.B48
Gross, John J., 1951.B79; 1956.
  B33, B66; 1959.B68
Grossman, James, 1949.B7
Guérard, Albert, 1940.B7; 1948.B12
Gulick, John Thomas, 1932.B9
Gurko, Leo, 1946.B20

H

H., E.B., 1956.B79
H., R.M., 1949.B78
Haber, Tom Burns, 1951.B85
Hale, Phillip, 1932.B48
Hall, James B., 1950.B45
Hall, Lawrence Sargent, 1944.B5
Halleck, Reuben Post, 1934.B7
Halsband, Robert, 1949.B116
Hamalian, Leo, 1950.B48
Hamilton, Charles, 1950.B117
Hanley, James, 1952.B11
Hansen, Harry, 1950.B82
Harada, Keiichi, 1956.B44, B75
Haraszti, Zoltan, 1947.B41, B46
Harcourt, John B., 1951.B36
Harding, Walter, 1951.B24
Harkness, Bruce, 1955.B12; 1959.
  B15
Hart, H.W., 1950.B41
Hart, James D., 1937.B24; 1941.B9;
  1947.B53; 1950.B12; 1955.B13

Hart-Davis, Rupert, 1952.B12
Hartman, Carl, 1960.B37
Hartwick, Harry. 1936, B8
Harvey, Evelyn, 1955.B41
Harvey, Sir Paul, 1932.B10
Hasley, Louis, 1937.B39
Hastings, Louise, 1938.B14
Hatch, Robert, 1951.B44
Hatcher, Harlan, 1935.B7
Haun, Eugene, 1950.B87
Hawthorne, Hildegarde, 1932.B11
Hawthorne, Julian, 1938.B15
Hawthorne, Nathaniel, 1932.B12,
  B20; 1941.B10
Hayford, Harrison, 1944.B16; 1945.
  B19; 1946.B33; 1949.B67, B93;
  1950.B92; 1951.B30, B73, 1952.
  B81; 1958.B75; 1959.B16, B78-
  79
Hazlitt, Henry, 1933.B10
Healy, J.V., 1945.B25
Hearn, Lafcadio, 1939.B4
Helfin, Wilson L., 1948.B71; 1949.
  B51; 1951.B8, B25; 1953.B9;
  1956.B82
Heilman, Robert B., 1956.B9
Heiser, M.F., 1953.B10
Hellman, George S., 1941.B32
Hemingway, Ernest, 1935.B8
Hendrick, George, 1960.B50
Herzberg, Max, J., 1933.B5; 1937.
  B7
Hetherington, Hugh W., 1953.B11;
  1955.B72
Hewett-Thayer, Harvey W., 1958.B13
Hicks, Granville, 1933.B11; 1941.
  B38; 1948.B82; 1958.B14, B49;
  1960.B64
Higgins, Paul Lambourne, 1952.B120
Hillway, Tyrus, 1944.B32; 1945.
  B12, B26, B29, B32; 1946.B21,
  B29; 1947.B29, B63, B70; 1948.
  B62; 1949.B24, B46, B53-54,
  B122; 1950.A2, B49, B75-76,
  B93; 1951.B37, B63, B86; 1952.
  B54, B76, B82, B103, B116;
  1953.A2-3, B12-13, B51-52, B62-
  65, B79; 1954.B30, B48-49, B57-
  58; 1955.B37-38, I40-47; 1956.
  B34-35, B51-54, B67-68, B83-84;
  1957.B13-16, B64-65, B72, B85;

Mabbott, T.O., 1932.B32; 1939.B11; 1941.B35; 1946.B38; 1949.B108; 1951.B66, B87

McAvoy, Mary Carey, 1938.B28

McCloskey, John C., 1946.B16

McCormick, John, 1957.B22

McCorquodale, Marjorie Kimball, 1954.B12

McDermott, John Francis, 1957.B78

MacDonald, Allan, 1935.B30

McDowell, Tremaine, 1933.B13

McElderry, B.R., Jr., 1955.B43; 1960.B26

MacFall, Russell, 1949.B84, B130

McFee, William, 1931.B12; 1949.B57

McGraves, Donald E., 1946.B25

McGreal, Ian, 1952.B77

Macy, George, 1943.B9

MacShane, Frank, 1958.B29

Maddox, Notley S., 1942.B15

Mailer, Norman, 1948.B19

Male, Roy R., Jr., 1957.B87

Malone, Ted. See Russell, Frank Alden

Mansfield, Luther Stearns, 1937. B26; 1938.A2, B26; 1944.B27; 1945.B21; 1950.B54; 1952.B17; 1953.A3, B13; 1956.B46

Marie Theresa, Sister, 1954.B13

Marsden, Walter, 1951.B46

Marshall, Margaret, 1951.B35

Martin, Edwin T., 1946.B23

Martin, Harold C., 1959.B22

Martin, Pete, 1952.B59

Marx, Leo, 1952.B104; 1953.B68; 1956.B40

Masefield, John, 1941.B14; 1952. B18

Mason, Ronald, 1951.A5, B80; 1955. B50

Mather, Edward, 1940.B8

Mather, Frank Jewett, 1938.B34

Mathews, Chesley J., 1949.B124; 1958.B67

Matthiessen, F.O., 1941.A1; 1944. B8; 1952.B19

Maugham, W. Somerset, 1940.B22; 1948.B20, B56; 1949.B10; 1955. B19

Mayberry, George, 1947.B36

Maynard, Theodore, 1947.B76

Mayoux, Jean-Jacques, 1960.A4

Mead, David, 1951.B12

Members of the Federal Writer's Project of the Works Progress Administration for Massachusetts, 1939.B6

Menard, Wilman, 1933.B27

Mencken, H.L., 1936.B13

Merchant, Norris, 1957.B23

Metcalf, Eleanor Melville, 1948. B21; 1949.B11; 1953.B5

Michener, James A., 1951.B13

Miles, Dudley, 1943.B11

Miller, Edwin L., 1933.b14

Miller, F. DeWolfe, 1951.B14

Miller, James E., 1955.B40; 1958. B41, B54; 1959.B23, B44-45, B59, B69, B80; 1960.B57

Miller, Leon, 1933.B15

Miller, Paul W., 1958.B71

Miller, Perry, 1949.B123; B19, B66; 1956.B15; 1957.B44; 1959.B24

Millett, Fred B., 1950.B19

Millhauser, Milton, 1955.B54

Mills, Gordon H., 1942.B16; 1950.B20; 1951.B59

Milne, Gordon, 1956.B16

Molyneux, William, 1953.B57

Montague, Gene B., 1956.B17

Montale, Eugenio, 1960.B58

Moore, Geoffrey, 1958.B61

Moore, Harry T., 1960.B66

Moorman, Charles, 1953.B44; 1956. B29

Mordell, Albert, 1931.B33; 1960. B27

Morison, Samuel Eliot, 1955.B60; 1956.B60

Morley, Christopher, 1931.B27, B34; 1937.B31; 1949.B12

Morpurgo, J.E., 1950.B95

Morris, Lloyd, 1931.B35, B37

Morris, Wright, 1958.B19

Mosier, Richard D., 1952.B20

Mott, Frank Luther, 1938.B19; 1947.B9; 1948.B8

Mulgan, John, 1939.B2

Muller, Herbert J., 1937.B33

Munford, Lewis, 1945.B14; 1947.B38, B68; 1955.B20

Targ, William, 1936.B18; 1940.
  B13; 1955.B26
Taylor, Houghton Wells, 1935.B10
Taylor, Robert S., 1951.B77
Taylor, Walter Fuller, 1936.B18
Tedlock, E.W., Jr., 1948.B29
Tharp, Louise Hall, 1950.B25
'Thersites,' 1949.B60
Thomas, Russell, 1932.B23; 1936.
  B25
Thomas, W.D. 1940.B29
Thompson, Francis J., 1952.B89
Thompson, Harold W., 1941.B18
Thompson, Lawrance, 1952,A2; 1953.
  B15; 1955.B73; 1960.B67
Thompson, Marjorie, 1953.B32;
  1954.B19; 1957.B29
Thompson, Ralph, 1936.B19
Thompson, W.R., 1957.B30
Thomson, Virgil, 1952.B87
Thorp, Willard, 1937.B30; 1938.
  B22, B27, B50; 1941.B19-20;
  1942.B25; 1944.B19, B33, B37;
  1945.B22; 1947.B16, B44; 1948.
  B30, B40, B75;1949.B49, B75,
  B90, B111; 1950.B26, B37, B77
  B108-110; 1952.B96, B113; 1953
  B33; 1957.B55, B67, B70; 1960.
  B36, B43, B69
Thurber, James, 1957.B31
Thurston, Jarvis, 1960.B37
Tillyard, E.M.W., 1958.B24
Tilton, Eleanor M., 1949.B30;
  1959.B75
Tindall, William York, 1955.B27;
  1956.B23
Tinker, Edward Larocque, 1937.B41
Tomita, Akira, 1955.B28
Tomlinson, H.M., 1934.B12; 1949.
  B113; 1950.B27
Townsend, Harvey Gates, 1934.B13
Treeman, Elizabeth, 1953.A6
Trilling, Lionel, 1947.B17; 1948.
  B38; 1950.B28; 1957.B32

U

Untermeyer, Louis, 1931.B22; 1934.
  B14; 1942.B6; 1945.B9; 1955.B29
Uzzell, Thomas H. 1947.B18

V

Vance, Thomas H., 1952.B27
Vancura, Zdenek, 1959.B27-28
Van Doren, Carl, 1933.B18; 1935.
  B13; 1936.B20; 1940.B14; 1942.
  B7; 1943.B16; 1949.B21
Van Doren, Mark, 1932.B21; 1957.
  B33
Van Patten, Nathan, 1934.B15
Varley, H. Leland, 1949.B27
Viereck, Peter, 1956.B24
Vietor, Alexander O., 1942.B18;
  1948.B50
Villiers, Alan, 1958.B25; 1959.B29
Vinal, Harold, 1953.B49
Vincent, Howard P., 1947.B19, B48;
  1949.A3, B28, B61, B91, B96,
  B114; 1950.b50, B59; 1951.B99;
  1952.B17, B61; 1954.B55; 1959.
  B47
Virtanen, Reino, 1948.B78
Visiak, E.H., 1941.B36
Vittorini, Elio, 1960.B62
Vogel, Dan, 1958.B83
Vogelback, Arthur L., 1952.B43
Von Abele, Rudolph, 1947.B64
Von Hagen, Victor Wolfgang, 1940.
  B15; 1948.B31; 1949.B22

W

Wade, Mason, 1948.B80; 1949.B128;
  1950.B84
Wagenknecht, Edward, 1950.B51;
  1951.B95, B115; 1952.B28, B46,
  B64; 1953.B75
Waggoner, Hyatt Howe, 1942.B12,
  B23
Wagner, Vern, 1958.B26
Wainger, Bertrade M., 1932.B24;
  1939.B25
Wainwright, Alexander D., 1952.B24
Walbridge, Earle F., 1947.B33
Walcutt, Charles Child, 1944.B22;
  1952.B98; 1956.B25
Walpole, Hugh R., 1941.B21
Wann, Louis, 1953.B53
Warbuton, T., 1936.B33
Ward, A.C., 1932.B22